Ball Perennial Manual:

Propagation and Production

by

Jim Nau

Ball Publishing
Batavia, Illinois USA

Ball Publishing
Post Office Box 9
335 North River Street
Batavia, Illinois 60510 USA

Library of Congress Cataloging-in-Publication Data
Nau, Jim, 1958–
    Ball perennial manual : propagation and production / by Jim Nau.
      p. cm.
    Includes bibliographical references and index.
    ISBN 1-883052-10-6
    1. Perennials—Handbooks, manuals, etc. 2. Floriculture-
-Handbooks, manuals, etc. I. Title.
SB434.N37 1995
635.9'3253—dc20

                        95-20481
                         CIP

Cover photo: *Taken at the production facility of T&Z Nursery, Inc., Winfield, Illinois.*

Photographer: *Chris Beytes.*

DEDICATION

Tulips and peonies were about the only flowers that one of my two grand-mothers would allow anywhere near her house. Maude's idea of a garden was one filled with tomatoes and peas, among other, less preferred, vegetables. "You don't eat flowers," she would say. On the other hand, my other grandmother, Vera, prized her blooming plants equally with her vegetables. Her garden was adorned with hostas, rambler roses, lilacs, bedding plants, lily-of-the-valley and, especially, sweet peas. Vera and Raymond also had the traditional victory garden where apple trees, straw-berries, and sweet corn lined the outer reaches of a garden planted to capacity with vegetables meant for the kitchen table as well as for freez-ing. Raymond actually planted it and took care of it, though Vera provided direction at every turn. Helen and Harold cared and tended their hybrid tea roses, Pat and Hope grew the biggest potatoes, while Cheryl and Bill have given me a new perspective on peppers. My family have all taught me something about gardening and growing, and, while not really trying to do so, changed a hobby into a profession. For that, I will always be grateful.

TABLE OF CONTENTS

PREFACE

Over the past 10 years, the Ball Seed Co. has been conducting detailed tests in germination, hardiness, adaptability, performance, and usage of a broad range of herbaceous perennial plants. This book was born in response to the many questions that we receive on how to grow and use these crops. We provide it only as a place to start. While not a feeble resource, it is also not definitive.

It is well known that no one reads a technical or cultural manual from cover to cover. Browsing through the index to the page number of the specific crop and then thumbing the pages to the exact spot where the information can be found is the preferred way to use such a manual—including this one. I would challenge you, however, to read the several chapters preceding the cultural information when you have an opportunity. Growers grow differently. While I am not a grower, I have peered over the shoulders of our growers for over a decade asking questions, taking notes, and commenting (well, maybe it was more like bossing) on the performance of various crops. My sincere appreciation to Jim Folgers, Maureen Safarik, and Janice Strayve for being so patient with my intervention and always providing insight into the problems of the various crops that we grew.

The culture in this book is based on a number of criteria, but the information is taken primarily from our own data collected from 1982 to 1990. Additional information came from respected growers, many of them my friends, who helped me to unravel certain mysteries of seed germination, divisions, cuttings, and other forms of propagation, production, and hardiness (both winter and summer).

Since no two growers use the same techniques, use the information in this book as a starting point—a cultural cookbook, if you will—to see the needs of a crop, as well as its limitations. Crop times are relative and change because of local conditions and personal experiences. If nothing else, I hope that I have given you information to perfect a crop you are currently growing or encouragement to try one for the first time.

ACKNOWLEDGMENTS

Few technical manuals are completed without the help of a number of professionals in the trade. This is true of this book as well. The following individuals and companies have generously offered their plants, their time, and their assistance in helping me complete this project. I extend my deepest appreciation.

Ball Seed Co., West Chicago, Illinois.

Benary Seed Company, Hann Muenden, Germany.

Shirley and Harlan Hamernik and their staff at Bluebird Nursery in Clarkson, Nebraska.

The many friends of the Perennial Plant Association who have offered their input in helping me solve propagation and production problems.

There are a number of companies noted in the book. To them and to the following companies, I also give my thanks for their assistance:

Addison Gardens, Vergennes, Vermont.

Donahue's Clematis Specialists, Fairbault, Minnesota.

Klehm Nursery, Champaign, Illinois.

Walters Gardens Inc., Zeeland, Michigan.

A work of this complexity could never be completed without the able assistance of the wordsmiths—the editors who helped translate manuscript pages into a finished book. My special thanks go to: Kathy Pyle, Meredith Publications, Des Moines, Iowa; Anne Brennan, Chilton Co., Radnor, Pennsylvania; and Liza Sutherland, Ball Publishing, Batavia, Illinois.

How to Use This Book

The *Ball Perennial Manual* is designed with a template that follows the same pattern from crop to crop. Each main heading on this template is noted below in headline type. Some crops may have additional notes or headings pertinent to just that one crop.

■ Botanical name

This is the genus and species of the crop being covered. All the information that is written is strictly for the genus and species named. If additional species are covered under **Related material**, all cultural, descriptive, usage, and handling information on the related crops is noted in that section.

Occasionally a crop has undergone a name change, and additional botanical names are provided in parenthesis. The first name may have been recently registered, though some crops may be referred to by two botanical names depending on which nomenclature reference you use.

For this book, *Hortus Third* is the primary nomenclature authority used. Since the current edition was last updated in 1976, there have been a number of changes to both genera and species. In these cases, other references including *The Royal Horticultural Society Dictionary of Gardening*, *Hardy Herbaceous Perennials* by Leo Jelitto and Wilhelm Schacht and *Index Hortensis* have been used.

Additional notes are provided under **Varieties**.

■ Family name

This is the family to which the genus belongs. In most cases, certain family characteristics such as petal counts, reproduction similarities, and other phenotypical criteria are common to all plants within a family. Production issues, however, such as crop time, propagation requirements, etc., are not necessarily the same between genus or even species. Therefore, you may find several crops (like *Dianthus*) covered in more than one crop outline. Review the index for the crops you want to grow.

■■ COMMON NAMES

The common names of the crops are noted under this heading. How the common name came into being may be discussed as well.

It is important to note that common names differ based on the region of the United States you are selling in. There are nationally accepted common names, but regional authors, growers, and home owners may know the plant under a different name.

Additional comments are provided under **Varieties**.

■■ DESCRIPTION

The description is a layman's interpretation of what the plant looks like. I have omitted the usual botanical terms in lieu of more universally understood ones without jeopardizing detail and significance. The emphasis is on flowers (type, size, whether scented or not, and color), as well as plant height, habit, and foliage attributes.

■■ HARDINESS

Few books ever review the concept of persistence in the garden along with the other cultural aspects of perennials. You could call it a taboo subject with good reason. It is conceivable that you could grow a plant in the garden by this or any other book and have it last only one or two years even though the information provided would suggest that the plants are extremely hardy. On some of the more challenging crops, I have included the reasons for short-term performance.

A USDA Hardiness Zone map is provided on pages 454 and 455. It gives approximate annual minimum temperatures expected throughout the United States and Canada. The lower the zone number, the colder it gets during the winter months. Most perennials perform well in Zones 4 to 8 but they vary in their hardiness due to other factors, such as soil type and sensitivity to persistent wet weather, snow cover, alternate freezing and thawing conditions, or dry, cold winds.

The term hardiness is often used when dealing with winter's worst, but few consider summer hardiness to be an issue. Nothing could be further from the truth. The farther south you go in the United States, you will find that a plant may live through the winter months without even dying back. However, in the high heat and humidity climates of a southern summer, the plants may readily die out or collapse to the ground. Comments on this are provided with each crop under the hardiness heading and **In the home garden**.

■ SEASON OF BLOOM

I have included the month in which the plants will flower in our Chicago area location, which is in Zone 5. While not directly helpful to my southern friends, the cultural information is still valid.

The detail provided under **Season of bloom** pertains to plants that are established in the garden and does not apply to plants that have been recently planted. If a perennial is sold and planted in the garden in the spring, it will most likely not flower during its normal period. After a year in the garden, the plants will resume their normal flowering period.

■ PROPAGATION

This gives you a nutshell approach to the common and not so common methods of propagating various perennial plants. They are highlighted here and detailed within both **Germinating** and **Growing on**.

While seed germination is a form of propagation, its detail is kept separate to highlight other common propagation methods. These common ones include cuttings, division, and root propagation. If available as tissue cultured plants or other forms, these are noted as well.

■ GERMINATION OVERVIEW

This information is specific to seed propagation and includes topics such as number of seeds per ounce, number of days to germinate, light or dark requirements during germination, and temperatures to use for best emergence. If germination is difficult, more detailed information is provided on how to increase the overall percentages. The number of days it takes before seedlings can be transplanted is provided as well. Note that transplant dates are from sowing until ready to pot up. In other words, 20 to 25 days to transplant means that the seedlings can be transplanted between 20 to 25 days from the day you sow.

Most of this information is straightforward, and no further definitions are necessary—except for pretreatments. In a number of perennials that are sown from seed, it's imperative that you sow the seed in the fall or early winter after the seed has been harvested or received. If the seed is stored to be sown later, it can go into a dormancy period that has to be broken before the seed will germinate. This is covered in more detail in the **Propagation Techniques** chapter.

The germination temperatures are constant from sowing until seedling emergence. The majority of easy-to-germinate perennials take three to seven days to emerge. However, many varieties may take from seven to 21 days to show first emergence. Maintaining a warm germination environment at the temperatures noted here until seedling emergence is imperative for a good seedling stand.

Seedlings that first emerge are susceptible to stretching and need to be moved from the germination chamber the first day they are seen. Seedlings emerging from an open flat upon the greenhouse bench are less susceptible but are still prone to stretching. Limited light and high soil temperatures will also encourage stretching. Although the percentage of visible seedlings may only be 10%, seedling emergence will continue as it does in bedding plants. A number of the common herbaceous perennials do not emerge as uniformly as annual or bedding plant crops. You may notice a random appearance of a group of seedlings developing over several weeks. This is more common in seeds that are being germinated without pretreatment, seeds that have been improperly stored, old seed, or seed that has a tough outer seed coat. Read more on this in the **Propagation Techniques** chapter.

Once seedlings are removed from germination temperatures, grow on until transplant at 60F to 65F (16C to 18C) nights and 70F to 80F (21C to 27C) days, out of direct sun. If seedlings appear to be growing too quickly or are starting to stretch, drop the night temperatures to no lower than 55F (13C) to slow plant growth prior to transplanting.

■■■Growing on

This section covers the crop time and scheduling of plants from seed or vegetative propagation. Growing temperatures, containers, and special needs are addressed here. All of the crop times are based on a production schedule for spring sales unless otherwise noted.

A note about pot size: Metric equivalents in most instances are provided in parentheses wherever English units of measurement are used in this book. However, container sizes such as quart and gallon may not be meaningful when expressed in liters, since you wouldn't transplant your perennials into 3.8 l pots.

So in this text no metric equivalents are included for quart- and gallon-sized pots, but the following measurements are what we used for producing our crops:

- A quart pot measures approximately 3½ to 4 inches (9 to 10 cm) in diameter and 4 to 5 inches (10 to 13 cm) deep.

- A gallon pot measures approximately 6 to 7 inches (15 to 18 cm) deep and 6 to 7 inches in diameter.

Crop times. All crop times noted within the crop cultures are inclusive from the day you sow your seed, transplant a plug, or pot up a purchased division or bare-root transplant until you can sell the plant. The culture will state whether the plant is sold green or in bloom and the container that the plant is grown in. Night temperatures are provided as well.

In this manual, I am assuming (and encouraging) that only rooted cuttings (as in the case of purchased liners or plugs) and purchased divisions or bare-root transplants be used to follow each crop's schedule for spring sales. If taking your own cuttings or divisions, the best plants for spring sales are those propagated during the previous year and overwintered as young plants in their final containers. Keeping active stock plants to take cuttings from during the winter, as well as trying to dig up field-grown plants to divide or transplant in mid to late winter, is not recommended unless you are dealing with only a limited number of cultivars or you are a commercial propagator.

As for seed, selected cultivars can be sown during the winter and early spring for April to June sales in cell packs and small 3- or 4-inch (7.6 or 10.2 cm) pots. The best plants are achieved from seed sown the previous summer until early autumn, potted when ready, then sold the following spring. Sowings made from June to early September will produce quart or gallon pots from summer to midautumn that can be overwintered dormant at 32F to 35F (0C to 2C) until March.

Sowings during November and December will produce quart and gallon pots that can be grown on cold, 38F to 45F (3C to 7C), for the remainder of the winter. This method is for cold season plants (mostly early and midspring bloomers that tolerate cold temperatures). Warm season plants will have to be grown at no lower than 50F (10C) for active growth.

Time for cell packs. Within the cultures provided in this book, I frequently give the crop time from seed to a finished flat of 32 cells per flat. I am not advocating or promoting the sale of perennials in cell packs. Instead, many growers or commercial companies sow seed during the warmer months (summer and early autumn) to produce plantlets in cell packs that can either be sold commercially or transplanted to larger containers (quart or gallon pots) for overwintering. These plants are then sold the following spring.

I have provided the crop time for cell packs as an indicator of what to expect based on the plant's rate of growth. When provided, the crop time to salable green flats means when the plants are leafed out and well rooted. These plants can be transplanted to quart or gallon pots now, or even a week or two earlier than the weeks noted, and grown on for sales at a later date—whether it be several weeks or months.

Crops that require 14 weeks and less to be salable in a 32-cell pack are often fast growing plants that will finish in a quart container between 16 and 19 weeks after sowing. In many plants, the key difference between the weeks noted is the increased amount of root activity and not the amount of foliage on top.

After winter- and early spring-sown crops are sold green in small pots during the following spring and summer, many plants often appear to "rest" once they are planted to the garden. Some crops will not grow much larger than the original crown of foliage that was present when they were planted to the garden. In many cases, the root growth will develop the first summer at the expense of the foliage. The following year, the plants will grow to the height noted in the manual. While some crops do grow well the first summer from a winter sowing, develop a strong crown of foliage and even flower, the majority of seed-grown cultivars are best sown the prior year, overwintered as small plants, and then sold in the spring.

Bare-root divisions or transplants. Whether you purchase bare-root divisions or transplants from commercial propagators or dig and divide your own plants, you need to keep the following information in mind.

- Many plants will flower during the summer from roots potted up from October to March depending on the size of the root and the amount of the cold storage the plants received. These plants will need as much time as possible to develop both the roots and foliage. Whether potted in October or March, many will flower the following summer either in the garden or left in the pot. However, the earlier potting helps develop a stronger root and shoot system, encouraging not only flower buds but more profusely flowering plants that will become more mature in size and habit during their first summer.

- In a number of cases, purchased bare-root plants can be divided or separated when they are received. The later in the year it is and the fewer vegetative buds you leave on each division, the smaller the overall plant will be at selling time in the quart or gallon pot. When these plants are placed in a retail sales area, consumers may view the variety as weak or inferior compared to other plants that were produced by different production and propagation procedures.

Plugs. Commercial propagating companies offer a wide range of herbaceous and some woody perennials from late summer to spring as plugs or liners. In the greenhouse industry there is some confusion over these two terms. I am using the word plugs to define flats designed to hold 125 plantlets or more, ranging all the way to 800. Commonly, 125 to 400 cells or plugs per flat are available from commercial companies. These are potted up into various container sizes. In some cases when using small plugs, several plugs (three or four) are used for large containers (2- or 3-gallon). As for liners, mostly 32 to 125 cells per standard flat, they are just large plugs. Liners are most commonly potted one liner per quart or gallon pot.

Many growers purchase either liners or plugs during mid or late autumn and throughout the winter for transplanting directly into the final container. Plugs purchased in the late summer months are usually planted into quart and gallon containers. Trays delivered in February or March are potted up into 4- to 6-inch (10 to 15 cm) pots.

Crops transplanted to quart and gallon pots during summer and autumn will be salable the following spring after being held dormant or grown cold during the winter. Most of these will flower their first year. Note that when purchasing and/or potting plugs or liners in the winter or early spring, many crops can be sold between eight and 15 weeks after potting when grown in 4-inch (10 cm) or quart containers at 50F to 55F (10C to 13C) nights.

Media. There are many books and reference guides to walk you through soil science. In this manual I am providing the media and fertilization practices we use for the plants we grow in our gardens.

There are a number of possible media mixtures that are equally as effective as the ones provided. Local or regional amendments that are more cost-effective than those I have written about but still provide the same consistent growing performance should be considered as well. As for fertility, it depends on your media and water quality, though the basics still apply. Before potting up your crop, you need to review criteria for your media: high or low pH, high or low fertility, amendment with slow release fertilizers, etc.

Soil test. While you've heard it before, a soil test that reports pH, cation exchange capacity, and fertility levels is the place to start. The information should include nitrogen, phosphorous, potassium, and key micronutrients. Combined, the results of a soil and water test will give you an idea of the fertilizer requirements you will need and any additional soil or water amendments required for successful crops.

Media amendments. When choosing a medium for your operation, consider your production cycles. For instance, regardless of the propagation method, plants potted during midwinter and spring can be treated differently with regard to their media than those potted up in the late summer or autumn. When potting up various perennials in the late summer or autumn for sales the following spring, I add in a percentage of pasteurized field soil to the media if growing in quart or gallon pots.

In my opinion, the added buffering capacity, weight, and mineral features of soil help in overwintering perennials and growing a superior crop. The quantity can vary from 10 to 20% of the total makeup of the mix. Many growers, however, rely on commercial soilless medias instead of incorporating soil into their production regimes. Commercially, there are a number of soilless medias available to use. From Ball Seed Company, we use Ball Growing Mix 2, a blend of bark, peat, vermiculite, and perlite. This is a coarser mix useful when potting up perennials in the late summer and fall for overwintering. It also is the media that we used to provide all the crop times in this manual. Other companies sell comparable products that can be used successfully when following the culture provided within the manual. When potting up during autumn, it is best to avoid starter fertilizers containing slow release urea, as they promote soft, succulent growth that is more prone to dying if frosted. For plants potted up in the winter or spring, especially to 4-inch (10 cm) containers and cell packs, I prefer only commercial soilless medias instead. In these cases, I use a similar blend, bark, peat, vermiculite, and perlite, to what I use for overwintering, though in a smaller particle size. Ball Growing Mix is the product I used to provide the cultural data noted within this book. When used in smaller containers, this media helps to minimize voids, allowing for faster root formation.

Media components. The components of a good medium for perennial plant production include, but are not limited to, commercial soilless mixtures, peat moss, composted pine bark, field soil, sharp sand (construction grade, not fine), Styrofoam, perlite, and vermiculite. While these make up the greatest percentage by volume of the medium, there are a number of other components to consider as well. These include lime, wetting agents, micronutrient packages, slow release fertilizers, and gypsum.

If you are not prepared to evaluate the various components of a make-your-own-media, then start with a commercial soilless mix and add additional components as necessary. Companies specializing in commercial soilless mixes offer them in bulk as well as individual bags. These companies can provide suggestions of additional amendments based on various crops and production methods, including perennials.

Another service these companies may offer is a customized blend based on your region within North America and the available selection of local materials. This helps reduce costs for your media mix.

Fertilizer. Fertilizer applications are equally as varied as media mixtures. First, start with both a soil and water test to verify the quality of both. From here, you can proceed in one of several directions. If you have mixed your own media, you may want to add a slow release fertilizer such as Osmocote, a micronutrient package, and various pH modifiers such as limestone. A high or low pH will affect the fertilizers you are using by making them unavailable to the plant or present in such high concentrations as to cause damage.

If you are purchasing commercial bulk mixes, review the information provided by the company you are working with as to the starter charges within the media. If you are unfamiliar with what you can add or do with the media, contact the supplying company with additional questions prior to potting up your plants.

Water soluble fertilizers. Once potted, we adopt a normal fertilization program by injecting water soluble fertilizers into our irrigation water. We usually purchase commercial blended fertilizers to provide consistent performance. During spring and other periods of active growth we often apply 200 to 250 ppm of nitrogen and potassium at every watering to pots without slow release fertilizers.

On plants overwintered dormant in our cold frames, fertilization does not begin until warm weather is expected to remain and regrowth has begun. Fertilizing during periods of warm days and cold nights can lead to soft growth that is readily frosted back at night. Instead, we wait until late March or early April before we begin a normal fertilizing schedule.

For late summer and autumn potted perennials we avoid slow release fertilizers in favor of water soluble ones that are applied through our injector. We avoid introducing high amounts of fertility into the media at this time so that we don't have crown foliage growth at the expense of roots. We concentrate on establishing roots to increase the plant's potential for winter survival.

Temperatures. The temperatures noted under each crop in this book are minimum *night* temperatures for active growth. Daytime temperatures are expected to be higher by 8F to 20F (4C to 11C). Temperatures can be used to manage the growth of herbaceous perennials. Depending on the type of plant (cold versus warm season plants) as well as your purpose, perennials can be subjected to temperatures ranging from 30F to 80F (-1C to 27C). With perennials, manipulating temperatures can be used to your advantage as long as you know your plants' needs.

Temperatures for seed germination through transplant are provided under **Germination overview**. Upon transplanting, perennials are often grown on at no lower than 55F to 58F (13C to 14C) nights for the first week or two to allow the roots to establish and the top growth to develop. After this time, night temperatures can be lowered as necessary to no lower than 48F (9C) for active growth especially on winter-sown seed.

We have gone as low as 45F (7C) nights with limited problems, though time to finishing has been longer on some plants. The foliage may turn from green to shades of purple and crimson but not to black, frozen leaves.

Stressful temperatures. Note that perennials being grown in small 2- or 3-inch (5 or 7 cm) pots, and especially those in cell packs, may be stressed at temperatures of 48F (9C) and lower. While appearing hardened off and healthy looking, the plant may "sit" in the garden upon planting and not develop much more that year. In other cases, the plants may prematurely flower on small, undersized plants. In both instances, the plants may not overwinter in the home garden. On plants produced from cell packs and small 3- and 4-inch (7 and 10 cm) pots, keep the night temperatures at no lower than 50F (10C) for best performance, and pot to larger containers as they become rootbound.

There are a number of perennials that do not tolerate cold temperatures well and, depending on the crop, their foliage may yellow and drop, or they will try to go dormant, or in severe cases, the plant may die. Summer Sun heliopsis, hibiscus cultivars, and *Asclepias tuberosa* are three examples of warmth-loving crops that prefer night temperatures of 55F (13C) and higher.

If sowing seed during the summer for overwintering pots for sales the following year, heliopsis will emerge by mid-May here in our Chicago climate and look healthy with no yellowing when the night temperatures are still 40F to 50F (4C to 10C).

However, from sowings made during December or January, plants subjected to 50F (10C) nights during March have resulted in loss of lower leaves and leaf yellowing. The plants seldom die or go dormant, but aesthetically the plants are not attractive. *Asclepias tuberosa*, on the other hand, will lose all its leaves and appear to attempt dormancy. In some cases, the plant will die.

Note: This book does not cover the issues of overwintering perennials in a dormant state between 30F and 34F (-1C and 1C). Keep in mind that some of the highest losses in perennials are due to warm winter or early spring days and cold nights below 38F (3C). Alternate freezing and thawing of developing green growth and plant roots usually leads to rot and eventually death. The term most often used to define this is "winterkill."

Special needs. Under each crop culture, details have been provided on crops that have special needs that should be addressed. In some cases, these are related to temperatures; in others, it is pH, media, container size, cultivar selection, or some other need.

■ VARIETIES

In my opinion, this is the most challenging area in growing perennials. Most perennials are known by their botanical names along with common names. Since many people have a hard time with the botanical name, you and your staff should also be familiar with regional common names. To capture the perennial plant enthusiast, you have to talk in his or her language—and the botanical name is the controlling authority. However, to the home gardener looking for that "something different" plant, the common name will be more readily used.

One area of horticultural mysticism that I have noticed is three words that are often used interchangeably—in error—variety, cultivar, and clone. Though this section is headlined **Varieties**, I am not making references to nomenclature. Instead, I am providing a breakdown of the available selections of a genus and species.

Botanically the word *variety* is used to separate slight differences between selections within a species, and though the plants can be propagated vegetatively, they will also come true-to-type when sown from seed. The term *cultivar* was penned by Dr. Liberty Hyde Bailey in the early 1920s to define crops in cultivation that were of unknown origin and not naturally occurring. Short for cultivated variety, the term is not that different in definition from variety and many horticulturists today, regardless of historical significance, use the two terms interchangeably.

For a number of years, the term cultivar was used incorrectly to define plants that were vegetatively propagated as opposed to being raised from seed. Today, the term *clone* is used to define these crops. A clone is considered to be an individual from which all additional plants are vegetatively propagated. In general, all subsequent plants are developed from pieces of the original plant. This is especially true in plants that are unable to set seed; or when seed is produced, the resulting plant would not be true to the mother plant.

Plant names in horticulture are governed by the International Code of Botanical Nomenclature, which serves as the authority in the taxonomic order of plants. While it has no legal power to enforce its findings, taxonomic changes are internationally endorsed, though not without some grumbling, as in the case of the more recent name change of the genus *Chrysanthemum* to *Dendranthema*.

If we were to hold to our own view and endorse *Chrysanthemum* as the only true name of the genus as a whole instead of adopting *Dendranthema*, *Tanacetum*, and *Leucanthemum* as noted by the Code, it is possible that we could confuse particular crops when trying to place orders or talking to people about a plant, whether it be someone inside or outside of the United States. It is imperative therefore that we have a common ground, an internationally accepted agreement, for the correct botanical names of plants.

In this book, the available selections on the market, both popular and less known, are provided under the heading of **Varieties**. Height, habit, flower color, other descriptive information and whether the crop is propagated vegetatively or from seed are noted.

■ Related material

In some cases there are a number of other species worth mentioning. If so, I have either covered them in the manual as separate crops, or I have included them in this section. Any growing information provided is specific to the crop covered under **Related material**. All other information under the remaining headings is specific to the genus/species that begins each crop culture.

■ Uses

In an attempt to provide the many uses of the class as a whole, this category is based on what has shown promise over the years in various settings. The most common use of these plants is within the perennial border. Border here implies a bed of any length with a 3- to 6-foot (0.9 to 1.8 m) depth, planted with various complimentary perennials arranged in mass.

Other uses include plants that are suited to the rock garden, used as cut flowers, or planted in the commercial or home landscape, or possibly planted in a container or basket.

▬▬▬ IN THE HOME GARDEN

For those of you in retail, this section can give you some ideas on how the variety will perform when planted to the garden. Comments are provided on staking, deadheading, rebloom, spacing (if not provided under the description), where to plant (full sun, partial shade, etc.), plus other topics.

Without lessening the impact of this information, let me remind you that the details provided use our Chicago area test gardens as the primary focal point unless stated otherwise.

Propagation Techniques

Propagating plants is not a difficult procedure once you know the techniques and the ways to improve your germination or rooting performance. The larger concern is identifying the reasons for failure in the first place. Growers measure propagation success in a number of ways. The more technologically advanced a greenhouse operation is, the higher the expected percentage for seedling emergence or rooted cuttings.

The reasons for propagation failure vary from too cool a rooting temperature to dormancy. With perennials, one year you can get over 80% germination or 70 to 90% rooting on a crop, and the following year, using the exact same procedures, you can get nothing more than 50%. At this early stage, handling care and quick response are keys to attaining superior performance.

This chapter is broken down into the primary forms of propagation including divisions, cuttings, and seed as well as their subparts. Other forms, such as tissue culture, grafting, budding (or bud grafting) and other highly specialized procedures are noted under the crop cultures to better inform you. They are not, however, covered in the propagation section of this book.

Appendix 3 provides propagation methods for the crops. The crop cultures offer additional details.

A more thorough understanding of all forms of propagation is available in the fifth edition of *Plant Propagation* by Hartmann, Kester, and Davies. Review the **Reference List** in this book if you are not familiar with their work.

■ Propagation by Division

A number of horticultural references discuss propagating plants by divisions. Depending on which one you use, the definition of the term may differ slightly, but the result is the same—a plant is vegetatively increased by taking a portion of the root along with a plantlet or section that includes a vegetative shoot. In some cases, the root can be rather large, awkward in shape, and somewhat difficult to handle.

The success of a division is, in my opinion, knowing the time of year to divide a crop, how old a planting should be to get the greatest number of transplants, and how small a transplant can be to be successful in rooting and growing. Dividing plants is expensive and labor intensive where nursery beds are maintained with stock plants that are systematically lifted, divided, and stored. The field itself is then prepared for replanting from transplants or from seedling or vegetative plugs.

If you sell a wide assortment of herbaceous perennial plants, maintaining and propagating your own plants by division is usually not practical. Labor, digging and planting equipment, as well as maintaining a large acreage, are key factors to consider before doing your own divisions. Time and storage are high on the list as well. Do you have the time to lift and divide the crop efficiently when it should be done?

If you are in an area of the country where the winters are cold and/or wet, such as Chicago and most sections of Zone 6 north, field digging is difficult from mid-November to early March. Late summer and autumn digging is common, and the bare roots are held in cold storage until shipped or potted.

When to divide

Dividing plants is commonly done either in the late summer or early spring. An old rule of thumb is that you divide spring flowering plants in the late summer or autumn and the summer flowering plants in the early spring. While this is still practiced, there are a number of exceptions. Plus a number of spring flowering plants root well when divided during June or July and actually perform better the following spring than those divided in the late summer.

Review the information provided in **Appendix 3** on the crops that can be divided and the appropriate season of year. Spring digging is more applicable for home gardeners due to the availability of time and field conditions in March and April. Regrettably, spring dividing refers to plants that can be divided up until June, but commercially they should be dug no later than May 1 to be available for spring container sales.

Sources

Nursery operations and commercial propagators offering divisions are usually set up in such a way that they already have an educated labor force, appropriate equipment, and/or the facilities for dividing and separating herbaceous perennials. Woody and herbaceous perennials do not differ as much in their needs from a nursery perspective as they do when looking at them from a commercial greenhouse point-of-view. While greenhouse growers may have the knowledge and facilities to finish off their product, they are more adept at propagating by seed or cuttings, since these crops can be greenhouse or cold-frame grown or maintained for their entire lives.

Maintaining stock beds

If you are in the commercial greenhouse business selling either wholesale or retail, there are a number of advantages in keeping a limited number of stock beds of perennials to divide. Some of these include:

1. You are selling retail and a difficult to find or frequently backordered perennial commands top dollar at the cash register. However, there is a "catch." A number of times this may be a slow growing crop that requires three or more years to propagate. Be sure to check the crop time required by the plant you are considering.

2. A select few, possibly native or regional herbaceous perennial favorites, are not readily available. In these cases the crop offers your operation a promotional and marketing opportunity.

3. You have found the "trick" to successfully divide and increase a perennial that your competition still has to purchase in.

4. You have found a sport or mutation occurring on a plant that you cannot find commercially available in the trade. On these crops, however, keep in mind that some plants commonly sport and may already be available commercially from another or several growers.

5. You want to sell wholesale and have the acreage, equipment, facilities, methods of shipment, knowledgeable labor, and the understanding of a crop's needs to be successful.

Commercially, companies like Walters Gardens, DeVroomen, and others sell their field-grown crops as divisions or as bare-root transplants. Regardless of the title, the bare-root plants are one-, two- or three-year-old field-grown plants that are dug, washed of their soil, sold "as is" or divided, and then either cold stored or shipped immediately. Upon receiving these plants, they can be potted up into quart or larger containers depending on the root size.

In the various lectures I have attended, the propagation books I have read, and the pamphlets that I have reviewed, divisions can be listed more broadly than I have done. In some cases, division has a broad definition that encompasses many of the aspects of ground or below ground propagation, including rhizomes, runners, stolons, and offsets. For my part, I have included them in this chapter under the heading of **Other propagation methods**.

■ PROPAGATION BY CUTTINGS

Like divisions, the term "cutting" is equally broad in its scope. The process of taking a cutting is not limited to removing a section from the stock plant and sticking it into a media to root. Though this may define the process, it is far more involved. The degree to which a cutting will root, as opposed to rot, depends on a number of factors. The age of the cutting, the place on the plant that you took the cutting from, and the portion of the stem that you use are just three factors that can drastically change the performance of a crop in rooting quickly or even rooting at all.

When someone says he produces a crop from cuttings, he is usually referring to stem cuttings taken from actively developing growth, which is the most popular form of cutting propagation. Other types of cuttings that can be taken include basal cuttings, leaf cuttings, and root cuttings.

STEM CUTTINGS

Stem cuttings range from taking only the terminal tip (tip cuttings) to removing an entire stem and cutting it up into sections, each with two or three nodes and a pair of leaves. These are then stuck into a propagation medium and allowed to root. The practice itself is simple and straightforward except for the importance of the stem's age. Terminal cuttings taken off of herbaceous perennials are usually supple and easily bent; the woody tissues have yet to form. This is not the case for all herbaceous perennials, nor is it true the farther down the stem from the tip that you go. In these cases, some additional terms are necessary.

1. **Softwood stem cuttings.** Softwood cuttings are the primary source of herbaceous perennials cuttings. During the spring and other periods of active growth, the plant stems are supple, easily bent, with recently developed leaves. The plant has yet to bud or flower nor has it developed any woody tissue at the stem's base. Some authors use the word juvenile to define these tissues. Once cut, the cuttings are handled in a number of ways.

   If a crop wilts easily, the cuttings are taken from the stock plants, the leaves are trimmed, and the cuttings are immediately stuck into a propagation medium for rooting. For those that are not as sensitive, the leaves may still be trimmed, but the cuttings are allowed to "dry" or "harden" prior to sticking. This can range from minutes to several hours, depending on the crop. In some cases, the cuttings can be moist chilled for several days at 40F (4C) before they are stuck.

   Softwood cuttings are susceptible to disease—primarily rots. However, waiting for these shoots to harden or stiffen to lessen the suppleness of the cutting may lead to a longer rooting time for the cutting. Softwood cuttings are taken during active growth from midspring through the early summer.

2. **Semihardwood stem cuttings.** Semihardwood cuttings are taken on plants where the stem has started to stiffen and auxiliary and terminal buds are forming or are present, but the stem is not yet woody. Sometimes referred to as semiripe cuttings, these are taken mid to late summer to allow them to root prior to the onset of cold weather. They can be rooted in greenhouses or cold frames and potted up into

4-inch (10-cm), quart, or gallon containers depending on the crop and the size of the plant being transplanted.

While not as popular for herbaceous perennials as softwood cuttings, semihardwood cuttings can be made on a number of broad-leaved evergreen perennials. They are especially useful if these crops cannot be propagated earlier due to time, labor, or both.

3. **Hardwood stem cuttings.** These are not frequently done on herbaceous perennials and are usually reserved for woody trees and shrubs. There are a limited number of perennials that fall between the herbaceous and woody plant categories. While they may have woody stems, the stems may be wiry and/or thin in appearance, and most often the plant lacks the definition reserved for our impression of a tree or shrub. Some clematis varieties can be propagated in this manner. This propagation method is used as a last effort.

4. **Basal cuttings.** In the late winter or early spring as plants are emerging from their winter dormancy, the crown of the developing plant has many single-stemmed shoots. These are harvested as described for a softwood cutting and will usually root quickly. In some cases, the stem piece removed may already have a developing adventitious root. For the flowering perennials that emerge first in the spring, cuttings should be taken as soon as they are ready, but prior to bud set. If you wait until the stem starts to elongate, flower buds may have already started to form. If flower buds start to develop, wait until after flowering to take your stem cuttings.

5. **Leaf cuttings.** Leaf cuttings are used least for propagating perennials. For those plants (whether perennial or not) that produce small, rooted, or nonrooted plantlets at the base of a leaf or along its outer margin, the procedure is easy and rewarding. In most cases, however, the process is far more involved. Some plants will form a vegetative bud and shoot from a rooting leaf section. In other cases, an individual leaf is laid flat on the propagation media and its midrib and veins slashed to allow for the exposed ends to touch the medium. A vegetative bud will then develop a shoot. In a third scenario, a leaf is removed along with its petiole, and the latter is stuck into the propagation medium to allow it to root and send up a vegetative shoot.

These methods are more commonly done by the home gardener. If the leaves have yet to form buds or root—as in the case of the first example above—it means a long propagation time. The plants may take so long to root that you may forget you did the procedure in the first place.

Rooting the cuttings

1. **Nodes.** Additional factors need to be considered for effective rooting when propagating by cuttings. Nodal cuttings (places along the stem where new shoots and

leaves develop) and internodal cuttings (the elongated portions in between the nodes) may root equally on a particular crop, though in others the newly developing roots may arise primarily from the node. On softwood and semihardwood cuttings, I allow for at least two nodes per cutting so I can plunge one node below the medium surface and leave the second one exposed, preferably with at least a leaf or two attached. Notice that I did not mention the length of the cutting in relation to the nodes. While I prefer a cutting of 2 or 3 inches (5.1 or 7.6 cm), I am looking for at least two nodes on a stem as well. This is a personal preference, not a scientific one.

2. **Leaves.** I like to have several leaves on a cutting for effective rooting. Even with only one leaf, cuttings root faster for us than if they were totally leafless. Research work by both Mahlstede and Haber as well as Hartmann, Kester, and Davies supports this theory. While their work focuses primarily on woody perennials, herbaceous perennials will show similar results.

The number of leaves and their size is another criteria I review when taking my own cuttings. Again, for me personally, I take cuttings with either two or three individual or pairs of leaves per stem on plants with medium-sized, 1- to 2-inch (2.5 to 5 cm) long leaves. On those plants with large, robust leaves, I trim the foliage back one-third to one-half its size. On those plants with numerous leaflets that are small (less than 1 inch [2.5 cm] long and longer than they are wide), I sometimes leave a number of leaflets on the cutting—five to eight leaflets or more, depending on the crop.

Regardless of the number of leaves, I attempt to keep a leaflet above the propagation medium during rooting, while the node where a leaf is attached may be below the medium surface. The leaflet itself is above the soil line. Leaves buried in the propagation medium often rot before the cutting roots, increasing your chances for disease problems with the cutting itself.

3. **Media.** There is no one propagation medium for all crops, though many growers use a standard mix that they adopt since it has been successful in the past. Some use commercially prepared mixes, while others may mix in one or more additional components to their purchased bag mix. Still others use their own blend of components to make their own propagation media. Regardless, the basics are still the same.

The primary components of a good propagation medium are peat, sand, vermiculite, perlite, and bark. Other components include rock wool, field soil, and polystyrene. Additional detail can be found in propagation books about the use of these and other products. Growers vary in the amount of each component that they use in their mix. Some use straight sand or peat while others use blends, including peat-perlite, peat-vermiculite, peat-bark-sand, peat-sand, etc. The percentage of each component varies with the crop, previous success, and time of year.

There is no one pH range that fits all plants. Mahlstede and Haber found a range of pH 7.0 to 7.2 to be most effective in rooting softwood cuttings. However, they also commented that there was limited callus formation from which the roots arise [6]. They also said that plants growing in lower pH areas would possibly root better in peat moss.

4. **Temperature, moisture, and humidity.** Media that is kept between 65F to 70F (18C to 21C) with an air temperature of 55F to 60F (13C to 16C) is best for herbaceous cuttings. Cuttings should be thoroughly moist around their stem ends but not wet. The medium should be well drained but should not dry out, and the relative humidity should be 95% or above. However, keep in mind that gray-green foliage plants like lavender, *Artemisia*, and others often rot with high relative humidity and overhead misting or watering. It is helpful to move these crops out of the propagation house as soon as roots start to emerge.

Fog is another method that you can employ in rooting and managing your cuttings. Gray-green or pubescent (hairy) foliage plants are less apt to rot, and plants usually root faster in a propagation house incorporating fog.

Now that you have your cuttings, you can stick them into a propagation area to allow for rooting. Another method is to stick your cuttings directly into a liner or plug tray of 50 to 200 cells with your propagation medium. The trays are placed over bottom heat and sometimes covered with a Reemay or Kimberly Row Cover type of material to reduce transpiration (water loss through the leaves), while some crops are given mist.

Fog, however, often replaces mist in commercial operations specializing in perennials due to the various cultural needs of the multitude of plants that they are growing. In most cases, cuttings are stuck one stem per cell pack, though with selected crops (varieties of sedum, thyme, etc.), two to four cuttings are stuck per plug.

Factors that determine rooting of cuttings. Cuttings are easy to take but require special attention on some crops. Here are a few tips to consider.

1. **Timing.** In general, cuttings of summer and fall flowering material are taken during the spring before the plants have started to send up flower buds. Spring flowering plants are trimmed back after flowering and fertilized to produce a mass of new growth. This growth becomes the parent material that cuttings are taken from. Cuttings can be taken off of field grown plants, leftover perennials from the sales area, or stock plants in a greenhouse.

Greenhouse stock plants (the way poinsettia stock plants are grown) are common in perennial plant propagation but are usually maintained by commercial propagators rather than the greenhouse grower due to cost of production, labor, and the vast array of plants. Only plants that are particularly hard to find, frequently unavailable, or sold at a volume that justifies devoting greenhouse space, should be considered for stock production.

2. **Rooting agents.** Many growers use a rooting agent or compound to encourage the quick development of roots. Both IBA (indolebutyric acid) and NAA (naphthaleneacetic acid) are common rooting hormones, and they are sold either mixed together or separately. A number of trade names and formulations are available in the United States including Hormex, Hormodin, and Rootone. While most of these contain only IBA or NAA, some have fungicides and other ingredients as well to protect the cuttings from rotting initially.

   If you are mixing your own compound, start with a 2:1 ratio of the two hormones (1.0% IBA to 0.5% NAA). The ratio can differ based on the plant's ease of rooting plus the type of cutting (softwood versus hardwood) taken. Experienced propagators vary the percentages based on these factors and personal experience.

3. **Stock plants.** When maintaining plants in a greenhouse for cuttings, be sure to grow the plants with ample water and, if necessary, feed prior to taking the cuttings. Some growers use a preventative fungicide spray over the tops of the plants several days before cuttings are taken to reduce the chances of rot in the propagation bench. Prior to taking cuttings, maintain stock plants with a high carbohydrate level and a low nitrogen level. To achieve this, reduce the amount of nitrogen-based fertilizers and use formulations higher in potassium.

ROOT CUTTINGS

There are a number of herbaceous and woody perennials that will produce a vegetative shoot from a root. Granted, there are far more plants that will produce adventitious roots (roots arising from any plant part other than by normal development of the seedling root) than adventitious shoots. In other words, the plants possess the ability to develop rootlets from their own stems. Once cut and stuck to a propagation medium, a cutting develops rootlets at the base of what used to be a rootless stem. Developing adventitious vegetative shoots is a different matter.

Few plants have roots that can be cut into sections, placed in a propagation medium and successfully rooted to produce vegetative shoots. Unlike stem cuttings, root cuttings require more time to develop these buds and grow into a salable plant. Taking root cuttings is one of the harder and less successful methods of propagating perennials and is only recommended when other methods haven't worked or for crops where this is the only reliable replication method known.

1. **Timing.** Root cuttings are taken during the fall and winter. We have had the best success taking root cuttings during fall and early winter in our Chicago location. Identify the crops you will propagate this way in the autumn prior to overwintering and put the plants where you can get to them easily during winter. We keep our stock plants either in ground beds or large pots within the cold frame during the winter so that the plants can be lifted when we want. Regardless of the way

you store the plants for the winter, be sure that you can get to them when you want to start propagating by root cuttings.

Plants from which root cuttings are to be taken are lifted from stock or nursery areas in late winter or early spring. There are some exceptions, *Papaver orientale* for example, and these should be taken during August or September when the plant is dormant in the field or garden. Avoid taking root cuttings once dormancy has broken since stored food may be depleted, which will result in smaller roots.

2. **Root type.** Plants with either fine or fleshy roots are most commonly used for root cuttings of herbaceous perennials.

Thin, delicate roots are cut into lengths of 1 or 2 inches (2.5 cm or 5 cm) and scattered across the propagation medium surface. These are then covered with a one-half-inch layer of media and moistened. Cover with a layer of plastic or glass to maintain moisture. Callus tissue will form, and both root and shoots will develop from adventitious buds along the root section.

Fleshy roots are cut into lengths of 2 to 3 inches (5 cm to 7 cm) and inserted vertically into the propagation medium (often coarse sand or peat moss). As you take the cuttings, be sure to maintain the correct polarity (which end is up and which is down).

Hartmann, Davies, and Kester provide the following information: "To avoid planting [the roots] upside down, the proximal end (nearest the crown of the plant) may be made with a straight cut and the distal end (away from the crown) with a slanting cut. The proximal end of the root piece should always be up. In planting, insert the cutting vertically so that the top is at about soil level. With many species, however, it is satisfactory to plant the cuttings horizontally 1 to 2 inches (2.5 to 5.1 cm) deep, avoiding the possibility of planting them upside down."[4]

Once stuck, follow the same conditions as noted for fine-rooted plants.

3. **Temperature.** Regardless of the type of root you take, once it is stuck into the propagation medium, grow on cool between 50F and 60F (10C and 16C) until rooting and shoot emergence. Root cuttings taken from January to early March will start to develop small plantlets within four to eight weeks. The increasing day and night temperatures of warmer weather will help to promote steady growth, and small plants will be sized up to 3- or 4-inch (7 or 10 cm) pots from June to August depending on the crop. Some fast growing perennials can be sold in 4-, 5- or 6-inch (10, 12, or 15 cm) pots in the autumn. Slow growing plants can be potted up into gallon containers when ready, grown for the remainder of the summer, and then overwintered dormant in a cold frame or other structure for spring sales the following year.

Be sure not to strip the mother plant of all its roots, otherwise it will die. A general rule of thumb is to leave up to 6 inches of root growth after pruning.

The following crops can be propagated by root cuttings. This is only a partial list.

Crop type*	Root
Acanthus	fleshy
Achillea	fine
Anchusa	fine
Anemone	fine
Asclepias	fleshy
Dicentra	fleshy
Dictamnus	fleshy
Echinops	fleshy
Eryngium	fine
Gaillardia	fine
Geranium	fine
Gypsophila	fleshy
Limonium	fleshy
Monarda	fleshy
Oenothera	fine
Papaver orientale	fleshy
Phlox	fine
Primula	fine
Salvia	fine
Stokesia	fine
Verbascum	fine

*Not every species under a genus can be propagated by root cuttings. Review the crop cultures for the best and most economical vegetative propagation methods.

Source: Adapted from A.C. Hottes, *Plant Propagation* [5].

■ SEED PROPAGATION AND GERMINATION

Seed is not a revered method of propagation in herbaceous perennial production, but it is a common one. Propagating plants by seed is the standard method in many classes of plants including perennials.

Seed is the cheapest way in terms of production costs to propagate perennials, though it comes with its own limitations. The following points on seed propagation will give you a better idea of what to expect.

22

ADVANTAGES OF SEED PROPAGATION

- Seed can be sown almost any time of the year (there are limitations provided later) while other propagation methods are usually seasonal—some plants produce their best cuttings when taken during the spring and summer; divisions in the spring or fall, etc.
- Most seed varieties are initially disease free, which is especially valuable if purchasing or treating seed with fungicides.
- Seed is easier to import from or export to other countries than vegetative material.
- While rates vary, many herbaceous perennials will consistently germinate at 70% or better.

DISADVANTAGES OF SEED PROPAGATION

- Many seed-propagated perennial varieties will produce off-types or rogues. These can be sources of new varieties. Off-types can be as unimportant as a shaded flower color or as significant as variable habit and height, which can result in nonuniform cropping. It is this latter problem that tarnishes the reputation of seed-propagated perennials.
- Though many crops germinate readily at 70% and greater, germination rates of a minimum of 85% are necessary for plug production. Germination rates of 80% and lower limit the acceptance by plug growers due to the amount of replugging later, as well as the amount of available material. In these cases, crops propagated by cuttings may be more economical.
- Difficulty in obtaining the varieties you are looking for. Most U.S. and Canadian seed companies carry a minimal selection of the thousands of perennials that are available from seed. European sources offer the best selection, though some U.S. firms, Germania in particular, also carry a wide variety.
- Difficulty in germinating. Purchased seed of some perennials may be dormant, requiring extensive germination techniques. For these you should maintain your own stock plants and gather your seed at the appropriate time.
- Nonuniformity of cropping. Bedding plants as a group germinate within a narrow range of temperatures and will be salable in cell packs from eight to 20 weeks, depending on the crop. Perennials are far more variable with some requiring 20 weeks just to germinate.

So why grow from seed? There are literally hundreds of species or varieties that can be sown from seed with limited problems. Many lend themselves well to commercial production and can be sown, germinated, grown, and sold with ease. However, an equal number of crops require special handling or often fail to reach 70% germination. This is the opportunity of perennials.

23

Along with herbs, perennials have yet to achieve the favor in the professional breeder's eye that bedding plants, cut flowers, and vegetables have received. There are many things to discover, challenges to overcome, and a multitude of opportunities that exist to propel your operation above your competition. To this end, propagating by seed can be very rewarding.

Unlike annual plants, perennials vary widely in how the various genera are germinated. Some perennials can be sown in a similar fashion to annuals and grown along with them for sales in the spring. However, perennials are better sold retail in 3-inch (7 cm) pots and larger rather than in cell packs. You will need to employ several germination procedures if you intend to have a wide selection of perennials from seed.

The challenge of germinating perennial seed goes beyond knowing the right soil temperature, whether the seed should be covered or left exposed, and other common factors affecting seed germination. The inability for a perennial seed variety to germinate may also be due to empty seed coats, immature or improperly conditioned embryos, or unique environmental conditions found within the plant's native habitat.

EASY-TO-GERMINATE PERENNIAL SEED

There are a number of herbaceous perennial plant varieties that will readily germinate from seed, and in many cases seedlings will emerge one and two weeks after sowing. In other plants, the seedlings will emerge after two to four weeks. Here "easy to germinate" refers not only to a short period from seed to seedling but also 60% or greater germination. The list of these items is the longest of the classifications noted here, and details are provided in the appendices located at the back of the book.

Seeds are generally germinated in commercial propagation mixes in a temperature range of 60F to 72F (16C to 22C). In some cases the seed is covered, and in other cases it is left exposed. Specifics are found in the crop culture section of this book.

Some perennials will germinate readily yielding 60 to 70% germination in only seven to 10 days. Regardless of when the seedlings emerge, once germination begins, remove the flat or plug tray from the germination bench or chamber to an environment where the seedlings are protected from direct sun and grown on at 58F to 65F (14C to 18C) nights and 68F to 80F (20C to 27C) days.

PERENNIALS REQUIRING PRETREATMENT

Unfortunately, there are other perennials that germinate randomly, not all at once. Termed "flushing," a group of seedlings (from 5 to 15% or slightly higher) appears over a period of time. This can range from days to several weeks; in severe cases it can extend over several months. The tricky part here is knowing whether the seed is dead, dormant, or convalescing (about ready to emerge). Under such circumstances, the faster growing seedlings will need to be transplanted as they are ready. After the seedlings are removed, the germination tray is then returned to the bench or chamber to allow for additional seedlings to emerge.

This condition is most severe in those crops that require pretreatments. If seen in normally easy-to-germinate perennial crops, the flushing may be the result of old seed or improperly stored seed, or it may identify crops requiring "moist chilling" or scarification (nicking or slight abrasion to allow the seed to soak up moisture).

Frequently throughout the culture profiles you will find the term "pretreatment" used. It is most often found under the heading of **Germination overview** and occasionally under **Propagation**. Pretreatment is a catchall word that I use to refer to those crops that require some additional methods to attain good germination rates of 50% and higher. Pretreatments can vary from seed that requires a moist-cold period (cold stratification), a warm-moist period (warm stratification) or both, to those that require scarification.

Moist chilling/cold stratification/cold conditioning. I find this propagation method the most challenging. Some may consider root cuttings to be close, but I do not find them as challenging as I do this class.

Historically, stratification was the term used to define the process of placing repeated layers of seed between moistened sand within a wooden box. The box would then be buried out in a nursery row or unheated cold frame and kept in a temperature range of 35F to 40F (1C to 5C) for the winter. Sowings would be made during November or December and the boxes removed in February or March depending on the species, temperatures, and grower experience. This method was normally reserved for woody perennials, but there were a number of herbaceous perennials that benefited from this period of moist chilling as well.

The term "stratification" is occasionally used, but moist chilling is a more accurate and expressive term when discussing herbaceous perennials. Another term, "conditioning" is also occasionally used as well. While the procedure is slightly different than stratification, the results are the same—the exposure of moistened seed to a period of cool/cold temperatures to aid in the germination process.

In some references, the term "frost germinator" is also used but is misleading. Frost germinator implies that seed will germinate if exposed to freezing temperatures for a period of time. This is incorrect since freezing temperatures are often used to store seeds to maintain their germination rates between sowings as opposed to germinating them.

The process of moist chilling seed is easy to do though it requires time. This is not a method that yields quick results. Instead it allows growers to germinate crops that gave them zero or limited seedlings with conventional germination methods.

In its simplest form, moist chilling includes placing seed within moistened peat moss or vermiculite inside a small plastic bag with a sealable top. A clear plastic bag is easy to see through should germination start; it also helps to maintain a high relative humidity and decrease the chances of the medium drying out. The bag is then placed in a home refrigerator and left at 40F (4C) for one to two weeks. When used as a pretreatment, this method helps to improve the overall uniformity and emergence of many herbaceous perennials. It works best on old seed, seed that germinates but the emergence is not uniform, seed that was shipped in paper packets, or any seed that historically has given you mediocre germination rates.

If the seed fails to germinate at all or you have less than 10% germination, the following will be of greater value.

For those crops that need a longer moist chilling to germinate than just one to two weeks, the process is more involved. On difficult crops, subjecting the seed to moist chilling may require up to 12 weeks depending on the crop. If given only one to two weeks of moist chilling, the seed will not germinate freely and overall germination percentages would still be low. In these cases, the seed is said to have an immature embryo and needs to be conditioned prior to germinating. This conditioning is most often done on perennials native to alpinelike habitats.

Sow seed from October to December to a winter-ready flat (wood, reinforced plastic) filled with peat moss. Water the flat in, allowing the seed to be covered lightly but not deeply. Place the flat in an area such as a warm cold frame or greenhouse germination bench that will yield soil temperatures from 55F to 65F (13C to 18C) for a period of four to eight weeks, depending on the genus. This period allows for the seed to absorb or imbibe water and reduce the initial conditions, usually chemical, affecting germination. After four to eight weeks and once the weather turns cold, the flats are ready to be moved from the greenhouse or cold frame.

Move the flats to a sheltered, ground-level or below location, such as an unheated cold frame, to brave the elements. The individual flats are covered with plastic and protected from rapid temperature swings. In a cold frame, the flats can be covered with several layers of the foam insulation used to overwinter perennials in pots.

In ground beds, where flats are placed down inside a chamber covered with a sash, flats can be covered with snow to protect them. It is important to keep the flats protected from daily temperature swings while maintaining a soil temperature of 33F to 38F (1C to 3C) for a period of four to eight weeks.

In February or March the trays can be uncovered and put in an unheated cold frame protected from freezing temperatures. For the first week or two after being put in, keep the soil temperatures between 40F and 50F (4C to 10C) until acclimated. Seedlings will emerge in a range of temperatures from 45F to 60F (7C to 16C) depending on the variety. They may take up to a month to germinate as long as the days are warm and the nights are cool, though no less than 45F (7C) in the cold frame. Temperatures above 70F (21C) cause stress, shock, elongated seedlings, or death. Keep germination temperatures below 68F (20C) as seedlings emerge.

Seeds that benefit from moist chilling are highlighted within the crop profiles and the appendices.

Warm-moist stratification/warm conditioning. The lesser known process of warm-moist stratification is an extremely useful way to germinate those seeds that are double dormant. Not many herbaceous perennials require this treatment.

Double dormancy implies both that the seed coat is impermeable and the embryo is not fully developed. Some argue this latter statement, saying that until water can be absorbed, the seed will not or cannot germinate. It has been theorized that the moisture helps to dilute certain chemicals, thus allowing the process of germination to begin.

Crops that benefit from this method include selected members of the Ranunculaceae family and other woodland plants where the soil becomes dry during the summer months after the mother plant has dropped the seed. The seed is conditioned by its environment to allow for moisture uptake when available. In temperate climates when the weather is favorable, seedlings may start to emerge as early as autumn or winter after a moist-chilling period.

Our Chicago weather is not the same, so we cannot afford to let nature take its course. Seed is collected fresh during June, July, or August, depending on the crop. The seed is immediately placed into wooden trays of moistened peat moss and exposed to daily temperatures of 68F to 86F (20C to 30C) for the remainder of the summer. The media is not allowed to dry out. Once the weather turns cold, we treat them as noted in the section on moist chilling, allowing for 10 to 12 weeks of 35F to 38F (1C to 3C).

Crops that have benefited from this include *Helleborus niger*, *Asarum europaeum*, *Mertensia virginica*.

Scarification. In larger seeded varieties, like many of the pea family, the outer seed coat has a hardened layer that is impermeable to moisture. By nicking, filing, or chipping away a portion of the outer coat, you will allow the flow of moisture to reach the embryo and start the germination process. This nicking is called scarification.

One of the most common suggestions is to pour hot, not boiling, water over the seed. Allow the seed to sit and soak for a period of 12 hours or less for most herbaceous perennials. Seeds that are floating or not swollen after this period will seldom germinate, indicating that the process needs to be repeated, the seed is dormant, or the seed is dead.

For large volumes of seed, consider using a tumbler with coarse, small stones or gravel inside. The seed is poured in, allowed to tumble, and then separated from the stones and sown within several days. Be sure not to damage or expose the embryo during this process. An exposed embryo would cause the seed to die, rot, or affect seedling emergence.

If a smaller volume of seed is to be scarified, rub them between two layers of coarse sandpaper followed by the hot water treatment.

Crops responding to this type of treatment include *Baptisia*, *Lupinus*, and *Lathyrus*.

■ OTHER PROPAGATION METHODS

I am using this category as a catchall to encompass several additional methods of propagation, including runners, stolons, and offsets. Propagation manuals differ in their placement of these three categories. Some place them as their own entity, while others treat them as subgroups under either divisions or cuttings. No matter—within the following paragraphs you will see the relationship to other propagation forms already covered in this chapter. You will also see how these differ, and why they are the easiest of the propagation methods listed in this chapter.

RUNNERS

Runners are above-ground stems. They grow along the soil surface or trail over rocks and are not part of the root system. Runners develop from the crown of a plant producing long sections of stem (called internodes) between two nodes, each with a bud from which leaves can develop. While still attached, leaves may develop at some nodes and, if touching the ground, may form roots.

If left untouched, another stem will develop out of the crown of this satellite plant and produce another plant at the next node. *Fragaria* (strawberry) and *Duchnesa indica* are two plants that exhibit this characteristic.

An interesting feature of runner-producing plants is the rapid movement the plants have across the garden. Take care not to let these plants grow into nearby slower growing plants. During autumn and winter, interconnecting stems may die, but the roots developed at each plantlet will protect the plant through the winter. In the spring, these individual plants can be dug and potted up into 4-inch (10-cm) or quart pots for sales that spring and summer.

STOLONS

Sometimes referred to as runners, stolons differ in that they can be either above or below ground. Above ground the stems grow horizontal to the soil surface, developing a long, rooted stem. This can be lifted, cut into sections, and each piece potted up.

Below ground, stolons are involved in the formation of tubers—as in a potato. While not the tubers themselves, stolons are the lifeline between the tubers and the plant crown. Often white, they are usually smooth and thinner than a pencil.

RHIZOMES

Like stolons, rhizomes are stems, but they only grow below the soil surface. They are thickened stems often knobby in appearance due to the nodes from which shoots and rootlets arise. Rhizomes tend to have one of two growth habits. They may spread rampantly under the ground producing a large spread of vegetative shoots like *Convallaria majalis* (lily-of-the-valley). Or they have a constricted rhizome with a short development like iris. On those rhizomes that spread vigorously, the rhizome itself is often thin, while in plants with constricted rhizomes you will find the stem thickened.

For propagating, rhizomes are treated like a division. Lift the crown, divide the rhizome into sections complete with both root and shoot, and pot immediately.

OFFSETS OR OFFSHOOTS OF ROSETTES

Rosette-forming plants are easily propagated by removing a small crown portion, including several shoots, along with a root piece. These shoots are often small plantlets complete with several stems and an already developing root system. These can be removed from the mother plant and transferred to a propagation area to fully root in two to three weeks and then are potted up. *Armeria* is a good example of this method.

■ REFERENCES

[1] Bird, R. 1993. *Propagation of hardy perennials.* London: B.T. Batsford, Ltd.

[2] Gillette, R. 1983. Propagating perennials. *GrowerTalks* December.

[3] Hartman, H.T., and D.E. Kester. 1983. *Plant propagation: principles and practices.* 4th ed. Englewood Cliffs, New Jersey: Prentice Hall, Inc.

[4] Hartman, H.T., D.E. Kester, and F.T. Davies, Jr. 1990. *Plant propagation: principles and practices.* 5th ed. Englewood Cliffs, New Jersey: Prentice Hall, Inc.

[5] Hottes, A.C. 1947. *Plant propagation.* New York: A.T. De La Mare Co.

[6] Mahlstede, J.P., and E.S. Haber. 1957. *Plant propagation.* New York: John Wiley & Sons, Inc.

[7] Perennial Plant Association. In *Proceedings*, Bulletin 717. Herbaceous Perennial Symposium.

[8] *The New Royal Horticultural Society dictionary of gardening.* 1992. London: The Macmillan Press Limited. New York: The Stockton Press.

[9] Swift, S., and D. Koranski. 1987. A how-to guide to producing perennials. *Greenhouse Grower* April.

[10] Thompson, P. 1992. *Creative propagation.* London: B.T. Batsford, Ltd.

[11] Van Hees, G., and C.D. Hendricks. 1987. Summer Cutting Propagation Workshop. Perennial Plant Symposium. Baltimore, Maryland.

HERBACEOUS PERENNIALS

---■---

149 GENERA, 300 SPECIES

A

■ ACANTHUS MOLLIS

FAMILY: Acanthaceae

COMMON NAME(S): Bear's Breeches

DESCRIPTION

Acanthus mollis is a robust and striking specimen noted for its deep, glossy green leaves on plants from 3 to 4 feet (90 to 120 cm) tall in full bloom. Plants are rather bushy or shrublike in appearance, and each leaf surface can be 1 foot (30 cm) or longer and 6 to 10 inches (15 to 25 cm) wide. The leaves are held singly, radiating out of a basal crown on thick stalks. One plant has an overall spread from 32 to 40 inches (81 to 102 cm) wide. In our cold winter climate in Chicago, however, the plants are often smaller and only marginally hardy.

Flowers are white with purple-rose highlights, single, fluted, and scentless and have been used as dried cut flowers. Unlike other varieties of *Acanthus* that tend to bear imposing thorns on the leaf edges, *A. mollis* lacks thorns and its leaves are less jagged than other varieties. The bracts surrounding the flowers, however, are sharp-edged and can causes minor scratches.

HARDINESS: Zones 6 to 10.
Plants tend to be reliably hardy in Zone 7 and farther south but require winter protection from southern Missouri and Kansas northward. In our Chicago-area gardens (USDA Zone 5), we can reliably overwinter the plants but they seldom flower. Apparently the foliage is hardier than the flowers, although we can only get two to three years of reliable hardiness with increasing losses each season. If our autumn weather in the North is wet and cold, followed by a harsh, cold winter, we will have 100% kill by spring. (Look to related species for additional, hardier varieties.)

SEASON OF BLOOM: June and July.

PROPAGATION

Seed, division, and root cuttings are the preferred propagation methods. Divide in spring or, if done in the fall, be sure that roots have developed before overwintering.

If not properly rooted, plants can heave more easily out of the container during winter. Root cuttings are usually taken after a cold treatment but when the plant is still dormant (January or February). See additional information in the **Propagation Techniques** chapter for further details on root cuttings.

GERMINATION OVERVIEW: 142 seeds per ounce/5 per gram.
Germination temperatures: 65F to 72F (18C to 22C).

No pretreatments are necessary to get germination percentages of 60 to 70% or higher, although on older seed an overnight soaking is suggested. Using fresh or recently harvested seeds will give you the best results. Seeds will germinate in 16 to 21 days, but we have had seedlings appear in as few as eight to 10 days after sowing. Seedlings can be transplanted four to five weeks after sowing.

GROWING ON

Crop time: From seed, *A. mollis* is a vigorous plant that is best transplanted from a germinating or plug flat to a 3-inch (7 cm) pot or comparable cell pack (18 cells per flat). While it may take some time to transplant seedlings, the plants grow quickly once they are established and will need to be transplanted again to a quart, gallon, or other container within a short period of time. The final container size depends on how long you plan to keep the plants in your greenhouse.

A mid-February sowing produces salable 6-inch (15 cm) standard pots by mid-May when grown at 60F (15C) nights using one plant per pot. This is one of the few crops we grow on the warm side since it responds so well to high temperatures. Once outside night temperatures reach 50F (10C) and above, we move the plants to a cold frame for several weeks of hardening off before planting to the garden. Plants will not flower the same season from seed.

Root cuttings taken during January will start to develop in March and April and can be potted into quart or gallon containers once fully rooted. In smaller containers these plants will often not reach salability until mid or late summer (allow six months for 4-inch [10 cm] pots). If selling larger plants, you may have to grow them a full year before sale, especially in northern zones.

VARIETIES

A. mollis is available from seed through several European and American seed companies, but it isn't easy to locate. Plants are available from a number of American nurseries although they may be offering *Acanthus mollis* Oak Leaf as opposed to the species.

A. mollis Oak Leaf is very similar to the species with dark glossy green foliage on large, robust plants. The leaves are more deeply lobed, however, like oak tree foliage. Plants are otherwise similar in habit, height, flowering time, and other aspects.

Plants can be found from a number of nurseries across the country, although they are more readily available from companies on the West Coast and farther south, due to winter hardiness.

RELATED MATERIAL

A. balcanicus (*A. longifolius*) is harder to find from started plants and even more so from seed in the U.S. trade. Plants are hardy from USDA Zones 6 to 9 and grow 4 to 5 feet (1.2 to 1.5 m) tall with a purple corolla that shades to a purplish pink color. Plants are similar to *A. mollis* but bear more deeply lobed leaves. Seed is available from European sources. Propagation, regardless of method, is similar to *A. mollis*.

A. spinosissimus (*A. spinosus*) is a beautiful but potentially dangerous plant best admired from a distance. As the name implies, this selection of *Acanthus* bears thistlelike rigid spines at the end of each leaf lobe, which arm the plant at every turn. Frequent handling of this plant will require gloves. *A. spinossimus* is more reliably hardy than *A. mollis* and will flower from Zones 5 to 8. Plants grow to between 3 and 4 feet tall with flowers in shades of purple to rose, though the flower can vary considerably. Propagate as suggested under *A. mollis*.

As in the case of *A. mollis*, these two plants will spread from 32 to 40 inches (81 to 102 cm).

USES

The plants bear such deep green, glossy, slightly lobed and large leaves that they make excellent specimen plants for the home perennial garden or landscape. *A. spinosissimus* is often underused because of its spines. *A. mollis* is spineless and can be used as a home container plant mixed with other perennials or annuals in the North due to its quick cropping and excellent outdoor performance.

IN THE HOME GARDEN

A. mollis works well in the home garden or landscape. Plants prefer a well-drained location and often fail in cold winter areas where wet weather has prevailed throughout the autumn. Plants are often long lived, however, as foundation plantings or where they receive protection from fall rains, severe winters, and unusually hot summers. In our Chicago climate, a hot summer that starts in June and lasts until September can considerably weaken the plants. When planted in full sun they're often short, with burned leaf margins. We often plant in locations where the plants receive morning sun but are shaded by early afternoon. Provide a mulch during winter for best results in Zones 5 and 6, although the plants will be short lived at best.

■ ACHILLEA FILIPENDULINA (A. EUPATORIUM)

FAMILY: Asteraceae

COMMON NAME(S): Fernleaf Yarrow, Yarrow

DESCRIPTION

Flowers are held in platelike clusters lying flat on the top of the plant. The clusters, which measure to 3½ inches (8 cm) across, are gold to golden yellow in color, scentless, and used in dried flower arrangements. The strongly scented foliage is deeply cut and fernlike in appearance. Plants grow from 2 to 4 feet (60 to 120 cm) tall in bloom (depending on the variety), and from 2 to 3 feet (60 to 90 cm) across. The plants branch only from the crown and the flowering stems are void of branches.

HARDINESS: Zones 3 to 8.

A truly reliable perennial with few overwintering problems.

SEASON OF BLOOM: June to July.

If plants are trimmed back after flowering, they will rebloom about a month later—although with less free-flowering performance.

PROPAGATION

Seed, cuttings, and divisions are the most common methods of propagating this species. Seed-propagated varieties are variable and often rank in appearance. The plants, however, often grow uniform in a cell pack or pot as they are growing. Propagate the named cultivars by taking cuttings in summer after flowering or as basal cuttings as shoots develop in the spring from the crown. Division is also easy once the plants reach maturity, about two to four years after planting. One-year divisions can be taken, although the number of transplants will be limited.

GERMINATION OVERVIEW: 200,000 seeds per ounce/7,000 per gram.

Achilleas germinate readily, requiring no special pretreatments to improve overall germination percentage. Seedlings emerge 10 to 15 days after sowing at 65F to 70F (18C to 21C) and faster if the temperatures are higher, but no more than 75F (24C). You can lightly cover seed or leave it exposed to light during germination. Transplanting can begin 18 to 24 days after sowing.

GROWING ON

From seed: Many *Achillea* species will germinate, grow, and develop flowers the same season from seed. *A. filipendulina*, when sown in January or after, will flower sporadically the same season. Sowings after March are less likely to bloom. The best flowering can be expected from plants sown from seed or taken as cuttings the previous year and overwintered in quart or gallon containers.

Winter or spring sowings can be sold in 4-inch (10 cm) pots within 12 to 14 weeks or a 32-cell pack in 10 to 12 weeks. Night temperatures of 50F to 55F (10C to 13C) are best. A February sowing produces sporadically flowering plants in either July or August.

Purchased liners or plugs from a 72-cell pack will root into 4-inch (10 cm) pots in six to eight weeks when grown at 55F (13C) nights. If the plants are vernalized (given a cold treatment), then the plants will flower during the summer. It's best to purchase your plug trays by February here in the North, to get some growth underneath the plants prior to retail sales. This will help improve overall flowering performance. One final point: 72 cells delivered during January can easily be potted up into quart or gallon containers instead of 4-inch (10 cm) pots for late April or May sales.

VARIETIES

All of the following varieties are species types and can grow to 5 feet (1.5 m) once established in the garden. In my opinion, these varieties appear to be very similar in all aspects of habit, flower color, and overall height. Although there may have been more differences in earlier years, the variety names may be used interchangeably for the same seed. Careful selection is advised.

Cloth of Gold is a tall selection that is also sold under the name of Parker's Variety. I've seen some catalogs listing this variety as 3½ (105 cm) feet tall, but it grows to 4½ feet (1.3 m) easily by the third year for us. Flowers are golden yellow in color and measure up to 4 inches (10 cm) across. One other note: This variety was originally propagated vegetatively. It's possible some growers—especially those dealing with European suppliers—may have shorter selections that are vegetatively propagated.

Gold Plate is also a large variety reaching 4 feet (1.2 m) with plate-like blooms of 5½ inches (14 cm) across. Flowers are a deep mustard yellow. In a number of trials over the past eight years, Gold Plate and Parker's Variety started separately from seed appeared to be the same plant.

RELATED MATERIAL

Achillea × Coronation Gold is a hybrid cross between *A. filipendulina* and *A. clypeolata*. It is the best achillea for landscaping, as plants get only 3 to 3½ feet (90 to 100 cm) tall with tight clusters of 3-inch (7 cm) blooms. The scented foliage is gray green in color. It is smaller flowered and shorter overall in habit than the other varieties listed above but very uniform. This variety is recommended for the perennial garden in mass plantings or as a specimen. Seed isn't available on this variety and should be avoided—it doesn't look the same. This variety is usually propagated by divisions taken in the spring and by cuttings taken in the summer after flowering.

Moonshine is related to other achilleas only by genus and not by species. Moonshine is the result of a cross between *A. clypeolata* and *A. taygetea*. The plant has sulphur yellow flowers on plants that grow to 2 feet (60 cm). Foliage is gray green and fernlike. See Color Plate 1 for photo of *Achillea* Moonshine.

An excellent variety, Moonshine is recommended for brightening up a sunny spot or, once the flowers have faded, the foliage can provide a contrast to the bright green foliage of companion plants. Moonshine is propagated by division and cuttings.

USES

This is definitely a good plant for the home perennial garden, either for specimen planting or massing. Use the taller varieties as a short, seasonal hedge with Hibiscus Southern Belle behind to flower once the achillea is spent. The flowers, which are on long, stiff stems, are excellent for dried cut flowers. Pick at any stage of development before the pollen sets. Flowers will dry the same way they are picked, and flower color lasts over the years. The herblike odor disappears as flowers dry. Any of the species types have more flowers on longer stems than Coronation Gold, however, they may not be as tightly held.

For commercial landscape planting, varieties like *A.* × Coronation Gold are recommended for accents and specimen plantings. I feel this is a good variety for golf courses as well. If a tall perennial planting is needed, consider using some of the species varieties noted earlier. Plant these along with one of the hibiscus varieties or Goldsturm rudbeckia for summer to fall color.

IN THE HOME GARDEN

Note that established plantings can become rank after several years, primarily in protected locations with ample water and yearly feedings. If grown out in the open, braving the elements of winter, the plants will often stay about a foot shorter here in Chicago, but will still be vigorous farther south. I suggest that *A. filipendulina* be planted 15 to 18 inches (38 to 46 cm) apart.

Plant in full sun locations in a well-drained but not overly fertile soil. Water as needed to establish and fertilize sparingly—the taller, ranker varieties will respond by becoming more so. Divide plants in spring or fall.

■■■ ACHILLEA MILLEFOLIUM

FAMILY: Asteraceae

COMMON NAME(S): Common Yarrow, Yarrow, Milfoil

DESCRIPTION

A familiar relative of *A. filipendulina*, this species also differs in several ways. *A. millefolium* has white or rose-red flowers that lie in clusters 2 to 3 inches (5 to 7 cm) across at the stem's terminal end. The cultivars, however, range in color from lavender to buff yellow, cherry, and other pastel shades. The flower clusters are less disklike and more open than *A. filipendulina*. Unfortunately, all the flower colors, except white, will readily shade to an off color, most often to a dull or off-white.

However, this class has garden merit for its long flowering period, uniformity in height, and longevity in the garden. When blooming, plants grow from 2 to 3 feet (60 to 90 cm) tall and 15 to 24 inches (38 to 61 cm) wide. The foliage has a strong herb-like odor. Like *A. filipendulina*, *A. millefolium* branches only from the crown, and flowering stems are void of any side-shoot development. Leaves are also fernlike as on *A. filipendulina*.

HARDINESS: Zones 3 to 8.

SEASON OF BLOOM: June and July.

If plants are trimmed back after flowering, they'll rebloom, although less vigorously, about a month later.

PROPAGATION

This species is propagated by seed, cuttings and divisions. Keep in mind that seed varieties are lighter and more variable in flower color than their vegetatively propagated counterparts. Named cultivars can be propagated by summer cuttings after flowering or basal cuttings as shoots develop from the crown in the spring. Division is also easy once the plants reach maturity, two to four years after planting. Two-year divisions can be taken, although the number and size of transplants may be undesirable.

GERMINATION OVERVIEW: 140,000 seeds per ounce/4,900 per gram.

Achilleas germinate easily and don't need special pretreatments to improve the overall germination percentage. Seedlings emerge 10 to 15 days after sowing at 65F to 70F (18C to 21C); faster at higher temperatures but don't exceed 75F (24C). Seed may be lightly covered or left exposed to light during germination. Transplanting can begin 18 to 24 days after sowing.

GROWING ON

From seed: *A. millefolium* will germinate, grow, and develop flowers the same season from seed as long as the seed is sown by March. Sowings after March will still flower the same season, but you'll miss having sizable plant material to sell in June.

Winter or spring sowings will be salable in 4-inch (10 cm) pots within 12 to 14 weeks, and a 32-cell pack in 10 to 12 weeks. Temperatures of 50F to 55F (10C to 13C) nights are best for growing on. A February sowing will produce flowering plants in either July or August and, unlike *A. filipendulina*, *A. millefolium* is a more prolific bloomer the first summer after sowing.

Plugs and/or liners of *A. millefolium* are also available from commercial propagators. Purchased liners or plugs from a 72-cell pack will root into 4-inch (10 cm) pots in six to eight weeks when grown at 55F (13C) nights. Many times these are vernalized plugs that have been exposed to a cold treatment to encourage blooming. While

A. millefolium will still flower from a spring sowing with only nominal cold conditions (55F or 13C nights), vernalized plugs have a strong, healthy root system and an evenly formed rosette which encourages a uniformly developing plant when the plug is potted up into a 4½-inch (10 cm), quart or gallon pot. The earlier in the year you bring in your plugs, the larger the container you can grow them in to allow for proper rooting prior to May sales.

VARIETIES

Cerise Queen is a cerise-red flowering variety more aptly described as rose red in its flower color. Plants can be 3 feet (90 cm) tall once they're established in the garden, but plants we've grown have been only 2 to 2½ feet (60 to 75 cm) tall. Both seed and vegetative forms exist. Seed-propagated plants are more vigorous, and the flower colors change in shade more readily than those vegetatively propagated.

Red Beauty, like Cerise Queen, exists in both seed and vegetative forms. Flowers are held in open clusters to 3 inches (7 cm) across, with carmine-rose flowers that fade to off-white regardless of how they're propagated. This cultivar reaches 2 feet (60 cm) in height.

White Beauty has pure white flowers on plants up to 2 feet (60 cm) tall. Plants flower in July and August. Both seed and vegetative material are available in this variety as well. Vegetatively propagated plants are more uniform in appearance.

Summer Pastels, a mix of colors, won an All-America Selections Award in 1990. Plants grow to 16 inches (41 cm) and spread to 16 to 18 inches (41 to 46 cm) across. Flower colors include salmon, cream, soft blush pink, and primrose yellow. Other colors will appear as more of the mixture is grown, but these are the predominant colors. This is an excellent variety especially recommended for landscaping. Summer Pastels is propagated by seed.

RELATED MATERIAL

The Galaxy hybrids are the result of a cross between *A. taygetea* and *A. millefolium*. In appearance, the plants look similar in habit and performance to *A. millefolium* but also tend to have some of the gray-green foliage that *A. taygetea* possesses. Some of the varieties in this line include:

Heidi grows from 15 to 20 inches (38 to 51 cm) tall with an equal spread. The flowers are rose pink.

Hoffnung (Hope) is slightly taller than Heidi, growing from 18 to 22 inches (46 to 56 cm) tall with about the same spread. The flowers are primrose.

Paprika is also a taller variety from 20 to 24 inches (51 to 61 cm) tall in flower and a similar spread. The red flowers have a yellow center. See Color Plate 2 for photo of *Achillea* Paprika.

All of the above and the additional varieties within the Galaxy hybrids are vegetatively propagated.

USES

A. millefolium is often slower to emerge in the spring than *A. filipendulina*. However, it makes up for lost time by producing a larger clump than the taller growing varieties of *A. filipendulina*. Plants can become invasive in areas where it has little competition. In the perennial border, divide as necessary and plant around other not-so-intimidated classes like *Rudbeckia fulgida* or *Echinacea purpurea*.

For cut flowers pick varieties that hold their color longer when harvested. Obviously, trial and error is necessary, but pick when color first shows, not when the plants are in full bloom. White varieties are best since they hold their color while red ones will shade to a soft pink or off white. Flowers are also often used dried.

For commercial landscapes the cultivated varieties are best for a strong show of color and overall uniformity. They also will keep their shape and not become as invasive as some species types. The species types, however, work well in large open areas like golf courses or parks. Combine this species with either ornamental grasses or other achilleas for a full season of interesting contrasts. Beware of mixing with dark or bright colors—it can make the more pastel shades appear muddy and unattractive.

IN THE HOME GARDEN

Note that established plantings can get rank after several years, though this is more common in seed-propagated varieties than the hybrids or vegetative selections. I suggest that *A. millefolium* be initially planted 12 to 15 inches (30 to 38 cm) apart. Even if spaced farther apart, most varieties will eventually grow in anyway. Plant in full sun locations in a well-drained but not overly fertile soil. Water as needed to establish, and fertilize sparingly since the larger, less uniform varieties will respond by becoming more so. Division in the garden can be done in spring or fall. Staking hasn't been necessary for us in Chicago, although a number of people do it to keep the plant habit more shapely during flowering.

▄▄▄ ACHILLEA PTARMICA

FAMILY: Asteraceae

COMMON NAME(S): Sneezeweed, Sneezewort

DESCRIPTION

A. ptarmica differs from its relatives by producing only white flowers. Plants grow 24 to 28 inches (61 to 71 cm) tall with a spread of 18 to 24 inches (46 to 61 cm). The flowers are primarily double, with some degree of singleness expected, especially from seed-propagated plants. The slightly fragrant flowers measure up to three-quarters of an inch (2 cm) across. *A. ptarmica* can become invasive and is often viewed as a weed—especially late in the season when the plant can fall open after flowering. Some staking at this time can remedy the problem.

HARDINESS: Zones 3 to 9.

SEASON OF BLOOM: June to early August.

PROPAGATION

Achillea ptarmica is propagated by seed, cuttings, and divisions. This species is relatively true from seed although doubleness within the flower is not consistent. Vegetatively propagated forms are more even in habit, larger flowered, and more fully double than their seed-sown counterparts. Propagate cultivars by stem cuttings taken in summer after flowering or as basal cuttings since the shoots develop from the crown. Division is also easy once the plants reach maturity, which is two to four years after planting.

GERMINATION OVERVIEW: 90,000 seeds per ounce/3,150 per gram.
Achilleas don't require any special pretreatments to improve germination percentages. Seedlings emerge 10 to 15 days after sowing at 65F to 70F (18C to 21C), faster if the temperatures are higher—but no more than 75F (24C). Seed may be lightly covered or left exposed to light during germination. Transplanting can begin 18 to 24 days after sowing.

GROWING ON

From seed: *A. ptarmica* is an easily grown crop that will readily root in a 32-cell pack in 10 to 12 weeks when grown at 55F (13C) nights. Seed sown anytime after Christmas until April will produce flowering plants during the summer. In our trials, seed sown during early February was salable green in early May (cell pack), and plants started to flower in mid- to late July.

Plugs or liners are also available in a wide variety of sizes. Plants are quick to finish in 4½-inch (10 cm) pots when using 100 or larger sized plugs. When potted in March, plants were ready in six to eight weeks at 55F (13C) nights.

Stem cuttings are easily taken and rooted, but plants will develop roots first before producing several strong stems. Some growers pinch back the original shoot after the roots have formed to encourage branching.

VARIETIES

The Pearl is the standard *A. ptarmica* variety with plants that grow 21 inches (53 cm) tall with spreads of 24 inches (61 cm). I want to point out, however, the variation that exists even in this one variety. The seed selection will have 10% to 30% double flowers and the rest mostly single. If you want to maintain your own stock plants, you'll have to select out the double flowering plants the first year or two to provide a mother block from which to take cuttings. See Color Plate 3 for photo of *Achillea ptarmica* The Pearl.

An easier way to get double flowering plants is to contact your favorite plant producer and ask whether his selection is fully double or has a percentage of single flowering plants. Don't be misguided in thinking that if you purchase started plants of this, or any crop, it was automatically propagated asexually. Your supplier does matter. To complicate matters, double, single, and everything in between are often listed as The Pearl variety.

USES

We have used the double-flowering varieties for years in our gardens with dependable performance. The plants are uniform in habit and, I think, easily contained to reduce their potential invasiveness.

As a cut flower, some growers have used these in place of matricaria (*Tanacetum parthenium*). Use the fully double-flowering varieties for the best color and overall performance.

In the commercial landscape, any of the varieties can be used in parks, shopping centers, natural plantings and on golf courses. Granted, in some cases, the material can become invasive, but if used in a large open area or where there is high traffic, this plant will work well.

IN THE HOME GARDEN

Note that established plantings can become rank after several years. However, if well fed, frequently watered, and placed in full sun, we seldom have any problems. We plant in a well-drained, full-sun location where the plants get one to two applications of fertilizer a year and have excellent success in keeping the plants under control in our Chicago location. Farther south, where the extended summer and less severe winters may not be as limiting to the plants, digging around the plant's crown in the spring prior to the start of new growth may be necessary to keep plants under control.

In general, it's suggested that *A. ptarmica* be planted 14 to 15 inches (35 to 38 cm) apart. Plants will fill in rapidly, but the stress from planting close clumps will also help keep them more manageable. Staking isn't necessary unless you are in the southern U.S. and/or are frequented by late summer rains that can help to lodge (push open) the plants. Trim plants back after flowering and they'll reflower, although not as freely as the first bloom. Achilleas can be divided in the home garden either in spring or late summer.

■ ACONITUM NAPELLUS

FAMILY: Ranunculaceae

COMMON NAME(S): Aconite, Wolf's Bane, Monkshood
The name of Wolf's Bane was given when *Aconitum* was used to poison wolves.

DESCRIPTION

The most common monkshood varieties on the market are, according to one source, the most poisonous of the genus [1]. Flowers are mid to deep blue, borne helmetlike (hence the name "monkshood") on erect stems between 2 and 3 feet (60 to 90 cm) tall. In warmer winter climates than Chicago, the plants may reach up to 4 or 5 feet (1.2 to 1.5 m). The plants will spread from 1 to 2 feet (30 to 60 cm) across. All plant parts (seeds, roots, stems, and leaves) are poisonous and should not be used in any situation where children may be playing around them. The roots are large, tuberous in shape, and could be mistaken for horseradish. Therefore, keep this plant out of the vegetable garden where the root might be harvested accidentally.

HARDINESS: Zones 3 to 8.
Plants are hardy in Chicago, but they'll do better when covered with a 2-inch (5 cm) winter mulch. Fall dug and divided plants need extra protection in the field or garden so they won't heave out of the ground during the winter.

SEASON OF BLOOM: July and August.

PROPAGATION

Division is the most common way to propagate, but seed can be done as well. Due to *Aconitum* roots' poisonous nature, use care and rubber gloves when working on divisions. While the roots don't appreciate being disturbed, autumn divisions every three years will yield enough salable transplants to make it worth your time. These plants will be salable the following spring.

GERMINATION OVERVIEW

Seed germination is an involved process when fresh seed isn't used. It's mainly for those growers who don't have an available source of divisions. I have had limited or no germination success when using seed stored for any length of time and then sown at 60F (16C) or warmer. Fresh seed does yield better results, although subjecting the seed to a warm-moist period followed by a moist chilling gives the best germination.

If, after sowing, the seedlings don't emerge, treat them to a warm-moist period and a moist chill. It's important to use all the seed you gather or buy, since seed seldom lives beyond one year. Follow the procedures for both warm-moist pretreatment and moist chilling noted in the **Propagation Techniques** chapter of this book.

GROWING ON

Crop time: Divisions taken in the fall are slow to root and grow. Roots are commonly divided and potted up into 2- to 4- quart containers, depending on size. Over the winter, these roots will develop at the expense of the vegetative shoots but will be salable the next spring with only one or two green shoots.

Commercial propagators will offer *A. napellus* and the other species listed as small divisions during the fall and winter. These can be potted up into 1- or 2-quart containers for spring sales. Allow seven to nine weeks at 55F nights, and remember that the plants will produce only one or two erect, nonbasal branching stems, regardless of the variety. For this reason larger containers are usually avoided because they will require additional weeks for the roots to fill out.

Since most seed-propagated plants first emerge from their seed coats in the late winter or spring, developing seedlings will not produce a salable plant in a quart or gallon pot for the spring season. Instead, grow the plants on in the summer for sales during late summer or early fall, or overwinter plants for spring sales the following year. *Aconitum* grown in this manner will not flower the first season from seed, which allows for better root development.

VARIETIES

A. napellus is available as seed or as transplants from a number of nurseries around the country.

A. album grandiflorum is a white-flowering selection listed by a number of perennial nurseries in the United States. It can also be listed as *A. napellus Albus*. Flowers are pure white on plants between 4 and 5 feet (1.2 to 1.5 m) tall.

Carneum is a soft pink variety suggested for more cool weather locations. In areas with long, hot summers, the variety will fade and appear dull or washed out in color. It grows 4 to 5 feet (1.2 to 1.5 m) tall and is propagated vegetatively.

RELATED MATERIAL

Some botanical confusion exists about the true development of some *Aconitum* selections on the market. When looking for varieties, be aware that the following may be listed differently, depending on the references used by your supplier.

A. × bicolor is a class probably made up of crosses between *A. variegatum* and *A. napellus* and is synonymous with any of the following species: *A. stoerkianum*, *A. cammarum*, and *A. napellus bicolor*.

All of the following are **vegetatively propagated** although Newry Blue seed is sold. Included in this group are all of the following:

Bicolor grows to between 3 and 4 feet (90 to 120 cm) with white flowers edged with violet blue. Leaves are deep green and glossy. In the trade it is sometimes listed as × *bicolor*. Plants flower from June to August.

Bressingham Spire by Alan Bloom ranges in height from 3 to 4 feet (90 to 150 cm), with deep violet-blue flowers. Plants flower from July to August.

Newry Blue is a tall variety, up to 5 feet (1.5 m) tall with deep navy-blue flowers. Plants have an erect habit and flower in July and August.

Spark's Variety is often listed botanically as *A. henryi* and may be listed by perennial nurseries simply as Spark's. Growing between 3 and 5 feet (90 to 150 cm) tall, the variety is common among western U.S. perennial nurseries. It's an upright, very erect variety and may require staking. Flowers are a deep purplish blue.

A. carmichaelii (syn. *A. fischeri*) is shorter than many of the other *Aconitum napellus* species. Ranging in height from 2½ to 3 feet (70 to 90 cm) tall, the plant grows erect with midblue flowers. Plants bloom from September to October, making it one of the latest to flower in the genus.

Arendsii (syn. *A.* × *arendsii*) is a hybrid between *A. carmichaelii* and *A. wilsonii*. Flowers are deep blue and richer than *A. carmichaelii* on plants that are between 30 and 40 inches (76 to 102 cm) tall. It flowers in July and August.

IN THE HOME GARDEN

Plants are often slow to emerge in the spring and should be labeled well in the fall since you will be able to plant the area around the roots and crown prior to the shoots emerging in May or June. Plants are impressive in bloom and should be planted with three to five clumps spaced 15 to 20 inches (38 to 51 cm) apart to get the best effect. Aconitums perform best in rich soil where they get shade in the afternoon and their roots can be kept moist but not wet. Plants are slow to establish in warm, dry soils. After three to four years an established clump needs to be divided to encourage a greater number of flowering stems.

The comment that *Aconitum* is poisonous isn't overstated—it's a beauty to be enjoyed in the garden, though from a distance. When using as a cut flower, keep house pets, small children, and unwary nonhorticulturalists at a distance. It is the plant's sap or resin that's poisonous, not the flower scent.

Plants don't require staking unless during the first season from transplant when plants may be weak from pot growing or if growing in too fertile a soil. Established plants will grow erect but may be taller than 3 feet (90 cm) if fertilized and well watered.

REFERENCES

[1] Clausen, R.R., and N.H. Ehstrom. 1989. *Perennials for American gardens*. New York: Random House.

■ ADENOPHORA LILIFOLIA
(sometimes listed as *A. lilifolia*)

FAMILY: Campanulaceae

COMMON NAME(S): Ladybells, Lilyleaf Ladybells

DESCRIPTION
Adenophora lilifolia is a hardy perennial resembling a campanula with which it's often confused. The fragrant flowers are midblue, bell-shaped, and measure from three-quarters to 1 inch (2 to 2.5 cm) across and up to 1 inch long. Flowers hang downward in open sprays. Plants grow from 18 inches to 2 feet (46 to 60 cm) tall and spread from 15 to 24 inches (38 to 61 cm) across. This selection is more heat tolerant than *Campanula* and thus is preferred for full-sun locations.

HARDINESS: Zones 3 to 8.

SEASON OF BLOOM: July and August.

PROPAGATION
Seed is the most common way to propagate, although cuttings can be taken as well. Division of the fleshy roots is difficult, and they'll rot if not properly handled. For both seeds and cuttings, treat the plants as you would a campanula. Basal cuttings are taken in the early spring after emergence but before the plants have had a chance to bud up.

GERMINATION OVERVIEW
Germination time: Seed sown into a peat-based media, left uncovered, and germinated at 70F (21C) will take one to two weeks to germinate. Older reference sources indicate that germination temperatures should be 55F (13C) for alpines like *Adenophora*, but seedlings often don't emerge for two to four weeks at lower temperatures.

GROWING ON
Crop time: Basal cuttings taken in spring will root easily and provide salable plants by late summer, or the pots can be overwintered for sales the following spring in gallon containers.

From seed, green cell packs will be salable in 12 to 15 weeks when grown at 55F (13C) nights. For 4-inch (10 cm) pot sales, allow 13 to 16 weeks at the same temperatures. As suggested above, sow and grow as you would campanulas for best performance. Seed sown during the winter and spring of the year will not flower until the following year.

Comment: The fleshy roots are difficult to handle when dividing this crop. Likewise, when starting from seed or cuttings, try not to let the crop become totally root-bound within a container. If completely rooted within the pot, the plant will take longer to establish in the home garden after transplanting.

VARIETIES

The species is available from seed, but only a limited number of companies readily provide it here in the United States. European sources are more dependable.

RELATED MATERIAL

A. confusa (syn. *A. farreri*) is a taller selection than *A. lilifolia* with a similar appearance, although the flower color is usually darker. A number of people say it's rather difficult to tell the two plants apart when height is the only factor that's noticeably different. Plants are not as heat tolerant as *A. lilifolia* but can be propagated from seed or cuttings and treated in a similar fashion. It reaches 2 to 3 feet (60 to 90 cm) tall with a 2-foot (60 cm) spread.

USES

Adenophora makes an excellent woodland plant, and its blue flowers compliment any setting. Interplanted with low growing ferns, hostas, or in a mass, *Adenophora* works well. Like *Campanula,* it's not used extensively in landscaping since the foliage provides little value once the flowers have gone.

As a woodland planting, *A. lilifolia* prefers a moist, though well-drained, location.

IN THE HOME GARDEN

Since the flowers are small and may be lost if planted close to brightly colored, larger flowering annuals and perennials, use several plants together to create a mass effect. *Adenophora* prefers a rich and moist environment, but one that's well drained, in either full sun or where it's shaded during the hottest part of the day. *Adenophora* will be free flowering in the garden once it becomes established and the roots have grown out of the pot form created by container constraints. Roots resent transplanting—so do so only if necessary.

▄▄ AEGOPODIUM PODAGRARIA VARIEGATUM

FAMILY: Umbelliferae

COMMON NAME(S): Variegated Goutweed, Silveredge Goutweed, Bishop's Weed
The common name of Bishop's Weed also belongs to the annual *Ammi majus*, which has similar flowers to *Aegopodium* but is very invasive.

DESCRIPTION

Though not as aggressive as the green-leaved form, *A. podagraria* Variegatum is still sometimes considered a weed due to its rhizomes' fast growth. The plant is noted for variegated foliage of light to medium green irregularly splashed with creamy white.

In flower it reaches 10 to 15 inches (25 to 38 cm); 6 to 8 inches (15 to 20 cm) the remainder of the summer. The spread or width of a single plant depends on its location in the garden. More fertile soils will produce a large mass from 12 to 20 inches (30 to 51 cm) across. (See **In the home garden** for additional information.)

The flowers are white, one-eighth inch (0.3 cm) across, and held in umbels (numerous short stalks radiating from a common point and each terminating with a flower) with 10 to 15 individual blooms. Flowers are rather insignificant and appear in June. See Color Plate 4 for photo of *Aegopodium podagraria*.

HARDINESS: Zones 4 to 8.

SEASON OF BLOOM: June. Plants flower for one to two weeks.

PROPAGATION

Aegopodium is easily propagated by division in either spring or fall. Plants taken with even a small piece of root will root easily. Seed is another way to propagate, though it is seldom done except by growers selecting out improved cultivars to vegetatively propagate.

GROWING ON

Crop time: The production of *Aegopodium* is what older propagation references call "simple culture," meaning crops that are easy to propagate and grow, with few problems.

Divisions taken in early spring will root readily and be salable in a 6-inch (15 cm) or gallon pot in six to eight weeks depending on the division's size. The crop time also reflects whether the root was dormant or if shoots already had started to emerge. Divisions can be taken during the summer, although high heat and humidity often hinder quick rooting. Once rooted, plants should grow on at no less than 50F (10C) for active growth.

This crop is also available from commercial propagators in a liner or plug. (For additional information on this production method see the **How to Use** chapter, page 6 of **Growing on**.)

VARIETIES

A. podagraria Variegatum is the only variety offered to any extent by the perennial trade. It's readily available from a number of sources and is the only cultivar of any merit in this listing. Seed-propagated varieties are of little value except for selection work or if you just happen to like doing it that way.

You can collect your own seed and make selections from the resulting plants since few U.S. seed firms will carry this seed. Variegation will vary in seed-grown plants; check plant vigor to avoid supplying your customers with potential weeds.

RELATED MATERIAL

A. podagraria is the green-leaved form of this crop and is grown like the variegated one. Height, bloom time, hardiness, and other factors are also similar. It differs in one key category, however. It's known for its invasiveness and ability to overrun weaker plants. If you need a plant to fill out an area where other plants cannot become established, then *Aegopodium* holds promise. In the right environment, it will succeed beyond your wildest expectations.

Grow as you would the variegated form.

IN THE HOME GARDEN

Catalogs describe this plant as "easy and quick to fill in," which is an understatement if the ground is fertile and/or moist and the plants are in partial shade. In one season plants can easily suffocate smaller plants around their base; this is more common with the green-leaved form. On the other hand, the plant is subject to attack by spider mites. If plants appear ragged looking, cut them back to the ground and water. The plants will develop new leaves within several weeks. *Aegopodium* is perfect on embankments, sloping or jagged hillsides and other places where other plants may be difficult to establish.

We have planted the variegated form in poorer garden locations to brighten up difficult spots. In locations with a well-drained soil, limited organic matter and a shady exposure, you will be rewarded with a slower growing version of *Aegopodium* with limited flowers. Remember that both the seeds and the rhizomes can pose similar problems with invasiveness: Trim off seedheads, especially if there are many of them. Some people like to use the flowers for cutting although *Ammi majus* provides a better, more free-flowering cut.

■■■ AETHIONEMA CORDIFOLIUM

FAMILY: Cruciferae

COMMON NAME(S): Lebanon Stonecress, Stonecress

DESCRIPTION

As a group, *Aethionema* is compact, growing less than 15 inches (38 cm) tall; *A. cordifolium* will grow to only 10 inches (25 cm) tall and spread to 12 inches (30 cm) across. The flowers are light pink, single, four lobed and measure less than one-half inch (1 cm) across. Foliage is blue green and relatively evergreen during cold winters. They are considered subshrubs with a woody stem.

HARDINESS: Zones 5 to 8.

Plants do better in Mediterranean climates than our Midwest winters. In our Chicago location, the plants are often short lived. If you are successful growing either *Arabis* or *Iberis* in your location, *Aethionema* should fit in well.

SEASON OF BLOOM: May and June.

PROPAGATION

Seed and cuttings are two preferred propagation methods. Dividing the woody root-stocks is almost impossible without damaging the plant. Seed, however, can yield various off-types in color and habit and seldom produces true-to-type plants. Either basal or summer stem cuttings can be taken. Plants should be lightly trimmed after flowering to produce a flush of new growth that yields short-stemmed cuttings during the summer.

GERMINATION OVERVIEW

Sources differ as to the best temperatures for adequate germination percentages. In general, seed sown to a peat-based media, left uncovered but watered in, and given temperatures of 65F to 70F (18C to 21C) will yield the best results. Seedlings emerge in four to eight days, but visually the flat or plug tray won't appear filled out for one to two weeks. Seedlings can be transplanted in two to four weeks after sowing. If germination percentages are low, seed may require a moist chilling. Additional information is provided in the front of this book.

GROWING ON

Crop time: From seed, make sowings during the summer prior to the year when you want to sell these plants. Aethionemas aren't slow to grow but will not flower from seed until the plants are vernalized (exposure to cold to form flower buds). Grow *Aethionema* as you would *Arabis* or *Iberis* and allow 13 to 15 weeks to fill out a 2- to 3-inch (5 to 7 cm) pot when grown at 50F to 55F (10C to 13C) nights. Although tolerant of colder conditions, plants will slow their growth if night temperatures drop below 50F (10C).

If sown in November and initially grown warm at 60F (16C) nights until potted into a 4-inch or quart container, plants will be salable in May. After potting, continue subjecting plants to 60F (16C) nights for a week or two and then move to a cold frame or similar environment where the night temperatures are 50F to 55F (10C to 13C).

Cuttings taken during the summer will be sizable enough to pot up into larger containers by late summer and overwintered for next spring sales. Propagate cuttings as you would *Iberis*.

VARIETIES

The species is sold in the trade without any variety or selection names. Seed is available from some U.S. firms but is more readily available from European seed houses.

RELATED MATERIAL

A. grandiflorum (syn. *A. pulchellum*), Persian stonecress, is an erect, sometimes spreading plant that will grow to no more than 18 inches (46 cm) in bloom. Its pink flowers appear in May and June. Plants are commonly propagated by seed or cuttings.

A. × warleyense (A. Warley Rose) is probably the result of a cross between *A. armenum* and *A. grandiflorum*. The foliage is steel blue with rose-pink flowers on plants to 10 inches (25 cm) tall. It is most commonly propagated by cuttings.

IN THE HOME GARDEN

When planted to the garden, the plants are initially prostrate but will mound more the following year. As the common name would suggest, stonecress means the plants are at home in the rock garden, tucked into the soil between rocks where roots are well-drained. Plants will suffocate in moist locations and often die out. The plants are native to Mediterranean regions where they grow on limestone cliffs; therefore, avoid acidic soils in locating them into the garden. In severe winter areas, cover with evergreen boughs rather than leaves to provide air circulation around the plant foliage. Wet leaves in the fall can introduce *Botrytis* or powdery mildew on the plants and kill them before next spring.

Plant to any spot that is shaded during the hottest part of the day. However, in coastal California and similar climates, full sun is preferred. Plants are not invasive but are often not long lived here in the Midwest.

▬▬ AJUGA REPTANS (A. REPENS)

FAMILY: Lamiaceae

COMMON NAME(S): Bugle Weed

DESCRIPTION

Ajugas are quick to establish and will move rapidly across the garden when the correct conditions are present. Plants grow from stolons and can become invasive, but it is possible to control ajugas. In the Midwest, the plants are seldom a problem. Many gardeners select them for their creeping or trailing habit, placing them in the front of the perennial border as an edging to keep sloping embankments from eroding.

Also, *Ajuga* foliage is attractive to the gardener's eye. It's smooth or puckered and can be green, variegated, or bronzed. The primary flower color is either violet or blue, though additional flower colors including pink, rose, and white are also available. Plants in flower grow 8 to 10 inches (15 to 25 cm) tall, otherwise they're usually less than 6 inches (15 cm) tall for most of the summer. Plants can spread from 15 to 24 inches (38 to 61 cm) across.

HARDINESS: Zones 3 to 9.
Winter kill is possible, especially with raised beds planted away from winter protection. In such cases not using a mulch only compounds the problem.

SEASON OF BLOOM: May and June.

A

PROPAGATION

Division and cuttings are the most common propagation methods. A crown can be lifted and divided any time of the year, although spring or autumn are best for quick rooting. *A. reptans* forms stolons (stems that grow horizontally on or just below the soil surface), and individual plantlets can be removed, along with their developing rootlet, and planted to a 50- or 72-plug/liner tray for rooting. There are some other ajuga species whose varieties form rhizomes. Instead of trailing across the ground, an individual plant will expand its spread. These plants should be divided and individual plantlets propagated in 50- or 72-plug/liner trays. In both cases, the crown can be divided into sections, potted up, and plants sold within three to four weeks.

As for stem cuttings, the easiest rooting occurs in midsummer after flowering, though plants will root anytime of the year, and quickly. Many times basal cuttings taken in the spring will already have small rootlets attached.

GERMINATION OVERVIEW

Ajuga is often propagated by cuttings and divisions. Seed propagation is usually for perpetuating a species or developing new hybrids, but it's not a commercial practice.

GROWING ON

Ajugas that are dug, divided, and potted in the spring will be quickly salable. Plants dug from a field bed in early March, cut into sections, and potted to a 3-quart or gallon pot will root in four to six weeks at 55F (13C) nights.

Plants are also available as liners from commercial propagators. A number of sizes are obtainable, although 50 and 72 trays are probably the most common. Plants can be finished off in 4-inch (10 cm) pots in six to eight weeks at 55F (13C) nights. Larger pots, such as a quart, will take about the same time, although two more weeks are usually required for the plants to fill out.

VARIETIES

A. reptans var. *alba*. Cream-white flowers on 6-inch-tall (15 cm) plants with light to medium green foliage.

Bronze Beauty is a metallic purple variety, 6 inches (15 cm) tall, with violet-blue flowers.

Burgundy Glow has four colored leaves in shades of rose, pink, green, and white. As the summer progresses, leaves will turn dark bronze (especially if in brighter light). Blue flowers form on plants to 6 inches (15 cm) tall. See Color Plate 5 for photo of *Ajuga reptans* Burgundy Glow.

Catlin's Giant has larger foliage than most of the other cultivars with glossy deep green to purplish leaves growing to almost 2 inches (5 cm) across. It has blue flowers on 6-inch-tall (15 cm) plants. See Color Plate 6 for photo of *Ajuga reptans* Catlin's Giant.

Silver Beauty has silver-green foliage edged in white. Flowers are a light blue on 6-inch-tall (15 cm) plants.

RELATED MATERIAL

A. pyramidalis Metallica Crispa. The foliage is bronze-purple in color with a metallic luster. Blue flowers form on 6-inch-tall (15 cm) plants. Propagate as suggested for *A. reptans*.

USES

In the perennial landscape, use *Ajuga* as a border plant, in mass, or as a rock garden plant. They are occasionally invasive enough to escape into the yard, which gives rise to suggestions of ajuga lawns. Plants are mowed to keep them in check, but the mower is raised so as not to trim too low.

In the landscape, the foliage and spreading characteristics are what are most prized. Plants will grow together quickly and become well established the first season after planting.

IN THE HOME GARDEN

If left unattended for the summer, selected varieties can easily fill in and take over, though this not a problem for us. Ajugas seldom are this invasive in our Chicago location. Plant in full sun to partially shaded locations, especially during midafternoon when the heat and humidity are highest. Space plants 12 to 15 inches (30 to 38 cm) apart and they will fill in quickly if the weather is favorable. The foliage will give a strong show from spring to frost.

Plants don't require mulching over the winter, although on raised berms or when planted in open areas, a winter mulch is suggested. In our Chicago climate, even with ample snow coverage, raised plantings are severely knocked back, especially in late winter or early spring when the days are warm but the nights can freeze. If plants are hit by a freeze and appear dead, remember that the stolons below ground may still be alive. Plants may not have much active growth until June. A week after a spring freeze, dig down close to the crown to see if there are any white rootlets. If so, plants will probably return, but late.

■■ ALCEA ROSEA

(formerly *Althaea rosea*)

FAMILY: Malvaceae

COMMON NAME(S): Hollyhock

DESCRIPTION

Alcea rosea is offered both as a annual and biennial. Plants are often short lived and work better in home gardens rather than professional landscapes. Both single- and double-flowering forms are available. Flowers may reach a size of up to 3½ inches (8 cm) across. Flower colors include yellow, white, carmine, crimson, pink, and various shades in between. Petals may be smooth edged or lightly fringed and slightly scented, especially on the single-flowering varieties.

Plants are taller than they are wide and grow 6 to 9 feet (1.8 to 2.7 m) tall with a spread of 2 to 3 feet. The plants produce a large rosetting crown from which two to four upright stems will develop. The foliage is large as well, with individual leaves measuring 8 to 12 inches (20 to 30 cm) across on mature plants.

HARDINESS: Zones 3 to 7.

Treated as hardy annuals in the North, the plants will often come back at least one time. Experts suggest that the plants overwinter better in containers (gallon pots stored for spring sales) than they do in the garden. It's the diversity of their enemies—and their persistency—that often makes these plants short lived, however.

SEASON OF BLOOM: Northern U.S.—July and August.

PROPAGATION

Hollyhock seed yields fairly good germination, even if seed is a season or two old. Propagation by cuttings is also possible, though it's not common and the amount of cutting stock produced is usually limited.

GERMINATION OVERVIEW: 3,000 to 6,000 seeds per ounce/105 to 210 per gram. Germination temperatures are 72F (22C), and seeds should be lightly covered during germination. Seedlings emerge in five to 10 days and are transplantable in 20 to 30 days. If you read the *Ball Culture Guide*, you'll note that the temperatures and number of days to emergence differ. Warmer temperatures of 70F to 73F (21C to 23C) will allow germination to begin earlier, while temperatures of 60F to 65F (15C to 18C) slow down emergence, although the final number of usable seedlings will be the same.

GROWING ON

Crop time: Regardless of whether you use annual or perennial varieties, the crop time from seed is the same—the only difference is that perennials may or may not flower the same season, depending on when they were started. In general, hollyhocks require 10 to 12 weeks to be salable green in 4-inch (10 cm) pots when the seed is sown during mid or late winter. Finish the plants in 4-inch (10 cm), quart or gallon containers for best root formation, allowing 11 to 13 weeks for green plant sales in quart containers.

It's not practical to count on having these plants in bloom at the time they're sold. The best that can be done is to grow them in 6-inch (15 cm) containers (from seed, allow 15 to 18 weeks) and have the pots ready for early or midspring sales. These larger plants establish themselves faster, rewarding the gardener with earlier and higher quality plants and flowers.

February sowings of the perennial varieties seldom flower profusely the first season; in fact, they usually don't flower at all until the second year. Plants often develop a strong clump by summer's end and will grow to 2 feet (60 cm) tall with a 2-foot spread. These plants will then flower the next year. If flowering plants are preferred, make November or early December sowings, transplant to gallon containers and move to a 50F to 55F (10C to 13C) cold frame for April/May sales.

VARIETIES

Seed varieties: Mixes dominate the market in popularity although separate colors are also available. There are no vegetative varieties commercially sold on the U.S. trade at this time.

Annual seeded varieties

Indian Summer Mix. A mixture of single-flowering varieties with 3½-inch (8 cm) blooms in primarily yellow and white shades, though pink and several other pastel colors are also available. Plants grow to 6 feet (1.8 m) tall. It requires staking, but it's stronger stemmed than other selections.

Summer Carnival Mix. Also a mixture and winner of an All-America Selections Award. Flowers are double, in rose, pink, white, yellow, and carmine. Plants grow to 6 feet (1.8 m) tall.

Additional annual varieties include both Silver Puffs and Majorette. Flower colors are silver pink on the Silver Puffs while Majorette is a mixture of pastel colors. Both varieties bear 3- to 3½-inch (7 to 8 cm) double flowers on plants that are about 2 feet (60 cm) tall. Both varieties were All-America Selections Award winners, but they're not as readily available as the other two selections.

Perennial seeded varieties (short lived or biennial)

Chater's Double series is sometimes called Chater's Prize—especially when referring to the mixture. This is the premier series in the U.S. trade, known by growers over the past several decades. It develops 3½-inch (8 cm) double blooms on plants to 6 feet (1.8 m) tall. It may well be the only variety sold in separate colors on the market today. Ten separate colors are available, but only a few seed companies carry more than five or six colors. Colors include rose, scarlet, pink, yellow, white, violet, purple, and others.

Powderpuffs Mixture. A double-flowering variety to 5 feet (1.5 m) tall. The blooms are claimed to be the largest of any hollyhock on the market today—4 inches (10 cm) across. Flower colors include yellow, pink, white, salmon, and scarlet. This is an excellent variety.

USES

Hollyhocks can be used in any number of settings in the home garden, although these plants personify the cottage garden or old-fashioned perennial garden look.

They're stately plants valued for their background performance and ability to fill in quickly and provide color throughout the summer. I suggest offering both annual and perennial varieties, concentrating on the double-flowering selections. Once the annuals finish flowering for the year, the perennials take over the next season and flower. Plant in areas where the plants get six hours of light or more daily and stake to at least 3 feet (90 cm) tall when they're flowering. Don't plant in areas that are not well drained or plants may succumb to disease.

IN THE HOME GARDEN

The fast growing nature of this plant and its ease of cultivation have made it a popular plant throughout America. Yesteryear's gardens were not complete without the towering spires of color that hollyhocks could provide. Sometimes these were cut, the foliage stripped, and the flowers arranged with other blooms. However, they were often short-lived, wilting in the vase by the end of the second day.

Plant to any full sun location and don't crowd. One plant will need 2 square feet (1800 sq. cm) to fill in. Plant in any well-drained but moist soil, avoiding areas with standing water. Plants can be used up against the house or in island beds in the middle of the yard. However, they're best visually when planted at the side of a barn, storage building, or other structure where they can be viewed from the house. If the building lacks a coat of paint, hollyhocks look even better.

Staking is usually not necessary if the plants are grown as noted above. After fertilizing in the spring, plants shouldn't be fertilized again. Ample water, fertile soils and no protection from the wind will make these giants lean. In this case, suitable support is suggested.

ALCHEMILLA MOLLIS (A. VULGARIS)

Alchemilla mollis (referred to by English experts) and *Alchemilla vulgaris* (*Hortus Third*) are treated alike in the following text. In growing plants from seed from several suppliers, we have seen little, if any, differences. See additional details provided under **Varieties**.

FAMILY: Rosaceae

COMMON NAME(S): Lady's Mantle

The common name is derived from folklore that suggests the plant was used to adorn the Virgin Mary.

DESCRIPTION

A low-growing perennial, *Alchemilla mollis* displays pubescent, lobed leaves on plants from 12 to 18 inches (30 to 46 cm) tall in bloom and from 18 to 24 inches (46 to 61 cm) across. Flowers are yellow green in color and dull in appearance. It's the foliage that is the primary focus of this crop since it is unusual in appearance and has no equal for form, height, and show in the perennial garden. The leaves are covered with a dense mass of fine hairs, giving the plant a velvety texture. During a rainstorm, water droplets dot the leaf surfaces. Eventually the droplets coalesce and, due to the weight, the leaf will bend towards the ground allowing the water to spill out.

The flowers are actually apetalous (without petals) and measure between one-eighth to one-quarter inch (0.3 to 0.6 cm) across. Due to their small size, the flowers, from a distance, appear to hang like a cloud or fog wavering above the plants in a breeze. As they age, the flowers turn a dull brown, which adds appeal to the mid-summer garden. See Color Plate 7 for photo of *Alchemilla mollis*.

HARDINESS: Zones 4 to 7.

SEASON OF BLOOM: May and June.

PROPAGATION

Alchemilla is propagated by seed and division. Divisions are taken on large, established clumps in the early spring (late March or April). In order to harvest the greatest number of divisions, plants should have some age on them (three to four years) before they are dug and divided.

GERMINATION OVERVIEW: 95,000 seeds per ounce/3,325 per gram.
Germination temperatures of 70F to 72F (21C to 22C) are suggested. Seed can be left uncovered during germination.

Pretreatments: None are needed with recently harvested seed. If seed is older or has been kept around from the previous sowing season, test 100 seeds to see what the germination is and prechill the seed flat if necessary. For more information, look under the moist-chill propagation section at the front of this book.

Seedlings will emerge in seven to 12 days and are transplantable five to six weeks after sowing. If seeds are fresh, seedling vigor will be slightly enhanced, and transplanting can be done a week or so sooner.

GROWING ON

Crop time: Spring-dug divisions potted up with a good root portion will be salable in 2- or 4-quart containers in two to four weeks depending on how much root growth you want prior to selling the plant. Or the crowns can be divided in the fall into individual plantlets, allowed to root in 2-inch-deep (5 cm) pots, overwintered, and sold the following spring.

Seeds sown in mid-February will produce salable green plants (32-cell pack) by early to mid-May when grown at 55F to 58F (13C to 15C) nights. These plants will flower sporadically the first season. For 4-inch pots, allow 13 to 15 weeks for a fully leafed-out plant when sowing from seed.

This crop is also available from commercial propagators in a liner or plug. These plugs can be shipped during winter and potted up into 4-inch (10 cm), quart, or gallon containers depending on when you bring in your plants. From a 72-plug tray, a 4-inch pot will finish off in four to six weeks when potted up in March and grown on at 55F (13C) nights.

VARIETIES

Variation can be expected from many seed-grown perennials and annuals when they're produced in open fields and allowed to cross-pollinate prior to seed set. *Alchemilla*, however, is a difficult crop to identify in the trade due to its apomictic nature (the flowers do not require fertilization to produce seed; therefore the resulting plant will be identical to the mother plant). In the trade, depending on the seed producer, it's conceivable that *A. mollis* may have merely been a variant of *A. vulgaris*; hence the confusion over nomenclature.

A. mollis (*A. vulgaris*) is available from a number of U.S. seed firms or from European seed companies. Plugs are easily found from various suppliers.

IN THE HOME GARDEN

When purchasing plants at the garden center you will find that the first season after growing from seed or being divided, the flower stalks tend to be weak and produce blooms only to the sides of the mounded foliage rather than upright from the center. After the plants become established, flowers can still be expected to lie close to the ground but initially will be held more upright and arch to the side as they age. Some authorities suggest that the plants reseed themselves freely and often become weedy. This occurs primarily in fertile soil under moist conditions—which is what these plants prefer, though we have never had a problem.

Plant *Alchemilla* in areas where the plants get morning sun and afternoon shade and where the soil is moist but well drained. If planted in full-sun locations, the plants will perform well but wilt in the hot afternoon sun, lasting only three to four seasons before the crowns burn out. Some plants may die. Flowers can be cut for fresh or dried arrangements.

▬ ALYSSUM MURALE (SYN. A. ARGENTEUM)

For *Alyssum saxatilis* (Basket o'Gold), see *Aurinia saxatilis*.

FAMILY: Cruciferae

COMMON NAME(S): Madwort, Yellow Tuft

The botanical name is of Greek origin, denoting a cure for madness.

DESCRIPTION

Closely related to the popular garden plant *Aurinia saxatilis*, *Alyssum murale* differs in having smaller flowers (one-sixteenth inch) on more mounding plants with smaller leaves than *A. saxatilis* Compacta. The flowers are a buff or light yellow color on plants that reach 18 inches (46 cm) tall when blooming. The plants are more erect than most other species in the genus but possess the same gray-green foliage.

HARDINESS: Zones 3 to 7.

Since it suffers in high heat and humidity, *Alyssum murale* is usually a short-lived plant in our northern locations. It is more sun tolerant than *A. saxatilis* but will still die out in three to four years.

SEASON OF BLOOM: May and June.

PROPAGATION

Cuttings and seed are the two most common methods to propagate alyssums. Take cuttings in early spring before bud set or in summer after flowering. The plants need to be sheared back, fed, and allowed to rejuvenate after flowering before cuttings are taken. Divisions are possible but difficult and seldom produce reliable results. Seed is the most common—and easiest—form of propagation, but the plants may vary in performance. We've observed that the habit and vigor of seed-propagated plants are usually uniform, though bud set and flowering may differ.

GERMINATION OVERVIEW

Seed will germinate readily and requires no pretreatments to get germination rates of 70% and higher. *Alyssum* will germinate in three to eight days in a 68F to 72F (20C to 22C) temperature range without being covered. After germination, drop the night temperatures to 58F to 60F (14C to 16C) to reduce stretching. Seedlings can be transplanted within two weeks after sowing.

GROWING ON

Crop time: Seed sown in mid-February will be salable as a green, 32-cell pack by mid-May. Grow on at 50F (10C) once plants have become established in the final container. Avoid long, cold, wet periods, however, as the plants are susceptible to root rot and will die. If disease problems persist, transplant to larger, individual containers. Plants will grow and fill in quickly in cool weather and continue to develop even as temperatures rise. The plants will not flower, however, until the following spring.

Sowings made in autumn, transplanted to quart or larger containers and overwintered in a cold greenhouse or cold frame, will have had sufficient cold weather exposure to flower the following spring. When starting this late in the year, don't allow plants to go dormant during the winter, and keep temperatures between 38F to 40F (4C to 5C) once the plants are firmly established in the their pots. In our trials, sowings made in November flowered in April.

You can also sow the seed the previous spring or summer for potting up. These can be transplanted to quart or larger pots for overwintering in a cold greenhouse or cold frame or allowed to go dormant for next spring sales. If you don't allow them to go dormant, keep temperatures cold during the winter to prevent plants from getting too robust.

VARIETIES

A. murale is not readily available from U.S. seed companies. While I wouldn't tell you it is something you have to have, it is worth trying once. European seed companies usually offer this and several of its related species.

RELATED MATERIAL

A. montanum (*A. pedemontanum*) is more prostrate in habit than *A. murale*, with plants growing to no more than 10 inches (25 cm) tall. Somewhat similar to *Aurinia saxatilis* (the Basket-of-Gold perennial alyssum) with its gray-green leaves, *A. montanum* is neater in appearance, however, and its flowers are fragrant.

A. spinosum (*Ptilotrichum spinosum*) is distinct from other genus members in bearing white to light pink flowers that are lightly fragrant. They appear in June and July. This plant is a subshrub with a spiny look to its mounding foliage and white stems. The leaves have a silvery cast and are about 2 inches (5 cm) long. Plants grow to 12 to 15 inches (30 to 38 cm) tall in the garden. Protect during winter to avoid windburned foliage.

A. spinosum Roseum is superior to the species in having lavender-rose flowers on shorter plants. The color shades more readily from plant to plant when grown in sun and when propagated from seed rather than cuttings.

All of the varieties noted here are propagated like *A. murale*.

IN THE HOME GARDEN

Plants from winter-sown seed that are purchased from a nursery in mid to late spring will develop into handsome, uniform plants by midsummer and then will flower profusely the following spring. If planted in locations where they get long, warm or hot summers, the plants will be short lived. In more northern areas, the plants live longer, especially when planted to soils on the lean side with a morning exposure but protected from the sun during the hottest and most humid part of the day. Once flowering is over, trim the plants back to encourage new growth, water, and lightly fertilize.

When planted to moist and fertile locations, *A. murale* will reseed, though not invasively. The resulting seedlings can be kept under control with limited labor.

▄▄▄ AMORPHA CANESCENS

Amorpha is derived from "a"=without, "morphe"=form, referring to the lack of form of the flowers.

FAMILY: Leguminoseae

COMMON NAME(S): Leadplant, Indigo Bush, False Indigo

DESCRIPTION

Amorpha canescens is a native plant of the United States found in dry, sandy knolls or gravelly areas where the soil is well drained. Plants are woody and shrublike in form, although the stems die back to the ground each winter. Flowers are a purplish blue and borne in 6-inch-long (15 cm) spikes at the branch ends. The scentless flowers somewhat resemble the blooms of *Veronica spicata*. Plants grow to a 2- to 4-foot (60 to 120 cm) height with spreads from 3 to 4 feet (90 to 120 cm), but cultivated plants are often shorter in height and spread more than the wild types. Plants have many leaflets arranged similarly to locust trees. In the early evening, leaves fold down but open up again by morning. The upper surface of the foliage has a downy gray cast that adds an interesting quality.

HARDINESS: Zones 3 to 8.

SEASON OF BLOOM: June and July.

PROPAGATION

Seed is the most common form of propagation, though softwood cuttings taken during the summer after flowering will root readily.

GERMINATION OVERVIEW: 17,000 seeds per ounce/595 per gram.

Pretreatments: *Amorpha* is a legume and, typical of the genus, germinates more readily if the seed is used fresh. If seed has been stored, seedcoats will require scarifying or chipping and soaking overnight in warm water to germinate readily. Some authorities have used a short moist-chilling period with good results.

Sow seed onto moistened sand and chill in a refrigerator at 34F to 38F (1C to 4C) for up to 14 days. Check regularly for germinating seed and remove to a germination bench when seed begins to sprout. Germinate between 62F to 68F (16C to 20C). Fresh seed germinates more rapidly and can be transplanted within three to four weeks after sowing, while seed stored until spring germinates over a period of several weeks to several months and thus requires multiple transplant dates.

GROWING ON

Crop time: Fall-sown seed will produce salable transplants in 1-gallon containers the second year after sowing. According to Michael Dirr in his book, *Manual of Woody Landscape Plants*, cuttings taken in July and dipped in 480 ppm Ethrel rooted well in a peat moss and perlite mixture [1].

VARIETIES

A. canescens is available from U.S. seed companies specializing in native flowering plants.

RELATED MATERIAL

A. fruticosa is taller than *A. canescens*, from 6 to 18 feet (1.8 to 5.4 m) in the wild. Flowers are insignificant and very small. The dull purple blooms are borne in spikes from 2 to 7 inches (5 to 18 cm) long, usually flowering in July. Foliage is locustlike and gray green in color. The seed pods are covered with glands that emit a pleasant odor as they open. Propagate as indicated under *A. canescens*.

USES

Recommended for the native woodland and wildflower garden and where heat-tolerant plants are preferred. Some of the species, especially *A. fruticosa*, have been suggested as good soil-holding plants for steep slopes.

IN THE HOME GARDEN

Plants aren't of high value or impact for the traditional home garden but are probably better for poorer full-sun locations where common summer annuals and perennials would fail. The purple flowers combine well with the gray-green foliage, but beware of planting overly colorful companion plants close by.

Plants don't require staking or special care of any kind. Once established the crop is long lived and can be used as a cut flower.

REFERENCES

[1] Dirr, M. 1983. *Manual of woody landscape plants*. Champaign, Ill.: Stipes Publ. Co.

▄▄ AMSONIA TABERNAEMONTANA

FAMILY: Apocynaceae

COMMON NAME(S): Willow Amsonia, Bluestar

DESCRIPTION

Light blue, one-half to three-quarter-inch (1 to 2 cm), star-shaped flowers are held terminally atop 2- to 3-foot (60 to 90 cm) tall foliage. Once in flower, plants remain in bloom for two to three weeks but seldom reflower during the summer. The plants grow from a small, 12- to 15-inch (30 to 38 cm) wide clump at the bases, but the slightly arching stems spread from 3 to 4 feet (90 cm to 1.2 m) across at the crown all summer. Later the stems become woody, and the plants die back to the ground each winter to emerge again the following spring. Its foliage is deep green and glossy. *Amsonia* is native to Virginia, the central United States, and south to Georgia and Texas. See Color Plate 8 for photo of *Amsonia tabernaemontana*.

HARDINESS: Zones 3 to 9.

SEASON OF BLOOM: May and June.

PROPAGATION

Seed, terminal cuttings, and division are the most common ways to propagate this crop. Seed can be harvested from plants in September or purchased. From seed, allow two years to flower plants and three years for profuse bloom. Cuttings taken in the spring prior to flower bud initiation will root more easily than those taken in July or later. Those require more time to root. In general, allow five to six weeks for spring cuttings to root.

Take divisions in the fall on strongly established clumps of amsonia. Clumps that are three-years-old or less will not yield as many transplants as older clumps, which tend to be more woody.

GERMINATION OVERVIEW

Pretreatments: If seed is sown in the spring in the traditional methods noted for annuals (70F or 21C, little or no cover, and mist), germination rates will be low or zero. *Amsonia* requires a moist-chilling prior to germination. Sow the seed in a peat-lite media, cover the germination tray with a piece of plastic, and then expose the flat to temperatures of 41F (5C) for five to six weeks. Once the treatment is over, bring the flat back into the greenhouse and grow on as you normally would.

In some cases, the seed needs to be exposed to the chilling for a longer period of time. For additional details, review the information about moist-chilling in the **Propagation Techniques** chapter.

Harry Phillips, in *Growing and Propagating Wild Flowers*, writes "... rapid and uniform germination will be obtained if you cut away a small piece from one end of each seed with scissors and then soak the seeds in water for two or three days. Cutting off the end of the seed allows more water to be absorbed quickly and germination to occur, usually in two or three days [1]."

GROWING ON

Crop time: On seed-propagated plants, the roots will develop quickly but will not produce flowering plants until the second year; more profuse bloom can be expected the third year. Plants will grow larger and bloom more with each year.

At the time of this writing, a new type of liner has become available. From Summersun Greenhouse Company in Washington state, a bottomless, 3-inch pot with a 6- to 10-month-old transplant is shipped to growers. The root ball is removed from the pot, scored (vertical surface cuts to encourage faster rooting), and then potted up into gallon (or larger) containers. Many of these plants, including amsonias, are salable in six to eight weeks as gallons, depending on your night temperatures and how well rooted you want your plants.

As for divisions, work with the plants when dormant. As they're lifted, look for the "eyes" on the crown where stems will emerge next spring. As you divide, take a piece of the crown with an eye and a portion of the root mass and pot up into 2- to 4-quart containers.

Cuttings will root relatively quickly when taken as spring shoots rather than during midsummer. Allow five to six weeks for rooting, and pot up into gallon pots for sales the following spring.

VARIETIES

A. tabernaemontana is more readily available from U.S. wildflower seed houses than at any of the commercial seed companies. Seed can also be gathered from your own stock plants.

A. tabernaemontana var. *montana* is a shorter variety than the species and grows to only 18 inches (46 cm) tall with blue flowers.

A. tabernaemontana var. *salicifolia* (*A. salicifolia*) has long narrow leaves, a less erect habit, and fewer flowers. Plants bloom one to two weeks later than the species.

RELATED MATERIAL

A. ciliata is a thin-leaved variety with a feathery appearance, hence the common name of Feather Amsonia. It is hardy to Zones 7 through 9, with blue flowers on plants to 2 feet (60 cm) tall. Propagate as you would *A. tabernaemontana*.

USES

Highly recommended for the wildflower or woodland garden where it becomes larger in habit as the seasons pass. Use it in the landscape where you can emphasize its shrublike performance in summer (it will die back to the ground during winter). Limited problems and excellent hardiness are trademarks of this plant.

IN THE HOME GARDEN

This is an easily grown perennial for sunny and well-drained locations. Avoid heavily shaded areas, especially when combined with fertile soil, since the plants tend to be too open and often don't flower freely. Once flowering is completed, lightly trim the plants back for a second flush of blooms. This second flush is not as full as the first but yields satisfactory results. Plants are low maintenance and have few insect or disease problems. Only when plants are stressed for a period of time do problems develop. In the fall, the foliage turns a butterscotch or yellow color.

REFERENCES

[1] Phillips, H. 1985. *Growing and propagating wildflowers*. Chapel Hill, N.C.: The University of North Carolina Press.

◼ ANACYCLUS DEPRESSUS

FAMILY: Asteraceae

COMMON NAME(S): Atlas Daisy

DESCRIPTION

A low-growing, rosetting perennial, *Anacyclus depressus* grows from 10 to 12 inches (25 to 30 cm) tall and spreads 12 to 15 inches (30 to 38 cm) across. The dissected leaves look fernlike and are gray green in color. The 2-inch (5 cm) white flowers are backed with a rich crimson to purple coloring; each bloom has a small but pronounced yellow eye in the center of the bloom. Flower heads will close up at night or on cloudy afternoons but remain more open than a portulaca under the same conditions. See Color Plate 9 for photo of *Anacyclus depressus*.

HARDINESS: Zones 6 to 8.

Anacylus doesn't tolerate hot, humid weather and under long-term exposure, the plants become more susceptible to diseases and insect pests. In our Chicago location, we can expect losses of nearly 100% in the spring from a planting the previous year. When plants do survive the winter, they are often languid and seldom produce more than three or four blooms. This plant is more suitable for the coastal United States or grown as a hardy annual in other parts of the country.

SEASON OF BLOOM: June.

PROPAGATION

Seed is the most common way to propagate and can be done at any time of the year. Seed lots are shipped fresh from U.S. seed companies annually, and the resulting germinations are greatly improved over stored seed.

GERMINATION OVERVIEW: 50,000 seeds per ounce/1,750 per gram.

Pretreatments: Seed will often germinate readily at 70 to 80% without any special handling. Older seed may require a period of moist chilling (see additional information under the **Propagation** chapter in this book). If using seed harvested within several months to a year, germination problems are limited. If rates are low, moist chill the seed at 37F (3C) for three weeks and then germinate as indicated below. Don't cover the seed, but water it in so that only the top of the seed is exposed to light.

If no pretreatments are necessary, seed will germinate in five to 10 days at 65F to 70F (18C to 21C). The seed doesn't need to be covered. Seedlings can be transplanted 12 to 20 days after sowing.

GROWING ON

Crop time: While the seeds are quick to germinate, the seedlings often sit after transplanting until they start to develop their basal rosette, which can take one to two weeks. From seed, *Anacyclus* will take from 12 to 14 weeks to fill out a 32 pack. The plants will flower sporadically, but not reliably, from a midwinter sowing.

Sowings in November/December, transplanted to a 4½-inch (11 cm) or larger container and grown on at 50F (10C) received enough exposure to cold weather (vernalization) to flower more freely than those that were sown later. In the northern United States, our best plants are those that were treated in this manner. Since *Anacyclus* is not reliably hardy here, sowings done the previous autumn for 4½-inch (11 cm), quart or gallon pots for spring sales offer us the best opportunity. Due to its limited hardiness, however, we treat it as a short-lived perennial or hardy annual in our climate.

This crop is also available from commercial propagators as a liner or plug. (Additional information is provided on this production method in the **How to Use** chapter under **Growing on**.)

VARIETIES

A. depressus is available from several U.S. seed firms as well as from Europe. The most common cultivar, Garden Gnome, exhibits all the attributes noted under the description and has had limited success here in our West Chicago gardens during the winter. Plants grown from seed are true to type and show limited variation from plant to plant.

IN THE HOME GARDEN

A short-lived plant in our Chicago gardens but one worthy of trying. Plants prefer full sun and being close to a lake or other areas around water where the cool nights bring out the plants best. Away from water and cool weather, choose a location where the plants receive morning sun but are shaded during the hottest part of the day.

Planting sites should be well drained with a pH of 7 to 8, although several authorities differ as to what is best. Some suggest that a slightly higher pH is better. When planting in Zone 5, choose a site close to a building with an eastern exposure and wind protection to improve the chances of this plant coming back from the winter.

▬ ANAPHALIS MARGARITACEA

FAMILY: Asteraceae

COMMON NAME(S): Pearly Everlasting

DESCRIPTION

This plant is valued equally for its flowers and foliage, but its foliage is a stronger element in the perennial garden. Prolific, basal branching stems produce an upright and mounded plant that tapers to either side. Plants can grow to 15 or 18 inches (38 to 46 cm) without blooms and up to 2 feet (60 cm) in bloom. Plants often spread to

20 inches and fill in well. The leaves are covered with a mass of fine white hairs, similar in appearance to dusty miller but not as rich in color. The flowers are small—up to one-quarter inch (6 mm) across—and the surrounding bracts are covered with fine gray hairs. Flowers look somewhat like strawflowers (*Helichrysum*) when in bloom and can have a light scent. See Color Plate 10 for photo of *Anaphalis margaritacea*.

HARDINESS: Zones 3 to 8.

SEASON OF BLOOM: July and August.

PROPAGATION

Seed, cuttings, and divisions are methods of propagating *Anaphalis*. Seed can be sown in the fall or winter for flowering plants the following summer. Seed produces relatively pure lines without a high percentage of off-types. Cuttings taken of newly developing shoots from the crown are easy to root. Divisions are done in the spring or fall on well-established plants (at least three years old) so that yields will be high enough.

GERMINATION OVERVIEW: 600,000 seeds per ounce/21,000 per gram.
Pretreatments: None needed. Germination should be above 70% with normal germination procedures.

Germination temperatures of 68F to 70F (20C to 21C) are ideal for a good seedling stand. Seed can be left exposed or lightly covered during germination. Light does aid in germination and produces stronger seedlings than covered seed. Germination begins in four to eight days, and transplanting can be done four to five weeks after sowing.

GROWING ON

Crop time: Seed sown in mid-February, transplanted in late March to a 32-cell pack, will be salable 10 to 11 weeks after sowing. After the plants have become established, grow on at 55F to 58F (13C to 15C) nights for May sales. Plants can be grown cooler but often don't attain a full size and look small and unproductive. Plants will flower the same season from seed, but if grown cool at 48F to 50F (9C to 10C), flower bud initiation takes place early, and plants may be only 5 to 7 inches (13 to 18 cm) tall when bud set begins. Plants almost look disproportionate.

If 4-inch (10 cm) or quart containers are desired from seed-propagated plants, sow seed in the late fall or early winter to allow 12 to 14 weeks for a fully developed 4-inch container (quart containers require two weeks extra). Grow on at 55F to 58F (13C to 15C).

Problems: The only major pest of *Anaphalis* is worms, which may attack plants grown outside. If this occurs, use Dipel or similar products containing *Bacillus thuringiensis*.

Varieties

A. margaritacea is sold in the United States by numerous seed companies under its botanical name, its common name (Pearly Everlasting), or as the cultivar New Snow. These are all equal in their development and habit.

Related material

A. cinnamonmea is very similar to *A. margaritacea*, although it is shorter with smaller blooms. Some of the seeded selections may be this species or *A. margaritacea*, however. Since I'm not a taxonomist, it's hard to say, but some of the aspects of New Snow are very close to this species, and many U.S. seed companies carry this latter selection in their catalogs.

A. triplinervis has been described as having a more pristine appearance than the species but may tolerate more shade. It, too, looks like *A. margaritacea* although it doesn't do as well in drought. Summer Snow has been written up in a number of publications as being an excellent cultivar, although few U.S. firms carry this selection either as plants or as seed. If located, it may be of value due to its compact nature—it's only 10 to 12 inches (25 to 30 cm) tall.

Uses

Primarily a plant for home garden use, but some professional growers do carry the plant as a dried cut flower.

In the home garden

Anaphalis is an easy perennial for the home garden whether in full sun or partial shade. However, too much shade produces weak stems, which may cause the plant to fall open at the crown. Plants prefer a well-drained location but will be more persistent in moderately moist environments than other gray-leaved foliage plants. Plants have been accused of becoming invasive, but we see this more in sandy loam soils rather than in our midwestern clay loam.

During the summer, check the terminal areas of the stems to see if they are bound together in a weblike fashion. This is a sign of worms. Apply Dipel or similar *Bacillus thuringiensis* products to eradicate the problem.

Anchusa azurea (A. italica)

Family: Boraginaceae

Common name(s): Italian Bugloss, Italian Alkanet

Description

Anchusa azurea is prized primarily for its bright blue flowers, but its acceptance in the marketplace is rather limited. Plants are durable, in fact, some selections border on the obnoxious in terms of surviving and returning year after year. But don't mistake my comment as totally negative. Some perennial forms of *Anchusa* have the uncanny ability to fill in an area and live for years, while others may live for only a few seasons. Some newer forms are not as aggressive and may be preferred. Leaves are coarse and hairy, and plants grow to between 4 and 5 feet (1.2 to 1.5 m) tall in our midwestern gardens. A single plant will spread from 15 inches to 2 feet (38 to 60 cm) across. The single, five-petaled blue flowers are up to three-quarters of an inch (2 cm) across, and plants bloom for three to four weeks.

HARDINESS: Zones 3 to 8.

SEASON OF BLOOM: May and June.

PROPAGATION

Seed, division, root cuttings, and basal cuttings are the usual ways to propagate this genus. You can divide plants either in the spring or fall; root cuttings are usually taken during dormancy in late winter or early spring. See the **Propagation Techniques** chapter in the front of the book for additional details on how to propagate root cuttings. As for seed, remember that the named cultivars seldom flower true to type when propagated from seed; division and root cuttings produce more reliable results. Basal cuttings are taken in the spring.

GERMINATION OVERVIEW: 1,200 seeds per ounce/42 per gram.
Pretreatments: *Anchusa* seed will germinate easily regardless of whether it's three months old or a year; germination will be around 70% either way.

Given soil temperatures of 70F to 72F (21C to 22C), the seeds will germinate five to 10 days after sowing. The seed doesn't need to be covered during germination. Seedlings are transplantable 12 to 18 days after sowing.

GROWING ON

Crop time: Plants will not flower the same season from seed. Seed sown in March will produce green salable cell packs 11 to 12 weeks later. Grow on at 50F to 55F (10C to 13C) once established in the final pack.

For quart and gallon containers, sow 15 to 18 weeks prior to sales and transplant to larger containers as the plants size up. Grow on at 50F to 55F (10C to 13C) nights. Depending on the length of exposure to cool temperatures, plants may flower sporadically the first year. For more dependable flowering, sow the previous summer, pot up when ready, and overwinter for sales the following spring.

Root cuttings are taken in mid to late winter from primarily dormant plants. See the **Propagation Techniques** chapter for further details. Root cuttings taken during winter will produce plants that can be sold in autumn or overwintered for sales the following spring.

VARIETIES

Dropmore is a 30- to 36-inch-tall (76 to 91 cm) cultivar with bright blue flowers that bloom in June. Leaves are rounded and gray green. While seed for this cultivar can be found in the European trade, vegetative propagation is most preferred and maintains uniformity and purity of the line. Seed-propagated plants grow and flower but they often become rank.

Little John is a shorter variety, 18 inches (46 cm) or less. Flowers are deep blue and have a long flowering period from June through late summer. Plants are reported to be evergreen to Zone 6. Propagate vegetatively only.

Loddon Royalist is another vigorous performer, 36 inches (90 cm) tall, with an intense blue flower richer and deeper in color than Dropmore. Plants are basal branching. Vegetatively propagate this cultivar.

Royal Blue (also called Dropmore Royal Blue) is an intense blue-flowering variety, similar in color to Loddon Royalist, between 2 and 3 feet (60 and 90 cm) tall. Plants have a triangular or pyramidal habit and nice form. Vegetatively propagate Royal Blue.

RELATED MATERIAL

Anchusa capensis has been listed as a biennial in a number of references, although its best performance is as an annual. Early February sowings will germinate within four to eight days and can be transplanted to the final container 15 to 20 days after sowing. Choose either packs or small pots, and use a 10- to 12-week crop time for first bloom in a 32-cell pack, with an additional week or two for full bloom. Plants aren't uniform in bloom times but don't usually require more than two weeks from first bloom to full flower. Plants will not live through a winter in Zone 5. Advise your retail customers to cut seed heads off as they form and reshape the plant by trimming; the plants will bloom again in three to four weeks.

Anchusa myosotidiflora. See *Brunnera macrophylla.*

IN THE HOME GARDEN

The taller selections are used at the back of the border and are excellent when combined with pink and yellow flower colors. The coarse foliage and blue flower color will remind you of an upright *Myosotis sylvatica* (forget-me-not); the latter can be used sparingly in the front of the border to relate the two groupings. Beware of overfeeding or planting in a rich and fertile soil. Some selections can become overgrown quickly, and the taller ones will require staking before midseason. In some cases, they'll overgrow small and weak plants if the area is too rich. Plant in full sun or partial shade. Space the larger varieties 2 feet (60 cm) apart and the shorter varieties 12 to 15 inches (30 to 38 cm).

■■■ ANEMONE × HYBRIDA (A. JAPONICA)

Many of the varieties sold under the common name of Japanese anemones are actually hybrids resulting from crosses, especially *A. hupehensis var. japonica* × *A. vitifolia*.

FAMILY: Ranunculaceae

COMMON NAME(S): Japanese Anemones

DESCRIPTION

Anemones are graceful background plants for the late summer perennial garden. They rate as some of the most beautiful additions you can have. Deep, dark green foliage adorns the slender and erect, to sometimes drooping, flowering stems. Plants are robust and command as much as 4 or 5 feet (1.2 to 1.5 m) in the garden, especially when grown in a deep, rich soil. Plants can spread from 15 to 24 inches (38 to 61 cm) across. Flowers are white and various shades of pink, ranging in size from 2 to 3 inches (5 to 7 cm) across. Cultivars are available in both single- and double-flowering forms.

HARDINESS: Zones 3 to 8.
Some cultivars are only marginally winter hardy.

SEASON OF BLOOM: September and October.

PROPAGATION

Division and root cuttings are the two most common methods of propagation, although root cuttings are preferred. The time to take divisions is in spring, while root cuttings should be taken during the late winter or early spring when the plants are still dormant.

GERMINATION OVERVIEW

Seed is available in Europe but is seldom found here. Seed isn't practical for propagating Japanese anemones; it's used only as a means of perpetuating the species or developing new hybrids, but it is not for commercial production. However, if you want to try it, use fresh seed only and subject the seed to a warm-moist period followed by a cold-moist period. See the **Propagation** chapter for details.

GROWING ON

Crop time: Spring divisions produce salable plants within a matter of weeks depending on the division size and the container used for transplanting. Care has to be taken in dividing the crowns of field-grown plants. The roots are easily injured and, if wounded during dividing, will require time to heal and produce a plant. If roots are severely damaged, plants may die.

As for root cuttings, roots removed from the mother plant during the winter require six months for sales in quart pots during autumn, though they can be overwintered in quart or gallon pots for sales the following spring.

Commercial propagators have both small pots or roots available for shipping during fall and winter for spring sales. A number of companies offer pot sizes ranging from 2½ inches to a quart depending on your market and the price you're willing to pay. If you purchase quart or 4-inch (10 cm) pots wholesale, plants are probably ready for retail sales immediately or within one or two weeks once you've hardened the plants off. Pot up 2½-inch pots into 1- or 2-quart containers and grow on at 55F (13C) nights for sales in five to six weeks.

Bare-root transplants are shipped in milled peat moss in a plastic bag. They can be potted up immediately or stored in a cool, dry place for several weeks until ready to use. Pot up into 1- or 2-quart containers, water in thoroughly, and grow on at 55F (13C) nights. Every year I hear complaints about this crop when the roots are grown too cold and too wet. After the initial watering, water as needed but not heavily until new growth starts to emerge. In general, it takes seven to nine weeks to produce a salable plant depending on how full you want it for retail sales.

VARIETIES

All of the following are **vegetatively propagated**.

var. *alba* (also listed as Alba) has single white flowers to 3 inches (7 cm) across on plants 2 to 3 feet (60 to 90 cm) tall.

Honorine Jobert (occasionally Honorine Joubert) is a free-flowering, pure white selection to slightly over 3 feet (90 cm) tall and just about as wide. It is a prized and recommended variety due to its stature and graceful appearance. Flowers are 2 to 3 inches (5 to 7 cm) across.

Krimhilde (sometimes listed as Kriemhilde) has a salmon-pink flower and grows to less than 30 inches (76 cm) tall.

Margarete (Margarette in some books and catalogs) is a semi to fully double-flowering pink selection, from 2 to 3 feet (60 to 90 cm) tall. Flowers measure 2 to 3 inches (5 to 7 cm) across.

Max Vogel is free flowering, with semidouble, bright pink blooms, growing to less than 2 feet (60 cm) tall. Flowers are between 3 and 4 inches (7 and 10 cm) across, but some authorities suggest they can be as large as 5 inches (13 cm).

Prince Henry (also listed as Prinz Heinrich and, less frequently, Prince Henryi) is a deep rose selection with semidouble to double flowers. Plants grow from 2 to 3 feet (60 to 90 cm) tall.

Queen Charlotte is a semidouble, delicate pink-flowering cultivar with blooms to 3 inches (7 cm) across. Plants grow to 36 inches tall and often have a similar spread.

September Charm is a single-flowering pink with a satinlike sheen or cast to the overall petal. This variety isn't as vigorous a grower—usually about 2½ feet (75 cm) tall.

Whirlwind is an older American-bred variety from late in the last century. Plants are robust and grow upright to between 3 and 4 feet (90 to 120 cm) tall. The pure white flowers are semidouble to between 2 and 3 inches (5 and 7 cm) across. Plants have an equally large spread to them, so space plants accordingly.

RELATED MATERIAL

A. hupehensis is a 2- to 3-foot (60 to 90 cm) variety with a light red or crimson tint to the flower bud, which then opens into 3-inch (7 cm) blooms of a dusty rose pink. It is admired by many horticulturists for its garden performance. Occasionally—though incorrectly—it may be labeled as the botanical name for the hybrids listed previously. This species also bears the common name of Japanese anemone, however. Propagate as you would *A.* × *hybrida*.

A. vitifolia (syn. *A. tomentosa*) Robustissima, like its name, is a robust-growing plant to between 3 and 4 feet (90 to 120 cm) tall when in flower. Blooms are bright pink in color and can start blooming in September, maybe earlier. Often hardier than the Japanese types, this plant develops large, deeply veined leaves that are wooly gray underneath. Propagate as you would *A.* × *hybrida*; seed is available from several European sources.

USES

This plant is primarily used for the home landscape and cutting garden. Plants often flower too late for professional landscapers, although the plants are worthy if used with proper companions. While I feel this is a gem in the home perennial garden, it has potential as an up and coming plant for commercial landscapes.

IN THE HOME GARDEN

This is a backbone plant for the late summer garden that adds a great deal to the home landscape. It is excellent for backing up against red brick or wood siding, especially natural or weathered wood that hasn't been painted. Plants do best in eastern exposures where they are shaded during the hottest part of the day. With a rich and moisture-retentive location, however, plants also perform well in full sun, usually in higher elevations or where the nights are cooler than our Chicago summers. Here we always give them some daytime shade.

Gallon-sized plants put in the ground in spring will establish roots over most of the summer at the expense of leaves. Keep the plants well-watered during this time and beware of allowing prolonged wilt. Plants seldom flower profusely the first autumn after planting, and may not flower at all if spring and summer weather was too severe. Drought and high heat are the biggest initial concerns after planting for up to one or two months, depending on the climate.

Northern winters can wreak havoc on these plants as well, especially when the previous summer's weather was hot and dry. Once every few years we experience a cool and wet fall in Chicago, followed promptly by a cold snap. This is usually the death of these plants, especially exposed plantings. A light to medium mulch is always a benefit. If planted where they get cold and dry winter winds, plants covered with evergreen boughs combined with a layer of mulch are well-protected.

▬▬ ANGELICA ARCHANGELICA
(also *A. officinalis* and *Archangelica officinalis*)

FAMILY: Apiaceae

COMMON NAME(S): Angelica, Archangel, Wild Parsnip
The common name of angelica was given due to its supposed angelic virtue as a medicinal herb.

DESCRIPTION
Angelica archangelica is an erect growing plant to between 4 and 6 feet (1.2 to 1.6 m) tall with strong, medium green stems that turn a bronze or crimson color as they age. The leaves are doubly or triply compound and large in appearance, often over a foot (30 cm) long and arching toward the ground. The single, greenish white flowers are small in size—less than one-half inch (1 cm)—and held in 4- to 6-inch (10 cm to 15 cm) umbels. The plants are considered biennials, although the plants act as short-lived perennials if flowers are removed before the seed develops. If the plant is allowed to set seed, it will die. Both plants and seed are aromatic.

Note: While some authorities suggest that angelica can be used as a culinary herb, others refute this notion, saying instead it is a suspected carcinogen. Also, be cautious about collecting seed from the wild if you are not trained in plant identification. An extremely poisonous look-alike, *Cicuta maculata* (the water hemlock), has been gathered in error.

HARDINESS: Zones 4 to 9.

SEASON OF BLOOM: July and August.

PROPAGATION
Angelica is commonly propagated by seed, although divisions have been mentioned by some authorities. Divisions are not always successful, however, and seed-propagated plants are more uniform. Divisions are more for home gardeners.

GERMINATION OVERVIEW
Pretreatments: Many authors reflect on the short viability of angelica seed, noting that it often dies within six months after harvesting: Few seedlings emerge when sown after this time. It's possible that the seed is actually dormant and requires a stratification period if stored prior to sowing. Seed gathered from the plants as it matures yields good germination percentages but these will be lower if the seed is

stored for six months first and then sown. If you have seed that has been stored for awhile, follow the suggestions in the **Propagation** chapter for moist chilling to help improve germination.

Germination temperatures of 68F to 70F (18C to 21C) work well on freshly harvested seed. Don't cover the seed during germination. They'll emerge either quickly or over a period of time, depending on freshness. In our trials, seedlings emerged in 10 to 20 days. Seedlings develop slowly, however, and can take up to eight weeks to transplant to a cell pack or pot. One additional method is to allow the seed heads to develop and disperse. The following spring, in April, numerous seedlings can be dug up and potted to 4-inch or quart containers for May sales.

GROWING ON

Crop time: Seed is often sown early in the year or late the previous year for quart sales of one plant per pot the following spring. If you're working with cell packs for green flat sales or intermediate containers before transplanting, the plants require 14 to 16 weeks for a 32-cell tray to reach the salable point. If grown on at 60F (16C) nights, the plants will be less than 5 inches (13 cm) tall when ready to sell. Plants will not flower the same season from seed but will grow surprisingly fast in the garden after transplanting. By mid-July the plants will be already 8 to 10 inches (20 to 25 cm) tall, with a 15- to 20-inch (38 to 51 cm) spread, when transplanted in June from a February sowing.

VARIETIES

A. archangelica is available from a select group of U.S. seed firms that specialize in herbs. While this variety is the most common, some companies may also carry some other selections.

IN THE HOME GARDEN

Angelica is an imposing background plant that adds a great deal to the landscape with both its foliage and flowers. Several plants are necessary, however, to create a full effect as the plants will be both tall and wide when in flower. Be sure to cut flowers off prior to seed formation to keep the plants from year to year; otherwise the plants will die. After three or four years, the plants will weaken and should be replaced. The flowers have been used both as solo cut flowers and in mixed bouquets where the muted light green flowers work well with both pastels and bolder colors.

Plants don't require staking and work well in a slightly acid (pH 5.5 to 6) soil. Plant in full sun to partial shade, although the plants tend to wilt during our late, hot summer days when the humidity is high. In USDA zones farther south where the plants get shade during the hottest part of the day, superior specimens will result. Plants will reseed readily if seed is allowed to develop.

ANTENNARIA DIOICA

FAMILY: Asteraceae

COMMON NAME(S): Everlasting, Pussy-toes, Ladies' Tobacco

DESCRIPTION

A. dioica is a rock garden plant prized for its gray foliage on mat or carpetlike plants that reach 1 inch (2 cm) tall when not in flower. During the spring, erect stems, growing from 5 to 7 inches (13 to 18 cm) tall, hold three to eight light green flowers with pink tips. The flowers are small—about one-quarter inch (6 mm) across—and resemble pussywillow flowers except that antennarias have a papery bract around the entire bloom.

The plants develop from basal rosettes that spread by stolons. In some climates, the plants can become quite large, spreading 12 to 24 inches (30 to 61 cm) across.

HARDINESS: Zones 4 to 8.

SEASON OF BLOOM: May and June.

PROPAGATION

Antennaria is usually propagated by seed and division. Stolons can be divided anytime during active growth, but the best results occur when plants aren't in flower or in the spring. Divisions can be taken in the summer; however, there's the potential for foliage rot during hot, humid weather. Overhead watering to encourage faster root set can lead to excess moisture on the hairy foliage. After prolonged exposure to heat and humidity the foliage can rot.

GERMINATION OVERVIEW: 65,000 seeds per ounce/2,275 per gram.
Antennaria will germinate in four to eight days at 70F (21C). Lightly cover the seed for better germination. Seedlings will usually develop quickly and can be transplanted about four weeks after sowing.

When we've grown the variety, we've gotten 50% to 70% germination using this method.

GROWING ON

Crop time: *Antennaria* will not flower the same year from seed if sown in January or later. The plants require vernalization (cold treatment) to develop flower buds. The plant's foliage is usually more appreciated than its flowers, however.

For commercial propagators, a 32-cell pack will not be salable for 11 to 13 weeks when grown at 55F (13C) nights. If you're sowing from November to March, the resulting plants will grow and root faster if grown at 60F (15C) nights, although the added heating cost may not warrant this. Cooler nights help to maintain the rosette and keep the plants more uniform.

For May sales in a 4-inch pot (10 cm), allow 15 to 18 weeks from seed when grown at 55F to 58F (13C to 14C) nights. Quart containers can also be grown, but it's better to start from divisions than from seed or else sow the previous year and overwinter for spring sales. Stock plants kept in cold greenhouses or cold frames will provide plantlets during the winter, although plants divided the previous summer, potted up by autumn, and overwintered for spring sales provide the biggest plants.

VARIETIES

Antennaria dioica can be found at seed houses both in the United States and in Europe. Although not widespread in the states, the plant can be seen on either coast and in the South.

A. dioica var. *rosea* is similar to the species, but the flowers are a darker rose-pink color.

USES

Antennaria, an underused perennial in the United States, has merit for rock gardens or where it can be tucked into the open spaces in rock walls, between paving stones, and other locations where its low-growing performance and gray foliage add color and form.

Plants can spread but are less apt to do so in full-sun and well-drained locations. Infertile soil will help keep plants contained, too. In some cases people use the plants as a "lawn" (similar to ajuga) where plants can be mowed to keep them from spreading too far.

IN THE HOME GARDEN

Antennaria can be grown either in full sun or in an area that is shaded during the hottest part of the day. In our Midwest gardens outside Chicago, the plants have never filled in or spread more than 5 to 6 inches (13 to 15 cm) in width. It isn't the heat, humidity, or soil fertility that's the limiting factor—it's the depth of planting. Antennarias and other low-growing plants need to be raised above depressions where water can collect and slow their growth. Since the plants are so compact, even a minor shower can flood the plants when they're planted in a low area. Repeated flooding can lead to rot.

Although short stemmed, the flower stalks can be removed, dried, and used in wreaths and for other crafts.

■ ANTHEMIS TINCTORIA

See comments under **Varieties**.

FAMILY: Asteraceae

COMMON NAME(S): Hardy Marguerite, Golden Marguerite

DESCRIPTION

Anthemis tincoria is a very common perennial with a vigorous habit. Its reseeding traits border on being obnoxious when the plant is grown in an uncontrolled environment. Plants bloom over several weeks bearing single, yellow, daisy-like flowers on plants up to 3 feet (90 cm) tall and 2 feet (60 cm) across. Selections from seed tend to produce blooms whose outer petals reflex or droop down when blooming—they're fine for natural or wildflower gardens but not for the professional landscape. Flowers measure up to 1½ inches (4 cm) across and the stems, when cut or brushed, emit a medium to strong haylike scent.

HARDINESS: Zones 3 to 7.

When grown in fertile soils with ample moisture, plants flower so freely that they're often short lived, even though they reseed freely.

SEASON OF BLOOM: June to August.

PROPAGATION

Seed, divisions, and cuttings work equally well in propagating this crop. Sow seed at any time of the year: Winter sowings work best for sales the same season. Divisions may be taken in the spring and cuttings in the early spring when new shoots are relatively short and the plants haven't reached budding stage.

GERMINATION OVERVIEW: 60,000 seeds per ounce/2,100 per gram.

Pretreatments: A very easy perennial from seed requiring no pretreatment.

Germination temperatures of 70F to 72F (21C to 22C) are excellent for this crop. Lightly covered seed will germinate in three to seven days and can be transplanted in 12 to 18 days after sowing.

GROWING ON

Crop time: Seed produces a fast crop of blooming plants in the first season. If using *A. tinctoria* Kelway, mid-February sowings will be salable green in nine to 10 weeks in a 32-cell pack. Plants grow so fast that they border on weedy, so be prepared to keep them cool at 50F to 52F (10C to 11C) after they've established roots in the final pack or pot. You might also consider using growth regulators. Plants can be grown in 4-inch (10 cm) or quart containers for first season sales although they tend to grow upright without a pinch or growth regulator or both. Plants flower in July from a February sowing.

Divisions will take readily and produce a salable plant in a short period of time (four to six weeks) for either quart or gallon sales.

Cuttings root within 10 to 14 days at 70F (21C) in either sand or vermiculite. Be sure to take cuttings from new vegetative shoots in the spring since the plants bud up fast—once in bloom, it will be difficult to take cuttings later in the season.

VARIETIES

A. tinctoria and *A. sancti-johannis* have readily hybridized, and it's possible that some of the following cultivars may be crosses of the two. When sourcing for varieties you wish to buy, keep in mind that nurseries may list them under either of the two names, depending on which nomenclature they use or where they purchase their seed or plants.

E.C. Buxton grows to 2½ feet (75 cm) tall and has off-white flowers with yellow centers. It resembles a Shasta daisy in appearance, but the foliage is more deeply cut with a gray-green overtone to it. Propagate vegetatively only.

Kelway (listed also as Kelwayii or Kelwayi) can grow to a height of 3 feet (90 cm) with 1½ to 2-inch (3 to 5 cm) yellow blooms. Propagate vegetatively or from seed. Seed propagated plants, however, are more uneven and rank in growth. Flowers can be more drooping in form than those selected vegetatively.

Moonlight has butter or light yellow flowers on plants to 2 feet (60 cm) tall, which is unusual for the species. Propagate vegetatively only.

RELATED MATERIAL

Anthemis sancti-johannis, as noted above, readily hybridizes with *A. tinctoria* and this has probably given rise to the cultivar of *A. tinctoria* St. Johannes. While both bear golden orange flowers, St. Johannes may be slightly shorter, but that's splitting hairs. Grown from seed, the results are very close, and I would even venture to say that they're the same thing. When looking through seed catalogs, keep in mind that either species may be used to define this plant.

One additional, but critical, point to make is that plants produced vegetatively are different than those propagated by seed. In the U.S. market you have an extremely high chance of buying St. Johannes as a seeded variety, which has led me to write this long digression on the potential for confusion when purchasing this variety. St. Johannes flowers from June to September on plants that can reach 30 inches (76 cm) tall.

USES

Plants can be used for cut flowers, in the landscape, or a wildflower meadow. They also help to prevent hillside erosion and have been used successfully as highway plantings.

IN THE HOME GARDEN

A full sun location with ample water and food may actually be the death of these plants. Under such healthy conditions they often flower to the point of being weakened. In this state, the plants can't make it through the winter and will die. If this is the environment that the plants have in your yard, they will last for three or four years, with the best growth and show the first two years after planting. Another trait that I've found unfortunate is the reseeding capabilities of some anthemis. If smaller, less aggressive plants are planted close by, anthemis can easily grow around these plants and choke them out. It's to your advantage to remove these seedlings as they emerge in the spring.

▰▰ AQUILEGIA × HYBRIDA

FAMILY: Ranunculaceae

COMMON NAME(S): Columbine

DESCRIPTION

Aguilegia is one of the most well-known and beautiful garden perennials. Many popular varieties today resulted from crosses between species within this genus; others will soon follow. Due to the intercrossing between species and varieties, there are a number of flower colors available: carmine, blue, lavender, yellow, pink, rose, and white. Flower colors are often two-toned or bicolor—petals are one color and the sepals another, although from seed, pure yellow, white and violet blue are also available.

Most varieties on the market are single flowering, but double-flowering forms are also available. The scentless flowers can measure up to 3 inches (7 cm) across. Plants grow from 18 to 30 inches (46 to 76 cm) tall, depending on the variety; they'll spread from 10 to 24 inches (25 to 61 cm) across.

HARDINESS: Zones 3 to 8.

SEASON OF BLOOM: May to June.

PROPAGATION

Columbine is usually propagated by seed. It's best to use fresh seed since columbine seed goes dormant as it ages. Prechilling techniques are noted below.

GERMINATION OVERVIEW: 15,000 to 22,000 seeds per ounce/525 to 770 per gram.

Aquilegia will germinate within 10 to 20 days when fresh seed is used. Leftover seed stored in a refrigerator between uses may take from 21 to 28 days to germinate, however. Temperatures of 70F to 75F (21C to 24C) are best; the seed should be left exposed to light during germination. Seedlings can be transplanted 30 to 40 days after sowing.

Pretreatments: None are usually needed. If you're using old seed or notice poor germination in purchased seed, however, there are some additional steps you can take to improve overall germination. First, one important reminder: When sowing a number of columbine varieties, you may notice various germination dates across the plug trays or flats. If one variety fails to germinate when the others do, it may require from seven to 21 days longer. If the variety fails to germinate within four weeks from the sowing date, move the tray into a refrigerator for two to three weeks at 40F (5C). When stored in the refrigerator, water trays only when necessary—don't saturate. Some growers cover the tray with plastic, while others do not cover the trays at all.

GROWING ON

Crop time: From seed, *Aquilegia* is a long crop that will not flower the same year when sown in January or later. Spring or winter sowings (January to April) are often sold as midsummer or fall pot crops for flowering the following year. *Aquilegia* needs a cold period in which to bloom.

If you prefer to sow your own seed, the sowings you make during the winter and grow on at 55F (13C) nights will be fully rooted within a 32-cell pack in 15 to 18 weeks. The three-week range of finishing time is based on the multitude of varieties within the class; vigorous varieties (such as McKana's Giants and selected Songbird varieties) are often one to three weeks earlier to finish. One other note: Both F_1 and dwarf varieties will be mostly uniform in appearance while older, more vigorous varieties like McKana's Giants will be rather open and lanky.

For 4-inch (10 cm) or quart container sales in May, allow 16 to 19 weeks at 50F to 55F (10C to 13C) nights. This crop time works well on more vigorous varieties as noted above, although we give 17 to 22 weeks for dwarf and slower growing varieties and species when growing in quarts. If plants are growing too fast, we drop the night temperatures to between 48F and 50F (9C and 10C) to slow them down. Regardless, plants will not flower the first year.

Obviously with crop times like these, the seed would need to be sown the previous year to get flowering plants ready for spring sales. This can be accomplished in several ways: Seed can be sown in late spring or early summer for fully rooted plants in quarts or gallons before November. These plants can be overwintered dormant at 30F to 32F (-1C to 0C) in a cold greenhouse or cold frame for spring sales.

Seed can also be sown later, during August or September, and plants overwintered in a 40F (5C) greenhouse or cold frame. In our trials, we sow the last week of August, transplant to a cell pack in mid to late September, pot into 6-inch (15 cm) or gallon containers in mid to late November and then move the plants to a cold frame about 10 to 14 days after potting. The temperatures are dropped to a soil temperature of

40F to 45F (5C to 7C) at night and 45F to 50F (7C to 10C) during the day. Once the plants are well-rooted, we drop the temperatures to 38F to 40F (3C to 5C) continuously for the remainder of the winter. The major problem with this growing method is warm late winter or early spring temperatures. When the days are naturally 55F (13C) and higher, plants can flower in April, which is too early for the majority of the country. If you prefer, the plants can be allowed to go dormant, once rooted, with continuous temperatures of 30F to 33F (-1C to 2C) to avoid early flowering.

This crop is also available in liners and plugs from commercial propagators. In our trials, we have transplanted vernalized 72-plug trays from 4½-inch (11 cm) pots in mid-March. These plants were salable by early May (six to seven weeks), although the root ball and foliage were not filled out. If larger, more lush plants are preferred, add one to two weeks more when growing at 50F to 55F (10C to 13C) nights.

Regarding forcing, over the past 10 years we've successfully flowered columbine for spring sales from August and later sowings (the latest was mid-October). We've also flowered plants during the winter with the intention of using the cut flowers for the long stems they produce during the shorter days of the year. We had to stumble on the best flowering method, however, and found some interesting results when we attempted to force columbine out of season.

After sowing during August and September, we exposed plants between 10 and 12 weeks old from seed to temperatures of 40F to 45F (5C to 7C) at night and 45F to 48F (7C to 9C) during the day for a period of four, six, eight, 10, and 12 weeks. Plants that were never exposed to below 50F (10C) temperatures never flowered for us at all during the winter or spring. As for those plants exposed to only four weeks of cold, depending on the variety, most didn't flower at all, but several varieties bloomed sporadically.

With the remaining exposures, we found that columbine would bloom after only six weeks of the temperatures noted. More importantly, the longer the treatment at approximately 45F or 7C (primarily the 10 and 12 weeks of cold), the earlier the plants would flower once returned to a warm greenhouse, with more profuse blooms and better uniformity in bloom count and plant habit. Once removed from the cold treatment, the plants were subjected to 73F to 75F (23C to 24C) during the day and 60F to 65F (15C to 18C) at night with no artificial lights. Using these temperatures, plants exposed to 12 weeks of cold and removed from the cold frame the last day of January showed their first blooms March 10, with full bloom during the next 10 days.

The total crop time from seed to first bloom is approximately 28 to 30 weeks when using both a cold treatment at 45F (7C) and a forcing temperature as noted above. This may lend some value to the idea of forcing columbine as a spring-flowering pot plant. In short, the best performing (in regard to bloom count) were the eight-, 10-, and 12-week cold-treated plants when exposed to an average 40F (4C). The plants were robust, tall, and free flowering—excellent as cut flowers but not as pot plants. Additional work needs to be done on growth regulator use or colder temperatures to keep the plant shorter if pot plants are preferred. If we moved the plants at visible bud stage to a cooler night temperature of 58F to 60F (14C to 16C), the plants were shorter overall, with a longer shelf life.

We have used this method a number of times, with similar results (plus or minus two weeks). Since there are so many varieties, the important point to remember is various cultivars will grow differently and, if all are sown on the same day, will not grow equally. In a number of cases, the varieties would differ as much as two weeks from the start of the cold period.

By no means is this experiment conclusive or absolute, since the temperatures within the cold frames weren't constant. The information is provided only to show you what we've found. Our results would be more valuable had the plants been placed within a refrigeration unit as opposed to the natural winter cold. It's conceivable that you could get similar results in a shorter number of weeks than what took us eight weeks to achieve. Use the information provided here as a starting place, comparing your results to ours. Several universities are trialing forcing methods as well, and more definitive information will be available as soon as their work is completed.

VARIETIES

All of the following are seed propagated and are offered from seed companies across the country.

Biedermeier is most often sold as a mix here in the United States with pure white, rose-pink and deep blue 1½-inch (3 cm) flowers. Plants make excellent quart or gallon pots, growing 8 to 10 inches (20 to 25 cm) tall, slightly taller in the garden.

McKana's Giants is a mixture of colors on plants up to 30 inches (76 cm) tall. This is one of the earliest varieties to flower and is one of the best known on the market.

Music series is an F_1 hybrid with many separate colors, blooming the same time as McKana's Giants. Plants are shorter, however, growing from 18 to 25 inches (46 to 61 cm) tall in flower.

Nora Barlow is a double-flowering variety from seed with lime green and rose flowers on plants to 3 feet (90 cm) tall. The flower color can be described as "interesting" or "unique"—either you like it or you don't.

The Songbird series is also an F_1 hybrid available in a number of flower colors as well as heights and habits. Blue Bird, Blue Jay, and Goldfinch are taller and can be used as cut flowers. Dove and Robin have an excellent habit in 6-inch (15 cm) and gallon pots for spring sales while Bunting is especially striking when tucked into the rock garden to highlight the smaller blooms. Cardinal isn't discussed in detail here since the variety has been removed from the market. It will probably be re-introduced during the next several years. Cardinal has deep scarlet sepals with scarlet and white petals on

18-inch tall plants. The remaining varieties, their colors, and heights include:

Blue Bird with white petals and midblue sepals. Plants grow to 24 inches (61 cm). This is vigorous variety in the cell pack, larger than most of the other varieties in the series at this stage.

Blue Jay with dark blue sepals and white petals. Though not as vigorous in the pack as Blue Bird, it is taller in the garden, growing to 30 inches (76 cm).

Bunting has the same flower color as Blue Bird with smaller flowers on shorter plants that grow no more than 20 inches tall (51 cm).

Dove has pure white flowers on plants that grow to 24 inches 61 cm) tall in the garden. See Color Plate 11 for photo of *Aquilegia* × *hybrida* Dove.

Robin has white petals with soft pink sepals. Plants grow to 24 inches (61 cm) tall.

RELATED MATERIAL

A. chrysantha is a yellow-flowering variety with 3-foot (90 cm) stems and a free-flowering habit. The variety most often sold in the United States is Yellow Queen. It's also offered under the species name as well.

A. flabellata is a short variety, excellent for quart or gallon pots and for the rock garden. Flowers are smaller than most varieties, ranging in size from 1 to 1½ inches (2.5 to 3 cm) across in either a bicolor white and blue or a pure white flower color. Flowers are slightly nodding. The foliage has a silver-green appearance, unique in columbines. The plants grow from 5 to 8 inches) 13 to 20 cm tall.

The Mini-Star series is available from numerous seed companies both here and in Europe. Colors include the blue and white as well as the pure white—though the blue and white is the most popular.

As for propagating and growing on, follow the culture noted for *A.* × *hybrida*.

USES

Aquilegias are used primarily in the perennial garden and as cut flowers. In the commercial landscape, the plants flower during May and early June but won't reflower again until the following spring. Some landscapers are promoting gardens or borders with seasonal color using a multitude of perennials that may flower for only two or three weeks. The plant list includes crops that flower during June, July, August or September, complemented with ornamental grasses and foliage as accents while waiting for the next burst of color.

As cut flowers, aquilegias will shatter within a day after being cut. For this reason, the stems are conditioned to help retain the flower on the stem for up to 10 days. These conditioners formerly had silver as one of the primary ingredients, but the treatments of today are using different compounds as well as silver. Companies like Floralife, Chrysalis and Gard-Rogard carry these products.

In the home garden

Space plants 15 inches (38 cm) apart in locations exposed to morning sun and afternoon shade. Plants don't require staking, but some varieties will get as tall as 3 feet (90 cm) in moist and fertile spots. Plants prefer soils that are well drained; they will rot if their roots are within too moist an environment for an extended period of time.

While the more dwarf varieties work well in rock gardens, most selections fit best into the perennial border or garden. The plants can be long lived, although they often tire and die out by their fourth or fifth year here in our Chicago gardens. If allowed to set and disperse seed, plants can reseed, however. To overwinter, plants don't require mulching unless planted in beds with wide-open exposures. In these cases, a layer of pine branches, leaves, or other mulching material is suggested. Note that in the spring, leaf miners will leave numerous tunnels visible on leaf tops. There's usually no long-term effect, but the foliage appearance won't be as desirable.

■ Arabis caucasica

(sometimes listed as *A. alpina* or *A. albida*)

Family: Cruciferae

Common name(s): Rock Cress, Wall Cress

Description

Arabis caucasia is a low-growing, gray-green, rosetting perennial that grows to 6 inches (15 cm) tall in bloom. Flowers are either white or rose-pink. The plants spread from 6 to 8 inches (15 to 20 cm) across in our climate, slightly larger in cooler climates. The flowers are four-lobed, fragrant, and about one-half inch (1 cm) across. Double and single flowering varieties are available as well as variegated leaf types. The plants do not become invasive. See Color Plate 12 for photo of *Arabis caucasica*.

Hardiness: Zones 3 to 7.

Season of bloom: April and May.

Propagation

Arabis is commonly propagated by seed, although cuttings are also popular in early spring, especially on the double-flowering and variegated leaf varieties. Take either basal or stem tip cuttings in the late spring after flowering. Plants may be sheared back after flowering, watered and fed, and new shoots allowed to develop to provide the cutting stock.

GERMINATION OVERVIEW: 70,000 seeds per ounce/2,450 per gram.

Seeds germinate at 65F to 70F (18C to 21C) temperatures. Seed can be lightly covered or left exposed to light. Germination occurs in six to 12 days, and transplanting can begin 14 to 21 days after sowing. *Arabis* is easy to germinate: percentages of 70% and higher can be expected.

GROWING ON

From seed: Winter or early spring sowings will produce green, salable cell packs or small pots within 10 to 11 weeks when grown on at 50F (10C) nights. Add one to two weeks for 4½-inch (11 cm) pots. These plants will not flower in spring if started in January or later.

For spring-blooming plants, sowings should be made early enough so that the plants can be exposed to a cold treatment (vernalization) for flower bud formation. Since plants are very cold hardy, sowings can be made as late as October for late winter- or spring-flowering plants. If sown this late, however, the plants need an initial warm period to get some roots underneath them before temperatures fall below 50F (10C). Once roots have become established in the final pot, you can drop the temperature to 48F (9C) or lower for overwintering.

This crop is also available from commercial propagators in a liner or plug. Additional information is provided on this production method in the **How to Use** chapter under **Growing on**.

One additional point: In the cold frame the foliage frequently has a purple or bronze coloring during cold temperatures and short days of spring. This is also evident in the garden but may not be as prevalent. Regardless, as night temperatures warm up to 50F (10C) and above, the plants will show less coloring.

VARIETIES

Compinkie is a rose-pink flowering variety available from a number of sources as either seed or plugs. Plants are 4 to 6 inches (10 to 15 cm) tall. In production, the plants will finish about the same time as white-flowered varieties although in the greenhouse and garden, the plants often have a smaller habit with a weaker performance.

Snow Cap (Snowcap) is the most popular variety on the market and is readily available from a number of seed and plug companies. Flowers are white, single, and poised on stems no taller than 6 inches (15 cm). Snow Cap is extremely hardy for us here in Chicago.

A. caucasica var. Plena has double-flowering white blooms on plants from 8 to 10 inches (20 to 25 cm) tall.

A. caucasica var. *variegata*. This is a variegated leaf form with cream-colored margins on medium green leaves. Flowers are white. This variety is vegetatively propagated and is hardy from Zones 4 to 7.

RELATED MATERIAL

A. blepharophylla Spring Charm is a single-flowering, rose-colored variety that we treat as a short-lived perennial. While plants are hardy from Zones 3 to 7, we get two to three years of good color and performance before the plants die out. We haven't trialed this variety enough to say conclusively, but it appears the plants have about the same hardiness as Compinkie here in Chicago. Sow and grow on as you would *A. caucasica*.

USES

The primary use is as a rock garden plant or border perennial.

IN THE HOME GARDEN

Plant in full-sun locations, or if in hot and humid areas, plant where *Arabis* gets morning sun and midafternoon shade. Plant in a well-drained soil such as sandy loam, and space plants 10 inches (25 cm) apart to fill in. Leaves are woolly; under hot, humid conditions they can rot during the summer, especially if overhead watered. Plants will probably be short lived, lasting three to four years at best, if cooler conditions aren't present. For us, the white-flowering selections have the best overwintering performance and are longer lived.

▄▄ ARMERIA MARITIMA

FAMILY: Plumbaginaceae

COMMON NAME(S): Thrift, Sea-Pinks

DESCRIPTION

Armeria maritima is a low-growing, evergreen perennial with blue-green, grassy foliage in rounded clumps. Plants grow from 6 to 15 inches (15 to 38 cm) tall when in bloom, although the foliage is often no more than 3 to 5 inches (7 to 13 cm) tall when the plants aren't blooming. The plants spread from 6 to 10 inches (15 to 25 cm) across.

The flowers are often white, rose, pink, or pastel colored. When in bloom, the flowering stalks are leafless and will wave back and forth in a light breeze. The scentless, single flowers form globes to 1 inch (2.5 cm) in diameter.

HARDINESS: Zones 4 to 8.

SEASON OF BLOOM: May and June.

PROPAGATION

Armeria is often propagated by seed, divisions, and offsets. Seed can be sown anytime of the year with equal results. Clump division can be done in the spring on two- or three-year-old plants but is more of a home gardening than commercial practice. Removal of a section of the basal rosettes (offsets) is the most common way to propagate named cultivars. This can be done spring to fall except during flowering.

GERMINATION OVERVIEW: 15,000 to 20,000 seeds per ounce/480 to 700 per gram. Pretreatments: Seed will germinate readily without special treatments. For best results, try to use seed within two years of harvest. If you purchase seed, it will already be cleaned for easier handling.

Germination temperatures of 68F to 70F (20C to 21C) are suggested for best results. Seeds can be lightly covered or left exposed during germination, but we've gotten slightly better germination with uncovered seeds. Seedlings emerge in four to 10 days and can be transplanted to cell packs 15 to 22 days after sowing.

GROWING ON

Crop time: Plants grow slowly from seed; even two months after sowing the plants will have only a small tuft of leaves with shallow roots that will not fill out the container. To have salable, green plants in quart or gallon containers for spring, you'll have to sow the previous year. Sow seed during winter or spring a year in advance for seedlings that can be transplanted to a final container by midsummer and grown on. During the following winter, the plants should be protected in a cold greenhouse or cold frame. Because of their evergreen foliage, care must be taken to avoid foliar diseases.

Commercial propagators offer liners or plugs during winter or spring for potting up into 4-inch (10 cm) or quart containers. A 72-cell tray, will be ready for sale approximately eight to 10 weeks after potting when grown at 50F to 55F (10C to 12C) nights. Gallon containers can also be grown, but the extra crop time may not warrant the sale. For salable plant, the crop requires 12 to 15 weeks; even then, plants seldom are fully rooted.

If you prefer to offer spring cell packs, seed sown in February will produce salable transplants in 14 to 17 weeks when grown on at 55F (13C). Don't expect the plants to flower; however, sporadic bloom may be seen.

Sections of the basal rosette can be removed and allowed to root. Take these in spring or during active growth but not when flowering. These can be potted up once they are rooted fully. Spring propagated, these plants aren't sold until late summer, or they are overwintered for sales the following spring.

About temperatures: If sowing seed during the fall or winter, grow the seedlings on at 50F (10C) and higher for the first three months after sowing. This will keep the plants actively growing so they'll fill out faster in a container. Plants will tolerate temperatures down to 45F (7C) in this stage but are slow to develop. When grown colder, the plants are more susceptible to overwatering and often rot. Also, due to their slow nature, avoid putting small transplants in large containers; many times the plants don't live long enough to grow into the container.

VARIETIES

A. maritima (sometimes listed as *A. maritima splendens*) sold as seed here in the United States is often listed botanically as *A. maritima* Laucheana. While this isn't taxonomically correct, it highlights the confusing problems of intercrossing these forms from seed. Vegetatively propagating such plants helps to maintain their distinct features.

Alba is a white-flowering form growing to less than 8 inches (20 cm) in our gardens here in West Chicago. It is seed and vegetatively propagated.

Dusseldorf Pride (Dusseldorfer Stolz) has wine-red flowers on plants to 8 inches (20 cm) in height. It flowers in June and intermittently throughout the summer. Propagate vegetatively.

Laucheana (sometimes listed as *A. maritima* var. *laucheana*) has deep rose-pink flowers on dark green foliage. Plants grow from 6 to 8 inches (15 to 20 cm) tall. It is often confused in the seed trade with *A. maritima* Splendens, which the seed may actually be.

Ornament is a hybrid mixture of white, rose, and pink flowers on plants growing to 10 inches (25 cm) tall in flower. It is available from seed.

Splendens is 8 to 10 inches (20 to 25 cm) tall with carmine flowers. It is often confused with Laucheana when propagated from seed. See Color Plate 13 for photo of *Armeria maritima* Splendens.

Vindictive is a free-flowering, deep pink variety that grows to 6 inches (15 cm) tall when flowering. The plant is only grown vegetatively and flowers in May and June.

RELATED MATERIAL

A. pseudoarmeria (*A. latifolia*) has broader, longer foliage giving the plant a more substantial appearance than *A. maritima*. Plants grow and develop as *A. maritima* and should be treated in a similar fashion.

Bees Ruby is a rose-pink flowering variety between 12 and 18 inches (30 to 46 cm) tall when flowering. Plants flower in June. It is vegetatively propagated.

Formosa hybrids are a seed-propagated strain that flowers in a mixture of rose and pink shades along with white. Plants grow to 18 inches (46 cm) tall and flower in June.

Follow the cultural methods noted under *A. maritima* for propagation.

IN THE HOME GARDEN

Armeria is used primarily as an edging or border plant in the perennial or rock garden. Once the flowers fade, the blue-green, grassy foliage is a season-long accent, especially when combined with white, primrose, or soft blue flower colors.

Plants grow best in a sandy loam; they're often short lived in heavier soils. In a better drained and more porous media, the plants' shallow roots will provide a stronger anchoring. Regardless, armeria is a short-lived plant here in our gardens outside Chicago. Plants live for three years at best and never attain their true performance. Our humid summers and wet, though often snowless, winters are usually the death of these plants. In our location, the plants prefer morning sun and afternoon shade.

During winter, we cover the plants with pine boughs or other evergreen branches to keep the foliage from being matted down. Heavier mulches like leaves increase the chances of keeping too much moisture next to the crown, killing the plant.

▄▄▄ ARTEMISIA LUDOVICIANA

FAMILY: Asteraceae

COMMON NAME(S): White Sage

DESCRIPTION

Artemisia ludoviciana is a perennial prized for its rich, silvery gray, aromatic foliage—a richer color than that of the dusty miller. The gray sheen is created by a mat of fine hairs that cover the surface and leaf undersides. As with dusty millers, artemisias are more prized for foliage than flowers.

Plants grow erect, from 2 to 3 feet (60 to 90 cm) tall, and can spread quickly due to a creeping habit. The flowers are off-white in color, one-eighth inch (3 mm) across, and held in clusters towards the stems' terminal ends.

HARDINESS: Zones 4 to 9.

SEASON OF BLOOM: August.

The flowers are rather unimpressive, and they often bloom and die unnoticed.

PROPAGATION

Divisions and cuttings are the most preferred methods for propagating this genus. Divisions are more common for home gardeners, while cuttings are the commercial propagators' preferred method. Divisions are taken primarily in late summer. Farther south they can be successfully taken until early fall.

Stem cuttings should be taken during late spring and summer, although with the multitude of varieties and hybrids, results may vary by season.

GERMINATION OVERVIEW

All the ornamental varieties on the market today are vegetatively propagated.

GROWING ON

Cuttings can be taken as noted above as long as the stems are supple and soft. Sometimes the stems will turn woody as you get closer to the crown of the plant—avoid these. Cuttings can be taken from spring until midsummer and root best with bright, indirect light and 75F (24C) media temperatures (70F or 21C air temperatures). Many growers use intermittent mist to root the plants, but care should be taken to avoid foliar diseases and rots. Some growers use high heat and fog for a week or two on the cuttings to encourage rooting. As they root, cuttings are removed to a greenhouse and watered as necessary. Cuttings take 14 to 20 days to root; late season or stressed cuttings may take up to four weeks.

Once rooted, pot and grow on the plantlets during the summer for late season sales or hold them over the winter for sales the following spring in quarts or gallons.

During the winter or early spring commercial propagators will have liners or plugs available that can be potted up into 4-inch (10 cm) or quart containers. These will be ready for spring sales within seven to 10 weeks at 55F to 58F (13C to 15C) nights, depending on the variety.

If you prefer to take divisions in the spring for potting up into 2-, 3-, or 4-quart containers, the plants will be ready for sales in four to six weeks depending on the container size versus the division size. In some cases, plants are allowed only a week to become conditioned or acclimated in their container after being divided. If you prefer the plant to be lush and fully rooted in the container, allow six to eight weeks in a 3-quart container with a division one third the size of the container.

VARIETIES

Silver King is the most well known of the cultivars. Silver-gray foliage develops on plants from 2½ to 3 feet (75 to 90 cm) tall. In our gardens outside Chicago, this variety is the most invasive of the selections we've tried.

Silver Queen also has silver-gray leaves and is similiar in habit and performance to Silver King but is not as invasive. Plants grow from 2 to 3 feet (60 to 90 cm) tall.

Valerie Finnis is showier than the first two varieties and shorter, often growing less than 2 feet (60 cm) tall. The foliage has slightly jagged leaf edges.

RELATED MATERIAL

A. absinthium (common wormwood) grows from 2 to 3 feet (60 to 90 cm) tall with an equal spread. While gray leaved, the plants don't possess the intense gray foliage color of the other varieties. Not as ornamental as the varieties listed above, however, *A. absinthium* does work well in woodland gardens providing a prominant, but not overpowering, coloring to the more sunny locations.

Powis Castle is a possible hybrid of *A. absinthium* and *A. arborescens* with a rich gray foliage color similar to *A. ludoviciana* varieties. Powis Castle has more deeply cut foliage, however, on plants that aren't as invasive. The variety has been listed as being hardy only to the southern United States and not our northern Chicago locations. While not as hardy as the varieties listed above, Powis Castle is hardy with winter protection—similar to Silver Mound. See Color Plate 14 for photo of *Artemesia* Powis Castle.

A. schmidtiana Silver Mound is a mounded perennial growing from 12 to 15 inches (30 to 38 cm) tall here in the Midwest, with about the same spread. The foliage is gray in color, soft to the touch, and prized for its ornamental value rather than its flowers. It's not as invasive as *A. lucoviciana*. Like the other varieties and species, the blooms are unspectacular—yellow or sometimes white in color, small in size, and appearing during July and August. The variety is hardy from Zones 3 to 7 but not long lived in our Chicago gardens, especially when planted in open locations away from surrounding winter protection.

Both species are propagated primarily from cuttings and can be grown in a similar manner to *A. ludoviciana*. With Silver Mound, however, be aware that the variety is often more susceptible to foliage rots during rooting than other varieties. Powis Castle should root more easily.

USES

The foliage is most often used as a perennial garden accent or to soften the effect of other perennials. *Artemisia* is especially effective when used to provide continuous foliage color as other seasonal perennials go in and out of bloom. The dried stems can also be used in floral arrangments or wreath work.

In the commerical or home landscape, artemisias work very well. Quick to fill in and establish themselves, plants have no special requirements while providing a continuous show all summer long.

IN THE HOME GARDEN

Artemisia works well in the garden but, like other plants covered with soft hairy foliage, the plants don't tolerate wet, humid conditions for very long. In our gardens this is more of a problem with Silver Mound than with any of the other varieties listed here. Extended hot and humid weather can take its toll on Silver Mound plants, and we usually lose the plants by the third and fourth year.

Plant in any full-sun location or where the plants get shade for a short period of time each day. Extended or deeply shaded locations tend to encourage weaker growth and a more sprawling habit. While the plants don't require staking, shadier locations may cause the crowns to fall open.

As for divisions, *A. ludoviciana* spreads by creeping rootstocks that can be easily lifted any time during the summer and moved. Better rooting occurs, however, when divided and replanted in the spring.

■ ARUNCUS DIOICUS

(formerly *A. sylvester, Spirea aruncus*)

FAMILY: Rosaceae

COMMON NAME(S): Goatsbeard

DESCRIPTION

Aruncus dioicus is a bold and dramatic plant noted for its arching plumes and vigorous habit. *Aruncus* resembles *Astilbe*—especially from seed while the plants are still small. The plants later grow to between 4 and 6 feet (1.2 to 1.8 m) tall with a 2-foot (60 cm) spread. The foliage is light to midgreen and deeply cut or fern-like in appearance.

The flowers are star shaped, cream white, less than one-eighth inch (3mm) wide, and bunched in feathery plumes. Plants are dioecious (each plant is either male or female); male plants are showier in appearance.

HARDINESS: Zones 3 to 7.

SEASON OF BLOOM: June and July.

PROPAGATION

Plants come true from seed; keep in mind that they may flower either male or female. If you prefer the showier males, then propagate by divisions. Divisions can be difficult to take, however, since the rootstocks can become woody with age. Therefore, use plants between two and four years old for best performance. Take divisions in spring or autumn.

GERMINATION OVERVIEW

Seed germinates in 15 to 25 days at 70F (21C). It can be lightly covered during germination. Once germinated, the seedlings are slow growing and will require 50 to 70 days from sowing until they are transplantable.

Pretreatments: Fresh seed is imperative to easily germinate this crop. Sowing seed as soon as it ripens or using seed that has been moist chilled during the winter are the two methods that will yield high germination counts. Seed that has been held and then germinated at 70F (21C) will often germinate at 25% or less.

See additional notes in the **Propagation Techniques** chapter on how to germinate seed using the moist-chilling method.

GROWING ON

Crop time: From seed, sowings should be made a full year before sales to get good growth and an established root system.

Sowings made of fresh seed during the summer will be slow to grow and develop. After germination, grow the plants warm in the greenhouse initially and then, once established in their final pots, put them into a cold frame for overwintering.

If using the moist-chilling technique, seedlings will emerge in spring. These can be potted up into quart and larger pots for midsummer or fall sales. If you have no market for perennial sales at this time, plants can be overwintered for sales the following year. This method adds another full year to growing the plants prior to sales.

Divisions can be taken in the early spring, although they are best taken before bud set and warm weather have started. Initially plants will wilt and should be treated like astilbes—protect them from all exposure to sun. This is especially true if you take divisions late in the spring. While plants can be divided in the summer after flowering, marginal leaf burn often occurs as the plants struggle against heat and humidity to form new roots.

If you purchase roots from commercial propagators during the winter for potting up into 2- or 4-quart containers, you can grow the plants like astilbes, with similar results expected. Based on a 55F (13C) night temperature, the plants will be salable in eight to 10 weeks in a gallon pot.

VARIETIES

Aruncus dioicus is easier to find as a liner or obtain from perennial nurseries than from seed. Few American seed companies carry this product although a number of British and European sources do.

Kneiffii grows to between 2 and 3 feet (60 to 90 cm) tall with finely cut, fernlike foliage. Flowers are cream white and bloom in June. This variety is harder to find than the species. Because Kneiffii is vegetatively propagated only, there is no seed available.

RELATED MATERIAL

Aruncus aethusifolius also has finely cut foliage resembling a fern, but the plants are substantially shorter, growing to only 12 inches (30 cm) tall. Flowers are also creamy white and appear in June. Seed is available on this crop, but it is more readily found in Europe. Propagate and grow on as suggested for *A. dioicus*.

USES

Aruncus is a dramatic plant for the back of the shady border where it is allowed to fill out and grow. Plants are especially recommended for the woodland garden and damp shade, although plants tolerate drier locations as well.

IN THE HOME GARDEN

A long-lived perennial, *Aruncus* can substitute as a shrub. It dies back to the ground every winter, only to reemerge the following spring, attaining its full size once again. The range of heights noted under the **Description** refers to the plant's location in the garden. If given morning sun and a rich and moist (no standing water) soil, these plants will grow to the full height noted. This size is too large for small gardens—the plants will overtake the space quickly. Instead, plant where the soil is not too rich, avoiding fertilizers and frequent waterings to keep the plants in check. This doesn't mean to plant them in well-drained, sunny locations, because the tender foliage will burn, and the plant will suffer from this mistreatment.

Even though the plants are big, they seldom need staking to keep them upright and require no winter mulching.

ASCLEPIAS TUBEROSA

FAMILY: Asclepiadaceae

COMMON NAME(S): Butterfly Weed, Butterfly Flower
Butterflies, especially monarch butterflies, are attracted to this plant's rich flower nectar.

DESCRIPTION
Asclepias tuberosa is a premier native perennial with one of the most vivid orange flowers available, though red and yellow colors are common, too. The individual, crown-shaped blooms are one-eighth to one-quarter inch (3 to 6 mm) across and form irregular clusters measuring 1 to 2 inches (2.5 to 5 cm) across. In late summer as the flowers fade, an elongated, tapered 4-inch (10 cm), seed pod develops from which seeds parachute to earth with silky, featherlike appendages.

Plants grow primarily upright, from 1½ to 2 feet tall (45 to 60 cm), and spread 12 to 18 inches (30 to 40 cm) across. Their stems contain a white, milky sap that exudes when the plant is wounded or cut.

HARDINESS: Zones 4 to 9.

SEASON OF BLOOM: June to August.
The best flowering is in July, continuing for up to six weeks. Cut off the dead flower heads for additional color four weeks later.

PROPAGATION
Seed and root cuttings are the most common ways to propagate. Divisions are possible but yield less reliable results since the rootstocks are brittle, and the plants are slow to emerge in spring.

GERMINATION OVERVIEW: 3,500 seeds per ounce/1,225 per gram.
Germination temperatures are 70F to 75F (21C to 24C). Seed can be covered or left exposed during germination.

Pretreatments: If seed is purchased during late fall or winter, it's most likely fresh seed. If germination is irregular or the percent of emerging seedlings low, moist chill the seed for several weeks for greater results.

Germination takes 21 to 28 days, and transplanting can be done 35 to 55 days after sowing.

See additional notes on moist-chilling seed in the **Propagation Techniques** chapter at the front of the book.

GROWING ON

From seed: Winter and early spring sowings will produce sporadically flowering plants the following summer. For full flowering and profusely blooming plants, however, sow seed the previous year, and transplant seedlings to quart containers by mid or late summer for overwintering. These containers can then be sold the following spring.

If you prefer pack sales, a mid-February sowing produces salable, green cell packs (32's) by mid-May when grown at 58F (14C) night temperatures. Plants flower sporadically mid to late July in the garden.

A comment regarding temperatures: If sown from seed during the winter, the plants should be grown warm at no lower than 55F or 13C nights until they are sold in the spring, regardless of the container size. When winter sown, plants grow erect with mostly one, sometimes two, stems void of basal or side branches. If growth temperatures fall below 50F (10C) for a period of time, plants will slow and the leaves may fall off. This is especially true when growing in December and January's short, dark days.

One final comment: I've grown this plant for years in our West Chicago gardens and have never seen the same performance as those that grow as weeds along Illinois roadsides. *Asclepias* hates transplanting, becoming weak and languid as its roots become bound into the container. For best performance, sow the seed into plug trays and transplant only once into a final container before planting into the garden.

VARIETIES

There are no cultivated varieties of *A. tuberosa* that I'm aware of. Instead, the orange variety is the most commonly offered variety in the United States. A mixture, Gay Butterflies, is available from seed and has orange, yellow, and red flowers on plants to 3 feet (90 cm) tall.

USES

Asclepias is an excellent plant for the perennial border, espcially where orange is a desired flower color. As a cut flower, it performs well from two-year-old plantings, which have longer stems. Sear the cut area to prevent the sap from bleeding or oozing. Seed pods can be used in dried cut flower arrangements or as Christmas ornaments.

IN THE HOME GARDEN

Plant in a full-sun location where soils are well-drained. *Asclepias* isn't invasive and will become a reliable planting that stays well contained. Unlike many other perennials, it is slow to emerge in the spring, so mark where you situated the plants last year. Space 12 inches (30 cm) apart in staggered rows. *Asclepias* doesn't produce large clumps requiring division. If needed, however, plants can be divided in spring, but care should be taken to avoid wounding the fragile rootstock. Well-established root-stocks damaged during division often rot and may die.

One additional point: Our plants suffer annually from an aphid infestation concentrated at the terminal 1 to 2 inches (2.5 to 5 cm) on each stem. If aphids are left unchecked, the plants will die out in two years.

■ ASPHODELINE LUTEA

COMMON NAME(S): King's Spear, Jacob's Rod

FAMILY: Liliaceae

DESCRIPTION

A stately, erect perennial, *Asphodeline lutea* grows to 4 feet (1.2 m) once established. However, in our Chicago area it grows only 2 to 3 feet (60 to 90 cm) tall. The foliage is gray green in color, grasslike in appearance, and develops a rosette from 10 to 12 inches (25 to 30 cm) across. The foliage is more arching in form than upright. The plants are 8 to 10 inches tall when not in flower.

Plants form a clustered, rhizomatous root at the plant's base. The first season from seed or division, the plants will form the primary rosette but usually will develop several secondary rosettes close to the crown. These secondary rosettes are more predominant the second year and give the plant a tuftlike appearance. These secondary rosettes can also be removed from the mother crown for propagating.

The flowers are single, lightly scented, yellow in color, and measure 1 to 2 inches (2.5 to 5 cm) across. They develop a raceme (similar to a spike, except there are short appendages holding the flower to the main stem). Something unusual about this plant: The flowers open intermittently along the floral stem, not from bottom to top or vice-versa.

HARDINESS: Zones 6 to 8.

The plants are marginally hardy here in the Chicago area, lasting from two to four years. Since the plants are Mediterranean natives, they are more long lived along the West Coast and similar climate areas of the United States. However, we have had them in our Zone 5 gardens for several years with success.

The plants are not fond of high heat and humidity. Although they will tolerate both for a period of time, extended exposure will eventually kill the plants. While hardy to Zone 8, *Asphodeline* will probably be short lived. For additional information, read the section **In the home garden.**

SEASON OF BLOOM: May and June.

PROPAGATION

Seed and division are the most common propagation methods. You can sow the seed any time, and a small collection of plants will produce enough seed for future needs.

Divisions are taken in the spring of the secondary rosettes, as noted earlier under **Description**. These can be removed along with a piece of the root and used to propagate the species. Careful attention needs to be given, however, to ensure getting both growing points. When selecting plants for dividing, use clumps that have been in the ground at least two to four years. Established plants resent dividing.

GERMINATION OVERVIEW

Seed germinates in eight to 15 days at 68F to 72F (20C to 22C). Seed can be covered lightly to germinate, and seedlings can be transplanted to cell packs 25 to 35 days after sowing. We have found that germination occurs over a period of time, however, yielding various-sized seedlings between eight and 35 days after sowing. In general, plan on transplanting at least two to three times for 200 plants.

As for pretreatments, additional work has to be done. In our trials, germination ranges of 40 to 60% were achieved by the end of the germination period, but we don't understand the reasons for the variability. The possibility of old seed, the need for testing alternative temperatures, moist chilling, and other opportunities have yet to be studied.

Note: As seeds germinate, the resulting seedling is an erect, elongated stem that looks like an onion or chive seedling as it develops.

GROWING ON

Crop time: Seedlings are slow to develop and will require time to fill out a cell pack or small pot. The leaves are long, almost filamentous, in the way they develop. The first season from seed, the leaves will proliferate around the plant's crown but will not flower until the second season.

Sowings made in late February, with the resulting seedlings transplanted to cell packs at the end of March, are salable green when grown at 58F to 62F (14C to 16C) nights. The plants actually prefer cooler temperatures of 50F to 55F (10C to 13C), although they are slower to grow and fill out. Sowings can be made in the autumn for potting up into quart containers during the winter, but the plants need to be grown at no less than 50F (10C to 13C) during this active growth stage. I wouldn't call the plants high maintenance, but they are definitely a high value crop and should reflect this in the price when grown east of the Rockies. Not surprisingly, *Asphodeline* will be more common in the western United States and Canada (specifically along the coast) than anywhere else in North America.

Beware of overwatering. In general, *Asphodeline* should be allowed to dry out slightly between waterings during cool weather to avoid root rots.

VARIETIES

Asphodeline lutea is not a common perennial and has a limited number of sources in the U.S. trade, if at all. European sources are more dependable, and you'll probably have to buy the variety only once. If you have stock increase beds, this variety breeds true from seed so you'll be able to collect your own for the future.

RELATED MATERIAL

Asphodeline liburnica is very similar to *A. lutea* with pale yellow flowers, although it only grows to 2½ feet (75 cm) tall, and the basal foliage is closer to the ground. Plants often flower a little later in the summer but have a hardiness and cropping performance equal to *A. lutea*.

USES

Asphodeline is a unique perennial that adds an attractive combination of foliage and flower to the perennial garden. The chivelike foliage remains throughout the season and the bright, single, yellow blooms on upright stalks have few rivals for form. Though some have suggested that *Asphodeline* can be used for a cut flower, I couldn't find any information on that.

Asphodeline can be used in landscaping, but due to its erect stature it may require staking if used in open areas such as golf courses or commercial plantings. Small clumps are suggested as a start to test the site's suitability for growing a good crop.

IN THE HOME GARDEN

As noted under **Hardiness**, these plants will perform better in year-round mild environments, avoiding extremes in heat/humidity and severe cold. They will be a challenging plant for anyone outside of these areas, although we have fared well in overwintering these plants. They're much longer lived, however, if used as foundation plantings where they can be mulched during winter and protected from winter winds. Often when a midwestern winter has been particularly severe, a number of plants will die out from root rots by midspring.

Stems tend to arch slightly when the plants are in full bloom but usually don't require staking, especially if they're planted out of direct wind or if the secondary rosettes have started to form around the base of the plant. These secondary rosettes provide additional support to keep the plants upright. Plant in a sunny location and avoid heavy clay loams, concentrating instead on more well-drained soils. Plants are native to regions where they grow in rocky, lime-rich outcrops in a 6 to 7.5 pH range or higher.

■■ ASTER ALPINUS

FAMILY: Asteraceae

COMMON NAME(S): Alpine Aster

DESCRIPTION

Aster alpinus is a small, bushy plant that grows to 8 inches (20 cm) tall in flower and spreads 10 to 12 inches (25 to 30 cm) across. The 2- to 3-inch (5 to 7 cm) flowers are pastel colored—purple, white, pink, rose, and blue. The foliage is gray green in spring, changing to medium green by midseason. Flowers are lightly fragrant. *Aster alpinus* is the earliest of the aster species to flower in the spring.

HARDINESS: Zones 4 to 7.
Usually short lived in hot, humid climates.

SEASON OF BLOOM: May and June.

PROPAGATION

Propagation by seed, divisions, and cuttings are the most common methods. Sow fresh seed for best results. Divisions should be taken in the spring or fall but use a stock plant that's two to three years old. Take cuttings off the plant during the summer after flowering.

GERMINATION OVERVIEW: 24,000 seeds per ounce/840 per gram.
Germination temperatures are 65F to 70F (18C to 21C). Seed should be left exposed during germination, but pressed firmly into the media. Germination occurs in 14 to 21 days and transplanting can begin 21 to 30 days after sowing.

Comments: Seed is notoriously slow to germinate if old or improperly stored seed is used. If seed is not sown within a short time after harvesting, it can go dormant. Germination rates of 25% and lower are common without pretreatments.

Pretreatments: *Aster alpinus* will respond to a moist chilling with overall improved germination. See the **Propagation Techniques** chapter at the front of the book for additional information.

GROWING ON

From seed: Winter sowings will flower only sporadically during the summer and aren't reliable. Sow seed in the late spring or summer until early July to allow time for the plants to develop. Then shift the plants into quarts or gallons and overwinter them in a protected shelter (cold frame). These plants will flower the following spring.

If you prefer to sell green cell packs in the spring, packs grown at 55F to 58F (13C to 15C) nights and 63F to 68F (17C to 20C) days will be salable in 15 to 19 weeks in a 32-cell pack when winter sown.

One other suggestion for northern gardeners is to sow seed in the spring and sell the plants in September and early October along with fall bulbs for autumn planting. Plants are cold tolerant and will flower the next spring with the bulbs. Consider this for a number of perennials including biennials and spring-flowering varieties.

For cuttings, shear plants back after flowering to encourage new growth. When the new shoots reach 1 to 2 inches (2.5 to 5 cm) long, they can be cut and stuck into peat and/or sand. They will root in one to two weeks. These can be potted up into 4-inch (10 cm) pots for late summer sales or quarts for overwintering and sales the following spring.

VARIETIES

Aster alpinus is often sold in a mixture of colors including pink, blue, and white. Flowers are 2 inches (5 cm) across and 8 inches (20 cm) tall.

Goliath has 3-inch (7 cm), medium blue flowers on plants up to 10 inches (25 cm) tall. Seed is available but produces more variable results than vegetatively propagated plants.

Dark Beauty has deep violet-blue flowers on plants growing to 12 inches (30 cm) tall. Seed is available but produces variable results.

Happy End has semidouble flowers; plants grow to 12 inches (30 cm) tall. Flowers are lavender pink and compact. It is available from seed.

RELATED MATERIAL

Aster divaricatus (commonly called white wood aster). This crop grows from 1 to 2 feet (30 to 60 cm) tall with white flowers from one-half to 1 inch (1 to 2.5 cm) across. Flowers in July and August. Propagate by division and seeds.

Aster × frikartii (Frikart's aster, hardy aster) is the result of a cross between *A. amellus × A. thompsonii*. The foliage is more mildew tolerant than other classes noted here. Flowers are lavender blue, 2½ inches (6 cm) across, and fragrant. Plants grow from 2 to 3 feet (60 to 90 cm) tall and from 12 to 15 inches (30 to 38 cm) across. We mulch plants to protect against our northern winters. We also pinch the plants one or two times in spring to increase the bloom count. Plants will probably need staking, especially if pinched. Bloom time is July and August. Cuttings are the standard way to propagate, although bare-root divisions and small pots are also available from commercial propagators.

Wonder of Staffa has 3-inch (7 cm), light blue flowers on plants up to 3 feet (90 cm) tall. Plants have excellent basal branching and fill out well. They're also free flowering. Wonder of Staffa is more commonly available than Monch, listed below. See Color Plate 15 for photo of *Aster × frikartii* Wonder of Staffa.

Monch is often listed as an *Aster frikartii*, but some authorities contest this. The flowers, which are deeper in color than Wonder of Staffa and with sturdier stems, grow to 3 feet (90 cm) tall. Monch is more free flowering, although slightly later to bloom than Wonder of Staffa.

Aster novae-angliae (commonly called New England aster) is a late summer flowering variety that blooms from late August until frost here in Chicago. When spring comes, pinch the variety in the garden and again several weeks later to encourage larger plants—although they are free branching without a pinch. The 1½-inch (3 cm) flowers appear terminally on plants up to 3 feet (90 cm) tall with a 2-foot (60 cm) spread. Propagation is mostly by division and cuttings, but seed is available. Seed-propagated varieties are vigorous and sometimes rank plants that are excellent for the woodland and wild flower gardens rather than mixed in with less obtrusive plants. The cultivars listed below are more uniform and shorter but will not come true from seed. They offer a strong show of color for fall performance.

Alma Potschke is a bright rose flowering variety that grows up to 3 feet (90 cm) tall. Flowers are 2 inches (5 cm) across. The blooming period is long—from four to five weeks.

Harrington's Pink is a large, robust variety reaching 4 feet (1.2 m) tall. It's one of the latest of this class to bloom. Clear pink flowers reach 1½ inches (3 cm) across.

Purple Dome grows from 14 to 20 inches (35 to 51 cm) tall, with 2-inch (5 cm) violet flowers. Reportedly it is powdery mildew tolerant.

September Ruby has 1-inch (2.5 cm) ruby-red flowers on 3-foot-tall (90 cm) plants. It is also called September Glow.

Aster novi-belgi is commonly called New York aster or Michaelmas daisy, with plants growing as tall as 5 feet (1.5 m). The standard flower color is violet blue, although cultivated varieties are available in a number of colors: pink, white, lavender, and salmon. Flowers can be either single or double and measure up to 2 inches (5 cm) across. Like the other classes (except for *A. alpinus*), a pinch when planting in the garden will increase this plant's flowering capacity. Fertilize in the garden or greenhouse when needed, but too much promotes long, lanky growth which can lead to problems. The taller varieties may require staking. Cultivars listed below are all propagated vegetatively, either by cuttings or divisions.

Alert is a deep crimson flowering variety up to 15 inches (38 cm) tall. It blooms in late August and September.

Professor Kippenburg blooms in September in Chicago on plants reaching 15 inches (38 cm) tall with semidouble, midblue flowers.

Patricia Ballard has semidouble, pink flowering blooms on plants to 3 feet (90 cm) tall.

Winston Churchill has violet-rose flowers on 2-foot-tall (60 cm tall) plants. Plants are compact and bushy; flowers extend to 1½ inches across.

Aster tongolensis (East Indies aster) has 5-inch-long (13 cm long), dark green leaves with 2-inch (5 cm) violet-blue flowers. Plants grow up to 24 inches (60 cm) high and flower in July and August. It is recommended for Zones 5 to 8. Propagate by division or cuttings after the plants have flowered.

Wartberg Star (also Wartburg Star) has lavender-blue flowers on plants ranging in height from 18 to 24 inches (46 to 61 cm). It can be used for cut flowers.

IN THE HOME GARDEN

Plant *Aster alpinus* in a well-drained area with afternoon shade; otherwise, in the Chicago area, plants tend to literally melt from August heat and humidity. Space 8 to

10 inches (20 to 25 cm) apart in the garden for plants to fill in. In cool summer areas, plants will grow larger than their Midwest counterparts.

Place in a full-sun and well-drained location. Plants don't require staking or special care but will look better during the summer if sheared back after flowering.

One final note: Asters, as a group, are susceptible to powdery mildew. While this is more noticeable in the home garden, it's also prevalent during active growth on the greenhouse bench. *A. novae angliae* and *A. novi-belgi* are the most susceptible. Chemical sprays are available to control this problem, and more disease tolerant variety selections are being made. One variety, Purple Dome, and others not listed here, show less tendency to mildew.

ASTILBE × ARENDSII

FAMILY: Saxifragaceae

COMMON NAME(S): Astilbe, False Spirea

DESCRIPTION
Astilbe is an ideal plant for dappled shade and damp, but well-drained, locations. Astilbes are medium height, ranging from 24 to 36 inches (60 to 90 cm) tall, and spreading 15 to 24 inches (38 to 61 cm). Thanks to breeders there are a multitude of varieties and colors available. *A. × arendsii* involves a number of crosses including *A. japonica*, *A. chinensis* var. *davidii*, *A. astilboides*, and *A. thunbergii*. While these are known parents of various varieties, other species and cultivars were probably involved as well.

With such a vast lineage, it's no wonder the flower colors cover such a spectrum, including red, carmine, rose, pink, white, and lavender, plus shades in between. The individual flowers are small, but numerous, and held aloft in erect, sometimes nodding, plumes. Flower plumes measure anywhere from 4 to 10 inches (10 to 25 cm) long, depending on the variety. While not richly scented, astilbe blooms are slightly fragrant. Although preferred for the perennial garden, astilbes can also double as pot plants and cut flowers.

HARDINESS: Zones 4 to 8.

SEASON OF BLOOM: June and July.
With the various species and hybrids involved, it's possible to have flowering astilbes from June to August.

PROPAGATION
The colorful hybrid astilbe selections available are only propagated by division, not by seed. Divisions can be taken from the plants in spring or fall; roots are available commercially during September, October or until late winter for potting. Seed can be

sown but only mixtures are available, and their flower colors are muted in shade and rather lackluster in appearance. The plants are often grown for breeding use, however, when cell packs and small pots are needed or when the more expensive hybrids are out of the consumer's price range.

GERMINATION OVERVIEW: 380,000 to 384,000 seeds per ounce/13,300 to 13,440 per gram. Germination temperatures are 60F to 70F (15C to 21C); seed should be left exposed to light during germination. Germination takes place in seven days, but seedlings emerge over a period of time ranging from 14 to 21 days after sowing. Seeds are ready to transplant 40 to 50 days after sowing.

Pretreatments: Additional techniques and methods usually aren't necessary for germination rates of 70% or better. Seed that has been stored for a long time or improperly, however, may germinate poorly. Expose stored seed to a moist chill for several weeks to improve germination.

GROWING ON

From seed: A key point in seed growing is to remember that plants will not flower during the summer from fall- or winter-sown seed. A January sowing won't flower until June or July of the following year (18 to 19 months later). Worse yet, for free-flowering plants, *add another whole year (a total production time of 30 to 31 months after sowing).*

Green, 32-cell packs, however, will be ready 14 to 16 weeks after sowing when grown at 55F to 58F (13C to 15C) nights. These plants can either be sold or moved up into quarts or gallons to sell in fall. If you're growing over the winter, it will probably be more cost-efficient to purchase roots and grow plants on for only three to four months versus the time consuming raising from seed.

From division: If you dig your own divisions, spring or fall is the best time. In the spring let the plants grow to between 1 to 2 inches (2.5 to 5 cm) and then divide the crown. Plant one individual clump to a 1- to 3-quart container, depending on root size—although astilbe roots are often too large to fit into a quart container. Plants can be sold in June, but most varieties won't flower until late June or July.

Bare-root transplants purchased from commercial growers can be potted up into a number of container sizes based on the variety. Large, robust growing selections can be potted to gallon pots and smaller varieties to 2- or 3-quart containers. If potted up in February or March and grown on at 55F (13C) nights, most varieties will be salable green in seven to eight weeks. However, the roots will not fill the pot, and the growth will only be 4 to 5 inches (10 to 13 cm) tall on most varieties. For more well-rooted and fuller looking foliage, allow nine to 11 weeks. At this point, a number of varieties will be starting to bud up, but few will be flowering.

For potted plant sales in flower during late winter and spring, bring the crowns (try to have three to four "eyes") in around September. Pot up into 6-inch (15 cm) or gallon pots, and let the plants become established in the container. Chill the containers for 10 to 12 weeks at 35F to 40F (2C to 5C). They can be overwintered with your other perennials and brought in when needed. Once the containers have been moved into the greenhouse, place the pots out of direct light and allow them to warm up gradually over a period of several days. Then increase temperatures to no less than 58F (14C) at night, with days 8F to 10F (5C to 6C) higher than the night temperature. Allow 12 to 16 weeks for flowering, depending on the cultivar. In general, the early and midseason varieties will flower about the same time; the late season varieties tend to take their time and flower two to four weeks later.

VARIETIES

Since the various astilbes on the market have a broad parentage behind them, the following chart will help you keep track. All varieties listed below are vegetatively propagated. The only seed varieties offered are mixtures under such names as Spires and Arendsii Mixed. With regard to the flowering season, "Early" refers to June and July flowering, "Mid" refers to early mid-July and "Late" refers to late July and August.

All of the following are **vegetatively propagated**.

Variety	Color	Height inches (cm)	Flowering time
Bridal Veil (also called Brautschleier)	White	20 (51)	Mid
Cattleya	Rose pink	36 (91)	Late
Deutschland	White	24 (61)	Early
Diamond (also called Diamant)	White	30-36 (79-91)	Late
Erica (also spelled Erika)	Pink	30 (76)	Mid
Etna	Crimson	20 (51)	Mid
Fanal (has bronzed foliage; one of the most popular varieties)	Deep red	22 (56)	Mid
Federsee	Carmine rose	24 (61)	Mid/Late
Feuer (also called Fire)	Coral red	24 (61)	Late
Glut (also called Glow)	Bright red	30 (76)	Mid
Irrlicht (flowers fade from rose pink to white)	White	24 (61)	Mid
Ostrich Plume (also listed as a variety of *A. thunbergii*)	Bright pink	30 (76)	Mid
Peach Blossom*	Pink	24 (61)	Mid
Red Sentinal	Scarlet red	24 (61)	Late
Rheinland	Pink	24 (61)	Early
Spinell	Carmine red	24 (61)	Mid
White Gloria	White	18-20 (46-51)	Mid/Late

*See Color Plate 16 for photo of *Astilbe × arendsii* Peach Blossom.

RELATED MATERIAL

Along with the hybrid varieties noted above, the following selections can be mixed and matched with them in the shade garden to provide plants of all heights, flower colors, form, and habit.

A. chinensis var. *pumila*. A dwarf astilbe growing from 10 to 12 inches (25 to 30 cm) tall in flower, spreading 15 to 18 inches (38 to 46 cm) across. The plants can be deceiving—the more damp and shady the exposure where they're planted, the larger they become. The lavender-rose plumes are more upright and formal in appearance than the hybrids but are also the smallest overall of the species and cultivars mentioned here. *A. chinensis* var. *pumila* prefers a well-drained though moist soil in the garden. Plants start to flower in July and continue into August. Plants are excellent as a border or edging and also for the rock garden. They can be propagated by division or from seed, with methods noted for the hybrids. From seed, however, the plants aren't as variable in growth and color as *A. × arendsii*. Zones 5 to 8. See Color Plate 17 for photo of *Astilbe chinensis* var. *pumila*.

A. simplicifolia is also shorter than the hybrids listed above, though it is usually taller than *A. chinensis* var. *pumila*. The foliage is more fern-like in appearance, while the plumes are more open and less formal than the hybrids. In full bloom, the plumes appear to radiate out of a central point, like the burst of color from exploding fireworks. This is a beautiful and underused astilbe with excellent potential. Plants grow from 1 to 1½ (30 to 45 cm) feet tall with a 15- to 20-inch (38 to 51 cm) spread.

As for propagation and growing on, keep in mind that many of the varieties sold under the name of *A. simplicifolia* are actually hybrids from crosses between this and other species. That's why their culture and care is also a little different. Upon potting a bare-root division, the following varieties are a little slower in setting roots than the varieties of *A. × arendsii* noted above. For this reason, they're often overwatered and eventually rot, especially if kept too cool below 55F (10C). Upon potting, water in thoroughly and then water as needed.

As a guideline, we give these plants one to two more weeks of growing to get them to size up in their pots. Eight to nine weeks at 55F (13C) nights will yield a better looking plant though they will be smaller in appearance than the *A. × arendsii* hybrids noted above. For a fully rooted and broader foliage plant, allow 12 to 14 weeks at 55F (13C) nights if you can afford the time and money.

Hennie Graafland has rose-pink flowers atop shiny, bronzed foliage. Plants grow 14 to 16 inches (35 to 41 cm) tall in flower. Some consider this variety the taller version of Sprite.

Sprite is the most popular variety and a Perennial Plant Association "Perennial of the Year." The flowers are shell-pink on plants measuring from 12 to 14 inches (30 to 35 cm) tall. See Color Plate 18 for photo of *Astilbe simplicifolia* Sprite.

William Buchanan has cream to white flowers on dark green foliage. Plants reach 8 to 12 inches (20 to 30 cm) tall in flower.

A. taquetii Superba (*A. chinensis* var. *tacquetii* Superba). Fall astilbe. A taller growing variety from 3 to 4 feet (90 to 126 cm) tall in bloom. This variety usually flowers later than the hybrids noted above, blooming in July and August. The lavender-rose plumes measure from 10 to 12 inches (25 to 30 cm) long. Propagate by division. Zones 4 to 8.

USES

Astilbes are primarily used in the home garden as a specimen, in groups and/or as a cut flower. In the commercial trade the plants are occasionally massed in damp, shaded locations along with hostas. While an individual variety will flower for a two- to three-week period, the multitude of hybrids give the professional landscaper varieties that will flower from June until late August. Astilbes are highly valued for their plumes of color.

For cut flowers, harvest the spikes as the lower half opens up. Once cut, flowers last seven to 10 days in the home. Some varieties work well dried—harvest when the flowers have almost fully opened.

IN THE HOME GARDEN

Space astilbes 15 to 18 inches (38 to 46 cm) apart in the garden in an area where they can get morning sun while being shaded late morning until evening. Since the plants prefer damp though well-drained locations, water the plants when placing them in warmer situations. Astilbes are shallow rooted and often dry out faster than the other plants around them. They're not drought tolerant.

Astilbes don't require special care or winter mulching to remain hardy in our West Chicago gardens. Divide the plants as needed, though we find they don't require digging for up to four years in our location. If you notice your overall plant size and number of blooms starting to decrease, however, dividing the plants will help. Plants are very long lived and don't require staking.

AUBRIETA DELTOIDEA
(sometimes listed as *A. deltoides*)

FAMILY: Cruciferae

COMMON NAME(S): False Rockcress

DESCRIPTION

Aubrieta deltoidea is a low-growing perennial sometimes confused with *Arabis*. Overall, the plants grow from 6 to 8 inches (13 to 20 cm) tall in flower, half that height when out of bloom. *Aubrieta* will spread from 5 to 7 inches (13 to 18 cm) across. The flowers measure less than three-quarters of an inch across and develop on upright stems over rosetting foliage. Flower colors include lavender, blue, and purple. Deep rose flowers are also sometimes present, but the colors often appear to have blue or lavender overtones.

HARDINESS: Zones 4 to 7.

SEASON OF BLOOM: April and May.

PROPAGATION

Aubrieta is propagated by seed, division, and cuttings. Seed and cuttings are the most common methods, however, due to the ease of rapid multiplication. Basal cuttings are taken in the spring while stem cuttings are taken in late spring or early summer after the plants have flowered. Divisions are done mostly by home gardeners in the early spring.

GERMINATION OVERVIEW: 85,000 seeds per ounce/2,975 per gram.

Germination temperatures are 65F to 70F (18C to 21C). Leave seed exposed to light during germination, which occurs in 14 to 21 days. Transplanting can begin 20 to 25 days after sowing. Germination will be faster if you raise the germination temperatures to 70F to 72F (21C to 22C). Germination can be retarded by temperatures over 75F (24C).

Comments: There are differing opinions on the best germinating temperatures for this crop. Some authorities recommend 60F (16C) and note germination rates decrease at 65F (18C) or above. In our trials, 70% germination rates have been obtained in summer sowings germinated at 70F or 72F (21C to 22C).

GROWING ON

From seed: Seed sown during winter or spring will not flower until the following year. *Aubrieta* requires a cold treatment (vernalization) before the plants will bud up and flower.

Winter sowings will produce green, salable cell packs and 4-inch (10 cm) and quart containers in the spring. In general, allow 10 to 12 weeks for 32-cell packs to be filled out and ready for sales. Four-inch and quart containers require 12 to 14 weeks, one to two weeks more if you want the roots filling the pot.

To have blooming plants for spring sales, sow in summer. These plants should be transplanted to quarts and overwintered dormant in a cold frame. Another method is to sow in early October, transplant to 4-inch (10 cm) or quarts and grow at 40 to 45F nights (4C to 7C) during the winter. These plants will flower in May.

VARIETIES

Purple Gem has three-quarter-inch (2 cm) purple flowers on plants that grow up to 6 inches (15 cm) tall. This variety is vegetatively propagated. The seeded form is similiar; it's called Whitewell Gem.

Large Flowered Hybrids is a catch-all name for this seed-propagated variety in a mixture of colors, including lavender, lilac, purple, and dark rose. Plants reach 8 inches (20 cm) tall.

RELATED MATERIAL

Many of the names that appear to be botanical—*Leictlinii* or *Hendersonii*—are probably variations or intervarietal hybrids of this species. Therefore, all of the following are listed under the name of *A. deltoidea*. Some of these include:

Leichtlinii. 6 to 8 inches (15 to 20 cm) tall with carmine rose flowers; often called pink rockcress.

Hendersonii. Similar in habit and overall performance to *Leichtlinii* except flowers are light blue in color. Also called lilac rockcress.

USES

Best use is in the rock garden or as a border plant or edging.

IN THE HOME GARDEN

Space plants 10 inches (25 cm) apart in a well-drained location where the plants get morning sun and afternoon shade. Trim plants back after flowering to tidy them up; they will not flower again the same season.

In our midwestern location, these plants are often short lived, living from two to three seasons with losses expected each year. It seems that *Aubrieta* doesn't appreciate hot, humid summers and harsh winters.

■■ AURINIA SAXATILIS COMPACTA (ALYSSUM SAXATILE)

FAMILY: Cruciferae

COMMON NAME(S): Basket O' Gold, Gold Dust

DESCRIPTION

A spring-flowering perennial with bright golden yellow flowers on plants from 10 to 12 inches (25 to 30 cm) tall and 12 to 14 inches (30 to 35 cm) across. Plants will often trail as their thickened, wiry stems cannot support the weight of the foliage. The single flowers are sulphur yellow in color, one-eighth inch across, and bunched in terminal clusters. The gray-green foliage contrasts well with the yellow flowers. Although Aurinia's flowering season is short, its foliage provides continuous contrast with other garden plants throughout the summer.

HARDINESS: Zones 3 to 9.

Aurinia saxatilis is usually a short-lived plant in our northern locations since it suffers from high heat and humidity. If grown in full sun, the plants will die within two to three years.

SEASON OF BLOOM: April and May.

PROPAGATION

Seed, division, and cuttings are common ways to propagate, but seed is the primary method. Divisions, which are taken during spring, are difficult because the plants clump. Take cuttings during the late spring after flowering and before the stems turn woody.

GERMINATION OVERVIEW: 30,000 seeds per ounce/1,050 per gram.

Seed will germinate readily and requires no pretreatments for 70% and higher germination rates. In the *Ball Culture Guide* I wrote that *Aurinia* germinates in seven to 14 days in temperatures ranging from 60F to 70F (16C to 21C) and doesn't need to be covered to germinate. Transplanting can begin 18 to 24 days after sowing. If you increase your germination temperatures to 68F to 72F (20C to 22C), seedlings will emerge in three to eight days and can be transplanted within two weeks. Remember that aurinias are fast growers, so after the seedlings have emerged, drop the night temperatures to 58F to 60F (14C to 16C) to reduce stretching.

Some growers have sown the seed direct to the final container with good results, although sowing to a plug tray and transplanting to the final pot produces more uniform plants.

GROWING ON

From seed: Sowings made from midwinter on will not flower the same season. Plants are salable green in a 32-cell pack 10 to 12 weeks after sowing. Sowings made in autumn, transplanted to 4½-inch (11 cm) or larger pots, can flower in mid-April when grown on at 40 to 45F (4C to 7C) nights. The peak flowering period, however, is usually in late April.

There are several other production methods used on this crop. Vernalized (cold-treated) plugs are available from a number of commercial propagators during winter. These are potted up into quart or larger containers and will flower reliably in the spring. This is dependent, however, on the size of plug used, the duration of the cold treatment, and how early you receive and pot up the plugs. Trial and error will be necessary to settle on the right method.

Finally, you can sow the seed in spring or summer for potting up and overwintering in larger containers for sales the following spring. As with vernalized plugs, small pots are available in autumn from commercial propagators. These can be transplanted to overwinter in a cold greenhouse or cold frame or allowed to go dormant for next spring sales. If not allowed to go dormant, plants should be kept at cold temperatures during the winter to prevent them from getting too robust. In our cold frames, we grow the plants on at 38F to 40F (4C to 5C) during the winter once they're firmly established in their containers.

VARIETIES

The most common cultivar on the market is *A. saxatilis* Compacta, which is easily propagated by seed. It's often sold under the name of Gold Dust, actually the species' common name. Another variety, Citrina, has a softer yellow flower color on plants that reach 10 inches (25 cm) tall. Citrina is also sometimes labeled as Silver Queen or Citrinum.

Compacta is available from many seed companies across the United States and Canada. The other varieties are available only through selected companies. See Color Plate 19 for photo of *Aurinia saxatilis* Compacta.

USES

Aurinia is excellent as a trailing plant over rock walls, where the roots keep cool by growing into various nooks and crannies and the foliage is in bright sun. For best performance, however, plant *Aurinia* where it gets full morning sun but is protected for the rest of the day. Especially when trailed over rock, brick, or other heat-retentive materials, aurinias can be burned by these surfaces. This will shorten its life expectancy, so concentrate on northeastern and eastern exposures for best performance.

IN THE HOME GARDEN

Space *Aurinia* 10 to 12 inches (25 to 30 cm) apart in areas where the plants get full morning sun and shade by early afternoon. Once plants have flowered, trim them back lightly to encourage new vegetative shoots. Plants will not rebloom here in our Midwest location, though their gray-green foliage is a nice contrast to other garden plants. Aurinias don't require staking or dividing and perform best in cool, dry locations. They tolerate neither prolonged drought nor hot, humid weather.

B

▬ BAPTISIA AUSTRALIS

FAMILY: Fabaceae

COMMON NAME(S): False Indigo, Blue Indigo

DESCRIPTION

Baptisia australis is a shrublike, bushy plant that grows 3 to 4 feet (90 to 120 cm) wide and equally tall once it is established in the garden. Arching stems radiate out of a central, tightly clustered 15- to 20-inch (38 to 51 cm) crown that produces numerous stalks. The foliage is pealike, medium green in color, and persists all summer. The flowers, which measure about 1 inch, are deep blue in color, somewhat resembling lupines. They form 2- to 3-inch-long (5 to 7 cm) seed pods, dull black in color, which are sometimes used in dried arrangements.

HARDINESS: Zones 3 to 8.

SEASON OF BLOOM: May and June, over a period of two weeks.

PROPAGATION

Division and seeds are the two most successful methods of propagating this crop. Divisions will be difficult, due to the taproot. If it is damaged in transplanting, the resulting plants will be slow to establish in their transplant containers. In regard to seed, be sure to use freshly harvested seed since, like most pea family members, the seed coats harden as they age.

GERMINATION OVERVIEW: 2,000 seeds per ounce/70 per gram.
Pretreatments: *Baptisia australis* germinates best from freshly harvested seed. If you're using old seed (6-months-old) test a portion before sowing the whole packet. If only a limited amount germinates, scarify the seed coat by nicking or scraping away part of the coat. Don't cut into the seed—just remove a portion of the coat to allow moisture to start the germination process. Additional information is provided in the **Propagation Techniques** chapter.

Seeds will germinate within seven to 14 days at 70F (21C); cover during germination. Alternately, if using old seed in the spring, soak overnight in hot (not boiling) water, sow into a standard peat-lite media and moist chill for a week or two at between 40F to 45F (4C and 7C). This will help to increase germination rates, especially if the seed is scraped prior to soaking.

Fresh seed germinates more rapidly and can be transplanted within three to four weeks after sowing, while seed stored until spring germinates over a period of several weeks to several months, requiring multiple transplant dates.

GROWING ON

Crop time: When sowing from seed, be aware that like most pea family members, *Baptisa* doesn't like frequent transplanting due to its deep-rooted nature. The long tap root can be damaged if allowed to go too long in the seedling tray prior to transplanting to a larger container. If damaged, the resulting plants often are slow to develop and may produce inferior plants when the root is restricted in the container; plants can often languish for a period of time and eventually die.

As a guide, winter sowings will produce weak seedlings by spring, often only 3 to 4 inches (7 to 10 cm) tall by June. In West Chicago, we potted the plants into quart and gallon containers, grew them on through the summer, and then overwintered the pots in a cold frame. They went dormant but reemerged in late March. From seed, plants may not flower for two more seasons, although they're salable as quarts or gallons in spring from a previous year's sowing.

This crop is also available from commercial propagators as liners or plugs. Additional information on this production method is found in the **How to Use** chapter, under **Growing on**.

One final note: Grow on at 50F to 58F (10C to 14C) nights once potted. The plants tolerate cooler conditions (more than 40F or 5C for active growth), but since they're slow to begin with, grow warmer to develop both roots and stems, especially when sown in winter for spring or summer sales.

VARIETIES

Baptisia australis is the most commonly grown of the *Baptisia* genus as a garden perennial. It is a long-lived, reliable selection here in our Chicago location.

USES

Plants don't develop rapidly, often taking up to three years from a planting to reach a sizable state. Plants are very hardy here in Chicago, and their fountain or arching foliage adds an excellent form to the perennial garden or when used as a shrub—at the front of the house as foundation plantings that develop into handsome plants each spring and summer then die to the ground during winter.

This is an easy perennial to grow, and it enjoys either full sun or locations shaded in late afternoon. Plants like a well-drained or moderately moist soil and will persist in their location for many years without requiring any transplanting. Staking isn't needed, unless the plants are grown in heavy shade. Division isn't necessary; plants will continue to grow for many years.

Since one plant is so robust, only a few plants are needed to provide the full effect of what this crop can offer. If planted to a location where drought conditions prevail, the plants will be dependable and adapt well, although initially they will require care until established.

BEGONIA GRANDIS
(formerly *B. evansiana*)

FAMILY: Begoniaceae

COMMON NAME(S): Hardy Begonia, Evans Begonia

DESCRIPTION
Begonia grandis is an upright, basal branching plant with 1-inch (2.5 cm), blush-pink flowers held in open sprays. Plants are usually 13 to 18 inches (33 to 46 cm) tall and taller in warmer climates. The plants will spread 12 to 15 inches (30 to 38 cm) by the season's end. The angel-wing-shaped foliage has red veins while the leaf undersides are reddish as well. The plants have tuberous roots smaller in size than annual tuberous begonias like Nonstop. See Color Plate 20 for photo of *Begonia grandis*.

HARDINESS: Zones 6 to 8.
Begonia grandis is only marginally hardy in the central United States to Zone 6; mulching is necessary to keep the plant in the perennial garden from year to year. While the plants have been known to survive chills to 0F (-18C), and locations as far north as New York City and Washington, D.C., this is in well-protected situations with a winter covering. In our West Chicago gardens, plants have never survived a winter. Read additional comments under **In the home garden**.

SEASON OF BLOOM: From July to fall.

PROPAGATION
Seed, cuttings, and bulbils are three propagation methods that will work equally well on hardy begonias. Seed is often difficult to find here in the United States, but European seed companies usually carry the crop. Seed can be sown anytime and grown as you would tuberous rooted begonias. Bulbils are most often planted in the winter, while cuttings can be taken during the summer.

GERMINATION OVERVIEW: 1,500,000 seeds per ounce/52,500 per gram.
Sow seed on any peat-lite media and don't cover during germination. Germinate at 68F to 72F (20C to 22C); seedlings will emerge seven to 14 days after sowing. They can then be transplanted 30 to 45 days after sowing. On seed received in December

from a crop harvested the previous summer, you can expect 70% or higher germination. Older seed usually germinates at roughly 50 to 60%.

GROWING ON

Crop time: Allow plenty of time if sowing from seed. If sown in February or later, plants will not flower readily the same year. Instead sowings should be made the previous year, from October to December for 4-inch (10 cm) or 1- and 2-quart container sales in spring. Grow the crop with warm nights of no lower than 55F (13C) for active growth.

If you prefer having cell packs ready for spring, a 32-cell pack will not be salable green for 15 to 18 weeks. These plants are between 3 and 4 inches (7 and 10 cm) tall and will have only a limited amount of flower color on them the same season.

A word of caution on *Begonia grandis*: Plants are highly susceptible to sunburn if exposed to full sun and allowed to dry out between waterings. If plants are moved to the cold frame prior to sales, keep in mind that they may burn under normal poly that doesn't have a latex shade or shade cloth. Plants are more susceptible to sunburn than bedding begonias, so take precautions when finishing off the plants.

As for bulbils, *Begonia grandis* produces a number of these within the plant leaf axis. These can be gathered and stored during the fall for winter planting and spring sales. If left on the plant and not frozen during the winter, the bulbils will eventually drop off and produce small plantlets during the next growing season. These bulbils can be used to increase your populations. If gathered, stored, and then planted in mid or late winter, the plants will flower the same year.

VARIETIES

B. grandis is a soft to medium pink-flowering variety that follows the description noted above.

B. grandis Alba is a white-flowering version of the pink type. Plants grow between 1 and 2 feet (30 and 60 cm) tall with 1-inch (2.5 cm) white flowers.

USES

Not an overly important perennial for the garden, but it does provide a unique form, especially in the perennial shade garden where a begonia's angel-wing-shaped leaves would be appreciated. Consumers view most begonias as tender and unable to survive the winter without being dug up and stored, especially tuberous rooted varieties. The fact that one variety can live from year to year will provoke curiosity and interest.

In merchandising this variety to the consumer, remember that it's difficult to obtain and consumers need education on its uses and limitations. *Begonia grandis* is usually only available from perennial plant growers and not the discount or supermarket chain stores in their spring storefront displays. Also, since it flowers all summer, this variety could be sold along with bulbs and other perennials for fall planting in well-protected locations in the southern United States.

In the home garden

With regard to hardiness and overwintering in the home garden, review the information provided under **Hardiness**. This is the most critical point in planting this perennial. While the hardiness ratings indicate this crop can survive winters to Zone 6, it's probably hardier throughout most of Zone 7 and lower parts of Zone 6. Without mulching and an appropriate growing site, the plants may not even survive in these locations.

In selecting a site, choose a place that is moist but well-drained, where the plants will receive only dappled light and are shaded during the hottest parts of the day. I would not call this a plant for the deep shade. Instead, we plant it in eastern and northern exposures or in areas where the plants get bright light but not direct sun. The plants should be fed sparingly since soft growth can lead to weak stems that require staking. In general, plants don't need staking unless they've been given heavy shade and/or plenty of food and water. As the flower buds set, stems will arch gracefully, allowing the new stems clustered in the center more light to extend upwards and flower.

Since *Begonia grandis* is tuberous, it requires a resting period with steady winter temperatures around 45F (7C) in which it can go dormant. In warm but wet winter climates where low temperatures are 40F to 45F (5C to 7C), the tubers could rot, so it's advisable to dig and store them for replanting during late winter or spring.

▬ Belamcanda chinensis

Family: Iridaceae

Common name(s): Blackberry Lily, Leopard Lily

Description

Closely resembling the foliage of German iris to which it's related, *Belamcanda chinensis* has swordlike leaves (leaves that overlap at the base) ending in a pointed tip. The flowers are single and open, from 2 to 3 inches (5 to 7 cm) across. They bud terminally at the end of forked stems. Flowers are brightly colored, usually orange or yellow, splattered with red dots across the surface of the petal. Black fruits containing the seeds develop in a tight vertical cluster and resemble ripe blackberries—the common name. Plants grow from 3 to 4 feet (90 to 120 cm) in full bloom; and while narrow at the base, the crown can spread from 2 to 3 feet (60 to 90 cm) across when in bloom.

HARDINESS: Zones 5 to 9.

SEASON OF BLOOM: July and August.

PROPAGATION

Divisions and seed are two easy ways to propagate. Roots can be divided in the spring similar to German iris. Each division of the rhizome should have a fan or cluster where the foliage is developing. Unlike German iris, however, these rhizomes are smaller, less fingerlike in appearance, and more clumped in development.

Seeds can be sown anytime, but due to the long crop time for a quality transplant, spring or summer sowings for following year sales are suggested.

GERMINATION OVERVIEW

Pretreatments: None required.

Germination temperatures of 70F to 72F (21C to 22C) are optimum for germinating *B. chinensis*. Sow in any peat-lite mixture, and cover the seed when sowing. Germination occurs in 15 to 25 days depending on the age of the seed—freshly harvested seed germinates slightly faster into salable transplants. Seedlings can be transplanted from a plug tray or open flat into a small cell pack (48 or 72) six to seven weeks after sowing.

GROWING ON

Crop time: January sowings often are too small for May retail sales. Landscape quality plants require at least a year from seed to develop into fully flowering plants. In the southern United States, the longer warm season helps plants to develop faster than here in our northern greenhouses.

Winter or spring sowings will usually be salable green in a 3-inch (7 cm) pot by late summer but shouldn't be sold for fall planting. Pot up into larger containers for sales the following spring instead for the best quality plants.

If you purchase roots for delivery during the fall or winter, pot these up into 1- to 3-quart containers for sales eight to 11 weeks later, growing on at 50F to 55F (10C to 13C) nights. Plants will flower later that summer.

Temperature: Grow the seedlings and divisions in the winter and spring in a moderate environment to allow them to establish. Remember they grow slowly: If grown cold below 45F (7C), they may rot if overwatered. Conversely, temperatures above 70F (21C) may result in weak plants and additional disease problems.

VARIETIES

Belamcanda chinensis is available as seed from many U.S. seed companies. You'll find that more European firms carry it than do American companies, but the variety is not widely available, even from Europe.

RELATED MATERIAL

× *pardancanda norrisii* (Candy Lily) is the result of a cross between *Pardanthopsis dichotomus* (Iris dichotoma) and *Belamcanda chinensis*. Both the Candy Lily and

Blackberry Lily look similar in habit and form. This crop has a wider flower color range that includes red, white, cream, and yellow plus shades in between. Plants grow to 3 feet (90 cm) tall and flower at the same time as *B. chinensis*. Seed is available in the U.S. trade from Park Seed Company; vegetative selections have been introduced from Europe as well.

USES

As a landscape plant, *B. chinensis* is better in groups of four to five plants so that its open crown and wiry stems provide a bold look. It's effective in either the home or professional landscape, where its flowers and foliage are used closer to the front of the display rather than lost in the back. *B. chinensis* is exotic looking, and container plants used to adorn entry ways or decks will provide a spectacular color show.

Combine lower growing annuals or perennials at the base of the plants to fill out the container. As a cut flower, the plants last as long as German iris and are a colorful decoration for the first week after cutting. In the late summer the blackberry-looking fruit and tan capsule are a striking contrast. These pods can be used in either fresh or dried arrangements.

IN THE HOME GARDEN

This is an excellent plant for full-sun locations with moderately drained soil. Excessive moisture will not kill the plant but will make it larger and more robust in appearance. Staking isn't necessary unless plants are situated in a fertile and moist place or grown where they get too much shade.

Plants are hardy in our Chicago gardens without any winter protection. People in zones farther north may want to consider mulching this plant during the winter to give it some protection. × *pardancanda*, on the other hand, is only marginally hardy in northern winters, often dying out by the third or fourth year after planting if grown in the open ground without protection. When used as a foundation planting, both crops live a long time with few problems.

■■■ BELLIS PERENNIS

FAMILY: Asteraceae

COMMON NAME(S): English Daisy

DESCRIPTION

Bellis perennis is a low-growing, rosetting plant, 6 to 8 inches (15 to 20 cm) tall in bloom, with an 8- to 10-inch (20 to 25 cm) spread. The dark green foliage is held closely to the crown. Flowers are either single or double, measuring $1\frac{1}{2}$ to 3 inches (3 to 7 cm) across. The scentless blooms come in white, pastel pink, and carmine red with several shades in between. Without blooms, the plants are between 3 to 4 inches (7 to 10 cm) tall.

119

HARDINESS: Zone 4 to 8.

Though called a "biennial" (plants that live for two years), *Bellis* is often treated as an annual here in the United States. Our severe northern winters or the intense heat of a southern summer can quickly kill these plants.

The best areas of the United States to grow this crop as a perennial are those with Mediterranean or English climates, such as the central East and West Coasts.

SEASON OF BLOOM: May to June.

PROPAGATION

Seed is the common way to propagate, but cultivated varieties need to be vegetatively propagated by divisions in spring or fall.

GERMINATION OVERVIEW: 140,000 seeds per ounce/4,900 per gram.

Seed germinates in seven to 14 days at 70F to 75F (21C to 24C) and can be left exposed to light during germination. Transplant seedlings 15 to 22 days after sowing.

GROWING ON

Crop time: If you're growing from seed, treat the plants as you would pansies. In general, pansies require from 12 to 14 weeks from sow to flower to bloom, 50 to 100% in a 32-cell pack. Grow this as a spring crop in the same fashion, allowing 14 to 15 weeks for a full-flowering crop at 50F to 55F (10C to 13C) night temperatures. This is based on using the variety Super Enorma Mix; Pomponette will flower up to a week earlier. Their best performance however, is in a 4- to 5-inch (10 to 13 cm) pot using one plant per pot. For flowering in 4½-inch (11 cm) pots, allow 14 to 17 weeks.

Varieties are cold hardy but will not tolerate severe cold as in a northern winter. For February sales, Pomponette was sown in October, producing flowering 4-inch (10 cm) pots in February, and grown at 45F to 50F (7C to 10C) nights in the North. While additional work needs to be done to test flowering under winter days, we didn't provide any additional lighting. *B. perennis* has potential use in the southern U.S. as a fall crop for winter and spring color. Due to the heat sensitivity of the crop, however, it would be best to buy in plugs available from commercial propagators as opposed to sowing your own seed in July for late southern summer sales. It is not suggested as a northern fall crop.

VARIETIES

There are a number of varieties available other than the two listed below, although these are the most common ones. While most of these other varieties are propagated from seed, some are vegetatively propagated; however, they're not commonly available in the United States due to our climate. Nursery catalogs seldom list varieties other than those noted here, but don't let that stop you from searching out new selections.

Pomponette is a seed variety noted for its buttonlike quilled blossoms in carmine red, pink, or white. Flowers are semidouble, measuring up to 1 inch (2.5 cm) across. In the United States, the mixture is most common, although separate colors are available as well. Plants grow to between 4 and 5 inches (10 and 13 cm) tall when in bloom.

Super Enorma Mix is a large flowering mix from seed with double flowers in white, carmine, pink, and several shades in between. Flowers are 3 inches (7 cm) across and somewhat ruffled in appearance. Plants grow to between 6 and 8 inches (15 and 20 cm) tall in bloom. Separate colors are also available though less frequently found in the U.S. trade than Pomponette's separate colors.

Although these two varieties can be grown in the same containers, Pomponette does better in cell packs and 4-inch (10 cm) pots, while Super Enorma is excellent in 4½- and 5-inch (11 and 13 cm) pots due to its larger size.

USES

With the advent of southern fall markets for pansies and other cool weather crops, *Bellis* has a potential for a small share. Unfortunately, due to their limited color range and heat intolerance, the plants have a limited market here in the United States, although they will do well as long as temperatures are cool. Pansies are more heat tolerant.

IN THE HOME GARDEN

In England the plants grow and develop freely but can stray and self-sow in lawns. Since they seldom breed true from seed, however, resulting plants are often more vigorous than the original variety and are weeded out. Here in the United States and Canada, our colder climates usually take their toll so reseeding isn't a problem, though coastal climates (especially the West Coast) may be more prone to reseeding.

Plants do best when given full sun in coastal locations, morning sun in hot summer climates, and a moist (but not wet) soil to grow in. Plants are best used in small groupings at the front of a bed but can also be easily used as a border or edging.

In West Coast gardens, the plants do very well, filling in when spaced 8 to 10 inches (20 to 25 cm) apart, and blooming the majority of the winter into late spring. In hot summer areas, plants are best treated as a spring annual mixed in with bulbs where they can be removed as bulb foliage deteriorates. At that time the plants can be replaced with warm season selections.

▬ BERGENIA CORDIFOLIA

FAMILY: Saxifragaceae

COMMON NAME(S): Heart-Leaved Bergenia

DESCRIPTION

These are beautiful accent plants with glossy, deep green, sometimes bronzed or purple foliage that is cabbagelike in texture and thickness. The foliage is evergreen and very hardy. In our Chicago-area gardens, new growth begins to appear in March. Last year's foliage will remain healthy and burn-free, although brushed with a bronze or purple highlight throughout the winter.

Plants grow 15 to 18 inches (38 to 46 cm) tall when in bloom; without flowers they seldom get above 14 inches (35 cm) tall and are often shorter. The roots are rhizomatous but not invasive. Flowers are single, rose-pink in color, and held in clusters on thickened stems.

HARDINESS: Zones 3 to 8.

SEASON OF BLOOM: April and May.

PROPAGATION

Propagate *B. cordifolia* by seed and the named varieties either by division or basal cuttings. Sow seeds anytime with equal results assured from year to year.

Field or nursery dug divisions can be done either in spring or summer, and bare-root divisions purchased from commercial propagations can be potted either fall or winter for spring sales. Basal cuttings are the shoots that develop at the base of the plant, either at the crown or slightly below the soil surface, during the spring or early summer.

GERMINATION OVERVIEW: 110,000 seeds per ounce/3,850 per gram.

Seeds germinate in four to eight days at 72F (22C) and don't need to be covered during germination. Seedlings are slow to develop and will be transplantable in seven to nine weeks (depending on the time of year). Since they're slow growing, you may want to try growing this crop in plug trays.

Sowing direct to a 290 or larger plug cell would help to speed up production, or at least, remove the tedious job of transplanting individual seedlings. From a 290 tray, move the plugs into small pots for growing before potting up into quart or gallon pots. Some can be transplanted to a large cell pack (18 or 24 per flat) instead of the small pot, but some growers feel the plants are too slow growing at this time and may tend to overwater. Therefore, they prefer individual pot production as opposed to flats.

GROWING ON

Crop time: From seed, bergenias will require time to grow into salable plants. In general, a February sowing will produce salable, green 32-cell packs in 16 to 18 weeks when grown at 58F to 60F (13C to 15C) nights. These plants can be sold as is or transplanted to quart or gallon pots, which can then be sold in the late summer for planting. We have transplanted bergenias as late as early October to our gardens without winter mulching. The plants rooted well before the worst of our winter cold set in, and we have never lost more than one or two plants. For your customers, however, mulching is suggested especially if planting in autumn. If seed is sown from December on, the plants will not flower the following summer from seed although they will reach their mature height. Instead, the plants will flower the following spring.

If you're selling bergenias in the spring from seed started in fall or winter, remember to keep the plants warm and continuously growing until the roots have fully developed. While bergenias flower under cool weather, as seedlings they prefer to be kept warm at 58F to 60F (14C to 15C) nights until the roots are firmly established in the cell pack or pot. The foliage will be deceiving as it is often twice the size of the roots massed in the pot. If roots aren't firmly anchored, cool or cold temperatures and overwatering will lead to root rots.

This crop is also available as liners and plugs from commercial propagators. Additional information is provided on plug production on page 6 of the **How to Use** chapter.

As for bare-root divisions, roots are available from a number of commercial propagators during the winter and spring for potting up into 2-, 3-, or 4-quart containers and selling in the spring. In our Chicago location, March-dug divisions potted into 3-quart pots were salable in mid-May, fully rooted.

VARIETIES

Bergenia cordifolia is available from seed under the botanical name and other poetic names like Cambridge Rose. There is no difference—they're the same thing. Color mixtures are also available, although rose and red shades predominate. Plants grow to 15 inches (38 cm) tall in bloom.

The following varieties are probably the result of a cross between *B. cordifolia* and *B. purpurascens* (the purple bergenia) and are listed as varieties under *B. cordifolia*, as a hybrid under the name of *B. × smithii* and, occasionally, under *B. purpurascens*. Most references list these varieties as either one of the first two examples. All of these are vegetatively propagated, in some cases from tissue culture, and are not available from seed.

Bressingham White may flower light pink at first, prior to turning to pure white. The variety grows to between 12 and 15 inches (30 and 38 cm) tall.

Bressingham Salmon is a salmon-pink flowering variety to 1 foot (30 cm) tall.

Morning Red (sometimes listed as Morgenrote) has red flowers on plants to 15 inches (38 cm) tall. This is a choice cultivar and one of the better ones on the market.

Silver Light (sometimes listed as Silberlicht) is a pink-tinted, white-flowering variety to 12 inches (30 cm) tall.

RELATED MATERIAL

Bergenia purpurascens (sometimes listed as *B. delavayi* var. *purpurascens*) is a variety that grows to between 12 and 15 inches (30 and 38 cm) tall with pink (sometimes magenta) flowers in the early spring (April). Plants are noted for their deep purple foliage in cool weather, equally as glossy but deeper in color than the foliage of *B. cordifolia.*

USES

One of the earliest perennials to return and flower in the spring, bergenias work well in clumps or as a border or edging.

IN THE HOME GARDEN

Bergenias do best in a partially shaded location. Plants are long lived in the garden and have few requirements as long as the soil they're planted in is well drained and not overly fertile.

Plants never require any staking. Even though rhizomatous, they've never become invasive in our gardens. The foliage is reliably evergreen and looks its best under cool temperatures in both the fall and spring here in Chicago.

■■■ BOLTONIA ASTEROIDES

FAMILY: Asteraceae

COMMON NAME(S): Boltonia, False Chamomile

DESCRIPTION

Boltonia is a premier plant for the midsummer garden with its scentless, daisylike, pure white, sometimes purple or lilac flowers. Single blooms measure about 1 inch across. The plants form clumps spreading 3 to 4 feet (90 to 120 cm) wide and grow erect to between 5 and 6 feet (1.5 to 1.8 m) tall in flower. Foliage is dull gray green in color.

HARDINESS: Zones 4 to 9.

SEASON OF BLOOM: August and September.

PROPAGATION

Seed, division, and cuttings are the usual ways to propagate boltonia. All are equally easy to perform, depending on which method fits into your production schedule. The most common white-flowering variety, Snowbank, should be propagated by either cutting or division since seed-propagated plants can be uneven or nonuniform. The seed, however, is available from European seed companies.

Divisions can be taken in the spring or fall and successfully rooted, while cuttings are taken in spring or summer before the plants have budded up.

GERMINATION OVERVIEW

Seed germinates in four to eight days at 70F (21C); cover lightly with peat or vermiculite. No special treatments are necessary to obtain 70% or better germination rates on purchased seed. From sowing, allow 22 to 30 days before transplanting the seedlings.

GROWING ON

Crop time: From seed, plants will produce a green basal rosette with six to 10 elongated leaves the first year after sowing. If you prefer green cell packs for spring sales, allow 10 to 12 weeks at 55F (13C) for plants 1- to 1½-inches (2.5 to 3 cm) tall. Plants don't flower the same season from seed, and the rosettes are slow growing. Instead, sow seed during summer for overwintering in quart or gallon pots for sales the following spring.

Divisions can be taken in both spring or fall, but spring-dug and divided plants root better than those cut after the plant flowers. A single clump of boltonia contains a number of rosettes that can provide quite a few divisions.

Take cuttings in 3-inch-long sections in either spring or early summer. Stick them into sand or peat moss within a warm propagating environment (74F/23C) and high humidity. Cuttings will root in about a month and can be transplanted to individual pots for late summer sale or for overwintering for sale the following spring.

VARIETIES

Boltonia asteroides seed is available from a limited number of U.S. seed firms specializing in native perennial plants. There is also a dwarf variety of this crop, but it may be harder to find. *B. asteroides* var. *latisquama* Nana is a white-flowering variety that grows to only 3 feet (90 cm) tall.

Snowbank is an excellent variety vegetatively propagated by either divisions or cuttings. Plants grow to 4 feet tall (120 cm) and produce numerous 1-inch (2.5 cm), white blooms on erect plants. They flower in the late summer. See Color Plate 21 for photo of *Boltonia asteroides* Snowbank.

USES

Boltonia works well in the mid and late summer garden, providing tall background impact when in full bloom. Plants are long lived and seldom require any special treatment, such as staking or winter mulching. They're a good choice for commercial landscape plantings, or as a summer backdrop for front-of-the-border plants, and their late season color is a welcome addition.

In wildflower or meadow settings both the species and Snowbank can be used, although I would use Snowbank only in commercial plantings.

The flowers also work well as a filler for late season bouquets. No special postharvest treatment is necessary; they should be cut and treated like asters. Their vase life is about as long as asters.

IN THE HOME GARDEN

A number of perennials reliably return year after year without requiring constant pampering or control. Likewise, there are a number of perennials that don't require special care in overwintering, staking, or insect/fungal treatment. Boltonia in general, and Snowbank in particular, fit all of these descriptions.

While still climbing the popularity ladder in the central United States at the time of this writing, Boltonia has potential for becoming a better known plant for the home garden, despite its limited color range.

Boltonias perform best when planted in a moist environment in full sun, but they also tolerate drained soils. Don't plant in rich soil since this can lead to tall and robust plants that lose their shape and might require staking.

▬ BRUNNERA MACROPHYLLA
(formerly *Anchusa myosotidiflora*)

FAMILY: Boraginaceae

COMMON NAME(S): Siberian Bugloss, Heartleaf Brunnera

DESCRIPTION

Brunnera macrophylla is a woodland plant with a vigorous, spreading habit. The foliage is heart shaped, medium green and lush. Azure to medium blue in color, the flowers are starlike in shape and resemble the blooms of either *Anchusa* or *Myosotis*; hence the former name *myosotidiflora* (flowers that look like myosotis). Brunnera plants reach 15 to 18 inches (38 to 46 cm) in height and spread about 2 feet (60 cm) wide.

HARDINESS: Zones 4 to 7.

SEASON OF BLOOM: April and May.

PROPAGATION

Seed, division, and root cuttings are the preferred methods of propagating this crop, but root cuttings and division are the most common. Divisions can be taken in the spring or late summer. Additional information on root cuttings is provided in the front of the book in the **Propagation Techniques** chapter. Any of the variegated-leaf cultivars are propagated vegetatively, not by seed.

GROWING ON

Crop time: If digging and dividing your own transplants, do so in late summer. Place transplants in individual quart or larger containers, trimming the foliage back, and then cover the crop with shadecloth until rooted. Plants should be treated tenderly the first several days until rooting begins, especially if dug from under trees or other shaded locations. The foliage wilts frequently after dividing when grown in brighter greenhouse and cold frame exposures.

These transplants will be salable in the late summer as fall plants for the home garden, but you can also overwinter the crop and sell it the following spring.

You can also purchase divisions or roots from a number of commercial sources in the fall or winter. These can be potted up into 1- to 3-quart containers, grown on at

50F to 55F (10C to 13C) nights, and sold in the spring. Brunnera will finish off in approximately nine to 11 weeks, while its variegated forms can take several weeks longer. These variegated varieties will also be slower growing in the garden.

VARIETIES

Brunnera macrophylla is the most available cultivar listed here. It is commonly sold as a transplant or division from a number of commercial companies. Read the comments provided under **Description** for additional details. If you are looking for seed, contact American seed exchanges or European seed companies. Additional selections include:

Hadspen Cream, which has light green, variegated foliage with an irregular, cream-white border around each leaf. The flowers are midblue. This variety isn't as tolerant of sun as the green-leaf types, and it, along with Variegata, isn't as easy to find in the U.S. trade. Maximum height is 15 inches (38 cm). Hadspen Cream is only propagated vegetatively.

Langtrees is another blue-flowering, variegated-leaf variety. Leaves are covered with small dots of silver grey at the border, which extends towards the center of each leaf. Plants will tolerate more sun and drier conditions than either of the two variegated varieties listed here. It grows 15 inches (38 cm) tall. Propagate vegetatively.

Variegata has variegated foliage similar to Hadspen Cream, but the variegation is bolder and can sometimes cover the entire leaf. Most of the light coloring extends from the outer margin around an island of green in the middle of the leaf. The plant prefers a shaded and moist location out of direct light. Maximum height is 10 to 15 inches (25 to 38 cm). Propagate Variegata vegetatively.

USES

This is an especially good plant for woodland settings or shaded locations, either in the home garden or commercial landscape. Plants can be used to carpet large shaded areas but won't have as dramatic an impact in dark shade; instead, they prefer morning sun or dappled light during the day.

IN THE HOME GARDEN

As suggested under **Uses**, choose a location where the plants get morning sun and afternoon shade. The farther south you go from Chicago, the more shaded and moist the location should be to avoid drying out the plants, especially the variegated forms. In the southern United States, plants tolerate more shade than in the Midwest where sun and high temperatures aren't as intense.

If grown under a canopy of tree limbs, the plants seldom require winter mulching. If planted in more open locations away from the protection of buildings or trees, the plants are more susceptible to winter drying, and an organic mulch is suggested. Be sure to remove the mulch in the spring to encourage the plants to come back uniformly.

■ BUDDLEIA DAVIDII

In older reference books, the genus is spelled Buddleja or Buddleija.

FAMILY: Loganiaceae

COMMON NAME(S): Butterfly Bush, Summer Lilac

DESCRIPTION

Buddleia davidii is an imposing plant with species reaching 10 to 15 feet (3 to 4.5 m) tall, although most of the clones sold seldom get above 8 feet (2.4 m), especially in severe winter areas where the plant dies back to the ground. In southern locations, however, it can achieve a height of 10 to 12 feet (3 to 3.6 m) depending on location. In width, plants can spread from 4 to 6 feet (1.2 to 1.8 m) across by August.

While plants are sometimes treated as shrubs here in the North, they have a vigorous, mostly erect habit, making them a good seasonal hedge. In warm winter areas, it can be evergreen.

As one of its common names suggests, *davidii* blooms resemble lilacs. The individual flowers measure up to one-quarter inch (6 mm) across and are arranged in a long spike from 6 to 10 inches (15 to 25 cm) long, but they are narrower at the base than lilacs. Flower colors include purple, white, lavender, and lilac. Individual flowers are often accented with an orange throat. The flowers are very fragrant.

HARDINESS: Zones 5 to 9.

Zone 5 hardiness depends on location. Moist, poorly drained soils can cause winter kill. In our gardens outside Chicago, however, the plants have been long lived.

SEASON OF BLOOM: July and August.

PROPAGATION

Softwood cuttings can be easily taken during late spring while hardwood cuttings are taken in late summer or fall. Although seed is available for the species itself, named varieties are propagated from cuttings only.

GERMINATION OVERVIEW

Seed germinates readily and no pretreatment is necessary. Germination occurs in eight to 12 days at 72F (22C). When sowing, cover seed lightly. Seedlings can be transplanted 28 to 35 days after sowing.

GROWING ON

Crop time: *Buddleia* grows quickly regardless of whether it is grown from seed or cuttings. For seed-grown plants, allow 10 to 12 weeks for salable green plants in a 32-cell pack; 14 to 16 weeks for a 4-inch (10 cm) pot. I want to stress, however, that sowings made anytime during the late winter or spring will produce primarily single-stemmed vigorous plants 10 to 15 inches (25 to 38 cm) tall, with limited basal branching. Seed-propagated plants can be visually unacceptable when sold in a cell

B

pack. In quarts or gallon pots, the plants can be pinched to encourage branching but avoiding high temperatures and low light are essential to control the growth.

Keep in mind that these plants grow quickly under warm conditions of 65F (18C) nights and above and more slowly under cooler temperatures of 50F (10C) nights and below. Make sure plants are firmly established in the final container first, and then drop the night temperatures to slow their growth. However, night temperatures below 48F (9C) can curl and lighten the foliage. While not sickly, the plants are not aesthetically pleasing either.

One final comment on seed-propagated plants: If sown anytime during the winter or early spring, the plants will flower in July or August, but by the second year, the plants will be more uniform and stronger flowering.

With regard to cuttings, softwood cuttings root easily during the spring and summer months: A gallon plant will be ready for overwintering if the original cuttings are taken in June. Just be sure to take your cuttings early enough so that they can grow sufficiently to survive a winter.

Hardwood cuttings don't root as easily and are more practical for southern growers than northern growers. While cuttings can be taken as late as autumn, you'll have to overwinter them in a warm greenhouse since they will drop their foliage and go dormant in cool temperatures. If taking hardwood cuttings in the autumn, take your cuttings a month or less after leaf drop to encourage better rooting. Treat *Buddleia* as you would any other warm season perennial, avoiding night temperatures below 45F (7C) unless you're trying to make the plants go dormant.

Hardwood cuttings can also be taken in the late winter in the South where plants don't die back to the soil line. Cut stems with three to four buds (approximately 4 to 6 inches [10 to 15 cm] long), and propagate them in a peat-based media with bottom heat. Plants will root by May. This method, however, is not as successful, or as easy, as using softwood cuttings.

VARIETIES

The cultivated forms of *Buddleia* are more uniform and less vigorous than any of the seeded varieties and are more preferred in the trade.

Buddleia davidii isn't readily available from seed in the U.S. trade. Seed is primarily available in mixtures containing violet, lilac, and white flower colors. The plants will grow between 5 and 6 feet (1.5 to 1.8 m) tall.

All of the following are the result of sports and crosses between *B. davidii* and other species. When looking through various nursery catalogs, you'll find that these are listed botanically under *B. davidii*. All of these are **vegetatively propagated**.

Black Knight grows between 4 and 6 feet (1.2 to 1.8 m) tall with deep purple flowers.

Empire Blue is a rich blue-flowering variety considered by some experts to be the best. Plants grow to between 4 and 6 feet (1.2 to 1.8 m) tall.

129

Harlequin has variegated yellow and green foliage with purple flowers. This variety isn't as hardy as nonvariegated cultivars in Zone 5.

Lavender Beauty has lavender flowers on plants to 6 feet (1.8 m) tall.

Nanho Blue is a more dwarf variety to 3 feet (90 cm) or sometimes as tall as 5 feet (150 cm) with blue flowers on silver foliage.

Nanho Purple has a similar height to Nanho Blue with violet-purple flowers on silver-leaved plants to 3 or 4 feet (90 to 120 cm) tall.

Petite Indigo has a lavender-blue flower on 3-foot-tall (90 cm) plants.

Petite Plum develops reddish purple flowers on plants to 3 feet (90 cm) tall.

Petite Purple is between 2 and 3 feet (60 to 90 cm) tall, with purple flowers.

Pink Delight has pink spikes on plants between 4 and 6 feet (1.2 to 1.8 m) tall.

Royal Red is reddish purple flowering plant growing between 4 and 6 feet (1.2 to 1.8 m) tall.

White Profusion has pure white flowers on plants that reach 4 to 5 feet (1.2 to 1.5 m).

RELATED MATERIAL

Buddleia alternifolia, commonly called the fountain bush, has distinctive lance-shaped foliage. Plants can reach 10 feet (3 m); in California they can grow to 12 feet (3.6 m). As the common name suggests, fountain bush arches or cascades to the ground like a weeping willow. The one-half-inch (1 cm) flowers are lilac purple and fragrant. Plants are hardy from Zones 5 to 9. The flowers grow on old wood, that is, stems that developed the previous year and overwintered to leaf out again the following year (the opposite of *B. davidii*). So do not prune the plants until after they have flowered in June.

USES

These shrubs are deciduous in cold winter areas, and they die back to the ground, re-emerging the following spring. Therefore, if you need a seasonal shrub to fill in an area during the summer only, consider using *Buddleia*.

Buddleia plants are large and robust and should not be planted in small, formal gardens where their form may overpower. But don't deny yourself the opportunity to landscape with these plants if you have the space for them. In the commercial plantings or large areas where they have adequate space, the plants will have few problems and will attract both hummingbirds and butterflies.

IN THE HOME GARDEN

Plant in full sun in well-drained locations. Plants will not tolerate wet soil, especially in cold winter areas where this is the leading cause of winter kill. Plants will die back to the ground in Ohio and Illinois for the winter, but farther South they will remain a woody shrub.

With regard to pruning, *B. davidii* produces flowers on new growth, so prune hard in the spring to encourage more uniform growth. For those gardeners in the southern United States, prune down to 10 inches (25 cm) from the crown in the late winter to keep the plant in check and to maintain its shape. Plants will develop quickly, regardless of whether they're growing in the South or the North. They can grow to 8 feet (2.4 m) tall or more by the season's end.

As for fertility, plants will tolerate a number of soils but a fertile—not rich— location is best. Plants don't need staking but if fed too well, they can get taller and more robust in habit. A pH of 6 to 7 is best.

▄▄ BUPHTHALMUM SALICIFOLIUM

FAMILY: Asteraceae

COMMON NAME(S): Oxeye Daisy

DESCRIPTION

The epitome of a wildflower performer, *Buphthalmum salicifolium* has single, 2½-inch (6 cm) daisylike, golden yellow flowers, often with a dark center. The blooms are scentless and held upright on plants that are 1 to 2 feet (30 and 60 cm) tall and wide. The foliage is dark green, toothed and narrow, resembling that of a weeping willow—hence the name "salicifolium."

HARDINESS: Zones 4 to 7.

SEASON OF BLOOM: July and August.

PROPAGATION

Most daisies are usually propagated by seed and division, and *salicifolium* fits in with its relatives. Take divisions in the spring and again after flowering if the plants are trimmed back, watered, and fed to encourage a proliferation of new stems.

GERMINATION OVERVIEW: 30,000 seeds per ounce/1,050 per gram.

Seed will germinate in four to six days at 72F (22C) and can be covered lightly. Transplant seedlings 15 to 20 days after sowing.

Pretreatments: Like many daisies, *Buphthalmum* needs no special pretreatments for germination and growing on.

GROWING ON

Crop time: *B. salicifoluim* is fast growing and will be salable green in a 32-cell pack in nine to 11 weeks. Grow initially at 65F (18C) to establish in the cell pack after transplanting. Once established, grow on in a cold frame environment where night temperatures are 50F to 55F (10C to 13C) and days are warmer by 10F to 15F (5C to 9C).

It's important to harden the plant off prior to sales, otherwise you'll have to use a growth regulator to keep the plants in check.

February sowings will be salable green in April and May; the plants will flower in July and August. Sporadic and uneven flowering is what you can expect the first year, with more profuse blooms the second year. For more reliable color, sow earlier in the season or the previous summer for larger plants ready for spring sales.

VARIETIES

Sunwheel is the only commercially available variety of any importance. It's commonly available from seed in Europe and the United States. Plants grow to 18 inches (46 cm) tall.

USES

Buphthalmum can be used as a border to accent other plants but really shines in wildflower gardens or as a meadow planting. Unfortunately, due to its "wild" nature, this perennial is often overlooked for use in mass plantings.

It can be planted in a cutting garden; commercially, however, there are other yellow daisylike flowers of greater value as cut flowers.

IN THE HOME GARDEN

Plants work best in full-sun locations in moist but well-drained soil. Plants do not require staking, but if given ample feed and moisture, the plants can become more sprawling in their performance. In these cases, staking will be necessary to maintain the shape. If grown on the lean side in a drier environment, plants will grow more upright.

Plants have a short flowering period here in Chicago. *B. salicifolium* flowers in July but will often be out of bloom by the month's end. Plants should be trimmed and shaped at this time and a second, though less profuse, set of blooms will appear in three weeks.

C

■ CALTHA PALUSTRIS

FAMILY: Ranunculaceae

COMMON NAME(S): Marsh Marigold
Caltha is the old Latin name for marigold. Linnaeus applied it to this genus.

DESCRIPTION
Caltha plaustris is a native perennial found most often along or in streams, in wet soils or shallow water 3 to 6 inches (7 to 15 cm) deep. It has single or double bright yellow (sometimes white) blooms, 1 to 2 inches (2.5 to 5 cm) across. The flowers are apetalous—that is, they lack petals—and the blooms are made up of sepals only. Leaves are glossy green and rounded in appearance, measuring up to 3 inches (7 cm) across. Caltha plants grow 12 to 15 inches (30 to 38 cm) tall and from 12 to 15 inches (30 to 38 cm) across.

HARDINESS: Zones 3 to 8.

SEASON OF BLOOM: May

PROPAGATION
Division and seed are two ways to propagate this plant. Divisions work best after flowering in either May or June, earlier in the southern United States. Seed should be fresh for best results, although it will still germinate in winter from seed collected the previous summer. You'll have to pretreat older seed, however, to achieve good germination.

GERMINATION OVERVIEW
Pretreatments: For best results sow only fresh seed, although it should germinate well for a limited time after collecting. To avoid pretreating, use the seed within a month or two after ripening.

If purchasing seed, test a 100-seed sample prior to sowing the whole packet. If seedling emergence is poor after 20 days, follow the procedures in the front of this book for moist chilling to improve germination.

We've found that *C. palustris* will germinate in 15 to 20 days after sowing, sooner if using fresh seed. Late summer sowings of collected seed had the best germination. Seed stored dry until winter and then sowed has repeatedly yielded 15% to 30% germination stands. Germination temperatures of 70F (21C) work best, and you can cover the seed lightly during germination. Transplant seedlings in four to six weeks after sowing.

GROWING ON

Crop time: From seed, *Caltha* takes time to develop into strong green transplants that can either be sold green or moved up into quarts for sales a year later.

For 4-inch (10 cm) or quart containers, you'll have to sow seed the previous year to achieve plants large enough for spring sales. Many crops listed in this book will easily finish in less than 20 weeks in a 4-inch (10 cm) pot, but *Caltha* grows very slowly at first.

We've often transplanted the seedlings to small cell packs to allow for easier rooting. Seedlings will not fill out a 32-cell pack for 13 to 15 weeks after sowing. They are often small and can be rather weak. Instead, try to gather seed from local sources to verify a fresh crop and sow immediately. Transplant as necessary and overwinter for quart sales the following spring. Be sure to keep the plants moist and shaded during the hottest part of summer to allow for as much vegetative growth as possible. Plants will not flower the same season from seed.

VARIETIES

Caltha palustris is more common in Europe than it is here; few companies carry the seed. It's easier to find started plants, and companies specializing in aquatic plants will often carry several different selections.

Alba is a white-flowering form with yellow stamens. It flowers about as profusely as the species. Plants grow to 10 inches (25 cm) tall and are vegetatively propagated.

Flore Pleno (Multiplex) is an excellent, free-flowering selection that's more common than the species. Flowers are fully double to 1½ inches (3 cm) across on plants to 10 inches (25 cm) tall. Flowers April and May. Propagate vegetatively only.

Monstrosa is sometimes confused with Flore Pleno. However, while Monstrosa also has fully double flowers on plants about the same height, the foliage is darker in color. Propagate vegetatively only.

USES

Caltha can be planted in shallow water, small pools, and ponds. It also works well in poorly drained locations.

IN THE HOME GARDEN

Caltha works best when exposed to morning sun, but it needs to be protected by afternoon shade. Read **Uses** in regard to site location. Remember that while some references state that the plants can take drier locations, they're often short lived, especially when grown in warmer, full-sun locations.

Plant in clumps around stream beds and in shallow water; protect initially if the stream can swell during a rainstorm and potentially tear the plant out of its site. Once well rooted, plants will take care of themselves and often don't require any additional handling or care. The single forms will reseed.

▬ CAMPANULA CARPATICA

FAMILY: Campanulaceae

COMMON NAME(S): Carpathian Harebell

DESCRIPTION

Campanula carpatica is a popular perennial noted for its blue or white, bell-shaped flowers. Growing up to 2 inches (5 cm) across, the scentless blooms are often held singly at the plant's crown. With light to medium green foliage, the plants are rounded or ball shaped in appearance and reach 8 to 15 inches (20 to 38 cm) in flower. *C. carpatica* maintains a relatively tight habit, measuring 8 to 10 inches (20 to 25 cm) across for the dwarf varieties and up to 15 inches (38 cm) for the standard selections.

HARDINESS: Zones 3 to 8.

SEASON OF BLOOM: June to August.

The most profuse color appears in June, but even without trimming *C. carpatica* will be dotted with some color across the crown intermittently throughout the summer. In our gardens in West Chicago, we've seen several blooms on the plants all summer long.

PROPAGATION

C. carpatica can be easily propagated by seed, division, and cuttings. You can sow seed anytime of the year. Divisions can be done early in the year once the ground is workable, but while the plants are still dormant, then again in late summer (August). Take basal cuttings early in the spring before bud set or flowering.

GERMINATION OVERVIEW: 200,000 seeds per ounce/7,000 per gram.

Provide germination temperatures of 70F (21C), and cover the seed lightly upon sowing. Germination occurs in 14 to 21 days, and transplanting can be begin 20 to 30 days after sowing.

No special pretreatments are necessary to get good germination percentages. Even seed held over from the previous year will often yield a 70%-plus germination rate.

GROWING ON

From seed: *Campanula carpatica* will fit into a bedding plant schedule for growers who want to produce large cell packs for spring sales. January or February sowings finished in 32-cell packs will be ready for May sales when grown on at 50F to 55F (10C to 13C) nights. In general, allow 11 to 12 weeks to sell green transplants, adding an additional week to 10 days if using jumbo type packs with deeper root cells but still at 36 cells per flat.

For quart sales in the spring, sowings can be made during the previous summer up until October. After transplanting, grow on at 45F to 50F (7C to 10C) nights. Our October sowings start to flower in late April in quart containers. By raising night temperatures earlier, you can force the plants into full color by midmonth (April). This is an excellent plant for a late Easter or Mother's Day crop.

Sowings made anytime before March will produce plants large enough to flower during the summer. The only exception are the dwarf selections, which will not bloom as profusely as the standard varieties during the first summer. This is especially true if sowings are made in late winter (March) and later.

Basal or stem cuttings taken from developing clumps in the spring from either field or off-stock plants from a cold frame or greenhouse will root within two to three weeks and can be potted up accordingly. Grow these plants on during the summer for late summer sales, or overwinter them for sales the following spring. Consider taking cuttings in late summer or autumn if you can take afford the time and space to size them up for spring sales.

Commercial propagators offer *Campanula carpatica* in various cell pack sizes, although 50 and 72 cells per flat are most common. These are available during winter and early spring for potting up into 4-inch or quart containers. They can also be potted up into gallon pots, but be sure to request your plants early enough to get the roots well established by April and May. In general, a 72-cell pack will finish off in a 4-inch (10 cm) pot in eight to 10 weeks when grown at 50F (10C) nights. This is based on using the dwarf Clips variety; the species will finish off faster.

One final note: In university and commercial grower tests, *C. carpatica* responds to Cycocel applications when used at label rates. Beware, however, of using it on the Clips varieties since the selection is already dwarf and may be retarded too much.

VARIETIES

Campanula carpatica is available in both blue and white flowering plants. It's hardier for us than the Clips series, especially if planted out away from a house foundation or other protective winter structure. Plants flower well the first season. Maximum plant height is 15 inches (38 cm) tall.

Blue Clips and White Clips are similar to the species although more dwarf in all respects. The Clips series has smaller leaves, flowers, and overall habit. When planting in the garden, space plants closer together to have them fill in. Plants grow 6 to 8 inches (15 to 20 cm) tall. Seed is available for both varieties and comes true with limited off-types. This variety is often vegetatively propagated as well.

Uniform Blue and Uniform White are intermediate cultivars between the previous two selections. They'll grow faster than the Clips series but not as tall or vigorously as the species. We flowered the Uniform series in May in a 4-inch (10 cm) pot. In general, allow 15 to 18 weeks for flowering at no less than 50F (10C) night temperatures. See Color Plate 22 for photo of *Campanula carpatica* Uniform series.

RELATED MATERIAL

Campanula glomerata Superba (clustered bellflower) is an erect growing plant from 15 to 36 inches (38 to 91 cm) tall, spreading 15 to 24 inches (38 to 60 cm) across. Its small, bell-shaped flowers are violet-blue in color and held in dense terminal clusters. The plants bloom in June and early July. Hardy from Zones 3 to 7, glomerata can be short-lived in rich and poorly drained soils. See Color Plate 24 for photo of *Campanula glomerata*.

Seed germinates as readily as *C. carpatica*, but it often grows more quickly, ready for transplanting as much as a week to 10 days earlier, depending on the season. *C. glomerata* often develops into salable transplants more quickly too and needs only 10 to 11 weeks to form rosetting plants to 1 inch tall in a 32-cell pack. These can be transplanted to gallons for sales in late summer or for the next spring. January-sown seed can be sold as cell-pack-grown transplants for April retail sales, but the plants won't flower profusely the first season from seed. For larger containers and plants that flower during the summer, sow the previous year for overwintering. *Campanula glomerata* is also available from commercial propagators in a variety of cell pack sizes. These are potted up into quart or gallon containers and will finish off in eight to 10 weeks at 50F to 55F (10C to 13C) nights; days should be 8 to 10 degrees warmer.

USES

Another backbone of the American perennial garden, *Campanula carpatica* can be used in small mass plantings of five to eight plants or as an edging or border. The more dwarf selections work well in rock gardens. Also, since the plants will often flower repeatedly during the summer, they can be interplanted with annuals in hanging baskets or other containers.

Campanula carpatica is also worth trying in the commercial landscape. I've seen the plants used on golf courses, in public parks, and in business plantings around existing shrubs to add highlights.

IN THE HOME GARDEN

Space plants 12 to 15 inches (30 to 38 cm) apart in full sun to partial shade in a well-drained location. Not overly drought-tolerant, *Campanula carpatica* prefers moisture during extended dry periods. The plants often flower out during the summer heat when night temperatures rise above 80F (26C). Once the nights cool, however, the blossoms tend to return. Plants don't require any staking and are dependably hardy, requiring no winter mulch.

▬ CAMPANULA MEDIUM (C. GRANDIFLORA)

FAMILY: Campanulaceae

COMMON NAME(S): Canterbury Bells, Cup and Saucer

DESCRIPTION

Campanula medium is a biennial reaching 3 feet (90 cm) tall in full bloom, though usually no more than 2 feet (60 cm) for us here in Chicago. The plants rosette the first season from seed, and the flowering stems emerge after a cold period (winter). The flowers are scentless, single or semidouble, bell or cup shaped, to 2 inches (5 cm) long. Both white and blue flowering plants are common: rose pink is also available. Since Canterbury Bells are biennial, they have to be planted each year to have blooming plants in the spring. See Color Plate 25 for photo of *Campanula medium*.

The foliage is evergreen but susceptible to crown rot during the winter here in our Chicago location.

HARDINESS: Zones 2 to 8.

Though hardy to Zone 2, this crop is a marginal performer in our Chicago area gardens. As winter ends, alternating cold/warm temperatures plus excessive moisture around the foliage often lead to crown rot. Instead, these plants excel in coastal climates such as California, Washington, and Oregon.

SEASON OF BLOOM: June.

PROPAGATION

Seed is the most common.

GERMINATION OVERVIEW: 79,000 seeds per ounce/2,765 per gram.

Provide germination temperatures of 70F (21C), and cover the seed lightly when sowing. Germination occurs in 14 to 21 days, and transplanting can be begin 20 to 30 days after sowing.

GROWING ON

From seed: Mid to late winter sowings will only rosette during the summer, not flower. For best performance, sow the seed during spring or early summer for late summer sales in 4-inch (10 cm) or quart containers. These plants should be planted to the garden, mulched, and overwintered for flowering the next spring.

C

C. medium can also be overwintered in the cold frame for quart or gallon sales the following spring. Since Canterbury Bells are biennial, however, many growers avoid this method because consumers expect the plants to continue to grow and develop during the summer after they flower. Using this method, it would be better to sell *C. medium* as short-lived plants.

For green pack sales in a 32-tray, allow 13 to 15 weeks at 55F (13C) nights.

VARIETIES

C. medium is readily available in the United States, sold by color and not by named varieties. There has been some recent European breeding work to produce a dwarf pot-plant variety. At the time of this writing, it has had limited impact on the U.S. market.

C. medium var. *calycanthema* differs from the above by having an additional calyx at the base of the flower that gives this variety its common name of Cup and Saucer. This variety is often sold as a pink, blue, and white mixture. There are also separate colors available. Seed is the primary method of propagation for Calycanthema and is available but not as common as the standard *C. medium*.

USES

When flowering, plants are erect, standing like soldiers at attention. Use them in small plantings since they will die out once flowering is over.

C. medium makes a good cut flower. The flowers, especially the pink, are unusual and have no counterpart for color and form.

IN THE HOME GARDEN

Campanula medium performs best where temperatures are cool and the humidity low. They do not appreciate the drastic temperature swings that our Chicago latitude is known for. Our hot, sometimes sweltering late July and August weather, combined with high humidity, weakens the plants as they go into the cool days of the fall. In spring the reverse is usually the death of plants as dormancy ends, and rain is followed by warm days and cool/cold nights.

The best performance is from plants started late in the spring or early summer, protected from direct sun during the hottest weather, and overwintered in a protected spot in the garden. Since the foliage is evergreen, beware of heavy or thick mulches. These tend to keep the water around the crown, encouraging rot. Choose pine or other evergreen boughs instead to keep the crown aerated as well as protected during the winter.

Space plants 12 to 15 inches (30 to 38 cm) apart in partial shade in a well-drained location. Not overly drought tolerant, plants perform marginally when the night temperatures get above 80F (26C). Plants don't require staking.

▬ CAMPANULA PERSICIFOLIA

FAMILY: Campanulaceae

COMMON NAME(S): Peachleaf Bellflower

DESCRIPTION

Campanula persicifolia is an erect plant from 2 to 3 feet (60 to 90 cm) tall with a spread of 12 to 18 inches (30 to 46 cm). The evergreen plants have a mounded appearance when not in flower, with either midblue or white, bell-shaped flowers from 1 to 1½ inches (2.5 to 3 cm) long. While most available varieties are single-flowered, there are some double-flowered selections. See Color Plate 26 for photo of *Campanula persicifolia*.

HARDINESS: Zones 4 to 7.

SEASON OF BLOOM: June and July.

PROPAGATION

Seed and division are the two most common ways to propagate this crop. Sow seed in midwinter for same season sales or during the summer for overwintering in quarts or gallons for sales the following year. Spring is a good time to take divisions. An alternative method is to take cuttings of the basal shoots that develop around the outer part of the crown in early spring. Once rooted, these can be potted up and grown on during the summer for late summer sales or overwintered for sales the next spring.

GERMINATION OVERVIEW: 340,000 seeds per ounce/11,900 per gram.
Pretreatments: If storing seed from year to year, keep seed in an air-tight container at 32F (0C) to preserve this crop's germination performance.

 C. persicifolia will germinate in eight to 13 days at 72F (22C), and the seed does not need to be covered during germination. Seedlings can be transplanted four to five weeks after sowing.

GROWING ON

Crop time: Green, rosetting plants in a 32-cell pack are salable in 10 to 12 weeks when grown on at 50F to 55F (10C to 13C) nights. They will not flower the same season from seed. If they do, it's usually stress induced and the flowers can be removed to allow the roots to firmly establish themselves in the soil first.

 For quart or gallon sales in April and May, seed should be sown the previous year with transplanting by December or January. Seed can be sown during spring or summer for transplanting to the final container by August or September. These plants can be overwintered dormant for sales the next spring. Alternatively, commercial propa-

C

gators offer this crop in cell packs, mainly 52 and 72 plants per flat. If you want finished pots ready by May 15, allow seven to nine weeks in a quart container to finish unless otherwise instructed by the propagator. This is based on using 50F to 55F (10C to 13C) nights.

As they grow, the white flowering plants will have lighter green foliage on slower growing plants than those with blue flowers. Blue flowering plants can be ready for transplanting or green pack sales as much as seven days earlier.

VARIETIES

Campanula persicifolia is available in both white and blue flowering selections here in the United States. The species can be obtained from both seed companies and propagators specializing in started plants.

Telham Beauty is available in vegetative starts as well as seed. This variety is more uniform, with a richer, clearer blue color than the species from seed. The flowers measure up to 2 inches (5 cm) across on plants to 3 feet (90 cm) tall.

USES

This crop is best in groups positioned throughout a perennial garden, as opposed to a mass planting. The blue form is especially attractive when its height and color are contrasted with complementary crops like Zagreb coreopsis and ornamental grasses like *Phalaris*.

Campanula persicifolia is also the best campanula cut flower since it offers upright spikes earlier to flower than other erect flowering species in the genera. Flowers last longer than other members of the genera.

As a landscape plant, *C. persicifolia* has limited uses in commercial plantings due to its short flowering time and need for staking. While not requiring much special treatment, it is a higher maintenance plant than most commercial accounts are willing to invest in.

IN THE HOME GARDEN

C. persicifolia is an excellent plant for the center of the perennial garden where its long spikes of color can be enjoyed in June. Plant it in front of Summer Sun heliopsis where it will flower before the heliopsis comes into color. Keep in mind that even though the plant will flower at 3 feet (90 cm), it will be only 10 to 13 inches (25 to 33 cm) tall once the spent flowers are cut back.

Plant in any full-sun, well-drained garden location. The plants are dependably hardy even in rich soils as long as excess water moves away from its roots. Stake the spikes as they develop—this may be more challenging than you prefer. Staking the spikes, however, will help to keep the stalks more upright and visually more enjoyable.

■■■ CAMPANULA PYRAMIDALIS

FAMILY: Campanulaceae

COMMON NAME(S): Chimney Bellflower
The common name derives from vases of this bellflower in chimney landings during the summer in England.

DESCRIPTION
Campanula pyramidalis has one to three, 3-foot (90 cm) spikes with 1-inch (2.5 cm), midblue to white, star-shaped flowers. The blooms are arranged pyramid fashion, hence the species name. The foliage color is deep green in color with rounded, 2- to 4-inch (5 to 10 cm) leaves in rosettelike clumps. When not in flower, the plants are 10 to 14 inches (25 to 35 cm) tall with a spread of 2 to 3 feet (60 to 90 cm).

In climates like England, the plants can become large, almost monstrous. Spikes to 5 feet (1.5 m) tall and plant spreads of 3 feet (90 cm) or more have been recorded. In Chicago gardens, however, the clay loam soils help to keep the plant under control and also more short lived.

HARDINESS: Zones 3 to 7.
Treat *C. pyramidalis* as a short-lived perennial because of its intolerance to high heat, humidity, and severe winters. In our West Chicago gardens, only 20% of the plants we originally planted in 1991 are still alive in 1994. Many references suggest sowing every two years and treating the plants as biennials.

SEASON OF BLOOM: June and July.

PROPAGATION
C. pyramidalis is usually propagated by seed, and it can be sown anytime during the year.

GERMINATION OVERVIEW: 250,000 seeds per ounce/8,750 per gram.
The seeds germinate in eight to 12 days at 72F (22C) and don't need to be covered during germination, although they can be covered lightly to maintain uniform moisture. Seedlings will be transplantable 30 to 38 days after sowing.

No special pretreatments are necessary to get 70% and better germination rates.

GROWING ON
Crop time: From seed sown in February, green transplants will be salable in a 32-cell pack in nine to 11 weeks when grown on at 50F to 55F (10C to 13C). For larger container sales, sow the seed the previous year up until late summer for transplanting to gallon pots. If overwintered dormant, the plants will flower the following summer. Seed sown during winter and spring will produce garden-sized plants, but these sel-

dom flower profusely until vernalized (given a cold treatment to achieve bud set and flowering).

VARIETIES

Campanula pyramidalis is available from a limited number of U.S. seed firms. It's not as common as other selections noted in this text due to its unreliability in returning year after year.

C. pyramidalis var. *alba* is a white flowering counterpart to the variety above and grows and develops in a similar fashion. Treat it the same way as you would the blue flowering selection.

RELATED MATERIAL

Campanula cochleariifolia (*C. pusilla*) is a low growing perennial between 5 and 8 inches (13 and 20 cm) tall in full bloom, with small, three-quarter-inch, bell-shaped flowers in blue (var. *alba* has white flowers). Flowers are unscented. See Color Plate 23 for photo of *Campanula cochleariifolia*.

This variety makes a nice 4-inch (10 cm) pot item. A sowing in mid-January will yield flowering 4-inch (10 cm) pots in late April when grown at 50F to 55F (10C to 13C) nights in a cold frame. Plants will stay in sporadic flower for some time. In our trials, the plants came into flower during May and stayed in bloom, even after planting into the garden, until late July.

USES

C. pyramidalis can be used reliably in the home perennial garden, although it is shunned by commercial landscapers for its limited colors and lack of hardiness. In the home garden, however, its performance is more appreciated for its glossier, more rounded leaves compared to other campanula species. The plants bloom later than the equally tall flowering *C. persicifolia*, so the two can be grown together in a garden to increase the flower display's longevity.

Campanula pyramidalis can be cut and displayed in a vase, but the stalks should be cut as the blooms start to open. Once pollinated, a flower will fade and drop within three days.

IN THE HOME GARDEN

Plants are often called short lived, but if planted into a well-drained location with morning or late afternoon sun, plants have persisted for three to four years for us. In some cases, the plants will not die but will look ratty and unkept after three years of growth in our Chicago gardens.

When grown in open locations, *C. pyramidalis* should be staked for best performance. After a light shower, a heavily budded stalk will easily bend, spoiling the overall appearance.

■ CARLINA ACAULIS SIMPLEX
(formerly *C. acaulis caulescens*, *Cirsium acaule*)

FAMILY: Asteraceae

COMMON NAME(S): Carlina, Silver Thistle

DESCRIPTION

Carlina acaulis simplex is a thistlelike plant with small rosettes that may grow no more than 2 to 4 inches (5 to 10 cm) tall, though it often reaches 6 to 8 inches (15 to 20 cm) when grown in climates similar to its native Europe. Flowers are single to semi-double, measuring up to 4 inches (10 cm) across. Flower colors are most often silvery white with a red or pink tint or shading. The foliage is up to 6 inches (15 cm) long and extremely spiny—it will cause injury if improperly handled. Read the additional information under **In the home garden**.

HARDINESS: Zones 5 to 8.

While carlina is hardy in cold winter climates, rich soils and severe summers limit the long-term adaptability of this crop to U.S. soils. In our West Chicago gardens, however, the plants will live for three to four years but seldom flower. In our location, we are probably at the upper end of its hardiness adaptability.

SEASON OF BLOOM: July and August.

PROPAGATION

Carlina is easily propagated by seed and root cuttings. Plants come reliably true from seed, and the seed doesn't require any special treatments to germinate.

GERMINATION OVERVIEW: 7,000 seeds per ounce/245 per gram.

Carlina germinates in four to eight days at 72F (22C) and can be lightly covered. Transplant seedlings 16 to 24 days after sowing.

GROWING ON

Crop time: From seed, green transplants will be ready for sales in 12 to 14 weeks, grown at 50F to 55F (10C to 13C) nights. Sow the seed to a plug tray, or space seedlings liberally in an open flat. Carlina isn't fond of transplanting and often dies if frequently handled. Therefore, transplant from the plug tray or open flat directly to a 2-inch-square (5 cm square) pot or comparable cell pack. Plants sold green will be about 1 to 1½ inches (2.5 to 3 cm) tall at best and won't flower the same year as sown. Carlina can be grown in the same manner as *Echinops ritro*.

For growing on from root cuttings, see the **Propagation Techniques** chapter in front section of this book for additional information.

VARIETIES

Carlina acaulis simplex is a European seed-propagated variety seldom seen in the U.S. trade due to its short life in our climate. Plants often flower in July and August in the United States but from August to September in Europe. It grows from 2 to 4 inches (5 to 10 cm) tall with red-highlighted white blossoms. Few American seed firms carry this crop due to its raggedy appearance in our severe summer climates plus its spiny leaves.

USES

Spiny plants are a novelty in the garden; they are a unique addition especially when viewed from a distance. Carlina is best used as a limited group or specimen planting out of arm's reach at the front of the perennial border.

IN THE HOME GARDEN

This is a plant that's definitely not recommended for a children's garden or where the plant would be mistakenly touched. These plants have spines similar to Canadian thistle or *Acanthus mollis* var. *spinossimus* and are painful to the touch.

The best place in the United States to grow carlina is probably in Mediterranean-like regions such as California. Here in Chicago, if plants make it through the first season, they usually return for several years but seldom flower profusely, if at all.

For best performance and growth, place plants where they get morning and late afternoon shade, although they tolerate full sun with limited problems. I suggest placing them near a building or other structure where they receive both winter and summer protection. Also continuously high temperatures and humidity will often weaken the plant so that a severe winter will finish the job and kill the plant off. Plant into a well-drained soil; soils with a pH of 6 are preferable to those that are more acid.

One comment: It's my personal opinion that these plants are mainly a novelty for the U.S. perennial garden. Their culture is more time consuming than it's worth outside the West Coast and similar locales.

■ CATANACHE CAERULEA

FAMILY: Asteraceae

COMMON NAME(S): Cupid's Dart

Catanache was an ingredient in ancient Greek love potions.

DESCRIPTION

Catanache caerulea has a rosetting form and grows to about 3 inches (7 cm) high without flowers. Its elongated, notched leaves develop to between 8 and 10 inches (20 and 25 cm) long once established. The single, scentless, cornflower-blue blossoms, about 1½ inches (3 cm) across, are clustered in a papery calyx used in dried flower arrangements. Flowers open atop 15- to 24-inch (38 to 61 cm) tall, leafless stems. Plants spread from 8 to 12 inches (20 to 30 cm) across. See Color Plate 27 for photo of *Catanache caerulea*.

HARDINESS: Zones 4 to 8.

Perennial plant experts differ on this crop's hardiness—but we seldom have trouble with it here in Zone 5 near Chicago. Review **In the home garden** for additional information.

SEASON OF BLOOM: July and August.

PROPAGATION

Catanache caerulea is easily propagated by seed, but root cuttings taken in early winter will also work. Some experts suggest that divisions work best when taken in autumn, but these can be tedious to obtain and results are not as successful as yields from seed sowing. Additional information is provided on root cuttings in the front of this book. See the **Propagation Techniques** chapter.

GERMINATION OVERVIEW: 12,000 seeds per ounce/420 per gram.

Seed germinates in four to 10 days at 70F to 72F (21C to 22C) and doesn't need to be covered during germination. Plants can be transplanted 15 to 25 days after sowing.

GROWING ON

Crop time: From seed, green rosettes are salable in 32-cell packs 11 to 13 weeks from sowing when grown at 50F to 55F (10C to 13C) nights. For 4-inch (10 cm) pot sales, allow 13 to 15 weeks for fully rooted plants; one to two weeks more for quarts. Regardless, this plant flowers reliably during summer from a winter sowing.

Commercial propagators offer *Catanache caerulea* as plugs, liners, and/or small pots. Any of these can be potted up (the small pots can be left as is or transplanted to larger containers) and sold in the spring.

VARIETIES

Catanache caerulea is available from many U.S. seed companies. It has all the merits noted under **Description**.

C. caerulea var. *alba* is the white flowering version, but it isn't as showy. This variety isn't commonly found in the U.S. trade and is often vegetatively propagated, since seed is seldom available.

USES

The elongated stems and small flowers of *C. caerulea* are best used in mass plantings as opposed to single plants in the garden or perennial border.

Like its cornflower relative, *C. caerulea* makes a good fresh cutflower or it also can be dried.

IN THE HOME GARDEN

C. caerulea is sometimes described as only marginally hardy here in the Chicago area, but our plants have sometimes lived over seven years in the same location without division. It has been known to return year after year with only limited problems.

Plant *C. caerulea* where it will get full sun or only morning/late afternoon sun in a well-drained soil. The plants will provide you with color year after year. Heavy clay loams will hold too much water, rotting the plants, so be wary of using plants in such a site. *Catanache caerulea* doesn't require staking, frequent waterings, or special techniques—it's an easy crop to grow and maintain in the home garden.

■■ CENTAUREA MONTANA

FAMILY: Asteraceae

COMMON NAME(S): Mountain Bluet, Perennial Bachelor's Buttons

DESCRIPTION
Centaurea montana is a well-known and easily grown perennial with open, rather flamboyant blooms. The scentless, 2½-inch (5 cm) flowers are purplish blue with a reddish highlight in the center. The plants grow 15 to 24 inches (38 to 61 cm) tall and will spread 12 to 15 inches (30 to 38 cm) across. Plants spread by stolons and also easily reseed. For us, however, they haven't been difficult to maintain and control, but this isn't the case where the plants are in a more fertile soil. Mountain bluets are long blooming but not overly free flowering in performance. The unique flower form makes this plant well worth considering, however.

HARDINESS: Zones 3 to 8.

SEASON OF BLOOM: June and July.
Plants are not profuse bloomers. They will flower in June and then sporadically the remainder of summer.

PROPAGATION
Seed and division are two ways to propagate this crop; *Centaurea montana* can also be reproduced with root cuttings. Sow seed anytime of the year, but divisions are best either in the spring or fall. For additional information on root cuttings, see the **Propagation** chapter.

GERMINATION OVERVIEW: 2,200 seeds per ounce/77 per gram.
Seed germinates in seven to 14 days at 72F (22C); seed can be lightly covered during germination or left exposed. Seedlings will be ready for transplanting 14 to 21 days after sowing.

GROWING ON
Crop time: From seed, green cell packs (32 cells per flat) are ready in 10 to 12 weeks after sowing. February sowings will be salable in late April or May and can be sold in the cell packs for midsummer flowering. They can also be moved up into quarts or gallons for midsummer sales.

For quart or gallon pots, sow seed during spring or summer for transplanting to the final pot by August. These plants can be overwintered dormant and sold the following spring. One- and 2-quart containers can be sold in the spring from fall-sown seed as well. For fully rooted plants in a 1-quart container, allow 15 to 18 weeks when growing at no less than 50F (10C) nights. The day temperatures should be at least 10 to 15 degrees higher. In our trials, seed sown in October or November, transplanted to 1- or 2-quart containers and overwintered in a 50F (10C) night cold frame, were both salable and flowering by early May. These plants were never free flowering but once planted in the garden would stay in bloom for a period of several weeks to two months, depending on the weather.

Centaurea plants can easily be divided and transplanted to quart or gallon containers, depending on the size of the individual sections removed. Potted up, the plants will root quickly and fill in a 1- to 2-quart container in four to six weeks at 55F (13C) nights.

VARIETIES

Centaurea montana seed can be easily obtained from a number of U.S. seed firms. Plants come reliably true from seed without any special techniques for germination or growing on. They're an easy perennial to sow, grow, and use.

RELATED MATERIAL

Centaurea macrocephala is an easily grown perennial, between 3 and 4 feet (90 to 120 cm) tall in our gardens, but it is often wild in appearance. An unusual plant, it has golden yellow flowers formed from numerous filamentous petals protruding from papery brown bracts at the flower base. The blooms measure 3 inches across in full bloom, sometimes larger. Plants flower in June and July.

The plants germinate in four to eight days at 72F (22C). Seedlings can be transplanted in 15 to 22 days after sowing and grown on at 60F (16C) until established in the final pack or pot. Then harden plants off by growing at 50F (10C) nights for the remainder of the growing period. The leaves are strap-shaped on rosetting plants that will be between 2 and 4 inches (5 to 10 cm) tall 11 to 13 weeks after sowing. Since these leaves can become quite imposing, grow *C. macrocephala* only as a 4-inch (10 cm) or quart-grown plant for best performance. If sown in early February, transplanted late in the month, and sold green in pots 15 to 16 weeks after sowing, plants will be 3 to 5 inches (7 to 13 cm) tall in the garden but with a 1½- to 2-foot (45 to 60 cm) spread by late June. Plants will not flower the same season from seed, since they require a cold period before they will bloom.

Though hardy from Zones 3 to 8, *C. macrocephala* will weaken or die out by its fourth or fifth season here in our West Chicago clay soil.

USES

Consider grouping plants in small clumps in a home perennial garden; they may not be free flowering enough to warrant use in commercial landscapes. The beauty of these plants should be enjoyed up close, not from a distance.

The plants can be used for fresh cut flowers, although *C. macrocephala* will be a better choice since it has longer stems and a bolder flower color. It will stay in flower a shorter period of time, however.

IN THE HOME GARDEN

Plant *Centaurea montana* where it will get full sun and good drainage. Plants are long-lived and seldom have problems in the home landscape. When grown in shaded areas, the plants will be slightly shorter but, more importantly, have even fewer flowers than noted. So be sure to plant these where they get as much sun as possible.

Plants are weak-stemmed and will fall open readily during the summer. They don't require staking in the garden, however, unless they've been grown on the fertile side. While they can be staked, space should be provided to accommodate the plant's floppy habit. When the plant falls open, it exposes the crown to the sun. Within a short period of time, a multitude of vegetative shoots will develop to fill in the open spot. Snip off any spent flower blooms so that new flower buds may develop and open. If the seed pods are allowed to develop and scatter, the plants will reseed themselves in favorable conditions. In our heavy soils and severe winters, the plants are well controlled, although *C. montana* has been aggressive in some locations.

If planted into an open area without winter protection, the plants will survive if mulched with a 2-inch (5 cm) layer of leaves. Be sure to remove the mulch in late winter before the new shoots start to grow.

■■ CENTRANTHUS RUBER

(occasionally listed as *Kentranthus ruber* or *Valeriana coccinea*)

FAMILY: Valerianaceae

COMMON NAME(S): Red Valerian, Jupiter's Beard

DESCRIPTION

Centranthus ruber is a fast growing perennial with blue or gray-green glossy leaves. The pastel, rose-pink flowers measure one-eighth inch (3 cm) across or less. The four-petaled blooms develop in clusters that measure up to 2 inches (5 cm) across. Although I haven't noticed a fragrance, some growers and gardeners comment that the blooms do have a scent. *Centranthus ruber* grows 2½ to 3 feet (75 to 90 cm) tall in flower and 18 to 24 inches (46 to 61 cm) across. Plants have become naturalized in warmer climates, especially southern California hillsides.

HARDINESS: Zones 5 to 8.

C. ruber is not a long-lived plant in our Chicago area gardens. We've found that the plants live for three to four seasons at best in our clay loam soils.

SEASON OF BLOOM: June to frost.

C. ruber flowers best from June to July with occasional reblooming until frost. In cooler climates, especially where maritime weather prevails, the plants will flower more profusely through the summer.

PROPAGATION

Seed and stem cuttings are the most popular forms of propagating this crop, but some experts suggest divisions also work well. Sow seed anytime during winter until April, and plants will flower the same season as sown. Obviously, the more profusely blooming plants result from earlier sowings, but color can still be expected from later (March or April) crops. Plant them into the garden as early as possible.

Basal cuttings of the newly developing shoots in the spring offer the best opportunity to propagate vegetatively. We take these in the spring as the crowns are developing but before the plants have budded up for flowering.

GERMINATION OVERVIEW: 70,000 seeds per ounce/2,450 per gram.

Pretreatments: None are needed as *C. ruber* germinates readily from seed.

Germination temperatures of 65F to 70F (18C to 21C) are best, and the seed doesn't need to be covered to germinate. Seedlings emerge in five to eight days and are transplantable 15 to 25 days after sowing.

GROWING ON

Crop time: Seed will produce green packs in a 32-cell flat nine to 10 weeks after sowing. The plants will mostly grow upright, with limited basal branching, and can be as tall as 10 inches (25 cm) if not kept in check. Therefore, transplant to a 4-inch (10 cm) or quart container and let the roots establish for several days to a week; then grow on at 50F to 55F (10C to 13C) nights. Lower temperatures can be applied as well, but be sure the plants are well-established before you turn the thermostat much below 48F (9C).

For larger containers, such as 4-inch (10 cm) or quart containers, sow seed to open flats or plug trays in November or December. The seedlings can be transplanted to the larger containers when ready, and grown on during the winter and early spring in a cool greenhouse or cold frame at no higher than 55F (13C) nights. *Centranthus ruber* grows quickly and can become too large in a cell pack or pot if not properly grown. Avoid high temperatures, overfertilizing, and overwatering.

Commercial propagators offer *C. ruber* in many forms. If you want to grow plants only in the winter or spring, liners of 70 to 125 cells per flat are often available. Pot them up, using one plant per 4-inch (10 cm) or quart container and allow six to eight weeks at 52F to 55F (11C to 13C) nights. For quarts only, allow an extra two weeks for a well-rooted plant.

VARIETIES

Centranthus ruber is the standard seed selection sold in the United States, and it's easily available from numerous sources. The most popular variety, it outsells and outperforms any other available selection.

C. ruber var. *albus* is the white flowering version of the above. The plants grow and develop the same as *C. ruber* and can be found from a number of seed sources around the United States.

USES

Centranthus ruber likes a moist but well-drained soil and does best when planted in full sun. Plants will establish themselves in gardens and can reseed in warmer winter climates like California, but this is not often a problem in zones farther north. Staking is usually not required, but the plants can reach 3 feet (90 cm) tall in the garden or landscape, making *C. ruber* a prime candidate for a home or local commercial cut flower crop.

▬ CEPHALARIA GIGANTEA (SYN. C. TATARICA)

FAMILY: Dipsacaceae

COMMON NAME(S): Tatarian Cephalaria

DESCRIPTION

As the species name "gigantea" suggests, this is a large, robust plant growing 5 to 6 feet (1.5 to 1.8 m) tall in flower and spreading to 3 feet (90 cm) wide. The first year after sowing, the plants develop vigorous, dark green foliage but only grow to 2 feet (60 cm) or so. The following year they will flower and attain their mature height. The 2-inch (5 cm), scentless, soft yellow flowers resemble the perennial scabiosa in their form. To me, the flowers are more uniform and neater than scabiosa blooms.

HARDINESS: Zones 3 to 7.

SEASON OF BLOOM: July and August.

PROPAGATION

Seed, divisions, and root cuttings are three ways to propagate this class. Seeds need to be sown fresh after ripening, while divisions can be taken in the spring. Take root cuttings in late fall.

GERMINATION OVERVIEW

Seeds germinate in seven to 12 days at 70F to 72F (21C to 22C) and don't need to be covered for germination, although we cover lightly to maintain uniform emergence. Seedlings are transplantable 25 to 30 days after sowing.

No additional pretreatments are usually needed.

GROWING ON

Crop time: From seed, allow 10 to 11 weeks for green rosettes salable in a 32-cell pack. These cell packs can be potted up into 4-inch (10 cm), quart, or gallon pots if preferred. In general, we allow 12 to 14 weeks at 50F to 55F (10C to 13C) nights for 4-inch pot sales in the spring from a midwinter sowing.

You can also sow seed the previous year for potting up into gallons for overwintering. These plants can then be sold the following spring. Sow seed no later than June for established gallons by fall.

Plants don't flower the first season from seed.

VARIETIES

Cephalaria gigantea isn't readily found as seed or transplants in the United States, although it can be located—check with those seed companies specializing in wildflower seed.

USES

Cephalaria gigantea works best in gardens where its large habit can be appreciated. Cephalaria plants are wild in appearance but not invasive or obtrusive. They wouldn't fit a small or structured garden, but they excel in open or large perennial borders.

Blooms can be used as homegrown cut flowers, although they have little commercial importance in the flower market.

IN THE HOME GARDEN

For best growth, plant in full-sun locations in moist but well-drained soils. Plants don't usually need staking but may become weak and require it if grown on the lush and fertile side.

If you aren't familiar with this plant, be sure to read more about it first. It's our experience that this plant is more preferred by enthusiasts than the general public.

■■■ CERASTIUM TOMENTOSUM

FAMILY: Caryophyllaceae

COMMON NAME(S): Snow-In-Summer

DESCRIPTION

An easily grown and hardy perennial, *Cerastium tomentosum* displays leaves covered by a gray-white mass of hairs (tomentose). Plants are short and trailing, spreading as much as 3 feet (90 cm) across in our West Chicago gardens. The plants grow only 3 or 4 inches (7 to 10 cm) tall in bloom. The scentless, single white flowers measure up to 1 inch (2.5 cm) across. Plants are very free flowering.

HARDINESS: Zones 3 to 7.

SEASON OF BLOOM: May and June.

PROPAGATION

This crop is usually propagated by seed, although divisions and cuttings also work. Take divisions in either spring or fall and cuttings in early spring or summer after flowering.

GERMINATION OVERVIEW: 80,000 seeds per ounce/2,800 per gram.

Seed germinates in seven to 14 days at 65F to 68F (18C to 20C); leave it exposed to light during germination. Allow 15 to 23 days after sowing to transplant the seedlings.

GROWING ON

Crop time: When growing *C. tomentosum* from seed, consider sowing it directly to a plug tray using two to four seeds per cell, and then transplant the plugs to their final container. *C. tomentosum* grows quickly and can be salable without flowers in 12 weeks in a 32-cell pack or 15 weeks in a 4-inch (10 cm) pot. Grow on at 55F (13C) nights for rapid growth, 48F to 50F (9C to 10C) nights to slow growth but improve appearance.

Commercial propagators offer this variety in a range of cell pack sizes, although 50 and 72 are the most common. A 72-cell pack will produce salable, green, 4½-inch (11 cm) pots in six to eight weeks when grown on at 55F (13C) nights.

VARIETIES

Cerastium tomentosum is readily found in the United States under various names— Silver Carpet (Silberteppich) is one of the most common. The variety grows to no more than 8 inches tall in flower, 6 inches (15 cm) tall out of bloom. In some cases the variety is mistakenly called Silvery Summer, a name of no botanical standing. Seed of both varieties comes from the same bag.

Yo Yo is slightly smaller and tighter in habit than Silver Carpet. The variety tends to have more gray-green color than the previous selection. Maximum height is 4 to 6 inches (10 to 15 cm) tall.

Seed is available on all the varieties noted.

USES

This is a hardy perennial, long lived in the garden or landscape. It works well in the rock garden, in the perennial border, or nestled between garden stepping stones.

IN THE HOME GARDEN

Plant in any well-drained location in full sun or at least half-day sun. In such a location, the leaves will be more gray in color than in shaded areas. In fact, the plants are often short lived in shady areas, lasting only several seasons.

Plants don't require any special treatments for overwintering. If established in the garden or landscape prior to the onset of cold weather, the plants will overwinter without mulching. If a mulch is used, be sure it doesn't compact the plants. Beware of heavily mulching the plants for winter protection; if water stays close to the plant's crown for extended periods, the plant will soon rot and probably die.

After an initial spring fertilization, avoid repeating unless needed. Fertile locations cause accelerated growth and the plant's center may die out, leaving only the extended growth at the perimeter of the dead crown.

▄▄ CERATOSTIGMA PLUMBAGINOIDES (PLUMBAGO LARPENTIAE)

FAMILY: Plumbaginaceae

COMMON NAME(S): Leadwort, Plumbago

DESCRIPTION

Ceratostigma plumbaginoides is a low-growing plant with purple-highlighted foliage in the early spring (especially in unheated cold frames) that turns dark green as the temperatures increase. Leaves change color again in the fall to a bronze red as the temperatures drop. Plants grow from 8 to 12 inches (20 to 30 cm) tall and spread as wide as 15 inches (38 cm). The plants have spreading rhizomes directly below the soil surface, but they don't grow fast enough in our climate to become invasive. The single, unscented flowers are deep to violet-blue in color, measure up to one-half inch across, and are held terminally on the stems. See Color Plate 28 for photo of *Ceratostigma plumbaginoides*.

HARDINESS: Zones 6 to 9.

The plants are hardy in selected areas of Zone 5 if protected during winter around foundations or with mulch.

SEASON OF BLOOM: July and August.

PROPAGATION

Plants can be propagated by divisions or from cuttings taken in the spring. Either semiripe or softwood cuttings can be taken from first emergence in the spring throughout the summer. However, cuttings taken from nonflowering stems tend to root faster with less obstruction to good root formation. In the south, stock plants can be maintained in unheated cold frames during the winter. Farther north, you can let plants go dormant for a portion of the winter but allow for early growth during February that can be used for taking cuttings.

GROWING ON

Crop time: Both divisions and cuttings grow quickly and can be sold the same season they are propagated. However, the best plants are propagated in the spring, allowed to get a full summer of growth in a quart pot, and sold the following spring.

Commercial propagators sell *C. plumbaginoides* in small cell packs (usually 50 to 72 cells per flat). These are available during the fall and winter and occasionally in the spring. If purchased in the fall to midwinter, the liners can be potted to quart and gallon containers for spring sales. Liners received in March and April can be potted to 4-inch (10 cm) pots and also sold in spring.

One note of caution: Plants are available in the fall and winter. It may be tempting to pot a 50-plug or liner into the final container (quart or gallon) and grow on cool at 40F to 45F (4C to 7C) nights. In many cases, these plants would perform better if given heat during the coldest and darkest days of the winter. Otherwise only one or two active stems may develop instead of the plant becoming bushy and filling out the pot. In our greenhouses, we've potted up 72 liners into 4-inch (10 cm) pots in March and then moved to a cold frame with no less than 50F (10C) night temperatures. Plants were fully rooted in six to seven weeks. Visually, the plants were filled in, though if a full crown of foliage was needed, we added one to two weeks to the schedule.

VARIETIES

Ceratostigma plumbaginoides is readily available from a number of nurseries across the United States.

USES

Plants can be used as edgings, on embankments, and in mass in either the home garden or commercial landscape. Its dark blue flower color and semitrailing habit are attractive near the water's edge or tucked in between rocks. Plants are long flowering (but not really free flowering), and the blue flowers and deep green foliage provide color all season long. Plants can be used in raised beds, in concrete planters, and as a ground cover with equal success. Just a few plants in one bed may go unnoticed, so these plants are better used in mass plantings. Between their spreading stems, we plant tulips and other spring flower bulbs that can be cut back to the ground in June when *C. plumbaginoides* begins to warrant attention.

IN THE HOME GARDEN

Plants prefer full sun but will take some shade in the afternoon. Brighter locations encourage flowering and discourage a sprawling, open habit. If plants become woody at the base and don't die back in warm winter areas, trim the plants back in the spring to get more uniform growth during the summer.

In cold winter areas (Zone 5), a winter mulch is suggested for this perennial, especially when it is is planted away from foundations, overhangs, and other structures that offer wind protection. We mulch in the fall with leaves or, better yet, evergreen boughs. The boughs allow for aeration to keep our potentially wet autumns from rotting the plants' crowns.

■■ CHELONE LYONII

FAMILY: Scrophulariaceae

COMMON NAME(S): Turtlehead, Shellflower

DESCRIPTION

This native perennial grows from 1 to 2 feet (30 to 60 cm) tall and spreads 12 to 18 inches (30 to 46 cm) across. The plants are found in moist, woodland settings, as well as damp or marsh-filled areas of the southeastern United States. The unique blooms resemble the head of a tortoise: they measure up to 1 inch (2.5 cm) long and are rose-pink in color. The flowers are closely clustered at the top of the plant. The stiff, erect stems are often branchless and usually emerge singly instead of producing clumps.

HARDINESS: Zones 4 to 9.

SEASON OF BLOOM: August and September.

PROPAGATION

Spring divisions and soft tip cuttings are the easiest and most common ways of propagating *C. lyonii*, though seed propagation works, too. Take cuttings in June or anytime before bud set. Seed is not readily available, but firms specializing in seed of native plants may carry it or be able to recommend a source for this plant.

GERMINATION OVERVIEW

Pretreatments: My personal experiences with germinating this seed have been limited and mostly unsuccessful. Fresh seed that had been harvested within the past several months germinated better than seed that had been stored for longer than six months. The stored seed benefited from a moist chilling for five to six weeks prior to sowing. Read the information in the front of this book for additional details.

Our germination tests showed a 35 to 55% germination rate 21 to 28 days after sowing, though emergence was erratic. Germination continued over a period of several weeks, but we had to transplant every seven to 10 days since the plants were at various stages of development. Our sowings in the winter produced a salable crop 16 months later (in the spring of the *following* year).

GROWING ON

Crop time: Transplants can be taken in the spring by digging your own field-grown plants and potting them up into quart or gallon containers. Depending on the age

C

of the crown and the number of plantlets that you separate from the mother clump, the crop time can be as short as one to three weeks at 55F (13C) nights. However, single-stemmed transplants potted into gallon pots will seldom be rooted well in May from a March or April digging. In these cases, plants should be given one summer to get some growth under them prior to sales in the autumn or the following spring.

Bare-root transplants are also available early in the year, though they may be species other than *C. lyonii*. Regardless, the roots of these varieties can be potted to 3- or 4-quart containers, grown on at 50F to 55F (10C to 13C) nights, and usually sold in nine to 12 weeks depending on the visual impact of the plant you want. Longer crop times produce better rooted plants as well.

Cuttings taken in June will root quickly and can be transplanted three to four weeks later. Pot them up into quart or gallon containers and overwinter for sales the following spring.

RELATED MATERIAL

Chelone glabra (Turtlehead) is similar in many respects to *C. lyonii*, but it has white flowers and possesses different foliage. Plants are native to the eastern United States and can be found in wet areas like *C. lyonii*. The blooms appear in August, though they are often earlier to show than either of the other two species here. Plants grow to 3 feet (90 cm) tall with a 2-foot (60 cm) spread and can be propagated the same as *C. lyonii*.

Chelone obliqua has foliage similar to *C. glabra*, but the flower color is a rich rose purple, deeper in color than *C. lyonii*. Blooms appear in September, and plants grow from 2 to 3 feet (60 to 90 cm) tall with a 2-foot (60 cm) spread. Propagate the same way as *C. lyonii*.

USES

Chelones are used primarily in the home perennial garden but are not well known. Often long-lived, with few faults, these plants are somewhat underused in the American garden.

The flower spikes are cut for arrangements, since the blooms last from eight to 10 days once cut. The dried seed pods can be used for indoor arrangements as well, though some people complain that the seed coat causes irritation when handled.

IN THE HOME GARDEN

Plant where it gets full sun and a moist but well-drained location. Plants will tolerate shade, but if the soil is fertile and moist, they may get top heavy and fall over. In most situations, however, the plants require no staking to keep them upright.

C. lyonii hasn't required mulch during the winter here in our Chicago gardens. In fact, they often go overlooked until summer when they start to bud. It blooms during a period when most other perennials have already passed their peak.

■ CHRYSOGONUM VIRGINIANUM

FAMILY: Asteraceae

COMMON NAME(S): Green and Gold, Goldenstar

DESCRIPTION

Chrysogonum virginianum is a native, low-growing perennial from 8 to 15 inches (20 to 38 cm) tall with triangular to oval-shaped leaves. The plants spread by underground rhizomes but aren't invasive if kept in well-drained but moist locations. The 1-inch (2.5 cm) flowers are single, yellow in color, and daisylike. *C. virginianum* is semievergreen in the southern United States.

HARDINESS: Zones 5 to 9.

SEASON OF BLOOM: June to September.
Plants reach their flowering peak in June and bloom sporadically the rest of the summer. In the southern United States, plants flower primarily in March but often rebloom during the summer.

PROPAGATION

The easiest way to propagate this plant is to remove sections of the creeping rootstocks including a piece of the root. These pieces root quickly and can be potted up within several weeks.

Seed is often difficult to find, so check with companies that specialize in native blooming plants or perennial wildflower seed. *C. virginianum* can also be propagated by divisions taken in the spring or late winter. Southern growers can take divisions in the fall as well.

GERMINATION OVERVIEW

Seed is difficult to collect since the seed heads develop over a period of time due to the long-term flowering performance of the plants. If you have a nursery bed of this crop, collect seed heads in June or July after the main flush of flowering has passed. They'll turn brown as they ripen. Seedlings will emerge in flushes.

A simpler method is to allow the plants to self-seed, then transplant the seedlings into quart containers for growing on and selling the following year.

GROWING ON

Crop time: Cutting and removing a portion of the creeping rootstock and transplanting it to a propagation bed is relatively quick. Plants propagated in the spring may be sold the same season depending on the final size of the cutting removed, the final container size, and when you want to sell the plants. For the best looking and best rooted plant, propagate in the spring and sell from mid to late summer, or hold them over the winter for sales the following spring.

C

To make divisions, dig up the plants, reduce the top growth by half, divide, and repot immediately. Divisions wilt readily and need to be shaded and kept cool until new roots develop. Keep them protected for the first week or two to reduce water loss. Plants divided in the early spring (or fall in the South) perform the best, since the temperatures are cool and water loss is minimal.

Commercial propagators usually offer this perennial during the winter as a liner or plug, most often in 50- and 72-cell trays. Liners root quickly and can be sold in a 4-inch (10 cm) pot in six to eight weeks. For quart containers, allow eight to 10 weeks. In both cases the plants won't be fully rooted, but the soil ball will hold together. Keep temperatures above 50F (10C) at night and 5 to 15 degrees higher during the day.

USES

Since it's a native plant, consider using *C. virginianum* in wildflower plantings and in areas bordering woodlands that are mass-planted with chrysogonum as a ground cover. It also can be used in maintenance-free roadside plantings, but it needs to be established before performing well.

IN THE HOME GARDEN

These plants prefer a sunny location that's shaded during the hottest part of the day. With too much shade, the plants become more open and somewhat sprawling with less flower color. This perennial will tolerate soils low in organic material, but it isn't fond of heavy soils with poor drainage. Instead, plant in a porous, humus-rich soil for best results.

These plants don't need mulch in the winter, but a light mulching will accelerate spring growth, especially in snowless areas of the North.

CIMICIFUGA RACEMOSA

FAMILY: Ranunculaceae

COMMON NAME(S): Black Snakeroot, Cohosh

DESCRIPTION

Spirelike and impressive, *Cimicifuga racemosa* is a excellent plant to use in the summer garden. The erect, wiry, 2- to 3-foot (60 to 90 cm) spikes of cream-white, fragrant flowers are one of the attractive features of this crop. The spikes are often branched and bloom later than the majority of perennials, so they really stand out in the late summer garden. Native from the northeastern United States and Canada eastward to Wisconsin and then south, *C. racemosa* is a dramatic plant that's often underused in the North American garden. The plants grow to an overall height of between 4 and 8 feet (1.2 to 2.4 m) tall and spread from 2 to 3 feet (60 to 90 cm) across.

HARDINESS: Zones 4 to 8.

SEASON OF BLOOM: July and August.

PROPAGATION

Divisions are the easiest method of propagation and can be taken in the spring or fall. Seed can also be used but needs to be sown fresh; stored seed needs to be cold-treated for successful germination.

GERMINATION OVERVIEW

Pretreatments: If seed is harvested in the late summer, you'll need to consider the special treatments this crop requires for successful germination. If the seed is held in a packet and sown without any special pretreatments, germination rates of only 10% can be expected—if even that high.

Cimicifuga racemosa will germinate more readily after a cold-moist treatment. Seed germinates even better when given a warm conditioning first, followed by a cold treatment. Additional details are provided in the front of this book in the **Propagation Techniques** chapter.

GROWING ON

Crop time: From seed, winter sowings for seedling emergence during the spring won't produce salable plants the same season. Instead, pot up into 3- or 4-inch (7 to 10 cm) containers, then transplant to larger containers such as 2- or 4-quart pots to overwinter, and sell the following spring.

Take and pot up divisions in fall or spring. Plants divided and potted in the fall produce better looking and better rooted plants in our Chicago climate than those dug in the spring. Late snowfalls followed by spring rains often delay digging of this perennial until April or early May. Plants dug this late won't be big enough to sell until summer, probably beyond the time that customers are willing to purchase the plants.

Another way to use divisions is to purchase roots from commercial propagators (like Walters Gardens and DeVroomen) during the winter for potting up into 3- or 4-quart containers for spring sales. The plants develop quickly when grown warmer than 50F (10C) at night, and they'll be salable green in five to seven weeks.

Cimicifuga racemosa is available from a number of nurseries around the country, though it may be hard to find. Be prepared to try the germination techniques noted above for more reliable germination.

VARIETIES

C. racemosa var. *atropurpurea* is a purple-leaved plant that flowers from late August until October. It grows 5 to 6 feet (1.5 to 1.8 m) tall in flower and bears cream-white, spirelike wands of blooms. *Atropurpurea* is sometimes confused with Brunette. However, Brunette is darker in color, slower growing and less readily available.

RELATED MATERIAL

C. simplex grows to only 3 to 4 feet (90 to 120 cm) tall in flower. The blooms, which resemble those of *C. racemosa,* are cream white in color but shorter in length and held more closely to the crown of the foliage. This is a magnificent plant in the garden and certainly underused. As for propagation and production, bare-root divisions are available and the crop time will equal *C. racemosa.* It's our experience that roots planted in mid-March produce 18 to 24 inch (46 to 61 cm) tall plants in 4-quart containers in six to seven weeks when grown above 50F (10C) in a cold frame.

White Pearl (also called Armleuchter) is a white flowering selection of *C. simplex* known for its flower color and light green foliage. It grows to 3 or 4 feet (60 to 90 cm) tall in flower.

USES

C. racemosa is an outstanding plant for home gardens or commercial plantings due to its long-lasting performance. Established plantings can be left undisturbed for some time without fear that the plants will weaken or die out. Impact is greatest when this perennial is used as a specimen or small group planting instead of in mass. Dramatic and showy when viewed from a distance, the plants can also be used in a small backyard garden as a perimeter or background planting for summer color.

IN THE HOME GARDEN

Plant *C. racemosa* in shady locations where it's protected during the hottest part of the day. If you plant late in the spring from a gallon container, beware that plants won't do well initially if they're not protected from the sun. Once established, the plants do much better but still don't prefer a full-sun location in our locale. In fact, many cimcifugas we've planted in full sun with high heat and humidity have died.

These plants thrive in a well-drained but moist location. During the winter, they don't require any special care or mulching unless they've just been planted or divided. Staking is rarely necessary, either, since the stems are strong enough to support themselves and the flowers.

■ CLEMATIS SPP.

The many clematis hybrids and species on the market worldwide make it impossible to classify this group under one species. In the United States, Jackmanii is probably the most common, if not most well known, clematis variety available. Like most large-flowered hybrids on the market, it's the result of a possible cross between two species. Other clematis varieties are the result of many subsequent crosses. The large-flowered varieties derive primarily from crosses between one or more of the following four species: *C. patens, C. lanuginosa, C. viticella,* and

C. florida. It's quite probable that other species were involved in the crosses, but these four provide the bulk of the parent material. The following information is based on available selections of large-flowered—primarily hybrid—varieties, of which Jackmanii is a member.

FAMILY: Ranunculaceae

COMMON NAME(S): Clematis, Virgin's Bower

DESCRIPTION

Clematis is the leading perennial vine, having no rival for flower color, performance, and number of varieties available on the market. In the United States, the clematis is characterized by upright vining varieties like Jackmanii, which can stand alone in a yard or be mixed in with other plants. These large-flowered varieties are often grown up a trellis, arbor, lattice, or fence, although there are some varieties that will look their best when allowed to sprawl across the ground, over rocks or terraces. English gardeners have trained the plants onto the outer limbs of trees and over shrubs, a practice not common in the United States.

Plants climb by twisting their petioles (small stems between leaves and stems) around any stationary object the plants can hold onto. Unlike ivies—whose modified roots along the plant stems can affix to the sides of walls—clematis need poles, wire, or other structures for petioles to wrap around. Clematis are deciduous and, in our Chicago winters, die back to the ground. The stems are primarily, but not always, woody and possess large, single flowers from 4 to 6 inches (10 to 15 cm) across, although when grown under ideal conditions, there are some selections with flowers to 10 inches (25 cm) as well. The flowers are not a combination of petals and calyx as in the case of many other flowering plants, but instead are composed of sepals—since there is only one set of floral appendages instead of two. Flower colors include red, white, yellow, purple, blue, pink, and many bicolors. Plants can vine anywhere from 6 to 25 feet (1.8 to 7.5 m) long, depending on the variety.

There are a number of other hybrids and species that don't fit this description. Most commercially available or wild species will have a flower size of 3 inches (7 cm) or less and often a sweetly scented blossom. Some hybrids have a slight scent, but most lack it altogether. Double-flowering varieties are also available but are not as common as their single-flowering counterparts.

HARDINESS: Zones 3 to 8.

SEASON OF BLOOM: June and July.

PROPAGATION

These large-flowered hybrid varieties can only be produced by vegetative means—not by seed. Seed collected off the named varieties in the fall will produce plants dissimilar to the named cultivars. Cuttings are the most common propagation methods though home gardeners can also use layering, divisions, and grafts. Some of the more difficult species have been tissue cultured, but it's the least preferred of the methods noted.

C

Layering is a good way for home gardeners to have a limited number of new plants to trade with friends. A trailing stem is bent over to the ground with a portion of the length (two to three nodes) buried in moist soil. Put a broad rock over the area covering the stem so that it stays moist and rooting can begin quickly. Don't allow to dry out.

Divisions are done only on some selected species, not the large-flowered hybrids such as *C.* × *jackmanii*, and only by the home gardener.

Propagation by grafting once was common due to the difficulties of getting most varieties to root readily as cuttings. Two-year-old seedlings of either *C. vitalba* or *C. viticella* were used for the root stock. In general, nodes were selected from the appropriate variety and grafted onto the root stocks, tied, and allowed to take hold. When grown at 70F (21C), this occurred within a month. There were problems, however, with grafted varieties, including dieback, lack of hardiness, and disease, so the practice is no longer done.

Softwood cuttings are taken from young plants or shoots, not from old stock plants. Spring is the best time for cuttings: March in the southern United States, a month later in the North. Internodal cuttings should include a pair of leaves, the dormant buds at their base, and the piece of stem below. To understand this better, keep in mind that there should be no stem above the two leaves. Stick this cutting into soil just up to the point where the leaf meets the stem. Use sand and peat as the primary propagation media and keep the temperature at 75F to 78F (24C to 26C) until the clematis cutting roots, usually between four and six weeks, depending on the cultivar. Rooted cuttings can then be hardened off between 60F and 65F (16C and 18C) and kept at this temperature until potted up. Spring cuttings can be potted up in late spring or summer for late summer or early fall sales or overwintered for sales the following spring.

Additional comments regarding cuttings:

1. If the stem portion is woody, wound it by removing a section of the stem. The portion you remove could best be defined as a sliver measuring about 1 inch (2.5 cm) long and one-quarter-inch (6 mm) wide at the base of the stem.
2. Propagation media will vary from grower to grower. Some use straight, coarse sand; others use a mixture of peat and sand while still others use a vermiculite and peat moss blend. Cuttings root easily in any of these media, although rooting in straight peat has not been as successful as in the combinations noted. The pH should be 7.0 to 7.5 for the overall best rooting performance.
3. Avoid frequent misting due to the increase in disease when the cuttings are rooting. Once stuck, sprinkle cuttings with water during the day. Frequency is based on the heat and amount of light reaching the cuttings. Mark Roh of the New

Crops Research Program at USDA-ARS suggests a six-second mist every 15 to 20 minutes for one to two weeks.

4. Propagators often use rooting hormones to improve overall rooting. Specifically, a 2,000 to 3,000 ppm IBA dip for three to five seconds is common. However, research by Erwin and Schwarze at the University of Minnesota showed that IBA (indolebutyric acid) "...had no significant effect on clematis rooting." [1]

5. Some shading is essential to avoid burning cuttings as they root, although light is necessary to speed root and new shoot development.

If, after a week or so, the cuttings are turgid (erect and solid, without soft stems or wilted foliage), it's probable that callusing has begun. Rooting will start soon after. Cuttings can be potted up as early as three to four weeks after the cuttings were first stuck. Clematis rooting is not an easy feat, however, and should only be attempted if you sell large numbers of plants or are a commercial propagator. Some growers have reported as much as 50% losses on specific varieties they've attempted to root.

GROWING ON

Crop time: If you're taking your own cuttings in the spring, allow a full year of growth before retail sales. Spring cuttings will need the full summer to root into liner size pots measuring $2\frac{1}{2} \times 2\frac{1}{2} \times 3$ inches deep ($6 \times 6 \times 7$ cm). These can be overwintered in an unheated cold frame and will then be ready for sales in early spring—fully rooted. These can be sold as is or potted up into quart containers and sold in the spring. Since rooting losses can be high, many growers turn to commercial propagators for their plants instead.

Liners are commercially available in fall and winter from a number of propagators, including Donahue's Clematis Specialists, Faribault, Minnesota. Plants are shipped in deep pots, cell packs, or are individually wrapped in polyethylene bags. In some cases, the plants are dormant, while in other cases the plants will be shipped with growth reemerging. Clematis are also available as one- or two-year-old plants.

As for crop time and scheduling, we have used one-year-old plants that had already broken dormancy and were actively growing. We removed them from a 3-inch-deep (7 cm) container, potted them up into 1-gallon pots using one liner per pot, added a short trellis for climbing, and then grew them on at 55F (13C) nights. Plants were salable six to seven weeks after potting. The roots will not be massed through the soil below, however. Plants can be sold as is or add another two weeks for better root formation. Some plants flower sporadically, but most of the energy goes into root and stem development. Better flowering occurs during the summer, though free flowering performance won't occur for another year in the garden.

Clematis roots are elongated, somewhat thickened but still thinner than a pencil, and are slow at first to root into the media. Four weeks after potting the roots will only be starting to form into the media. For this reason, some growers pot up into

2- or 3-quart containers to decrease the crop time. Regardless, four weeks after potting the top growth will be developing.

Clematis have earned a reputation in this country for being difficult to grow and, indeed, plants can easily die back to the ground, looking as if they have rotted off. Closer inspection of the roots may show a strong and healthy system devoid of any problems, however. A fungus, *Ascochyta clematidina*, has been identified as the cause of the majority of clematis wilt diseases as well as leaf spot. The fungus can attack any part of the plant above ground down to just below the soil surface, which is why the plants may return a year later after early dying off the previous year. This is why it is especially important to bury the crown below the soil line. For additional information, see **In the home garden**.

As a preventative, some growers have used Chipco 26019 (iprodione) and reported success in keeping losses down. The product is used at the label rate.

VARIETIES

The large-flowered clematis varieties are sometimes classified in groups (as in Michael Dirr's book, *Manual of Woody Landscape Plants*, third edition) or by all the varieties within a color range (as in Christopher Lloyd's book, *Clematis*, revised edition). I've listed the large-flowered varieties in alphabetical order. These are all vegetatively propagated; there are no seed-propagated varieties here.

You'll note in the varieties below that the key months for flowering are June and July. Some varieties are noted for their September comeback, although they aren't as free flowering as plants that bloom in spring or summer.

Also, flower size is dependent on overall plant health and performance. Small plants with limited foliage cover aren't going to develop large flowers, regardless of the sizes indicated below. One year in the garden (sometimes two years) is needed before the plants will produce large flowers.

Barbara Jackman has 6- to 8-inch (15 to 20 cm) flowers in May and June in a bicolor bloom of medium blue to purple highlighted by deep carmine in the center. The stamens are cream white in color. May rebloom in September. Plants can grow 10 to 12 feet (3 to 3.6 m) in length.

Bees Jubilee has 7- to 8-inch (18 to 20 cm), light pink flowers with a deep red center to each sepal and yellow stamens. Plants bloom in May and June and may show color again in August. Grows 10 to 14 feet (3 to 4.2 m) long.

Belle of Woking (Bell of Woking) has double flowering, mauve-blue flowers. Some authorities say it is pink, others say light blue, and still others call it lavender. The color is a light blue and pink combination, thus the mauve description. Plants flower in May and June (may rebloom in September) and grow 4 to 6 feet (1.2 to 1.8 m) long.

Candida (*C. lanuginosa* Candida) has 7- to 9-inch (18 to 23 cm), pure white flowers on plants to 15 feet (4.5 m) in length. Plants flower in June, July, and sometimes in September.

Dr. Ruppel is a ruffle-edged, white-flowering variety with a deep red center down each sepal. Flowers measure 7 to 8 inches (18 to 20 cm) across and appear in May or June, often reappearing in September. Plants grow to 10 to 12 feet (3 to 3.6 m) long.

Duchess of Edinburgh has semi to fully double, 6-inch (15 cm) white rosettes with yellow stamens. They appear in May and June; there may be September reblooming. Plants can grow to 12 feet (3.6 m) in length.

Elsa Spath has 6- to 8-inch (15 to 20 cm), rich lavender-blue overlapping petals that give a double-flowering appearance. The plants can be vigorous in their growth, up to 12 feet (3.6 m) long.

Ernest Markham has 4- to 6-inch (10 to 15 cm), magenta-red flowers with gold stamens. Plants flower in July and August and sometimes again in September. Plants grow 12 to 15 feet (3.6 to 4.5 m) long.

Gypsy Queen is a rich violet-purple flowering variety with reddish stamens. Free flowering, the plants often have 6-inch (15 cm) flowers on up to 18-foot-long (5.4 m) plants. Plants flower in July and August—there's some reoccurring color in September.

Hagley Hybrid has 5- to 6-inch (13 or 15 cm), rich pink flowers with purplish brown anthers. It blooms in June and may rebloom in September. Plants grow 8 feet (2.4 m) long.

Henryi's blossoms of pure white with dark stamens are usually 4 to 5 inches (10 to 13 cm) in diameter, though they've been measured as large as 7 inches (18 cm) across. Often flowers in June and again in September if the plants aren't cut back from the previous year. It grows 12 to 20 feet (3.6 to 6 m) long.

Horn of Plenty is a light blue flower with dark blue highlights down the center of each petal. Plants bloom in June and again in September. Can grow to as much as 16 feet (4.8 m) in length. It is free flowering.

Huldine has 4-inch, iridescent white flowers in July with recurrent bloom until October. Plants grow to 20 feet (6 m) in length.

Jackmanii is the most profusely blooming, vivid purple clematis on the market. The flowers are 5 to 6 inches (13 to 15 cm) across and appear in June and July, and sometimes again in September. The variety is probably a cross between two different species (C. lanuginosa × C. viticella) back in the late 1850s by the Jackman family in Woking, Surrey, England. It is the most well-known clematis variety in the United States due to its ease of culture and vibrant color.

King Edward VII has 5- to 6-inch (13 to 15 cm) lilac flowers with sepals centered in deep pink. The stamens are brown. The plants flower in July and August on plants up to 8 feet (2.4 m) long.

Lady Betty Balfour has 5- to 6-inch (13 to 15 cm), violet-purple pointed flowers with cream-yellow stamens. Plants flower in July and again in September on 20-foot-long (6 m) plants.

Lasurstern has 7- to 9-inch (18 to 23 cm), lavender-blue flowers with cream-white stamens. The sepals are often wavy in appearance, giving a double-flowering look to the bloom. Plants bloom in May and June and again in September. The length is 10 to 12 feet (3 to 3.6 m).

Lincoln Star has raspberry-red pointed sepals with white edges and reddish stamens. Flowers can develop to 8 inches (20 cm) across and appear in May and June, reblooming in September. Plants reach 8 feet (2.4 m) or more in length.

Madame Baron Veillard has lilac-pink flowers to 6 inches (15 cm) across on plants to 12 feet (3.6 m) long. Plants are vigorous and free flowering, blooming in June and again in September.

Madame Edward Andre (Madame Edouard Andre) has 5- to 6-inch (13 to 15 cm), velvet red flowers with yellow stamens on plants up to 10 feet (3 m) long. Plants flower in June and July and may show color again in September.

Nelly Moser (Nellie Moser) has 5- to 6-inch (13 to 15 cm), pale pink flowers with a deep rose pink vein down the center of each petal. Plants flower in May and June and again in mid to late summer. This is a very popular variety.

Ramona has 6- to 8-inch (15 to 20 cm), lavender-blue flowers with dark anthers. Plants grow as long as 16 feet (4.8 m) and flower in July, August, and September.

Ville de Lyon has 4-inch (10 cm), carmine red sepals that are darker to the outer edge and cream stamens. Plants flower June through September and grow to 12 feet (3.6 m) long.

William Kennett has 6- to 8-inch (15 to 20 cm), lavender-blue ruffled flowers with dark purple stamens. It flowers June to September on 20-foot-long (6 m) plants.

RELATED MATERIAL

Clematis integrifolia is a short growing variety between 2 to 5 feet (60 to 150 cm) tall, with violet to medium blue or white flowers usually no more than 1 inch (2.5 cm) across. The flowers are often downturned. Plants will flower from June to July. *C. integrifolia* is hardy to Zone 3 and commonly propagated by cutting and seed. See Color Plate 29 for photo of *Clematis integrifolia*.

Clematis recta is commonly called "Ground Clematis" due to its sprawling but mounding habit. I've seen it used effectively along streams and waterfalls, planted so that its growth trails and tumbles over rocks down into the water. Plants can be trained to grow up a trellis, but they perform better when allowed to spread.

Clematis recta has numerous 1-inch (2.5 cm) white flowers on plants growing to about 5 feet (1.5 m) in length, although it's often 4 feet (1.2 m) long in various Chicago gardens I've observed. As the flowers fade, they're replaced by bright silvery seed heads that reflect the sun. Plants put on their strongest show of color in June and continue on into July. Seed heads will start to develop by the end of July.

Hardy to Zone 3. Propagate by seeds or cuttings.

Clematis maximowicziana (formerly *C. paniculata*) is an Asian variety known for its free flowering performance and ease of growing, both in landscape and home gardens. Commonly called "Sweet Autumn" clematis, an established planting will literally give hundreds, if not thousands, of fragrant, cream-white, 1-inch (2.5 cm) or so blossoms. Plants flower in late August until mid to late September. See Color Plate 30 for photo of *Clematis maximowicziana*.

Once flowering is over, the seed will start to develop. As it ripens on the plant, seed becomes a rose-red color. The seed is enclosed in a fattened casing that holds an elongated tail of light pink, giving the seed pod an almost whorled or pinwheel effect. After seeds ripen and fall to the ground, seedlings will start to emerge the following spring. These can be easily transplanted to other areas. Sweet Autumn clematis is the easiest of the clematis varieties to grow in our gardens and is long lived.

Clematis maximowicziana may be almost too good a grower in the South, but it's worthy of a place in the southern garden due to its overall performance and endurance. This variety is very easily grown and not in need of babying. Once established in the garden, it will perform reliably from year to year. In the central and southern parts of the South, the plants may be partially evergreen depending on the winter, but here in the North the plant readily dies back in cold weather. In the spring the plants can be cut back to 10 inches (25 cm) for a strong show of growth by late summer when the flowers bloom. Southern-grown plants appear more adept at reseeding than their northern counterparts.

Hardy to Zone 3. Propagate by seed or cuttings.

Clematis montana is considered to be one of the easiest and most prolific bloomers of the clematis group. This species often blooms early with 2- to 3-inch (5 to 7 cm) flowers. Some of the varieties and cultivars are exceptionally vigorous.

Elizabeth has soft pink flowers on vigorously growing vines. During one summer, the plants can grow 15 to 20 feet (4.5 to 6 m) long once established. The flowers have a scent of vanilla.

Grandiflora has numerous pure white, 3-inch (7 cm) flowers. Grandiflora is a solid mass of white when in full bloom. Blooms have a slight vanilla fragrance.

Marjorie is a profuse bloomer with 2- to 3-inch (5 to 7 cm) creamy pink blossoms highlighted by salmon or orange. Flowers may be single or semidouble.

Clematis montana var. *rubens* has purple highlighted foliage in the spring that will turn dark green or stay lightly bronzed during summer. The flowers can vary in color from soft or light pink to a deep rose pink depending on the season. The scent of vanilla is most predominant in the evening hours.

The species can be sown from seed, though it is easier to propagate both the species and the named cultivars from cuttings.

Hardy from Zones 5 to 8.

Clematis viticella is native to southern Europe and is one of the species used in developing the many hybrid varieties available today. *C. viticella* often is a vigorous grower with long blooming periods. Like *C. montana*, this species can also grow from 15 to 20 feet (4.5 to 6 m) per year; the cultivars below grow 10 to 15 feet (3 to 4.5 m). As a group, they are not as susceptible to clematis wilt.

Etiole Violette has starlike, 3- to 4-inch (7 to 10 cm) deep purple flowers. It blooms late June until September.

Kermesina (misnamed Rubra) has small crimson (sometimes called burgundy) flowers on vigorously growing plants.

Mme. Julia Correvon is a stunning variety with its true to rosy red, 3- to 4-inch (7 to 10 cm) blooms. The blossoms are slightly reflexed.

Purpurea Plena Elegans (syn. Elegans Plena) is an extremely showy, double-flowering, antique rose-purple selection that flowers July to September. It is not as vigorous in height as the other selections listed here.

All of these cultivars are hybrids and need to be vegetatively propagated. The species can also be propagated by seed. Hardy from Zones 5 to 8.

IN THE HOME GARDEN

If you've ever purchased a clematis from a garden center or received planting advice from an expert, you were probably told to locate it where the roots are kept cool but the vines are in full sun. Some gardeners, professional growers, and other informed horticulturists continue to live by this rule—I see no reason to change it. Some authors have suggested this practice is not necessary, but in the ever-changing summer weather experienced by most of the country, the plants do better when treated in this way than in stronger, full-sun locations.

From Chicago to the Carolinas and east to the Rockies, clematis is not fond of the big three summer stresses: full sun, high heat, and high humidity. If you place the plants in areas where the soil around the roots warms up (especially 80F/27C and above), the plants will struggle—without at least a mulch to keep the roots protected.

Conversely, too shady a location will decrease the plant's overall size and flower diameter.

What's the best location? Choose a site with ample room for the plant to grow up and out (or over or in—however you're using it), and where the roots are protected from direct sunlight heating the soil around the rootball. Mulching the crown, interplanting with other plants, or using rocks at its base will shade the roots. Plant where the foliage gets five hours or more of direct sun, but allow for some shade—an hour or two—from noon until late afternoon during summer's hottest days.

When buying plants in the spring, you may start with a slender, elongated pot with only a 2-inch (5 cm) opening or less at the top. This type of pot allows for good root development, although the top growth is often stringy and sparse. One or two active vining shoots can be expected, but these will not produce strong flowering plants the same season. From this type of growth, a full year or two will be needed to get the results that gardening magazines depict.

When planting in the garden, prepare a site as large as the width of your shovel or fork to work up. Add to this some compost, peat moss, or other organic material to enrich the surrounding area, and then plant the crown 2 inches (5 cm) deeper than it was in the pot. Allow for at least one pair of buds below the soil line to initiate regrowth should anything happen to the top growth.

For the home gardener, pruning is by far the most difficult aspect of home culture, outside of wilt. If you prune some varieties in the spring, you may be rewarded with no flowers or limited blooms during the summer. On others, prune in the spring and an abundance of color will appear during summer. Varieties differ in their pruning needs and commercial propagators such as Steffen's of New York and Donahue's of Minnesota provide detailed information on how to prune the various varieties they sell. Refer to these companies, or the brokers they sell through, for pruning suggestions on different varieties.

You may notice that the plant suddenly wilts one day, although the ground appears moist and additional watering does not correct the problem. Review the information provided previously under **Growing on** for a discussion of disease.

—In preparing the information, the author appreciates the help of Christopher Lloyd's book, Clematis, *a most thorough and definitive work in deciphering the mystery and confusion behind this impressive genus.*

The author sincerely appreciates the time that Richard (Dick) Donahue of Donahue's Clematis Specialists, Feribault, Minnesota, spent in reviewing and updating the information on clematis. Regrettably, Dick did not live to see the work's completion, but his insight and thoughts will be here in print for generations to come.

REFERENCES

[1] Erwin, J., and D. Schwarze. 1993. *Factors affecting Clematis rooting.* Minnesota Commercial Flower Growers Association Bulletin 41 (4).

▰ COREOPSIS GRANDIFLORUM
(sometimes called *C. lanceolata*)

FAMILY: Asteraceae

COMMON NAME(S): Tickseed, Coreopsis

DESCRIPTION
Coreopsis grandiflorum displays single to double, golden yellow flowers on plants 18 to 24 inches (46 to 61 cm) tall. It is a dependable perennial with excellent color that remains stable throughout its flowering period. The flowers are 1¾ to 2½ inches (4.4 to 6 cm) across, mostly pure in color, although some varieties have red flecking towards the base of the flower. Plants spread 12 to 16 inches (30 to 41 cm) across.

HARDINESS: Zones 4 to 9.

SEASON OF BLOOM: June and July.

PROPAGATION
Seed is the most popular form of propagation due to its ease and the uniform plants it produces. Divisions can also be taken in the spring or fall.

GERMINATION OVERVIEW: 10,000 seeds per ounce/350 per gram.
Germination temperatures are 65F to 75F (18C to 24C). Seed can be left exposed or lightly covered during germination; no pretreatments are necessary. Germination takes nine to 12 days, and seedlings can be transplanted 20 to 25 days after sowing.

GROWING ON
From seed: If Sunray or Sunburst coreopsis seed is sown in winter, plants will not flower profusely the same season. In fact, if sown as early as February, planted up into cell packs, and grown at 50F (10C) nights, plants will remain vegetative the following spring and summer when planted into the garden in May. In the case of Early Sunrise, however, March sowings transplanted to cell packs, grown on at 50F (10C) nights, and planted to the garden in May/June, flower profusely from mid-July until late August. All varieties will fill in equally well and their foliage will look similar.

For Sunray or Sunburst, sow seed in July or August for overwintering in gallon containers, one plant per pot. These will flower the following spring. I suggest that you grow Early Sunrise from seed sown early in the year as opposed to trying to overwinter this variety. It's more cost-effective to sow and grow it as a 4-inch (10 cm) or quart bedding plant than trying to overwinter it. For all varieties allow 11 to 12 weeks for green cell packs. For blooming 5-inch (13 cm) pots of Early Sunrise, allow 16 to 18 weeks.

VARIETIES

Of the following, only Early Sunrise will flower the same year from seed when sown from January to March. It's probable the variety will flower from sowings made even later. When I tried sowing it as late as March, plants flowered in mid-July. See Color Plate 31 for photo of *Coreopsis grandiflorum* Early Sunrise.

Baby Sun has single, 1- to 2-inch (2.5 to 5 cm), golden yellow blooms with a red fleck at the base of each petal. The plants grow 12 to 16 inches (30 to 41 cm) tall in flower.

Early Sunrise reaches a height of 2 feet (60 cm) with semidouble, golden yellow blooms. Flowers are 2 inches (5 cm) across. Early Sunrise plants can bloom in just 100 days when sown during midwinter or later for spring sales. Early Sunrise is a 1989 All America Gold Medal winner from Burpee Seed Company. It was the first Gold Medal award winner in 15 years.

Sunburst is a vigorous performer growing to 3 feet (90 cm) tall with an open, rank habit in the garden. Its flowers are yellow and 2 inches (5 cm) across, with either a single or semidouble appearance.

Sunray is an excellent double-flowering variety growing to 2 feet (60 cm) tall. It has a neater habit than Sunburst, with flowers to 2½ (6 cm) inches across. The flower color is a rich golden yellow.

USES

In the perennial garden, mix coreopsis with hardy annuals like Victoria Blue *Salvia farinacea* or dwarf perennial veronicas for an outstanding color combination. Coreopsis works well in the middle of the perennial border.

As a cut flower in the home, use long-stemmed, taller varieties like Sunburst for the best arrangements.

IN THE HOME GARDEN

For your customers to maintain long-lived plants, tell them to divide coreopsis as needed. It's worth noting here that we've had no problem maintaining mass plantings of both Early Sunrise and Baby Sun, while the remaining varieties have died out within two or three years. Space coreopsis 12 to 15 inches (30 to 38 cm) apart, depending on whether you want them to fill in completely or leave space around them. Plant in full-sun locations. While staking isn't normally required, you might warn customers that Sunburst may need it, especially if it's planted in an area where it's kept moist, partially shaded, or well fed.

■ COREOPSIS VERTICILLATA

FAMILY: Asteraceae

COMMON NAME(S): Threadleaf Coreopsis, Whorled Tickseed

DESCRIPTION

A native perennial noted for its thin, 2- to 3-inch-long (5 to 7 cm), dark green leaves and bright flower color. The scentless flowers are single, golden or lemon yellow, and held upright on mounded or spreading plants. The drought-resistant plants range in height from 10 inches (25 cm) to 2½ feet (75 cm) and spread 2½ to 3 feet (75 to 90 cm).

HARDINESS: Zones 3 to 9.

Some sources suggest the plants are hardy only to Zone 6. In our West Chicago gardens (Zone 5), however, we haven't had any problems in overwintering either of the Moonbeam or Zagreb varieties.

SEASON OF BLOOM: June to August.

Only Moonbeam is a recurrent bloomer; the other varieties listed below will bloom in June and early July and won't repeat unless trimmed back after the first flowering. While the secondary blooms are not as prolific as the first, Moonbeam will flower repeatedly during the summer months.

PROPAGATION

The named varieties are propagated either by division or cuttings; only the species can be propagated by seed. Plants reach maturity two to three years after planting and can be divided either in spring or fall.

GERMINATION OVERVIEW

Seed varieties of threadleaf coreopsis are inferior to the clones and are of limited value in commercial trade. If you have seed you want to try, sow it on a peat-based media and cover lightly. Germination temperatures are 68F to 70F (20C to 21C) and germination occurs in two to three weeks.

GROWING ON

From cuttings: This is the most popular way to propagate *C. verticillata* cultivars. They should be taken in spring or anytime the plants aren't flowering. For Moonbeam this will be almost an impossibility since the plants flower most of the summer. Cuttings will root within two weeks under mist, and if stuck into a 72-cell pack or plug tray, the transplants will be fully rooted in five to seven weeks. These can be potted into 4-inch (10 cm), quart, or larger containers for growing on during the summer. Cuttings taken during the summer are potted up and grown on for overwintering and sales the following spring. Cuttings taken the previous fall or from stock plants during winter will produce plants large enough to sell by the next spring. It may be cheaper to buy in started liners and finish them, however, than to maintain plants over the winter.

Commercial propagators have liners (72 cells per flat) available during winter and spring. These can be potted up into 4-inch (10 cm) or quart containers and sold in the spring. If purchased early enough, the plants can be sold in 2- or 3-quart containers as well. For a 4-inch (10 cm) pot, allow eight to 10 weeks for a fully rooted plant when grown at no lower than 50F (10C) nights. The plants can be sold as early as six weeks, however, depending on the age of the liners received and how much growth is visually acceptable prior to selling.

From divisions: Plants can be divided as noted under **Propagation** and potted up into quart or gallon containers for spring sales. The named varieties noted below will all flower the same year from divisions depending on the size of the division taken.

Commercial propagators will also have roots available during winter. These bare-root pieces can be potted to quart or gallon pots and grown on at no less than 50F (10C) nights for salable plants in seven to nine weeks. These plants will flower during the summer.

VARIETIES

All of the following are vegetatively propagated and are not available from seed.

Golden Showers (also called Grandiflora). Flowers are a bright golden yellow, the deepest yellow of the three cultivars noted here. Plants are 20 to 36 inches (51 to 91 cm) tall—taller than Zagreb.

Moonbeam. A 1992 Perennial Plant of the Year award winner and for good reason. This excellent cultivar has light or buff yellow, 1- to 1½-inch (2.5 to 4 cm), single blooms on plants from 18 to 24 inches (46 to 61 cm) tall. The plants are more spreading than upright with finely cut leaves on plants measuring up to 3 feet (90 cm) across. Today it's the most popular of these types due to its long flowering season, but it is not a true *C. verticillata* variety. While its heritage is not fully known, a number of species, including *C. verticillata*, have been crossed to yield this superior garden performer. See Color Plate 33 for photo of *Coreopsis verticillata* Moonbeam.

Zagreb. This cultivar has a deeper yellow color than Moonbeam. While the foliage is as deeply cut, the plant is upright, and it grows to 12 to 15 inches (30 to 38 cm) tall in the garden. See Color Plate 34 for photo of *Coreopsis verticillata* Zagreb.

RELATED MATERIAL

C. rosea is a pink flowering plant sometimes listed as *C. verticillata rosea*. The blooms are single, 1½ inches (3 cm) across on plants with foliage similar to Moonbeam. *C. rosea*, like Moonbeam, has a more upright than spreading habit and can become invasive in moist, fertile locations. In some cases the plant will have to be controlled to avoid overtaking other plants around it. See Color Plate 32 for photo of *Coreopsis rosea*.

Propagate by division or cuttings and grow on as noted under *C. verticillata* types. Hardy from Zones 3 to 8.

USES

This class of perennial plant material performs very well in either home or commercial landscapes. Plants are known for their upright or spreading performance, and Moonbeam will flower repeatedly during the summer. In the landscape, *C. verticillata* is an excellent choice for those warm, dry locations that are well drained. For the other varieties, flowering starts in late June in the North and continues in full show throughout July. Trim the old flowers off in early August, and rebloom will occur in three to four weeks.

IN THE HOME GARDEN

Plant in full sun locations or where plants will get morning shade in a well-drained location. Coreopsis plants don't like to have their roots wet for an extended period of time. Space plants 12 to 15 inches (30 to 38 cm) apart, allowing them to fill in; even the taller varieties won't need staking to stay upright. Spreading types are best when allowed to arch gracefully over streams, steps, or small slopes.

No special care is required during the winter to protect the plants from dying out. We don't cover or mulch our plants and have little problem getting all of them to return in our gardens near Chicago.

CROCOSMIA × CROCOSMIIFLORA

The common varieties of this crop on the market today come from crosses between a number of species and varieties. The first cross by Messrs. Lemoine of Nancy, France, in 1882, set the stage for the development of additional introductions into the market. They crossed *C. aurea* and *C. pottsii* and named the resulting hybrid *C. crocosmiaeflora* (*Montbretia* × *crocosmiaeflora* by other authorities). Neither name was officially endorsed; instead the name *C.* × *crocosmiiflora* became the accepted botanical reference for the crop.

Since then, additional crosses have been made between this variety, other species and the related genus *Curtonus*. Therefore, some references note other species for the various varieties listed in the market. Sometimes they're listed as varieties of **C. masonorum** or they're simply termed hybrids to reflect the varied parents used to produce the plant.

While the names can get confusing, it's important to be aware of the various botanical references that have developed since the first crosses were made and to realize that one botanical name does not encompass all of the selections available. The plants or corms you receive from various sources may be one and the same, depending on which botanical reference each company uses.

FAMILY: Iridaceae

COMMON NAME(S): Crocosmia, Montbretia
Crocosmia, roughly translated, means "saffron-smell," which refers to the saffron scent emitted by the dried flowers when soaked in warm water.

DESCRIPTION
These erect, upright plants with swordlike, medium green leaves look and grow similar to gladiolus. The flower stalks develop out of the crown on wiry stems that gently nod in the breeze. The flowers are single, rather open in form, brightly colored in shades of red, orange, and yellow and measure from 1 to 1½ inches (2.5 to 4 cm) across. Plants grow 3 to 4 feet (90 to 120 cm) tall in full bloom and spread 8 to 12 inches (20 to 30 cm), narrow at the base and filling out more at the crown.

HARDINESS: Zones 6 to 9.
Crocosmia is not hardy in Chicago (Zone 5), so we dig up the corms in the late summer or autumn for overwintering as we would gladiolus. Since the varieties are hybrids between two or more unlike (though related) plants, their hardiness is determined by their parents.

SEASON OF BLOOM: July and August.

PROPAGATION
Planting corms is the easiest way to propagate crocosmia. You can also remove and plant the offsets that develop around the base of the corm by the end of the summer to increase the population.

GROWING ON
Crop time: Crocosmia is grown like gladiolus, except that glads are often planted where they are to flower, while crocosmias can be greenhouse grown and transplanted to the garden when weather permits. Since crocosmia plants are narrow at the base and usually develop only one (sometimes two) stems, it's common to plant two or three corms per gallon container, buried 2 to 3 inches (5 to 7 cm) beneath the soil level.

Crop time is based on your preferred plant size for green plant sales in the spring. Corms planted in the middle of March in a gallon container will be 12 to 20 inches

(30 to 51 cm) tall, depending on variety, by the first of May if greenhouse grown with warm (68F/20C) nights. A higher quality crop is produced at 60F (16C) nights, since the cool temperatures help keep the plants from becoming top heavy. However, plants grown cool may be an inch or two (2.5 to 5 cm) shorter. These plants are sold green in May and will start to flower in June or July.

Like gladiolus, crocosmia doesn't appreciate cold weather and can't be planted outdoors until all danger of frost is passed, especially if entirely greenhouse grown prior to retail sales. If you're selling retail in the northern United States, the additional information provided later in **In the home garden** may assist home gardeners in the digging, storing, and eventual replanting of the corms in cold winter climates.

VARIETIES

All of the commonly grown varieties on the market today are hybrids rather than a single species. Of these hybrids, Lucifer is the easiest variety to find in the United States. You may have trouble finding the other cultivars, but they're worth the search when you're looking for something different. The following is only a partial list of cultivars that are available.

Emberglow (*Crocosmia masonorum* × *Curtonus paniculatus*) is an upright, scarlet-red variety that reaches 3 feet (90 cm) in flower. The calyx is often bronzed or dark in color. Hardy from Zones 5 or 6 to 9.

Lucifer is by far the most common variety available on the U.S. market. Lucifer is popular due to its cold tolerance (Zones 5 to 8) and adaptability. The plants are larger than most other varieties, growing as tall as 4 feet (120 cm) in some climates. In our Chicago location, the plants often reach 3 to 3½ feet (90 to 105 cm) tall in full bloom. The flowers are bright fiery red and measure up to 1½ inches (3 cm) across. Lucifer is highly recommended as a focal point for its flowers and foliage. Note: Lucifer is more reliably hardy in the southern areas of Zone 5 or near the various lakes than it is farther inland in northern areas of the zone. The crop suffers from the cold, damp autumns and springs in these harsher areas, though it may overwinter if sufficiently mulched.

Spitfire (*C. masonorum* × *C.* × *crocosmiiflora* Jackanapes) is a vivid orange flowering variety that grows 3 feet (90 cm) tall. Spitfire is hardy from Zone 5 or 6 to 9. See Color Plate 35 for photo of *Crocosmia* Spitfire.

IN THE HOME GARDEN

The above information might lead you to believe that you can leave crocosmia in the ground in cold climates if you mulch heavily. Frankly, this works best on crocosmia used as a foundation planting around a home or other building where the ground doesn't freeze and thaw as much as open ground (such as in a commercial landscape). To be blunt, I've had little luck in successfully overwintering crocosmia in the ground during a Chicago winter.

In mid to late September the leaves will start to die back, and all the flowers will have faded. We wait until the ground has been dry for several days before we dig the corms up. The soil around the corms is allowed to dry before being removed. The corms are stored in basements or other frostproof environments in peat moss for the winter. In the spring, the corms can be planted during the week of the last expected frost, at the same time you plant gladiolus. The corms should be planted about 3 inches (7 cm) deep in a light, sandy, organic soil rather than heavy clay/loam and watered.

If you prefer, you can start the corms indoors in a standard potting mix in a 6-inch (15 cm) pot using three corms per pot. Place the containers in a warm area and transplant to the garden in about four to six weeks. Take care to avoid letting the media fall away from the corms during transplanting. To keep the media in place, be sure the roots have started to mass around the inside of the container, and water the plants well the day before. A moistened soil ball will hold together better than a dry one.

When starting your own corms or transplanting purchased containers from a nursery or greenhouse, plant in a sunny, well-drained location. Plants started indoors in the home are often lanky and will probably require staking. Plants purchased from a greenhouse may also require staking, especially during flowering in open, windy locations.

D

Delphinium elatum (D. × elatum)

The garden varieties available today resulted from intercrossing between species and/or other varieties, including *D. elatum* and *D. exaltatum*. Botanical names have been used to describe these crosses, most notably, *D. × cultorum*. This collection of hybrids is listed under **Varieties**. While not definitive, many consider *D. elatum* to be the primary parent of the taller varieties of which Pacific Giant is the most well known.

Family: Ranunculaceae

Common name(s): Delphinium, Bee Delphinium, Bee Larkspur, Perennial Larkspur, Candle Larkspur

Description

True *D. elatum* is seldom grown and not easily found in the trade. Therefore, the following description represents the cultivars that are most commonly available.

Delphiniums are among the tallest and stateliest of the garden perennials. Plants grow erect with limited or no basal branching and usually with only one stem the first year. The second year there will be two to five emerging shoots, but only one or two at a time will develop into flowering plants; the others at the base of the plant remain vegetative until the first stems have bloomed.

Delphinium flowers are single to fully double, depending on cultivar; the bloom itself is made up of five petal-like sepals. In the center of the bloom are a number of true petals, one-quarter to one-third the size of the sepals. These are fluffy and commonly called "bees," giving rise to one of the common names. These "bees" are often white or black while the sepals are primarily blue and blue-tinged shades, as well as white. The flowers are scentless.

Hardiness: Zones 4 to 7.

Delphiniums are rather short-lived perennials in most of the United States. High summer heat and humidity followed by wet, alternating cold/warm winters will often lead to crown rot and death. Read **In the home garden** for suggestions on maintaining these plants from year to year.

SEASON OF BLOOM: June and July.

If plants are cut back after the first bloom, a second flowering will occur during late August and September.

PROPAGATION

Delphinium is usually propagated by seed, but divisions and cuttings can also be taken from stock plants. Use only fresh seed—avoid any seed older than one year. See additional notes under **Germination overview**.

Divisions can be taken in the spring, but fall-dug plants often winter kill here in the Midwest. Fall-dug plants survive better when moved to cold storage and then divided and potted during the winter. However, this method is usually uneconomical.

Take only a 3- to 4-inch-long (7 to 10 cm) *solid* stem cuttings (delphiniums have hollow stems on mature growth) in the spring as plants first emerge from the ground or as shoots develop on stock plants. Plants will also produce new shoots at the base after they've flowered. These cuttings will root within two or three weeks and can be potted up for sales the same year if taken early enough.

GERMINATION OVERVIEW: 8,000 to 10,000 seeds per ounce/280 to 350 per gram. Pretreatments: Delphiniums have a reputation for being poor germinators. If you receive seed from your supplier during the fall and winter, no pretreatments are usually necessary. Seed is harvested in late summer for fall and winter sales. The best germination, ranging from 70 to 90%, is within the first four to six months after harvesting. Like larkspur, delphinium often germinates at less than 50% by the following summer. Seed that's purchased in winter and held for summer sowing should remain in its sealed packet and be refrigerated until needed.

There has been a lot of conflicting directions on germination provided over the years. Most methods accomplish the same job but over a broad range of times. If the seed is fresh, germination temperatures of 70F to 75F (21C to 24C) with a light covering of coarse vermiculite usually works well for us. Even with a fresh seed crop, however, this method might yield only 40 to 55% final germination. When this is the case, we use an alternate day/night temperature of 80/70F (27/21C). It's our experience that low germination is more common for the Pacific Giant varieties than for the *D. × belladonna* types. A constant germination temperature of 65F to 70F (18C to 21C) works well for the latter.

Germination takes 12 to 18 days. Seedlings can be transplanted 20 to 28 days after sowing.

GROWING ON

From seed: Delphiniums grow rapidly from seed and will produce flowering plants during the summer from seed sown anytime from December to March. To get the best growth and quality flowering spikes, however, sow early and grow cool. Regardless of whether you're selling large cell packs (18 cells per flat) or 3-quart containers, the seed should be sown from late December to mid-January into plug trays or open flats.

Transplant the seedlings into small pots or cell packs and grow on in the greenhouse until they're well rooted. (In our greenhouse, the temperatures are no less than 58F (14C) nights for rapid—but not weak—growth.) Then pot the plants, one per 3- or 4-quart container. Allow them to root and then move them to a cold frame for the remainder of the season.

We transfer our plants to the cold frame in early March when the night temperatures are no less than 50F (10C) and days are 8F to 10F warmer (4C to 6C). These plants will produce salable green plants by mid to late April. Dwarf varieties like Blue Fountains or the Magic Fountains will flower earlier than the Pacific Giants. Dwarf varieties may flower in late May or June. With the taller varieties, like the Pacific Giants, plants don't bud as early and won't flower until June or July.

From liners: Commercial propagators usually carry a wide list of varieties that are available in many different liner or small cell pack sizes. These can be transplanted into quart or larger containers for spring sales. In general, allow seven to nine weeks at 50F (10C) nights for a quart pot to be salable after transplanting from a 52-cell tray.

From division: Plants dug and divided in early spring can be shifted into 1- or 2-gallon containers and sold four or five weeks later with several strong canes. Grow on at 50F (10C) nights.

VARIETIES

All of the following are seed propagated and come reliably true to type, although some off-types can be expected. Some cultivars are also vegetatively propagated. These are not as common in the United States or Canada, however.

Blue Fountains is a mixture of blue shades plus white. The 2-inch (5 cm) flowers are single to semidouble with few fully double blossoms. The plants grow 3 to 4 feet (90 to 120 cm) high, taller than Magic Fountains. In our Chicago climate, Blue Fountains is also hardier and earlier to emerge in the spring than Magic Fountains.

Blue Springs is a double-flowering mix of lavender and blue florets on separate plants. It reaches 2½ to 3 feet (75 to 90 cm) tall.

Magic Fountains contains seven separate colors plus a mixture. The plants are shorter than either the Pacific strain or Blue Fountains, growing 2½ to 3 feet (75 to 90 cm) tall. The 2¼-inch (5.7 cm) semi to fully double flowers appear on upright spikes 10 to 20 inches (25 to 51 cm) long.

Pacific Giant Strain (also called Round Table strain). A premier collection of upright and erect hybrid perennial delphiniums with 17- to 28-inch (43 to 71 cm), spirelike flower stalks. Developed in California in the late 1930s, this series grows 4 to 5 feet (1.2 to 1.5 m) tall the first season from seed and 6 feet (1.8 m) tall once established. Flowers are semi to fully double and measure up to 2½ inches (6 cm) across. Used either as a cut flower or a garden perennial, plants should be staked. The separate colors in this series are named after the legendary characters of King Arthur's

court in early Britain. They include the following, all of which have white "bees," except for Astolat and Black Knight, which display black "bees."
- Astolat, orchid-lavender blooms.
- Black Knight deep or dark blue flowers.
- Cameliard, lavender-rose flowers.
- Galahad, a pure white flowering variety.
- Guinevere, lavender-blue flowers.
- King Arthur, royal violet-blue flowers.
- Round Table Mix, a mixture of the above colors plus several others.

Additional Pacific Giant colors are available under non-Arthurian names such as Blue Bird (midblue flowers) and Summer Skies (light blue flowers).

RELATED MATERIAL

D. × belladonna (also called belladonna hybrids). The belladonna hybrids are the premier commercial cut flower selections. Plants are short, growing only 2 to 3 feet (60 to 90 cm) tall in our gardens. The flowers are single, 2 inches (5 cm) or less across, and don't have a scent. Free flowering and well branched, these plants can easily be grown from seed. Propagate and grow on as noted for *D. × elatum.* Hardy from Zones 4 to 7.
- Belladonna, light blue flowers.
- Bellamosum, a dark blue flowering variety.
- Casablanca, pure white flowers.

D. grandiflorum (also *D. grandiflorum* var. *chinensis*) is a perennial but is treated as an annual in North America. Plants grow quickly and can be sold as small flowering pot plants in the spring from a winter sowing. The flowers are single, from 1 to 1½ inches (2.5 to 4 cm) wide, in blue, violet, or white. These are dwarf-flowering delphiniums that reach a maximum height of 15 to 20 inches (38 to 51 cm). Rather than producing upright spikes of color, *D. grandiflorum* varieties often have a more rounded shape and can be used as a border in perennial and annual gardens for summer color. Plants readily die out in midwestern winters but may live on in temperate regions.

D. grandiflorum varieties are propagated by seed. The seed is smaller than any of the other delphiniums, with as much as 29,000 seeds per ounce (1,015 per gram). *D. grandiflorum* varieties can be sown with the other varieties listed above and will be salable in the same amount of time. One additional note: We sowed seed to a 220-plug tray in mid-January and transplanted one plug per 4-inch (10 cm) pot a month later. Growing them on at 65F (18C) nights and 72F (22C) days until early March, we then moved the plants to a cold frame at 45F to 50F (7C to 10C) nights.

The plants flowered at 10 inches tall the first week of May. Since we first ran that trial, we've moved up to 4½- and 5-inch (11 to 13 cm) pots.

Blue Mirror (Blauer Spiegel) has deep blue flowers on plants to 16 inches (41 cm) tall.

USES

Delphiniums are shunned in commercial landscapes in most parts of the country since they seldom provide enough color or look exceptional enough in mass plantings to justify the upkeep. However, I've seen some beautiful specimens along the coastal areas of the United States and Canada that were grown in large containers as accents in an outdoor shopping mall. Combined with other cool season plants like digitalis and verbascum, the effect was spectacular.

In the commercial cut flower trade, the most common varieties are the belladonna hybrids. These include Belladonna, Bellamosum, and Casablanca. In the home garden, however, any of the varieties listed above will work as cut flowers except for *D. grandiflorum* types because of their short stature. All varieties suitable for cutting can be used fresh or dried.

IN THE HOME GARDEN

Plant in a sunny location that's well drained and slightly raised to avoid excess water around the crowns of the plants. Plant hardiness depends on location in the garden. In general, delphiniums, mass-planted in island beds here in Chicago where they're exposed to the full elements of summer and winter, will seldom last more than two seasons. Instead, plant delphiniums around buildings, high shrubs, and other places where they'll get morning or midday sun but are sheltered from afternoon sun. They should also be protected from any buffeting winter winds.

In our West Chicago gardens, plants given this special care have lived three to six years. However, one to three years of life is common for the plants out in our fields, away from protection.

Plants don't need mulching or special treatment during the winter, and you definitely want to avoid covering them with materials that pool water around the crown. Some gardeners place evergreen boughs over the plants to provide aeration, decreasing the heaving/thawing of a northern spring.

Staking is usually required on the taller varieties, which get top heavy during flowering. The stems of all varieties are brittle and break easily. Don't pinch the plants back when planting but do remove any spent flower heads. Secondary flowers will develop on these plants, although they'll be noticeably smaller in spike length and flower size. If cut back after plants have flowered, a number of new shoots will emerge from below the soil surface. These will flower in about a month.

■ DENDRANTHEMA × GRANDIFLORA

(formerly *Chrysanthemum × morifolium*)

The genus *Chrysanthemum* has undergone major nomenclature revisions. Most U.S. growers know this crop by its former botanical name rather than this newly assigned genus. However, it's important to note that these updates are not done to confuse the issue but to identify the complex relationship of plants.

The garden chrysanthemum does not represent one species but a multitude of hybrids. The varieties on the market are the result of a number of crosses between various species, other varieties, and cultivars.

FAMILY: Asteraceae

COMMON NAME(S): Garden Chrysanthemum

DESCRIPTION

A range of flower forms, bloom sizes, habits, and colors contribute to the popularity and diversity of fall-flowering mums. Plants have leathery, aromatic, gray-green foliage on stems between 1 and 3 feet (30 to 90 cm) tall. The flowers vary in shape and size from 1 to 4 inches (2.5 to 10 cm) across and display the colors most often associated with autumn: bronze, crimson, red, gold, copper, yellow, white, purple, and lavender. Plants can spread from 12 to 15 inches (30 to 38 cm).

HARDINESS: Zones 5 to 9.

Depending on where they were planted and the clone you choose, chrysanthemums will probably be short lived in Zone 5 and north. Selection is the key to long-lasting chrysanthemums.

SEASON OF BLOOM: September and October.

PROPAGATION

Both divisions and cuttings are used to propagate this crop. Make divisions in the spring, and take cuttings in the spring and early summer. Seed is available but produces plants that are often weak in stature, short lived, and uneven in development.

GERMINATION OVERVIEW: 70,000 seeds per ounce/2,450 per gram.

Pretreatments: Seed germinates readily and requires no special treatments. Seed germinates in five to 10 days at 70F (21C) and can be left uncovered. Transplant seedlings in 15 to 25 days after sowing.

GROWING ON

Yoder Brothers of Barberton, Ohio, and Ball Seed Co. of West Chicago, Illinois, have provided growers with extensive notes on the production of garden mums over the years. Due to the depth of the information already available from these companies, I suggest you contact them for detailed culture sheets.

Note: Chrysanthemums are short day plants. They require days shorter than 12 hours to flower. By providing more than 12 hours of light, you can keep the plants vegetative to provide bigger plants for pot sales or stock plants for cutting material.

Crop time: Propagation from seed is discussed here, but the resulting plants are often of low quality. I've tried a number of times, but the plants aren't as pleasing to the eye as those that are propagated vegetatively. However, if you do grow from seed, seedlings develop quickly, and salable green transplants are ready for retail sales in a 32-cell pack in 10 to 11 weeks after sowing. If you prefer to sell plants green in 4-inch (10 cm) pots, allow 13 to 15 weeks from sowing for fully rooted plants. Like the vegetatively propagated varieties, garden mums grown from seed will branch better if pinched. However, to sell seed varieties green in the spring rather than in late summer, one pinch is all that is suggested, although it isn't really necessary. Granted, plants are not freely basal branching, but the price of the crop at the cash register doesn't usually justify the added work and crop time of a pinched crop.

If left unpinched, plants will grow 3 to 4 inches (7 to 10 cm) tall, with limited (if any) basal branching. If planted to the garden in May, they'll flower in September and October as the day length naturally decreases.

Take divisions in the spring, pot them up into quart or gallon pots, and sell them in the fall in full bloom. As for cuttings, you can purchase either unrooted stems or rooted liners from a number of companies in the spring for summer production. If you prefer, take your own cuttings in the spring and sell blooming plants in late summer in gallon pots.

VARIETIES

Dendranthema × *grandiflora* seed produces marginal plants and availability is limited in the United States. Varieties like Autumn Glory and Fashion are sold by a number of seed companies. Vegetative selections are far too numerous to discuss in detail, so I'd suggest you contact both Yoder Brothers and Ball Seed Co. for their listings.

RELATED MATERIAL

Chrysanthemum nipponicum (Nippon Daisy, Montauk Daisy) has large, single, 3- to 4-inch (7 to 10 cm) white flowers on plants from 2 to 3 feet (60 to 90 cm) tall—taller in southern locales. The foliage is deep green and somewhat thickened, and the leaves often drop from the lower one-third of the plant by the time it blooms in September. Propagate from tip cuttings taken in the spring, grow on through the summer, and sell green the following spring. However, this crop often dies out in Zone 5, preferring the less severe winter of the lower parts of Zone 6 instead.

Chrysanthemum pacificum (*Ajania pacifica*) is commonly called Gold and Silver Chrysanthemum. This plant grows from 12 to 24 inches (30 to 61 cm) tall and from 14 to 20 inches (35 to 51 cm) across. *Chrysanthemum pacificum* has dark green foliage highlighted with a ribbon of white around the outer edge of each leaf. The light yellow flower clusters develop late in the season, usually October, but the plant will be hit by frost before the crop has a chance to flower profusely in our West Chicago gardens.

Chrysanthemum pacificum is listed by many manuals as being hardy from Zones 5 to 8, but it rarely survives a winter here in our Zone 5 gardens when planted in the open. When planted next to the foundation of a home, under an overhang or other protective winter structure, the plants have a greater chance of living through a winter.

Propagate by tip cuttings during spring or summer, or home gardeners can divide the plants in the spring.

USES

Mums provide bright late summer and autumn color in the garden and add life at a time when most perennials are retiring for a winter's rest. Though most varieties are late summer or fall flowering, a number of varieties flower from June until September. The fall-flowering varieties are the best known. Home gardeners plant both types in the spring. For commercial plantings, however, most companies don't want them planted until they're showing their first color, usually around Labor Day or after.

IN THE HOME GARDEN

In our West Chicago gardens, mums grow best in full sun in a well-drained soil. They need to be divided once every three to four years. The faster growing varieties can be divided annually to increase the populations or share with friends. Mums don't normally require staking, though support is handy if plants are grown in fertile, moist soil and the new growth becomes weak.

Plants don't require any mulching for winter protection, but they don't appreciate water around the crown of the plant. In these cases, plants often rot and die out by spring.

■■ DIANTHUS BARBATUS

FAMILY: Caryophyllaceae

COMMON NAME(S): Sweet William

DESCRIPTION

This perennial is better known by consumers than many other dianthus species because of its reseeding performance, which provides color for years on end. Most varieties are biennial, flowering the second spring after planting. Annual flowering varieties are also available; in some cases, they rival the biennial ones in colors but often not in stature. The biennial varieties are often taller, stockier in habit, and more free flowering.

Sweet Williams grow 12 to 20 inches (30 to 51 cm) tall and from 14 to 20 inches (35 to 51 cm) wide with deep green foliage. They exhibit a basal branching habit. The flowers are one-half to three-quarter-inch (1 to 2 cm) wide, although some varieties grow larger (seldom over 1-inch [2.5 cm] wide). The numerous flowers are bunched together in a cluster at the top of the stem. Flowers are scentless but show some of the most vivid colors and markings available in *Dianthus*. Flower colors include red, rose, pink, violet, lavender, white, and also shades in between. The flowers often have "rings" or strands of deep carmine or another uniquely contrasting color around the inside of each blossom.

D

HARDINESS: Zones 4 to 9.

Sweet Williams enjoy cool conditions but are either biennial or annual. That means the plants often give one or two seasons of color but seldom last longer. However, they do reseed fairly easily.

SEASON OF BLOOM: May and June.

PROPAGATION

Seed is the usual method for propagating Sweet William, although cuttings taken during the summer from nonflowering stems work well also.

GERMINATION OVERVIEW: 25,000 seeds per ounce/875 per gram.

No pretreatments are necessary to get 70% or better final germination for this crop. Seeds sown onto a peat-lite media, lightly covered, and given 70F (21C) soil temperature will germinate in seven to 10 days. Seedlings can be transplanted in 13 to 18 days after sowing.

GROWING ON

Crop time: Crop times for green, salable plants in packs or pots don't differ between annual and biennial varieties. You should review the varieties listed below and those in seed catalogs to determine which you're getting, however. If all the plants bloom the same season as sown (summer flowering from a February or March sowing), they're annuals and will seldom overwinter here in the Midwest. Due to stress from a number of causes, biennial varieties may flower only sporadically the same year as sown. Depending on how much they flowered the first year, the plants often return at least one more spring.

The key point in growing is to consider your market. If you sell this plant in quarts or gallons after overwintering the plants in a cold frame, your customers are going to get one season of color. If the variety reseeds, the plants will return the following year, but this cannot be quaranteed. In general, allow 10 to 12 weeks for green packs (32 cells per flat). For quarts and gallons, sow directly to plug trays (72 or 112), or transplant your cell packs into the larger containers for green sales 13 to 15 weeks after sowing (gallon containers will require an additional two weeks to size up).

To reemphasize a previous point: January through March sowings of the biennial varieties for green sales in April through June won't flower that same year.

One final note on growing: The Ball Seed Co. conducted vernalization, or cold treatment, studies during the 1980s to test the number of weeks to get flowering on plants, which without the treatment, would not bloom. The variety Double Midget Mix was used. The following results are provided as a guideline and aren't suggested as standard practice. Sowings were made in late August. Seedlings were transplanted to cell packs in early September, potted to 4-inch (10 cm) round pots in late September, and then moved to a cold frame October 11. Plants were left on the floor of the cold frame where the daytime temperatures ranged from 50F to 58F (10C to 14C), and the nighttime lows ranged from 40F to 43F (4C to 6C). Eight pots were removed after four weeks of cold, and eight more were removed every two weeks after that so that we had plant material exposed to these temperatures at four, six, eight, 10, and 12 weeks.

The only important results were those observed from the 12-week treatment. To clarify the treatment, 12 weeks of the temperatures noted were given from October 11 until January 3. At the time the plants were brought into the greenhouse, there were no blooms or buds. After six to seven weeks of 73F (22C) days, 67F (19C) nights, however, we had budded or blooming plants on all eight pots. Remember that this study was conducted on a particular mixed variety, and single colors may react differently. Full bloom was achieved on all eight pots between February 15 and March 1.

By contrast, none of the other plants exposed to zero, four, six, or eight cold weeks flowered or budded up at all. However, three plants out of eight did bud up and flower after exposure to 10 weeks of the temperatures noted above.

The following August we duplicated our trial with similar results the following February and March. While the time frame may not offer you any sales possibility for March, manipulating the culture for your particular needs may prove valuable. One final comment: When in bloom, the plants were 4 to 6 inches (10 to 15 cm) tall (not including the pot) with an 8-inch (20 cm) spread. No growth regulators were applied, although during the greenhouse forcing period after the cold frame treatment, plants were grown under HID lights.

VARIETIES

All of the following varieties have the traditional Sweet William appearance: a primary flower color highlighted with a ring of deep rose towards the center of each petal. This ring can be as broad as half the length of the petal or as thin as a thread. But this variation is what's so distinctive about Sweet Williams.

The following varieties represent only a limited number of selections. There are many more listed by seed and plant companies. Often these are cut flower varieties, which are taller, but they work well in the perennial border.

Double Midget Mix is a dwarf-flowering variety, 8 inches (20 cm) tall in bloom. Flower colors are lavender, rose, pink, and white. This variety makes excellent quart pots, either green or in color. The blooms measure one-eighth to one-half inch (3 mm to 1 cm) across, in 2½- to 3½-inch-wide (6 to 9 cm) clusters. Unfortunately, the variety is close to being removed from the market due to low seed sales. In part, this may be due to lack of doubleness within the variety. At present, we've seen the variety flowering with 50% single flowers.

Double Mix is a taller variety to 18 inches (46 cm) in flower, with colors of of deep red, pink, rose, and white. Blooms are one-half inch (1 cm) across and reliably double.

Indian Carpet Mix is a dwarf-flowering variety to 8 inches (20 cm) tall in bloom, with all flowers exhibiting a prominent eye of either rose or red.

USES

Dianthus barbatus can be used in the perennial border as a specimen or border plant. It's seldom used for mass plantings since it has a limited flowering period in all parts of the United States except for temperate coastal climates like California. It doesn't bloom for more than two months even in these climates.

As a cut flower, *Dianthus barbatus* is frequently seen in mixed floral bouquets. The flowers are used fresh and can be harvested when 10% of the color shows. Strip off the bottom leaves and plunge the stems into water. The flowers last seven to 10 days, longer with a floral preservative.

IN THE HOME GARDEN

Dianthus barbatus is a traditional, old-time variety that has fallen out of favor. But what other crop presents such wonderful two-tone colors on plants that can be used either as an accent or for cut flowers, and one that will reseed year after year? And although not heavily scented, they do have a pleasant, light fragrance.

Unlike their cousins the carnations, taller Sweet William varieties seldom require staking because of their stockier habit, even though the plants are often freer to flower. Plant them into any well-drained location where the plants get morning and/or late afternoon sun but aren't exposed to sun during the hottest and most humid part of the day. If you're growing them out in the open—away from buildings or other similar protection—be sure to watch the plants in the spring. When grown in this environment, they're often prostrate due to snow compaction and winter rains. In the early spring, trim back the plants to encourage new growth and upright stems, especially on the tall varieties. If not trimmed, the plants will stay prostrate and produce flowers at the stem ends only several inches off the ground.

■■■ DIANTHUS CARYOPHYLLUS

Read the information under **Varieties** prior to sowing and growing this crop, especially if you aren't familiar with it.

FAMILY: Caryophyllaceae

COMMON NAME(S): Carnation

DESCRIPTION

Seldom reliable as a perennial in the central United States, carnations are best in climates with cool weather and bright sun. California and selected areas of the southern United States offer the best growing opportunities. See **In the home garden** for additional information.

Carnations have gray-green foliage with thickened leaves and nodes (areas where the leaves are attached) on basal-branching plants from 12 to 18 inches (30 to 46 cm) tall. Flowers are double in appearance, 2 to 3 inches (5 to 7 cm) wide, and spicily fragrant, often with the scent of cloves. Carnation varieties sold as annuals in the United States are easier to obtain and often outperform the perennial varieties in a number of traits. Annual types have better habits and suitability for pots, are more free flowering, have more blooms, and are available in more separate colors than the perennial varieties. In the cooler climates of Europe and England, perennial carnations in separate flower colors are available, but in the United States the short-lived nature of the plants is usually not worth the cost. Flower colors include red, white, pink, rose, salmon, and shades in between.

HARDINESS: Zones 6 to 8.

In our Chicago-area gardens (Zone 5), carnation plants frequently die out during a severely cold winter. Plantings seldom survive more than two years in our climate.

SEASON OF BLOOM: June and July.

PROPAGATION

Perennial carnation varieties are usually propagated by seed, but cuttings can be taken on vegetative shoots during the summer as well.

GERMINATION OVERVIEW: 14,000 seeds per ounce/490 per gram.

There are no pretreatments necessary for this crop. Germination rates of 70 to 96% are usual, depending on the year of harvest. Seed will germinate in five to 13 days at 65F to 70F (18C to 21C) and can be transplanted 15 to 20 days after sowing. It can be left exposed or lightly covered during germination.

GROWING ON

First and foremost, carnations love cool temperatures below 60F (16C) and bright light, which limit their best performance to only a few areas of this country, including the southern United States as a winter crop and the California coast.

Crop time: From seed, plants will not flower reliably the first season. February and March sowings seldom produce a flowering plant before autumn. Occasionally, sporadic plants will bloom during the summer, but they will ultimately suffer during August heat and humidity.

As for crop time, allow 11 to 13 weeks for 32-cell packs to be large enough to transplant or sell green. For flowering plants in quarts or gallons, sow seed in the late summer or early fall for overwintering in cold greenhouses. Don't allow the plants to go dormant.

D

VARIETIES

Carnations aren't reliably hardy in the United States and are often overrated as a cold-hardy perennial. They are actually tender perennials that tolerate cool weather with repeated frosts, but the severe cold and wet conditions of a northern winter or the intense heat and humidity of a southern summer make carnations more of a seasonal planting. Although the perennial selections are more reliably hardy in Europe and England, this isn't the case in the United States outside of selected areas of the West Coast and New England where plants may live throughout the year. In southern states from the Carolinas west to Texas, carnations will perform best when sown in late summer for fall, winter, and spring flowering.

Following this definition, the dwarf, compact plant varieties from 8 to 10 inches (20 to 25 cm) tall that are included in the **annual** section of any seed catalog could be substituted for the Grenadin series noted below. Varieties like Essence, Lillipot, Monarch, Knight, and others are better suited for 4- and 6-inch (10 to 15 cm) pot sales instead of summer bedding, although they can be used as such. Chabaud has been treated as a tender perennial with success, and since it's about 20 inches tall (51 cm), it makes a better show in borders than the annual varieties.

Chaubaud series. This variety has been available in many separate colors, but the mixture is usually sold on the market today. The flowers are fully double and make good cut flowers. Chabaud is propagated by seed.

Grenadin series. The predominant perennial carnation seed variety in the United States, Grenadin was readily available in both separate colors and as a mixture. Its popularity, however, has waned since it's not reliably hardy, so the mixture is more commonly seen these days. Separate colors, when found, include King of the Blacks, a deep burgundy red; Red, a truer shade than the previous variety; Pink, a medium rose pink; Golden Sun, a golden yellow; and White. Plants grow to 22 inches (56 cm) tall with $1\frac{1}{4}$- to $1\frac{3}{4}$-inch (3 to 4.4 cm) flowers with a heavy, clove-like fragrance.

RELATED MATERIAL

Dianthus × *allwoodii* (sometimes listed as a *D. plumarius* variety) [Border Pinks] is the result of crossing *D. caryophyllus* and *D. plumarius*, yielding plants with gray-green

191

foliage and mostly double flowers to 2 inches (5 cm) across. It provides the carnation color range but on more dwarf, more heat tolerant and longer-lived plants. In our Chicago climate, this class resembles carnations but on more spreading plants. Unlike the carnation, however, this crop grows in full sun, is winter hardy without mulch or other protection, and still returns year after year, flowering consistently in May and June. If the old flowers are removed, we often get return bloom during the summer, although sporadic. Cool nights in July and August greatly improve the chances for repeat flowering.

Dianthus × allwoodii, hardy from Zones 4 to 9, is propagated by cuttings. Our plantings have been in place since 1989, and we've never divided them. While divisions can be taken in either spring or fall, in our experience they don't yield enough plants for the commercial propagator. Cuttings are your best opportunity and can be taken in June after flowering is over.

In the home garden plants prefer a well-drained location where they will tolerate full sun, although afternoon shade is beneficial.

Aqua is a double-flowering, pure white selection on plants to 12 inches (30 cm) tall in our gardens. The blooms are 2 inches (5 cm) across and scented.

Dianthus gratianopolitanus (Cheddar Pink) develops dense mats of gray-green foliage growing to 12 inches (30 cm) tall in flower. The single or double blooms are 1 inch (2.5 cm) across and in shades of either rose or pink. Like some of the other dianthus species presented here, this one also varies in form and habit when grown from seed. Allan Armitage, in his book *Herbaceous Perennial Plants*, comments that the species is "almost indestructible" in the southern United States.

The following varieties are propagated by terminal cuttings taken after flowering. There are seed varieties available readily from a number of U.S. seed companies, but these are all mixtures flowering in June.

Spotty is a rose-red cultivar speckled with white on plants to 5 inches (13 cm) tall. It displays fairly consistent summer blooming, which first appears in June.

Tiny Rubies (Tiny Ruby) has double, deep rose blooms on plants to 4 inches (10 cm) tall. It flowers in May and June.

Dianthus plumarius (Cottage Pink) has a similar appearance to carnations but is shorter. Foilage is gray green on plants to 18 inches (46 cm) tall in flower. Cottage Pink plants are hardier than carnations for us in Chicago and more reliable during our summer heat. While plants are longer lived than carnations, varieties sown from seed vary in habit and height, and there can be both double and single flowers in the same crop. Flower colors include white, pink, and rose, although light lavenders are also present. The flowers are often banded with deep rose on the lighter flower colors for a bicolor effect. Flowers are 1½ inches (4 cm) across and scented. Plants bloom in May and June and, while variable, they show consistent color.

Seed sown anytime in the winter or spring will produce about 50% blooming plants the same year. Seed germinates in three to six days, and the seedlings can be transplanted 15 to 25 days after sowing. Green, 32-cell packs will be filled out and ready for sales or transplanting in 10 weeks. If grown during cold weather at 48F (9C) nights and days of 8F to 10F higher (4C to 6C), plants will branch basally and stay relatively compact. In warm temperatures—especially when planted in gallon pots—a growth regulator may be needed to keep plants in check.

January-sown seed, shifted to 4-inch (10 cm) pots for spring sales and planted into the garden by May or early June, will often flower in August of the same year, although sporadically. Once established, the plants will flower in spring rather than late summer.

In the home garden, plants will stay evergreen during the fall and winter in the Midwest. In early spring we cut the foliage back to remove all the brown and allow for new growth.

IN THE HOME GARDEN

In the northern United States, plant carnations in a location where they'll get morning sun and afternoon shade, especially during the hottest part of the summer. Staking will be needed to keep the plants upright when flowering, but other plants can be spaced closely to support leaning carnations. If this is your goal, choose erect and stocky plants as supportive neighbors, such as marigolds or physostegia.

As an alternative, choose one of the related varieties noted above—especially Aqua. These are enduring, uniform plants that deserve more attention from the American gardener.

DIANTHUS DELTOIDES

FAMILY: Caryophyllaceae

COMMON NAME(S): Maiden Pinks

DESCRIPTION

These dwarf, spreading plants grow to 12 inches (30 cm) tall. The commonly grown varieties in the United States are usually 8 inches (20 cm) or less. Single blooms appear in shades of pink and rose, although cultivars are also available in salmon, white, and crimson. The flowers are scented and cover the plants in the spring. Some varieties flower sporadically the remainder of the summer, but others put on a strong show of spring color and then remain green the rest of the summer. Plants spread 12 to 20 inches (30 to 51 cm), although some varieties grow a little larger on either coast of the United States.

HARDINESS: Zones 3 to 9.

SEASON OF BLOOM: June and July, longer for some varieties.

PROPAGATION

Seed is a common propagation method and will yield similar results from year to year, although a limited number of off-types can be expected. Cuttings can be taken during the spring or summer from nonflowering shoots.

GERMINATION OVERVIEW: 48,000 seeds per ounce/1,680 per gram.
No pretreatments are necessary to get uniform germination. Seeds will germinate in seven to 10 days at 68F (20C), seven days or sooner if germinated at 72F (22C). Lightly cover seed during germination or leave it exposed. Seedlings will be transplantable 20 to 25 days after sowing.

GROWING ON

Crop time: Production for salable green or flowering transplants varies by cultivar. Varieties like Zing Rose will grow and develop faster than Brilliant. Zing Rose will fill out a 32-cell pack in 10 to 12 weeks. A mid-February sowing yields salable green plants in late April or May, which flower by late May. Plants aren't free flowering, but rather are sparsely covered with deep, vivid, carmine-rose flowers (see additional information under **Varieties**). Brilliant will require one to two additional weeks to fill out the same cell pack, and plants will appear thinner when grown side by side. This variety doesn't flower for us the same season from seed and requires vernalization before plants will bloom.

For quart and larger container sales in the spring, sow seed the previous summer, transplant to the final container, and overwinter dormant for flowering plants the following spring. For pot sales of Zing Rose in the spring, sow in December or January and grow on cool, alongside annual dianthus or pansies.

Commercial propagators have many cell pack sizes available in a wide range of varieties. When purchased in winter, these can be potted up into 4-inch (10 cm), quart, or gallon containers for spring sales. Depending on the variety, crop time ranges from six to nine weeks to fill out a quart container from a 72-cell tray when grown on at no less than 48F (9C) nights, with day temperatures 8F to 10F higher (4C to 6C).

Like most dianthus varieties, this crop prefers cool growing temperatures of 50F to 55F (10C to 13C) in order to stay low growing and basal branching. Avoid warm temperatures of 65F (18C) and above, especially at night, which produces excessive soft growth and ruins later performance.

VARIETIES

D. deltoides is available from numerous retail and commercial seed companies across the United States, but it's not as popular as the following selections. Plants grow 6 to 8 inches (20 to 25 cm) tall and have one-half-inch-wide (1 cm), clear pink flowers.

Brilliant is a single-flowering, rose-red variety on 6- to 8-inch-tall (15 to 20 cm) plants. The flowers only develop in the spring, and the plants seldom bloom longer than three weeks. Winter sowings usually don't produce flowering plants the same year.

Flashing Light (Leuchtfunk, Fanal) is a deep scarlet-red flowering variety to 6 inches (15 cm) tall. The plants have dark or bronzed foliage arranged tightly around the crown. Sowings made in winter seldom produce flowering plants the same year.

Zing Rose is a vivid carmine-rose variety about 8 inches (20 cm). It's larger leaved with a broader spread than either Brilliant or Flashing Light. The flowers are single, 1 inch (2.5 cm) across, and appear all summer long from June to September. While plants flower the first season from seed, bloom is more profuse the second year. Some report that the plants are short-lived, but our plants have survived for two years without problems, even the ones on raised berms that are exposed to winter's worst weather without a mulch.

RELATED MATERIAL

Dianthus arenarius is a low, ground-hugging variety that appears to spread across the ground like icing spreads across the top of a cake. The foliage is gray green. Plants grow between 2 and 3 inches (5 to 7 cm) when not in flower, 7 to 10 inches (18 to 25 cm) when in full bloom. See Color Plate 36 for photo of *Dianthus arenarius*.

The single flowers are 1 inch (2.5 cm) across and pure white with a carmine-rose thread or thin band positioned around the entire blossom, one-eighth inch (3 mm) from the flower center. This line of color isn't dramatic looking but does give an unusual highlight to the variety.

Winter or spring sowings will flower only sporadically the same season from seed. Sow seed in March for green transplants in a 32-cell pack 11 to 12 weeks later. Grow at 55F (13C) night temperatures. These can be sold as is or moved into quart or gallon pots for sales during late summer or overwinter for sales the following year. In general, you can expect 10 to 15% first-year flowering when sown from January through March. While normal flowering is in May, seed sown in February will flower in July of the same year. In subsequent years, *D. arenarius* flowers in May.

Dianthus knappii may be the only yellow-flowering variety within the *Dianthus* genus. The flowers are light yellow or buff colored, scentless, and between one-half and three-quarter inch (1 to 2 cm) across. Blooms are single and rather open in appearance. The stems are primarily upright, weak, and can require staking in a pot if not kept cool and controlled by a growth regulator. Plants grow 15 to 20 inches (38 to 51 cm) tall but can get taller when grown in a gallon pot under warmer temperatures. Ours have grown as tall as 26 inches (66 cm) in pots when raised in a cold frame during summer.

Winter sowings through April will flower the same season from seed, although the plants will not be free flowering. This is true of established plants as well. When sown as a winter crop in February, seedlings emerge in four to eight days and can be transplanted into a cell pack or small pot in 20 to 25 days. These packs can be transplanted into quart containers for sales in another seven to nine weeks. The total crop time from seed to 50% in bloom is 16 to 19 weeks when grown the first six months of the year. If sown from seed during late summer or autumn, flowering is less assured within the provided time frame, as the plants don't flower well under short days.

While the variety may be hardy in Zones 3 to 8, we have treated it as a tender perennial due to its unreliability in returning from year to year in our Zone 5 gardens.

USES
Plants make perfect borders or edgings where a semitrailing plant is wanted. *Dianthus deltoides* isn't invasive and is easily controlled when planted around the outer edges of landscapes. The plants can also be used in rock gardens as well, but for this use, Zing Rose may be too large.

IN THE HOME GARDEN
Plants prefer well-drained, full-sun sites in our Chicago location. Like many dianthus species, the plants will tolerate sunnier exposures but prefer afternoon shade during the hottest and most humid times of the year. The farther south you go, the more important this is. Full-sun exposures here in Chicago will result in short-lived plants. Dianthus plants often succumb to the summer heat in Zones 8 and 9 since there's seldom enough time for them to recover before winter arrives.

Plants often remain evergreen during winter, so we lift up the foliage at the crown and trim away the dead growth prior to the regrowth in the spring. No special care or treatment is necessary, including mulching.

■ DICENTRA SPECTABILIS

FAMILY: Fumariaceae

COMMON NAME(S): Japanese Bleeding Heart, Common Bleeding Heart

DESCRIPTION
Graceful and elegant, *Dicentra spectabilis* arching wands of heart-shaped flowers are unmatched for form. The leaves are not as deeply cut as in other *Dicentra* species and are often larger. Individual blooms are 1-inch (2.5 cm) high and mostly pink to rose, although white is also available. The foliage dies back to the ground during mid or late summer. Plants grow 24 to 30 inches (61 to 76 cm) tall, spreading from 15 to 20 inches (38 to 51 cm) across.

HARDINESS: Zones 3 to 9.

SEASON OF BLOOM: May and June.

PROPAGATION

Division is preferred for propagating *Dicentra spectabilis*, although both cuttings and seed can also be used. Named cultivars have to be propagated vegetatively to maintain the integrity of the variety, while seed can reproduce the species. *D. spectabilis* can also be propagated by root cuttings taken during the winter. Additional information is provided in the **Propagation Techniques** chapter regarding this method. Take divisions in the spring or fall; while stem cuttings are best taken during the spring. Some growers have succeeded with stem cuttings taken after flowering as well.

GERMINATION OVERVIEW

Dicentra spectabilis germinates best when using fresh seed. Seed can be collected in August and September and sown immediately to protected cold frames for overwintering for spring emergence.

Commercial growers need an easier method of seeding, though time and patience will still be required. Upon gathering your own seed, follow the procedures for warm-moist stratification as noted in the **Propagation Techniques** chapter. In some cases, we can take the freshly harvested seed, sow it into moistened peat moss and chill in a refrigerator for six to eight weeks at 40F (4C). Following this we remove the germination tray to the greenhouse bench and germinate the seeds at 60F to 65F (16C to 18C). Regardless, emergence is erratic and transplanting is done over a period of time (starting seven to 10 weeks after raising the temperatures to 60F to 65F [16C to 18C]). If germination is low (20 to 40%), return the germination tray to the refrigerator for another two to four weeks and repeat the above. If germination is lower than 10%, you should treat as a warm-moist germinator, as noted earlier, and follow those procedures.

Some additional points: We have never gotten over 60% total germination on this crop. Transplanting was done over a three-week period resulting in plants of various ages on the greenhouse bench, yielding different crop times. Finally, seed collected or received during late summer and then stored dry until February or March before sowing has repeatedly given us 0% germination with some type of pretreatment.

GROWING ON

From seed: Seedlings emerging in the winter or spring will require up to a year before they fill out a gallon container. It will take one full summer to develop a plant large enough to produce blooms the following spring.

Commercial propagators have bare-root divisions available during late fall and winter. Many times these are already precooled so the roots can be planted to produce flowering pot plants for the winter and early spring holidays or potted up during mid to late winter for spring perennial plant sales. The roots are potted up into 3- or 4-quart containers and grown on at 50F to 55F (10C to 13C) nights. *Dicentra spectabilis* will develop quickly, and February or March potted roots will yield flowering plants in five to seven weeks. If grown under cooler night temperatures or under prolonged, cloudy springs, the plants will require up to one to two weeks longer to flower.

The crop time for a flowering pot plant for an early Easter or for Valentine's Day is from six to seven weeks at 50F to 55F (10C to 13C) nights. For plants that are to flower during winter and early spring, research by Thomas Weiler and Pamela K. Markham suggests that a 1,250 to 2,500 ppm B-Nine application is effective when applied early. They suggest that the ideal time is when "...the emerging sprout(s) begin to unfold, 10 to 19 days after planting at 50F to 55F night temperature(s)." [1]

VARIETIES

D. spectabilis is readily available from commercial propagators across the United States as a bare-root division or potted perennial. Some commercial seed houses carry this crop as well, though seed exchanges and societies are more reliable in shipping fresh seed.

D. spectabilis var. *alba* is not as vigorous as the species but has pure white flowers on plants from 20 to 30 inches (51 to 76 cm) tall. It flowers in May and June on light green foliage.

RELATED MATERIAL

Dicentra eximia (fringed bleeding heart, plume bleeding heart, eastern gray-green bleeding heart) is a native perennial with deeply cut leaves that are almost fernlike in appearance. The flowers are pink to lavender in color, although several other colors are available too. The blooms are heart shaped to an inch (2.5 cm) and nod in the breeze on flowering scapes to 15 inches (38 cm) long.

You're most likely to find this selection from seed companies specializing in native perennials or through seed exchanges. Conversely, you can also gather your own from stock plants. Fringed bleeding heart purchased from commercial propagators' plants could either be from bare-root divisions or from seeds. Mature height is 15 inches (38 cm).

The following cultivars may be seen as selections of *D. eximia* or *D. formosa*. While both species are available, confusion exists as to the proper parentage of the cultivars. Therefore, suppliers may list their selections differently depending on which botanical reference they used or from whom they bought their plants.

Except for the species, the following cultivars are more tolerant of sun and can be put in areas with some afternoon sun.

Luxuriant is considered by many to be a hybrid of the two species, *D. eximia* and *D. formosa*. Plants have cherry-rose flowers and bloom from May until frost (though not always free flowering), on plants to 15 inches (38 cm) tall. Luxuriant is probably the most popular variety due to its long flowering period. In our gardens, first year potted roots produced flowering plants in eight weeks. These plants sporadically flowered in the garden all summer long. It is vegetatively propagated.

Zestful is also considered to be the result of a cross. It has large pink flowers from May until frost. It's vegetatively propagated.

Snowdrift is vegetatively propagated only. It displays pure white flowers in May with repeat bloom during the summer. It grows 12 to 15 inches (30 to 38 cm) tall.

The cultivars of *D. eximia* are commonly propagated vegetatively or by seed, though the clones are vegetatively propagated only. In both cases, treat as you would *D. spectabilis*. One additional comment on growing on: When potting up *D. eximia* and *D. spectabilis* cultivars on the same day, some *D. eximia* selections—especially Luxuriant—are more filled out but shorter in the pot, and they may take from one to two weeks longer to flower. Conversely, if used as a pot plant for winter sales, the plants seldom need a growth regulator to keep their shape.

USES

The unusual flower form is the highlight of these two species. Ferny foliage is an additional quality in *D. eximia*. Plant these two varieties in the shaded perennial border.

Plants can also be used in the home cut flower garden. I prefer the blooms of *D. spectabilis* over *D. eximia*. They have longer stems and fit better in arrangements.

In the commercial landscape, avoid large uses of *D. spectabilis*, especially in areas where summers are hot and humid—this tends to speed up the plant's decline. *D. eximia* will continue to flower during the summer and autumn but usually stops blooming when night temperatures are above 80F (26C). At this point the foliage will be the key attribute until the flowers reappear.

IN THE HOME GARDEN

Plant in areas where the plants get morning sun and afternoon shade. As pointed out above, the cultivated varieties of *D. eximia* can take more sun but require moisture and a tighter spacing than their shade-grown counterparts. Space plants 15 to 18 inches (38 to 46 cm) apart, and plant in groups of three or four to create a mass.

D. spectabilis will go dormant by summer's end. Here in our Chicago gardens, the plants often go downhill during August. If the summer has been particularly hot and humid, most of our plants disappear by Labor Day. Otherwise, late September is when plants usually die back to the ground.

All varieties prefer a moist, though well-drained, site and will not tolerate wet winter soils. Conversely, the plants are not drought tolerant and will either die out or die back prematurely.

REFERENCES

[1] Weiler, T.C., and P.K. Markham. 1986. Eight steps to better Bleeding Hearts. *Greenhouse Grower*. January.

▄▄ DICTAMNUS ALBUS (D. FRAXINELLA)

FAMILY: Rutaceae

COMMON NAME(S): Gas Plant, Burning Bush, Dittany, and Fraxinella

DESCRIPTION

Dictamnus albus is a long-lived perennial. Its common name derives from the release of volatile oils that can ignite at the light of a match (additional information is provided under **In the home garden**). Both flower and foliage possess glands that release the oils; the foliage, when crushed, will have the smell of citrus. Flowers are white, single, fragrant, rather open and from 1 to 2 inches (2.5 to 5 cm) across in size. The flowers develop in spikes from 10 to 12 inches (25 to 30 cm) long on plants from 2 to 3 feet (60 to 90 cm) tall in flower. This is a hardy and dependable plant.

HARDINESS: Zones 3 to 8.

SEASON OF BLOOM: June.

PROPAGATION

Dictamnus albus is propagated by seed. Divisions are also possible but difficult, so they're done mostly by the home gardener, not the commercial grower. Seed may offer the commercial grower a challenge as well, since it's not easy to germinate. If you specialize in easy perennials, *D. albus* will not be one of your choices.

Divisions are difficult due to possible crown damage. In dividing and moving this plant, we've noted that clean cuts to the roots result in the best performance. A spade plunged straight down through the plant's center, cutting the roots cleanly without severe bruising, gave us the best results.

GERMINATION OVERVIEW

Pretreatments: Seed gathered off the plant in the late summer and sown immediately to a cold frame, nursery bed, or other protected site will germinate the following spring. Seed stored in a packet and finally sown during winter at 70F usually doesn't germinate at all.

Moist chilling will help to improve overall germination. In our tests, germination rates of 50 to 65% were common when using this method. Additional information is provided in the front of this book regarding moist chilling. See **Propagation** chapter.

There are some authors who suggest sowing to a flat, allowing the seeds to absorb moisture for a period of several weeks, and then placing seed flats in a cooler or refrigerator. I, too, have found some value in this, but I've often observed repeated "flushes" of germination over a period of time. Follow the procedures for warm-moist stratification followed by moist chilling as noted in the front of this book in the **Propagation Techniques** chapter.

One final comment regarding seed: If you're collecting seed from your own plants, cover the seedheads with cheesecloth bags, nylon stockings or similar materials because the ripening seed pods will explode open upon maturing, spewing seed all over.

D

GROWING ON

Crop time: From seed, seedlings will not develop into salable plants the first year. Since the seeds are sown in the autumn and germinated during March and April of the following year, they're not large enough to sell until the fall a full year after sowing, and even then they will be small. Once seedlings have emerged, transplant them into quart or gallon containers for growing on during the summer. These plants are overwintered and sold the following spring.

This perennial will not flower at all the same year it germinates and will have limited bloom the second year. The best color will occur the third year after germination.

VARIETIES

Dictamnus albus isn't readily available from most U.S. seed companies due to its germination difficulty. It is more available from seed companies specializing in perennial seed varieties.

D. albus var. *purpureus* (var. *rubra*) is a beautiful plant that I grew for many years on my parents' farm in Iowa. The flowers are soft pink in color highlighted with red veins. Plants grow from 2 to 3 feet (60 to 90 cm) tall and flower in June and/or July.

IN THE HOME GARDEN

This is a reliable and hardy perennial that's long lived in the perennial border or flower bed and requires little maintenance. The plants perform best in full sun. While not overly drought tolerant, the plants do better in well-drained locations. It doesn't require staking or any special treatments for active growth and development.

Most garden authors suggest you leave these plants undisturbed after planting and avoid moving them from spot to spot within the garden. It has been necessary for us to move our plants around to various beds. Granted, digging up plants that have been firmly established in their previous spot for three years or more will provide a challenge, but plants located in the garden only for two or three years have been more easily moved. Dividing the roots, however, can lead to plant death and needs to be done carefully. A sharp spade quickly forced deeply down the center of plant to slice the roots cleanly in half without injuring them has been successful for us. If you're struggling with the roots as you divide—twisting, turning and forcing your way down the crown—you'll be assured of failure.

Many people have tried unsuccessfully to hold a lighted match to this plant's blossoms on a calm night to see the puff of blue flame that many a text claims will appear. Some references state the oils are more readily released from the flower while others say it is the stem. In one meager, but successful, attempt of mine, I held the flaming match near the stem below the inflorescence and noticed a sudden flare of the match. Granted, it was short, more humorous in appearance than awe-inspiring, but, nonetheless, it happened. Regrettably, these same oils have been known to cause dermatitis in some people.

▰▰ DIGITALIS PURPUREA

FAMILY: Schrophulariaceae

COMMON NAME(S): Foxglove

DESCRIPTION

A premier plant, *Digitalis purpurea* is fondly remembered by older gardeners but used less today than it was just 20 years ago. The plants are true biennials, rosetting the first season from seed with vertical spikes the following spring. Plants grow to 4 or 5 feet (1.2 to 1.5 m) tall and 3 feet (90 cm) across.

The 1½-inch (3 cm) flowers are purple, pink, or white in color and muted or pastel in shade. Flowers are tubular, up to 3 inches (7 cm) long, and the throats are spotted with crimson or lavender shades. This is a dramatic and imposing plant in bloom.

HARDINESS: Zones 4 to 8.

SEASON OF BLOOM: June.

PROPAGATION

Seed is the most reliable method for propagating foxglove: it yields relatively high germination percentages for a perennial and is easy to do. Due to the plant's biennial nature, seed also offers the most consistent cropping of any propagation technique.

In some climates, *Digitalis purpurea* may act like a perennial, so a few references mention division as an accepted form of propagation. However, this method is for home gardeners and not commercial growers.

GERMINATION OVERVIEW: 126,000 seeds per ounce/4,410 per gram.
Pretreatments: Seeds will germinate readily and no pretreatments are necessary. Germination temperatures of 60F to 65F (15C to 18C) have been recommended for decades as the best for overall germination on this crop. While this is true, it will also germinate just as well—and several days faster—when temperatures of 70F to 72F (21C to 22C) are used. Above these temperatures seedlings will stretch. Seeds shouldn't be covered during germination. Seedlings emerge in five to 10 days and are transplantable 15 to 20 days after sowing.

GROWING ON

Crop time: On most varieties, winter sowings will not produce flowering plants the following spring or summer—until plants receive a cold treatment. If seed is sown December through March, the plants will not flower until the following year. However, one variety, Foxy, will flower as an annual if started early enough from seed.

For spring flowering plants, *Digitalis purpurea* can be sown any time the previous year until November. Sow seed during July or August for seedlings large enough to transplant to 4-, 5-, or 6-quart containers. Plants are fast growing and we've sown as late as September for gallon pots large enough to overwinter dormant by Christmas.

Sowings made during the late summer or fall can be transplanted to their final container (a 1- or 2-gallon pot) during December or January and grown cold (but not dormant) during the winter. Remember that *Digitalis purpurea* responds well to cold temperatures, so to keep the plants from growing too large, keep the night temperatures between 40F to 45F (5C to 7C). In our northern location, plants will be salable quickly—possibly before the weather warms up enough to plant to the garden. Therefore evaluate this method before pursuing. When these plants are placed in the garden in late April or early May, they will flower sporadically during late spring or early summer. Often foxglove lives through one more winter and will flower more profusely the following spring.

This culture is based on Giant Excelsior; other varieties may perform differently. Foxy should be sown during December, potted one plant to a 2-, 3- or 4-quart container and grown on at 45F to 48F (7C to 9C) nights once established. These plants often flower during June, either in the pot or in the garden.

VARIETIES

Foxy is a mixture—rose, lavender, cream, yellow, and white. Plants reach 36 inches (91 cm) or less. In our Chicago climate, the plants seldom grow over 2 feet (60 cm) tall when sown January or later, though I have seen them grow taller on both the East and West Coast. Plants should be treated as hardy annuals or tender perennials since they often flower the same year as sown from seed but seldom overwinter.

Giant Excelsior is the best-known foxglove mixture. It is also sold as Excelsior Hybrid or Excelsior Mix. Plants are large and stately, growing to between 4 and 6 feet (1.2 to 1.8 m) tall the second year after sowing. Flowers are primarily pink or cream with spotted throats, but additional colors of white, purple, and pale primrose are sometimes seen in the mix.

RELATED MATERIAL

Digitalis × *mertonensis* (strawberry foxglove) grows from 2½ to 3 feet (75 to 90 cm) tall although taller in warmer climates. The common name is derived from the light rose pink flowers. *D.* × *mertonensis* is a result of crossing *D. grandiflora* with

D. *purpurea* and is more long lived than D. *purpurea* in our Chicago climate, lasting from two to three seasons.

Seed is readily available in North America and can be treated the same as D. *purpurea*.

USES

Cottage and home gardens have long used this crop. Since the plants are biennial, they're considered uneconomical by landscapers because they're short lived. The best areas in the United States for landscaping with foxgloves are coastal California and other temperate climate areas. The plants perform well when night temperatures are cooler and in the long days of spring. High temperatures and humidity lead to rapid flower decline, and once flowering is over, the plants seldom flower again the same season.

IN THE HOME GARDEN

D. *purpurea* is at home in full sun and a well-drained but moist location. In our Chicago gardens, however, we avoid planting it out in open locations away from buildings or other unprotected sites. In these locations, the plants are often short lived, dying out from crown rot or winter kill. Instead, we place the plants in the back of the border close to the foundation or under an overhang for best performance. Plants don't require staking during flowering, but if planted to open areas, staking may be necessary. If the ground is left undisturbed around the base of the plant, self-sown seedlings often emerge during the late summer after seed drop.

■ DORONICUM CAUCASICUM

Botanical references differ on the species. Most of the American trade recognizes D. *caucasicum*, although both D. *cordatum* and D. *orientale* are sometimes used to define this species as well.

FAMILY: Asteraceae

COMMON NAME(S): Leopard's Bane

DESCRIPTION

One of the earliest perennials to flower, *Doronicum caucasicum* is a hardy but often short-lived plant in Midwestern gardens. The scentless flowers are single to semi-double, golden-yellow, with a daisylike form. They measure up to 2½ inches (6 cm) across. The flowers are held terminally on plants to 2 feet (60 cm) tall. Foliage is kidney shaped, deep green in color, and spreads to 15 inches (38 cm) across.

HARDINESS: Zones 4 to 7.

SEASON OF BLOOM: April and May.

PROPAGATION

Doronicum caucasicum is frequently propagated by seed and division. Most plants on the market come from seed. Divisions can be taken either in fall or spring.

GERMINATION OVERVIEW: 26,000 seeds per ounce/910 per gram.

Historically, I've often had trouble getting good germination rates on *D. caucasicum*. My own germination percentages have ranged from a disgusting 10% all the way to a meager 45% over the years. In my book, *The Ball Culture Guide*, 2nd edition, I went so far as to say that "...Germination for doronicums is always low; order seed accordingly." [1] Since then, however, we have tried several techniques that have proved beneficial in raising our percentages.

Seedlings will emerge in 14 to 21 days after sowing when germinated at 68F to 72F (20C to 22C). If the seed has been stored for any length of time, germination occurs over a longer period of time. Winter- or spring-sown seed in the greenhouse yields germination percentages of 70 to 85%, but the time extends from 14 to 35 days. Seed that is sown fresh yields the same percentages but usually in two to three weeks.

Seeds can be lightly covered or left exposed during germination. If covered, use a thin layer of coarse vermiculite over the media.

GROWING ON

From seed: This perennial flowers in spring once its cold requirement has been met. If seed is sown in December and grown on in 4-inch (10 cm) or quart containers, plants won't flower until spring of the following year. For spring-flowering plants, sow seed the previous July, transplant to quart containers using one or two plants per pot during late summer, and overwinter dormant in a cold frame.

VARIETIES

D. caucasicum. Sometimes sold as *D. cordatum*, this variety is available from numerous seed companies and will be easy to find.

Finesse has larger, fuller blooms than the species and with longer stems. It's sometimes listed as a variety of *Doronicum orientale*. Maximum height is 20 inches (51 cm) tall.

Magnificum is more uniform than the species but similar in overall appearance and habit. It grows to 20 inches (51 cm).

USES

Doronicum is effective in the perennial border as an accent planting. Large mass plantings should be avoided due to the short duration of flowering and expected heat stall during the summer.

It can be used as a home cut flower lasting five to 10 days once cut.

IN THE HOME GARDEN

Space 8 to 10 inches (20 to 25 cm) apart and plant in full sun or partially shaded areas where summers are excessively hot. Plants do best in cool summer climates and can go completely dormant in areas with long, hot, and humid summers—primarily in the South. In our Midwest location, plants don't go completely dormant but often suffer in mid to late August without some midafternoon shade.

This perennial prefers a moist but well-drained site. Plants have a two-week flowering period and won't rebloom during our midwestern summers. Plants are reliable but summer drought can kill them. Staking isn't necessary.

REFERENCES

[1] Nau, J. 1993. *Ball culture guide.* 2nd ed. Batavia, Ill.: Ball Publishing.

■ DUCHESNEA INDICA (FRAGARIA INDICA)

FAMILY: Rosaceae

COMMON NAME(S): Indian Strawberry, Mock Strawberry

DESCRIPTION

Duchesnea indica is an aggressive, trailing plant similar in habit, size, and overall form to the common strawberry, thus its common name. *Duchesnea indica* differs from *Fragaria indica* in its yellow flowers and its prostrate runners' rampant movement across the soil surface. These plants are extremely invasive in our Chicago gardens and have become naturalized in selected areas of the eastern United States. In milder winters, the bright green, three-lobed foliage is evergreen. The blooms are single, one-half to 1 inch (1 to 2.5 cm) across and, once pollinated, they give rise to small, bright red fruits. Plants grow 4 to 6 inches (10 to 15 cm) tall but can spread 6 to 8 feet (1.8 to 2.4 m) across in three or four years after planting.

HARDINESS: Zones 4 to 8.

SEASON OF BLOOM: April to June.
Plants flower sporadically during the summer.

PROPAGATION

Duchesnea indica is easily propagated by removing the already rooted runners that develop so vigorously. A single prostrate runner or stem can develop as many as six shoots along its 18-inch (46 cm) length, each with a root system. You can cut off the stem at the crown, separate each plantlet, and either allow them to root further, or pot them up into 2-inch (5 cm) pots. Once these are fully rooted, they can be potted up into either quarts or gallons.

GROWING ON

Crop time: Runners can be separated anytime during the growing season, although early spring and late summer propagation will offer the best performance. In early to mid-March in Chicago and other areas of Zone 5, it's easy to go through the nursery bed and remove started plants, probably enough for your spring sales without the work of overwintering the plants in a cold frame.

Pot these up into 4-inch (10 cm) or quart containers and grow on in a cold frame or other protected area at 50F to 55F (10C to 13C) nights, days that are warmer by 8F to 10F (4C to 6C). If the plants are growing too slow, raise the night temperatures to between 58F and 60F (15C to 16C). In general, pots finish in five to eight weeks depending on how well rooted you want the finished products to be.

If you prefer, you can dig up or transplant rooted plantlets in the late summer for potting to their final container by the first of October. Allow these to fully root into a quart container (usually by Thanksgiving) and then overwinter them in a cold 32F (0C) cold frame or similar structure for spring sales.

VARIETIES

Duchesnea indica is so vigorous that many growers keep their own plants and propagate as needed. While not difficult to find, this plant is sometimes considered a weed, so be prepared to handle it appropriately.

USES

An excellent plant for ground cover use in difficult areas, especially on sloping embankments, hillsides, and rocky outcrops. The plants also work well in bright woodland settings. Once firmly established, the plants will grow profusely.

IN THE HOME GARDEN

Most references suggest that this plant is best in semishade in a moist but well-drained location. However, the plants we have are in full sun on a raised berm 6 feet (1.8 m) high. While they get irrigated once every two weeks if needed, they have always grown rampantly.

No special winter or summer care is required for long-term performance. I would suggest, however, that every late winter (early March) you look over the planting and remove any runners that have grown into any companion plantings. If left undisturbed, at least six new plantlets will develop from each stem left from the previous summer.

E

■ ECHINACEA PURPUREA (SYN. RUDBECKIA PURPUREA)

FAMILY: Asteraceae

COMMON NAME(S): Purple Coneflower

DESCRIPTION

A perennial native to the American prairie, *E. purpurea* is a uniformly branching plant growing from 2½ to 3 feet (75 to 90 cm) tall and 20 to 28 inches (51 to 71 cm) wide. The 4- to 5-inch (10 to 13 cm), single flowers are a vivid rose-purple color highlighted by an orange and brown center when in full bloom. The leaves are deep green and don't attract powdery mildew as easy as their cousins, the Gloriosa daisies. This wilder selection has recessed petals (instead of laying flat or horizontally, the petals fall downward), while the newer cultivars on the market have a flat petal arrangement more preferred for cut flowers or for mass planting in the garden. See Color Plate 37 for photo of *Echinacea purpurea*.

HARDINESS: Zones 3 to 9.

In our climate, hardiness of the rose-purple flowering varieties isn't in question. These are often long lived and can even reseed. However, the white-flowering varieties, specifically White Swan, are often short lived for us, dying out within two seasons after planting. See additional comments under **In the home garden**.

SEASON OF BLOOM: July to September.

PROPAGATION

E. purpurea can be easily propagated from seed, divisions, or cuttings. Seed yields similar germination percentages regardless of what time of the year it is sown. Divisions are mostly the province of home gardeners, not commercial growers. Divisions are done in the spring or fall, while basal cuttings are best taken in spring.

GERMINATION OVERVIEW: 8,000 seeds per ounce/280 per gram.

Germination temperatures are 65F to 70F (18C to 21C); you can leave the seed exposed to light or lightly cover it during germination. Seeds germinate in 10 to 15 days; transplanting can begin 20 to 28 days after sowing the seed.

GROWING ON

Crop time: From seed, sowings made of any of the named seed varieties will flower during summer when sown in winter. Regardless of whether they were transplanted to the garden from cell packs or pots, seed-propagated varieties are quick to flower.

January sowings transplanted to small packs to get some growth and then transplanted to 4-inch (10 cm) or quart containers will be salable in May. For well-rooted quarts or gallons, sow in December or purchase in started plugs. Grow on at no less than 50F unless plants are growing too fast.

Allow 10 to 12 weeks for green packs for sale in early May; these plants will then flower during the summer. Plants in 4½-inch (11 cm) pots will need 13 to 15 weeks.

Commercial propagators often have *Echinacea* varieties available in a number of liner or plug sizes for faster finishing. These are primarily produced from seed and will finish in a 4-inch (10 cm) or quart container within a matter of weeks. Some companies sell in larger pack sizes to allow for deeper rooting. These plants can be sold as is or potted up into 1- to 4-quart containers for sales later in spring or summer depending on when purchased.

Cuttings are best taken in the spring on new growth emerging from the plant's crown. The cuttings can be snipped and stuck like a chrysanthemum and will root in two to three weeks.

VARIETIES

E. purpurea is easily found from both seed companies and plug firms around the country. In many cases, varieties offered as a plug or liner are one or more of the selections noted below as opposed to the true species.

Bravado has rose-purple flowers on plants to 28 inches (71 cm) tall.

Bright Star (Leuchstern) has rose-purple flowers on plants up to 28 inches (71 cm) tall. Bright Star has 4- to 5-inch (10 to 13 cm) blooms that lie flatter than the species.

Magnus is a basal-branching variety to 26 inches (66 cm) tall with 4½-inch (11 cm), rose-purple, single blooms. The petals lie flatter than the species or other cultivars.

Magnus, Bravado, and Bright Star are all well known in the U.S. trade for their intense flower color and uniform habit. Debate exists over the differences these three varieties display. However, when sown from seed, the three varieties can look strikingly similar. For plants propagated by vegetative means, the difference among the three is more noticeable.

In reviewing trials of the three over the years, either Magnus or Bright Star has been the best performer. In some trials, Bright Star will be taller and more vigorous but still performs well. Magnus has repeatedly been the favorite in our gardens—it's long lived and uniform, needing little to look exceptional en masse or as a single planting.

White Lustre is a white-flowering variety with a dark center. It is often vegetatively propagated because seed is seldom available. It grows to 3 feet (90 cm).

White Swan is the white-flowering variety with a similar growth habit though often shorter for us than the rose-purple flowering varieties. Mature height is 18 to 22 inches (46 to 56 cm).

USES

Echinacea purpurea is an excellent landscape or home garden plant or a cut flower. These plants provide an unusual color and behave like restrained wildflowers in a landscape setting. The cultivars noted above maintain a uniform habit throughout the season and are long lived, requiring only an occasional spading to divide the plants when they become crowded.

IN THE HOME GARDEN

Plant in full-sun locations in well-drained soil; white-flowering varieties appear more sensitive to excess water than the purple forms. Plants have few pest and disease problems, require no staking unless heavily fed, and seldom become invasive. Plants are easy to divide and require division only when the centers begin to die out or in four years. Some experts suggest dividing every three years. This can be done to increase your stock, but it isn't necessary unless the plants appear crowded.

Other gardeners in the Chicago area and farther south have reported few problems specifically with the white-flowering varieties. It's possible that our open island beds, unprotected from the elements, may be the limiting factor along with our heavy clay loam. We have noticed very few problems with white-flowering cultivars planted close to houses or other buildings where they're protected year-round and receive shade for two to three hours during the day.

ECHINOPS RITRO

FAMILY: Asteraceae

COMMON NAME(S): Globe Thistle

DESCRIPTION

An impressive perennial, *Echinops ritro* displays metallic blue flowers on thistlelike plants from 24 to 36 inches (61 to 91 cm) tall, expanding from 18 to 24 inches (46 to 61 cm) across. The flower heads are spherical or ball shaped, ranging from 2 to 2½ inches in diameter. The spheres are massed with single, one-eighth-inch (3 mm) flowers that open from the top down. Leaves are distinctively thistlelike with deeply lobed edges complemented by spiny ends. Unlike other spine-bearing plants, however, echinops aren't as prickly as they might appear and are more easily handled. See Color Plate 38 for photo of *Echinops ritro*.

HARDINESS: Zones 4 to 9.

SEASON OF BLOOM: July and August.

PROPAGATION

The species is available as seed, while the clones can be propagated by division or root cuttings. More vigorous than the clones, the species can grow to 4 feet (1.2 m) after three years. Take divisions in the spring. You can divide the clones after three or four years—they tend not to be as vigorous as the species.

Review the information in the **Propagation Techniques** chapter at the front of this book for additional details on root cuttings.

GERMINATION OVERVIEW: 2,600 seeds per ounce/91 per gram.

Germination temperatures are 65F to 72F (18C to 22C), and the seed should be left exposed to light during germination. Germination occurs in 14 to 21 days; transplanting can begin 20 to 31 days after sowing.

GROWING ON

From seed: If you're sowing from seed, plants will not flower during summer from seed sown during winter or spring. Green cell packs or 4-inch (10 cm) pots transplanted into the garden in May will rosette for the first year and then flower the following year.

Sowings are more often made in spring or summer and transplanted directly to quart containers. *Echinops ritro* doesn't appreciate numerous transplantings and can often die out. In some cases the die-out is from burying the crown too deeply. In others, root damage is the cause. Regardless, plants from seed sown to plugs and transplanted to the final pot have given the best performance over the years.

In general, for green plants in the spring, sow seed in January or February, transplant directly to 3-inch (7 cm) pots, and sell in spring. Allow 11 to 13 weeks from sowing.

Commercial companies will offer the species (*E. ritro*) in a number of plug or liner sizes. These will be ready for winter shipping for potting up into 4-inch (10 cm), quarts or gallons to be sold in spring or summer, depending on when you received your plugs. Plants are relatively quick to finish in a 4-inch (10 cm) or quart container, however, when using 50 liners or larger per tray.

As for divisions, the plants can be dug, divided, and potted up in the early spring, then sold. Transplants are available from numerous firms for winter or early spring delivery. Once potted up, these can be sold the same spring.

Root cuttings taken during winter won't produce plants large enough for retail sales until the end of summer. To get some size under them, the plants are often left over the winter for sales the following spring.

One final comment: Temperatures can be a limiting factor in growing *Echinops*. Avoid cold temperatures below 48F (9C) on actively growing seedlings. Low temperatures combined with excessive watering often lead to crown and root rots. For seed or plants potted during our often cloudy and cold late winters, we keep the night temperatures no lower than 55F (13C).

VARIETIES

E. ritro is relatively uniform although some variability exists when large numbers are grown. I'd especially recommend them for the cut flower grower due to their vigor. Note: The cultivar Royal Globe is the same as the species, and there is no difference between them. Both are propagated by seed.

Taplow Blue is the most popular cultivated selection today. It is an excellent plant with steel blue flowers to 3 inches (7 cm) across. Plants are 3 to 4 feet (90 to 120 cm) tall once established. It is vegetatively propagated only.

Veitchii's Blue is a darker blue than Taplow Blue and is earlier to flower in the garden. It's becoming more popular in North American gardens. It is vegetatively propagated only.

USES

In the perennial border, *Echinops* adds both a unique color and form not often found within the garden. Due to its spiny nature and Canadian thistle similarities (to a limited degree), it's not often planted by the novice. *Echinops* and *Acanthus* are excellent garden performers but should be put out of hand's reach for the sake of any children.

In the cut flower garden, this variety can be used either fresh or dried. As a fresh cut, harvest when the top flowers emerge. As a dried cut, harvest when about one-third of the flower has opened and before the top blooms have faded or died. Hang in a warm, dry place. This plant should be used when you want to attract bumblebees to your garden.

In the commercial landscape, *Echinops* provides an excellent show. With its spiny nature, the globe cluster in which the flowers are borne, the silver-grey undersides to the leaves, and the deeply cut leaves, this plant lends character unmatched in professional settings.

IN THE HOME GARDEN

Plantings made from seedling transplants take up to three years to attain the vigor noted above. The first season, plants are often 2 to 2½ feet (60 to 75 cm) and can be spaced 12 to 15 inches (30 to 38 cm) apart. Once they reach 4 feet (1.2 m), plantings do best on 20- to 24-inch (51 to 61 inch) centers. Plant in full sun or at least where the plant can get afternoon sun and a dry location in the garden or border. It is drought tolerant. Be careful of placement if there are children or play areas nearby because the plants have spines.

▬ EPIMEDIUM × RUBRUM

(also listed *E. alpinum* Rubrum. For additional details see the notes under **Varieties**.)

FAMILY: Aceranthus

COMMON NAME(S): Barrenwort

DESCRIPTION
Epimedium × rubrum is a commonly grown variety resulting from a cross between *E. alpinum* and *E. grandiflorum*. The 1-inch (2.5 cm) blooms are crimson highlighted with light yellow. Rising above the foliage on flowering stalks, there are 10 to 20 blooms per stalk. Epimediums will often flower as foliage starts to develop at its crown; other times the leaves will not show up until flowering has started or is almost complete. The heart-shaped leaves are redtoned in the spring and fall, less so or not at all during summer.

Epimediums, in general, are considered semievergreen, although this condition is seldom seen in severe winter areas. *E. × rubrum* will not retain green foliage during the winter. In colder locales, the foliage will turn brown and stay so during the winter. *E. × rubrum* is a clump-forming plant while other epimediums can form rhizomes that help to speed the plant's spread into a larger, more filled-in appearance. Plants grow up to 12 inches (30 cm) tall although often slightly less in climates like Chicago. Their spread is about the same, but they require time to fill out.

HARDINESS: Zones 4 to 8.

SEASON OF BLOOM: May and June

PROPAGATION
Divisions, the most common propagation method, can be done in the spring or fall. Seed can be sown for some species but not any of the hybrids.

GERMINATION OVERVIEW
The following is for germination of the genus in general, not *E. × rubrum*. Seed propagation isn't a standard method due to problems with seed viability. Fresh seed improves the chances of higher germination percentages. In general, sow seed after harvesting to a peat moss/vermiculite blend; allow six to eight weeks of 68F to 86F (20C to 30C) temperatures, followed by a cold period where the seeds are protected from direct frost and the temperatures are lowered to 38F to 45F (4C to 7C). The seed cannot be allowed to dry out during either temperature regime.

Seeds can be sown during the summer for natural cold treatments during the winter. The emerging seedlings will start to show during the winter or early spring as temperatures increase in the cold frame or other protected structure. Quarts and gallons will take another full year to develop for green sales. Plants may flower, although they'll bloom more profusely three years after sowing.

GROWING ON

For *Epimedium × rubrum*, commercial propagators offer bare-root transplants during fall and winter that can be potted to 1-, 2-, 3- or 4-quart containers, depending on the size of the root. Plants often grow slowly, requiring 10 to 12 weeks to look visually salable—that is, with enough foliage to fill out the container. In contrast, the root growth will not be fully massed, but it will be filled out enough to plant in the garden. This is based on 45F to 50F (7C to 10C) night temperatures.

For faster growth, pot the roots up during winter and grow on initially at no lower than 55F (13C) nights. Plants will grow faster and still be salable in 10 to 12 weeks but will be fuller in habit and more well rooted.

VARIETIES

E. × rubrum is easily available in the United States from various propagators as bare root or growing plants in liners or containers. It's occasionally sold as *E. alpinum*, although that's the result of a cross between *E. alpinum* and *E. grandiflorum*. Rubrum is also considered to be one of the most free-flowering epimediums [1]. The description above provides more details on its performance.

RELATED MATERIAL

E. grandiflorum (syn. *E. macranthum*) grows 12 inches (30 cm) tall with bicolor blooms of white and reddish pink highlighted by purple on various parts of the flower. The flowers measure 1 to 2 inches (2.5 to 5 cm) across and somewhat resemble a columbine flower. Leaves are crimson to bronze in both spring and fall cool weather. The plant forms clumps and should be propagated by divisions.

Rose Queen is one of the showiest of the varieties. The flowers are carmine rose with spurs that fade to white at the outermost tip. The flowers are larger but are often fewer in number than other selections.

E. perralderianum Frohnleiten is a yellow-flowering variety between 8 and 10 inches (20 to 25 cm) tall. The flowers are held erect above the foliage, and when flowering, appear open and butterfly-like in a mass. The foliage is dense green but may be edged or highlighted with red or crimson during cool weather in spring or fall, especially on young plants. Foliage may be evergreen in the South, but not so in a northern winter. This variety is a clumping type.

E. × versicolor Sulphureum is a cross between *E. grandiflorum* and *E. pinnatum* var. *colchicum* with yellow flowers on plants to no more than 12 inches (30 cm) tall when flowering. Plants spread by rhizomes and are considered one of the more reliable epimediums.

One additional way to propagate this plant is to take any rhizomes that are present just underneath the soil and section them. Lay these sections in a peat-based media to root, then pot them up, and if large enough, sell them the following year from a quart container. This method is often used before flowering during the month of May. The clump-forming varieties are better propagated by division.

IN THE HOME GARDEN

These perennials are shade plants, preferring a moist, well-drained location with dappled daylong or morning sun. Protect well during the hottest parts of the day—especially in a southern or midwestern summer.

E. × rubrum is a clump-forming variety that doesn't spread rapidly to fill in a landscape. Therefore, don't expect a groundcover in the sense of a trailing plant that blankets the ground. Instead, use this plant in rock gardens and small gardens as a specimen for edging or borders all summer long. This variety works well with naturalized bulbs in woodland locations.

REFERENCES

[1] Hayward, G. 1990. The elegant Epimedium. *Fine Gardening*. March/April.

[2] Weaver, R.E., Jr. 1987. In praise of Epimediums, Part I. *Perennial Plant Association Quarterly Newsletter*. Vol. XI.

[3] ———. 1987. In praise of Epimediums, Part II. *Perennial Plant Association Quarterly Newsletter*. Vol. XII.

ERIGERON SPECIOSUS

(also called *E. × hybridus*)

Most of the varieties offered are the result of hybridization including one or more crosses of the following: *E. speciosus, E. speciosa* var. *macrantha, E. aurantiacus,* and *E. glaucus.*

FAMILY: Asteraceae

COMMON NAME(S): Fleabane

DESCRIPTION

Erigeron speciosus is an upright perennial with excellent lasting power in our gardens over the years. It has scentless, pale, double flowers, 1 to 2 inches (2.5 to 5 cm) across, with prominent yellow centers. The blooms appear similar to the fall-flowering asters and bloom in pink, rose, lavender, purple, and shades in between. The plants will spread 18 to 24 inches (46 to 61 cm) apart.

HARDINESS: Zones 4 to 8.

Various references point to a differing number of hardiness zones for this plant. In Zone 5 the plants have proven themselves very hardy with few problems related to our severe winters. Our plants are not mulched and are in island beds away from the protection of trees, shrubs, or other windbreaks.

SEASON OF BLOOM: June and July.

Depending on the references you read, *Erigeron* is listed as a sporadically flowering plant blooming from summer until fall. In our observations, the main flush is in late spring or summer with some possible rebloom in late summer, although this depends on whether the plants were cut back or not during the summer. Regardless, the plants aren't noted for their ability to provide color throughout the season.

PROPAGATION

This perennial can be propagated from clump divisions, basal cuttings, or seed. All three forms are easy, and plants take readily regardless of the method. Divisions and basal cuttings are often taken in the early spring.

GERMINATION OVERVIEW: 99,000 seeds per ounce/3,465 per gram.

Pretreatments: Several authors suggest that fresh seed is imperative to this crop's success. The information was compiled using Pink Jewel and Azure Fairy as the templates for the seed-propagated crops. These two varieties have shown repeated, excellent germination results when sown within a year after harvest without special pretreatments.

Erigeron will germinate in four to eight days at 68F to 70F (20C to 21C) and can be covered lightly during germination. Seedlings can be transplanted 18 to 24 days after sowing.

GROWING ON

Crop time: *Erigeron* will not flower reliably the same season if sown from seed in February or later. Green packs will be salable 10 to 11 weeks after sowing when grown at 50F (10C) night temperatures. If planted into the garden from cell packs in May, the plants will often flower during July and August with more free-flowering plants the following year.

Instead, sow seed during spring or summer for transplanting up into quarts or gallons for sales the following spring. Plants will flower during June or earlier depending on night temperatures and the farther south you go.

Commercial propagators will offer selected varieties in various plug or cell pack sizes. Some of these are in 2-inch square (5 cm square) cells either 2½ to 3½ inches (6 to 8 cm) deep. As long as the plants were sown the previous year and vernalized (given a period of cold), they will flower the same year. If received in February or after for May sales, pot up into 1- or 2-quart containers. For 3- to 4-quart container sales, pot up in January. Grow on at no less than 50F (10C) nights.

VARIETIES

Erigeron speciosus is seldom seen in the U.S. market. Varieties resulting from its crossing with other species, however, are more readily available. (See the information under the botanical name above.) The following cultivars reflect this hybridization.

Azure Fairy is a semidouble flowering variety displaying midblue flowers with a prominent yellow eye. Plants grow between 2 and 2½ feet (60 and 75 cm) tall. Some authorities have suggested that the variety will shade from mid to light pink, although in our gardens, the plants have been reliably true from plant to plant with limited color variations. This variety is available from seed.

Darkest of All is a vegetatively propagated variety developed by Bressingham Gardens of England by perennial plantsman Alan Bloom. The flowers are purple with bright golden yellow centers. The plants grow between 24 and 30 inches (61 to 76 cm) tall. This variety is listed by many nurseries as one of the best overall. It is vegetatively propagated only.

Pink Jewel is a medium pink flowering variety on plants 18 to 24 inches (46 to 61 cm) high. Like Azure Fairy, Pink Jewel has been noted to color between mid to light shades of pink. As with Azure Fairy, we have seldom seen any problems in shading with this variety. However, the plants have not been as hardy as Azure Fairy for us. This variety is available from seed.

Rose Jewel (reportedly the same as Rosy Gem) has medium rose flowers on plants less than 24 inches (61 cm) tall. This variety is vegetatively propagated.

RELATED MATERIAL

Erigeron karvinskianus is an annual flowering variety that will not overwinter and dies out readily in cold weather. Plants grow 10 to 14 inches (25 to 35 cm) tall and trail over the side of a container. Plants don't trail like a morning glory or clematis, instead, they "bunch trail" by producing a multitude of shoots proliferating from the numerous nodes available along the stem. The plants trail down the first 5 to 7 inches (13 to 18 cm) of a container, weighed down by the new growth on top, similar to how some nasturtiums or nierembergia behave.

Plants grow quickly from seed. The variety Profusion is the only one I've seen available in the trade. It will be salable green in 10 to 11 weeks after sowing when grown at 55F (13C) nights. If planted in a garden in May, the plants will consistently flower in two to three weeks as long as nights are above 60F (15C).

USES

Erigeron can be used to extend the flowering period of asterlike plants and colors. Since asters flower naturally in late August or September, the late spring or summer flowering *Erigeron* provides a similar flower form earlier in the season.

Plants aren't used as commercial cut flowers, but they are suited for home cut flower gardens. Treat as you would an aster.

IN THE HOME GARDEN

Be sure to review the information noted above under **Hardiness** and **Season of bloom** for information pertinent to this crop's culture.

Erigeron should be grown in full sun in a moist but well-drained location. Plants are weak stemmed if grown in rich, moist environments and frequently fall over; they can also fall over if they get above 20 inches (51 cm) tall. Plants are long lived and don't require any special overwintering techniques in our Chicago area gardens. Some varieties are more hardy than others (see **Varieties**).

▬▬ ERIOPHYLLUM LANATUM

FAMILY: Asteraceae

COMMON NAME(S): Woolly Sunflower, Oregon Sunshine

DESCRIPTION

Eriophyllum lanatum is a rather plain, mounding plant from 12 to 15 inches (30 to 38 cm) tall with a 15-inch (38 cm) spread. The leaves are a wooly white underneath, midgreen on top, about 1½ inches (3 cm) long and notched. The single, yellow, scentless flowers are daisylike and less than an inch (2.5 cm) across.

HARDINESS: Zones 5 to 7.

Plants are native from British Columbia to California and often don't do well east of the Rockies in hot and humid locations; they prefer drier regions. In Chicago, however, we've had several plantings that have returned reliably after three consecutive winters with limited problems.

SEASON OF BLOOM: May and June.

PROPAGATION

Seed and divisions are the best ways to propagate. Divisions work well when taken in the spring, and seed should be sown fresh or within several months after harvesting.

GERMINATION OVERVIEW: 70,000 seeds per ounce/2,450 per gram.

Seed will germinate in four to eight days at 68F to 72F (20C to 22C) and doesn't need to be covered. Seedlings can be transplanted 20 to 25 days after sowing.

GROWING ON

Crop time: From seed, the plantlets grow erect with limited (if any) basal branching during the first few months after sowing. Seed sown January to March will produce green, salable 32-cell packs in 10 to 12 weeks. Eighteen cells per flat or 4-inch pots

(10 cm) require 12 to 14 weeks when grown at 55F (13C) nights and higher. Plants flower sporadically the first summer from a winter or spring sowing. For dependably flowering plants, sow the previous summer, pot up into quart or larger containers, and then overwinter for spring sales.

Eriophyllum lanatum is seldom available as a plug or liner on the North American market.

VARIETIES

Eriophyllum lanatum isn't commonly available from commercial seed companies.
Instead, try those companies selling native wildflower varieties or seed exchanges.

IN THE HOME GARDEN

Plants aren't long lived in areas with hot and humid summers. Add wet and cold winters with limited snowfall to that and the plants often die out in two or three years. Plant in locations where shade is available during the hottest part of the day. A protected site with well-drained soil media (sandy loam) will lengthen plant life. On the West Coast, plants don't need as much care, although a sandy soil, especially a moist one, will encourage more rapid growth.

No staking is required: *E. lanatum* will keep its mounded habit throughout the summer with few problems.

███ ERYNGIUM YUCCIFOLIUM

FAMILY: Umbelliferae

COMMON NAME(S): Rattlesnake Master

DESCRIPTION

Eryngium yuccifolium is an impressive native perennial with one to three erect stems rising out of yuccalike foliage. The stems are essentially bare except for several tightly clasped, small leaves along the stem. The leaves, stems, and flower stalks all have a glaucous (bluish white) coloring. The white flowers are small and clustered in a tight, round flower head seldom measuring larger than three-quarter inch (2 cm) in diameter. Flower heads can be off-white in color. Plants grow from 3 to 4 feet (90 to 120 cm) in flower and spread 12 to 18 inches (30 to 46 cm).

HARDINESS: Zones 4 to 8.

SEASON OF BLOOM: July.

PROPAGATION

Root cuttings and seed are the most frequently used methods to propagate this genus. For seed to be successful it should be fresh and cannot be stored. Root cuttings are taken in late winter while the plant is still dormant. Divisions can also be done, although they are challenging.

Eryngiums possess a long taproot that develops over time once planted to the field or nursery bed. Divisions have to be taken when plants are young, a year or two after planting; however, this is no guarantee that the individual transplants will take and produce healthy plants. Divisions are most often left to the home gardener rather than the commercial grower.

GERMINATION OVERVIEW

Eryngium is noted for notoriously low germination rates. While this isn't always true, a short review of germination needs will prove useful. Eryngiums are one of the class of perennials that provide horticulturalists with the most challenging requirements for average to good germination results. Once the seed ripens on the plant and starts to shed, it can be gathered, allowed a week or two of dry conditions to fully ripen, and then sown. Allan Armitage notes in his book, *Herbaceous Perennial Plants*, that he got 55% germination with seeds of *E. planum* "...[when] collected fresh and sown within two weeks but plummeted to 5% or less after three months."

While Allan only speaks of *E. planum*, most other species will yield similar results. If the seed you have is not germinating, however, the seed may only require conditioning prior to germinating, as long as you have patience and time. Refer to the **Propagation** chapter in the front of this book for information on those crops that prefer a warm moist stratification treatment followed by a moist-chilling period.

GROWING ON

Eryngiums will require a full year for quart or gallon plants to be salable from an aesthetic point of view. If you use 4-inch (10 cm) pots, however, the plants will finish out earlier and be salable the first year—although often small—depending on how and when you germinate the crop.

Seed allowed to germinate during the winter will produce green, 4-inch (10 cm) pots in 16 to 18 weeks, although there's usually only a limited number of leaves (six to eight), and the plants are often two-sided instead of filling out a pot. Plants will vary in crop time in the pot, some finishing two to three weeks ahead of others. Those plants held over a winter in quart or gallon containers will be more uniform in habit and performance than those plants sold the same year after germinating. Avoid cell packs for finishing—when the roots start to hold the soil ball together, the leaves will start to yellow. Eryngiums, as a group, dislike the stress of being rootbound.

Spring-germinated crops often flower during August and September the same season as germinated (the flowering isn't anything to write home about), whether pot grown or in the garden. The second-year plants are showier and often produce a multitude of flower heads.

Root cuttings taken during winter won't be salable until autumn or later. Allow for a full summer's growth, and sell in the fall or hold over the winter for spring sales the following year.

VARIETIES

Eryngium yuccifolium is difficult to find in the United States as either plants or seed. This is true for some other *Eryngium* species as well, although they're more common in perennial nurseries than *E. yuccifolium*. I suggest that you grow your own stock plants, gather your own seed, and sow it immediately after harvest in a protected area—a cold frame or similar environment. European seed houses carry a number of other varieties not found in the United States. If you purchase seed, you'll need to follow the methods noted for conditioning.

RELATED MATERIAL

E. alpinum (Bluetop Sea-Holly, Alpine Sea-Holly) is one of the most free flowering as well as largest flowering of the eryngiums listed here. The 1- to 1½-inch (2.5 to 3 cm) flower heads are cone or pineapple shaped in appearance with blue flowers subtended (directly beneath the cone) by blue, supple (rather than stiff) bracts. The flowers are more frilly than other species.

Plants grow mostly erect with primarily one, sometimes two, stems between 2 and 2½ feet (60 to 75 cm) tall. They branch at the crown and not at the base—typical of eryngiums. The plants also possess a blue coloring in the stems and flower stalks at the crown. *E. alpinum* tolerates light shade and heavier soils but too much of either makes the plants short lived and often in need of staking, especially in exposed or open areas.

E. amethystinum (Sea-Holly, Amethyst Sea-Holly). Mostly erect with branching at the crown during flowering, *E. amethystinum* is a spiny plant noted for its steel blue flowers and milky blue stems, especially at the crown. The single flowers are less than an inch across, although the pointed blue bracts directly beneath the flower head give the appearance of much larger blooms. Plants grow to no more than 2 feet (60 cm), but they can be slightly shorter. The plants are taller than they are wide, so expect a 1½-foot (45 cm) spread on this plant.

E. giganteum (Stout Sea-Holly) has a blue-gray appearance with leaves more closely resembling holly than the other species. The plants are large, growing from 3 to 4 feet (90 to 120 cm) or sometimes as tall as 5 feet (150 cm), but are short lived, dying out in three years or less in most cases. Plants often reseed.

E. planum has blue-gray flowers to three-quarter inch (2 cm) across and is one of the better known varieties. Plants grow to 3 feet (90 cm) tall and have fewer spines than the other species (and sometimes none at all).

Propagation and growing on is similar to *E. yuccifolium*.

USES

Eryngiums are versatile as cut flowers, specimen plantings, or in naturalistic or wild-flower gardens. *E. yuccifolium* is often underused in American landscapes because it doesn't fit in easily. It can be effective in mass plantings since the plants have a unique overall form and habit that are often overlooked. Using limited numbers (even in large areas) will still have a dramatic impact.

   E. yuccifolium isn't as hardy as the other eryngiums listed above. While hardy to Zone 4, it has questionable winter/summer tolerance all across the country in Zone 4 or 5. It's more reliable in Zones 6 and south, while the other varieties will be more reliable in our Chicago-style Zone 5.

IN THE HOME GARDEN

Plant in full sun in a well-drained location and avoid heavy clay soils. While *E. yuccifolium* will tolerate shade during the afternoon, it isn't fond of prolonged shady conditions and prefers the heat to look its best. It doesn't require staking, and I have seldom needed to apply support of any kind during the summer, even the first year after planting when the roots haven't yet fully established. If the soil is more fertile or moist, some support may be required, although the plants are usually not moderate or heavy feeders.

■■■ EUPATORIUM PURPUREUM

FAMILY: Asteraceae

COMMON NAME(S): Joe-Pye Weed

DESCRIPTION

Eupatoriums are American natives and are prized for their large, vigorous habits. They tower 4 to 6 feet (1.2 to 1.8 m) tall in full bloom and 3 to 4 feet (0.9 to 1.2 m) across. The flowers are clustered in dense terminal bunches much like an ageratum. The single blooms are one-half inch across, purple in color, and scentless. Plants produce a large clump of stems which, along with the statuesque height, give it a dramatic presence in the summer garden. In the winter it dies back to the ground. The stems are sometimes highlighted with purple although the nodes are the most richly colored. In the spring, the plants have deeper coloring, resulting from the warm days and cool nights.

HARDINESS: Zones 4 to 9.

SEASON OF BLOOM: August and September.

PROPAGATION

Seed, cuttings, and divisions are all equally easy ways to propagate eupatoriums. Seed can be sown any time of the year, but seedling uniformity will vary with the season. Tip cuttings can be taken on nonflowering or budded shoots and will root quickly. Divisions can be cut in spring to early summer and again in early fall.

GERMINATION OVERVIEW

Pretreatments: Fresh seed germinates more readily and produces more reliable results. If you gather your own seed in the fall but don't sow it until spring, chill the seed in the meantime. If the germination isn't what you expect, follow the information in the **Propagation** chapter for moist chilling.

In general, fresh seed germinates in 10 to 13 days at 70F (21C) and can be transplanted 22 to 27 days after sowing.

GROWING ON

Crop time: From seed, plants develop rather quickly and are transplantable from a 32-cell pack in 10 to 12 weeks. Plants will grow erect without basal or side branching and, if sold out of cell packs, will not be in bloom when sold. Some growers have kept the plants dwarf by using B-Nine, but 50F (10C) nights also suffice if plants are properly established in the pack or pot when cooled down.

It should be noted, however, that seed-propagated varieties will produce plants of various habits and heights. Care should be taken when using this method as your primary means of propagation. Seed-propagated strains are better grown in a nursery bed so you can select the best performers to increase by cutting or division. If seed is sown by early March, with the resulting plants transplanted to the garden by mid-May, they'll start to flower by July. Toss the inferior plants, and use the nursery beds to keep your mother stock for future divisions or cuttings.

If sowing in the winter for spring sales in 4-inch (10 cm) pots or quarts, allow 12 to 16 weeks for a fully rooted plant when grown at 55F (13C) nights.

Stem tip cuttings taken in the spring will root readily and can be potted into quarts within a few weeks. If cuttings are taken from emerging shoots in early spring, the plants can be sold in summer. Plants will be small their first season but will usually root well enough by early to midsummer from cuttings taken in early April. However, it is better to wait until late summer for sales to ensure a well-rooted plant.

The best plants for divisions are those that have vigorous undergrowth to yield numerous plantlets. Plants can be divided after one year, although you get greater yield by leaving the plants in the nursery bed for up to two years prior to dividing. Plants dug, divided, and then potted up during late winter will soon be salable (four to eight weeks), depending on how well rooted the soil ball is and how lush the top growth has to be.

VARIETIES

Eupatorium purpureum is more readily available as started plants than as seed from U.S. nurseries. You can find seed more easily from companies specializing in native perennial seed, from European sources, or by gathering your own. From seed, plants will vary in the amount of purple highlights. Some plants will lack any purple coloring at the nodes.

Eupatorium purpureum Atropurpureum has rich purple flowers (deeper, more vibrant than *E. purpureum*), stems, and leaves on plants between 4 and 6 feet (1.2 to 1.8 m) tall. Propagate by divisions to retain the coloring.

RELATED MATERIAL

Eupatorium coelestinum is a shorter plant, 2 to 3 feet (60 to 90 cm) tall, with one-half-inch single, purple flowers. Plants aren't as hardy as *E. purpureum* and often fail in the upper North when grown in areas without winter protection. As with *E. purpureum*, seed is available, although started plants can be located and are more reliable in growth and performance. If seed is the way for you to go, however, it will be more difficult to find commercially.

Eupatorium maculatum is another vigorous grower—from 4 to 6 feet (1.2 to 1.8 m). It's similar in form and habit to *E. purpureum* but has more purple stem coloring than the predominantly green background of *E. purpureum*. Plants are more cold hardy as well, extending as far north as Zone 3 as a reliable overwintering plant. The "Joe-Pye weed" offered in the trade is more often this selection than anything else.

For propagation and growing on, follow the procedures noted for *E. purpureum*. Vegetatively propagate to maintain the cultivar's integrity and uniformity.

USES

This plant is an excellent choice where native perennials are preferred. Don't short-change this crop because it's so common in its native habitat. Plants reliably return year after year and have limited needs.

Golf courses are just one landscape where these plants can be used effectively both as a specimen plant and seasonal shrub. Plants will grow dependably once established but are intolerant of extended drought. They prefer moisture when planted in order to become established, but they will tolerate dryness for a short period.

IN THE HOME GARDEN

Eupatoriums prefer full-sun locations in drained but moist soil to be at their best. If planted into a drained clay loam, however, the plants are often shorter (3 to 4 feet [90 cm to 1.2 m] tall) and less invasive. Some experts suggest the plants do better in afternoon shade, although we've never seen the need for that here. As you go farther south, afternoon shade may be of significant benefit. I would be concerned, however, that the plants could become weak stemmed if planted in a dim location.

Plants are weak their first season and look better if staked, especially as they bud up and start to show color. In full bloom, they may fall over in an unexpected rain shower. We've never had to stake them to keep them upright the second and additional years. However, if grown in a more lush and moist environment, staking is suggested.

■ Euphorbia polychroma (syn. E. epithymoides)

Family: Euphorbiaceae

Common name(s): Cushion Spurge

Description

Euphorbia polychroma is a dependable, long-lived perennial growing 18 to 24 inches (46 to 60 cm) tall and up to 2 feet (60 cm) across. It grows in a clumps with stems radiating out of the crown. In fall, the foliage turns a bright crimson color as temperatures cool. The flowers are unattractive and can go unnoticed because of their nondescript color, shape, and earliness. The "flowers" are actually bracts that turn bright yellowish green in full bloom. The single blooms are clustered terminally on the stem. Like all euphorbias, cushion spurge produces a white, milky latex that will exude out of the stem when it's injured. This exudate is an irritant and should be avoided by those who suffer from dermatitis. See Color Plate 39 for photo of *Euphorbia polychroma*.

Hardiness: Zones 4 to 8.

Season of bloom: May.
If a cool spring prevails, the plants will flower into June.

Propagation

Seed, divisions, and cuttings are all popular ways to propagate euphorbias. Seed may require some special handling; techniques and additional information are provided under **Germination overview**. Divisions can be taken in the spring or fall, but beware of older clumps in which the central, woodier clump should be discarded. Cuttings consist of terminal cuttings taken in April or May before buds set. However, semimature stems can also be used as cutting material in July.

Germination overview: 3,500 seeds per ounce/122 per gram.
It's best to use fresh seed when germinating this crop—germination rates can drop to less than 30% within several months after ripening. If you're gathering your own seed, remember to cover the seedhead with a mesh bag. When ripe the seedhead explodes and scatters the seed across the ground.

Consider your options in buying seed for this crop. In a number of germination tests performed at the Ball Seed Company, we haven't achieved over 40% germination when using seed recently imported from European harvest sites. You may need to give your seed a moist-chilling period for three to four weeks to increase overall germination rates. Additional information is provided in the **Propagation** chapter.

Generally, seeds will germinate in eight to 15 days at 70F (21C) and don't need to be covered during germination. Seedlings can be transplanted 20 to 25 days after sowing.

GROWING ON

Crop time: The first several months after germinating, the plants will produce one shoot that will grow predominantly upright without basal or side branching. Early January sowings will yield 8-inch (20 cm) tall, erect plants with roots that will fill out a 32-cell pack by the first to third week of May when grown at 50F (10C) nights. The plants aren't salable at retail, however, because of their weak and elongated growth. Pot to gallon containers instead, and grow on for sales the following year. It's not necessary to start early in the year if you're growing from seed, although all sowings should be finished by April in order to have a strong gallon- or quart-sized root ball by fall (to survive northern winters).

Don't let its wimpy beginnings fool you, however. If some of the plants started in January were put into the garden after rooting out in a 32-cell pack, the plants would basal branch rapidly, growing 14 inches (35 cm) tall with a 15-inch (38 cm) spread by the end of July. Plants would also flower erratically the first season from seed.

Commercially, *E. polychroma* propagators carry a wide range of container sizes, from plugs up to prefinished plants. If a large plug or liner is purchased for winter potting, plants will be salable green in the spring. If plants are vernalized, they will flower at the time they're sold.

VARIETIES

Euphorbia polychroma is available from numerous seed companies and nurseries across the United States. See comments under **Description**.

RELATED MATERIAL

Euphorbia myrsinites is a interesting plant, with whorled, gray-green foliage on plants under 10 inches (25 cm) tall. Plants can spread 10 to 15 inches (25 to 38 cm) and are evergreen during the winter. However, the plants need to be protected from winter winds for best performance. In late winter or early spring before growth begins, cut the plants back to get more uniform growth. Like *E. polychroma*, these plants have inconspicuous flowers appearing in early spring. Plants are hardy from Zones 5 to 9 and reliably hardy in northern winters and summer heat.

When dividing this crop, beware that *E. myrsinites* has several long taproots that often snap in two when dug up. The remaining fibrous roots are so fragile that you're often left holding a whole plant with only a broken taproot and few root hairs making it impossible to effectively divide this crop. However, seed and cuttings can be taken with more reliable outcomes. Seed germinates easily without pretreatments, while cuttings can be taken as they are for *E. polychroma*.

Seed germinates in seven to 14 days at 70F (21C) and doesn't need to be covered. Seedlings can be transplanted in 16 to 22 days after sowing. They initially grow erect without basal branching and are as slow to develop as *E. polychroma*. From a February sowing, when grown in a cold frame at 50F (10C) nights, the roots will not fill out a 32-cell pack for 13 to 14 weeks. As day length and temperatures increase, however, the plants grow more quickly and basal branching occurs more readily. Winter and spring sowings can be transplanted to gallon containers for sales the following spring.

USES

Euphorbias are reliable perennials returning year after year with limited fuss. Plants work well in groups, but you should avoid mass plantings in commercial landscapes unless combining them with flowering plants. *Euphorbia myrsinites* can be used as a border around daylilies or other yellow-flowering perennials for an excellent effect, but *E. polychroma* is better when grouped in a border. If growing for seasonal displays, use *E. polychroma* in your fall plantings for its bright autumn color.

IN THE HOME GARDEN

Plants require limited care and handling and will live indefinitely as long as they get basic care. Euphorbias like full sun and a light spring feeding. Be cautious of over-feeding and excess watering as the summer progresses. If grown lush, the plants will often fall over and require staking to stay upright.

    E. polychroma doesn't require any pinching, but the faded flower heads can be removed. On *E. myrsinites*, trim the foliage to within 6 inches of the crown after winter or after flowering, whichever you prefer. This helps plants look more uniform and be less apt to sprawl across the ground in a languid fashion.

F

◼ FILIPENDULA ULMARIA

FAMILY: Rosaceae

COMMON NAME(S): Queen of the Meadow

DESCRIPTION

Filipendula ulmaria has elmlike leaves and grows 3 and 4 feet (90 to 120 cm) tall by the second season from seed. Leaves are deep green on top with a white tomentose underlayer. The plants basal branch and fill in well. Flowers are a creamy white, measuring one-quarter inch across in plumes 5 to 6 inches (13 to 15 cm) tall that resemble a duster in shape. The blooms are scentless.

HARDINESS: Zones 3 to 9.

SEASON OF BLOOM: June.

Some perennial authors suggest the plants will bloom sporadically throughout the summer after the main flush of color in June. In our Chicago gardens, plants flower once in the spring and then will not flower again the same year. Even when the plants are cut back after the first flowers fade, blooming does not reoccur later in the summer.

PROPAGATION

Seed and division are the two most common methods for propagation. Seed should be sown as soon as collected. If purchasing seed, buy it in early fall from reputable suppliers. Seed becomes increasingly difficult to germinate as it ages. Divisions can be cut either in the spring or fall and are preferred by many over the hassles of seed germination.

GERMINATION OVERVIEW

Pretreatments: *Filipendula ulmaria* can be a difficult crop to germinate from seed. If, after sowing, the seed does not germinate or if you have poor stands, treat the seed to a cold-moist period as noted in the **Propagation Techniques** chapter.

In general, seedlings emerge in five to 10 days at 70F to 72F (21C to 22C). The seed doesn't need to be covered. Seedlings can be transplanted 22 to 28 days after sowing.

GROWING ON

Crop time: Seed-propagated plants won't flower the same year from seed even if started in December or January. Plants resulting from seed sown during winter will be up and down in habit, and it will be difficult to finish flats or pots uniformly. In general, allow 12 to 14 weeks for green rosettes in a 32-cell tray when grown at 50F to 58F (10C to 14C) nights. Don't be concerned that the leaves appear more rounded to slightly lobed during this time. As the plant ages, the leaves will become pinnate like an elm. If sold green, the plants will remain small throughout the season. It's better to sow in spring or summer and plant up into quarts or gallons for following spring sales.

Divisions of three- or four-year-old plants or older work the best for potting into quarts or gallons. If spring digging, you won't get large size plants until summer; they can be dug for sales in the fall or for next spring.

VARIETIES

F. ulmaria. This can be found both as seed and as started plants, but it isn't readily available. Several U.S. seed companies have the seed, but you are more apt to find it through European firms. See Color Plate 41 for photo of *Filipendula ulmaria*.

F. ulmaria Aurea is a plant valued for its golden yellow foliage. It grows to between 2½ and 3 feet (75 to 90 cm) tall. Plants can grow taller but tend to be short since they're often grown in bright, direct light. The flowers are small and insignificant and do not detract from the foliage. When planting into the garden or landscape, position Aurea in a moist soil amended with organic matter in a morning light exposure. The foliage burns easily whether you're growing it in Chicago or Tennessee and, while hardy, the leaves may burn or fade to cream yellow if given full sun in soils that are too well drained. The golden yellow foliage is more pronounced in the coolness of spring. Several expert sources suggest trimming off the flower buds as they develop to keep seeds from forming, since the germinating seedlings have deep green foliage that doesn't color up to a golden yellow. Aurea is vegetatively propagated only.

F. ulmaria Flore-Plena is a fully double, creamy white flowering cultivar on plants 28 to 40 inches (71 to 102 cm) tall. Plants aren't as tolerant of full sun and may be slower to develop, especially when grown in well-drained soils. Plants perform similar to the species. They are vegetatively propagated.

RELATED MATERIAL

F. rubra Venusta (sometimes labeled as *F. venusta*) is a large plant commonly called Queen-of-the-Prairie. It's native to the United States from west of the Mississippi, east to Pennsylvania, and then south to Georgia. Plants grow 6 to 8 feet (1.8 to 2.4 m) tall when fully established, but they'll be 4 to 6 feet (1.2 to 1.8 m) tall in areas where they compete for nutrients and moisture. They're definitely not for a small, intimate home garden since they take up a large space and make a commanding display. Flowers are medium pink in color and fragrant. Plants prefer moist conditions and full sun and often flower in June and July. See Color Plate 40 for photo of *F. rubra* Venusta.

Seed and divisions are the most common forms of propagation. Seed can be as difficult as *F. ulmaria* to germinate, so it's often fall-sown for spring germination in a outdoor nursery bed or cold-moist treated as previously suggested. Divisions can be taken in the fall, then potted and overwintered in a cold frame for sales the following spring.

REGIONAL COMMENTS

Green-leaved forms of all of the above do best in light shade in the South, especially when grown in soils that are more well drained. Farther north, the plants will tolerate more sun.

USES

The foliage of either of the above two species works well in landscaping, home gardens, or in any large open area where plants with stature are desired. These plants can offer a dramatic setting—in sites with lakes, ponds, or streams—especially when in flower. If the areas are well drained and lightly shaded, *F. ulmaria* will grow more upright in form, especially the first two to three years after planting. *F. rubra* will become more robust and dominate an area more quickly, filling in faster than *F. ulmaria*.

IN THE HOME GARDEN

Filipendulas are excellent plants for growing in areas where moist soils are prevalent throughout the season. They're not for submerging in water, but they can take standing water that will drain away within several hours, leaving behind a moist soil. Plants can withstand soils more drained than this, but I suggest a soil rich in organic matter or one that has been amended with compost or other comparable media. Plants are taller and have a fuller habit in media that has more available moisture.

Plants don't require staking anytime during the summer. The stems are erect, strong, and upright and have been used for home cut flowers. Plants don't require winter protection to be hardy. If planted or divided late in the summer or early autumn, however, mulching is suggested to keep the root ball from heaving out of the ground.

■ FILIPENDULA VULGARIS
(formerly *F. Hexapetala*)

FAMILY: Rosaceae

COMMON NAME(S): Dropwort

DESCRIPTION
The finely cut leaves of *Filipendula vulgaris* are similar in form to the foliage of carrots. Plants won't appear as full as *F. ulmaria* since the leaves are clustered at the plant's base and the 3- to 4-foot (90 to 120 cm) flowering stalks are mostly void of leaves. Flowers are primarily cream white in color, measuring individually to one-quarter inch (6 mm) across in heads 5 to 6 inches (13 to 15 cm) tall. *F. vulgaris* will flower about two weeks earlier than *F. ulmaria*. Once in bloom, plants flower for two to three weeks and then can be trimmed back.

HARDINESS: Zone 4 to 8.

SEASON OF BLOOM: Northern U.S.: June.
Some authors suggest that filipendulas will bloom sporadically throughout the summer after their main flush of color in June. Once my plants have flowered they seldom produce significant color later in the season, even if they've been cut back.

PROPAGATION
Seed and division are the two best propagation methods. Seed can be sown at any time, since the resulting plants won't flower until the following year. *F. vulgaris* seed germinates more readily than *F. ulmaria* or *F. rubra*, as long as it's properly handled and stored. Seed becomes increasingly difficult to germinate as it ages. Divisions can be made either in the spring or fall and involve less hassle than seed germination.

GERMINATION OVERVIEW
F. vulgaris requires germination temperatures of 70F to 72F (21C to 22C). Seed doesn't need to be covered for germination, though a light covering of vermiculite helps to maintain moisture.

Germination time: Seedlings emerge in five to 10 days and are sizable enough to transplant 22 to 28 days after sowing.

GROWING ON
Crop time: Seed-propagated plants won't flower the same year from seed even if they're started in December or January. Compared to *F. ulmaria*, *F. vulgaris* produces uniform rosettes the first season from seed. Seedlings develop into salable green plants in about the same amount of time *F. ulmaria* takes—12 to 14 weeks to produce green rosettes in a 32-cell tray. If sold green, the plants will remain small throughout

the season. Therefore, it's better to sow in spring to plant into quart or gallon containers for sales the following spring.

Divisions of at least three- or four-year-old plants are easiest to divide and pot up into quart or gallon containers. Plants dug in the spring won't be large enough to sell until fall or the following spring.

Temperature: *Filipendula* prefers temperatures between 50F and 58F (10C to 14C) in the spring. If the plants are stressed in the summer by high temperatures and limited water, they'll be more prone to powdery mildew.

VARIETIES

F. vulgaris is available both as seed and as started plants. Several U.S. companies carry the seed, but you're more apt to find it from European firms.

F. vulgaris Flore Plena is a double-flowering variety with cream white blooms on plants to 15 inches (38 cm) tall. It's not as hardy in Zone 5 as the species, but it will survive if protected from fall rains and winter winds.

REGIONAL COMMENTS

F. vulgaris is more tolerant of dry soils than either *F. ulmaria* or *F. rubra* and grows uniformly throughout the season. For our gardens here in the Chicago area, the plants do better in full sun than does *F. ulmaria* and will flower two weeks earlier. However, the two varieties' flowers appear almost identical, and the species differ mostly in their foliage appearance.

USES

In general, *F. vulgaris* is grown and used like *F. ulmaria*, though *F. vulgaris* can tolerate more well-drained locations. Since the foliage is located at the base, the plants bloom tall but can be trimmed down to 8 inches (20 cm) or so after flowering. Plants seldom flower again the same year.

IN THE HOME GARDEN

Read the comments provided in the *F. ulmaria* chapter for additional details about that species' characteristics. Of all of the Filpendula species, *F. vulgaris* offers the most versatility in the garden, especially the more dwarf, double-flowering *F. vulgaris* Flore Pleno. It can be used even in small gardens, and the flowering stalks can be trimmed back after flowering to show off the foliage.

G

▬ GAILLARDIA × GRANDIFLORA
(previously *G. aristata*)

FAMILY: Asteraceae

COMMON NAME(S): Blanket Flower

DESCRIPTION
An easily grown and hardy perennial, *Gaillardia × grandiflora* displays single flowers in bright yellow, crimson, and in-between combinations. The scentless flowers are 2 to 4 inches (5 to 10 cm) across in an open, daisylike habit. The plants are mounded, although some varieties can be more upright. Plants reach 12 to 30 inches (30 to 76 cm) tall and spread 18 to 24 inches (46 to 61 cm) across.

HARDINESS: Zones 3 to 9.
Blooming is heavy at first and then provides better than average color the remainder of the season.

SEASON OF BLOOM: June to frost.

PROPAGATION
Seed, stem and root cuttings, as well as divisions can all be used to propagate gaillardias. You can sow seed anytime with equal results. Stem or basal cuttings can be taken from newly developing shoots as the plants reemerge in the spring or from root cuttings while the plant is dormant. Divisions can be made in either spring or fall.

GERMINATION OVERVIEW: 7,000 seeds per ounce/245 per gram.
Provide germination temperatures of 70F to 75F (21C to 24C); leave seed exposed to light. Germination takes five to 15 days, and transplanting can begin 30 to 42 days after sowing.

Note: You can sow seed directly to the final container, but plants may become lanky if not transplanted once to slow them down.

GROWING ON

Seed-sown plants are quick to grow and develop into salable green transplants in a 32-cell pack or 4-inch (10 cm) pot. Winter-sown seed will produce green cell packs in 10 to 12 weeks when grown at 52F to 55F (11C to 13C) night temperatures. If sowing in December, 4-inch (10 cm) or quart containers will finish in 13 to 15 weeks. For better rooted quarts, allow an additional week or two. Gaillardias will flower sporadically the first year after sowing, blooming more profusely the second season.

Commercial propagators offer a number of varieties in liners or large plug sizes transplantable to 4-inch (10 cm) and larger containers for same season sales. These plugs are usually available year-round but are mostly purchased for potting up during the winter months.

Stem cuttings taken in spring will root within a week or two and can be potted up into 3- or 4-inch (7 to 10 cm) pots for late spring or summer sales. These cuttings can also be potted up into quart or larger containers for mid to late summer impulse sales or overwintered for sales the following spring.

Root cuttings taken from January to March are given four to five months at 50F (10C) nights or higher to root into a 4-inch (10 cm) or quart container. Depending on variety and culture, plants are allowed to fully root over the summer for late summer sales, or the pots can be overwintered. These plants are then sold the following spring.

VARIETIES

Keep in mind that many or all of the following may be listed under *G. aristata* or *G. grandiflora*. All of the following are propagated from seed except for Baby Cole, which is vegetatively propagated.

Baby Cole is a dwarf variety with yellow-tipped red flowers. The plants grow from 8 to 10 inches (20 to 25 cm) tall in full bloom. This variety is vegetatively propagated only.

Burgundy is a rich wine-red flower on 2- to 2½-foot (60 to 75 cm) plants. Although I haven't seen the vegetatively propagated form of this plant, the seeded variety is dull in color, and the flowers can get lost in the foliage.

Dazzler has crimson-red petals tipped with yellow. It is a more vigorous version of Goblin. Plants grow 14 to 16 inches (35 to 41 cm) tall.

Goblin is a dwarf variety mounding to 12 inches (30 cm) tall. The flowers measure 3 to 4 inches (7 to 10 cm) across on established plantings, and the flower color has a red base with yellow tips. This is the most preferred variety for uniformity and overall garden performance. Vegetatively propagated plants are more uniform than those propagated by seed. Plants produced from seed, however, are also good garden performers.

Golden Goblin is the pure golden yellow flowering variety, growing 12 inches (30 cm) tall in flower.

Monarch Strain is a upright and vigorous variety to 30 inches (76 cm) tall. The flower colors are primarily red and yellow combinations. This variety is suitable for cut flower gardens. It may require staking.

USES

Gallardias are true performers in the perennial garden or when used as a specimen planting within the garden. They also can be used at the front of a perennial border or planted along with annuals or native perennials in wildflower displays. For home cut flowers, choose only the taller varieties like Monarch Strain, although its stems are rather wiry and weak. Even though the dwarf varieties can grow to 15 inches (38 cm), you'll find that Goblin and Dazzler flowers tend to stay low, close to the foliage.

Goblin offers the best landscape performance. Use vegetatively propagated plants to provide the uniformity that landscapes require. The seeded varieties aren't as uniform and while they flower profusely, the unevenness can make the display look untidy.

IN THE HOME GARDEN

Growing this genus will prove one of the highlights of your summer color. Gaillardias' daisylike blooms will provide color all season long (pick off spent blooms for better performance) and work well in mass plantings. Plant in full-sun locations where the plants get excellent drainage, and they'll reward you by being long lived. Our plantings have been established for over six years without winter protection or dividing. Staking is needed only for the taller varieties like Burgundy and Monarch Strain. Space the plants 15 inches (38 cm) apart to fill in.

■ GALIUM ODORATUM (ASPERULA ODORATA)

FAMILY: Rubiaceae

COMMON NAME(S): Sweet Woodruff, Bedstraw, Woodruff

DESCRIPTION

This crop's trademark is its whorl of six to eight, 1-inch (2.5 cm) or larger leaflets at every node. The leaves and stems, when crushed, emit the odor of freshly mowed lawns. In the spring the plants are in bloom with single, fragrant, white blooms to one-quarter inch across. This is a low-growing and spreading perennial between 6 and 10 inches (15 to 25 cm) tall with erect, sometimes ascending, stems that are often termed weak by other authors. In our climate, the weight of the leaves may cause the stems to nod in the wind or after a rain.

HARDINESS: Zones 4 to 8.

SEASON OF BLOOM: June and July.

PROPAGATION

Plants are most commonly grown from spring divisions of the stoloniferous roots. While seed has been noted as a way to increase plants by numerous authorities, it is not a common practice here in the United States and, if used, needs to be sown fresh. Seed stored for any length of time will be slow to emerge, if it germinates at all.

GROWING ON

Crop time: Stolons taken in the spring and summer will be well rooted in a liner or small pot in two to three months depending on the size of division taken and the pot used for sales. Plants are quick to fill out a quart or gallon container and appear to grow fastest under cool conditions around 50F to 60F (10C to 15C) with indirect but bright light. Well-drained but moist media (peat moss) are preferred for rapid development of the roots and top growth.

Galium odoratum is also available from many commercial propagators as a liner during the winter. These can be potted up into 4-inch (10 cm) or quart containers for sales in May. Depending on the liner size (50 to 72 cells per flat are common), the crop time is seven to nine weeks at 55F (13C) nights to fill out a quart container. For visually filled-out crowns and a well-rooted soil ball, allow nine to 10 weeks.

VARIETIES

Galium odoratum is available from numerous nurseries across the United States. If seed is your preference you won't find it readily either here in the United States or in Europe. Other selections are available, but they can escape and become invasive. These species are described below. They're seldom preferred by gardeners due to their insignificant bloom and nondescript appearance—they're not as novel as *G. odoratum*.

RELATED MATERIAL

G. boreale (Northern Bedstraw) has small white flowers during June and July, although it grows to between 2 and 3 feet (60 to 90 cm) tall. The flowers are fragrant. Plants will fill in well, but the stems can become top heavy and will often "lodge" (fall any which way, opening the crown of the plant), although I personally prefer its garden performance over *G. verum*. *G. boreale* plants will tolerate more shade than *G. verum*.

G. verum (Yellow Bedstraw) is a European native that has escaped into U.S. cultivation and has become a noxious weed in certain states. It is highly praised in legend, however, as the bedding (as in mattress) the Virgin Mary rested on, while the yellow flowers signify Jesus Christ's birth. This gives rise to another common name, Our Lady's Bedstraw.

If kept under control the plant does have its merits: *G. verum* has yellow flowers instead of white. The blooms are small—one-eighth to one-quarter inch (3 to 6 mm) across—on wispy plants that some have compared to asparagus. The blooms appear in June and July and are fragrant. *G. verum* grows to 2 feet (60 cm) tall and does very well in full sun and dry locations in our Chicago garden.

G. verum seed is not commonly found in the United States—European sources will be more reliable. Once sown, the seedlings will emerge in five to 10 days at 68F to 70F (20C to 21C) germination temperatures and be transplantable in 15 to 20 days. After the seedlings start to emerge they'll develop quickly and become vigorous. Remove them from the germination house and slow their development by growing on at 58F to 60F (15C to 16C) nights and days that are warmer by 5F to 7F (3C to 4C).

If sown in early February, the plants will be salable green from a 32-cell tray in 10 to 11 weeks when grown at 45F to 50F (7C to 10C) nights. It would be better to sell them in 4½-inch (11 cm) pots when started in the winter for spring sales. These containers will be salable green in 12 to 13 weeks. Once planted in the garden in May, the plants develop quickly and will be close to 8 inches (20 cm) tall with a 12-inch (30 cm) spread by the end of June. The plants will also flower sporadically during July the same year as sown.

USES

G. odoratum is a premier plant for woodlands, shady areas or anywhere the plants get protection from the sun and the benefits of cool exposures. When planted into full-sun areas, especially the hot, early afternoon sun, the plants often falter and burn. Even in December, plants grown under the protective shroud of trees and shrubs will still be a dark green, while those planted in more open locations without overhead protection will be brown or dormant.

IN THE HOME GARDEN

As described under **Uses**, be sure to grow the plants in shade for best performance. Combine this with a moist but well-drained location, and the plants will live long and fill in fast but not to the detriment of other plants around them.

Plants don't tolerate prolonged dry spells or hot sun locations but will flourish when grown without either condition. While plants are well known for their garden performance, they've also been utilized in the kitchen for centuries. *Galium odoratum* "...has been collected and cultivated since the Middle Ages at least, ... to flavour apple jellies, sorbets, creams and fruit salads. As a tisane (allow to wilt slightly), it has a fresh grassy flavour and a gently sedative effect." [1] For the freshest flavor, harvest before the plants flower since blooming will change the overall taste.

REFERENCES

[1] *The New Royal Horticultural Society dictionary of gardening.* 1992. Vol. 2. New York: The Stockton Press.

▰ GAURA LINDHEIMERI

FAMILY: Onagraceae

COMMON NAME(S): Gaura

DESCRIPTION

Gaura lindheimeri is a tall-growing American native with an airy habit and white butterfly-like blooms. Initially vase shaped in habit but spreading outward as the season progresses, it reaches 2 to 3 feet (60 to 90 cm) in height and spreads up to 3 feet (90 cm) across in our Chicago location. Farther south, however, the plants are known to grow as tall as 4 feet (1.2 m) with a spread of 4 feet (1.2 m) across. The 1-inch (2.5 cm), single, white flowers (sometimes blushed with rose or pink) are borne along the stem and are held well above the foliage. The plants are seldom free flowering, although they are in bloom for most of the summer.

HARDINESS: Zones 5 to 9.

Plants are classified as short-lived perennials that usually live for several seasons and then die out, especially farther north. Zones 5 to 6 are the borderline where they can live in our Chicago gardens (Zone 5), but they seldom survive for two years or more in open, unprotected locations.

Plants are usually hardy in the Midwest, but a wet fall followed by a cold winter can kill our crop in Chicago. It would appear, though not conclusively, that a heavy clay loam is the most limiting factor in getting reliable returns from year to year. Review the information under **In the home garden** for more details.

SEASON OF BLOOM: Late June to August.

PROPAGATION

Seed and cuttings are the primary propagation methods. Commercial propagators prefer cuttings to maintain trueness to type, but seed-propagated plants also come reliably true. Summer is the time to take cuttings.

GERMINATION OVERVIEW: 1,700 seeds per ounce/60 per gram.

Gaura seed requires no special pretreatments for germinating. Seed will sprout in five to 11 days at 70F (21C) and doesn't need to be covered. Seedlings can be transplanted 21 to 28 days after sowing. They can become vigorous, so transplant as soon as the plantlets are ready.

GROWING ON

Crop time: From seed, green salable 32-cell packs will be ready nine to 10 weeks after sowing when grown at 50F (10C) nights. The plants will initially rosette, stretching to about 3 or 4 inches (7 to 10 cm) tall. As the plants grow out of the rosette they will get 7 to 8 inches (18 to 20 cm) tall. Sowings made as late as March have produced flowering plants the same year from seed. In general, early February sowings were salable green around the first of May. Planted in the garden during the next several weeks, these plants were showing 90% color by late June.

A better way to handle this crop is to sow seed to plug trays (190 or comparable) or cell packs (72 cells per flat) during December, thinning to one or two seedlings. Move these plantlets into 4-inch (10 cm) or quart containers and grow on cool at 50F to 55F (10C to 13C) nights, then sell in the spring. Plants produce a stronger root system, and the rosette will develop more uniformly than when grown in a cell pack.

Commercial propagators offer this crop as a liner or plug during winter and spring. These plantlets are often vegetatively propagated from cuttings the previous summer, kept cool/cold during autumn, and then shipped in various plug sizes ranging from 50 to 72 cells per flat. If potted to 4-inch (10 cm) containers, the plants will be salable in six to eight weeks when grown on at 55F (13C) nights.

While gauras have limited problems, there is one that growers encounter as the crop develops. In the winter and spring, the plants are cold-frame grown in our climate where the night temperatures can dip into the upper 40s and the days may be cloudy with limited light. During these periods the plants exhibit small, sometimes round, purple blotches of one-quarter inch or so in diameter across the surface of the leaves. These are more noticeable on the leaves of the rosetting plants and less frequent on those that have started to develop some stem length. The plants will eventually grow out of this condition, and the leaves will turn fully green.

VARIETIES

Gaura lindheimeri is available from many U.S. seed firms. It's sometimes sold under the name "The Bride," although this variety's performance is equal to the species and little differences, if any, are noticeable.

USES

Due to this crop's continuous flowering performance, you can plant it along with other perennials or annuals to provide spotted color within a flower bed for some time (in our garden we can expect two months of color). It's not a freely flowering plant, however, and never appears "loaded with color," which is why it is better mixed with other plants for its effect to be fully appreciated. The flowering spikes are long and arching and literally lie on or through the foliage of other plants.

IN THE HOME GARDEN

Winter hardiness in our Chicago location is based on the site that gauras occupy. More well-drained locations seem to ensure survival, while a clay-loam soil in an area with little or no protection from winter's fury can often lead to a full die-out. Late planting or poor site preparation will guarantee die-out after the first winter.

Plant gauras in a full-sun location in areas where its flowering stems can arch over or through surrounding plants or structures. When planted in open areas where they can't lean on other plants, gauras will be tossed about by the wind and require some reshaping as the summer progresses. We have seldom ever needed to stake this crop, although some major untangling has been called for after a summer storm.

▬ GEUM QUELLYON (SYN. G. CHILOENSE)

FAMILY: Rosaceae

COMMON NAME(S): Geum, Avens

DESCRIPTION

Geums offer a lot of charm for a short period of time. Flower colors are either red or yellow, and blooms appear for one to two weeks in the spring. They are scentless, semidouble to double, from 1½ to 2 inches (3 to 5 cm) across. The plants produce a mass of foliage from which the flowering stems develop up to 20 inches (51 cm) in length. Overall, plants can grow 18 to 24 inches (46 to 61 cm) tall with a 14- to 18-inch (35 to 46 cm) spread, but they're often a short-lived perennial for many American gardeners.

HARDINESS: Zones 4 to 8.

SEASON OF BLOOM: May and June.

PROPAGATION

Geum can either be propagated by seed or by divisions taken in the spring or fall.

GERMINATION OVERVIEW: 10,000 seeds per ounce/350 per gram.
Provide germination temperatures of 65F to 70F (19C to 21C). Cover the seed for germination. Seedlings emerge eight to 15 days after sowing. While no pretreatments are usually necessary, seedlings can be slow or irregular to emerge. If using fresh seed or seed that has been harvested within the last six months, germination will be adequate, but percentages can range from 65% to 80%.

If, however, the seed has been stored dry in its package from the previous year, alternating day and night temperatures by 8 to 10 degrees (4C to 6C) has proved beneficial in increasing the overall germination percentages.

Seedlings can be transplanted 18 to 28 days after sowing.

GROWING ON

From seed: Sowings made during winter and later for green pack or 4-inch (10 cm) pot sales in the spring will not produce flowering plants that summer. Instead, the plants will flower once they're exposed to a cold treatment and bloom the following spring.

For plants that will flower in the spring, seed can be sown the previous summer with the resulting seedlings transplanted to cell packs or small pots. Once well rooted, these can be potted up into quart or gallon pots and overwintered dormant for spring sales. Another method is to sow seed in autumn for plugs or liners and then transplant to quarts or gallons when ready. The plants are allowed to root in initially at 50F to 55F (10C to 13C) nights until they are established, and then they're exposed to 40F to 45F (5C to 7C) nights for the remainder of the winter. These plants will flower sporadically during the spring if given at least eight weeks of cold.

An easier method is to purchase vernalized (subjected to a cold treatment) plugs or liners from commercial propagators during the fall or winter. These can be potted up into quarts or larger containers and grown on at 48F to 50F (9C to 10C) nights for green plant sales in spring. Plants will usually bud and flower during June. In general, geums will be salable green in a quart container from a 72 plug within nine to 11 weeks at 52F to 55F (11C to 13C) nights.

For green, 32-cell packs, allow 10 to 11 weeks at 55F (13C) nights. These can be sold as is in the spring (they won't flower that summer), or the plants can be moved into larger containers and sold later.

VARIETIES

Some authorities have noted that many varieties available today under the botanical name of *G. quellyon* are actually hybrids of *G. quellyon* and *G. coccineum* (this latter species has red blossoms). Therefore, you may see the following varieties listed as *G. hybrida* or just simply "Geum hybrids" in other listings.

Mrs. Bradshaw is the most common geum variety on the market. It has bright red 1½-inch flowers held on mostly upright plants in May. Plants range from 18 inches to 2 feet (46 to 60 cm).

Lady Stratheden has deep golden yellow flowers to 1¾ inch (4.5 cm) across that are semidouble or double. Plants bloom in May.

IN THE HOME GARDEN

Often short lived in our gardens near Chicago, geums aren't fond of our wet autumns and cold, dry winters. While plants can tolerate summer heat and humidity, they prefer more shade during the hottest part of the day. Plant into any well-drained location, around building foundations or taller plants. These provide winter protection and help to increase the plant's longevity. Since geums primarily stay short and mounded, staking is not required.

In our gardens, plants flower during June and then sporadically during the summer if night temperatures are below 70F to 80F (21C to 26C). The plants seldom get more than three or four flowering stems at one time, however.

▬ GONIOLIMON TATARICUM
(sometimes listed as *Limonium tatarica*)

FAMILY: Plumbaginaceae

COMMON NAME(S): German Statice, Statice

DESCRIPTION
A well-known and hardy perennial, *Goniolimon tataricum* has small, dark green, basal rosettes that are less than 4 inches (10 cm) tall when not flowering. The foliage is evergreen and persists throughout the winter. Flowering stems are rigid, requiring no support. The open, branched flower heads are made up of multitudes of small, one-eighth-inch (3 mm), lavender to rose-red flowers held by papery white calyxes. As the bloom ages, it will fall out, leaving the dried calyx behind for use as a dried flower. In bloom, the plant grows from 15 to 24 inches (38 to 61 cm) tall and from 15 to 20 inches (38 to 51 cm) across. When not flowering, the plant will spread only 3 to 6 inches (7 to 15 cm) across.

HARDINESS: Zones 3 to 9.

SEASON OF BLOOM: June and July.

PROPAGATION
Seed is the most common propagation method. Divisions work but plants are slow to spread. Divisions are most often left to the home gardener.

GERMINATION OVERVIEW: 22,000 seeds per ounce/770 per gram.
Germination temperatures are 65F to 75F (19C to 24C), and seed needn't be covered with media. Seeds sprout within 14 to 21 days and can be transplanted 24 to 36 days after sowing.

GROWING ON
From seed: While this crop is related to *Limonium latifolium* and germinates in the same number of days, the cropping schedule is entirely different. *Goniolimon tataricum* grows more slowly from seed and should be sown in spring for transplanting to 1- or 2-quart containers by late summer. These can be overwintered for spring sales and will flower during the next spring or early summer in the garden. In general, a green 32-cell pack will require 15 to 18 weeks to fully root when grown at 50F (10C) nights. German statice does not flower the same year as sown.

Commercial propagators offer this crop as bare-root transplants, in small pots or as a liner or plug. Primarily available during the autumn and winter, any of these can be potted up into quarts and gallons and sold in spring.

VARIETIES

Goniolimon tataricum is readily available from seed and plant companies across the United States.

USES

In the perennial border, the bunching habit of the flowering stalks produces an almost mounded or round form in June. The white calyx will stay on the plant for the remainder of the season but becomes dingy as the summer progresses. As a cut flower, German statice is excellent in either dried or fresh arrangements.

In commercial or home landscapes, two-year-old transplants will offer a strong, noninvasive show for years. Plants tolerate various conditions and offer longevity in return for minimal care.

IN THE HOME GARDEN

This extremely hardy plant is often overlooked for home perennial gardens. Its primary use is as a dried cut flower. Allow a number of the flowering stems to remain all summer long after the lavender flower dies. As the season progresses, some staking may be required, although the flowering heads are equally happy if allowed to lean on their neighbors to stay upright.

This variety is somewhat deceiving in its budding and flowering. Most plants bud and then flower during the following week or two. German statice, however, tends to bud in late April or May and does not become free flowering until mid-June. Space plants between 12 and 15 inches (30 and 38 cm) apart and plant in a full-sun, well-drained location.

GYPSOPHILA PANICULATA

FAMILY: Caryophyllaceae

COMMON NAME(S): Baby's Breath

DESCRIPTION

Upright and full, *Gypsophila paniculata* is a tried and true perennial admired for years as a fresh or dried filler in floral arrangements. A multitude of one-eighth-inch (3 mm), scentless, single pink or white flowers are held terminally in open sprays on plants to 3 feet (90 cm) tall in flower. The airy, gray-green foliage can spread 2 to 4 feet (60 to 120 cm) across.

HARDINESS: Zones 4 to 8.

This is not a long-lived perennial here in our gardens, mostly due to our wet autumns (causing crown rot) and dry winters.

SEASON OF BLOOM: June and July.

PROPAGATION

Propagation methods depend on the variety. Cultivars that do not come true from seed—Perfecta and Bristol Fairy—are propagated by cuttings or tissue culture to preserve their double-flowering performance. Other selections, like *G. paniculata* Double Snowflake, are seed varieties and can easily be found from various seed sources. These varieties are inferior to the vegetatively propagated ones, however.

Grafting was a common method in the past but seldom practiced today. It had its merits since some varieties would not readily root when taken as a cutting. *G. paniculata* was the rootstock and other varieties were grafted onto it.

GERMINATION OVERVIEW: 26,000 to 30,000 seeds per ounce/910 to 1,050 per gram. Gypsophila will germinate readily without pretreating. Seedlings emerge in five to 10 days when germinated at 70F to 80F (21C to 26C). Seed doesn't need to be covered to germinate. Seedlings can be transplanted 15 to 20 days after sowing.

GROWING ON

From seed, green 32-cell packs will be salable 10 to 12 weeks after sowing. Plants flower the same season from seed when winter sown. At best they flower sporadically, however, and there's no guarantee of much color the first year. Regardless, don't spend alot of time on seed varieties—they lack the grace and appeal of their vegetative counterparts.

Commercial propagators offer a number of plug and liner sizes in autumn or winter that can be potted up into quarts and sold green in the spring. Crop times can vary due to the multitude of sizes, but six- to 10-week finishing times are commonplace with a growing regime of 55F (13C) nights.

Cuttings can be challenging—expect losses. As explained under **Propagation**, grafting was used because of the slow or nonexistent root formation on some varieties. Heel cuttings (those that include a portion of the stem) appear to work better but this, too, isn't always reliable.

Photoperiod: *G. paniculata* is a long-day plant. It needs more than 14 hours of light to grow and flower. In our tests, early October sowings were slow growing under short days and cool night temperatures of 48F (9C). Plants grew columnar without basal branching and never filled in. When planted into the garden in early May, the plants were only 4 to 6 inches (10 to 15 cm) tall without a growth regulator. The plants flowered in June but weren't free flowering until the second year.

VARIETIES

The seed-propagated cultivars of *G. paniculata* are inferior to the clonal material that is vegetatively propagated.

G. paniculata. This is the single-flowering species from seed. Sometimes the word "single" will appear in quotations next to the species name. It is a small, white-flowered plant reaching 3 feet (90 cm) tall that reliably produces tiny, one-sixteenth-inch (less than 2 mm) flowers.

Double Snowflake (Snowflake). Don't let the delicate name fool you. This is a vigorous plant to 30 inches (76 cm) tall with 50% double and 50% single blooms when grown from seed. The flowers are no larger than one-sixteenth inch (less than 2 mm) across. This variety is rather open and weedy in appearance.

Perfecta is a beautiful variety with double white blooms on plants to 36 inches (91 cm) tall in the garden. This is now the standard cut flower selection over Bristol Fairy in California and Florida. Flowers can measure to one-quarter inch (6 mm) or larger and make excellent dried cut flowers. It is definitely more free flowering than either of the two previously noted. Propagate by tissue culture or from cuttings.

Bristol Fairy is another double white-flowering variety, both smaller flowered and weaker stemmed than Perfecta. However, it often produces more cut flowers than any other variety listed here. When grown as a cut flower, it's also less susceptible to *Botrytis*. Plants are often propagated by tissue culture or cuttings. It grows 24 to 28 inches (61 to 71 cm) high.

Pink Fairy. Plants reach 20 inches (51 cm) with double pink flowers. It has a similar habit and overall performance as Bristol Fairy. Propagate vegetatively.

Red Sea. A beautiful variety with deep pink flowers on plants with 3- to 4-foot (90 to 120 cm) stems. Flowers are double but aren't as free flowering as Pink Fairy. Propagate by tissue culture or cuttings.

RELATED MATERIAL

G. repens (creeping baby's breath) is a dwarf trailing variety producing a large mat of foliage that works well in rock gardens. Flowers are mostly single, but double-flowering varieties are available. Plants grow 5 to 7 inches (13 to 18 cm) tall in bloom and 12 to 18 inches (30 to 46 cm) across.

Seed and division are two common propagation techniques. Divisions can be made in spring and summer after flowering; seed can be sown anytime. Winter sowings of *G. repens* are salable green in 10 to 12 weeks. Plants will flower in June for two or three weeks with a stronger show the following year. *G. repens* is sold 45,000 seeds per ounce (1,575 per gram). Most often the seeded varieties are offered as either white (Alba) or pink (Rosea).

Like *G. paniculata*, *G. repens* is often available from commercial propagators in various liner and plug sizes during autumn and winter. These can be potted up from January to March for mid or late spring sales.

G. pacifica has been confused as a variety of *G. paniculata* although it's a separate species. This seed-propagated variety is the longest lived, however, and the overall best performing of any gypsophila in our Chicago gardens.

G. pacifica has one-quarter-inch (6 mm), single-flowering pink blooms on plants that grow 3 to 4 feet (90 to 120 cm) tall. From seed, it's been more uniform in habit and performance than seed varieties of *G. paniculata*. It is also used as a fresh cut flower and is hardy to Zone 3.

Propagate by seed or cuttings and treat as you would *G. paniculata*.

USES

Baby's breath's predominant use in the United States is as a cut flower—either dried or fresh. Beware of using seed-propagated varieties for this purpose since they're not the same as that sold in floral arrangements. As a fresh cut flower, *G. elegans* Covent Garden Market is preferred, but the variety can't be dried. It's also an annual and will die after the first flush of flowers.

IN THE HOME GARDEN

Plant in full sun, 12 inches (30 cm) apart, in a well-drained but moist location. In bloom, the plants often look billowy and will be self-supportive. Staking may be necessary if planted in open locations away from other plants where the flowering branches could fall over. *Gypsophila* prefers a slightly alkaline soil and won't be long lived in acidic soils. Once flowering is over, plants seldom rebloom profusely, although spotted color returns if old flower heads are removed.

H

■ HELENIUM AUTUMNALE

FAMILY: Asteraceae

COMMON NAME(S): Sneezeweed

DESCRIPTION

Vigorous and erect, *Helenium autumnale* grows semicolumnar, reaching 4 to 5 feet (1.2 to 1.5 m) in height and spreading no more than 2 feet (60 cm) wide. The 2-inch (5 cm) flowers are single, scentless, daisylike and pure yellow, reddish brown, orange, or in combinations of these colors.

HARDINESS: Zones 3 to 8.

SEASON OF BLOOM: August and September.

PROPAGATION

Seed can be used to propagate the species, although there are many fine cultivars vegetatively propagated by divisions in the spring or by cuttings taken in spring and early summer.

GERMINATION OVERVIEW: 140,000 seeds per ounce/4,900 per gram.
Seed germinates in eight to 12 days at 72F (22C) and doesn't need to be covered. Seedlings can be transplanted 28 to 35 days after sowing.

GROWING ON

Crop time: Seed-propagated varieties are quick to grow and maintain a decent uniformity from plant to plant when produced as either quarts or gallons or even when sold green in cell packs in the spring.

With green cell packs, allow nine to 11 weeks from sowing for strong transplants that can be planted in May or June for late summer color the same year. When grown using this method, plants will be 2 feet (60 cm) tall by the end of July and blooming a month later. The plants will be taller and more filled out in later years as roots become more firmly established.

When growing from seed the first year, be sure to harden the plants off in the cold frame prior to sales. This helps keep the plants in check without growth regulators. Temperatures can be 48F to 55F (9C to 13C) during the nights and 10 to 20 degrees (6C to 12C) warmer for days.

For 4-inch (10 cm) pot sales the first year from seed, allow 11 to 13 weeks at 50F (10C) nights; for quart containers, add two to three weeks for rooting into the pot. These plants will also flower the first season from seed.

Cuttings taken during spring and summer will root in two to four weeks at 72F (22C). These are potted up when ready and grown on during the summer for late season sales or held over the winter for spring sales.

Divisions are easy to take in the spring as the growth is first emerging, and the crown will yield many transplants. Once potted to quart containers, these will be quickly salable in two to four weeks.

VARIETIES

There are many varieties commercially available, but the Red and Gold Hybrids noted below are the most common.

Butterpat has bright yellow flowers and grows to 4 feet (1.2 m) tall. It is an excellent and reliable performer from year to year. Propagate vegetatively.

Red and Gold Hybrids grow to 4 feet (1.2 m) tall in yellow and various shades of red, including mahogany, crimson, and bronze. A popular variety, it is readily available from U.S. seed companies.

Riverton Beauty has lemon-yellow flowers with a dark center. Plants grow to 4 feet (1.2 m) tall and are propagated vegetatively.

RELATED MATERIAL

Helenium hoopesii is a rather short-lived perennial that bears 3-inch (7 cm), single, scentless, bright yellow flowers. Plants reach 2 feet (60 cm) tall in the garden and may need staking if grown in fertile locations. The plants flower in June and July but don't have a very impressive overall appearance and should be used sparingly the first year as the gardener evaluates their usefulness.

Seedlings will germinate in seven to 10 days and are transplantable 18 to 24 days after sowing. *H. hoopesii* is faster to germinate than *H. autumnale*; however, it often requires up to 12 weeks to fill out a 32-cell pack before the roots mass up the side of the container. Plants will not flower the same season as sown.

USES

Helenium autumnale works well in gardens where late summer color is desired in a landscape or display. It's most effective when massed at the back of the border where its height is valuable and its flowering is a fresh addition against the green foliage.

In the landscape, *H. autumnale* is hardy in the open and rarely needs any special

——Selected Perennials——

1 *Achillea* Moonshine

2 *Achillea* Paprika

3 *Achillea ptarmica* The Pearl

4 *Aegopodium podagraria*

5 *Ajuga reptans* Burgundy Glow

6 *Ajuga reptans* Catlin's Giant

7 *Alchemilla mollis*

8 *Amsonia tabernaemontana*

9 *Anacyclus depressus*

10 *Anaphalis margaritacea*

11 *Aquilegia × hybrida* Dove

12 *Arabis caucasica*

13 *Armeria maritima* Splendens

14 *Artemisia* Powis Castle

15 *Aster × frikartii* Wonder of Staffa

16 *Astilbe × arendsii* Peach Blossom

17 *Astilbe chinensis* var. *pumila*

18 *Astilbe simplicifolia* Sprite

19 *Aurinia saxatilis* Compacta

20 *Begonia grandis*

21 *Boltonia asteroides* Snowbank

22 *Campanula carpatica* Uniform series

23 *Campanula cochleariifolia* ➤

24 *Campanula glomerata*

26 *Campanula persicifolia*

25 *Campanula medium*

27 *Catanache caerulea*

28 *Ceratostigma plumbaginoides*

29 *Clematis integrifolia*

30 *Clematis maximowicziana*

31 *Coreopsis grandiflorum* Early Sunrise

32 *Coreopsis rosea*

33 *Coreopsis verticillata*
Moonbeam ➤

34 *Coreopsis verticillata*
Zagreb ▼

35 *Crocosmia* Spitfire

◄**36** *Dianthus arenarius*

38 *Echinops ritro*

37 *Echinacea purpurea*

39 *Euphorbia polychroma*

40 *Filipendula rubra* Venusta

41 *Filipendula ulmaria*

43 *Hibiscus acetosella*

44 *Hibiscus moscheutos* Dixie
Belle White

42 *Heliopsis helianthoides* var.
scabra Summer Sun

45 *Lamiastrum galeobdolon* var.
variegatum

46 *Lamium maculatum* White Nancy

47 *Lathyrus latifolius*

◄ **48** *Leontopodium alpinum*

49 *Liatris spicata*

◄ **50** *Ligularia dentata* Desdemona

51 *Ligularia stenocephala*

52 *Lobelia siphilitica*

53 *Lupinus polyphyllus*

54 *Lysimachia nummularia* Aurea

55 *Papaver orientale*

56 *Perovskia atriplicifolia*

57 *Phlox paniculata* Mt. Fuji

58 *Phlox subulata* Emerald Blue

59 *Physostegia virginiana*

60 *Platycodon grandiflorus*
Sentimental Blue

61 *Pulsatilla vulgaris*

62 *Sagina subulata*

64 *Saxifraga × arendsii* Purple Robe

63 *Saponaria ocymoides*

65 *Sedum* × Vera Jameson ➤

66 *Sedum reflexum*

67 *Sedum spectabile* Brilliant

68 *Tradescantia* × *andersoniana*
Zwanenberg

69 *Veronicastrum virginicum*

70 *Viola odorata*
◄ White Czar

care from year to year to look its best. The long-lived plants can be massed with other perennials or annuals for full summer color. People seldom notice the green foliage of a nonflowering plant until its full color regalia is noticeable in late summer. Few perennials—and few plants in general—reach their peak of color in the late summer. *Helenium*'s flowering is quite dramatic when used effectively in the landscape. It's a refreshing change from the normal, static color present only a week or two before.

H. autumnale can also be used as a fresh cut flower. It's best when mixed with some foliage greens or small-flowered crops like gypsophila. Cut the stems when the first color starts to unfold, and flowers will last up to a week.

IN THE HOME GARDEN

Helenium autumnale is a long-lived plant in the garden and seldom requires any special winter coverings, summer treatments, or techniques to keep it happy. Due to its height, it can be placed at the back of perennial borders or gardens or tucked in among other perennials, shrubs, or annuals. Its color will add a new dimension to the garden plants when in full bloom.

Plants don't require any staking but appreciate full-sun locations to keep the stems erect and strong. Too fertile an area will cause weak stems and short-lived plants that often grow and flower so continuously that the roots weaken to the point where they succumb to winter conditions.

Helenium works well in reclaiming embankments and other hard-to-plant areas where a hardy, flowering plant is needed to add some late season effects.

HELIANTHEMUM NUMMULARIUM

FAMILY: Cistaceae

COMMON NAME(S): Rock Rose, Sunrose

DESCRIPTION

A Mediterranean native, *Helianthemum nummularium* is a low-growing, spreading perennial. Maximum height is 8 to 12 inches (20 to 30 cm) tall, although the plants will grow taller in warm winter climates. They possess woody stems with green to gray-green evergreen foliage on branches that spread to 20 inches (51 cm) across. The flowers are single (sometimes double), mostly an inch across, but some grow as large as 2 inches (5 cm) across. Common flower colors are rose, pink, and yellow; some are orange, red, and white as well.

HARDINESS: Zones 5 to 7.

In our Chicago climate plants can be short lived when a wet fall or warm/cold and wet winter occurs. Review **In the home garden** for clarification.

SEASON OF BLOOM: May and June.

PROPAGATION

Seed and cuttings are the standard propagation methods. The named cultivars (see **Varieties**) need to be propagated by semiripe cuttings taken after flowering in summer and early autumn. Some authors suggest dividing the plants in the spring—I find this a rather meticulous process, with serious consequences and limited yields if not done correctly. It's better done by the home gardener, not the professional grower.

GERMINATION OVERVIEW: 14,000 seeds per ounce/490 per gram.

Pretreatments: Fresh seed is essential in achieving good germination results. If seed is gathered in the late summer and sown in November, germination results will be relatively high. For us, fresh seed has germinated at 75% to 85% over the years. Seed held until the following summer and then sown has germinated between 60% and 70%.

Sow seed to any peat-lite media, covering lightly. Seed germinates in five to 15 days, and transplanting can start in 20 to 30 days after sowing. In the *Ball Culture Guide*, I state that *Helianthemum* seed germinates in 15 to 20 days. This is true when using seed older than one year.

GROWING ON

Crop time: When sowing from seed, keep in mind that helianthemums are shallow-rooted perennials, often not filling out a container with a massive root system. In general, 4-inch (10 cm) pots are ready for green sales 18 to 20 weeks after sowing when grown at 55F to 58F (13C to 14C); however, plants won't flower the same year.

Sow seed in the fall or winter for 4-inch (10 cm) or quart sales the following spring. These plants will be sold green and flower a year later. For larger plants as well as flowering ones, you can sow during spring for gallon or quart sales the following year. These plants will flower the same year as sold.

Cuttings taken during the summer can be potted up into their final containers by late summer and grown dormant over the winter. Because of the foliage's evergreen nature, plants shouldn't be cut off down to the crown; shearing them lightly to maintain their shape is acceptable.

Commercial propagators often have a number of vegetatively propagated cultivars available for winter shipping. If shipped then, plants will probably be vernalized already (exposed to a cold treatment), so they'll flower during the coming spring. Liners or large plugs can be potted one plant per quart container and grown on at no lower than 50F (10C) nights. As for crop time, a liner or plug from a 72-cell tray will finish in a quart container in nine to 13 weeks when grown at 55F (13C) nights and warmer.

VARIETIES

There are many cultivars that should be vegetatively propagated to maintain the plant's color and form. Seed is sold in mixtures only and is listed below under the name of Mutabile. With the exception of this one variety, all of the remaining varieties listed here must be vegetatively propagated to maintain plant integrity.

All of the following varieties are single flowering unless otherwise noted.

Buttercup is 6 to 10 inches (15 to 25 cm) tall with golden yellow flowers.

Cerise Queen is 10 to 18 inches (25 to 46 cm) tall with double red flowers.

Fire Dragon (sometimes Firedragon) has orange flowers on plants 10 to 12 inches (25 to 30 cm) tall. Foliage is gray green.

Mutabile is a seed-propagated variety most often sold as a mixture, although rose and pink flower colors tend to predominate. Plants grow to 10 inches (25 cm) tall.

Raspberry Ripple grows 8 to 10 inches (20 to 25 cm) tall with raspberry red and white flowers. It has gray foliage.

Wisley Pink (*H. rhodanthum carneum*) has soft pink flowers on plants to 10 inches (25 cm) tall. The foliage is gray green.

Wisley Primrose has lemon-yellow flowers on plants less than 10 inches (25 cm) tall.

H

USES

Helianthemum is at home in the rock garden, tumbling over walls, as a border or edging, or where the dainty flowers and foliage can be appreciated at close quarters, such as in a small garden or tucked in a patio corner. Plants don't work well when massed, since the color shows strongly for only one to three weeks depending on the coolness of the spring. The flowers only last for one day and new flower buds open daily.

The plants aren't recommended for use massed in commercial landscapes because of their limited blooming period and dwarf habit. For the home garden and selected commercial sites, however, they shouldn't be overlooked. The blooms have a wild roselike appearance (even the single-flowering ones), and their evergreen foliage colors early in the spring.

IN THE HOME GARDEN

Helianthemum grows best where it gets full sun, warm days, and cool nights. The plants are often long lived (four years or more) when grown in our hot Midwestern summers. The key to survival is a well-drained soil and protection from frequent autumn rains and drying, cold winter winds. The autumn rains may seem an odd thing to avoid, but even with a well-drained soil, excess water around the roots from October to early December followed by a cold, hard freeze, will be the death of most of your plants especially when planted out away from buildings or other protection.

Once planted, use a light mulch around the crown year-round to protect the plants and allow for good moisture retention. Plants perform better in a neutral pH to slightly alkaline soil. They don't require any special techniques or treatments to grow other than the mulch.

▬▬ HELIOPSIS HELIANTHOIDES VAR. SCABRA

The following notes are specific to the cultivar Summer Sun.

FAMILY: Asteraceae

COMMON NAME(S): False Sunflower, Hardy Sunflower, Sunflower Heliopsis

DESCRIPTION

This is an excellent perennial with a long flowering period. It grows between 3 and 4 feet (90 to 120 cm) tall and has a 15- to 24-inch (38 to 61 cm) spread. Stems grow erect, without branching, from a central crown. As many as 10 stems will develop, each one producing a flower canopy at its terminal point. The dark green foliage measures up to 4 inches (10 cm) long. The scentless flowers are yellow, single to semidouble, and 3 to 4 inches (7 to 10 cm) wide.

HARDINESS: Zones 3 to 9.

This extremely hardy perennial requires no mulching or special care for garden longevity.

SEASON OF BLOOM: June to September.

PROPAGATION

Heliopsis is propagated in three ways, from seed, cuttings, and division. Plants started from seed are reliably true and will flower the same season as sown when started in winter or early spring. Divisions are easily taken during spring or fall, and cuttings are best taken in early spring prior to flower buds developing.

GERMINATION OVERVIEW: 8,000 seeds per ounce/280 per gram.

Seed germinates in three to 10 days at 70F (21C), uncovered. Transplant seedlings 11 to 20 days after sowing.

Note: This an easily grown perennial from seed. You can expect germination rates of 70% or better.

GROWING ON

Crop time: From seed, plants grow quickly and are salable green eight to 10 weeks after sowing. Four-inch, quart, or gallon containers are equally easy to ready for spring from seed sown in late fall or early winter. Plants will start flowering in June or July from a winter sowing.

Heliopsis prefers warm conditions and bright light when started from seed during winter. If temperatures are too cool, the lower leaves will yellow around the margins, then across the entire leaf until it falls off. To avoid this condition, keep temperatures above 55F (13C) day and night. Once night temperatures are consistently in the upper 50s (13C to 15C) and the roots have fully formed, less yellowing will occur.

If plants grow too rapidly under warmer weather, give the plants a soft pinch prior to sales. That will force two stems to develop and keep the plant shorter in the garden the first season.

Cuttings are easy to take and root. To increase your cutting material, allow the plants to emerge in the spring, shear them off, and use the snipped shoots as your cutting material. Be sure to take cuttings early (May) to avoid budding.

As for divisions, they're easy to take and numerous plantlets can be obtained from a 2-year-old crown. March/April-dug crowns, divided to allow for two to three active stems, will root within two weeks into a gallon pot. That's at least enough to hold the root ball together in retail sales. The plants will grow erect without basal branching, but you can help the plant to fill out and look more attractive if you pinch the stems back at the same time you take the division.

VARIETIES

All of the following varieties prefer full sun and warm conditions.

Summer Sun is the most common variety within the species and the best performer across the country of all the varieties noted here. Hardy and dependable, it's uniform to flower and tolerates various soil and climate conditions. The **Description** section provides all the detail on this variety. It is available from seed. See Color Plate 42 for photo of *Heliopsis helianthoides* var. *scraba* Summer Sun.

Vegetative varieties

Golden Plume grows to 3½ feet (105 cm) tall with free-flowering, double yellow flowers from June to September. It is the best of the fully double-flowering selections on the market.

Gold Greenheart (also listed as Goldgreenheart) also bears double yellow flowers, but each flower has a midgreen center. Plants grow to 3 feet (90 cm) tall.

Incomparabilis grows from 2 to 3 feet (60 to 90 cm) tall with semidouble, deep gold-yellow flowers. The blooms have dark centers.

Karat bears 4- to 5-inch (10 to 13 cm) single, deep yellow flowers on plants to 4 feet (1.2 m) tall.

Patula has semidouble yellow flowers on plants from 2 to 3 feet (60 to 90 cm) tall.

USES

Heliopsis is a long-lived perennial with an excellent performance in the home garden or in general landscaping. The plants fill in quickly but may require staking the first season after planting since the flowers develop and bloom faster than the roots have time to set and establish the plant.

Consider using heliopsis in golf courses and other large commercial plantings where a herbaceous hedge is needed for the summer. It dies to the ground in winter.

While not commercially important, heliopsis does make a very good cut flower variety.

IN THE HOME GARDEN

Fast growing and dependable, heliopsis requires very little care. It yields numerous yellow flowers for a good portion of the growing season—longer than most perennials.

Heliopsis should be planted where it gets full sun in a well-drained soil. If the plants moved to your garden are elongated, pinch the tops back to encourage branching. You should stake the plants the first season until they become established; in subsequent seasons they seldom require staking unless overfed or heavily watered.

▬ HEMEROCALLIS SPP.

FAMILY: Liliaceae

COMMON NAME(S): Daylily

DESCRIPTION

The grand dame of the perennial border, the daylily excels in performance across the United States. While some perennials prefer coastal areas, others the heat of a southern summer, and a few the chill of a northern winter, daylilies cross all regions and climatic conditions, performing equally well regardless of the climate. Granted, there are extremes that even daylilies will not tolerate, but they are still one of the most versatile and widely distributed of the garden perennials.

Only a few of the hemerocallis species are grown in American gardens. Instead, it is the hybrids that have helped this class become one of the backbones of the perennial plant trade. The plants are clump-forming perennials with enlarged, white tuber-like growths at the end of the thickened fibrous roots. Plants can grow from 2 to 4 feet (60 to 120 cm) across with gracefully arching leaves providing a fountain-like look to the planting. Leaves can elongate to 1 inch (2.5 cm) wide and up to 2 feet (60 cm) long once established.

There are dormant, evergreen, and semievergreen daylily varieties available, but the evergreen varieties are for our southern gardeners while the semievergreen varieties do better in more temperate climates. Here in Chicago, all the varieties that we have tried go dormant in winter. Flowers are held upright on stems that range from 12 inches to 3½ feet (30 to 105 cm). Flowers are in a variety of colors, primarily in bold and bright shades of yellow, orange, red, pink, rose, purple, maroon, and crimson. Ivory, white, and blue aren't available. The blooms range in size from 2½ to 6 inches (6 to 15 cm) wide and deep. Flowers are trumpet shaped (lilylike), sometimes fragrant, and usually last only one day.

HARDINESS: Zones 4 to 9.

In Zones 6 to 8, lilies with evergreen foliage will be more persistent during the winter months. If you live in the upper regions of Zone 7 or in Zone 6, covering the plants during extended cold weather may be advisable. The cold hardiness of the roots, however, is not in question. Hemerocallis, as a group, is very hardy and will return year after year.

SEASON OF BLOOM: June to frost.

One variety may flower only during a one-month span. However, there are now many varieties that flower summer to frost—Stella de Oro is one of these.

PROPAGATION

Daylilies are commonly propagated by division. Tissue-cultured plants are also available. Spring or fall is the time for digging and division. Most commercial sales are done on 2-year-old plants. As you separate the clumps, divide the roots to have two to three shoots. Many commercially propagated pieces you'll receive will have one or two. Seed propagation is strictly for finding new cultivars and growing the species. Many times, however, the resulting plants are then replicated by either of the two methods noted.

Occasionally some references note that hemerocallis is propagated by cuttings. Technically, cuttings taken from any of the species or hybrids will not root. Instead, small plantlets develop around the base of the stems. These can be removed, along with a root portion, to a propagation bench to fully root. It can take from two to three years to get a strong flowering plant.

GERMINATION OVERVIEW

Seed for the various species is available, although not readily found in the United States. You can collect the seed yourself to try the methods below. Since you can readily propagate the various hemerocallis selections by division, the following notes are provided only as a point of reference:

Sow the seed into an open flat and cover with a layer of propagation media (peat, vermiculite, mixtures, etc.), and keep media temperatures at 68F to 70F (20C to 21C). Germination starts in two to three weeks but seedlings may appear in flushes ranging from two to seven weeks after sowing. Dr. Norman Deano in his book, *Seed Germination Theory and Practice*, got germination rates of 91% between two and nine weeks at 70F (21C). My germination rates were 20% or less.

If germination is slow, more erratic than noted above, or non-existent, a cold/moist period may be of benefit. Sow seed in a peat-based media, cover as noted above, moisten and store at 40F (4C) for a period of six weeks. Then germinate as above. Seed will germinate very irregularly over a period of three to eight weeks, and seedlings will need to be transplanted as they are ready—don't throw the tray out until germination is complete. From seed, plants will take two to three years to flower.

GROWING ON

From division: In August and September, hemerocallis plants are dug, divided, and immediately shipped as roots to growers, or stored. Commercial propagators such as DeVroomen, Walters Gardens, Klehm Nurseries, etc., will have roots available for shipping from late summer until early or midwinter. The roots can be potted up anytime during this period for overwintering; the developing plants can be sold the following spring.

As for crop time, most varieties will be salable green between eight and 10 weeks after potting up in gallons and growing on at 55F (13C) nights. In general, bare-root transplants potted up in February and March will be rooted enough in the container to sell in May. These divisions will usually produce from one to no more than three active shoots. Obviously, the more shoots produced, the faster the plant will root and the quicker the crop time. Also, the plant will be more filled out on a three-stem base than those that have only one. With one potting date, therefore, it's conceivable that salable plants from a visual standpoint will reach the same point over a two- or three-week period.

Hemerocallis, like gladiolus, usually grow in a one-sided formation. Instead of leaves positioning themselves all around the developing stem, the leaves are two-ranked, opposite one another. If there is only one active stem, the plant will not appear visually full at the time it's sold, especially if a small root is potted to a gallon pot. When using roots with one shoot or if potting up dwarf varieties, you might try a 2- or 3-quart container—retail customers may consider it a better value. A 4-quart or gallon pot will work better for larger growing varieties.

Hemerocallis varieties will flower the first summer in the garden if started early enough. Plants overwintered from a fall potting produce the best flowering plants the following summer; roots potted up in March yield the least flowering plants. Dwarf varieties readily flower and can often be sold blooming in a gallon pot, even when the division is potted up in March or April. Most sales are in April and May, however, so allow 11 to 14 weeks for flowering plants on selected varieties when grown at 55F (13C) nights.

Sometimes varieties won't flower at all and will develop a foliage canopy instead. In some cases, the problem is that the plants are from one-year-old divisions and are too small for flowering. Many growers pot these up into 2-gallon containers and grow them on during the summer for fall or next spring sales. Granted, this increases your costs and won't be applicable for everyone's business.

If roots are planted in the fall, make sure the plants have firmly rooted before temperatures drop consistently below 40F (4C). Otherwise, 45F (7C) night temperatures are best to establish plants in pots before the onset of cold weather. While cold hardy, daylilies need special care to avoid root rots when brought out of winter treatment. Here in Chicago, hemerocallis plants can be brought out with limited problems when night temperatures are still dropping below 40F (4C). If thawed out after being overwintered in a cold frame, however, the bulbous roots are susceptible to absorbing excess water and then bursting if allowed to freeze again.

VARIETIES

With over 20,000 daylily selections registered, this crop is much too detailed to be properly represented here. Some commercial propagators—like Walters Gardens, Klehm Nursery, DeVroomen, etc.—carry a broad listing based on variety, chromosome count, or color. Check with these companies for complete available variety listings.

One additional note: Daylily varieties are often categorized by their chromosome count. As you read through the various catalogs, notice the information on each plant's hybridization. Diploid daylilies have two sets of chromosomes with 3- to 6-inch (7 to 15 cm) blooms and softer colors. Tetraploid varieties have four sets of chromosomes, usually with a larger plant and flower size than the standard hybrids and often with frilled or ruffled petals. Tetraploids are usually more expensive but make a bigger, bolder show in the garden. Another class—miniature daylilies—are so-called due to their small flower size of 3 inches (7 cm) or less. While the flowers may be smaller, some varieties can grow as tall as 24 inches (61 cm).

To do justice to the multitude of hemerocallis varieties that are available on the market, I feel that a minimum of four pages of varieties would be needed. While this would take care of most of the commercial varieties offered by various companies across the United States and Canada, there are some regional or local favorites that you would miss. To that end, I am not including a cultivar list in this book. Many of the varieties that I thought of listing are now antiquated, and you would be missing newer, more refined selections that you should consider. Contact the various nurseries noted in this section or provided in the **Perennial Source List** at the back of this book for additional addresses.

USES

In the daylily perennial border, little can match some of the larger types for arching habits and long-lasting color. Use as foundation plantings, massed outside the home, or as specimen plantings around the yard.

Hemerocallis makes a good cut flower if you take a stem with open blooms and a mixture of opened and opening flower buds, since the blooms generally last only one day.

In the commercial landscape, daylilies work very well. A number of varieties will rebloom once initial flowering is over. In the interim, the foliage provides a softening and formal appearance to the planting.

IN THE HOME GARDEN

Daylilies are a welcome addition to any garden, providing bold and dramatic colors, especially yellow. The perennial border can literally dance with the vibrance of these hues. Plant daylilies in a full-sun location, although they can tolerate partial shade.

However, remember that hemerocallis needs six hours of sunlight daily to produce strong stems and a profusion of flower color. Plant them where their foliar fountain of leaves can arch unhindered to the ground. Don't plant tight up against shrubs or large, robust, herbaceous perennials. However, we've seen an excellent performance in our garden by combining them with upright, spiring plants that project through and above the foliage. Plants like *Lobelia cardinalis*, some of the dwarf delphinium species, *Asphodeline lutea*, and other nonintrusive varieties combine well.

Space plants 15 to 24 inches (38 to 61 cm) apart, depending on the variety, in a well-drained location. Soil pH should be between 6 and 7 for best performance. Plants don't require staking or any special treatment but should be fed during the spring to encourage a strong bloom set. They don't need regular division, but once planted, they can be lifted and separated every three or four years if you want to share plants with friends. Established clumps left undivided, however, can become robust (depending on the variety) and provide a dramatic background in your garden.

—The author appreciates the time that Roy Klehm of Klehm Nursery, Champaign, Illinois, took to read and edit this information.

■ HESPERIS MATRONALIS

FAMILY: Cruciferae

COMMON NAME(S): Dame's Rocket, Sweet Rocket

DESCRIPTION
The flowers of dame's rocket are sometimes scented, usually most strongly in the afternoon or early evening hours. It is a biennial plant, rosetting the first year from seed and flowering the following year with single, four-petaled, one-half to three-quarter-inch (1 to 2 cm) flowers in either purple or white. If seed is sown during the winter or spring, the plants will reach 5 to 7 inches (13 to 18 cm) during the summer. The following year, *Hesperis matronalis* will grow to between 2 and 3 feet (60 to 90 cm) tall, spreading 12 to 15 inches (30 to 38 cm). Plants reseed prolifically.

HARDINESS: Zones 3 to 8.

SEASON OF BLOOM: May and June.
If cut back after flowering, the plants will rebloom in the cooler days of summer.

PROPAGATION
Seed is the most common propagation method but often gives you both purple- and white-flowering plants from the same seed bag. If the packet reads *Hesperis matronalis* without noting that the color is purple, you will get both colors with purple predominating. Cuttings are taken from the double forms since seed doesn't come true to type.

GERMINATION OVERVIEW: 14,000 seeds per ounce/490 per gram.

Hesperis germinates readily, requiring only the basics to develop and grow. It will germinate in five to seven days at 70F (21C), and the seed doesn't need to be covered for germination. Seedlings can be transplanted in less than 17 days after sowing.

GROWING ON

Crop time: *Hesperis* is one of those crops that can be sown directly to the final container and allowed to develop and grow without a transplant, due to its quick growth. It's easily grown directly in the garden and can become a weed if the flower heads are allowed to fully mature and drop seed. In a greenhouse environment, I would suggest at least one transplanting to keep the plants in check. The seedlings grow quickly and can get away from you, requiring water, temperature, or growth regulators to slow them down.

Seed sown during winter and spring will produce green salable transplants (in a 32-cell pack) in 11 to 13 weeks when grown at 50F to 55F (10C to 13C) nights. The plants will only rosette their first season and flower the following year. If seed is sown during late summer to early October, transplanted to quart or gallon pots when ready, and grown dormant or with cold nights of 40F (5C) during the winter, the plants will flower by the end of June. A cold period is necessary to break the plants from their immature or rosetting state before they will mature or flower. If you want salable flowering quart or gallon plants in the spring, sow seed during the previous spring or early summer, transplant to quart or gallon pots, and overwinter in a dormant state at 32F (0C).

Under periods of extreme cold the lower foliage turns a bright burgundy or purple, but permanent damage will occur only after prolonged exposures.

Take cuttings from the double-flowering forms yearly to perpetuate the line. Since this crop is biennial, waiting a year may leave you without a mother block to take cuttings from. Stronger plants will grow from cuttings taken from shoots that develop when the plant is cut back after flowering. Feed and allow to grow vegetatively. Note: When cut back after flowering, plants can also bud up again. Be sure to take your cuttings before buds form.

Double-flowering varieties can also be divided in early spring. In the United States, however, there are few places that mimic England's weather patterns which yield plants big enough to take divisions from. Instead, in our more severe, hot climate, the plants are usually more dwarf or petite in forming a clump, so cuttings are often your best bet on the double forms.

VARIETIES

Hesperis matronalis is readily available from numerous U.S. seed companies. If a pure color line of purple or white is preferred, you can obtain the purple from certain

H

companies, but you may have to gather your own seed to get a consistent supply of the white.

H. matronalis var. *alba-plena* is a white, double-flowering variety. The double forms are seldom seen in the United States, and few companies carry the selections. While reviewing commercial catalogs from various nurseries and plant companies for this book, I wasn't able to find any that carried them.

USES

Hesperis is best planted where it can naturalize. If planted into a structured garden, this crop's reseeding can be a nuisance. Instead, plant into areas where low maintenance is needed or preferred, and a surprise seedling or two would be appreciated, not scorned. As a cut flower, the plants have a limited vase life and are better utilized as a garden flower.

Due to the plant's seasonality, *Hesperis* isn't recommended as a landscape plant unless you are working with wildflowers or meadow gardening. In the southern United States, the plants often die after flowering and set seed, while in the North the foliage often yellows as the seed heads mature. The plants seldom die out by the end of summer, however.

IN THE HOME GARDEN

Plant *Hesperis* where it gets full sun for most of the day—although it will tolerate afternoon shade. If planted in a moist and well-drained soil, it will produce good overall growth in a full-sun location. If planted where drainage or moisture are lacking, although it gets full sun, the plants often go downhill faster after flowering. In these exposures, a location with some afternoon shade is preferred. In naturalized settings, the self-sown seedlings will exhibit less of this pattern.

Once flowering is complete, trim the developing seed heads off and a second—though less showy—flowering can be expected, especially if the nights are less than 80F (26C). A reflush of color can be expected three weeks or so after cutting the plants back.

Plants are often weak stemmed during flowering, particularly when planted in moist open areas where they're not sheltered from the wind. Plants may require staking.

If purchased plants flower for you this year and you remove all the seed heads from the plants after they flower, you'll be heading to the nursery again the following year—if you want to see *Hesperis* again. As an option, allow one or two plants to set seed and allow seed to drop. In our gardens, the seeds ripened in July and August and were allowed to fall; developing rosettes were visible in late summer and flowered the following year.

■ HEUCHERA SANGUINEA

FAMILY: Saxifragaceae

COMMON NAME(S): Coral Bells, Alumroot

DESCRIPTION

Dwarf, low mounds of densely held foliage and elongated, spirelike flowering stems are the key attributes of this native perennial. *H. sanguinea* is the most common of the coral bells with rounded, lightly lobed foliage growing 6 to 8 inches (15 to 20 cm) tall and 8 to 12 inches (20 to 30 cm) across. Every spring, erect, arching, flowering stems develop out of the center of the crown reaching 12 to 18 inches (30 to 46 cm) high. The flowers are single, about one-half inch (1 cm) and resemble tiny campanulas on the stems. Flower colors are pastel shades of red and scarlet.

HARDINESS: Zones 3 to 8.

Plants are generally reliable from season to season here in the Midwest. If we have a particularly wet fall followed by a cold snap, however, the plants often die out during the winter due to crown rot.

SEASON OF BLOOM: June and July.

After the main flush of color, many varieties will sporadically flower until frost.

PROPAGATION

Heuchera is commonly propagated by seed but the cultivars can only be propagated by division. Divisions can be taken during spring or autumn.

GERMINATION OVERVIEW: 500,000 seeds per ounce/17,500 per gram.

Heuchera sanguinea germinates in 21 to 30 days at 65F to 75F (18C to 24C). Leave the seed exposed to light during germination. Transplanting can be done 30 to 45 days after sowing.

GROWING ON

The first year after sowing, this perennial is slow to develop and grow. Therefore, sowings made anytime during the winter will not produce lush quality plants for sales during spring or summer. Rather, these plants will be small, growing 2 to 3 inches (5 to 7 cm) tall with the same width. They will not flower the first year.

For 4-inch (10 cm) and larger container sales in spring, sow seed the previous year in the spring. From sowing, eight to 10 weeks are required for the plants to be rooted in a 32-cell pack or 50-liner tray when grown at 55F (13C) nights. These plants will be just large enough to handle, however. For more well-rooted plants allow 10 to 12

H

weeks. These transplants can be potted to their final container by mid-August and overwintered dormant for spring sales.

Commercial propagators offer many varieties propagated by either seed or crown divisions. These are available in a number of plug and liner sizes, although the seeded varieties are usually offered in tray sizes of 50 to 125 cells per flat while the vegetative ones are in 30 to 72 cells. Liners can be potted up one plug to a 4-inch (10 cm) or quart container during winter for spring sales. In general, eight to 10 weeks are required for a 50-plug to root into a quart container when grown at 55F (13C) nights.

From division: Crown divisions can also be taken. The crowns are made up of five to seven individual rosettes that can be divided and removed (along with roots) from the mother crown. When taken in the late summer or autumn, plants can be potted up into 1- or 2-quart containers for overwintering and sold in the spring. Divisions can also be taken in the spring and will fill out a 4-inch (10 cm) container, one plant per pot, in six to eight weeks, depending on plantlet size. Plants propagated in the spring, however, aren't the size and quality of those produced the previous year.

Commercial propagators also offer many varieties bare root for shipment in fall and winter. These can be potted up into 1- to 3-quart containers during January, February, or March for spring sales.

VARIETIES

Bressingham Hybrids. This seed mix of pastel shades includes scarlet and light crimson. Plants grow 18 to 22 inches (46 to 56 cm) tall in flower.

Chatterbox. Deep rose-pink flowers are displayed on stems from 18 to 20 inches (46 to 51 cm) tall. Propagate vegetatively.

Snow Storm and Snow Angel are two excellent cultivars with variegated cream-white-splashed foliage highlighted with soft pink flowers. Both varieties reach 15 to 18 inches (38 to 46 cm) tall and are vegetatively propagated.

Splendens (Spitfire or Firefly) is another seed-propagated variety with deep red flowers on uniformly growing plants. This is one of the most popular seed varieties. It's 12 to 18 inches (30 to 46 cm) tall in flower.

RELATED MATERIAL

H. micrantha Palace Purple (sometimes listed as H. americana) is an excellent cultivar with densely packed, maplelike leaves in more open clumps than H. sanguinea. The leaves are richly colored, with a bronze upper surface and a deep purple coloring beneath. The upright panicles hold a multitude of one-half-inch-long, cream-white to yellow flowers on 8- to 12-inch-tall (20 to 30 cm) plants, although when flowering the plants get 18 to 22 inches (46 to 56 cm) tall. Palace Purple will spread 12 to 15 inches (30 to 38 cm) across.

Palace Purple was a 1991 Perennial Plant Association variety of the year. Although it is a clone, it's also propagated by seed. Care needs to be taken, however, to remove all green and other off-types. While these off-types account for less than 5% of the total seedlings grown, vegetatively propagated plants are true to type.

When growing from seed, follow the information as provided for *H. sanguinea*. Since this crop tends to take longer from seed, we add two weeks to the above cropping information. This is only true for seed sown during winter for spring or summer sales when growing side by side with *H. sanguinea*. If sowing in summer for transplanting to overwintering containers, both species will grow equally.

USES

This is an excellent variety for the home garden, commercial landscapes, and for a container plant. The plants are ideal as a garden border or edging, grouped in threes or fours, and are appreciated by hummingbirds.

In the commercial landscape, the variegated forms of *H. sanguinea* or Palace Purple are of the most benefit since their foliage will provide continuous color all summer long. Note that *Heuchera* flowers primarily in spring but will sporadically flower until frost. In commercial landscapes, various colored foliage cultivars are recommended to fill in for sporadic flower color.

One additional comment regarding Palace Purple: Some consider the flowers to detract from the foliage and prefer to use only the foliage.

IN THE HOME GARDEN

Plants are shallow rooted and may need dividing by the third year. Here in our Midwest location, however, we wait for up to five or six years to divide depending on how large the plants have become and whether they require it. If planted in open beds away from winter protection (buildings, shrubs, etc.), our plants can be short lived. In these cases, we cover them with evergreen boughs or other mulch to get air to the crown and to avoid compacting the plants.

Plant *Heuchera* in a well-drained, semishaded area where it gets morning sun and shade by the hottest part of the day.

◼ HIBISCUS MOSCHEUTOS

FAMILY: Rosaceae

COMMON NAME(S): Hibiscus, Rose Mallow

DESCRIPTION

Dramatic and impressive in the midsummer garden, hibiscus has been more often associated with the South than the North. Hibiscus produces a small clump with three to six upright stems that develop from the roots every spring. Each stem produces a number of single, scentless flowers facing outward on plants from 2½ to 5 feet (75 to 150 cm) tall. Flower colors include red, rose-pink, and white, either pure colors or with dark-colored eyes. The flowers are huge and platelike, due to the flat appearance of the bloom. One bloom can measure 6 to 10 inches (15 to 25 cm) across and, while they last only one day, the plants will stay in flower until frost. Plants spread 2 to 4 feet (60 cm to 1.2 m) across.

HARDINESS: Zones 4 to 9.

Winter kill is the hardiness problem we face with hibiscus in the Midwest. If there are heavy rainfalls in autumn followed by a severe cold snap, we can lose the entire planting.

SEASON OF BLOOM: July to frost.

In the southern United States, these plants start to flower in June and continue until late summer. Here in our Chicago gardens, the plants begin flowering the last two weeks of July and stay in color until the weather cools.

PROPAGATION

Hibiscus can be propagated by seed, cuttings, and divisions. Stem cuttings can be taken during spring or early summer. Divisions are made in the fall or spring. Keep in mind that plants are slow to send up shoots in the spring so fall dividing will be easier. Tissue culture is another method of commercial propagation.

GERMINATION OVERVIEW: 2,100 seeds per ounce/735 per gram.

Pretreatments: Fresh seed offers the best germination and performance in the sowing flat. We soak the seed overnight before sowing, however, and nick or chip the seed-coats on seeds still floating the following morning. Germination takes seven to 10 days at 70F to 80F (21C to 26C); cover the seed for germination. Transplanting can be done 16 to 22 days after sowing.

GROWING ON

From seed: Winter- or early spring-sown seeds will produce flowering plants the same year. February sowings transplanted to 1- or 2-quart containers and grown on at 58F (14C) or higher nights will be salable green in May. Plants will start to flower in June or July.

Dwarf varieties can be forced into bloom earlier and as a pot plant. Seed sown in March yields flowering gallon or 6-inch (15 cm) pots in June when grown in a greenhouse using 60F (16C) nights. Using one plant per pot, cultivars like Dixie Belle and/or Disco Belle will flower 13 to 15 weeks after sowing. However, since plants are single stemmed, producing only one flower at a time, two or three plants per 6-inch (15 cm) pot are preferred for better flowering. The plants will be 12 to 15 inches (30 to 38 cm) tall during flowering, so a larger 8-inch (60 cm) pot is desirable when using three plants or when larger plants are preferred.

Divisions can be taken in either the spring or fall but are used primarily by the home gardener and not the commercial grower. Remember that plants are slow to reemerge in the spring.

Commercial propagators offer hibiscus varieties, both seed and vegetatively propagated ones, in a number of plug and liner sizes. These can be purchased during the winter for potting up into quart or gallon pots and sold in the spring.

Temperatures: If sowing from seed and growing on in winter, don't allow these plants to be hardened off with cool season annuals and perennials below 55F (13C) nights. Under extended periods of cool weather, hibiscus plants will lose their leaves and try to go dormant—especially in mid to late winter under short days.

Growth regulator: Cycocel is registered for use on hibiscus at 460 ppm in a foliar spray once new shoots are approximately 2 inches (5 cm) long. American Cyanamid suggests two or three applications 14 days apart. I have used Cycocel with success and found it especially useful on dwarf varieties to allow them to flower in the 6-inch (15 cm) pot, three plants per pot. Sowings made in mid-November and transplanted in early December were sprayed with Cycocel in January and again in February. In early April plants flowered in the 6-inch (15 cm) pot at 17 inches (43 cm) tall. Flower size was reduced—each bloom was 5 inches (13 cm) across.

VARIETIES

The following selections are common varieties. The seed varieties, however, are repeatedly in short supply since they are produced by one company and then brokered through a number of seed companies around the world. Order early.

Dixie Belle is a mixture of red, rose pink, and white on plants 2 to 3 feet (60 to 90 cm) tall. Flowers measure 6 to 8 inches (15 to 20 cm) across. This variety is seed propagated. See Color Plate 44 for photo of *Hibiscus moscheutos* Dixie Belle White.

Disco Belle is similar in all respects to Dixie Belle but is available in separate colors. Pink, Rosy Red, and White have 9-inch (23 cm) flowers on plants 2 to 3 feet (60 to 90 cm) tall. This is another seed-propagated variety.

Lady Baltimore is a pink-flowering hibiscus with a dark red eye. Flowers are 10 inches (25 cm) across and bloom in August. Lady Baltimore grows to 5 feet (1.5 m) and is vegetatively propagated.

Lord Baltimore is a brilliant red hibiscus with 10-inch (25 cm) flowers on plants up to 5 feet (1.5 m) tall. It flowers from August to frost and is a vegetatively propagated variety.

Southern Belle is a mixture of colors including red, rose pink, and white. Flowers are 10 inches (25 cm) across and are borne on plants to 5 feet (1.5 m). In the southern U.S. plants can get up to 6 feet (1.8 m) tall. Southern Belle is a seed-propagated variety.

RELATED MATERIAL

Hibiscus acetosella (*H. eetveldeanus*) has brilliant bronzed or maroon coloring over the entire plant. Upright and erect, *H. acetosella* grows from 5 to 7 feet (1.5 to 2.1 m) tall the first year from seed. Basal branching, often woody at the base, the plants are herbaceous and will die back to the ground each winter. The foliage becomes more lobed like a maple leaf as the season progresses, but initially it's more heart shaped in appearance. The single flowers are purple, red, or yellow. They will not appear on seed-propagated plants the first year in our Chicago location. Plants aren't hardy for us, preferring Zones 8 through 10 in the southern U.S. *Hibiscus acetosella* is especially recommended in mass landscapes due to its unfailing performance and uniform coloring. See Color Plate 43 for photo of *Hibiscus acetosella*.

We use the variety as a tender annual since it isn't hardy in Chicago. Seed is sown in March for green 32-cell packs in May. These are planted into the garden once the danger of frost has passed. For 4-inch (10 cm) pots, allow 11 to 13 weeks when sown in February/March using one plant per pot.

H. acetosella can be readily propagated by stem cuttings as well. These will root rapidly and can be potted up within two weeks after sticking the cutting. *H. acetosella* isn't easy to find through U.S. seed companies although it is available. Cuttings or started plants are easier to find.

Red Shield is a variety most often propagated from cuttings. In some cases, seed has been used to propagate the selection and little differences are noted. Red Shield grows from 4 to 6 feet (1.2 to 1.8 m) tall. Grow and propagate as you would *H. moscheutos*.

USES

Hibiscus, especially taller hibiscus, make excellent seasonal shrubs. Plants die back to the ground each fall and regain the heights noted each summer. The farther south you go, the more dependable these plants become, but there are still plenty of reasons to use hibiscus in Zone 5 locations.

In the landscape, hibiscus plants make a dramatic show of color from midsummer to fall. If green plants can be tolerated in the landscape for spring and early summer, then hibiscus will reward you with flowers for up to six weeks here in the North, once they start to flower in July.

IN THE HOME GARDEN

As noted previously, plants die back to the surface in the winter. Leave the stems throughout the winter to mark where the clumps are for the next spring. Plants are as slow as molasses in reemerging, usually mid to late May for us, and later if the spring has been cool. Space plants 15 to 24 inches (38 to 61 cm) apart when planting the taller varieties and 15 to 18 inches (38 to 46 cm) apart on the dwarf varieties. Plants haven't required staking from my experience and perform their best in full sun and well-drained locations. In partial shade, plants tend to stretch and have a smaller flower size and fewer blooms overall.

HOSTA SPP.

For species see **Varieties**.

FAMILY: Liliaceae

COMMON NAME(S): Plantain Lily, Funkia, Hosta

DESCRIPTION

Hostas are king of the shade garden and have few, if any, rivals in foliage color, form, habit, and overall performance. In the landscape, hosta foliage can provide a bold presence while softening the features of even the most defined area. In total number of available varieties, hostas outrival petunias, but I would venture to say that when you see one white petunia, eight others don't differ much. That's not the case with hostas; Variety selections cover the spectrum of foliage color, leaf texture, size, and mounded versus upright habit. Foliage comes in gold, blue-green, and green. A number have white or yellow margins.

Most varieties will flower midsummer to early fall, although it's the foliage that has gained the attention of landscapers and home gardeners alike. Flowers are borne in spikes (racemes), growing from 6 inches (15 cm) up to 6 feet (1.8 m) long although when in bloom plants can grow from 5 inches to 3½ feet (13 cm to 1 m) tall. In spread, plants range from less than 12 inches (30 cm) to over 9 feet (2.7 m) across. Colors range from purple to white to various shades in between, such as cream, lilac, and lavender. Some selections are fragrant, but hostas, in general, are scentless.

HARDINESS: Zones 3 to 8.

Hostas perform best in Zones 3 through 7 but are reliably used in Zones 8 and 9 if planted in more shade than here in the North.

SEASON OF BLOOM: July to September.

The best time for blooms is July and August, but with the multitude of varieties and species available, flowering can start in June and extend well into fall.

PROPAGATION

Both tissue culture and division are ways to propagate hostas, but division is the most common. Additional detail on tissue culture is provided under **Growing on**. Seed propagation is strictly for breeding work. New cultivars are then replicated by division or tissue culture.

GERMINATION OVERVIEW

Seeds are available for a number of hosta species. Germination temperatures are 68F to 72F (20C to 22C), and the seed is covered during germination. Germination takes about 15 to 21 days. Seed dormancy is possible and can be broken by giving two to three weeks of moist chilling at 40F (4C), such as in a home refrigerator. The seed is mixed with moist sand or peat or a mixture of both and placed in a small plastic bag. Plants require four to five years to be large enough to divide when grown from seed, but it depends on the species.

GROWING ON

From division: If you're growing your own plants in the field, you can divide the plants in the spring when new growth is still dormant or less than 1 inch (2.5 cm) tall. A division should have one or two active shoots. Pot these up into quart or gallon containers using one division per pot. Crop time is two to four weeks depending on the transplant size and container size. If you want a plant that's well rooted, the crop time will be four to six weeks for a gallon pot with three active shoots grown at 55F (13C) nights.

Purchased roots are readily available for either fall or winter shipping, depending on the variety. These varieties can be a species or represent hybrid crosses or sports (mutations)—crop times will differ. It's difficult therefore to give a general crop time for all hosta cultivars. If potted to a gallon container, however, most varieties will be salable in seven to nine weeks for roots potted up in late February and March and grown at 55F to 58F (13C to 14C) nights and days warmer by 8F to 15F (4C to 8C). For larger plants, as well as the slower growing varieties used as borders or edging, allow eight to 11 weeks in a 3- to 4-quart pot and the same night temperatures.

Tissue-cultured plants are often sold in liners or trays with 72 plants per flat. If potted up into 1-quart pots, they'll finish off in five to eight weeks depending on the variety. Grow on at 55F to 58F (13C to 14C) nights.

Notes regarding finishing off: If your goal is to have a plant with limited leaf number (usually less than eight) with a "just rooted" rootball, then these crop times and temperatures will suit your needs. If you're looking for a well-rooted plant with full and lush foliage, you will need to add two more weeks to the crop time above and four more weeks for more compact varieties. Or better yet, pot up your divisions or transplants in the autumn and overwinter dormant for spring sales. The crop times are based on a quick turnover rate for mass merchandising. If you can afford the time and labor, give the plants some additional time to improve their appearance.

VARIETIES

This is worth a chapter in itself. There are so many varieties on the market that this small section couldn't possibly address them all. For your benefit, it's important that you spend some time with your favorite supplier to make sure you get the hostas you really want. A problem we've encountered with some companies offering bareroot divisions is that the off-type percentage within one variety can be as high as

10%. The firms are reputable, but blocks of growing plants can become intermixed within a field.

There are 14 different species from which the plant trade offers multitudes of varieties to the grower. Some of the following cultivars are naturally occurring; others are the result of species crosses, while still others are sports or mutations that were found growing alongside the parent plant. Even though we've listed many varieties here, there are still pages of additional varieties not included. If you're interested in a wide variety of cultivars, I suggest you contact several commercial propagating firms for their listings.

Note: In all the following, the heights refer to the mound of foliage only. Flowering plants can be two to three times the height of the foliage when blooming. Most varieties, however, are chosen for their foliage, flowers being secondary. For more details and color photographs, review *The Hosta Book* by Paul Aden.

The following information is provided as a guide only and can change based on climate and locale. For growers in Zone 5 without lake or ocean effects, these heights and flowering times will be close to actual. For those in the South, far West, or affected by maritime conditions, the information should be used as a guideline.

Production times and growth characteristics of selected hostas

Varieties	Foliage color	Margin color	Flowering time (months)	Height
Antioch	Green	White	July–Aug.	15–20 inches
Winner of the American Hosta Society Eunice Fisher Award and Alex J. Summers Distinguished Merit Award.				
H. fortunei Aoki	Blue/green	None	July–Aug.	15–20 inches
Flower color is lavender pink.				
August Moon	Green/yellow	None	July–Aug.	15–20 inches
Large plant with rounded leaves. Flowers are off white to soft lavender although the latter color isn't well pronounced. Winner of the American Hosta Society President's Exhibitor Trophy.				
Angel	Blue/green	None	July–Aug.	24–36 inches
Large type hosta similar to *H. sieboldiana*. Very free flowering.				
Blue Boy	Blue/green	None	June–July	6–12 inches
Low-growing variety useful in borders or edgings.				
Candy Hearts	Green	None	July–Aug.	10–20 inches
Lavender flowers.				
Crowned Imperial	Grey/green	Cream	July	3–6 inches
A Walters Gardens introduction. A sport of *H. fortunei* Hyacinthina. Pale lavender flowers adorn this fast growing variety.				

Production times and growth characteristics of selected hostas (continued)

Varieties	Foliage color	Margin color	Flowering time (months)	Height
H. fortunei Albo-picta	Yellow	Dark green	July–Aug.	15–20 inches

Some authorities believe this is the same as *H. lancifolia* var. *viridis marginata*. Albopicta is also written as one word and not hyphenated. The leaves are wavy edged with a light green margin. The plant will turn dark green during the summer and lose the yellow cast to its foliage.

H. fortunei Aureo-marginata	Green	Green/yellow	Aug.–Sept.	15–20 inches

Same as Obscura Marginata. Flower color is light violet to lilac.

H. fortunei Hyacinthina	Grey/green	White	July–Aug.	15–20 inches

The margin on this variety is a thin line around the outer leaf surface. The plant is one of the last to flower of the *H. fortunei* types and is slightly more vigorous than other varieties.

Francee	Green	White	July–Aug.	15–20 inches

The variegation remains stable within this variety. Winner of the American Hosta Society Eunice Fisher Award.

Frances Williams	Blue/green	Yellow	July–Aug.	15–20 inches

An *H. sieboldiana* type that is well known among hosta enthusiasts. Winner of the American Hosta Society Alex J. Summers Distinguished Merit Award. A recommended variety.

Gold	Yellow	Green	July–Aug.	15–20 inches

This variety developed from a seedling. As it grows in the spring, leaves are green, turning yellow as the season progresses. This golden yellow color intensifies with morning sun. Lavender to lilac flowers. Winner of the American Hosta Society Eunice Fisher Award.

Golden Sunburst	Green/yellow	None	July–Aug.	18–24 inches

This is the golden leaf form of *H.* Frances Williams, according to Walters Gardens. Bears white flowers in summer.

Golden Tiara	Green	Gold	July–Aug.	6–12 inches

Lavender flowers. Winner of the Nancy Minks Award by the American Hosta Society.

Honeybells	Green	None	July–Aug.	15–20 inches

Violet-white flower color.

Kabitan	*	*	July–Aug.	8–10 inches

*Color is in the eyes of the beholder on this one. It's often listed as green-leaved with a bright golden yellow vein down the center main vein. Some experts, however, refer to the whole leaf as being golden yellow with a dark green band around the outer margin of the leaf.

Krossa Regal	Blue/green	None	Aug.–Sept.	3–4 feet

One of the tallest of the hosta varieties. When in bloom in certain parts of the country, the plant can reach a height of 6 feet once it becomes established. Flowers are lavender blue and can extend to 2 feet long. Plant has a vase-shaped habit. Winner of the American Hosta Society Eunice Fisher Award.

Varieties	Foliage color	Margin color	Flowering time (months)	Height
H. montana Aureo-marginata	Green	Yellow	Sept.	24–36 inches

Large pointed leaves with broad yellow margins. Winner of the Alex J. Summers Distinguished Merit Award.

Northern Halo	Blue/grey	Cream*	July–Aug.	24–36 inches

A Walters Gardens introduction. Northern Halo is a sport of *H. sieboldiana* Elegans with rounded leaves.

*The margins of the leaves have a cream-yellow color that changes to a creamy white as the season progresses.

H. plantaginea var. *grandiflora*	Green	None	Aug.–Sept.	15–20 inches

This group is fragrant hosta and is often called August Lily. This variety is also one of the oldest. While the leaf color is green, it can shade to an off-green or green yellow.

Royal Standard	Green	None	Aug.–Sept.	24–36 inches

This is a selection of *H. plantaginea* with fragrant flowers. It was introduced into the United States by Wayside Gardens, Hodges, South Carolina. Although not as yellow as some other varieties, Royal Standard does have a light cast to the foliage.

H. sieboldiana Elegans	Blue/grey	None	Aug.–Sept.	24–36 inches

A strong garden performer, 4 or 5 feet wide. Flowers are either lilac or white.

Tall Boy	Green	None	July–Aug.	24–36 inches

Flowers can reach as high as 5 feet when flowering. Plants bear lavender flowers.

H. tokudama Aureo-nebulosa	Light yellow	Blue/green	Aug.	15–24 inches

Slow grower. Leaves are quite wavy.

H. undulata Albo-marginata	Green	White	July–Aug.	15–24 inches

Lavender flowers on these plants spread 14 to 18 inches.

H. undulata Erromena	Green	None	July–Aug.	15–24 inches

Light violet flowers on plants, with 15- to 20-inch flowering stalks.

H. ventricosa Aureo-marginata	Green	Cream white	Aug.–Sept.	15–20 inches

Alan Bloom of Diss, England, discovered this variety within a planting of *H. ventricosa*. The cream-white edge starts out a creamy yellow and changes color as summer progresses. Also called Variegata.

Source: Compiled from information provided by Walters Gardens, Inc., 96th Avenue and Business I-196, P.O. Box 137, Zeeland, Michigan 49464, and from *Herbaceous Perennial Plants* by Allan M. Armitage, Varsity Press, Inc., Athens, Georgia.

H

Uses

Hostas are a premier plant well known for their performance in the shade garden. The plants have equal value in brighter locations, especially with morning sun or dappled light all day long. In Chicago, hostas tend to do very well in areas that get morning sun but are shaded during the hottest parts of the day. Larger, more robust varieties perform better in the sun than the dwarf or miniature varieties. When planting in sunnier exposures, be sure to keep the plants well watered for the first two weeks to avoid drying out—eventually the leaves will expand over the soil and cool its surface, allowing water to stay around the tender roots.

Hostas are most noted for their foliage, but a number of varieties provide good cut flowers for the home garden. Long-stemmed varieties are preferred, especially the selected varieties of *H. plantaginea* or *H. ventricosa*. *H. plantaginea* varieties are considered the most fragrant.

In the landscape, hostas are a particularly durable and long-lived perennial in any setting. Plants take one to two years to fill into the area if you use only one-year-old divisions. If instant impact is important, consider using fully established 2- or 3-gallon plants for your display. These plants are stronger, especially those of the dwarf varieties, which take longer to grow and fill in.

In the home garden

Depending on the varieties you select, hostas can grow slowly or very quickly. Some varieties take years to grow into plants large enough to fill in an area while others may spread and fill in within one year. When planting, space hostas 15 to 25 inches (38 to 64 cm) apart. If you're using container-grown plants, space closer and divide or transplant within two to three years to allow for more uniform spread.

Follow the suggestions under **Uses** for the best sunlight exposure. One additional comment: If the soil is sandy or very well drained, light shade is preferred, which will keep moisture around the plant's roots. Hostas seldom wilt unless exposed to prolonged drought or too much bright, direct light.

Dwarf selections may not require dividing for up to four years depending on the rate of growth. Faster growing or more robust selections like Honey Bells and Krossa Regal can be divided within three years when planted from a gallon pot.

—The author appreciates the time that Mary Walters and her staff of Walters Gardens, Zeeland, Michigan, took in reviewing and correcting this information.

■■■ HYPERICUM CALYCINUM

FAMILY: Hypericaceae

COMMON NAME(S): St. John's-wort, Aaron's Beard, Rose of Sharon.

The common name of St. Johns-wort honors Balder, the sun god, with its golden yellow flowers. As Christian beliefs prevailed, this pagan day of honor became St. John's Day, and the plants were held in high regard as a deterrent for warding off evil spirits.

DESCRIPTION

A stoloniferous (trailing) plant with a handsome form and habit describes this wonderful plant. The leaves are simple in design, longer than wide and rounded at the outer edge. The foliage color is a dark green or blue green, and the plants tend to be evergreen during winter (see notes under **Hardiness**).

The flowers are golden yellow, 2 to 3 inches (5 to 7 cm) across, and single. Due to the mass of stamens towards the center of the bloom, however, the plants can have an almost double or roselike appearance. They will be 15 to 20 inches (38 to 51 cm) tall all summer long and spread from 15 to 24 inches (38 to 61 cm) across.

HARDINESS: Zones 6 to 9.

In the notes under **Description**, I indicate that the plants are evergreen. This is most often seen in climates where winters aren't severe and plants are sheltered from winter drying (Zone 7 and south). In zones farther north, the leaves may brown and die back during severe cold weather, but new shoots will develop in spring from the roots.

Some references indicate that *Hypericum calycinum* is hardy in Zone 5. In our gardens outside Chicago (the northern part of Zone 5), these plants aren't evergreen nor are they truly perennial. Over the past 10 years, plants in four different locations, all without winter protection, have died. Occasionally we've gotten three or four plants of the group to regrow from the roots, but these are often weak in stature. They usually succumb to summer heat and are dead by summer's end. However, covering with a layer of mulch during the winter has greatly increased their survival.

SEASON OF BLOOM: July and August.

PROPAGATION

Seed, cuttings, and division are the usual methods for propagating this crop. Seed can be sown any time after harvest but shouldn't be stored longer than a year for

H

best germination. Softwood cuttings can also be taken, rooted, potted to quarts or gallons, and overwintered in an unheated cold frame with protection in colder winter areas. Finally, divisions can be taken in the spring, although that's more commonly practiced by home gardeners than professional growers.

GERMINATION OVERVIEW: 26,000 seeds per ounce/910 per gram.

Pretreatments: None are usually necessary, but older seed won't be as reliable to germinate. If germination is slower than normal (see below), then treat *H. calycinum* as you would other perennial shrubs and moist chill the seeds for best performance.

Hypericum is not a fast germinating seed to sprout and grow. Seed covered lightly with coarse vermiculite, plus a 60F to 70F (16C to 21C) soil temperature, will result in first seedlings poking through media about 10 days after sowing; in all, 10 to 21 days are required for germination. A 60F (16C) temperature isn't too cool, but I've had quicker germination at 65F to 68F (19C to 20C), with good seedling quality—78F (25C) has caused stretched seedlings.

Seedlings can be transplanted 20 to 32 days after sowing.

One final note: Hypericum seedlings don't emerge uniformly and often yield lower germination rates when sown late. The number of germinated seedlings may be low (less than 50%) if the seed is old.

GROWING ON

Crop time: In the *Ball Culture Guide*, I state that a flat with 32 cells will be salable green in 12 to 14 weeks when grown at 50F (10C) nights.

While this is true for green pack sales, I would add that quart and gallon sales are preferred. Seed should be sown in November/December for 4-inch (10 cm) or quart sales in the spring. For gallons, sow seed during spring or summer for seedlings to be potted to gallons by late summer. These are overwintered in cold frames and sold the following spring.

Softwood cuttings can be taken during July and August, but because plants may still be flowering, take cuttings on nonflowering, semimature stems that are still green and not woody. Pot these cuttings up into the final container and overwinter in a protected, nonheated structure (cold frame) for green plant sales the following spring.

Commercial propagators offer *Hypericum calycinum* in a variety of plug and liner sizes. These are available in winter and can be potted one plug to a 1- or 2-quart container for spring sales.

VARIETIES

H. calycinum seed is usually in ready supply from a number of U.S. seed companies.

IN THE HOME GARDEN

H. calycinum does well when grown in a sandy rather than clay-based soil. If the pH is 6.0 to 7.0, and the plants are grown in shade with bright indirect light (not heavy shade) then *H. calycinum* will perform at its best.

If planted in an open area with limited winter protection, use evergreen boughs or similar materials to cover plants and protect them from drying out.

H

I

◼◼ IBERIS SEMPERVIRENS

FAMILY: Cruciferae

COMMON NAME(S): Evergreen Candytuft, Hardy Candytuft

DESCRIPTION
A perennial favorite for the home garden, *I. sempervirens* is a low-growing, woody-stemmed evergreen perennial. It grows about 9 to 12 inches (23 to 30 cm) tall and spreads 10 to 15 inches (25 to 38 cm) across. The flowers are single, pure white, scentless, and develop in clusters measuring 2 to 3 inches (5 to 7 cm) across in early spring. Plants are dependably hardy and are one of the first returning perennials to show color in the spring.

HARDINESS: Zones 3 to 9.

SEASON OF BLOOM: April to May.
Bloom longevity is limited. In Chicago, color lasts up to four weeks, longer if the spring is cool.

PROPAGATION
Candytuft is usually propagated by seed and cuttings. Seed germinates easily, but the purity of the white flower color and the flower size varies. Named cultivars are propagated by cuttings taken after flowering.

GERMINATION OVERVIEW: 10,000 seeds per ounce/350 per gram.
Iberis germinates in 14 to 21 days at 60F to 65F (16C to 18C); seed doesn't need to be covered to germinate. Transplanting can begin 25 to 38 days after sowing.

GROWING ON
From seed: For fully developed plants in quarts or gallons, sold budded or in bloom in early spring, seed should be sown the previous year. Late spring or summer sowings can be potted up into quart or larger containers. These can be left as is, although

some growers shape the plants towards late summer by lightly shearing them. The plants are overwintered dormant and sold the following spring.

Seed can also be sown in late summer or early fall with the seedlings potted to their final container when ready. These plants are kept cold but not dormant over the winter—40F to 45F (5C to 7C)—as they root and establish themselves in their final pot. Don't drop the temperatures until the plants have begun to root, especially when placing a small plug or transplant into a large soil volume. In our Chicago location, short days, extended cloudy periods, and cold weather combined with overwatering will lead to plant death. However, late season sowings are relatively easy to grow and finish in a cool/cold greenhouse during the winter months. These plants can be sold in the spring and will flower in April and May.

Seed sown anytime after the first of the year will not flower the same season from seed when grown at 50F (10C) nights. Green packs are salable 10 to 14 weeks after sowing; plants will attain their full height the same season from seed.

Commercial propagators offer this perennial in both a plug and liner size. These plugs come from either seed or vegetatively propagated plants. They can be potted, one plant per 1- to 3-quart container, and sold in the spring if received and transplanted early enough.

Bare-root divisions are also available from commercial propagators. These can be potted up into 2-, 3-, or 4-quart containers and sold in the spring. If potted up in February and grown on at 50F (10C) nights, the plants will be salable in eight to 10 weeks. For fully rooted plants, allow two more weeks.

Stem tip cuttings taken during the summer are easily rooted, potted up into quarts or gallons, and overwintered cold for spring sales.

VARIETIES

Iberis sempervirens seed will not be difficult to find. Occasionally the cultivar Snow White is offered in seed-propagated plants. Plants propagated by seed can vary in both purity of white flower color and darkness of foliage. It's an excellent variety with pure white flowers on plants to 12 inches (30 cm) tall. There are vegetative forms of this variety as well and most nurseries request the vegetative form.

Alexander's White is a low-growing variety to 10 inches (25 cm) tall. More compact than the species, Alexander's White is noted for its uniform habit and free-flowering performance. It is vegetatively propagated.

October Glory flowers first in spring and then again in fall. Usually the fall flowering is not as full as the spring, but it's unusual for *I. sempervirens* to flower again the same year. It grows to 8 inches (20 cm) and is vegetatively propagated.

Snowflake is another white-flowering variety with 2- to 3-inch (5 to 7 cm) clusters on 10-inch-tall (25 cm) plants. Its overall habit is shorter, but it is free flowering with dark green foliage. Snowflake is vegetatively propagated.

USES

Iberis works very well as a border or edging in the home garden but is shunned in commercial landscapes because of its short flowering season. The plants provide a deep green foliage all season, however.

If you're planning a fall or winter garden, remember that *I. sempervirens* evergreen foliage holds up well if properly maintained in summer by removing seed pods and spent flowers.

IN THE HOME GARDEN

Plants should be spaced 10 to 12 inches (25 to 30 cm) apart and placed in a full-sun location. The soil should be well drained and the plants trimmed back after flowering to keep their shape. Plant as early in the ground as possible—May 1 in Chicago—so that they can establish while the nights are still cool. Plants will do well even if planted in June but are slower to develop, often appearing wilted due to heat stress.

▬ IRIS HYBRIDS

Although formerly called *Iris germanica*, today's varieties are hybrids from a myriad of species and cultivars.

FAMILY: Iridaceae

COMMON NAME(S): Bearded Iris, Fleur de lis, Sword Lily, Garden Flag

DESCRIPTION

Every spring my Iowa hometown celebrates the iris. Mount Pleasant is a quiet community where family histories run three or four generations deep. Many have lived in the same house and have handed down their iris varieties through the generations. There's usually a clump or two to be found at every house in town and those scattered across the rolling farms that stretch in every direction, including the old farmhouse where I grew up. Our town is nicknamed the "Iris City." The local restaurant I used to work at displays artwork showing the many virtues of iris. Even its name is "The Iris." There is also the Iris Motel, Iris Realty, Iris Cleaners, Iris Bowling Center and, at one time, the Iris Beauty Shop. While the town's fondness for this flower may seem a bit overdone for such short-lived splendor, this is a testament to the iris and the beauty it possesses.

Often called bearded iris, the common garden iris came about through the breeder's art, the result of combining various species and cultivars together to derive new selections. Flower colors include purple, blue, yellow, pink, violet, gold, cream, white and shades in between. Blossoms can be all one color, bicolor, two-tone, streaked or frosted, and are either pastel in color or bold and bright.

Iris blooms are unique in the plant world. The flowers are held vertically with three outer petals that hang down, called "falls," and three central upright petals called "standards." The falls often have a tuft of hairs down the center of each petal that resembles a caterpillar or beard—hence the common name of "bearded iris." The flowers are fragrant, measuring from 3 to 5 inches (7 to 13 cm) tall and from 3 to 4 inches (7 to 10 cm) across, and usually last from three to six days. In their display of petals, irises are among the most flamboyant of flowers.

Plants range in height from as short as 5 inches (13 cm) to as tall as 4 feet (1.2 m). They often have one or two open blooms at once with a total of five to seven blooms per plant. The foliage is gray green and fan shaped in appearance. Leaves grow anywhere from 12 to 18 inches (30 to 46 cm) tall and the flowers are held far above. The foliage develops out of a rhizome that lies partially exposed on the soil surface.

HARDINESS: Zones 4 to 8.

SEASON OF BLOOM: May and early June.

Not a long bloomer, iris flowers first appear around Memorial Day here in Chicago, but most varieties have usually finished flowering by mid-June.

PROPAGATION

Iris is propagated by division. Today's hybrid varieties only come true if divided. Seeds collected from the hybrids and sown will produce plants, but they will be markedly different from their parents.

Plants can be dug in the summer, divided, and the plump, finger-like rhizomes cut into smaller sections, each with some root attached to the rhizome. Trim the leaves to 5 or 6 inches (13 to 15 cm). This division can be sold immediately for potting up or stored for sales during the winter. If you are digging and dividing your own plants, July and August are the best times. Commercial propagators will have rhizomes available for shipping in the fall and winter months, however, that can be potted up for spring sales.

GROWING ON

From divisions: One- and two-fan divisions are the most commonly available roots from commercial propagators around the country. When you receive them, pot them up to a 1- or 2-quart container for growing. Since many of these are received and potted during the winter, the plants often die due to overwatering and too cool a growing environment. Water sparingly instead, allowing fans to begin developing before feeding and frequent water applications. When using quart containers, some growers water thoroughly the first day and then as needed. Larger containers, such as gallons, often don't drain for the first week or two after watering begins. This allows moisture to concentrate in the upper part of the container, helping plants to start actively growing but avoiding excess moisture that could cause root rots.

When potting up the roots, be sure to plant the finger-like rhizome horizontally and no more than 1 inch (2.5 cm) deep in the media. Each rhizome top should be exposed and not covered. Remind your customers not to bury the crown in the garden either. See **In the home garden** for additional details.

Iris roots planted in 1- or 2-quart containers by February or March and grown on at 55F (13C) nights will be salable in seven to nine weeks, gallon pots two to three weeks longer. Plants will not be in flower when sold but should have one or two fans developing in the container. The growth is often one sided, however, and the pot will not be filled out when sold. Those of you who are familiar with growing iris may wonder at this comment, but some first-time iris growers have expected lush, pot-filled foliage ready for retail sales.

Plants will flower sporadically the first summer from a spring planting. If potted up late (March), however, there may not be any flowering at all. It depends on how long cooler temperatures last and how well the roots were allowed to mass before retail sales. Review the temperature comments below; remember that the longer the exposure to 48F (9C) nights with a well-massed root ball, the better the flowering will be during spring or early summer.

Regarding temperatures, 55F (13C) night temperatures are perfect to allow for root formation and initial foliage development. Once plants are up and growing, drop the night temperatures to no lower than 48F (9C) during the spring. This is assuming your day temperatures are 8 to 10 degrees (4C to 6C) higher, to allow for rapid growth. If days are cooler and dark, keep the night temperatures around 55F (13C) for active growth. Obviously, if plants are growing too fast, reduce night temperatures to 48F (9C) as prescribed to harden the plants off prior to retail sales.

VARIETIES

Iris varieties are divided into three categories based on growth: dwarf, intermediate and tall. Dwarf selections are 10 to 15 inches (25 to 38 cm) tall, flower the earliest, and are suggested for small areas or rock gardens. They work well as an edging or border plant. Intermediate varieties grow from 16 to 27 inches (41 to 68 cm) tall, will flower later than the dwarf selections, and are usually more upright in habit than the tall selections. Tall varieties are the most common on the market and usually grow taller than 27 inches (68 cm). If planted in open locations or if buffeting winds are frequent, the plants may require staking as they bud and flower. Dwarf varieties start to flower by mid-May, and the tall group will finish blooming by mid-June here in our Chicago gardens.

The number of iris varieties on the market is far too extensive to do proper justice here. Commercial propagators offer extensive lists of varieties and their offerings should be reviewed. Schreiner's Iris Gardens offers the most selections, although other companies like DeVroomen, Klehm Nursery, and Walters Gardens have large iris lists as well. Refer to **Perennial Source List** in the back of this book for addresses.

Related material

Iris ensata (Japanese iris, also called *I. kaempferi*) is the largest flowering of the iris species with blooms measuring from 6 to 10 inches (15 to 25 cm) across, although some are slightly smaller to no more than 4 inches (10 cm) across. Blooms can be single, double, or multipetaled. These latter types are sometimes called "peony-like." Japanese irises lack the so-called "beard" that other varieties have. Flowers are flat in appearance without upright "standards". The flowers can measure 10 inches (25 cm) across, but most are 4 to 7 inches (10 to 18 cm) when fully developed. Colors include burgundy red, violet, blue, and lavender; through hybridization other colors like buff yellow are also available. Plants flower during June and July.

The foliage is more clumping than the bearded iris and appears more graceful—a mass of thin, elongated leaves that radiate out of a central point, called a "fan." Many fans are produced across the rhizomes' crown; collectively, they give the plant a more filled-out appearance than the bearded types. The rhizomes are smaller in size and less knobby.

Japanese irises prefer moist conditions (though not wet during the winter) and an acid soil, and will work well around lakes and streams. Plants grow from 20 to 40 inches (51 to 102 cm) tall. They measure 8 to 12 inches (20 to 30 cm) across at the base, but their long leaves lean and then gracefully arch back towards the ground, providing a spread of 2 feet (60 cm) at each plant's top. Plants grow equally well in sun or partial shade and can be divided every four to five years or as needed. Zones 5 to 9.

Iris pseudacorus (Yellow Flag iris). This is another of the water-loving iris species with 2- to 3-inch (5 to 7 cm), beardless yellow flowers. The plants grow in large clumps of swordlike leaves and tend to be more upright in appearance than other varieties listed here under **Related material**. Rhizomes are smaller than those found on the bearded types. While plants grow in shallow water, they also tolerate more well-drained locations as well as full sun. Here in our Chicago location, the plants have grown in full sun for years without winter mulching. Yellow Flag is long lived and one of the most robust of the irises on the market. Plants grow from 3 to 4 feet (90 to 120 cm) tall but will be taller in warmer winter climates and when grown in shallow water where they may reach 7 feet (2.1 m) in flower. Zones 3 to 9.

Iris sibirica (Siberian iris). Like the previous two species, this class also appreciates moist conditions during the summer. Planted in full sun and given a moist location, the foliage will develop to a height of 2 or 3 feet (60 to 90 cm). Plants flower in June. The blooms vary in size up to 4 inches (10 cm) across, and the foliage is swordlike in appearance. Siberian iris are more free flowering than any of the other species noted here, although flowers tend to be smaller than the other classes.

Division can be done in the spring, but Siberian types, like the Japanese types, don't require dividing as soon as the bearded ones. Plants will need several years to get established first. Zones 3 to 9.

Caesar's Brother has deep violet-blue flowers and grows between 24 to 36 inches (61 to 91 cm) tall. Flowers have a velvety sheen.

Snow Queen is a white-flowering variety that's 24 to 30 inches (61 to 76 cm) tall.

With regard to cropping, all of the species mentioned can be grown in a similar fashion to the bearded types. Plant rhizomes to 1- or 2-quart containers (no larger than a gallon pot), using one rhizome per pot planted about 1 inch deep. Beware of overwatering, and follow the same procedures for the bearded types noted above. Crop time is approximately seven to nine weeks for 1- or 2-quart containers, with gallon pots taking eight to 10 weeks based on 55F (13C) nights and days 8 to 10 degrees warmer. For a fully-rooted plant and a filled-out canopy, you'll need to have 12 to 15 weeks at 55F (13C) nights. Remember that *Iris pseudacorus* will produce two or three fans, while both *I. ensata* and *I. sibirica* will usually have five to 10 and will fill out the container sooner.

USES

When using a number of iris cultivars and species, it's possible to have a succession of color from mid-May until July here in Chicago. With bearded iris alone, the flowering period is much shorter, although there are recurrent bloomers on the market. For this reason, commercial landscapers are selective about mass plantings of bearded iris. These landscapes capitalize on the swordlike foliage instead, for use in dotted clumps across a planting.

As a home cut flower, iris are truly prized for their large blooms and fragrant scent. In the central United States they are often used with peony flowers to adorn graves on Memorial Day.

IN THE HOME GARDEN

Plant in full-sun locations in a well-drained site. A soil pH of 6 to 7 gives the best plant performance. Plants don't require staking, but the taller types may need some support during flowering, especially in windy locations.

Whether you use purchased plants, divided roots, or a section of a friend's prized iris variety, be sure to plant the white, thickened rhizome slightly exposed. In fact, don't even mulch over it. With other plants, enlarged roots like these need to be covered for best performance, but with iris, covering up the rhizome decreases flower counts and can encourage insects and diseases. Only the rhizome's top needs to be exposed and the enlarged, fibrous roots below will help to anchor the plant. In our

Chicago location, we have never winter-mulched iris. Even with the rhizome exposed, the plants are cold hardy and require few amenities.

Iris varieties don't need regular lifting and separating. As your flower counts decrease and the plants become crowded, however, dividing your plants will encourage a stronger show the following year. When dividing, follow the comments under **Propagation**, except replant to a well-prepared spot in the garden. After flowering, we dig the plants, toss out any hollow roots or woody growth, and retain only the plump and healthy looking rhizomes with a portion of fibrous roots below and at least one set of leaves. On the spot where the roots are to be planted, dig the area to 8 inches (20 cm) deep, turning the soil till it's crumbly. Next, scatter bone meal across the site and rake it in and, finally, plant the rhizomes horizontally 1 inch (2.54 cm) deep but with the tops exposed. Water the plants in and mulch around the outer crown to retain moisture in the soil but avoid covering the rhizome. Rooting takes from two to three weeks; new growth will be seen within four weeks of replanting. The following year the plants will flower but only marginally. The second year after replanting, the iris clumps will be free flowering and profuse.

K

■ KNIPHOFIA UVARIA
(formerly *Tritoma uvaria*)

FAMILY: Liliaceae

COMMON NAME(S): Red Hot Poker, Torchlily

DESCRIPTION

Kniphofia uvaria is an impressive plant with coarse, thin long leaves radiating out of a central crown that grows from 15 to 20 inches (38 tp 51 cm) tall when not flowering. The foliage will develop out of the crown and arches back over to the ground but not necessarily gracefully. A large group planting may appear unkempt since the long, linear leaves sometimes bend to the ground.

When in flower, the plants will top out at 3 to 4 feet (90 to 120 cm) tall. The flowers are small, tubular, and droop or hang from the crown of an erect 3-foot (90 cm) stalk. Collectively, a mass of blooms occupy the top 4 to 6 inches (10 to 15 cm) of the spike. The blooms are often two-tone or bicolor in yellow and red or orange. If transplanted to the garden the previous year, one to three spikes of color can be expected with more in future years as the plants become established.

HARDINESS: Zones 5 to 9.

SEASON OF BLOOM: July and August.

PROPAGATION

Seed and division are the two primary propagation methods. Seed can be sown year-round, but read the notes below under **Germination** to achieve the best performance. Divisions are best taken during the spring and early summer when the anchor roots are forming and will establish readily after transplanting.

GERMINATION OVERVIEW: 9,000 seeds per ounce/315 per gram.

Pretreatments: Seed can be sown year-round, but seed germinates best (80%+) in autumn after harvest. Seed stored until spring will still germinate, but it may be slower with a decreased number of seedlings.

To achieve good germination and active growth, sow from December on until spring. If seed has been stored for an extended period, or has been stored improperly and fails to germinate readily, the seed may actually go through a two-part germination process typical of some lily family members.

Seed will develop a root radicle but will then form a small bulbil or round growth at the root crown. After a cold period, the shoot will actually develop from this. Seed starts to germinate in six to eight days after sowing, but a high percentage of seedlings will not be seen until 14 to 20 days after sowing when exposed to 65F to 75F (19C to 24C) temperatures. Seed will germinate whether it's covered or not and still give the same germination results.

As seedlings emerge they will be erect, 3-inch-long (7 cm), grasslike spikes, 20 days after sowing. Seedlings can be transplanted 30 to 45 days after sowing. When transplanting, be sure that seedlings are strong enough to be handled, but don't allow them to establish a strong root in the sowing tray prior to transplanting. Although they have a tap root, they're not as prone to transplant shock as other tap-rooted perennials. There is also no need to slow down the plants' growth and development by letting roots become restricted within the germination tray or plug cell.

GROWING ON

Crop time: From seed, plants develop slowly; cloudy weather or cool temperatures will accentuate this condition. Sowings made after the New Year will not be salable the same year from seed unless you're planning late summer sales here in the North.

For best performance, decrease the stress brought on by growing in small, restricted cell packs or small pots by potting up in containers that allow the tap root to develop. Cell packs are fine to establish seedlings into strong, rosetting plants after they are first transplanted. Transplanting the seedlings to a quart or similar container direct from the germination tray or plug will often be detrimental. Seedlings might not develop fast enough into the soil because of the plant's slow growth coupled with overwatering.

Seedlings, transplanted to a 32-cell pack 30 to 45 days after sowing in December or January, won't be large enough to transplant to quarts for as long as five to six months. Since seedlings develop so slowly, green plants can be sold later in the summer, but overwintering the plants for spring sales is your best bet.

For green quarts or gallons in the spring, sow seed the previous spring, allowing a full year of development before sales. Plants can be potted up into quarts or gallons, left to grow and root, and then sold the following spring.

Commercial propagators offer this perennial as bare-root transplants or started plug/liner trays. Both can be potted up during the winter for spring sales.

VARIETIES

Kniphofia uvaria is a common perennial readily found from various seed companies. It's most often sold as Novelty Mix, Early Hybrids, Royal Castle, Royal Castle

285

Hybrids or Pfitzer's Hybrids—all these varieties are the same when sold as seed. The plants have orange, yellow, and red flowers on plants to 4 feet (1.2 m) in bloom.

Pfitzeri (also listed Pfitzerii) differs from the seed strain by having scarlet-orange flowers on plants to 2 feet (60 cm) tall in flower. This variety is vegetatively propagated and available from commercial propagators as bare-root divisions.

IN THE HOME GARDEN

While some have used this plant to replace *Yucca filamentosa* because of its bold texture, I feel this exaggerates the possibilities of red hot poker plant. *Kniphofia uvaria* can be used in small or large gardens without fear of overpowering height or texture or clashing with other plants. For show and color, it has few rivals although it's only in bloom for several weeks.

Plant in a sunny site with good drainage for best results. *K. uvaria* is usually hardy in our Chicago location and requires no mulching or covering during winter. If we have a wet autumn quickly followed by a cold spell, however, it is marginally hardy and may winter kill. Even if the plants are in a well-drained soil with a heavy mulch, excess rain water and cold temperatures will damage this crop.

L

■ LAMIASTRUM GALEOBDOLON
(formerly *Lamium galeobdolon* and *Galeobdolon luteum*)

FAMILY: Lamiaceae

COMMON NAME(S): Yellow Archangel

DESCRIPTION
Lamiastrum galeobdolon is a ground cover that grows 10 to 12 inches (25 to 30 cm) tall in flower, sometimes taller farther south. Plants spread by stolons (surface runners), often spreading only 12 to 18 inches (30 to 46 cm) across, but they can become invasive in fertile conditions. Flower clusters arise from where the leaves are attached in whorls to the stems. The blooms are hooded, with the upper petals protruding over the lower portion, about three-quarter-inch (2 cm) long, yellow, and positioned along the stem from the terminal point to the fourth or fifth node.

    Lamiastrum galeobdolon's foliage is usually bright green with no markings, but there is a variegated form that is preferred for ornamental uses. The foliage remains evergreen in warm winter areas and dies back to the ground in the Midwest and Northeast.

HARDINESS: Zones 4 to 9.

SEASON OF BLOOM: June and July.

PROPAGATION
Lamiastrum is propagated by terminal cuttings and divisions. Divisions are easy due to the stolons' spreading habit, but cuttings are preferred for high yields.

GERMINATION OVERVIEW
L. galeobdolon is available from seed, but the variegated form and cultivars are vegetatively propagated. Seed is primarily available from Europe; U.S. companies sell the vegetative forms.

GROWING ON

Crop time: By removing a portion of the stolon along with a piece of the root, the plants will root quickly. Terminal cuttings will also root readily and be transplantable within several weeks. Cuttings collected during the summer can be potted up to their final container and overwintered for spring sales.

Commercial propagators offer *L. galeobdolon* in small pots or liners. Depending on their size, the small pots can be sold as is, primarily for commercial landscapes, or transplanted to gallon pots for spring sales.

VARIETIES

Lamiastrum galeobdolon from seed isn't a common variety in the U.S. trade. The following cultivars are the sought-after ones:

Herman's Pride has variegated silver and green leaves. The silver blotching or splashes are more pronounced than on Variegatum (described below), and the plants are more compact than either of the other two selections listed here. Flowers are yellow.

L. galeobdolon var. *variegatum* is more prolific than Herman's Pride, with silver blotched leaves and yellow flowers. This is the most common cultivar and an excellent choice for the perennial garden. The leaves possess a similar silver splotching as Herman's Pride, but a mass planting usually yields variable coloring, sometimes on the same plant depending on the age of the leaves. The flowers are bright yellow. See Color Plate 45 for photo of *Lamiastrum galeobdolon* var. *variegatum*.

USES

I prefer to use *L. galeobdolon* rather than *Lamium maculatum* for commercial plantings because of the partial die back or brown spots that lamium often suffers from. In a woodland setting or shaded border the plants will accent, but not suffocate, spring bulb displays. Developing bulb leaves will push through the web of lamiastrum stems and foliage, flower, and can then be trimmed back to the ground once dead. *Lamiastrum* flowers will often start to show color just as the bulb blooms start to subside.

IN THE HOME GARDEN

Grow *L. galeobdolon* in the same manner as *Lamium maculatum*, but it can tolerate drier locations. *Lamiastrum* tolerates more direct sun in the morning or early evening; especially avoid an afternoon sun location during the hottest and most humid parts of the summer.

Both *L. galebdolon* and *L. galeobdolon variegatum* can spread rapidly, often becoming invasive in fertile and moist sites. If plants grow out of line and look unkempt, they can be trimmed back in midsummer. They will basal branch, and the foliage will fill in, appearing more uniform in height than if left unpruned.

■■ LAMIUM MACULATUM

FAMILY: Lamiaceae

COMMON NAME(S): Dead Nettle, Spotted Dead Nettle

DESCRIPTION

Lamium maculatum is a premier plant for the shade that, under ideal conditions, can spread rapidly. The foliage has silver highlights mottled with green next to the midrib and across the leaf surface. The plants grow upright, are less than 12 inches (30 cm) tall in bloom, and fill in well when given a moist but drained location.

Lamium's lipped flowers are three-quarters to 1 inch (2 to 2.5 cm) long, pink to rose red or purple in color, and single in form. Flower quality is secondary to the plants' speckled foliage and ability to fill in readily.

HARDINESS: Zones 3 to 8.

SEASON OF BLOOM: May and June.

PROPAGATION

Cultivars common to the trade are vegetatively propagated and not available from seed. Seed is sown only for the species and not the cultivars listed below under **Varieties**. Cuttings and divisions can be easily taken in the spring.

GERMINATION OVERVIEW

Seed is not a practical production method since the resulting plants are weedy and unkempt and will not look like any of the listed selections under **Varieties**. For selection work to find new cultivars; however, seed can be sown in the greenhouse in summer for seedlings that can be moved up into quarts or gallons by late summer.

For the inexperienced breeder, your selections shouldn't necessarily be centered around the most vigorous plants. Remember that the cultivars listed below were preferred because they're all less vigorous in habit than the species. Concentrate instead on plants with unusual mottled foliage, flower color, and plant performance.

GROWING ON

The following is information for cultivars listed under **Varieties**, not the species.

Crop time: Divisions taken in the spring will, depending on variety, be sized up to fill out a 4-inch (10 cm) pot within six to eight weeks. If plants are to be sold the following year, pot the developing transplants into a quart or gallon container for overwintering.

From cuttings, roots will develop quickly, and the transplants can be potted into quart containers within two to four weeks, depending on when they were taken. The warmer it is, the faster rootlets develop. The quart pots are overwintered in an unheated cold frame for spring sales. If stock plants are maintained in a warm

L

greenhouse over the winter, cutting material will be available for potting to 4-inch (10 cm) pots or quarts for spring sales.

Commercial propagators offer *Lamium maculatum* in either small pots or as liners. Primarily available during the autumn and winter, either of these can be moved up into quarts and gallons and sold in spring.

VARIETIES

Lamium maculatum is available in the United States only as vegetatively propagated material. Look to the European seed companies for seed availability.

All of the following varieties are **vegetatively propagated** and don't grow as rampantly as the species.

L. maculatum var. *aureum* has light yellow to golden foliage with a white midrib down each leaf center. The flowers are pink and less sun tolerant than the silver- or green-leaf types. Aureum reaches a height of 6 inches (15 cm) tall.

Beacon Silver is a silver-leaved variety highlighted at the leaf edge with a deep green band. The pink flowers bloom in spring. It grows to 6 inches (15 cm) tall.

Chequers is a variety similar to Beacon Silver, although the foliage is marbled with more green than what you see in Beacon Silver. The flowers are deep pink to lavender and appear in the spring. Plants grow to 6 to 8 inches (15 to 20 cm) tall in bloom.

Shell Pink also has green and white foliage like the previous two varieties and displays pink flowers.

White Nancy is the white-flowering form of Beacon Silver, growing between 6 and 8 inches (15 and 20 cm) tall with the same silver mottling. See Color Plate 46 for photo of *Lamium maculatum* White Nancy.

USES

An excellent plant for the landscape, home garden, or anything in between. Plants can be used around house foundations, under trees, along walks, and around other plantings. In commercial plantings, it works well as long as it is protected from hot sun where the plants can burn out.

IN THE HOME GARDEN

The key to a healthy planting is a moist soil with no standing water and a shady area. With these two requirements, the plants will fill in and be striking in appearance.

The most common landscape problem is the brown patches that appear across a clump. Most often they occur when the plants are grown in brighter and drier locations. *Lamium maculatum* should only receive direct sun morning or early evening for good performance, especially during the hottest parts of the summer. As the weather warms up, be sure to keep the soil moist around the plants. If the soil around the plants dries out, plants wilt, weaken, and if dryness is repeated, the brown patches will die.

■■■ LATHYRUS LATIFOLIUS

FAMILY: Fabaceae

COMMON NAME(S): Perennial Sweet Pea, Hardy Sweet Pea

DESCRIPTION

Lathyrus latifolius displays nonfragrant blossoms, in deep rose or white (sometimes red or pink), on plants that can trail 6 to 9 feet (1.8 to 2.7 m) once established. The stems develop tendrils that grab hold of anything and twist and turn to reinforce the plant's weight as it develops. Considered a nuisance where it has escaped into the wild, *L. latifolius* is often seen growing among the porches and fence rows of older farms and cottage gardens but is seldom seen in garden centers today. Once planted, however, it often reseeds as well as returns from old rootstocks to flower year after year. Plants have become naturalized in many areas—from Georgia west to Texas and north to Missouri. The seeds are considered poisonous. See Color Plate 47 for photo of *Lathyrus latifolius*.

HARDINESS: Zones 4 to 7; selected areas of Zone 8.

SEASON OF BLOOM: June to August.

PROPAGATION

L. latifolius is usually propagated by sowing seed, although cuttings can be taken in early spring or fall after flowering is complete. Plants can also be divided, but according to many authorities, it's difficult to do, with most plants dying after divisions are taken. Based on economics alone, seed and cuttings are the preferred methods.

GERMINATION OVERVIEW: 625 seeds per ounce/22 per gram.

Seeds germinate at 62F to 70F (18C to 21C). Fresh seed germinates readily but if using old seed or seed of unknown age, an overnight soaking is suggested. If any seeds are floating by morning, these often will not germinate and can be nicked and allowed to soak again. Cover seed for germination, which can take anywhere from 10 to 20 days.

GROWING ON

Crop time: Seedlings may be transplanted, but most authorities and my own experience dictate that it's better to sow them into final containers. If transplanting, do it early and don't allow the roots to become firmly established within a germination tray. However, deep plug trays can be used. Sow three to four seeds direct to get two to three actively growing shoots. Transplant the plug into a 4-inch (10 cm) or quart container. If sowing direct to the final container, use three to four seeds per Jiffy pot to verify germination stand, and then thin to two plants if so desired.

Seeds sown in late February will produce salable green plants in May. These plants will spread only about 2 to 3 feet (60 to 90 cm) the first season and flower sporadically during late August and September. In general, 4-inch (10 cm) pots with two plants per pot will be salable 13 to 15 weeks after sowing when grown at 50F (10C) night temperatures. For quarts allow 15 to 17 weeks to fully root the plants.

VARIETIES

Most seed sold in the United States is available as a mixture and only under the botanical name. In the world seed trade, separate colors are also available primarily in white, red, and pink. It is sometimes sold under the name of The Pearl, but is more often simply sold as *Lathyrus latifolius* "alba," "rosa," and/or "red."

USES

An excellent climbing plant for old wagon wheels, porch railings, and in wildflower gardens or meadows. Plants are long lived and aggressive enough to kill out weaker plants below. Flowers are slightly larger than the standard sweet pea but lack the fragrance. However, the perennial pea can also be used as a cut flower and has a longer flowering season but fewer blooms than its annual flowering counterpart.

IN THE HOME GARDEN

Plant into full-sun locations in a moist but well-drained site where the plants are allowed to climb over a stable, upright support. *Lathyrus* doesn't require special care once established and can be grown easily in locations where it's neglected.

Plants don't require winter protection and will be free to flower once they've been planted into the garden for a year. Although they reseed, in our gardens they haven't become a problem.

■■ LEONTOPODIUM ALPINUM

FAMILY: Asteraceae

COMMON NAME(S): Edelweiss

DESCRIPTION

A small alpine or rock garden plant, *Leontopodium alpinum* grows no more than 8 inches (20 cm) tall in bloom. The leaves and stems are covered with gray hair similar to what you'd see on dusty miller leaves although not as silver.

The insignificant blooms are dull yellow and small in size. Directly beneath the flowers are a number of small leaves that, collectively, give a starlike appearance. See Color Plate 48 for photo of *Leontopodium alpinum*.

HARDINESS: Zones 6 to 8.

This crop's limited hardiness has more to do with soil type and the severity of both summer heat and winter cold/wet. Extremes of either are detrimental to this plant, and it will die easily.

In our Chicago Zone 5 location, the plants last only one to two years at best. Read the information under **In the home garden** for additional comments.

SEASON OF BLOOM: Late spring.

PROPAGATION

Seed is the preferred and easiest propagation method for this crop. Divisions can also be made in the spring but are more practical for home gardeners than professional growers since the plantlets from dividing are small and few in number.

GERMINATION OVERVIEW: 310,000 seeds per ounce/10,850 per gram.
Pretreatments: Fresh seed usually yields the highest germination with the best overall seedling quality. By contrast, if the seed is held until the following summer it will probably drop in germination but will seldom go below 50%. Seed that germinated at 90% in a greenhouse in November had dropped only to a low of 63% by the end of July the following year in our tests following the same methods.

To germinate, first test a small portion (50 seeds) for 10 days. A germination rate of 30% or greater is acceptable for this crop, especially if germinating in January or later. If the germination is lower than 10%, then a cold treatment will be necessary to get a higher germination.

Leontopodium alpinum germinates for me in July at between 60 and 70% final germination when subjected to temperatures of 70F to 73F (21C to 23C) for five to 11 days. Germination starts by the fifth day and is completed by the eleventh. Seedlings can be transplanted by 20 days after sowing. On the other hand, if you are getting only 50% germination or less, then a cold-moist treatment is your best bet. Refer to the **Propagation Techniques** chapter for more information.

GROWING ON

Crop time: *Leontopodium* is relatively quick to grow and develop into a plant ready for small pot and pack or quart container sales. If sown during the winter, the plants can be sold by May in cell packs of 32 cells per flat, but they will be small. From seed, the roots need 10 to 12 weeks to fill out a 32-cell pack. Late spring sowings can be transplanted by early summer to a quart container, which will be large enough by autumn for overwintering for spring sales.

Leontopodium isn't readily found from U.S. commercial propagators since the plants are seldom long lived. For sources, I would suggest contacting nurseries from Oregon and California to Colorado since selected areas of these states have regions that mimic alpine conditions.

This plant's hairy foliage can pose cultural problems. If grown in an area where moisture remains on the leaves daily, the plants often rot and eventually die out. Be sure to keep the plants in an aerated area where the foliage dries between waterings and humidity remains low. If overwintered in a cold greenhouse, cold frame, or under plastic, be sure to protect the plants, since wet foliage is often the leading cause of this plant's death. Your efforts in protecting the plants during winter may be futile, however. Read **In the home garden** for additional information.

VARIETIES

Leontopodium alpinum isn't commonly found in the United States due to its short-lived nature in our climate.

IN THE HOME GARDEN

This is not an easy crop to grow in the home landscape for any length of time because of its limited tolerance of extreme weather conditions. The high heat of a southern summer or a snowless and dry northern winter will lead to quick death. Plants under these conditions seldom live more than one to two years, if that long. The plants are well suited, however, for more mountainous regions.

To successfully grow plants in the garden, locate them in a sunny, well-drained spot with a pH of 6.0 and above; in winter, they need a layer of snow for protection. The plants are more winter hardy south of Chicago but high summer heat and humidity are just as limiting. Needless to say, this is a challenging plant to grow and should be carefully considered before purchasing.

▬ LEUCANTHEMUM × SUPERBUM

The genus *Chrysanthemum*, including Shasta daisies, has recently been divided between new and existing genera. This crop was formerly labeled *Chrysanthemum × superbum* and *C. maxima*.

FAMILY: Asteraceae

COMMON NAME(S): Shasta Daisy

DESCRIPTION

One of the best known of garden perennials, Shasta daisies have 3- to 4-inch (7 to 10 cm), lightly scented, pure white blooms with yellow centers. While single flowers are common, double-flowering varieties are also available. Plants vary from 10 inches (25 cm) high (Snow Lady) to as tall as 48 inches (122 cm) for Starburst and Alaska. Shasta daisies spread 15 to 24 inches (38 to 61 cm) across.

HARDINESS: Zones 5 to 8.

In the Midwest, these are most often treated as short-lived perennials. Shasta daisies need well-drained areas to avoid winter kill. Even then, Midwest winters are generally too severe for plants to last more than two to three seasons.

SEASON OF BLOOM: June to August.

PROPAGATION

The majority of the single-flowering varieties available on the market are propagated by seed. For 100% double-flowering varieties, the plants have to be propagated by cuttings or divisions. Divisions can be taken in the spring or autumn.

GERMINATION OVERVIEW: 15,000 to 35,000 seeds per ounce/525 to 1,225 per gram. Seeds germinate in nine to 12 days at 65F to 70F (19C to 21C); cover seed lightly during germination. Seedlings can be transplanted 20 to 25 days after sowing.

GROWING ON

From seed: Crop times and flowering response differ greatly for each variety. In general, seed sown in winter produces flowering plants in summer for many cultivars. However, Shasta daisies flower more profusely when exposed to six or eight weeks of 50F to 55F (10C to 13C) nights. There are exceptions, of course, and these are noted within the following varieties.

Alaska. Seed sown in mid to late winter will produce sporadically flowering plants the same season, most often flowering in late summer and early fall. Plants produce a strong clump that can be lifted the following spring or fall and then divided. Allow 11 to 13 weeks for green 32-cell packs and 14 to 16 weeks for 4½-inch (11 cm) or quart containers.

Snow Lady. For green, 4-inch (10 cm) pot or quart sales in May, sow in January and February; for flowering pots, sow in October or November. If sown in late February or March, plants can be sold green in packs in late May and will flower by early July.

Silver Princess. The previous two varieties will flower the same year from seed if sown by mid-March. Silver Princess will not do so reliably. We have sown this crop in early October, transplanted to packs in late October and to quart containers in February. Grown at 48F to 50F (9C to 10C) night temperatures, plants flowered in June; earlier flowering can be forced by raising the night temperatures to 60F (15C).

G. Marconi and Diener's Double. The double-flowering varieties from seed will not produce flowering plants the first year when sown in January or later. Instead, treat as you would Silver Princess for color.

From divisions: Plants divided in the spring can be moved up into 1- to 4-quart containers and sold once they become established. Fall divisions can be taken in September and moved up into quarts or gallons. Grow at 50F to 55F (10C to 13C) nights initially and then overwinter dormant with your other perennials.

Commercial propagators offer Shasta daisies as bare-root transplants in small pots or as liners/plugs, depending on the variety. Primarily available during the autumn

L

and winter, any of these can be potted up into quart and gallon containers and sold in spring.

VARIETIES

The single-flowering Shastas are the best known seed varieties in the trade. The doubles are best propagated from divisions or cuttings since those propagated by seed are only 50% semi- or fully double, the remainder being single.

Alaska grows 24 inches (61 cm) tall the first season from seed but can grow up to 30 inches (76 cm) tall the next year. Flowers are pure white to 4 inches (10 cm) across and are single to sometimes semidouble. This variety is propagated by seed.

Diener's Double is quickly vanishing from the trade. The variety boasted 3-inch (7 cm) blooms with frilled petal edges on plants to 2 feet (60 cm) tall. Unfortunately, the variety was offered as seed, which yielded flat petaled blooms in both double and single flowers. If you have stock plants, use them to propagate vegetatively.

G. Marconi (Marconi) has 3- to 4-inch (7 to 10 cm), pure white, semi- and fully double blooms on plants to 3 feet (90 cm) tall. The variety has been offered as seed for years, although single-flowering off-types are common. For fully double-flowering plants, propagate vegetatively.

Little Miss Muffet is a short, single-flowering variety similar in habit and overall appearance to Silver Princess. Plants are 12 inches (30 cm) tall with 2½-inch (6 cm) white flowers. Propagate vegetatively.

Silver Princess (Little Princess) is a seed-propagated variety that's taller and hardier than Snow Lady but shorter than Alaska. The variety makes better mounded and more uniform quart and gallon pots than Alaska but is stockier and more robust than Snow Lady. Grows to 15 to 17 inches (38 to 43 cm) tall.

Snow Lady is an F_1 hybrid for use in borders, edgings, or in pots. Plants bear single to semi-double white blooms to 3 inches (7 cm) across. An All-America Selections Award winner, this variety is seed propagated. It reaches 10 to 12 inches (25 to 30 cm) tall. Note: This variety is best treated as an annual since it seldom survives a winter.

White Knight has single, 3- to 4-inch (7 to 10 cm), pure white flowers on plants from 15 to 24 inches (38 to 61 cm) tall. It is taller, hardier, and slightly larger flowered than Silver Princess. Propagate by seed and grow as you would Silver Princess.

USES

The shorter Shasta daisy varieties work well as borders or edgings, while the taller selections can be used as specimen or mass plantings towards the middle or back of the garden. For the commercial landscape, choose the intermediate varieties like

Silver Princess or White Knight for best performance. They don't require staking and will reflower sporadically during summer after the main flush of color in spring.

Shasta daisies work well as a home cut flower. Choose any of the taller, long-stemmed varieties. Treat as you would a chrysanthemum.

As a pot plant, the best varieties are either Silver Princess or Snow Lady. Snow Lady has the quickest crop time from seed and is the shortest variety overall.

IN THE HOME GARDEN

Once planted, Shasta daisies tend to be short-lived perennials due to poor drainage. In our gardens near Chicago, an exceptionally wet autumn, quickly followed by a cold snap and freezing, usually leads to crown rot. Each spring numerous plants will die, with 100% losses expected by the third year after planting. Plant only in well-drained areas or raised beds. Place in a full-sun location and space 15 inches (38 cm) apart for the taller varieties, 10 inches (25 cm) apart for Snow Lady.

The double-flowering varieties from seed will have a better stature and overall higher flower quality if shaded during the hottest part of the day. The best cut flowers and brightest foliage come from plants given full sun, however. Staking isn't necessary, but it's best to plant the taller varieties where they are massed together or can lean against a structure (a fence, house, etc.). If this can't be guaranteed, providing at least one layer of support is recommended.

L

■■■ LIATRIS SPICATA

FAMILY: Asteraceae

COMMON NAME(S): Kansas Gay Feather, Blazing Star

DESCRIPTION

Liatris spicata is a tall and stately perennial with long tapered spikes of lavender-purple or white. The flowers are small, to one-quarter inch (6 mm) across and tightly arranged on 10- to 15-inch (25 to 38 cm) spikes. Blooms open from the top of the spike down instead of the bottom up as most spikelike flowers do. The foliage develops as a rosette of thin, elongated leaves. Liatris grows 1½ to 3 feet (45 to 90 cm) tall and 15 to 20 inches (38 to 51 cm) across. See Color Plate 49 for photo of *Liatris spicata*.

HARDINESS: Zones 3 to 8.

SEASON OF BLOOM: July and August.

PROPAGATION

Seed, corms, and divisions are the usual ways to propagate *L. spicata*. Divisions are taken either in the spring or autumn.

GERMINATION OVERVIEW: 9,400 seeds per ounce/329 per gram.

Germination temperatures are 65F to 70F (20C to 21C). Leave the seed exposed to light during germination. Reduce night temperatures by 10 degrees (6C) during germination if seedlings are slow to emerge. Germination takes 21 to 28 days; transplanting can begin 28 to 38 days after sowing.

GROWING ON

From seed: For plants that will flower in summer, seed should be sown during the previous summer for transplanting to the final container during August or early September. These plants are overwintered for green container sales the following spring.

For seed sown during the winter for green packs in spring, allow 12 to 14 weeks at 55F to 58F (13C to 14C) nights for rooted plants. Plants will flower the same season as sold, although seed should be sown by January or February for best performance. In trials, I have had March sowings fail to flower until the following year.

Commercial propagators offer *L. spicata* in small pots, liners or plugs. Primarily available during the autumn and winter, any of these can be potted up into quarts and gallons for green, budded, or flowering pot sales in the spring, depending on how early you transplanted the crop.

From corms: If planted one corm per quart container in mid-March, plants are saleable green in mid-May. Plants will flower in late June and July. If you have corms left over from spring planting, pot three corms up into a 6-inch (15 cm) pot in early July, and plants will flower in September. For spring production, keep the night temperatures between 50F to 55F (10C to 13C) or above.

Commercial propagators also offer it as bare-root transplants. These can be potted up into 3- or 4-quart containers in the winter or early spring for May sales.

VARIETIES

Kobold (also called Goblin) grows 18 to 24 inches (46 to 61 cm) tall. Flowers are lavender purple. The plants have worked well in our gardens. This variety is available from seed, corms, or division. Those propagated by vegetative means, however, were usually darker in flower color and more uniform in appearance.

One additional note: Kobold is a superior variety well known in the perennial trade. The plants you saw under this name five to 10 years ago were mostly vegetatively grown, which protected the line's integrity. While not a poor cultivar, the seed-propagated selections are not the same. Today, corms or divisions could have originated from seed. If this matters to you, contact your supplier to see if the corms or divisions you are buying originated from seed-propagated plants.

Floristan series is another spicata type available either in white- or blue-flowering plants—the blue offered as Floristan Blue or Floristan Violet. Plants are 3 feet (90 cm) tall and make excellent cut flowers. Floristan is propagated by seed.

USES

Tall, spirelike *Liatris spicata* spikes will give a military feeling to your perennial borders. For full impact, scattering several clumps of plants across the garden is suggested. Whether budded or in flower, the erect, rigid spikes add smooth lines to your landscape. When combined with soft-textured foliage, perennials such as *Liatris* provide a sharp contrast and unusual form.

As a cut flower, this is a prime choice. It is one of the perennials that's native to the United States. After hybridizing work in Holland, the plant has become a staple in the U.S. florist trade. For fresh cut flower use, harvest when the topmost florets begin to open. Flowers can also be dried.

IN THE HOME GARDEN

Plant in full sun and a well-drained location. *Liatris* does very well in drought conditions and doesn't tolerate wet roots for any great length of time. If kept overly moist, plants will suffer from a crown rot that turns the foliage black and kills the plant. I've never had to stake these plants, but some authorities recommend it. I've also planted them in partially shaded locations where they're in full shade by midafternoon. Those plants performed very well and flowered the same time as their full-sun counterparts. If a full-sun location is available, however, this is where they should be planted.

Protect from rabbits and deer in newly planted beds. The young shoots are particularly pleasing to these animals.

L

▬ LIGULARIA DENTATA

(sometimes called *Senecio clivorum* or *Ligularia clivorum*)

FAMILY: Asteraceae

COMMON NAME(S): Bigleaf Goldenray, Bigleaf Ligularia

DESCRIPTION

L. dentata is a clump-forming perennial with elongated stalks, each terminating in a rounded, kidney-shaped leaf. The flowers are daisy or rudbeckia-like in their form, golden or yellow orange in color, single or semidouble in shape, and $2\frac{1}{2}$ to 4 inches (6 to 10 cm) across.

Ligularias are shade-loving plants that often grow 2 to 3 feet (60 to 90 cm) tall in full bloom and spread 2 to 3 feet (60 to 90 cm) across when established in the garden. In gardens farther south than our Chicago area trialing station, however, the plants have been up to a foot (30 cm) taller or broader depending on location. Ligularias appear robust but are not invasive.

HARDINESS: Zones 5 to 8.

SEASON OF BLOOM: July and August.

PROPAGATION

Division is the most common form of propagating ligularias since clones are preferred over seed-grown selections. The species itself can either be grown from seed or propagated by divisions. According to Richard Bird [1], both Desdemona and Othello will often come true from seed as well. Plants that are allowed to flower and go to seed will produce self-sown seedlings that can be transplanted to containers and sold. Divisions can be made in spring or autumn.

GERMINATION OVERVIEW

Ligularia isn't commonly grown from seed in the United States, so the seed will be more easily found from seed exchanges and European seed companies.

When growing from seed, *Ligularia* achieves its best germination from winter-sown seed when the seed is exposed to a period of warm temperatures followed by a period of cold. Germination will often be 30% or less if not treated in this manner, especially on stored seed sown in January in the greenhouse. Information is provided in the **Propagation Techniques** chapter for warm-moist and moist-chill treatments.

GROWING ON

Crop time: Spring-dug divisions will take readily and can be sold in late spring after a late winter digging, depending on the size of the division versus the size of the container. Otherwise, divisions can be taken in the late summer, potted to any of the common containers, and held over the winter for sales in spring.

Plants will not flower the same year from a winter or spring sowing. For flowering plants, sow the previous year, potting to the final container by August or September. These plants are overwintered dormant for sales the following spring. As a guideline, *Ligularia* requires to 11 to 13 weeks from sowing to fill in a 32-cell pack. The plants can be transplanted to quart or gallon pots for green plant sales.

Commercial propagators offer ligularias as bare-root transplants. Primarily available during the autumn and winter, bare roots potted to 3-quart containers will finish in seven to nine weeks when grown at 55F (13C) nights.

VARIETIES

None of the following are seed propagated and require crown divisions to perpetuate the varieties named.

Note: Unless otherwise specified, all of the following have rich, vivid purple stems, petioles, and foliage when young. This coloring will persist as the plants emerge in the spring, though as summer approaches, the surface of the leaf will be green in color with a dark purple highlight. The undersides and leaf edges will remain purple, however.

Ligularia dentata is a green-leaved plant without any purple highlights or stem coloring during the summer. Flowers are golden orange and 3 inches (7 cm) or less across. Of all the varieties listed here, however, it's often shorter in stature than any of the purple-leaved types that follow. In our Chicago location the plants are often 3 feet (90 cm) or less in height with a spread of 2½ feet (75 cm) or less.

Dark Beauty is a tall cultivar, 3 to 4 feet (90 to 120 cm) in flower, with a 3-foot (90 cm) spread. Dark Beauty is shorter than Desdemona but similar in appearance. The flowers are golden orange and up to 3 inches (7 cm) across. Seed is available on this cultivar, although it will usually has a percentage of green or light purple off-types in it.

Desdemona is the most vigorous in spread and tallest in height of the varieties listed here. The plants grow from 3 to 4 feet (90 to 120 cm) tall but are closer to 4 feet (120 cm) in full bloom. The flowers tend to have more yellow in them than the other cultivars listed but they are still golden, not pure, yellow. Flowers measure up to 3½ inches (8 cm) across; plants will spread to 3½ feet (1 m). See Color Plate 50 for photo of *Ligularia dentata* Desdemona.

Othello is related to Desdemona but often grows into a mirror image of Dark Beauty in appearance. This is a good cultivar with a 3- to 4-foot (90 to 120 cm) height and a 3-foot (90 cm) spread. The flowers are golden orange and 2½ to 3 inches (6 to 7 cm) across. Othello has a dark leaf coloring similar to the previous two varieties.

RELATED MATERIAL

The species noted below develop spike-type flowers as opposed to the daisylike blooms on the *L. dentata*. Also, though they possess a dark stem coloring as seen on some *L. dentata* varieties, it's not as rich in color or as persistent.

Ligularia przewalskii has yellow flowers on plants to about 3 feet (90 cm) tall in bloom, taller in more fertile and moist locations. The flowers are held in spikes from 10 to 15 inches (25 to 38 cm) long, and they will flower before *L. dentata*. Plants will spread from 2 to 2½ feet (60 to 75 cm) across.

L. stenocephala is an interesting plant but it's the specific clone, The Rocket, that has gained the market's attention. The variety is named for its elongated flower spikes, broader at the base and tapered at the tip. The Rocket is often confused with *L. przewalskii* and is sometimes listed as its clone. One point of difference, however: The Rocket often has more flowering stems than does *L. przewalskii* in our trials—as much as three times more. The Rocket is a cultivar developed by Alan Bloom of England. It grows to a 3- to 4-foot (90 to 120 cm) height with a 3-foot (90 cm) spread. The yellow flowers are held in upright spikes from 10 to 15 inches (25 to 38 cm) long and, like *L. przewalskii*, will flower earlier than *L. dentata* varieties. See Color Plate 51 for photo of *Ligularia stenocephala*.

For both of the above species, hardiness, propagation methods, and cropping are the same as for *L. dentata*.

USES

Ligularias are excellent by the water's edge in shaded locations. Valued for their dark colored foliage and kidney-shaped leaves, the plants are effective in small groupings. Mass plantings should be reserved for landscapes that can handle them, such as commercial locations.

IN THE HOME GARDEN

Allan Armitage writes in his book that you should grow *Ligularia* "...in cool, moist conditions or not at all."[2] Although he gardens in Athens, Georgia, his comments are true for our Chicago location as well. In full shade the plants seldom perform as expected. However, in sunny locations the plants wilt by mid to late afternoon and recover in the early evening as the temperatures cool, although repeated exposure burns the leaves. Our best performance has been with plants that are given dappled light and a morning sun exposure but bright, indirect light for the remainder of the day. If planted to a moist location (but not standing water), such as beside a moving stream, the plants will even be more successful.

Ligularia can be divided in spring or late summer, but it has to be established in its new home before the onset of cold weather. The first winter following an autumn division, the new plants should be mulched to protect them.

REFERENCES

[1] Bird, R. 1993. *The propagation of hardy perennials*. London: B.T. Batsford Ltd.

[2] Armitage, A. 1989. *Herbaceous perennial plants*. Athens, Georgia: Varsity Press, Inc.

■■ LIMONIUM LATIFOLIUM

FAMILY: Plumbaginaceae

COMMON NAME(S): Wideleaf Sea Lavender, Sea Lavender, Statice

DESCRIPTION

Limonium latifolium has large basal leaves from 10 to 12 inches (25 to 30 cm) long radiating out of a central crown. The foliage is medium green and usually semitwisted or unkempt, less uniform in appearance than German statice (*Goniolimon tataricum*). The flowering stems are heavily branched and often weak stemmed, requiring support. The single, papery, lavender-blue flowers are small (one-sixteenth inch/1.6 mm) on stems up to 2½ feet (75 cm) tall. The plants will spread from 24 to 30 inches (60 to 76 cm) across.

HARDINESS: Zones 4 to 9.

In our Zone 5 garden outside Chicago, these plants aren't long lived. Refer to **In the home garden** for additional comments.

SEASON OF BLOOM: July and August.

PROPAGATION

Limonium latifolium is commonly propagated by seed, but divisions taken in the spring and root cuttings will also work. Seed and root cuttings are the preferred methods of commercial propagation, but bare-root transplants are available.

GERMINATION OVERVIEW: 28,000 seeds per ounce/980 per gram.

Limonium latifolium germinates in 14 to 21 days at 65 to 75F (19C to 24C) from uncovered seed. Transplanting can begin 24 to 36 days after sowing.

GROWING ON

From seed: For salable green quart or gallon sales in spring, sow the previous June and overwinter the plants. Seed sown after the first of the year seldom produces a plant large enough for spring sales unless you can sell green cell packs. Seed sown from January on will not produce flowering plants the same season from seed. For green pack sales, allow 10 to 12 weeks at 55F (13C) nights.

Commercial propagators offer *Limonium latifolium* as small pots, plugs, liners, or bare-root transplants. Available during the autumn and winter, any of these can be potted up to quarts or gallons and sold in spring.

One note, though: *L. latifolium* requires three years to become strongly established in the garden. While plants may flower the first year after planting, they require time to establish themselves and flower more profusely, regardless of the propagation method.

VARIETIES

Limonium latifolium is readily available from U.S. seed and plant companies.

RELATED MATERIAL

L. perezii is a tender perennial to 3 feet (90 cm) tall in warm winter areas. In our gardens near Chicago, it seldom grows more than 2 feet (60 cm) tall and never is as free flowering as those growing on the California coast. Flowers are mid to deep blue with a white throat, from which the common name Seafoam is derived. *L. perezii* does not survive cold winter areas, and 100% losses can be expected.

Readily propagated from seed, *L. perezii* is a fast grower that will flower the same season as sown. For spring sales in the Midwest, however, sow the seed in December for 5- and 6-inch (13 and 15 cm) pot sales in late April or May. If green salable cell packs are preferred, allow 10 to 12 weeks at 55F to 58F (13C to 14C) nights. However, while a fully grown 5-inch (13 cm) pot planted to the garden in

L

May will flower in July, the cell packs will not flower until August or September.

L. perezii is faster to grow than *L. latifolium* but only hardy from Zones 8 to 10.

USES

In the perennial border, the graceful flowering spikes add midseason color similar in form to gypsophila or baby's breath. As a cut flower, *L. latifolium* works well either dried or fresh.

In the commercial or home landscape, the planting of two-year-old transplants will yield a strong, noninvasive show of flower color for a number of weeks in mid-summer. Plants will tolerate various conditions and offer longevity in return for minimal care.

IN THE HOME GARDEN

The key here is that plants will not flower profusely until three or four years down the road after sowing. The second year after sowing, as many as five flowering stems will sprout, which is minimal compared to the eight to 15 stems on established plantings. Plant in a full-sun location in a moist but not wet area, and space 15 to 20 inches (38 to 51 cm) apart. Though staking isn't normally required, be cautious in applying fertilizer more than once or twice per summer. High fertility will produce tall, lanky growth requiring some staking late in the season.

As for hardiness, *Limonium latifolium* can be a long-lived plant, but care has be taken to avoid excessive water around its crown. This can lead to crown rot and death. It's also suggested that you avoid planting this crop in open locations away from winter protection, specifically in areas exposed to late autumn rain and dry cold. A combination of the two can seriously decrease your chances of plants returning from year to year.

◼ LINUM PERENNE

FAMILY: Linaceae

COMMON NAME(S): Flax, Perennial Flax

DESCRIPTION

Upright but arching at the crown, *Linum perenne*'s stems radiate out of a small, 8- to 10-inch (20 to 25 cm) base to a spread of 2 feet (60 cm) across the top of the plant in summer. The stems branch minimally but grow to 2 feet (60 cm) tall and possess a multitude of small, linear leaves. Flowers are single, soft sapphire blue and measure about an inch (2.5 cm) across. They last only one day, then the five petals detach themselves and fall to the ground. While new blooms replace the ones fading from the previous day, the ground is scattered with the spent color.

HARDINESS: Zones 4 to 8.

SEASON OF BLOOM: June and July.

PROPAGATION

Seed is the most reliable and consistent way to propagate perennial flax. *Linum* isn't a hard plant to germinate from seed and comes true, producing few off-types or rogues. Plants can be divided in the spring, but this isn't a common practice among professional growers. Home gardeners would benefit more from this method.

GERMINATION OVERVIEW: 9,000 to 24,000 seeds per ounce/315 to 840 per gram. Leave seed exposed or lightly cover it with coarse vermiculite for germination. When soil temperatures of 70F to 73F (21C to 23C) are reached, seedlings will emerge in four to eight days and be transplantable to cell packs 14 to 21 days after sowing. In the *Ball Culture Guide* I note that germination occurs in 10 to 12 days. When sowing under cooler temperatures of 65F to 70F (18C to 21C), germination is slower but will yield similar results in the number of usable seedlings.

GROWING ON

Crop time: From seed the plants grow and develop slowly. Seed sown in January will produce salable cell packs (32 cells per flat) by May, although a December sowing is better since the extra time makes a heftier plant. Keep in mind that these plants are producing erect, nonbranching stems out of a central crown. Since the foliage is wispy, the longer crop time will produce a larger plant both above and below the ground.

Seed sown as late as March will still produce a flowering crop the same year as sown. The later sowings obviously yield limited results, however, with the greater flower power on those stronger plants that were sown earlier.

If growing in a 32-cell pack, allow 13 to 15 weeks for green salable transplants for May sales. Flax should be grown warmer than other perennials at no less than 50F (10C) nights to keep it actively growing although 55F (13C) and above is better. Since it isn't an overly large plant to begin with, cold temperatures and common daily watering practices can eventually lead to rots and premature death due to the plant's slower growth.

For larger, more robust quart sales next year, sow seed the first four or five months of the year for transplanting to the final quart container by July. Plants are then over-wintered in a protected environment (cold frame or similar structure) where they can be kept dormant. Plants are sold the following spring.

Commercial propagators offer *Linum* as plugs or liners. Available in autumn and winter, they can be potted up into quart and gallon containers and sold in spring.

Growers frequently ask about the plant's temperature requirements. It's hard to understand why a plant that, once planted to the garden emerges in April and grows as tall as 16 inches (41 cm) by early May, should have such a problem with cool temperatures while growing. The answer lies in the plant's root development. When

L

started from seed, both the shoots and roots actively grow and develop but require warmer temperatures to get started and established. *Linum*'s thin, fragile roots take longer to develop than many other perennials they are often grown with, and due to their slower nature, can wind up dying. The second and third months after sowing are the most critical time: Warm sowing temperatures are a given—it's the cooler temperatures after transplanting that cause the problems.

VARIETIES

L. perenne is available from numerous U.S. seed firms. Of the cultivar selections listed here, this is one of the most dependable and long lived. *Linum perenne* has been reported to be short lived in the garden, but this is more common when it's grown in soils that are too wet or where the plants are repeatedly subjected to stressful conditions such as drought during the summer.

L. perenne Saphyr (Sapphire) bears the same flower color as *L. perenne* but is shorter in stature than the species. Plants will be the same in all other aspects such as culture, performance, crop time, and flower size, but the plants only grow to 20 inches (51 cm) tall or less.

USES

From the discussion above, you can see the limitations of this plant in regard to use as a cut flower or landscape plant. While the one-day life span of the blooms isn't suited to cut flower use, landscaping problems may not be as obvious.

Linum isn't fond of overhead watering or rain showers that help accelerate petal drop from the plants. While the water from above keeps the plants clean of dying blossoms, it also decreases the amount of color you see on the plants. It can be used in the landscape, however, especially where the plants are combined with other plant material to compliment the light blue flower color. Avoid companion plants with large, bright blooms that may take away from *Linum*'s lighter color. Smaller blooms of white, pink, and buff yellow all work well.

IN THE HOME GARDEN

Plant in full-sun locations where excess water will not puddle. Plants should be spaced apart in staggered rows to 14 or 16 inches (35 to 41 cm) apart for best effect. Remember, plants have a small crown that creates a vaselike habit with arching, almost fountainlike stems.

Plants don't require winter protection, although if you plant them out in the open with no winter wind barriers, you need to provide a light mulch at their base for added protection. If the fall has been unusually wet and cold here in Chicago, the plants can winter kill regardless of mulching, although the species has been reliably more winter hardy than the other cultivars.

▬ LIRIOPE MUSCARI

FAMILY: Liliaceae

COMMON NAME(S): Blue Lily Turf, Big Blue Lily Turf

DESCRIPTION

Liriope muscari is a dwarf plant growing to 18 inches (46 cm) in flower, with violet-blue or white flowers on evergreen plants. Flowers are held in spikes to 5 inches (13 cm) long above the foliage. Leaves can grow to 18 to 20 inches (46 to 51 cm) long but are no wider than three-quarter inch (2 cm) across. The foliage is fountainlike with the leaves arching over; colors can be green or variegated white and yellow. The roots are tuberous. Once the flowers fade, deep blue berries develop and persist until frost. The plants spread from 10 to 14 inches (25 to 35 cm) across.

HARDINESS: Zones 6 to 9.

Liriope is not reliably winter hardy in Chicago and easily dies out in our gardens 40 miles west after a severe winter. However, within the city of Chicago I've seen numerous plantings survive—the lake effect has helped to protect the plants during the winter. In areas farther south—St. Louis, for example—this plant does much better. Additional information is provided under **In the home garden**.

SEASON OF BLOOM: August and September.

PROPAGATION

Named cultivars are propagated by division, which can be done in either the spring or autumn. Numerous plantlets can be obtained from an established planting. Seed can be used to propogate the species.

GERMINATION OVERVIEW

Liriope germinates in 15 to 35 days at 70F (21C) and doesn't need to be covered to germinate. It isn't hard to germinate but emerges irregularly, meaning you'll have to stagger transplanting.

If seedling percentage is low, chill the germination tray at 40F (5C) for two to four weeks to help break dormancy. You can also soak the seed overnight to hasten germination.

GROWING ON

Liriope is available in both bare-root divisions and cell packs during the autumn and winter. Pot these up into quarts or gallons for spring or summer sales. Grow on at 55F (13C) nights.

L

VARIETIES

Big Blue grows from 12 to 18 inches (30 to 46 cm) tall with dark violet flowers.

Majestic is a larger flowered, violet-blue to lilac cultivar that grows to 18 inches (46 cm). Leaves are deep green.

Variegata (Variegated) has dark violet-blue flowers on plants with cream to light yellow striped foliage. It reaches 12 to 18 inches (30 to 46 cm).

RELATED MATERIAL

Liriope spicata (Creeping Lily Turf) is a rhizomatous species growing from 10 to 12 inches (25 to 30 cm) tall with narrow leaves and lavender flower spikes. Though the flowers are not as showy as *L. muscari*, plants of *L. spicata* are more winter hardy here in our northern location. As the flowers fade, dark purple fruit will persist throughout autumn. It is hardy to Zone 4.

Propagate as you would *L. muscari*.

USES

In warm winter areas (Zone 6 and south), the variety is an excellent ground cover, well known for its heat tolerance with few pest and disease problems. The plants can become invasive, however, if conditions are right.

In the commercial landscape, this crop offers a lot of potential for those semi-shaded areas where hostas or *Dicentra* may be growing.

IN THE HOME GARDEN

Liriope muscari is the liriope of choice for southern gardeners. The plants are tolerant of drought, humidity, and heat and are consistent performers for the shade garden. Plant in moist, well-drained soils, though plants will tolerate drier locations. In the deep South, plant where they get morning sun but are shaded in the afternoon. Farther north, plants can take more sun.

In the northern United States, plantings of either *L. muscari* or *L. spicata* should be protected during the winter from cold, dry winter winds, which are the death of these plants. Cover with leaves or other mulching materials. Remove them in April or earlier if the temperatures have warmed up.

In southern gardens, the plants will be evergreen, but they can be trimmed back from December to February if they appear ratty or unkempt. Here in our Chicago gardens, I trim the foliage back on *L. spicata* in the spring, though the foliage may have persisted throughout the winter here.

■ LOBELIA CARDINALIS

FAMILY: Lobeliaceae

COMMON NAME(S): Cardinal Flower, Red or Scarlet Lobelia, Indian Pink

DESCRIPTION

Lobelia cardinalis is a native perennial predominant in moist woodland settings and streamsides from eastern Canada, south through the United States to the Gulf of Mexico. Plants are erect, taller than they are wide, from 2 to 4 feet (60 to 120 cm), with a 2-foot (60 cm) spread when fully mature.

The flowers are a bright cardinal red on plants with medium to dark green foliage. Blooms are from 1 to 1½ inches (2.5 to 3 cm) long and more open in appearance than *L. siphilitica*. Flowers are held out and slightly up on racemes to 14 inches (35 cm) long, sometimes longer if the plants are self-sown or if they sprout within a naturally existing clump.

HARDINESS: Zones 2 to 9.

Although obviously hardy, the plants are short lived, lasting from two to four years depending on soil and exposure.

SEASON OF BLOOM: July to September.

PROPAGATION

Seed is the common propagation method, although plant clumps can be divided in spring or fall as well. Many lobelias produce a cluster of new basal growth in late summer after the central stem dies. These can be removed from the plant—along with their roots—and potted up or moved to the propagation bench to fully root for sales after the pots become fully established. Plants can be overwintered as well for sales the following year if they aren't subjected to below freezing temperatures that could cause die out.

GROWING ON

Information for germination and growing on is included under the notes for *L. siphilitica*; similar results will be obtained for this species.

One interesting fact: One perennial reference manual notes that *L. cardinalis* is one of only a few native plants bees can't pollinate due to the flower's elongated tubes. Instead, hummingbirds do the job since they can reach the nectaries located at the base of the corolla [1].

VARIETIES

L. cardinalis can be readily found at native wildflower companies and seed exchanges as well as commercial seed houses in the United States.

RELATED MATERIAL

L. × gerardii (*L. × vedariensis*) is a hybrid lobelia resulting from a cross between *L. × hybrida* Queen Victoria and *L. siphilitica*. Its deep green foliage often has a bright crimson shading to the stem as it develops and grows. The flowers are often larger than other lobelia species, in a range of colors from pink to violet purple. Colors are vibrant and will easily catch a gardener's eye. The plants aren't reliably hardy in the northern United States and are usually treated as annuals in cold winter areas since they don't appreciate severe winters. This wasn't the case during the winter of 1993-94 here in Chicago, however, when all the Butterfly Rose plants returned in the spring. I've always been told that these plants aren't winter hardy, so I usually pulled them from the gardens in the fall thinking that they were annuals in our climate. While one winter isn't conclusive proof for this crop's hardiness, I'm evaluating it for several more winters.

Plants grow quickly from seed, filling out a 4-inch (10 cm) pot in May from a February sowing. If planted to the garden before Memorial Day, these plants are often in flower by the end of June or July and stay in color throughout most of the summer when given bright shade or full sun.

Varieties aren't commonly sold here in the United States but some, like Butterfly Rose, will grow well and flower all summer long.

L. splendens (*L. fulgens*), commonly called Mexican Lobelia, is similar to *L. cardinalis*. The major difference is the bronze leaves on *L. splendens* varieties. The hybrids of the group rather than the species have gained much attention. They are propagated both vegetatively and from seed.

These hybrids are the result of *L. splendens*, *L. cardinalis*, and *L. siphilitica* crosses. (*L. amoena* is considered to be a parent as well by some authorities.) The hybrids are known by the botanical name of *L. × hybrida*. The plants aren't hardy in our Chicago location and readily winter kill. So they're often grown as annuals or protected "perennials," and divisions, offsets, or stem cuttings are taken from spring to late summer.

Seed is available and can be sown in winter for summer flowering. February sowings potted to 4-inch (10 cm) pots will be salable as vigorous growing plants in May. These, once planted to the garden before Memorial Day, will often be in flower in late June or early July.

The following cultivars are selections of the crosses noted earlier.

Bees Flame has bronze-red foliage with scarlet-red flowers. Plants grow from 3 to 4 feet (90 to 120 cm), taller in the southern United States.

Compliment series is available in scarlet, red, and deep blue separate colors. It's a youngster compared to some of the varieties in this group. While many have been around for over 10 years (Queen Victoria goes back to the 1930s), the Compliment series was introduced in the early 1990s. Plants grow from 2 to 3 feet (60 to 90 cm) tall with deep green foliage.

Fan series is also young by comparison—it was introduced to the trade in the late 1980s. Plants are often 2 feet (60 cm) tall, and separate colors of orchid, rose, scarlet, or deep red are available. The leaves are deep green except on scarlet-flowered plants, which have bronze leaves.

Illumination is often listed as a sister variety to Queen Victoria. Illumination is closer to the *L. splendens* species than the hybrids noted, however. Its foliage is dark green with large spikes of bright scarlet-red flowers. Illumination reaches 1½ to 2½ feet (45 to 75 cm).

Queen Victoria is often listed as a *L. cardinalis* variety and may have been listed as *L. cardinalis atrosanguinea* in older texts, referring to the bronze foliage. The plants possess brilliant red flowers similar to *L. cardinalis*, although the foliage is a consistently vivid bronze-red. Plants can grow as tall as 4½ feet (1.3 m) but seldom reach over 3 feet (90 cm) in our gardens in the first and only year after sowing.

One final note regarding these lobelias: Don't pinch the plants back as they're growing. Lobelias have a central stem with a number of basal side shoots that develop. By pinching back this primary stem, the secondary ones develop, increasing your crop time to first flower by as much as four weeks.

IN THE HOME GARDEN

Since the various species are so similar, read the following information on *L. siphilitica* for particulars.

REFERENCES

[1] Giles, F.A., R.M. Keith, and D.C. Saupe. 1980. *Herbaceous perennials*. Reston, Va.: Reston Publishing Co.

LOBELIA SIPHILITICA

(sometimes *L. syphilitica*)

FAMILY: Lobeliaceae

COMMON NAME(S): Blue Cardinal Flower, Great Lobelia, Great Blue Lobelia

DESCRIPTION

Lobelia siphilitica is a native perennial found in moist woodland settings in a sweeping range from Maine westward and south from the Dakotas to Louisiana. It is an erect and stately plant from 2 to 3 feet (60 to 90 cm) tall with a spread from 15 to

20 inches (38 to 51 cm) across. The plants will appear leafy in form and habit, either when growing in a pot or in the garden. The flowers are single, with a purple-colored upper lip and a lower set of blue petals highlighted in white. The flowers are tightly held and appear tubelike to about 1 inch (2.5 cm) long. They develop in upright racemes that measure from 6 to 9 inches (15 to 23 cm) long. See Color Plate 52 for photo of *Lobelia siphilitica*.

HARDINESS: Zones 4 to 8.

SEASON OF BLOOM: July or August to September.

PROPAGATION

This species is usually propagated by seed while the named cultivars are often propagated by divisions taken in the spring or early summer. Stem cuttings can also be taken.

GERMINATION OVERVIEW

The following information is applicable to *L. cardinalis* as well.

With no germination pretreatments, *L. siphilitica* germinates in a range of 65% to 85%. The seed isn't covered during germination, and emergence is usually eight to 12 days after sowing at 70F (21C). Seed used in studies involving using GA-3 (gibberellic acid) were covered with the media during germination and gave 100% germination in the second week after sowing at 70F (21C) [1].

Seedlings can be transplanted 24 to 30 days after sowing.

GROWING ON

The following is also applicable to *L. cardinalis*.

Crop time: From seed, plants grow quickly with a broad habit and large leaves. Sowings could be made to plug trays (72 to 105 cells per flat) and transplanted directly to the final quart or gallon pot. Pack sales aren't suggested due to this crop's quick growing nature. If green pack sales are needed, plants will be salable green (32 cells per flat) with well-rooted and leafy plants in 10 to 12 weeks when grown at 50F (10C) nights.

Lobelia siphilitica should be grown in nothing less than a quart container for growing in summer for sales the following year. Plants flower readily the first summer after sowing but are one-third the size of the full-grown specimens in the garden. They look, for lack of a better term, puny. Combined with the fact they're variable in color—they will range from light to mid blue, as well as produce a few white-flowering plants—you're better off growing them on for a summer to size them up; then you can select out the superior performing ones.

As for divisions, *L. siphilitica* will sometimes produce offsets that can be removed from the plant's crown. This is especially true when plants are grown in moist soils rather than well-drained locations. As the crowns enlarge, the centers may die out, producing offsets around the plant's outer perimeter. These also can be removed, potted up, and sold the same year or following year, if desired.

VARIETIES

L. siphilitica is available from many U.S. seed companies. Seed exchanges and European seed houses also carry this variety.

IN THE HOME GARDEN

L. siphilitica is a moisture-loving perennial for planting along streams and other areas with running water. It will not tolerate standing water but will live readily in moist or damp soils. In fact, the plants can become a reseeding nuisance in such an exposure, but they're shallow rooted and easily removed. If planted in well-drained locations that may frequently dry out between waterings, the plants aren't as productive nor as vigorous. In these dry areas, the plants prefer a more shady location where they're protected during the hottest part of the day. In the moist soils, the plants will appreciate sunnier locations, though the plants are often short lived.

The plants' crowns frequently rot out in our Chicago-area gardens in late winter or early spring. In February or early March as the days become warmer but the nights are still cool/cold, the plants prematurely leaf out and the leaves often frost and die. This is more common when they're planted in open locations away from winter protection, however. When planted by the side of a house or under an overhang, they'll have fewer problems.

In warm winter climates, the plants may not die back all the way to the ground—although they're herbaceous in cold winter areas and will reemerge in the spring.

During winter we mulch our plants, especially those in open and less protected areas, since severe cold and drying winds can decrease this crop's life. Plants don't require staking to remain upright and can be harvested as cut flowers. Many experts suggest searing the cut ends with flame to ensure a longer lasting cut.

REFERENCES

[1] Deano, N. 1993. *Seed germination theory and practice*. 2nd ed. Personally published.

■■ LUNARIA ANNUA (L. BIENNIS)

FAMILY: Brassicaceae

COMMON NAME(S): Honesty, Money Plant, Dollar Plant

DESCRIPTION

Lunaria annua is an old-time garden favorite known for its silvery, transparent, flat seed pods in the spring. *Lunaria* is a true biennial, rosetting the first year from seed and requiring a cold period to develop stems that bloom the following year. The flowers are single, less than an inch (2.5 cm) across, with little or no fragrance. The blooms are mostly purple, although 5 to 7% white plants often appear when growing the species. While the flowers are considered rather common by many gardeners, the developing seed pods are unique and useful as dried cut flowers. Plants can grow up to 2½ feet (75 cm).

HARDINESS: Zones 4 to 8.

SEASON OF BLOOM: May and June.

PROPAGATION

Seed is the easiest and most successful means to propagate *L. annua*.

GERMINATION OVERVIEW: 1,500 seeds per ounce/525 per gram.

Lunaria is an easy biennial to germinate compared to the other crops covered in this book. Over the past 10 years we've tried various sowing methods to germinate this crop with similar results. Seed that is used within a year after harvesting (new seed is available from seed companies in November or December), will germinate at 80% and above, as long as the seed is used within that first year.

Seed that has been covered lightly with a layer of coarse vermiculite or more heavily with a one-eighth-inch (3 mm) layer of peat moss has yielded germination stands of 80% or greater. When seed was sown without any covering, the germination percentage was 80% and more.

Therefore, to germinate *Lunaria*, sow in any peat-lite media, cover lightly and keep the soil temperatures at 70F to 72F (21C to 22C) for best results. Seedlings will start to emerge after six days, but 10 to 14 days will be required to get strong stands. Seedlings can be transplanted to cell packs or small pots 16 to 25 days after sowing.

One final note: The crop grows quickly enough for seed to be sown direct to the final container. This isn't a practice I recommend, since transplanting seedlings helps to slow their development and helps to keep them in check. *Lunaria* can grow too fast and become top-heavy and visually unattractive in a small 2- or 3-inch (5 or 7 cm) pot when sown direct and not allowed at least one transplanting.

GROWING ON

Crop time: Plants will be salable as finished green transplants in 32-cell packs or smaller, nine to 11 weeks after sowing. If growing 4½-inch (11 cm) pots from winter or spring sowing, allow 12 to 14 weeks at 50F (10C) nights. These plants will bloom the next year after overwintering.

From a retail point of view, consider several options in offering this plant to your customers. If plants have to show color to sell, sow the seed during the previous summer (June or July). These seedlings can be moved up into quart or gallon containers in late summer for overwintering in a cold frame or similar structure, then sold green in spring.

This crop is also available from commercial propagators in a liner or plug. If purchasing in the winter or early spring, be sure to order vernalized plugs, since these will have been exposed to cold temperatures and offer the best chance of flowering the same year.

One additional point: Plants can be treated as wildflowers by reminding customers not to remove flowerheads so that the seed can develop and fall back to the ground. This will provide blooming plants each year. The plants will not become invasive since individual seedlings can be pulled out or dug and moved to another location.

VARIETIES

Lunaria annua is offered by a variety of seed companies across the United States.

L. annua is a lavender or purple flowering variety, though 3 to 8% white flowering plants will be noticeable as well.

L. annua var. *alba* is the white flowering counterpart, similar in most respects to the purple flowering version. Though available, it isn't readily found.

USES

Lunaria is primarily used in the home garden due to its limited performance in a professional landscape. As a wildflower, the plants aren't strong enough to hold their position against an aggressive competitor, so don't count on planting in a meadow or such if native grasses and similar plants are grown nearby. *Lunaria* does best when unchallenged and will not become invasive. If a grouping of five to 10 plants is allowed to flower, and even one is allowed to produce seed, then the plants will usually reseed, producing plants for the following year. However, I haven't been that lucky in our gardens in West Chicago. I have to sow each year to assure flowering plants annually.

Lunaria makes a excellent dried cut flower.

IN THE HOME GARDEN

Lunaria is a plant that prefers morning and afternoon sun though it likes a break from summer heat if at all possible. The best place to grow *Lunaria* is where the plants are shaded during the hottest part of the day. Our plants look their best if given an eastern exposure and well-drained soil. With a heavy soil and full sun, the plants will often look good during the summer but die out in winter due to stress. We have lost full plantings of 40 or more plants when they were exposed to full sun and locations that were poorly drained.

Space plants 12 inches (30 cm) apart in staggered rows to allow for filling in. When the seed pods are starting to develop, plants will seldom need any staking unless the ground is fertile or the plants are growing in a windy area. Seed pods should be harvested when they are fully developed but before they have completely dried. The outer green appendage can be left on as the branches are cut. After the branches have dried for a few weeks, it can be easily removed.

▬ Lupinus polyphyllus

Family: Fabaceae

Common name(s): Lupine

Description

Lupinus polyphyllus is a striking plant with pea-like flowers arranged in erect spikes to 12 inches (30 cm) long. The flowers are small, somewhat rounded, to one-half-inch (1 cm) long and are held singly. Flower colors include white, soft blue, midblue, red, and pink. Plants are traditionally a biennial or short-lived perennial, seldom surviving beyond a second winter. Plants perform best in cool, moist conditions and don't take kindly to hot, humid weather. Overall height is 20 to 30 inches (51 to 76 cm) depending on the cultivar. Plants will spread 15 to 24 inches (38 to 61 cm) across. See Color Plate 53 for photo of *Lupinus polyphyllus*.

Hardiness: Zones 4 to 8.

Although we're located in Zone 5, established clumps of lupines are more a dream than a reality. See **In the home garden** for additional information.

Season of bloom: June and July.

Propagation

Lupines are commonly propagated by seed, although basal cuttings taken in early spring will also work. Divisions can be cut in early spring, a method used mostly by home gardeners.

Germination overview: 1,000 seeds per ounce/35 per gram.

Lupines germinate in six to 12 days at 65F to 75F (19C to 24C), and the seed should be covered when sowing. Various publications recommend different germination temperatures, but all tend to work depending on what's best for you. One variation includes using an alternate day/night temperature of 80F/70F (26C/21C), which can be effective on old seed (seed stored for a year or more). The seed may also need to be soaked overnight or scarified (the outer coat nicked with a razor or file) for good stands.

Growing on

From seed: Winter or early spring sowings will not flower the same season from seed. For spring-flowering plants, the normal method is to sow the previous summer, pot up to quarts or gallons when ready, and then overwinter dormant. Using this method, however, growers have experienced large losses in the spring due to rot.

Another method that we've used is to sow seed in early October, transplant mid-month to small pots, and then shift up into gallons (one plant per pot) in early February. Plants were grown at 45F to 48F (7C to 9C) nights and planted to the garden in May, flowered in mid-June. We grew them in the cold frame with normal (ambient) daytime highs and lows after April 1. It's conceivable that by raising the temperatures, you can flower the plants earlier. This method was especially effective on the Gallery series.

Commercial propagators offer lupine as a bareroot transplant in small pots or as a liner/plug. Primarily available during the autumn and winter, any of these can be potted up into quarts and gallons and sold in spring. If vernalized (exposed to a cold period), the plants will flower in the spring.

If green packs are preferred for spring sales, allow a deep enough container (nothing smaller than a 32 tray) or, better yet, use a tray with 18 cells per flat for best performance. For green packs in the spring, plants are saleable 10 to 12 weeks from sowing in A-18s (18 cells per flat) when grown on at 50F to 55F (10C to 13C) nights. One final note: If you're selling in packs or small pots, be sure to sell the plants before they become rootbound. If roots are restricted during active growth, lupines will be more susceptible to root rots. Allowing plants to become rootbound also spoils later performance—hot/humid summers only worsen this condition.

VARIETIES

All of the following are seed propagated.

Gallery Series is a shorter strain growing to 20 inches (51 cm) tall. The flower colors are similar to the Russell Strain but tend toward more basal branching. Overall habit is also smaller, making these a prime choice for late season sales in larger containers.

Minarette is a mixture of lupine colors similar to the Russell Strain. Plants grow 18 to 20 inches (46 to 51 cm) tall.

Russell Strain (also called Russell series) is often sold as a mix and is available as both seed and transplants. Plants grow to 3 feet (90 cm) tall with flowers to 1 inch (2.5 cm) wide. Colors include red, yellow, pink, blue, purple, and white. Separate colors are available and are sold under the following names:

> My Castle—brick red flowers
> Noble Maiden—white flowers
> Chandelier—yellow shades
> The Governor—violet-blue flowers
> The Pages—carmine rose
> The Chantelaine—pink and white bicolor

Nothing can beat a show of lupines with 20 to 30 plants of a single color in a planting. The variety isn't a single species but a cross between a number of species and types. It is often labeled as Lupine Russell Strain or Russell Hybrids.

USES

Lupines are often used as annuals in areas with hot, humid summers where the weather frequently kills the plants with diseases, which are intensified by the heat.

IN THE HOME GARDEN

Plant into a well-drained and sunny location, spacing the plants 15 inches (38 cm) apart. Plants don't require staking to remain upright. Lupines are best in perennial gardens along coastal areas or places with temperate climates. In our gardens outside Chicago in Zone 5, lupines don't tolerate our hot and humid summers nor wet/cold winters. We've experienced 50 to 80% losses within one year after planting into the garden, mostly due to root and crown rots.

One additional comment about using lupines: We've found more success with plants located next to a house or near shrubs and other objects providing protection from weather extremes. If covered with evergreen boughs or some other open, non-compacting winter mulch, the plants have a greater chance of survival in our climate.

■■■ LYCHNIS CHALCEDONICA

FAMILY: Caryophyllaceae

COMMON NAME(S): Maltese Cross

DESCRIPTION

Lychnis chalcedonica is an erect growing perennial that develops from a small clump. Plants are taller than they are wide, growing 18 to 28 inches (46 to 71 cm) tall with a 12-inch (30 cm) spread when flowering. Some authors suggest the plants can become taller and wider, but this is not our experience in midwestern gardens. In more fertile locations, however, it's possible that the plants could become taller and wider.

The single scarlet flowers are three-quarter to 1 inch (2 to 2.5 cm) wide, in clusters of 10 to 20 blooms. The clusters measure up to 3 inches (7 cm) across. Each stem developing out of the crown grows upright with limited branching, terminating in a cluster.

HARDINESS: Zones 3 to 9.

SEASON OF BLOOM: Late May and June.

PROPAGATION

L. chalcedonica is an easily propagated perennial from either seed or divisions. You can sow seed year-round with similar germination stands from sowing to sowing. Take divisions during the spring or later on in the summer after flowering.

GERMINATION OVERVIEW: 12,500 seeds per ounce/4,375 per gram.
Pretreatments: None are needed to maintain germination rates above 70%. When not sowing, store the seed in a cooler or similar structure at 35F (2C).

With a germination temperature of 70F (21C), and little or no seed covering, seedlings will start to emerge in five to seven days with enough developed to start transplanting in 15 to 20 days after sowing. The first edition of the *Ball Culture Guide* states that *Lychnis* requires 14 to 21 days to germinate. In the second edition, the number of days to germinate *Lychnis* was omitted completely and the number of days to transplant was incorrectly stated at 22 to 35. Alas, the foibles of book writing. Rest assured that you can transplant this crop within three weeks after seeding.

GROWING ON

Crop time: From seed, sowings made as late as February or March will still flower in June or July depending on how it is grown. Obviously, later sowings produce smaller plants with fewer blooms.

For 4-inch (10 cm) or quart sales in spring, seed would need to be sown in December or January and transplanted when ready. These are moved to a cold frame and grown on at 50F to 55F (10C to 13C) nights until sold. Four-inch (10 cm) pots will be salable in 14 to 16 weeks; quart containers require up to two weeks longer to fully root in. These plants will flower during June.

If green, salable cell packs are preferred for spring sales, allow 10 to 12 weeks for a fully grown 32-cell pack to be filled in. Grow on at 50F to 55F (10C to 13C) nights or, if the plants are growing too fast, drop the night temperatures to between 45F to 50F (7C to 10C), which also helps to keep *Lychnis* branching from the base.

Commercial propagators offer *Lychnis* as bare-root transplants, in small pots or as liner/plugs. Primarily available during the autumn and winter, any of these can be potted up into quarts and gallons and sold in spring.

VARIETIES

Lychnis chalcedonica is available from numerous U.S. seed and plant companies.

Hoarfrost is the white-flowering version of the above. It's similar in all aspects to the scarlet variety except for the pure white flowers. The variety is seldom seen in the United States but is available from seed and worthy of mention. Hoarfrost grows 15 to 20 inches (38 to 51 cm) tall.

RELATED MATERIAL

L. coronaria is commonly called rose campion. It's known for its woolly gray foliage on plants 15 to 30 inches (38 to 76 cm) tall in flower. The foliage is as gray as dusty miller or a mullein. *L. coronaria*'s single flowers open a dull white, turn to dusty rose and then a darker rose as they age. The flowers measure up to 2 inches (5 cm) across. *L. coronaria* is hardy from Zones 4 to 7 but falters under excessive moisture on leaves or at roots along with high heat and humidity, although we have had no problem growing them in our gardens. Plants frequently reseed but seldom become a nuisance.

Like *L. chalcedonica*, green transplants are ready for the garden 10 and 12 weeks after sowing. Unlike the Maltese cross, these plants will not flower the same year after sowing when sown in January or later. The plants rosette the first year and then flower the following year. Instead, sow the previous year, pot up into quarts and overwinter for spring sales. Since the foliage is woolly, handle like an

319

artemisia or other hairy-leaved foliage varieties, making sure there's no excess water on the leaves or around the roots in late autumn when overwintering—otherwise the plants may rot.

L. × *haageana* is the result of a *L. coronata* and *L. fulgens* cross. The bright scarlet or orange flowers are larger than *L. chalcedonica*, as big as 2 inches (5 cm) across. The variety is only marginally hardy but will return for several seasons here in our gardens with limited problems. It's not as dependable, hardy, or as long to bloom as the Maltese cross in our location, although it will flower the same year as sown.

As for propagation and growing on, the cultivars come true from seed and can be grown as indicated above for *L. chalcedonica*. The species in general, as well as the following cultivar, are probably better as pot plants; however, they're short lived and not as preferred as *L. chalcedonica* by either the public or growers.

Regarding my comment about treating these as pot plants: Sowings made to 220 plug trays in mid-January were potted up into 4-inch (10 cm) pots in mid-February. They were allowed to root first at temperatures of 60F (16C) nights in a greenhouse prior to moving to a heated cold frame with 50F (10C) nights for finishing off. Plants started flowering in early May. I want to stress that these plants only looked good—not great—and that we had a hard time with water mold (*Pythium*, *Rhizoctonia*, etc.) at the time of bud set.

Vesuvius has been listed as a variety of both *L. haageana* and *L.* × *arkwrightii* (this latter species is the result of a cross between *L. chalcedonica* and *L.* × *haageana*). The point is that this variety looks closer to *L. haageana* than *L. chalcedonica* when growing and flowering. The variety grows to no more than 12 inches (30 cm) tall for us, is short lived, and probably better as a pot plant than as a perennial. The variety comes true from seed and will flower in a 4-inch (10 cm) pot.

L. viscaria (*Viscaria vulgaris*) is commonly called the German catchfly due to its sticky (viscous) patch directly below the flower heads and internodes. On closer inspection you'll notice flies and other insects that adhered to this patch and weren't able to get free. The plants grow from 15 to 20 inches (38 to 51 cm) tall in bloom (taller in the southern United States), with magenta flowers in May and early June. They won't flower the same year as sown. *L. viscaria* is hardy to Zone 3, very dependable, and better looking (though shorter flowering) than *L.* × *haageana*. It's often short lived, however, acting more like a biennial than a true perennial.

As for propagation and growing on, the plants require 11 to 13 weeks to fill out a cell pack for green pack sales. For flowering plant sales, sow the previous year, overwinter in quart containers, and sell in the spring.

IN THE HOME GARDEN

Since many *Lychnis* species have a short flowering span, they're seldom used in mass plantings but instead are offered as old-time garden flowers for the home garden. Maltese cross plants are long lived, reliably returning early in spring.

Plants don't require staking, can be grown as home cut flowers, and will tolerate full sun to partial shade here in our northern location. In gardens in the deep and central southern United States, provide more afternoon shade to allow the plants to revive before nightfall for better long-term performance. Repeated stress from high heat, humidity, and rainfall will take their toll and reduce this plant's longevity.

Plants don't require winter mulching but need to be planted where the soil is well drained. Plants will flower in the spring but seldom rebloom during the summer. If the summer is cool or the plants are trimmed back after flowering, *Lychnis* may reflower in the late summer but not with the same performance as earlier.

■■■ LYSIMACHIA CLETHROIDES

FAMILY: Primulaceae

COMMON NAME(S): Gooseneck Loosestrife, Japanese Loosestrife, Shepherd's Crook
Note: Loosestrife is also the common name for *Lythrum*, a genus of well-known, and sometimes rampant, plants. *L. clethroides* can also become vigorous but is tame by comparison to *Lythrum*.

L

DESCRIPTION

Lysimachia clethroides is a stellar performer with running roots that will promptly fill in any open area and grow up through any weak-growing plants. Erect shoots develop from below the soil line and grow upwards to a height of 3 feet (90 cm) or slightly less for us in Chicago. The unscented flowers are single, pure white in color and about one-half inch (1 cm) across. The bloom is unusual because the flowering stalk isn't upright but angled or curved in a horizontal pattern resembling a goose's profile or a duck head in outline. The tapered tip (the duck's bill) gradually becomes broader and more rounded as you reach the "neck" of the flowering stalk. The flowerhead measures 4 to 5 inches (10 to 13 cm) long.

Keep in mind that the plants produce a single shoot with no basal or side branching development. Instead, each shoot terminates with a bloom. The plants fill in readily however, producing a multitude of shoots across the soil surface.

HARDINESS: Zones 3 to 8.

SEASON OF BLOOM: July and August.

PROPAGATION

Divisions and cuttings are common means of propagating *Lysimachia* due to the ample availability of new shoots produced. Both can be done in the spring. It can also be seed propagated, although few U.S. seed companies carry the seed.

GROWING ON

Crop time: Commercial propagators usually offer *Lysimachia* as a started plant in either a liner or plug that can be shipped during autumn or winter. These are potted up to quarts or gallons and sold in the spring.

As for stem tip cuttings, these can be taken anytime the plants are not budded or flowering. Plants will root in two to four weeks and can be transplanted to their final container.

From divisions, propagation is quick and easy. If you maintain your own stock beds for taking divisions, several clumps are all that's necessary to get the number of salable pots.

Plantings of *L. clethroides* to clay loam soils are less invasive than those planted to a sandy loam. The clay loam soil in our location is perfect for getting a multitude of shoots at any one time, but we can easily keep the plants from growing into other nursery rows nearby.

The roots spread actively during April and May, so we take our divisions at this time as the shoots become several inches long. If we wait until mid or late June, we can still take divisions, but the plants are already 10 to 16 inches (25 to 41 cm) tall, and we need to remove more top growth to reduce transpiration. When taking your divisions, those removed from the peripheral or outer edge of the spreading mass root are the best. We leave the center intact, since these usually have woody roots that have thickened with age due to overwintering. Divisions taken a year after planting to the nursery bed, however, are less likely to pose a problem.

Each plant's center is left undisturbed, but we circle the entire plant with a shovel or spade to take divisions as well as promote a rapid redevelopment of roots from the crown.

Since *Lysimachia*'s spreading nature is most rampant in the spring, this is also the time to keep the plants under control to avoid invasiveness. If we decide not to divide our crop, we rototill twice in early May around the clump's outer perimeter about 10 days apart. We rototill only the area where the new shoots are developing underground, leaving the original crown intact. In our clay loam soils we've never had new plantlets show up in any other area during the remainder of the season.

Once divisions are taken, they're potted up into quarts or gallons, allowed to root in, and then sold later in spring or summer. For spring sales of overwintered plants, divide in autumn, transplant the roots to gallon pots and overwinter dormant.

VARIETIES

Lysimachia clethroides is readily available from various greenhouse and nursery operations across the country as a started plant or liner. Seed isn't easily found in the
United States, but seed exchanges may offer it.

RELATED MATERIAL

Lysimachia nummularia (creeping Jenny) has dark green, rounded leaves on plants
with a trailing habit. Plants grow to no more than 8 inches (20 cm) tall in bloom
with a 2-foot (60 cm) spread. The flowers are bright yellow, 1 inch (2.5 cm) across,
and fragrant.

Unlike *L. clethroides*, this crop prefers a shadier location to perform best. It's fond
of damp or moist locations but will not live in standing water. While the dark
green variety is good, the following cultivar has gained a great deal of attention.

L. nummularia Aurea is the lime green or light yellow foliage variety for shadier
locations. It's prized for its foliage since its yellow blossoms get lost in the
foliage. Occasionally you hear that variegated plants are sometimes slower to
grow than their green-leaved counterparts. While maybe not as quick to fill in,
the growth rate is still respectable. We have grown the variety in full sun, but it
appreciates protection from afternoon sun—otherwise leaf scorch is common,
with leaves eventually turning white. This condition is compounded when the
plants are grown in well-drained locations or are allowed to dry out frequently.
See Color Plate 54 for photo of *Lysimachia nummularia* Aurea.

L. nummularia is hardy from Zones 3 to 8 and can be propagated by divisions or
stem cuttings. Take divisions in the spring or late summer and stem cuttings in
spring and summer.

L. punctata (yellow loosestrife) is an upright plant with three-quarter to 1-inch-
wide (2 cm to 2.5 cm), bright yellow flowers. The flowers are in whorls around
the leaf axis. Blooms are close to the stem but are large and colorful enough to
make yellow loosestrife a useful landscape plant or cut flower.

Plants are hardy from Zones 4 to 8 and, like the other species described here, will
be vigorous in fertile and moist locations. *L. punctata* also prefers the same sunny
location as *L. clethroides*. Plants are propagated by cuttings and seed. In the
United States, however, liners are more readily available than seed. The freshest
seed is found from seed exchanges here and more commonly in Europe.

USES

This is an exceptional landscape plant and cut flower variety for both the professional grower and home gardener. In the landscape, plants fill in freely. Care

needs to be taken on soil type, water, and fertility: Excesses of all three will turn several single plants into a mob scene within one year.

As a cut flower, *Lysimachia* supplies an abundance of blooms. For growers with nursery beds, a spring planting can yield as many as 40 stems per plant. This is a conservative number since we often rototill the areas directly around our plantings. It's our opinion that we could double that number in July from a planting made the previous year. Additional information on *Lysimachia*'s potential as a cut flower is presented in *Specialty Cut Flowers* by Allan M. Armitage.

IN THE HOME GARDEN

Lysimachias, in general, are an excellent crop to plant in the home garden. All of the above species will work in bright shade or sun, although *L. clethroides* and *L. punctata* do better with more sun than does *L. nummularia*, especially Aurea. If planted into a fertile, moist, and sunny location, plants often fill in amazingly fast. If planted next to small, unobtrusive or weak plants, *L. clethroides* will easily overgrow these plants, snuffing them out in a year or two.

L. clethroides doesn't require staking to remain upright nor does it need any winter protection here in our Chicago location to keep returning from year to year. Unlike many other perennials that form a central crown, its center doesn't die. Instead, the plants will develop a full appearance year after year and do not require frequent dividing to keep looking good.

■ LYTHRUM SALICARIA

FAMILY: Lythraceae

COMMON NAME(S): Lythrum, Purple Loosestrife

Note: *Lysimachia clethroides* is also commonly called loosestrife. The two plants do not resemble each other, however. While both can become rampant, it's the various lythrum species and cultivars that will become more invasive and kill out both weak and moderate growing plants.

A number of states including Arkansas, Colorado, Minnesota, Montana, Oregon, South Dakota, Washington, and Wisconsin have now banned sales of lythrum as a genus. In Arkansas, "...it is illegal to transport buy, sell, offer for sale or distribute *Lythrum* plants, plant parts and seed."[1]

The cultivars that are most often sold in the United States today are derived from crosses between several species but primarily *L. virgatum* and *L. alatum*. It was discovered that when grown singly, these plants will set limited or no seed since the sexes are incompatible on the same plant. If plantings of *L. salicaria* are grown nearby, however, then the cultivars can cross freely, producing seed at an elevated rate, higher than what's produced in nature. This is especially true across North American wetlands in both the United States and Canada.

On the other hand, if isolated plantings of *L. salicaria* are grown, it's possible to limit invasiveness. This is true of our plants. *L. salicaria* has been planted to several locations around our 40-acre (16 ha) demonstration garden since before 1990 and no invasiveness has been noted. The performance is the same whether the soil around the base of the plants has been disturbed or left unplowed.

If you're offering this crop for the first time, double-check with county extension agents or state officials to see if the crop is considered illegal in your state. Regardless, be responsible in your decision to offer this crop.

DESCRIPTION

These are upright plants growing 3 to 4 feet (90 to 120 cm), sometimes 6 feet (1.8 m) tall with a small spread—usually only 2 feet (60 cm) across on even three- or four-year-old plants. *L. salicaria* has naturalized itself in damp lowlands, marshes, and wetlands across the northern part of the country, from the plains to the East Coast. The flowers are single, magenta purple, and displayed in racemes. Many people call them flower spikes rather than racemes, though the correct botanical term is raceme. The difference? Flowers on a spike butt up against the main flowering stalk while racemes have a small appendage between the flower and the stalk.

HARDINESS: Zones 3 to 9.

SEASON OF BLOOM: Late June to August.

PROPAGATION

Seed is easily propagated on the species while the cultivars listed below under **Varieties** are propagated by division or tip cuttings. Seed will not come true to type on these selections. As for divisions, they're usually done in the spring when the plants are small and still manageable. Divisions taken in late spring may be budded but will also be 3 to 4 feet (90 to 120 cm) tall. Earlier divisions yield a higher quality transplant. Cuttings are taken on the rapidly developing shoots in spring until bud set starts.

GERMINATION OVERVIEW

Seed germinates in five to 10 days at 70F (21C), either left exposed to light or covered lightly with coarse vermiculite to maintain moisture. Seed doesn't need to be covered, however.

Seedlings will be transplantable 20 to 25 days after sowing.

GROWING ON

Crop time: From seed, plantlets develop rapidly and can be grown in 4-inch (10 cm) pots for sales in 11 to 13 weeks. Green 32-cell packs are salable in nine to 10 weeks when grown at 50F (10C) nights.

Divisions should be taken as shoot development begins, as soon as the ground has dried out enough to take the divisions.

Tip cuttings taken in the spring will root readily and can be transplanted to the container of your choice since they'll readily fill out a quart or gallon pot. Plants can be grown on during the summer, overwintered, and sold the following spring.

VARIETIES

Lythrum salicaria is getting harder to find in the United States as various states decide its fate. If a seed company is located in a state where the plant is banned, they cannot legally sell the seed to the greenhouse and nursery trade. However, it can still be found in those states where the seed isn't illegal.

For other crops covered in this book, I separate each genera's various species to show the differences. I'm diverging in the case of lythrum, since *L. virgatum* closely resembles *L. salicaria* in appearance and flower color. Some authors state that *L. salicaria* is between 2 and 3 feet (60 to 90 cm) tall, but I have seen it taller; other differences are hard to discern unless the plant is closely inspected.

One other point: All of the following are the result of either sexual or asexual propagation of these two species and *L. alatum*. All of them are vegetatively propagated, however, since seed will not yield plants true-to-type. The parentheses after each name refer to its parentage, either indicating the dominant parent or the crosses used to develop the variety.

Firecandle (*L. salicaria*) is sometimes called Feuerkerze; it has rose-red flowers on plants from 2 to 3 feet (60 to 90 cm) tall.

Gypsy Blood (*L. salicaria*) is also known as Zigeunerblut, a deep red variety to 3 feet (90 cm) tall.

Happy (*L. salicaria*) is a dwarf-flowering variety from 15 to 18 inches (38 to 46 cm) tall with deep pink flowers.

Morden series. The following Morden varieties were selections made at the Morden, Manitoba, Canada Agricultural Research Station. These varieties were derived from a *L. virgatum* sport or a cross between *L. virgatum* and other varieties or species. One final note: The following varieties are listed as Morden as well as Morden's. Both are acceptable spellings.

Morden's Gleam is a 3- to 4-foot (60 to 120 cm) tall variety with rose-pink blooms.

Morden's Pink is a rose-pink flowering variety on plants 3 feet (60 cm) tall or taller.

Morden's Rose is 3 feet (60 cm) tall with rose-red flowers.

Pink Spires (*L. virgatum*) is a 3-foot-tall (60 cm) variety with bright pink flowers.

Purple Spires (*L. virgatum*) is a 3- to 4-foot (60 to 90 cm) tall variety with purple flowers.

Robert (*L. salicaria*) grows from 18 to 24 inches (46 to 61 cm) tall with rose-red flowers. The foliage turns a bronze-red color in the cool of autumn.

USES

Plants work well if left undisturbed in the commercial landscape. They will return reliably year after year. Any of the cultivars listed above will work well, although it's important to identify stands of *L. salicaria* that have become naturalized. On open expanses of golf courses and other broad lawn commercial sites, it's possible that cross-pollination can take place, causing invasiveness. If these plantings are close to water, the problem is compounded twofold. In these cases, urge that the plantings be removed promptly.

Lythrum was also used as a cut flower during the early parts of this century, most often in funeral arrangements.

IN THE HOME GARDEN

By reading all the negative comments on lythrum's invasiveness, you'd assume that *L. salicaria* should be avoided. In many cases, I would agree. Woodland gardens with damp soils will only encourage the rampant growth of this crop. Instead, be responsible and plant only in well-drained locations in states that allow the planting of lythrum. The plants are noteworthy due to their uniform habit, long-term summer color, and reliable overwintering performance. When planted in full-sun locations, the plants don't require staking to remain upright.

L

REFERENCES

[1] Arkansas bans *Lythrum* as noxious weed. *Greenhouse Manager*. April 1990.

M

■ MACLEAYA CORDATA

FAMILY: Papaveraceae

COMMON NAME(S): Plume Poppy

DESCRIPTION

Macleaya cordata is a vigorous and stately woodland plant with limited garden suitability, although its height and foliage should not be overlooked. Plants can grow 4 to 9 feet (1.2 to 2.7 m) tall with buff yellow or cream, apeatalous (without petals) blooms occurring in upright and open plumes. The flowers are rather nondescript—it's this plant's lobed foliage and height that are the primary attractions. The rhizomes are creeping and can become invasive.

HARDINESS: Zones 3 to 8.

SEASON OF BLOOM: June and July.

PROPAGATION

Seed, divisions, and basal cuttings are the easiest ways to propagate *Macleaya cordata*. Divisions can be taken in spring as the plant is developing, and seed can be sown at anytime. But late, summer-harvested seed from a mother plant will yield its best results when sown soon after ripening. Basal cuttings can be taken in the spring using 2- to 3-foot (60 to 90 cm) long shoots. Root in sand. A less frequently used method is root cuttings taken in the winter. Additional details are provided at the front of this book under **Propagation Techniques**.

GERMINATION OVERVIEW

Seed germinates in 25 to 35 days at 72F (22C) when sown in the winter or spring. Lightly cover seed during germination. Seedlings are transplantable seven to eight weeks after sowing.

GROWING ON

Crop time: From seed, the crop is slow to grow and develop, although green 32-cell packs are ready for sales or potting up into gallons 15 to 17 weeks after sowing when grown on at 52F to 58F (11C to 14C) nights. Plants will not flower the same season from seed.

If you're making divisions, divide *Macleaya* in the early spring or when the ground can be worked. Find clumps that are three but no more than five years old. Older rootstocks can be woody or intertwined, and losses can be expected from divisions.

Commercial propagators offer *Macleaya* as a bareroot division that can be potted up into 3- or 4-quart containers during the winter for spring sales. Provide no less than 50F (10C) nights for active growth.

VARIETIES

Macleaya cordata isn't readily available from seed in the U.S. trade, but once you have a clump, all the seed you'll probably ever need will be at your fingertips. Plants will not be that hard to find though, and are available from a number of U.S. perennial nurseries.

RELATED MATERIAL

Macleaya microcarpa (formerly *Bocconia microcarpa*) grows faster than *M. cordata* and can reach 8 feet (2.4 m) or taller. The major visible difference between this and *M. cordata* is more compact plumes which give the plant a more uniform appearance. These varieties are similar in most other respects.

Propagate and grow as described for *M. cordata*.

USES

This is an excellent choice where annual shrubs or tall, background specimens are wanted. Plants die back to the ground in winter but are quick to fill back in the following spring and early summer. Consider planting in an area where a tall fence is wanted in the summer, but open space is preferred in winter.

With its unique habit and appearance, *Macleaya* is also suggested for woodland garden sites in bright shade. If planted in heavily shaded locations, the plants are often weak, shorter, and of limited value.

Macleaya is obviously not recommended for small and intimate gardens but rather for open expanses on large properties where impact is needed from a more distant view. It is excellent for commercial plantings when combined with seasonal blooming perennials, shrubs, and annuals. Plants require little maintenance and will return reliably year after year with limited mulching or other pampering.

IN THE HOME GARDEN

Plant in full sun in the North and in partial shade in the southern United States. When divided or transplanted to the garden, the plants will reach 2 to 4 feet (60 to 120 cm) the first season, taller with subsequent seasons depending on fertility and moisture. If the plants are grown in a fertile location with ample—but not standing—water, the plants will quickly reach for the stars. If not fertilized in clay loam soils, plants seldom reach higher than 4 or 5 feet (1.2 to 1.5 m) within four years after planting.

M

Even though tall, plants don't require staking unless grown on the fertile side. I've never seen such a situation, however.

■ MALVA ALCEA FASTIGIATA

FAMILY: Malvaceae

COMMON NAME(S): Mallow, Hollyhock Mallow

DESCRIPTION

An excellent garden performer, *Malva alcea* Fastigiata bears 2-inch (60 cm) blooms in a rich rose-pink color. Plants grow between 2 and 3 feet (60 to 90 cm) tall; and once in bloom they'll flower profusely for two to three weeks and then bloom sporadically for another three to five weeks, depending on weather and maintenance. The habit is erect—plants seldom require staking unless they are grown in rich environments. The foliage is deep green and provides a nice contrast to the flowers. Plants spread 15 to 20 inches (38 to 51 cm) across.

HARDINESS: Zones 4 to 8.

SEASON OF BLOOM: June and July.

PROPAGATION

Seed, tip cuttings, or divisions are the preferred methods to propagate this crop. Seed can be sown any time of the year with similar germination percentages. Tip cuttings taken in spring prior to budding will easily develop roots. If you can't take cuttings until summer, harvest from stems developing out of the crown as they first stand to emerge in the spring. Divisions can be taken in spring or fall.

GERMINATION OVERVIEW

Seed germinates in three to six days at 70F to 72F (21C to 22C); cover the seed lightly. Seedlings can be transplanted 15 to 20 days after sowing.

GROWING ON

Crop time: From seed, plants are salable green in nine to 10 weeks after sowing when grown one seedling per cell, 32 cells per flat, at 50F to 55F (10C to 13C) nights. Plants grow quickly enough to be transplanted into 3- or 4-inch (7 or 10 cm) pots for sales 11 to 13 weeks after sowing. If 1- to 2-quart containers are desired, it would be better to sow seeds into deep plug trays 15 to 18 weeks prior to sales, and then transplant plugs to the larger containers when ready. Regardless, as long as the seed is sown by March, *Malva alcea* will flower during the summer. In our trials, an early February sowing produced flowering plants in July when transplanted to the garden in May.

Cuttings will root relatively easily and can be potted up into quarts or gallons for sales in fall or the following year. Cuttings taken in May or early June will be salable green within six to nine weeks when grown in 4-inch (10 cm) pots. These cuttings often produce erect plants with limited basal branching their first season after propagation, however. Cuttings taken during spring or summer will look better when sold the following spring in 1- or 2-gallon pots.

Pot fall divisions up into 1- or 2-gallon containers. Malvas have a woody root system requiring a shovel to divide. If the plant you're dividing is several years old, you'll need a 2-gallon or larger container so as not to bend back the root stocks. Spring divisions will have enough top growth for sales the same season, although the roots seldom fill out the pot until midsummer.

Commercial propagators offer *Malva* in either small pots or as bareroot transplants. Primarily available during the autumn and winter, either of these can be potted up into quarts and gallons and sold in spring.

VARIETIES

M. alcea var. *fastigiata* is available from commercial propagators but may be difficult to find through U.S. seed firms. European companies, however, carry wider selections, including the malvas listed under **Related material**.

M. alcea is longer lived in northern gardens than in southern locations. Plants are often under attack from Japanese beetles and other insects throughout the South and even in northern areas like Ohio.

RELATED MATERIAL

M. moschata, commonly called musk mallow, grows between 2 and 3 feet (60 to 90 cm) tall in the garden. Flowers are single, cup-shaped to 2 inches (5 cm) across, and bloom in rose-pink or pure white. Hardiness ratings indicate the plants are hardy from Zones 3 to 10, although they often winter or summer kill here in our Zone 5 location. In the Midwest, the plants live from summer to summer when winter protected with cover or grown out of the way of direct winter winds. Even with protection, our plants have been short lived at best, often dying out within two to three years.

Like *M. alcea*, plants flower the same season from seed but will bloom earlier. From an early February sowing, plants will be budded in the cell pack or 3-inch (7 cm) pot in late April. If sold by mid-May, plants flower in the garden in June and continue flowering until August. Although not free flowering all summer, the "flower power" is not bad.

IN THE HOME GARDEN

Malva alcea is suited to many situations including general landscapes, golf courses, and the home garden. Plants can be utilized as a short screen around home air conditioners or to provide an excellent planting around shrubs. In the garden or landscape, plants may lodge (fall open) if given ample food and overhead irrigation.

M

Try to avoid overhead irrigating as it promotes flower decline and can lead to powdery mildew on the foliage. Plant in full sun to light shade, but avoid locations where the plants receive less than six to seven hours of sun since that decreases the bloom count and the number of weeks plants stay in color.

▬ MONARDA DIDYMA

FAMILY: Lamiaceae

COMMON NAME(S): Bee Balm, Bergamot

DESCRIPTION

Monardas are a native American perennial and an excellent garden plant. Flowers are composed of either single or double petals in a rolled or tubular arrangement, each to 1 inch (2.5 cm) long. The flowers measure up to 3 inches (7 cm) across; they can be either open or densely packed with florets, depending on the variety. Flower colors vary; scarlet-red blooms are most common although white, purple, blue, and shades of pink and rose are also available.

Monardas have creeping rhizomes which produce large clumps that send out individual, erect stems to 3 feet (90 cm) tall. The clumps can range from 15 to 24 inches (38 to 61 cm) across. Monarda foliage is simple in appearance, fragrant when crushed, and highly susceptible to powdery mildew. However, new cultivars have been selected that are more tolerant of the disease.

HARDINESS: Zones 4 to 9.

SEASON OF BLOOM: June and July into August.

PROPAGATION

Monarda is easily propagated by seed, divisions, or cuttings. Seed-propagated plants are of little value here in the United States since cultivars, except Panorama, do not come true from seed. Seed-propagated varieties are sometimes used for cell packs and small pots in retail and for selecting new breeding material, but seldom for wholesale production. Cuttings and division are the primary methods for commercial propagation in the United States. Cuttings taken in the early spring (before bud set) or fall root easily. Divisions can be made in spring or fall once the plants start to emerge from the soil in March and April.

GERMINATION OVERVIEW: 56,000 seeds per ounce/196 per gram.
Monarda germinates in five to eight days at 72F (22C), and seed can be lightly covered or left exposed for germination. Plants develop quickly, and seedlings will be transplantable 20 to 28 days after sowing.

GROWING ON

Crop time: From seed, monardas grow quickly and will be salable green in a 32-cell pack at eight to 10 weeks when grown on at 50F to 55F (10C to 13C) nights. Plants will not flower the same season from seed if started in January or later. If sown in the autumn, overwintered in a cold frame and sold in the spring, the plants will flower during summer.

Plants produced from seed will vary in height, darkness of foliage, flower color, and even in shades of a single color. Something unusual about seed-propagated plants—in most years, the plants that were started from seed in either winter or spring and planted to the garden once frost passed will not have any powdery mildew on their foliage for the entire season. These plants also will not flower as noted above. The following year, however, the plants will flower but will be laden with powdery mildew.

As for cuttings, 2- to 3-inch (5 to 7 cm) cuttings taken on nonflowering or budded stems will root within two to four weeks and can be potted up into quart or gallon containers. If propagated in the spring, the plants will be ready for sales by midsummer or fall. If cuttings are taken any other time, the plants are often overwintered and sold the following spring.

In most cases, a 72-cell tray of monardas received in February or March from a commercial propagator will be salable in a 4½-inch (11 cm) pot within six to eight weeks at 55F (13C) nights.

As for divisions, a two-year-old clump will produce a mass large enough to yield numerous plantlets, depending on division size. Potted to 4-inch pots or quart containers, these plants will be salable in two to three weeks when divided in March and grown on in a cold frame at 55F (13C) nights. For better rooted plants, allow six weeks.

VARIETIES

There are a number of good cultivars on the market worthy of adding to your garden, although many are susceptible to powdery mildew. Breeding and selection have brought about a new era for monardas in the development of mildew-tolerant strains. Both tolerant and intolerant selections are noted below.

All of the following are **vegetatively propagated** except for Panorama Mix, which is from seed.

Adam is a variety to 3 feet (90 cm) tall with dull ruby-red flowers.

Blue Stocking is a vivid violet-purple flowering selection from 3 to 3½ feet (90 to 105 cm) tall.

Croftway Pink bears pink blossoms on plants to 3 feet (90 cm) tall.

Gardenview Scarlet (Gardenview Red) is a mildew-tolerant monarda to 3 feet (90 cm) tall with scarlet-red flowers.

M

Mahogany has dark red flowers on plants to 3 feet (90 cm) tall.

Marshall's Variety has rose-pink flowers on plants to 4 feet (120 cm) tall. Plants are mildew tolerant.

Panorama Mix is a seed-propagated mixture in scarlet, bright red, pink, salmon and crimson. Although it would appear to be a nice color blend, all the colors are red based and can be uneven in height. This is the best seed-propagated mix marketed and grows to 2½ feet (75 cm) tall. Seed is available from a number of U.S. seed companies.

Prairie Night has lilac-purple blossoms on plants to 3 feet (90 cm) tall. It is also powdery mildew tolerant.

Snow White has cream-white flowers on plants to 3 feet (90 cm) tall.

Violet Queen has violet or purple flowers on plants from 3 to 4 feet (90 to 120 cm) tall. Plants are a hybrid of *M. fistulosa*.

RELATED MATERIAL

Monarda fistulosa is a purple-flowering variety that grows between 3 and 4 feet (90 and 120 cm) tall. Leaves are hairy. This plant is native to eastern North America and should be considered for wild and native flower collections or meadows. It has been used to breed some of the previously listed varieties.

Propagate as you would *M. didyma*.

USES

Monardas have many uses in the home garden and will live on from year to year. Plants can be grouped in small mass plantings with shrubs, other perennials, or annuals. Bee balm makes a good cut flower and is prized for attracting hummingbirds.

In the landscape, concentrate on the more mildew-tolerant selections, but avoid monardas if overhead watering is a practice. Plants usually don't die from the fungus, but powdery mildew's effects aren't a pretty sight.

IN THE HOME GARDEN

Looking through the myriad of plant catalogs received during the winter, you might notice some cultivar heights varying between companies. Monardas are generally about 3 feet (90 cm) tall but will grow taller and faster in fertile, moist, and drained soils. With these conditions, the plants will need dividing every two to three years and can become aggressive. Plants don't normally require any staking unless grown in rich, moist soil.

Plants don't tolerate drought conditions well. Monardas love full-sun locations. They will tolerate some morning shade but prefer to be in areas where the foliage can dry off by midday to decrease the chances of getting powdery mildew. Plant in any moist but well-drained location, and divide in the spring.

▬ MYOSOTIS SYLVATICA

A variable class of plants that often may be listed as *M. alpestris* and, less often, as *M. dissitiflora*. While these are two distinct *Myosotis* species, the cultivated forms offered under these two names are most often *M. sylvatica*.

FAMILY: Boraginaceae

COMMON NAME(S): Forget-Me-Not, Garden Forget-Me-Not, Woodland Forget-Me-Not

DESCRIPTION

Myosotis sylvatica is a low-growing plant, about 10 to 12 inches (25 to 30 cm) tall, dotted with one-eighth to one-quarter-inch (3 to 6 mm) flowers in light to midblue. Additional cultivars are available in both rose or white. It's more common, however, to find a blue-flowering selection than any other color at a seed house or garden center. Flowers are five-lobed with a yellow (sometimes white), star-shaped eye in the bloom's center. The foliage is usually coarse and somewhat hairy. Plants are often short lived in the garden and, although listed as biennials, frequently won't live beyond one season here in the Midwest. Plants prefer shaded, moist locations: This is probably the primary factor in their short life in the home garden. Native to Europe, *Myosotis* has naturalized itself in the eastern North American woodlands where the plants are larger flowered (to one-half inch/1 cm) and can be as tall as 16 inches (41 cm).

HARDINESS: Zones 5 to 8.

Usually hardy to Zone 5 and protected areas of both Zones 4 and 3 as well; short lived, lasting two seasons or possibly three.

M

SEASON OF BLOOM

May and June, with scattered bloom the remainder of the summer.

While this plant can naturalize itself as far south as central Georgia, it's not a full season plant out of the woodlands or other moist protected environments. *Myosotis* often disappears by July from a February planting, especially when grown in the home garden. Plants succumb to *Botrytis* and powdery mildew as temperatures and humidity rise.

PROPAGATION

Myosotis is most often propagated by seed, although both cuttings and divisions are also grown. Cuttings are most often taken during spring, while divisions are made mostly by the home gardener.

GERMINATION OVERVIEW: 45,000 seeds per ounce/1,575 per gram.

Seeds germinate in eight to 14 days at 68F to 72F (20C to 22C); you don't need to cover the seed when sowing. Seedlings can be transplanted 15 to 25 days after sowing.

GROWING ON

Crop time: Spring sowings seldom produce free-flowering plants the same season from seed. For pack sales, allow 10 to 12 weeks to fill out a 32-cell pack for spring or fall sales. For flowering plants, sow seed during the previous summer to have quart containers with one plant each by fall. These plants can then be overwintered in an unheated cold frame or similar structure for sales the following spring. We have sowed in early October, transplanted to cell packs on October 17th, and then potted one plant per 4-inch (10 cm) or quart pot for March bloom. These plants were grown in a 48F (9C) house and planted into the garden in early May. Once flowering began in February, they continued to bloom until late June. Flower color peaked in April and May.

Temperature: For spring and fall production, 48F to 54F (9C to 12C) nights are best. During the summer, grow on as cool as possible and provide shade during the hottest part of the day.

Preventative: *Myosotis* is susceptible to both *Botrytis* and powdery mildew. Apply control measures as necessary but allow for adequate air circulation around these plants, especially when growing pot to pot during summer. Shading the plants as noted is also helpful.

VARIETIES

All the following varieties are propagated by seed. In choosing a variety to sell, it isn't necessary to offer more than two blue-flowering selections from those listed below. A deep blue and mid or light blue will suffice. From the retail point-of-view, remember that the consumer sees the color of forget-me-nots as blue.

Blue Ball. A dwarf-flowering variety to 6 inches (15 cm) tall with deep indigo blue flowers on compact and mounded plants.

Indigo Blue. This selection is available in two different strains, differing primarily in height. Flowers are a royal blue color on plants between 10 to 14 inches (25 to 35 cm) tall; the other selection measures between 8 and 10 inches (20 to 25 cm) tall. Both strains are sold under the same name, although the more dwarf selection often has the name "compacta" attached either to the end of the name or within the description. Indigo Blue is sometimes listed under the name of Royal Blue.

Victoria series. A dwarf selection available in four colors including light blue, dark blue, white, and rose. Plants range in height from 6 to 8 inches (15 to 20 cm) tall in the garden but will be taller if given shade and a moist location. Often the variety may be listed simply as Victoria, which refers to the blue-flowering selection.

Ultramarine. Also a dwarf selection measuring 6 to 7 inches (15 to 18 cm) tall in flower with deep blue flowers.

RELATED MATERIAL

Myosotis scorpioides (true forget-me-not). Sometimes listed as *M. palustris*, this species is a true perennial but considered by many to be less important than *M. sylvatica*. The plant bears light to midblue flowers, although pink-flowering varieties can be purchased as well. Plants grow to about 15 inches (38 cm) tall and will spread by creeping rhizomes. Plants can have an unkempt habit, as they tend to grow more prostrate than *M. sylvatica*, but they perform well in our Midwest gardens. *M. scorpioides* prefers shaded, moist woodland environments and tolerates more swamp-like conditions. In such environments, however, the plants can become weedy and overgrow an area. Plants flower in June and continue with sporadic color most of July and August.

IN THE HOME GARDEN

Across the United States, the plants perform best where they are kept shaded from late morning throughout the hottest part of the day. Morning and evening sun exposures are fine for the plant's growth and development. Soils should be moist but well drained. *M. scorpioides* can become a weed in such an environment, but in a woodland setting, the effect may be acceptable. *M. sylvatica* can also become a nuisance when the conditions are perfect, but this is seldom a problem in the United States.

Plants are often short lived in Zones 5 and south due to heat and humidity stress, which weakens them and allows powdery mildew and *Botrytis* to develop. Leaf edges will start to brown and curl under, and the plants eventually die if conditions aren't changed.

M

In the landscape the plants perform best in woodland environments where they can spread and naturalize, often reseeding themselves and creating carpets of forget-me-nots scattered across the forest floor. *Myosotis* works well as an underplanting for spring bulbs when spaced 8 to 10 inches (20 to 25 cm) apart.

O

■ OENOTHERA MISSOURIENSIS

FAMILY: Onagraceae

COMMON NAME(S): Ozark Sundrops, Missouri Evening Primrose

O. missouriensis will flower during the day even though one of its common names would suggest otherwise. Although this plant possesses two common names, the term "sundrops" is often applied to day-flowering *O. missouriensis* while "evening" refers to those that flower only late in the day.

DESCRIPTION

A perennial native to the central United States, *Oenothera missouriensis* is well known for grand displays of funnel-shaped, bright yellow blossoms. The blooms range from 3 to 4 inches (7 to 10 cm) across and have a light fragrance. As the plants grow and develop, growing tips, sepals, and even the aging blossoms can be highlighted or brushed with red. Plants grow from 6 to 12 inches (15 to 30 cm) tall—in our gardens we've never seen them taller than 8 inches (20 cm) in flower.

Plants are often short lived (read the information under **In the home garden**) but can reseed to perpetuate the variety. Plants can produce a clump from 1 to 2 feet (30 to 60 cm) across. It's our experience, however, that the plants have a closely held crown and a spread of only 10 or 12 inches (25 to 30 cm) across. These are larger on plants in the wild.

HARDINESS: Zones 4 to 8.

SEASON OF BLOOM: June and July; sometimes August.

PROPAGATION

Oenothera is usually propagated by seed, although cuttings of either the spreading roots or basal shoots as they develop are also methods to consider. Divisions are made in the spring but mostly by the home gardener.

GERMINATION OVERVIEW: 6,500 seeds per ounce/227 per gram.

Oenothera is easy to germinate and doesn't require any special treatments or techniques to achieve germination rates of 70% or higher. In general, seed shouldn't be covered during germination and responds best to a bottom heat of 70F to 80F (21C to 27C), although we have seen more uniform and less stretched seedlings at 70F to 72F (21C to 22C). At higher temperatures the seedlings should be removed from the heat as soon as they start to emerge. Seeds germinate in eight to 15 days and can be transplanted 18 to 27 days after sowing.

Growing on

Crop time: From seed, plants will grow quickly but are often open in growth, seldom filling containers fully when grown for green pack sales in the spring. Cell packs will finish in 10 to 12 weeks when finished at 50F (10C) night temperatures. Plants are sold green but will flower sporadically during the summer after transplanting to the garden.

The best performance comes from a crop grown in 4-inch (10 cm) pots rather than cell packs. Overwatering is a possibility because plants aren't equal in their ability to dry out between waterings. If plant crowns are kept constantly moist, water rots tend to become established and can kill a number of plants.

When growing from seed, avoid late sowings in March and April for same-season sales. Instead, transplant to quart or larger containers for growing through the summer and then overwinter for sales the following year. March and April sowings seldom produce roots strong enough to keep the plants performing during the summer. This is primarily true of plants grown in cell packs, but any small container production is equally limiting.

For cuttings, avoid the woody rootstock at the plant's center and concentrate on the trailing roots just below the soil surface. These can be cut, removed, and potted up. Cuttings can also be taken from shoots as they emerge from the crown in spring. In references these are often called basal cuttings. Remove and root as you would a terminal tip cutting. Some growers wait until after flowering to take cuttings, but we get better performance from basal cuttings.

Commercial propagators offer *Oenothera* as a bare-root transplant, liner, or plug. Mostly available during the autumn and winter, any of these can be potted up into quarts and gallons and sold in spring.

Varieties

Oenothera missouriensis is an easy-to-locate native perennial carried by commercial seed firms, native seed companies, and companies offering young plants or plugs.

Related material

Oenothera fruticosa (commonly called sundrops) is a day-flowering native perennial with 1½-inch (3 cm) yellow flowers and reddish stems from 1 to 2 feet (30 to 60 cm) tall. Some books refer to a multitude of varieties supposedly available under this species. *Hortus Third* notes that "...references to *O. fruticosa* in horticulture literature apply to *O. tetragona*, with which *O. fruticosa* has been confused." [1] I'm not a taxonomist, and while I don't want to confuse you any more than I have already, I will point out that many U.S. plant companies sell these varieties under *O. tetragona* instead of *O. fruticosa*. Read the information under *O. tetragona* for details.

The species is the most common selection of *O. fruticosa* sold on the U.S. trade although there is a single variety occasionally seen as well. *O. fruticosa* Youngii-lapsley has yellow flowers on plants to 24 inches (60 cm) in June. Less common as the species, this variety can be found—but not easily. The species is seen occasionally in wildflower and native perennial seed catalogs. It can also be found from commercial propagators as started or young plants.

Hardy to Zones 4 to 8. Propagate as suggested for *O. missouriensis*.

Oenothera speciosa var. *rosea* (Mexican evening primrose) is often sold in the U.S. as just *O. speciosa* or *O. berlandieri*, and it's a plant to watch out for. While not a free-flowering plant, it does bloom with continuous and spotty color across the crown all summer. It is three times more persistent than *O. missouriensis* and less finicky when growing. Its stoloniferous root stocks are invasive, however, and will travel from one end of the garden to other if allowed to do so. Be prepared to control the plant if the soil is fertile and ample moisture is available. The plants have single, blushing pink blossoms to 2 inches (5 cm) across that will bloom during the day, though the common name would suggest otherwise.

To encourage more free-flowering plants, lightly trim the plants back after the first flush of flowers in the spring, and plants will bud up faster. Mexican evening primrose grows 12 to 15 inches (30 to 38 cm) tall in our gardens, taller farther south, with a spread of up to 15 inches (38 cm). We accidentally planted it in a bed amended with organic material and brother, did we get a surprise! At last check, it had grown under the 3-foot-wide (90 cm wide) groundcloth we use to keep the weeds down and had killed weaker plants growing in its path. In any case, when planted to a full-sun location in poor to not-so-fertile soil that drains well, the plants are long lived and valued for their blossoms dotting the crown all season long.

For propagation, treat as you would *O. missouriensis*. Mexican evening primrose is hardy from Zones 5 through 8.

Oenothera tetragona (also called *O. fruticosa* var. *youngii*, *O. youngii*, or *O. glauca*) invites confusion when you try to find it in the trade. It closely resembles *O. fruticosa* and is often confused with it; it also may be listed under a number of botanical names. Like *O. fruticosa*, *O. tetragona* is an upright variety to 2 feet (60 cm) tall with one-half-inch (1 cm) lemon-yellow flowers. It also exhibits red-tinged buds prior to flowering.

The following varieties are **vegetatively propagated**. Seed of the species is seldom seen in the U.S. trade although it can be found in Europe.

Fireworks (also listed as *O. tetragona* var. *fraseri*) is sometimes identified as the same variety as Illumination. It bears 2- to 3-inch (5 to 7 cm), bright yellow flowers on plants from 14 to 18 inches (35 to 46 cm) tall. The leaves are leathery and bronze tinged. Buds are highlighted in orange red while the stems have been described as purplish red, but reddish brown is more appropriate. Fireworks flowers June to August with additional, spotted color in the autumn.

Highlight (Hoheslicht) grows to 18 inches (46 cm) tall with reddish stems, orange-red buds, and bright yellow blooms.

Yellow River has 2-inch (5 cm), light yellow flowers on plants to 18 inches (46 cm) tall. The plants we've seen have green stems, although some references have described the stems as red in color.

USES

Oenothera, in general, works well in native perennial settings, wildflower gardens, and in the front of the border, providing sporadic color from June to August after the first flush. As for commercial landscapes, some *Oenothera* species, such as *O. speciosa* and *O. tetragona*, will work better than others.

IN THE HOME GARDEN

Although *Oenothera missouriensis* is a true perennial, the plants often struggle in the home garden, usually because of too much of a good thing. Plants prefer dry or well-drained soils to moist ones and will die quickly in wet environments, especially in cold winter locations. Plants should be located where they are allowed to dry out between waterings and where the crowns are slightly raised, especially in a fertile or organic soil where a ring of moisture might form close to the stem. Plants often rot in this environment.

Plant *Oenothera* where it will get full sun to partial shade. Although I have no scientific data to support this, it does appear that naturally occurring stands—that is, plants that have grown where the seed fell the previous year—are healthier, larger and have fewer problems than greenhouse-grown plants.

When grown in open expanses without protection from trees, shrubs, or overhangs, a mulching is suggested to help the plants through the winter.

REFERENCES

[1] Bailey Hortorium. 1976. *Hortus third*. New York: Macmillan Publishing Company.

P

■ PAEONIA HYBRIDS (GARDEN OR HERBACEOUS TYPES)

The following information pertains only to the herbaceous peonies, those that die back to the ground during winter. Tree peonies (woody plants) are discussed in the following chapter.

The common garden peony is derived from a number of crosses with *P. lactiflora* and *P. officinalis* being the primary parents. Additional breeding information can be found through the American Peony Society, 250 Interlachen Road, Hopkins, MN 55343.

FAMILY: Paeoniaceae

COMMON NAME(S): Common Garden Peony, Chinese Peony

DESCRIPTION

Peonies are a heritage perennial known for their durability and long-lived performance. Peonies found in the gardens of yesteryear were commonly double flowering, and the blooms measured 4 to 6 inches (10 to 15 cm) across. Historical accounts describe families moving westward across the country, taking their peonies with them. Peonies were easy to transport, easy to plant, and hardy through the coldest winters. Prior to the development of hybrids, there were two common species available in the early 1900s: One, *Paeonia officinalis*, was called the "Memorial Day peony" since its flowers appeared in late May and were used to adorn the graves of loved ones—a practice still followed in the central United States today. A second species, *Paeonia lactiflora*, had larger blooms that flowered later but were fully double. *P. officinalis* could have either single or double blooms, and both varieties had blooms in either white or red, although *P. lactiflora* also had pink-flowering blossoms.

The peony hybrids commonly promoted today, mostly developed in the 1930s, haven't tarnished any of the brilliant colors or fragrance that pioneer families appreciated over a century ago. F.F. Rockwell, in his book *Peonies*, describes peony colors best:

"In color, at least within the range which they cover, peonies do vie with the rose. Whites are as pure as one could wish: even where—as with such varieties as that wonderful old favorite Festiva maxima—a thread of crimson or scarlet

342

sometimes appears, it only serves to emphasize the purity of the white. The reds are not harsh, but deep and rich, and the pinks are as warm and soft and flowing as one may find anywhere in the flower world. It is among the cream and opal tints, however, that the peonies excel. This latter shade, as it is found in the peony, is difficult to describe; it ranges from old ivory to mother-of-pearl. Cold words in black type can give little idea of the living, glowing color." [1]

Peonies are clump-forming plants with erect to arching stems up to 3 feet (90 cm) in height that emerge from the plant's crown. Each stem will terminate in a flower bud with two additional buds on either side. After the first bud blooms, the secondary buds will then develop and flower. These blooms are smaller than the first but will produce flowers that are otherwise the same. The buds are the size of a large marble measuring from three-quarters to 1 inch (2 to 2.5 cm). As for the blooms, the American Peony Society has classified the blooms into five different flower types: single, Japanese, anemone, semi-double and double.

The plants reach 2½ to 3 feet (75 to 90 cm) tall with a rounded appearance and a subshrub type performance. While they don't become woody, plants have strong stems that are sometimes woody at the base. Plants grow upright, but some varieties may require staking during flowering. When mature, plants spread to 3 feet (90 cm) wide.

HARDINESS: Zones 2 to 7.

Peonies are also hardy in selected areas of both Zones 1 and 8 but are known to perform reliably within the zones noted. Peony plants do well where they receive enough cold to induce dormancy and aren't exposed to extended periods of high heat and humidity. Under such conditions some varieties can be short lived or die back to the ground prematurely during the summer.

Unlike many perennials, peonies tend to perform better the colder it is (within reason). At my family home in Iowa, the same peonies have been growing for at least two generations without dying out, and while I am not recommending it, the plants were never divided.

SEASON OF BLOOM: May and June.

Flowering is relatively brief, only two weeks. Early- to late-flowering varieties can be used to extend the flowering for a six-week period in our Chicago climate from mid-May until late June, depending on how long winter lingers.

PROPAGATION

Division is the most common way to propagate peonies. Seed is used only to continue a species or develop new hybrids by commercial propagation, but it is not a method for commercial growers.

GERMINATION OVERVIEW

Only peony species will come true from seed, and the various hybrids and selections can only be reproduced by divisions. If you prefer seed for either the challenge or for growing the species, you must follow several steps and be prepared for some time-consuming efforts.

First, fresh seed that's gathered, properly stored, and then sown will offer the best results. Collect the fully developed seed in the late summer as the pods open and store in moist sphagnum peat moss for late summer sowing. When temperatures start to stay cool (early to mid-October here in northern Illinois), seed can be planted from one-half to 1 inch (1 to 2.5 cm) deep and spaced about the same into a ground bed of an unheated cold frame or other protected area.

Germination usually occurs the following spring. If the emerging seedlings don't meet your expectations based on the number of seeds you sowed the previous year, leave the bed intact for another full winter and early spring since it may take several years to germinate the whole lot.

If the seed has been allowed to dry out, your germination difficulties may be compounded. Seed may require warm-cold-warm conditioning followed by another cold treatment to break dormancy and germinate. Regardless, germination is erratic, with seedling emergence occurring over a period of two to three years—the longest I've seen is four years. Patience and persistence in this form of propagation is a virtue—not to mention a necessity.

GROWING ON

Crop time: Commercial propagators provide divisions primarily from mid or late August through the fall and winter. The plants are dug, cleaned, and divided up into individual roots, usually with three to five pointed, red-capped buds called "eyes." After the wounds have calloused over, the sections are refrigerated or shipped immediately. If received in the fall, roots can be potted up and moved into a cold greenhouse or cold frame for the winter and held just above freezing until March. These plants can be sold in the spring.

Roots may be potted up anytime during the winter for spring sales. Most varieties received as bare roots during the winter can be potted up into 2-, 3-, 4-, or 5-gallon containers for spring sales in late April or May depending on the temperature, container, and root size. In general, a root with three buds, potted up into a 2- or 3-gallon pot and grown on at 55F (13C) nights, will be salable in seven to nine weeks depending on the variety.

Many times early flowering varieties will be budded or flowering when sold but the mid or late season varieties will probably not show color until planted in the garden. Usually there are only one or two blooms during the first season. If roots are potted up in the fall and overwintered in a cold frame, better flowering will follow in the spring. When sold, plants will have one stem per bud, growing erect without basal or side branching. A February/March potted root will produce plants almost 2 feet (60 cm) tall when sold, depending on the variety.

Regarding root shape and size versus the growing container, most peony roots shipped by commercial propagators are woody, large, and odd shaped. Many times the dormant buds or "eyes" are clustered and to plant them properly, the large roots must be buried in a variety of positions. Proper container selection is crucial to growing a uniform and healthy plant. In most cases, peony roots are too large for quart and many gallon pots. The larger rooted varieties that you receive often require a 2- or 3-gallon container, but surprisingly, they will root and grow to fill out the container by the middle of spring.

If you're taking your own divisions, lift the clumps in August or September based on the weather and plant performance. If the seed pods have opened or the plants are semidormant (most often mid to late August), the plants can be divided. The only exception is when the summer is wet. In such cases, the roots may not be fully developed or ready to go dormant. If dug and divided, the resulting plants may be slow to develop, become diseased, or die.

When taking your own divisions, use plants that have been in their current location three to five years. After five years the center core of the crown can become entangled in the roots and difficult to divide. Divisions can be taken from the outer perimeter of the clump and the center discarded. In general, a three-year-old division may yield two to three good divisions, each with three to five "eyes."

From seed, flowering usually is delayed for four to five years. Once a plant is old enough to flower, one to three more years are necessary to verify flower color and quality. This is only important if you're breeding for new cultivars, not for your own enjoyment and personal use.

Some additional comments about seed grown peonies: The first summer after emerging, most plantlets will produce only one leaf. During that first summer the plants should be protected from direct sun, or this new leaf will almost always burn back. Leave the seedlings in their current location for two or three years after emergence, and then transplant to a nursery row to flower.

VARIETIES

As was the case with hosta, iris, and hemerocallis varieties, this book cannot cover all the numerous peony varieties on the market. Many commercial propagators offer only a few varieties, although there are a number of companies (like Klehm Nursery of South Barrington, Illinois) that specialize in peonies, propagate their own plants, and sell the roots in the late summer or autumn to home gardeners or commercial growers. Klehm's offers a vast array of varieties by flower type and color. Refer to this company's catalog for variety listings.

RELATED MATERIAL

P. tenuifolia is a peony with finely cut foliage commonly called Fernleaf Peony after its botanical name. The foliage is soft and needlelike on 12- to 15-inch (30 to 38 cm) tall plants. Two types exist: *P. tenuifolia* has single blossoms while *P. tenuifolia* Plena has double flowers. Both are crimson red. Fernleaf peonies do best in a well-drained location in full sun. Like the other peonies noted here, plant with the "eyes" 2 inches (5 cm) below the soil surface. For additional protection, winter mulching is suggested the first winter after a fall planting. Divide as you would for the Chinese or garden peonies and grow on in a similar manner. Hardy from Zones 4 to 7.

USES

Without question, peonies are a welcome addition to any commercial or home landscape where permanent, but herbaceous, plants are preferred. Once planted, they will last for years—long beyond the generation of the person who originally planted them. For best growth and development, follow the comments noted under **In the home garden** along with one additional tip—in commercial landscapes, avoid locations with frequent overhead watering. This can lead to additional foliar disease problems and weak plants that require staking.

Peonies make excellent cut flowers as noted under the **Description**. For home use, remove the lateral buds and keep only the center terminal bud for larger blooms. Don't do this on every stem since it will greatly reduce the number of flowers. Cut when the buds crack open and the first petal starts to unfurl. The cut flowers can also be stored for later use. Cut as above, strip the foliage off and store dry in paper in a refrigerator. These will last from three to six weeks depending on the variety; when needed, recut them at the base of the stem and plunge into warm water. Flowers will open during the next several days.

If you're considering commercial cut flower production, additional information can be found in the Kansas State University publication, *Peonies*, as well as Allan Armitage's book, *Specialty Cut Flowers*, from Timber Press. The KSU publication is part of the *Commercial Specialty Cut Flower Production* series, article MF-1083.

IN THE HOME GARDEN

Like all plant enthusiasts who will always have a place for their chosen leafy "friends," I can't overstate the hardiness and longevity of this plant. It seldom balks at winter and seems to enjoy the wonderfully nasty dips to below-zero temperatures. It flourishes with full sun, a heavier rather than light soil, and limited staking.

Staking is more common on the double and semi-double flowering varieties than it is on single, Japanese, or anemone types. If flowers are fully developed and a spring shower comes along, the plants will become top heavy and bend over to the ground. Some gardeners apply twine just under the crown of the foliage as flower buds set while others use metal rods to assure plants stay in place all summer long. As the plants go dormant, remove the stakes and store for winter.

Peony plants don't require any special care or help, although they may get a number of foliar, root, and flower diseases. As the plants go dormant, cut the stems back to the soil, remove them along with any fallen leaves and destroy them. If a disease is present, using the stems and leaves as winter mulch will only increase problems the following year.

Plants don't require any dividing, but if you want to increase your populations or move the plants, they're easy to work with. Dig them up in late summer, trim away old growth, and cut the roots back to 5 or 6 inches (13 to 15 cm); then replant with 1 to 2 inches (2.5 to 5 cm) of soil over the top of the "eyes." Beware of burying any deeper—even at 3 inches (7 cm), some varieties take five years to flower, some don't flower well, and others won't flower at all. We take our divisions here in Chicago during late August and early September to allow plants to become established. In general, divisions will not flower profusely the following spring, but if they're dug in August, divided and transplanted immediately, there could be some color the following spring. Plants become more free-flowering, however, two to three years after the initial division.

REFERENCES

[1] American Peony Society. 1983. *Handbook of the Peony*. 4th ed.
[2] Laurie, A., and L.C. Chadwick. 1934. *Commercial flower forcing*. Philadelphia: P. Blakiston's Son & Co. Inc.
[3] Rockwell, F.F. 1933. *Peonies*. The home garden handbooks series. New York: Macmillan Publishing Company.
[4] Wister, J.C., ed. 1962. *The Peonies*. Washington, D.C.: American Horticultural Society.

—The author appreciates the time that Roy Klehm of Klehm Nursery, Barrington, Illinois, spent in reviewing and editing this material.

PAEONIA HYBRIDS (TREE TYPES)

Many of the varieties sold are hybrids from the various crosses of *Paeonia suffruticosa* (sometimes called *P. arborea* or *P. moutan*), *P. lutea*, and *P. delavayi*.

FAMILY: Paeoniaceae

COMMON NAME(S): Tree Peony
Occasionally you'll read of "moutan" peonies, a derivative of "mew tang," "mow tan," or "muh tang." Tree peonies were once botanically called *Paeonia moutan*, which is also their common name in certain circles.

DESCRIPTION

Called "tree peonies" due to their woody stems, these peonies are actually shrublike in their performance. They grow from 4 to 5 feet (1.2 to 1.5 m), or sometimes as tall as 6 feet (1.8 m) in full bloom. In or out of bloom, the plants spread 3 to 4½ feet (90 to 135 cm) across. Instead of dying back to the ground in winter, a woody, branched stem or trunk remains from which new foliage develops in the spring. Tree peonies are available in many flower colors including white, pink, crimson, maroon, purple, and red. There are also some blue varieties although they are muted or shaded, often appearing maroon. Yellow-flowering varieties are available in *P. lutea* hybrids as well.

Tree peony flowers are mostly semidouble or fully double, but singles are available, too. The flower size will vary depending on variety. Hybrids average from 4 to 8 inches (10 to 20 cm) across while some species can be as large as 15 inches (38 cm) across. When compared to garden peonies, tree peonies are larger in habit with slightly larger flowers and more colors, but they're not as common in the marketplace.

HARDINESS: Zones 3 to 7.
Read **In the home garden** for additional details.

SEASON OF BLOOM: May and June.
Tree peony blooming times range over a three- to four-week period in the spring.

PROPAGATION

While many references list various propagation methods, the standard for tree peonies is grafting. This is a tedious, complicated procedure that has a high rate of failure for the nonskilled propagator. The main reason for failure is lack of sanitation during the grafting process, which can lead to high losses due to disease, primarily *Botrytis*.

If you're interested in grafting your own varieties, the American Peony Society has detailed information in their handbook. Look for their address at the beginning of this section.

Other propagation techniques include dividing, layering, root cuttings and seed. Methods are the same as for the herbaceous peony but will yield various—if not completely different—results. Only tree peonies from nongrafted stock can be propagated by division. (After grafted plants have been growing in the garden for several years with the graft several inches below the soil, the plant will be rooted on its own, no longer dependent on the union for support. At this time, plants that originated from a graft may be divided.)

Seed can be sown, but only commercial propagators searching for new varieties pursue this method. Cuttings have reportedly been used by propagators to increase the species and some hybrids, but at the time of this writing, the results have been mixed.

GERMINATION OVERVIEW

Unlike garden or Chinese peonies, tree peony seed requires a warm temperature period followed by a cold period to germinate. Warm conditions help to develop the root systems while the cold encourages shoot development after exposure. If seeded in the fall without sufficient warmth to start germinating, the seeds will remain dormant until the following summer. They'll root, but it will be the effects of the subsequent winter that will allow the shoots to emerge in the spring. Information provided in 1932 by the Boyce Thompson Institute under the direction of Lela Barton suggested sowing the seeds as soon as they're ripe into a flat in a warm greenhouse for three months. Then move the flat to a cold environment for another three months, and then on to a cool greenhouse for germination. "Cold" refers to 32F to 50F (0C to 10C), although by today's standards it's usually 38F to 42F (4C to 6C), while a cool greenhouse is 52F to 58F (11C to 15C).

After germination, the seedlings should be relocated to a protected bed away from direct sunlight and grown on for a period of two or three years.

GROWING ON

Crop time: Purchased tree peony roots will be one of two types: Japanese-grown, usually from a one-year-old graft or U.S.-grown and harvested when two to three years old. You'll pay more for the U.S.-grown varieties than those from Japan, but the cultivars are more true to name. Both are available in the late summer, fall, and early winter months from various wholesale firms across the country and should be potted upon receipt.

For potting up, container size is based on the plant's root size. Like garden peonies, the larger rooted varieties are suited to a 2-gallon or larger container—slightly smaller if using one-year-old grafts. The roots are potted up with the graft just slightly below the soil surface and moved to a cold frame and sold the following spring for garden planting. These plants may flower sporadically during spring or early summer, but they'll require two to three years to become fully established and free flowering.

If you're digging your own tree peonies from a nursery bed, the appropriate time to do so is based on your locale. Here in Chicago, it's October or November. Unlike garden peonies, tree peonies aren't as dormant at the time they're dug for bare-root sales. The branches will still be leafed out, and the foliage will be dark green. Toichi Domoto of Toichi Domoto Nursery in Hayward, California, writes in the American Peony Society's *Handbook of the Peony* that he digs near the root ball's outer perimeter and looks for newly developed white rootlets. As the plant starts to slow down in late summer, these roots aren't common and dormancy is beginning. He continues by removing all the leaves from the plant and trims the stems back to 6 or 8 inches (15 or 20 cm) above the base. He further comments that this "...sacrifices stem length and flowers for one season, hoping that the dormant basal eyes are forced into growth which will produce buds that open to flower the second season." [1]

Move the roots to a cool environment out of direct sunlight to make them less brittle and more pliable. Check the roots for any damage, and trim off broken or splintered pieces as you look for cracks in the flesh. These too, should be removed, as they are an invitation for root rots later on. Pot up the roots; if not ready to plant, store them in moist sphagnum until ready to use.

P

VARIETIES

Since tree peonies are sold commercially as a grafted plant here in the United States, there are only a limited number of commercial propagators who specialize in offering a wide range of traditional as well as new tree peony varieties. Klehm Nursery, South Barrington, Illinois, and other wholesale firms carry varieties, although some companies offer unnamed varieties sold by color. Klehm's specializes in their own as well as other breeders' varieties. These selections are usually No. 1 grade transplants field harvested from Japan and shipped to the United States. In some cases, these are grown on to verify color and performance but most are immediately repackaged and shipped to growers for potting up.

Like herbaceous peonies, tree peonies are available in a long list of varieties. To do justice to them all, contact either Klehm Nursery or the American Peony Society. Look under **Perennial Source List** in the appendix for Klehm's address. You'll find the address for the American Peony Society in the **Herbaceous Peonies** chapter.

IN THE HOME GARDEN

Home gardeners not familiar with tree peonies may get "sticker shock" after reading the price tag of a container-grown plant. They're not inexpensive either when purchased by mail order directly from the propagator.

If a tree peony is sold bare root in the spring and appears small with only one or two buds atop a small cluster of roots, that plant will probably not flower for at least two years. Some require up to four years to bloom. Likewise, a small plant in a small container will yield similar results. If plants were grafted the year before, potted up, overwintered, and then sold in the spring, the surface roots are seldom massed and there are usually only one or two active stems developing. This plant isn't going to flower for several years. Plants will eventually flower, but if you want flowering plants in a short period of time, be prepared to pay for the variety and quality you really want.

When planting in the garden, dig a hole 2 feet by 2 feet (60 cm by 60 cm), add some organic matter, place the bare root or container-grown plant into the hole and adjust so that the graft union is below the soil line, 2 to 4 inches (5 to 10 cm) deep. By burying this union you increase the plant's survival chances from year to year as well as decrease the possibilities of suckering that may occur from the rootstock. Space plants 3 to 4 feet (90 to 120 cm) apart, depending on the design effect you want to create, but avoid crowding as this can lead to disease.

Unlike garden peonies, tree peonies' rewards will not be as quick. Many don't flower for two to three years after planting, sometimes more. Once established and grown on, the plants will be a welcome addition, drawing gasps of awe when viewed for the first time in full color.

Tree peonies tolerate more shade than garden peonies and will often look better because of it. Plant where they get morning or late afternoon sun but are protected during the hottest part of the day. Plant in any well-drained location since constantly moist soils lead to disease problems and early death later on.

As prescribed under garden peonies, remove and discard all leaves and clean the plants up in the fall prior to winter. Place a mulch over the crown of the plants in northern winter locations—in the lower parts of Zone 6 and south it's not as necessary. The first winter after planting bare-root peonies in the fall, however, mulch to protect the roots.

Finally, tree peonies are slower to grow than garden peonies. For this reason don't compare the two and expect equal performance from transplants. Instead, appreciate each plant for its own merits and both will reward you in different ways.

REFERENCES

[1] Domoto, T. 1983. Digging and shipping tree peonies. In *Handbook of the Peony*. 4th ed. American Peony Society.

[2] American Peony Society. 1983. *Handbook of the Peony*. 4th ed.

[3] Rockwell, F.F. 1983. *Peonies*. The home garden handbooks series. New York: Macmillan Publishing Company.

[4] Wister, J.C., ed. *The Peonies*. 1962. Washington, D.C.: American Horticultural Society.

—The author appreciates the time that Roy Klehm of Klehm Nursery, Barrington, Illinois, spent in reviewing and editing this material.

▬ PAPAVER ORIENTALE

FAMILY: Papaveraceae

COMMON NAME(S): Oriental Poppy

DESCRIPTION

Single, crepe-paper-like blooms measuring from 4 to 6 inches (10 to 15 cm) across highlight this plant. The blooms can be gaudy due to their large size and bold, vivid color. The flower colors, almost iridescent, are shades of scarlet and orange, although salmon, pink, and additional flower colors exist among some of the cultivars. Flowers are enhanced by a deep purple to black blotch around the petal base and a multitude of purple stamens around the center. Damaged or broken stems will exude a white latex. Plants grow from 2 to 3 feet (60 to 90 cm) tall and from 15 to 24 inches (38 to 61 cm) across. See Color Plate 55 for photo of *Papaver orientale*.

HARDINESS: Zones 3 to 7.

Oriental poppies can be deceiving. They are one of the earliest perennials to re-emerge in the spring but will often go dormant during late August. This is especially true during a hot and humid summer.

SEASON OF BLOOM: May and early June.

PROPAGATION

Seed, root cuttings, and divisions are the easiest propagation methods. Root cuttings are taken from dormant plants during the winter while divisions work best in mid to late summer.

GERMINATION OVERVIEW: 95,000 seeds per ounce/3,325 per gram.

Seed germinates in seven to 14 days at 65F to 75F (18C to 24C). It should be left exposed to light during germination. Seedlings can be transplanted 16 to 25 days after sowing.

GROWING ON

From seed: Oriental poppies are commonly sold in quart and gallon pots in the spring from seed sown the previous year. The seedlings are transplanted to cell packs to size up and then to the final quart or gallon pot during mid or late summer to establish before cold weather. Plants are overwintered and sold the following spring. Seed sown anytime after the first of the year will produce basal rosettes the entire summer; plants will not flower until after being vernalized (exposed to a period of cold).

If green, salable 32-cell packs are needed, allow 10 to 12 weeks at 50F to 55F (10C to 13C) nights. Be sure to transplant the cell packs to the garden or a larger container before they become root bound, however. If stressed at a young age, the roots often become entangled and gnarled, affecting later performance.

Root cuttings are described in the front of this book.

Commercial propagators offer *Papaver* as a bare-root transplant or as a liner or plug. Available during the autumn and winter, any of these can be potted up into quarts and gallons for spring sales.

VARIETIES

Allegro is a scarlet-orange flowering plant to 18 inches (46 cm) tall. It is more compact than the other cultivars noted below.

Beauty of Livermore is a deep-red-flowering variety on plants to 2½ feet (75 cm) tall.

Brilliant has bright scarlet flowers on plants to 30 inches (75 cm) tall.

Oriental Mix is a color mixture that includes red, scarlet, pink, and salmon. The red and scarlet shades make up the majority of colors in this mix, however. This is also called Benary's Special Mixture.

RELATED MATERIAL

P. nudicaule (Iceland or Arctic poppy) is sometimes sold as a true perennial although it's quite the opposite. Plants are annuals or tender perennials and flower in 4-inch (10 cm) pots 15 to 17 weeks after sowing. There are many varieties on the market, and many will be listed as perennials in catalogs. Plants prefer warm days and cool nights and excel in coastal areas such as California. In our Chicago climate, however, these plants are not summer tolerant and often "melt" in August from extremes heat and humidity.

USES

In the perennial border, these plants make a dramatic impact when flowering. Be prepared to have larger, later-flowering perennials surrounding Oriental poppies to make up for the brief flower show and eventual absence of foliage, since plants go dormant in July and August and die back to the soil. For this reason they aren't recommended for landscaping projects.

Oriental poppies make good cut flowers although they're short lived in the vase. Sear the stem's open end with a flame to seal it. This prevents the milky latex from seeping out.

IN THE HOME GARDEN

Plant in areas where poppies will get morning sun and afternoon shade in a well-drained soil, and they'll have a long life. They've been in our garden for five years with a strong show each season, and we haven't lost a plant. Oriental poppies are more tolerant of wet autumns than other perennials as long as it isn't prolonged and plants aren't flooded out. Note the comment under **Uses** about plant dormancy in midsummer. For first-time plant buyers, this is often an unexpected surprise and not appreciated. The problem is compounded by this plant's bigger size, requiring large growing material to cover up the open spots.

Winter covering isn't necessary to improve their hardiness nor is staking required to keep plants upright. One word of caution, though—for the best performance from the delicate flowers, avoid open, windy locations. In these exposures, the flowers are often battered around in the wind to the point of breakage. Also, the deep purple stamens will stain the brilliant flower color.

▬ PENSTEMON BARBATUS VAR. COCCINEUS

FAMILY: Scrophulariaceae

COMMON NAME(S): Bearded Tongue

DESCRIPTION

This unassuming native perennial displays bright, shiny green foliage and upright racemes of tubular, scarlet flowers. The flowers are 1 inch (2.5 cm) long, with a white line of color down the center of the throat. Flowers hang downward from the flowering stalk rather than horizontally and lightly sway back and forth on a windy day.

The foliage mats close to the soil and, when not in flower, may be no more than 4 to 8 inches (10 to 20 cm) tall. Plants develop a basal tuft of foliage rather than a rosette, although it may resemble a rosette when young. The leaves radiate out of this tuft from 4 to 6 inches (10 to 15 cm) in length. Plants grow from 2 to 3 feet (60 to 90 cm) tall in flower and spread 12 to 16 inches (30 to 41 cm) across.

HARDINESS: Zones 3 to 8.

Plants are reliably hardy here in our Chicago location, more so than the true *P. barbatus* varieties.

SEASON OF BLOOM: June and July.

PROPAGATION

Seed and cuttings are the two usual ways to propagate this crop. Seed can be sown anytime of the year while cuttings can be taken during the active growing period—spring to autumn—from nonflowering stems. Divisions also work and are best done in the spring.

GERMINATION OVERVIEW: 15,000 seeds per ounce/525 per gram.

Penstemon germinates readily without pretreatments, yielding 60% or greater germination rates from a spring sowing. Seeds will germinate in seven to 10 days at 70F (21C) and don't need to be covered. Seedlings will be large enough for transplanting 20 to 28 days after sowing.

GROWING ON

Crop time: From seed, plants will basal branch and appear as a rosette in either the pack or pot. Plants develop uniformly and produce glossy, deep green leaves shortly after sowing. In general, midwinter sowings transplanted to a 32-cell pack will be salable green in 10 to 11 weeks after sowing when grown at 50F (10C) nights. The plants are grown warm at 60F (16C) nights from just after germinating until they start to root in the cell pack. Then they can be moved to a cold frame and grown on at 50F (10C) nights until ready to sell.

From an early February sowing, plants will be salable green in May and, if planted to a garden by Mother's Day, will be in flower by the end of June or early July. Plants flower sporadically the first season from seed. You'll see variable blooming dates the first year from seed and a probable flowering response of 25 to 65%, depending upon when sown. The following year all plants will flower.

Seed can also be sown anytime during the winter and spring for potting into 4-inch (10 cm) or quart containers for sales the same year or the next spring. Allow 14 to 15 weeks at 50F (10C) nights to finish a green, 4-inch (10 cm) pot. For full-blooming plants during the summer, sow seed the previous spring or summer. Shift the seedlings to the final container during warm summer months and then overwinter for spring sales. Be sure to start the plants early enough and get them established in their final containers before cold weather. If they haven't grown in, the plants are often stressed and many can die, even when protected by a cold frame. This is especially true when the root ball is kept too moist.

Penstemon can also be rooted from cuttings. From the tuft of foliage at the crown, especially in the spring, a number of vegetative shoots can be removed, rooted, and potted up into quart or gallon containers for overwintering.

VARIETIES

P. barbatus var. *coccineus* is an up-and-coming selection. It's more readily found from seed houses specializing in native perennial plants than from a commercial source.

While the culture above is for *Penstemon barbatus* var. *coccineus*, there are *P. barbatus* varieties worthy of discussion. These include:

P. barbatus var. *praecox* (also listed as Praecox) is a mixture of colors including shades of scarlet, purple, carmine, and rose plus white and pink. It grows to 3 feet (90 cm) tall and flowers during June and July. A dwarf variety—*P. barbatus* var. *praecox nanus*—also listed *Praecox Nanus*—is a dwarf version growing 15 to 18 inches (38 to 46 cm) tall. You may see this variety also listed as Rondo.

These have a similar culture to *Penstemon barbatus* var. *coccineus*.

Elfin Pink has pink flowers on plants from 12 to 15 inches (30 to 38 cm) tall.

Prairie Dusk is a long-stemmed variety to 24 inches (60 cm) with rose-purple tubular flowers. Plants bloom in June and July.

Prairie Fire is a taller plant than Prairie Dusk, growing to 3 feet (90 cm) or slightly shorter. The flowers are scarlet red.

RELATED MATERIAL

P. digitalis Husker Red has bronze-purple leaves and white blossoms on plants that grow 2 to 3 feet (60 to 90 cm) tall. While seed is listed in several catalogs, the variety will only come true from vegetative propagation.

USES

As a group, penstemons are reliable performers in the landscape. They do best in natural settings rather than formal landscapes, providing several weeks of color during the early summer. Since the flower colors are usually pastel and the show of color is more visually rewarding up close rather than from a distance, plant in the front of a border or in large plantings at the back for greater effect. Flower colors combine well with scarlet, red, and yellow-flowered plants.

As cut flowers, penstemons are adequate for home garden use but impractical for the commercial trade. Occasionally you may see them in mixed wildflower bouquets at a farmer's market.

IN THE HOME GARDEN

While penstemons are usually hardy in cold northern winters, garden location is the key to their success. Plants tolerate full sun to high shade. High shade is the area around trees, houses and other light-blocking features. Several hours of direct sun

P

during the day and bright, indirect light at other times will keep the plants happy and long lived. If planted to dark shade, the flower stalks become flimsy and weak, often falling over during summer storms. Plant in any well-drained location for best performance. If plant crowns are kept overly moist or wet, the plants will rot, especially during the winter.

Plants don't need staking, but old flower stalks should be removed as the flowers age and die. If not, they become weak as the summer progresses and bend and fall over. If the flowering stalks are removed down to the crown, it's possible the plants will rebloom later in the summer.

■ PEROVSKIA ATRIPLICIFOLIA

FAMILY: Labiatae

COMMON NAME(S): Russian Sage

DESCRIPTION
A striking plant noted for its color and form as well as its fragrance, *Perovskia atriplicifolia* is a clump-forming perennial from 4 to 5 feet (120 to 150 cm) tall, though we seldom see it over 3½ feet (105 cm) in our Chicago gardens. The stems are covered with a glaucous (grayish white) waxy layer, and the foliage is light green or gray green on the top and grayish white underside. The flowers are light blue, approximately one-quarter inch (6 mm) in size and arranged in panicles which are branching flower clusters. Perovskia grows from 3 to 4 feet (90 to 120 cm) across once established. See Color Plate 56 for photo of *Perovskia atriplicifolia*.

HARDINESS: Zones 5 to 9.
Plants are marginally hardy here in our Chicago climate. Read the notes under **In the home garden** for further information.

SEASON OF BLOOM: July to September.
This is a midseason perennial with a long flowering performance.

PROPAGATION
Stem cuttings are the most common method used to propagate this crop, though the species can be grown from seed as well. During the last several years, a number of hybrids have appeared on the market, but none will come true from seed. Divisions are difficult and seldom produce enough plants to make it worth your time. Some propagators offer bare-root transplants that can be potted up. But in general, divisions are more often made by gardeners than by commercial growers.

Cuttings are the quickest and most reliable method for propagating this crop.

GROWING ON

Crop time: Cuttings can be taken on either immature or semimature stems. This means that cuttings can be taken anytime in spring, as shoots emerge from the crown and elongate in June. The cuttings will root easily in two to three weeks with bottom heat. When roots have developed, transplant to a quart or gallon container and grow through the summer for late summer sales or overwinter for sales the following spring.

Bare-root transplants are available from commercial propagators for potting up during autumn or winter into 3- or 4-quart containers for spring sales. Liners are frequently available for this crop as well. Pot them up into quart pots for spring sales.

VARIETIES

Perovskia atriplicifolia seed will be difficult to find in the United States, though started plants, liners, and divisions are readily available from various commercial propagators.

Perovskia × Longin (Longin) is a variety developed by Kurt Blumel of Maryland. Longin displays a more erect habit than the species and grows from 3 to 4 feet (90 to 120 cm) tall. It can only be propagated vegetatively.

USES

Don't underestimate the potential of this excellent perennial for the commercial landscape. Few plants can compare or compete with the unusual stem coloring, light blue flowers, open, airy flower heads, and noninvasive nature that this plant offers. To accent the flower color, combine with scarlet, rose, coral, and buff-yellow shades of other plants for a striking effect.

Remember the open habit of the flower clusters. From a distance, the blooms look like a hovering crown of scattered blue above the foliage.

IN THE HOME GARDEN

It's important to provide a well-drained soil for this crop. Our Chicago gardens are the northern boundary for hardiness of *Perovskia*. If the crowns are covered and stay wet during the winter, the plants seldom make it to the following spring. As you move farther south in the United States, winter moisture is less of a problem. Here in the North, we can lose large plantings after just one winter. However, foundation plantings and other protected locations greatly increase the survival chances of *Perovskia*.

We also plant to a well-drained, slightly mounded or raised location where the crowns are covered only lightly or not at all. We cover the plants with two to three evergreen boughs.

Perovskia does well in full sun and requires little fertilizer. Once transplanted to the garden, the plants will fill in slowly their first year depending on what size of container they were transplanted from. They'll grow larger and more open after the second year.

▬ PHLOX PANICULATA

FAMILY: Polemoniaceae

COMMON NAME(S): Perennial Phlox, Summer Phlox, Garden Phlox

DESCRIPTION

Phlox paniculata is a widely grown perennial commonly available in colors of white, pink, lavender, and salmon; red, purple, and light blue shades are also available. Many have dark-colored centers or bands around the flower center. The flower clusters grow from 8 to 10 inches (20 to 25 cm) across, with individual flowers measuring 1 to 1½ inches (2.5 to 3 cm). Some cultivars have scented flowers. Plants grow 2 to 3 feet (60 to 90 cm) tall and from 15 to 24 inches (38 to 61 cm) across.

HARDINESS: Zones 4 to 8.
Phlox performs best in warm and dry areas. Plants won't tolerate a long duration of hot and humid weather—they are extremely susceptible to powdery mildew.

SEASON OF BLOOM: July to September.

PROPAGATION

Division and root and stem cuttings are the most common ways to propagate. Seed isn't a common method of propagation, but some growers use it to produce green cell packs in the spring. Plants can also be divided in spring or late summer.

GERMINATION OVERVIEW: 2,000 to 2,500 seeds per ounce/70 to 88 per gram.
Pretreatment: Fresh seed yields the best germination results, but good germination rates for *P. paniculata* aren't common. Without pretreatment, 10 to 20% germination rates are to be expected. Instead, seed should be exposed to a moist chilling period during the winter. Additional information for using this method is provided in the front of the book.

Once pretreated, seed germinates in 15 to 25 days at 60F (16C).

GROWING ON

From seed: If sown during the winter, the developing seedlings will emerge erratically. Transplant to cell packs when large enough to handle. These plants will be salable green in late May and June when grown on at 55F (13C) nights. They won't flower the first season from seed.

From division: Divisions purchased from commercial propagators establish quickly, and most varieties are salable green in seven to nine weeks when grown at 55F (13C) nights. These plants will have two to four active shoots, 3 to 5 inches (7 to

13 cm) long at the time they're sold. Some varieties are naturally more robust performers and will be taller.

From cuttings: If taking your own stem cuttings in spring or summer, you can pot up the plantlets to quarts once they've rooted, in two to three weeks. These can be grown on for midsummer sales or held over the winter for spring sales. Commercial propagators offer a wide assortment of varieties in plugs or liners propagated from cuttings. These are most often available in 50 and 72 cells per flat, which can be potted up during the winter for spring sales.

Take root cuttings during the winter while plants are dormant. Root sections that are removed during January or February and allowed to develop into strong shoots during early spring will make 4-inch (10 cm) or quart sales by late summer. For fully rooted plants with several shoots per crown, however, overwinter the plants dormant and sell the following spring.

VARIETIES

There is a long list of available phlox varieties on the U.S. market today. While the bulk of these are powdery-mildew-susceptible, a number of varieties are mildew tolerant and are noted below. This list is abbreviated, however; there are far too many cultivars than space in this book. Be aware that many commercial propagators offering divisions or cell packs have their own selections, and you should read their lists for details.

All of the following are **vegetatively propagated**. Seed offered in the trade is a color mix of 2- to 3-foot-tall (60 to 90 cm) plants available under the name of Beltsville Beauty or New Hybrids Mixed. Several U.S. seed companies carry it.

Blue Boy is one of the phlox varieties that is closest to a true blue color. The plants grow from 2½ to 3 feet (75 to 90 cm) tall in flower.

Bright Eyes is one of my personal favorites with soft pink flowers highlighted by a maroon or red blotch on each flower. The flowering stalks are also dark colored. Bright Eyes grows 2½ to 3 feet (75 to 90 cm) tall.

David has pure white, fragrant flowers on plants 3 to 4 feet (90 to 120 cm) tall in bloom. It is mildew tolerant.

Fairest One has light pink flowers on plants from 18 to 24 inches (46 to 61 cm) tall.

Mt. Fuji has pure white blooms on plants 2½ to 3 feet (75 to 90 cm) tall in bloom. See Color Plate 57 for photo of *Phlox paniculata* Mt. Fuji.

RELATED MATERIAL

P. × chattahoochee (often called Chattahoochee) is a cross between *P. divaricata* var. *laphamii* and *P. pilosa*. The 1-inch (2.5 cm) flowers are midblue with a maroon eye in the center. Foliage is dark green. Plants do best when grown in shaded garden locations. It flowers in April and May and is hardy from Zones 4 to 9.

Propagate by stem tip or root cuttings or by divisions.

P. maculata (meadow phlox, wild sweet William) is a rhizomatous perennial growing from 2 to 3 feet (60 to 90 cm) tall in flower. *P. maculata* is more tolerant of powdery mildew than *P. paniculata* although it has a limited color spectrum. The species flowers pink, white, or purple, but it's the cultivars in this class that have merit.

Alpha has lilac-pink flowers from July to September on plants 2 to 3 feet (60 to 90 cm) tall in flower.

Delta is considered by some to be an improvement on Miss Lingard, with white flowers highlighted by a soft pink eye. Delta often blooms earlier than Miss Lingard and is more free flowering. Plants grow 2 to 3 feet (60 to 90 cm) tall in flower.

Miss Lingard (Mrs. Lingard) is sometimes labeled as a *P. carolina* cultivar or, less frequently, a cultivar of *P. suffruticosa*. Its exact parentage is confusing—some believe it's a cross between *P. maculata* and *P. carolina*. Regardless, be prepared to find this variety listed under either botanical name by the commercial propagator and distribution firms offering this selection. It features pure white, fragrant 1-inch (2.5 cm) flowers, occasionally with a light pink ring or band towards the petal base, plus a yellow eye. Miss Lingard reaches 2 to 3 feet (60 to 90 cm) tall.

Omega has pure white blooms highlighted with a violet-rose eye. Plants grow 2 to 3 feet (60 to 90 cm) in flower.

P. maculata is propagated by divisions, root cuttings, and stem tip cuttings. Commercial propagators offer this crop in various sizes that can be grown on as suggested under the *P. paniculata* heading.

USES

Garden phlox is used primarily in the perennial border for midsummer color in either home or commercial landscapes. The blooms can also be harvested for cut flowers; vase life tends to be short, though, only about seven days.

IN THE HOME GARDEN

Garden phlox is a long-lived crop, but it is frequently plagued by powdery mildew during the summer. Plant in full-sun locations in well-drained but moist soil for best performance. Avoid afternoon and evening waterings, because of the plants' sensitivity to powdery mildew. Be sure to avoid splashing the foliage before and after mildew starts—this only compounds the problem.

Plant in the middle of the perennial border without staking. Space on 18-inch (46 cm) centers. Phlox doesn't require mulching or any special treatment to survive the winter.

■ PHLOX SUBULATA

FAMILY: Polemoniaceae

COMMON NAME(S): Moss Pink, Creeping Phlox, Ground Phlox

DESCRIPTION

Phlox subulata is an excellent evergreen ground cover with needlelike, dark green foliage on plants 4 to 6 inches (10 to 15 cm) tall. Plants spread 15 to 24 inches (38 to 61 cm) across. The single, open flowers measure one-half to three-quarter-inch (1 to 2 cm) wide in colors of pink, blue, and white.

HARDINESS: Zones 2 to 9.

SEASON OF BLOOM: April and May.

PROPAGATION

Phlox subulata is usually propagated by division and stem tip cuttings. Layering is also effective but is more common with home gardeners than commercial propagators.

GROWING ON

From cuttings: Cuttings are easy to take and root—new plantlets will be ready by late summer to sell as 4-inch (10 cm) green plants along with bulbs and fall mums. They can also be overwintered for spring sales.

Choose only semimature shoots: Avoid any with woody stems when taking cuttings. Plants should be sheared after flowering to encourage new shoots. The cuttings can be taken during July or August, allowed two to three weeks at 72F to 75F (22C to 24C) to root in sand, and then potted up into 4-inch (10 cm), quart, or gallon containers when ready.

From divisions: Since cuttings are so easy to take, propagation by divisions is more common with home gardeners. Commercial propagators also offer a number of bare-root varieties that can be potted up into 1- to 4-quart containers during the winter for spring sales.

Besides divisions, *P. subulata* is available from commercial propagators in small pots or as liners or plugs. All can be potted up into larger containers during winter, grown on at 50F to 55F (10C to 13C) nights, and sold green or flowering in the spring. *P. subulata* requires a cold period for flowering. If purchasing plugs or liners during the winter, be sure that the plantlets were vernalized before they were shipped to you. If they weren't, pot up by January or February and grow on, once established, at 45F to 50F (7C to 10C) nights. This will help to promote a flush of color but not full bloom by April or May.

VARIETIES

All of the following are **vegetatively propagated**.

Emerald Blue (Blue Emerald) is a blue-flowering sport from Emerald Pink. Plants grow 4 to 6 inches (10 to 15 cm) tall in flower. See Color Plate 58 for photo of *Phlox subulata* Emerald Blue.

Emerald Pink has pink flowers on plants 4 to 6 inches (10 to 15 cm) tall.

Crimson Beauty's name would make you think that the flowers are a vivid color. The blooms are really rose red, on plants 4 to 6 inches (10 to 15 cm) tall.

White Delight has pure white flowers on plants from 4 to 6 inches (10 to 15 cm) tall.

USES

P. subulata is recommended for the perennial garden as an edging or border as well as for the rock garden. In the landscape, once plants have ceased flowering in spring, they won't flower again for the remainder of the year. Focus on their landscape value as a bright, low-growing evergreen plant. For best effect, plant them only in well-drained areas and out of the way of prevailing winter winds.

IN THE HOME GARDEN

Once in bloom, plants will flower four to six weeks depending on the variety and the weather, but the foliage will persist year-round. *P. subulata* performs best in a full-sun, well-drained location. I've enjoyed these plants for the past six years on the western side of my house, thriving in a clay-loam soil.

In the late winter, lift the mat of foliage off the ground and remove all the brown or dead needles on the soil underneath. Remove any dead stems as well. Next, *lightly* cultivate the soil surface under the plants and then lay the foliage back in place. This helps aerate the soil and keeps it from repelling water during the summer. After flowering, the plant's crown can be sheared back.

■■■ PHYSALIS ALKEKENGI
(syn. *P. franchetii*)

FAMILY: Solanaceae

COMMON NAME(S): Chinese Lantern

DESCRIPTION

This plant is well known for its large, bright orange, Chinese-lantern-shaped fruit often used in late summer and fall dried arrangements. The fruit is actually a berry enclosed within a papery husk. *Physalis* grows erect with no branching along the stem and with lanterns at each axis or set of opposite leaves. The flowers are single, small (one-half to three-quarter inch [1 cm to 2 cm]), white, and of limited value since they're tucked down in the foliage. Plants grow 18 to 24 inches (46 to 61 cm) tall, spreading from 15 to 30 inches (38 to 76 cm) across, and can become invasive.

HARDINESS: Zones 3 to 8.
Sometimes treated as an hardy annual in the northern United States.

SEASON OF BLOOM
Flowers appear in June and July, and fruits in August and September.

PROPAGATION
Seed and division are two common methods used to propagate this crop. Seed can be sown anytime during the year, but see **Germination** for additional details. Taking divisions involves digging up the underground stems, cutting them, and potting them up. Divisions can be made in spring or fall.

GERMINATION OVERVIEW: 17,000 seeds per ounce/595 per gram.
Pretreatments: Seed germinates readily, requiring no pretreatments unless stored for a long time. If in doubt, sow 100 seeds using the following suggestions, and count the seedlings. If less than 50% of the seeds germinate, the seed could be old and require a cold treatment. Follow the information under moist chilling in the front of this book.

Numerous articles and books I've read note that this crop may take months to germinate unless given a cold treatment. In our experience, *Physalis alkekengi* seeds will germinate readily (80%+) up to 10 months after harvest. They will probably germinate well after 10 months, but this is the oldest seed we've tried.

Seed will germinate in seven to 14 days at 72F (22C) and can be lightly covered or left exposed to light during germination. Seedlings can be transplanted 15 to 25 days after sowing.

GROWING ON
Crop time: From seed the young plants will develop quickly. Green pack sales in a 32-cell pack will be ready 10 to 11 weeks after sowing. We used warm temperatures of 60F to 65F (16C to 18C) after germination for a three- to four-week period to get active growth. During this time, the day temperatures were 5 to 10 degrees (3C to 6C) higher. After the plants established in the 32-cell pack, we moved them to a cold frame and finished off at 50F (10C) nights until sold.

The previous paragraph is based on a winter sowing for spring sales. Plants don't need 50F (10C) to flower the same year in the garden when started from seed. The lower temperatures encourage a compact and uniform plant. Since these plants are sometimes treated as annuals, however, it would be better and cheaper to sow them in the winter for spring sales. If you want to sell plants in 4-inch (10 cm) pots, sow in early January for early May sales.

As for garden performance, green transplants from cell packs planted to the garden in early May will be a foot tall by late June. Flowering will begin by mid-July, and stalks with orange pods ready for cutting will appear by mid to late September.

Commercial propagators offer *P. alkekengi* in either small pots or as liners. Available during the autumn and winter, both pots and liners can be potted up into quarts and gallons, then sold in spring.

VARIETIES

Physalis alkekengi is commonly sold in the United States as Chinese lantern, so look for both names when ordering. It may also be sold under the name of *P. franchetii*, its former name. All three names refer to same plant.

USES

Physalis alkekengi is an easy and excellent plant for use as a cut flower—its pods, once dried, will retain their medium to dark orange color for years. This plant is also recommended for children's gardens since it provides such an unusually shaped, bright pod. The stalks of plump orange lanterns make interesting fall decorations or tall centerpieces.

If harvesting for dried arrangements, be sure to hang several stems in various configurations to avoid a completely upright vase design. When hanging upside down, the stems will dry straight and erect; therefore, bend and tie the stems with twist-ties to help encourage different angles. The lanterns will hang down perpendicularly to the stem instead of against it on erect stems.

IN THE HOME GARDEN

Physalis is an easy-to-care-for plant, although its looks will initially be deceiving during the first few weeks after planting. Once established, plants will literally take off and, if planted in a fertile area, will grow and produce an excellent lantern crop. In the fall, however, warn your customers that the plants may come back with a vengeance the following spring.

We plant *P. alkekengi* in open locations in full sun where the soil is well drained. We're able to keep plants more contained and less invasive by not fertilizing more than once or twice during the summer. Organic and pliable soils offer the plants little resistance and stress, so their underground stems will travel freely. A lack of water may be the only restraining factor.

Plants don't require staking to keep upright unless they've grown quickly due to excess moisture and fertility. Space plants 12 x 12 inches (30 x 30 cm) apart to fill in. As for problems, beware of beetle damage, which can skeletonize the foliage and lanterns.

■ PHYSOSTEGIA VIRGINIANA

FAMILY: Lamiaceae

COMMON NAME(S): Obedient Plant

DESCRIPTION

A perennial native to the eastern United States, *Physostegia virginiana* has 12- to 15-inch (30 to 38 cm) flower spikes with 1-inch (2.5 cm), trumpetlike, rose-pink flowers. A clump-forming perennial, *P. virginiana* has rhizomatous roots that spread 2 to 3 feet (60 to 90 cm) across, with 3- to 4-foot (90 to 120 cm) tall upright stems. The plants branch freely at the base with each stem terminating in a floral spike. See Color Plate 59 for photo of *Physostegia virginiana*.

HARDINESS: Zones 2 to 9.

SEASON OF BLOOM: August and September.

PROPAGATION

Division, cuttings, and seed are three propagation methods, but cuttings and divisions are the most popular. Divisions are taken in the spring, while basal cuttings are clipped as young shoots emerge from the crown. Stem cuttings can be taken as well. Seed can be sown anytime.

GERMINATION OVERVIEW: 18,000 seeds per ounce/630 per gram.
Pretreatments: None are usually needed. If seedlings emerge erratically, the seed can be moist chilled. Read the additional information provided in the front of the book.

Seeds germinate in seven to 14 days at 65F to 70F (18C to 21C) and don't need to be covered. Seedlings can be transplanted 21 to 28 days after sowing.

GROWING ON

Crop time: After germination, plants develop and grow quickly. Midwinter sowings will be salable green in 32-cell packs 10 to 12 weeks after sowing. If sown in early winter, 4-inch (10 cm) pots as well as quart containers will be ready by early to mid-May. Any sowings after the first of the year to late March will flower reliably the same season. Obviously, those sown earlier will have larger rootstocks capable of producing stronger, more free-flowering plants.

Divisions are easy to take on this crop, and the yield off a single crown will be quite good on a 2- or 3-year-old, field-grown stock plant. The plants spread by rhizomes, so allow ample room in your nursery bed since the plants will spread readily under moist, fertile conditions in a sandy loam.

Basal cuttings can be taken from shoots in the spring as they emerge from the

P

crown, or stem cuttings can be taken later as the plants grow. Once rooted, move them into quarts, gallons, or similar containers and grow on for mid or late summer sales. Plants can be overwintered for green sales the next spring and will bloom abundantly the same summer.

Commercial propagators offer *Physostegia* as bare-root transplants, small pots, or plugs/liners. Any of these can be potted up during the winter for spring sales.

VARIETIES

P. virginiana var. *alba* is the same as the variety White Crown. Refer to the description below for details.

P. virginiana var. *rosea* is the same as the variety Rose Crown. Refer to the description below for details. (Rose Crown will not flower reliably the same season from seed.)

Crown series is a seed-propagated line with either white (White Crown, Snow Crown or Crown of Snow) or rose-pink (Rose Crown or Rose Queen) flowers. The plants grow 2 to 3 feet (60 to 90 cm) tall, but the white-flowering selection is slightly less vigorous. Even though these are varieties of the species, they're less invasive and vigorous than the species. Plants can also be propagated by cuttings or divisions.

Summer Snow is a white-flowering variety to 2½ feet (75 cm) tall with white blooms. It's reportedly less invasive than White Crown, but both varieties have displayed equal heights and habits in our gardens. Summer Snow is vegetatively propagated.

Variegata is an upright variety with cream-white blotched leaves. The flowers are pink on 2- to 3-feet (60 to 90 cm) tall plants. When purchasing plants from commercial propagators, be advised that the crop is usually in limited supply—so order early. It is vegetatively propagated variety.

Vivid is a lavender-rose flowering variety on plants reaching 18 to 20 inches (46 to 51 cm) tall in full bloom. Flowering can start as late as September but will continue until cold weather. Vivid is vegetatively propagated.

USES

Physostegia is an excellent crop for commercial landscapes, as a cut flower, and in the home garden. Plants are long lived and winter hardy, which encourages their use as a field cut or landscape plant. To make the most of their late-flowering habit and to show them at their best, mix this perennial with annuals or other perennials that finish flowering by late August. The plants provide upright stems that don't need unsightly staking. They can also be kept even after the weather turns cold. Some selections have russet to crimson foliage in the fall. As cut flowers, the spikes are in demand, and their popularity is increasing in the U.S. flower markets.

IN THE HOME GARDEN

P. virginiana is an extremely easy perennial to grow from year to year in the garden. Plants love full sun and a well-drained location. They don't require staking or autumn mulching. After planting in the garden, avoid ample fertilizer, soils rich in organic materials, and moist locations. Under these conditions plants can become a nuisance, especially the species.

■ PLATYCODON GRANDIFLORUS

FAMILY: Campanulaceae

COMMON NAME(S): Balloon Flower, Chinese Bellflower

DESCRIPTION

Platycodon grandiflorus is a clump-forming perennial noted for its inflated ballonlike flower buds in white, pink, and especially, blue. These buds will eventually split open, expanding to 3 inches (7 cm) when fully developed. The flowers are single, sometimes double, scentless and emerge terminally at the stem ends. Stems are erect and basal branching; they develop out of the center of the plant.

The stems, when broken, will exude a white, milky latex; sear them with a flame before placing in a vase. The roots are fleshy, so dividing the plants requires care. Dwarf varieties grow 10 to 12 inches (25 to 30 cm) while the cut flower strains reach 2 to 3 feet (60 to 90 cm) in height. Plants spread from 10 to 15 inches (25 to 38 cm) across.

HARDINESS: Zones 3 to 8.

SEASON OF BLOOM: Late June to August.

PROPAGATION

Platycodon is typically increased by seed and divisions, though seed is easier. As noted under **Description**, the roots are fleshy, somewhat elongated, and tapered from crown to tip. If these are torn in dividing, disease may enter the wounds and kill the roots before they have a chance to heal. Overwatering accentuates this condition.

GERMINATION OVERVIEW: 32,000 seeds per ounce/1,120 per gram.
Pretreatments: None are needed for germination percentages of at least 70% when sowing seed collected from harvests six to eight months past. Seed more than a year old usually germinates readily, but it depends on storage and the original germination of the batch.

Sow seed in any peat-lite media and germinate at 60F to 70F (18C to 21C). The seed doesn't need covering, but a light covering of vermiculite helps to prevent drying out if there's no mist system. Warmer germination temperatures of 72F (22C) are equally beneficial, but be sure to keep the seeds from dehydrating during germination. Seedlings emerge in seven to 14 days and can be transplanted 19 to 28 days after sowing.

GROWING ON

Crop time: Sown during the winter months, *Platycodon grandiflorus* will flower in summer with only limited problems. Some experts suggest that it takes a year to get flowering plants, but this may be based on older varieties or the species. Granted, first year plants are not as free flowering as two-year-old plants, but the first year bloom count is respectable. Double-flowering selections are not as free to flower.

For 4-inch or cell pack sales in April/May, sow in December or January and grow on at 55F (13C) nights. February sowings can be transplanted to 32-cell packs in March and will be ready for green pack sales in early May or transplanted into 4-inch (10 cm) pots for late May or June sales. For quart or gallon sales, sow the previous year and overwinter dormant. *Platycodon* is a plant that should be sold in 4-inch (10 cm) pots the same year as sown or sown the preceding summer for spring sales in quarts.

Platycodon, like *Hibiscus moscheutos*, will be late to emerge in spring in the garden or a container. If overwintering quart containers for sale in the early spring, be sure to move plants to a warm place. Plants are slow to come up when the soil and weather are cold. Therefore for sales in late April or May, plants will just be starting to emerge.

When planted into the garden during May, the more dwarf varieties will flower by late June and the taller ones in July if winter sown from seed. Plants overwintered in a cold frame will bloom in June.

Commercial propagators offer *Platycodon* as bare-root transplants in small pots or as liners/plugs. Although mostly sold during the autumn and winter, any of these can be potted up into quarts and gallons and sold in spring.

VARIETIES

All the following varieties are available from seed both here and in Europe. The varieties listed are summer flowering (June to August) once established.

P. grandiflorus var. *albus* has single white flowers on plants 18 inches (46 cm) tall in bloom.

Apoyama has violet-blue flowers on plants to 15 inches (38 cm) tall. There are white-flowering forms on the European market.

Fuji series. This is a cut flower variety available in white, pink, or blue. The single flowers are between 2 and 3 inches (5 to 7 cm) wide on 2- to 3-foot (60 to 90 cm) tall plants.

Hakone Blue (also called Double Blue) is a double-flowering blue variety to 20 inches (51 cm) tall that flowers from June to August. Although called "double flowering," the variety is often semidouble since it usually has only two layers of petals.

P. grandiflorus var. *mariesii* (sometimes listed as Mariessii) is a dwarf variety between 15 and 24 inches (38 and 61 cm) tall with blue flowers. It is an excellent variety known for its compact habit and flowering performance.

Sentimental Blue is a dwarf-flowering variety between 10 and 12 inches (25 and 30 cm) tall with 2- to 3-inch-wide (5 to 7 cm) purplish blue flowers. This plant makes excellent 4-inch (10 cm) pots. When started from seed the same year as flowering, usually only one flower opens at a time. Since the variety is so large flowered, however, just one bloom may be preferred. See Color Plate 60 for photo of *Platycodon grandiflorus* Sentimental Blue.

Shell Pink (same as Perlmutterschale) is a light or blush pink variety to 24 inches (61 cm) tall.

Uses

Platycodons are suited to the home garden or landscape, or use as cut flowers. When planted in the home garden, the more dwarf selections work well in decorative containers that can be moved to a cold attached garage close to the house's foundation for overwintering. If you're planting *Platycodon* in the landscape, keep in mind that while it flowers for several months, there's only minimal flowering the first summer after planting until the roots establish themselves. Also, use complementary companion plants of soft pink, yellow, and other colors to accentuate the blue color most platycodens are noted for.

In the home garden

Balloon flowers like a well-drained location in full sun. Never in need of staking, the plants will be long lived once established. Heavy autumn rains followed by a hard freeze can mortally damage the roots, but this is rare.

In the garden, be careful of digging around the vicinity where platycodons were situated last year. They are late sleepers, often not emerging here in our Chicago climate until early June. If you want to divide them, do so in the spring by slicing straight down across the top of the crown.

P

■ Plumbago auriculata

(formerly *P. capensis*)

Family: Plumbaginaceae

Common name(s): Plumbago, Leadwort, Cape Leadwort

Description

Plumbago auriculata is a subshrub with a semitrailing or vining habit that grows to 10 or 12 feet (3 to 3.6 m) in warm winter areas with support. Since the plants grow erect with no basal branching and only limited side branching, an individual stem becomes so elongated that plumbago has a reputation as a trailer. It doesn't wrap itself around upright structures or adhere to them, however. If you want it to grow upright, don't pinch off the crown and tie it to its display structure. If they aren't tied up, the plants will grow up and then fall over. Plants reach a height of 3 to 5 feet (90 to 150 cm). Plants will spread up to 8 feet (2.4 m) in warm winter areas like the Gulf South, central and southern Florida, southern Texas and southern coastal California. In other areas the plants may spread 2 to 4 feet (60 to 120 cm), depending on age.

The blooms have a corolla, which is a 1-inch (2.5 cm) tube between the calyx and petals. The azure-blue flowers are 1¼- to 1½-inches (3 to 3.5 cm) wide. Flowers are clustered together in groups of 10 to 20 and are often barbed with a sticky substance below the blooms. While not as painful as a rose thorn, the barb often surprises the unsuspecting.

HARDINESS: Zones 9 and 10.

Plants are also hardy in selected Zone 8 areas but will die back to the ground during the winter if temperatures repeatedly fall below 28F (-2C). The roots are more cold tolerant than the foliage, however, and shoots will emerge the following spring.

In zones farther north, plants will winter kill and not last from season to season. Plants require greenhouse protection to at least 45F (7C) for overwintering.

SEASON OF BLOOM: Spring to fall.

PROPAGATION

Cuttings and seed are the usual means of propagating *Plumbago auriculata*. Cuttings are taken from nonflowering, semiripe stems during early spring or summer, or as basal cuttings in the early spring. Divisions are more practical for the homeowner than the commercial grower due to plumbago's limited crown size and lack of numerous basal branches. I've propagated this species by both seed and cuttings with relative ease.

GERMINATION OVERVIEW: 2,000 seeds per ounce/70 per gram.

Plumbago is relatively easy to germinate, but final germination percentages will vary with the seed's age. Most companies offer only recently harvested seed since they seldom can keep the seed in inventory due to demand. It's important to note, however, that seed harvested from plants during the last eight months provides the best germination results.

Plumbago germinates in seven to 12 days at 70F to 72F (21C to 22C) and can be lightly covered although it will germinate anyway. Seedlings will emerge and develop irregularly and may occur in flushes over a period of one to two weeks. Yet even with this limitation, a final germination of 60% to 70% is common.

Seedlings can be transplanted 22 to 30 days after sowing.

GROWING ON

Crop time: Seedlings develop nonuniformly and will vary in height the first two months after sowing. Plants produce a single stem without basal or side branching. If transplanted to a 32-cell pack once plants are large enough to handle, the roots will fill out the container in 13 to 15 weeks after sowing here in Chicago. These plants need to be pinched to encourage side branches, but only three or four awkwardly placed branches appear directly below the point where the pinch was taken.

As for crop time, a February 1st sowing will yield flowering plants in 4- or 5-inch (10 or 13 cm) pots by mid-June here in our Chicago location. These plants are strictly greenhouse grown and are not subjected to any temperatures lower than 55F (13C) nights to keep them actively growing.

It may seem odd that I'm dwelling on the merits of a crop that can be difficult and of limited performance here in our location. I have seen beautiful specimens of five to seven plants grown in whiskey barrels in St. Louis (Zone 6), however, and farther south where the plants were grown from stock plants overwintered in the greenhouse or started from seed in autumn. Semiripe and tip cuttings were taken in the late summer and autumn, dipped in rooting hormone, and allowed to root in warm sand. Plants were kept warm during the winter for spring sales.

To be grown in northern locations, the plants obviously require a specialized market since their detailed culture doesn't fit typical perennial plant production.

VARIETIES

Plumbago auriculata is available from numerous U.S. seed companies, but it's rarely listed in catalogs since an ample supply cannot be guaranteed for the market. Contact your favorite seed supplier to verify whether they carry it and when it will be available.

P. auriculata var. *alba* is the white-flowering version of the above with a similar growth habit and performance. It's rarely seen and seldom found commercially from seed companies.

IN THE HOME GARDEN

Plumbago can be grown as a semihardy shrub in the lower United States or as a trailing plant that trellises to arbors, porches, and the like with good results. As for winter tolerance, be sure to read the information under **Hardiness**.

Plumbago is drought and heat tolerant if established before summer's onset. While it will grow in poor soils, it will be slower to start. Plants prefer full sun but will tolerate some afternoon shade as long as it's not heavy. Plant into any well-drained soil for best performance. It has some salt tolerance, but it's not known for handling long-term exposure to salinity.

For best impact, plant plumbagos en masse near freeways or embankments. Since the plants don't flower uniformly, a group planting is the best way to ensure blooming plants all summer long.

In warm winter areas plumbago should be pruned back in autumn or winter. Farther north, they can be cut back to the ground if the leaves and stems blacken after being frosted. Regardless, plumbago will not survive a northern winter.

■■ POLEMONIUM CAERULEUM

FAMILY: Polemoniaceae

COMMON NAME(S): Jacob's Ladder

DESCRIPTION

Predominantly upright in habit, *Polemonium caeruleum* has alternate leaves with 1-inch (2.5 cm) leaflets arranged like ladder rungs—hence the common name, Jacob's Ladder. The single, light or pale blue flowers are about 1 inch (2.5 cm) across on plants from 2 to 3 feet (60 to 90 cm) tall. *Polemonium* spreads from 10 to 15 inches (25 to 38 cm) across.

HARDINESS: Zones 4 to 7.

SEASON OF BLOOM: June and July.

PROPAGATION

Propagate from seed or clump divisions. Successful divisions can be taken in either spring or fall.

GERMINATION OVERVIEW: 32,000 seeds per ounce/1,120 per gram.
Germination is quick and no special pretreatments are necessary. Uncovered seed germinates in five to eight days at 70F (21C). Seedlings can be transplanted 18 to 24 days after sowing.

GROWING ON

Crop time: Plants develop quickly when grown from seed—salable green transplants will have filled out a 32-cell pack in 10 to 12 weeks after sowing when grown at 50F to 55F (10C to 13C) nights. Plants will appear to have rosetted as they grow, and heights of 4 to 7 inches (10 to 18 cm) can be expected by the time they are sold green.

An interesting note: The species is a blue-flowering plant but there are also white selections available from seed. These white varieties, when grown side by side with their blue counterparts, will appear lighter green and often develop more vigorously. In our trial gardens, however, the white-flowering selections tend not to be as long lived.

Since they initially rosette, plants will look better if sold green in a jumbo pack,

18 cells per flat, or 4-inch (10 cm) pots. If quarts or gallons are preferred, the seed can be started in the fall or, better yet, sown during the previous late spring or summer. Move plants up into gallons during the summer and overwinter for sales the following spring.

Commercial propagators offer *P. caeruleum* as a bare-root transplant, in small pots, or as liners/plugs. Available in autumn and winter, any of these can be potted up into quarts and gallons and sold in spring.

VARIETIES

Polemonium caeruleum is available from seed and as started plants from a number of seed companies and nurseries across the United States.

Polemonium caeruleum var. *lacteum* (also listed as album) is the pure white flowering form of the above description.

USES

Its primary value is as a home garden plant, although it does have some commercial value as well. My biggest concern with the plant is that it puts on a strong show of color initially and then slows down. Granted, this is true of many perennials, but in our climate there are other perennials that would be better choices for a strong color show.

IN THE HOME GARDEN

In our climate, plants survive in full sun but may tire in the afternoon heat. The plants prefer a well-drained and lightly shaded location. If given morning sun but shaded in the afternoon, they'll look their best. No staking is necessary, but plants can be trimmed back after flowering for reblooming several weeks later. This is more an aesthetic treatment than a requirement. If not trimmed back, plants will continue to flower sporadically during the summer but often stop blooming by late summer.

■ POLYGONATUM BIFLORUM

FAMILY: Liliaceae

COMMON NAME(S): Small Solomon's Seal

DESCRIPTION

Polygonatum biflorum is an elegant, native woodland plant often seen on embankments and other sloping ground where its unbranched, elongated stems develop from a slow-growing rhizome.

Each horizontal stem arches gracefully, bouncing or nodding on windy days. Leaf pairs develop along the stem, and the flowers hang down from under the leaves. The flowers are small, one-half to 1-inch (1 to 2.5 cm) long, tubular, and either greenish white or greenish yellow in color. They are lightly fragrant. After flowering, the plants develop black berries. Solomon's Seal grows from 2 to 3 feet (60 to 90 cm) tall.

HARDINESS: Zones 4 to 8.

SEASON OF BLOOM: June.

PROPAGATION

Divisions are commonly used to propagate Solomon's Seal, but seed can be sown for the species. The variegated varieties can only be reproduced by divisions since they won't come true from seed. Divisions can be taken either in fall or spring.

GERMINATION OVERVIEW

Seed isn't a common way to propagate *Polygonatum* as a genus. It requires a cold-moist period prior to germinating, best carried out by sowing the seed into a nursery row. Sown in the autumn, seedlings will emerge in late April or May. Additional information is provided in the front of this book.

GROWING ON

Crop time: Divisions can be purchased from commercial propagators in the fall or late winter for potting up into quarts or gallons. Their first season, however, the plants often produce only two to four shoots while growing in the pot. Therefore, many growers prefer to use a smaller container to de-emphasize the lack of foliage.

P. biflorum can be potted up from divisions or transplants planted in the autumn or winter. Plants potted up during the winter or early spring, however, will often produce only one to three erect branches their first season. In appearance, the plants will look sparse and not ready for retail sales. As a guideline, many plants propagated by bare-root transplants supplied commercially will be salable green in six to 10 weeks when cropped for spring sales. *Polygonatum* often develops small white rootlets from the main rhizome during this time. If planted into the garden, the foliage often persists for a month or two and then dies back to the ground; the roots continue to develop at the expense of flowers. If potting up divisions during the winter or early spring, grow on at 55F to 60F (13C to 15C) in a protected cold frame or greenhouse, avoiding lower night temperatures until the roots have established and the top growth has started. The top growth may be less than what your customers expect. One final note—winter-potted bare-root transplants may fail to develop a vegetative shoot, and yet the rhizome is intact without any sign of disease. If exposed to a period of cold, the shoots will develop. If these pots of undeveloped plants were planted to the garden in May, the shoots would develop the following May.

VARIETIES

P. biflorum is readily found at perennial plant nurseries across the country. There are no named varieties that I'm aware of.

RELATED MATERIAL

P. commutatum (also called *P. canaliculatum* and *P. giganteum*) is a larger version of *P. biflorum* growing from 3 to 4 feet (90 to 120 cm) tall. It's commonly called Great Solomon's Seal due to its vigor, but it can be cropped like *P. biflorum*. There's some confusion as to the species, however; some taxonomists say it's actually a type of *P. biflorum*.

P. odoratum Variegatum (also listed as *P. odoratum* var. *thunbergii Variegatum*), commonly called Variegated Solomon's Seal, has medium green, variegated leaves with a cream-white ribbon or band around the leaf's outer edge. This combination helps brighten up the planting area more than the previous selections, especially in heavier shade locations. The fragrant, bell-shaped flowers are smaller than the selections listed above and are white. Plants grow from 18 to 24 inches (46 to 61 cm) tall. This variety is propagated by division.

The previous two species are hardy from Zones 4 to 8 and can be propagated and grown on as noted under *P. biflorum*.

USES

Solomon's Seal is a landscape or home garden plant with excellent form and grace where a woodland planting is preferred. Combine with hosta, ferns, and other shade-loving plants for best effect. It isn't invasive but is easily divided if it spreads too much, although from an initial planting this will require many years.

IN THE HOME GARDEN

Since stems emerge singly and are unbranched, the plants often don't look like much when purchased in a 1- or 2-gallon pot in the spring. There's usually only one to three actively growing stems within the pot. Since *P. biflorum* will require a year to establish, in which the rhizome branches and fills in, you should plant three or more pots at the same time to encourage faster coverage of the area where they're planted. Plants prefer a shaded location and have readily died in our Chicago gardens in full sun or in the path of direct afternoon sun.

Instead, plant on a sloping hill or flat ground where the plants are protected from all but morning sun. *P. biflorum* prefers a moist but well-drained location—it will not do well in extended hot and dry periods. Plants don't need mulching, but I suggest you use a layer of leaves between the plants. This keeps the soil cool and moist but isn't thick enough to keep new shoots from emerging and developing. A light mulch also helps control weed seeds, but growing in the shade will slow the weed seedlings down.

■ POTENTILLA NEPALENSIS

FAMILY: Rosaceae

COMMON NAME(S): Potentilla, Cinquefoil

DESCRIPTION

Potentilla foliage is strawberry-like and grows to 2 feet (60 cm) tall in flower. The stems radiate out of the crown, spreading 2 to 3 feet (60 to 90 cm) across the plant canopy once established. The 1-inch (2.5 cm) flowers are single and two-toned, with a ruby-red center and a dark coral or salmon outer margin on each bloom. Each bloom's center has purple-to-black reproductive parts, giving the flowers an interesting and beautiful contrast.

HARDINESS: Zones 5 to 7.

These plants are very hardy here in our Chicago latitude when planted in a well-drained location.

SEASON OF BLOOM: June and July.

PROPAGATION

Seed is the usual way to propagate the species, while stem tip cuttings are more common for cultivars. Divisions can be taken in the spring as well. Growers usually purchase divisions rather than do their own. Lifting and dividing plants is more practical for the home gardener when a small number of transplants are desired.

GERMINATION OVERVIEW: 75,000 seeds per ounce/2,625 per gram.

Potentilla sown in winter or early spring from seed harvested the previous fall will germinate readily with good results. Seed germinates in five to nine days when sown to any peat-lite media; no covering is necessary, although a thin layer of coarse vermiculite has been beneficial when overhead mist can't be provided. Seedlings can be transplanted 18 to 23 days after sowing.

GROWING ON

Crop time: From seed, plants grow relatively fast with few problems. Allow 10 to 11 weeks for green, salable transplants in 32-cell trays. Plants will be less than 2 inches (5 cm) tall at this time since they rosette in the cell pack, so you may want to pot up to larger containers for sales later.

If 4-inch (10 cm) pot sales are preferred, allow 13 to 15 weeks for salable plants. Again, these will only rosette in the pot and garden the first year if sown during winter or spring. For flowering plants the first year, sow the previous spring for transplanting into gallons (quarts are also possible, but a gallon offers a larger, more free-flowering plant) during late summer. Overwinter the pots for spring sales.

Commercial propagators sell potentilla as bare-root transplants, small pots, or liners/plugs in autumn and winter. Any of these can be potted up into quarts and gallons and sold in spring.

In all the culture above, the seedlings are transplanted under warm conditions of 65F to 70F (18C to 21C) days and 60F to 65F (15C to 18C) nights. The transplants are then moved to a cold frame with 50F to 55F (10C to 13C) nights when started as a winter or spring crop. If sown during the late spring or summer, the seedlings are protected from hot, direct sun until established in the container.

VARIETIES

Miss Willmott is the most common variety on the market and is relatively easy to find from U.S. seed companies.

IN THE HOME GARDEN

In the garden, potentilla provides an unusual leaf shape and performance similar to strawberries. Plants are best in full-sun locations with a nonsoggy soil. As for longevity, some authors have stated that the plants are short lived, growing for two to four years at best before dying out. In our gardens outside Chicago, however, the plants have been long lived and dependably hardy. Our primary problem is deer, which eat the tender new shoots in the spring.

■■ PULMONARIA SACCHARATA

FAMILY: Boraginaceae

COMMON NAME(S): Bethlehem Sage

DESCRIPTION

Many of the cultivated varieties of *Pulmonaria saccharata* are known for their elongated, silvery, white-spotted leaves. In some locations the foliage of selected varieties will be evergreen depending on the weather's severity. The scentless flowers are single, trumpet-shaped and can change from rose-pink to blue as they age, although some can be pure white or pink in color. Flowers are about one-half-inch wide and from one-half to 1 inch (1 to 2.5 cm) long and often appear before the foliage. They're held aloft in clusters on 10- to 15-inch (25 to 38 cm) stems. Established plants spread from 12 to 15 inches (30 to 38 cm) in low-growing clumps. *Pulmonaria* grows from rhizomes.

HARDINESS: Zones 3 to 8.

SEASON OF BLOOM: April and May.

PROPAGATION

Division and tissue culture are the primary propagation methods. Bare-root transplants can be purchased from commercial propagators and potted up for salable plants in spring. If you prefer to dig your own divisions, take them in spring after flowering or in the fall. Larger, more established clumps that are two to four years old can be easily divided.

Tissue culture propagation is beyond the scope of this book. However, you will be able to find tissue-cultured plants from a number of sources. Commercial propagators offer many varieties that have been propagated in the lab (often their own). These are sold in small pots that can be retailed or wholesaled as is or transplanted into larger containers for spring sales.

Pulmonaria species can be propagated from seed, but be warned: Pulmonarias readily hybridize, yielding plants different from their parents. If you're growing a number of selections and you collect the seed from one, the resulting plantlets will give you various leaf spotting, flower colors, forms, and possibly habit.

GERMINATION OVERVIEW

Don't spend a lot of time trying to find U.S. companies that carry seed. Seed is sown primarily to select new cultivars which will be vegetatively propagated if introduced into the commercial trade.

If seed is your preference, contact companies or seed exchanges specializing in Alpine or rock garden plants, although you'll probably have to collect your own.

GROWING ON

Crop time: You can purchase *Pulmonaria* roots during the fall and winter for potting up into gallons. Roots potted up in mid-March, moved to a cold frame, and grown on at 45F to 50F (7C to 10C) nights will often flower first and then develop foliage. At this point, the plants appear weak and uneven in growth. Instead, once plants are potted, try growing them warmer to 55F (13C) nights, especially if potting up in February or earlier. Plants will still flower, but the warmer temperatures will encourage root set and a better foliage canopy. Notice that those plants that develop a flowering stalk first will be slow in developing a basal rosette of leaves, while those that are flowerless will be bushier, healthier, and earlier to finish. Plants that flower first can take up to two weeks longer to finish off than those that don't. Warmer night temperatures, initially, will help to produce a more uniform crop. Once plants are rooted within the pot, the night temperatures can be dropped to 50F (10C) to harden off the crop.

In general, roots potted up in mid-March and grown on at 55F (13C) will produce a salable, leafed-out plant in a gallon pot in eight to 10 weeks. Add one to two weeks more for well-rooted and leafed-out crops.

VARIETIES

Of the following, only *P. saccharata* var. *alba* can be propagated from seed. While the other cultivars can produce seeds, they are the result of free hybridizing between varieties. Therefore, the resulting seedlings will produce nonclonal plantlets (again, the only exception is *P. saccharata* var. *alba*).

One other note: Unless stated otherwise, all of the following have flowers that color up pink as they open, then change to blue.

P. saccharata var. *alba* is a pure white flowering variety that doesn't shade or fade to blue or any other color. Plants grow from 12 to 15 inches (30 to 38 cm) tall in flower. The leaves are lightly mottled with silver; the dark green foliage gives an excellent contrast to the pure white flowers. Seed is not easily found.

Janet Fisk is well known for its white mottled or marbled foliage with pink flowers that turn blue as they age. The variety grows 10 to 12 inches (25 to 30 cm) tall.

Margery Fish is more popular in Europe at the time of this writing but is becoming better known in the United States. It is considered to be a cultivar of *P. villarsae* by some authorities, although the Royal Horticultural Society's *Dictionary of Gardening* places the variety under *P. saccharata*. Margery Fish is a pink-flowering cultivar with broad, irregular blotches of silver-gray foliage on plants to 12 inches (30 cm) tall in bloom. Sometimes the mottling almost reaches from margin to margin on a leaf.

Mrs. Moon is a distinctive variety with numerous silver spots mottling the leaf surface. It reaches 10 to 12 inches (25 to 30 cm) tall. It is very popular selection here in the United States and Canada.

Pink Dawn has coral-pink blossoms that can become rose pink without the blue shading noted in other cultivars. The foliage is midgreen in color, lacking any mottling. It grows 10 to 12 inches (25 to 30 cm) tall.

Roy Davidson has longer, narrower leaves than the other cultivars listed here. Flowers turn from pink to blue. It is eight to 10 inches (20 to 25 cm) tall.

Sissinghurst White is usually listed as a selection of *P. saccharata,* although some authors list it as one of *P. officinalis*. Unlike the other cultivars described here, it has white flowers on plants from 9 to 10 inches (23 to 25 cm) tall in bloom.

RELATED MATERIAL

In the commercial trade, *P. saccharata* cultivars are the most easily found. While not uncommon, the following species are more difficult to find.

P. angustifolia differs from many other horticultural species by having dark green leaves that are unspotted. The plants look similar to cultivars listed under *P. saccharata* in all other respects including flower color. *P. angustifolia* flowers a rose pink that turns medium blue. It doesn't have the contrast other selections possess, but it is an otherwise excellent species. *P. angustifolia* isn't evergreen, even where *P. saccharata* is.

Horticulturists differ in their opinion of the various *P. angustifolia* cultivars. Azurea, Munstead, and Mawson's are considered by some to be very similar in habit, so not all are worth offering. Some consider Mawson a different species

(*P. officinalis*) based on foliage characteristics. In the United States the three are seldom found at the same wholesale house, but any one will suit your needs for the first time.

P. longifolia has vivid blue flowers on plants 8 to 10 inches (20 to 25 cm) tall. The narrow leaves are spotted with silvery gray. It's not as common as the previous two species but worthwhile in its own right. Depending on the season, it can flower later than the other species listed here. Bertram Anderson is a little easier to find and better known than the other cultivars in this group. The flowers are a violet blue and bloom a little later than the species.

P. rubra can be the earliest *Pulmonaria* species to flower, depending on your climate. The species has evergreen foliage, although this is more common in less severe winter locations than our Chicago gardens. The plants flower a coral red on light green leaves. The plants will grow to about 1 foot (30 cm) tall when in flower. The most commonly found selection, Redstart, has a deeper flower color than the species, on plants from 12 to 14 inches (30 to 35 cm) tall in bloom.

All the species provided under **Related material** can be propagated by division. Follow the same cropping as noted under *P. saccharata*. If preferred, the species can be propagated from seed, although seed isn't commonly sold in the United States—it's more readily found in Europe.

IN THE HOME GARDEN

Pulmonarias prefer a shaded location away from direct sun (unless it's morning light) to avoid a wilted and slow-growing performance. Plant in a moist, but not wet, area in a cool soil. It is excellent around the base of shrubs, in shade gardens with hostas, or in woodland settings where plants are protected by the tree canopy above them. Plants may reseed, although the plantlets seldom become invasive in the majority of our North American gardens. In locations with weather similar to Britain, reseeding may be more of a problem.

In severe winter areas, most cultivars will not be evergreen but will go almost or completely dormant from December to March. Plants will return and grow normally, so little concern should be given to this dieback. In the spring, many of the cultivars listed here will flower first and then develop their leaf canopy. Don't be alarmed. In some cases, leaves will start to develop, but the flower stalk will push through and start blooming with only a few leaves. The flowers often develop at the expense of the foliage. Once flowering has begun, the crown of foliage will fully develop and persist all summer long. Pulmonarias don't require staking or frequent watering, although they enjoy watering during extended periods of dry weather.

Divide as needed or every three or four years. A large clump divided in two parts will seldom cause you any problems. If you prefer to take smaller sections with one or two active growing points, be prepared to watch over the plants during the first three weeks after dividing and replanting. Mulch the area and protect from direct sunlight for the first week. Regardless, plants will continue to wilt. If taken before flowering, the small sections will try to bud up, so remove the buds to encourage root development. Water as necessary.

▄▄ PULSATILLA VULGARIS
(formerly *Anemone pulsatilla*)

Be prepared to find this variety in the trade under both names. This is due to discrepancies among various perennial manuals. Some have been updated recently while others list *Pulsatilla vulgaris* under the old name.

FAMILY: Ranunculaceae

COMMON NAME(S): Pasque Flower

Pasque flower is the common name of two related plants: *P. vulgaris* and *Anemone patens* (*Pulsatilla patens*). This latter variety is listed below under **Related material**.

DESCRIPTION

A spring-flowering perennial less than a foot tall, *P. vulgaris* has striking, cup-shaped blooms slightly smaller than 3 inches (7 cm) across. Flowers are purple, but they vary in shade. The flowers develop and bloom in spring before the foliage has fully emerged. Blooms open in the morning and close at night; they're often short lived, lasting only several days to less than a week. The foliage is soft and fernlike in its appearance. As the flowers fade, the seed pods develop into upright, off-white "mops" with numerous filaments projecting out from the seedhead. See Color Plate 61 for photo of *Pulsatilla vulgaris*.

HARDINESS: Zones 5 to 8.

SEASON OF BLOOM: April and May.

P

PROPAGATION

Seed is the common form of propagation on this variety, but divisions are also possible. Divisions normally aren't used by commercial growers, however, because it takes three to five years to produce a plant big enough to divide. Also the fragile roots often die from bruising. If you want the challenge, however, divisions can be taken in either spring or fall.

Bare-root transplants are available from commercial propagators during autumn and winter.

GERMINATION OVERVIEW

Pretreatments: Like many *Ranunculaceae* family members, *Pulsatilla* can be difficult to grow from seed if fresh seed isn't used. Test a 100-seed sample prior to sowing the rest to determine the germination rate. If germination is low or the sample fails to germinate, follow the procedures in the **Propagation** chapter for moist chilling.

Germination temperatures of 68F to 70F (20C to 21C) are perfect for starting *Pulsatilla*. Many experts suggest slightly lower temperatures, but don't go below 62F (17C). Since the seed shouldn't be covered, don't allow temperatures to rise above 72F (22C). Higher temperatures may cause the seed to dry out in the seed tray and fail to germinate. Fall-harvested seed sown shortly after gathering will germinate in 10 to 25 days and may take seven to eight weeks after sowing before plants are transplantable to cell packs. Purchased seed may take longer or require pretreating before germination levels are acceptable.

GROWING ON

Crop time: *Pulsatilla* from seed is slow to develop into salable plants. Seed sown in February and transplanted to cell packs in April won't be salable green until late June or July; 4-inch (10 cm) pots or quarts require additional time. Therefore, sow in fall for green sales in late spring or summer and sow again in early spring for quart sales the following year.

Commercial propagators offer *P. vulgaris* as a liner or plug for autumn or winter shipment from a 50 to 72 tray, plant one plug to a quart pot and grow on at 55F (13C) nights for spring sales.

Pulsatilla isn't known for producing massive plants worthy of the time spent taking divisions. Instead, plants are often dug and repotted as is—not divided. To this end, bare root transplants purchased from commercial propagators during the fall and winter can be potted one per 1- to 3-quart container and grown on at 50F to 55F (10C to 13C) for spring sales.

VARIETIES

P. vulgaris is available in the United States as seed, bare-root transplants, small potted plants, or plugs or liners. You should have little difficulty in finding this crop.

P. vulgaris var. *alba* is a white-flowering selection up to 8 inches (20 cm) tall.

P. vulgaris var. *rubra* is a rich rose-wine to magenta variety growing to 8 inches (20 cm) tall.

RELATED MATERIAL

Anemone patens (*Pulsatilla patens*). This plant is also commonly called the Pasque flower. Depending on your catalog or reference, you'll find that both these names are used in the U.S. trade depending on propagators' sources for naming. *Pulsatilla* differs from *Anemone* in the long filamentous styles atop the fruit. In many other visual respects the plants are similar.

Anemone patens is a North American native, 12 or 15 inches (30 to 38 cm) tall, with deeply divided and narrow leaves. Flowers are a purplish blue, measuring no more than 2 inches (5 cm) across. The flowers bloom and die before the foliage develops. Plants flower in April and May. Propagate and grow as you would *Pulsatilla*. Seed and transplants are available in this country from limited sources.

IN THE HOME GARDEN

This is an excellent, hardy perennial providing both interesting foliage and unusual flowers. Choose a well-drained location away from intense wind and afternoon sun, especially in hot and humid summer areas. Plants can tolerate sun but perform better when shaded during the afternoon. Plants seldom rebloom after flowering, but their cut foliage and dwarf habit are a fine addition to any perennial border or rock garden.

P

R

▄ RUDBECKIA FULGIDA

FAMILY: Asteraceae

COMMON NAME(S): Perennial Black-Eyed Susan, Goldsturm

DESCRIPTION

Rudbeckia fulgida is a premier, late-summer-flowering perennial noted for its single, 3-inch (7 cm), scentless, golden yellow flowers highlighted with a dark, contrasting center. Plants grow upright, each stem terminating in a flower. The foliage is dark green and uniform and reaches 2½ to 3½ feet (75 to 105 cm) tall. *R. fulgida* spreads 15 to 18 inches (38 to 46 cm) across.

HARDINESS: Zones 3 to 9.

SEASON OF BLOOM: July to September.

PROPAGATION

Goldsturm is the best-known variety on the market. How to propagate *R. fulgida* to maintain uniformity is widely debated. True-to-name plants are best propagated vegetatively. Goldsturm, however, is one of the few varieties for which seed is not only available, but yields plants similar to those propagated by cuttings or divisions.

Some growers have noted that seed-propagated plants have duller colored, smaller flowers than those propagated vegetatively.

Make divisions in spring or autumn and take cuttings in the spring.

GERMINATION OVERVIEW: 25,000 seeds per ounce/875 per gram.

Pretreatments: *Rudbeckia fulgida* is more difficult to germinate than any of the *R. hirta* varieties (discussed in this book as a separate crop) and can yield poor results. New research, however, has focused on the crop's temperature needs.

Most germination guides indicate that *R. fulgida* will germinate best once the seed is moist chilled at 40F to 45F (5C to 7C) for two to four weeks. Once exposed to these temperatures, the seed will germinate in 14 to 20 days at 72F (22C). However, research work done at Ohio State University under the direction of Dr. Steven Still noted that the germination percentage increased when the soil temperature was raised instead of lowered. In general, germination at 72F (22C) was only 2 to 27% after 14 days. With seed germinated between 82F and 88F (28C to 31C), yields ranged from 50 to 90% depending on the seed lot used.

In the second edition of the *Ball Culture Guide*, I wrote: "To improve germination for the Fulgidas, increase germination temperatures to 75F or 80F (24C to 27C) for five to six days." This will help to increase the germination rates but not as quickly nor with the percentage results of Ohio State's findings.

Seed doesn't need to be covered to germinate. Transplanting can be done 28 to 38 days after sowing.

GROWING ON

Crop time: Sowings made any time after the first of the year will not flower the same year from seed. *R. fulgida* requires a cold period (winter) before it will flower. Some spotted color in first-year crops has been reported, but it isn't uniform or of much value. Seed is often sown in summer for plants to be to be potted up during late summer and overwintered in the cold frame. These plants can be sold in quart or larger containers in the spring. For green pack sales, allow 11 to 15 weeks at 50F to 55F (10C to 13C) nights.

Commercial propagators offer *R. fulgida* Goldsturm as a bare-root transplant, in small pots, or as liners/plugs. Primarily available during autumn and winter, any of these can be potted up into quarts and gallons and sold in spring.

VARIETIES

Goldsturm is a superb variety, flowering midsummer to September. Compter's Gold is the same seed as Goldsturm, but concern that the seed-propagated strain wouldn't be as uniform prompted the name change. Goldstrum is a misspelled form, and Golden Storm is the English translation of Goldsturm.

RELATED MATERIAL

Rudbeckia fulgida var. *speciosa* (*R. speciosa, R. newmanii*) is a taller, smaller-flowered plant than Goldsturm, growing 30 to 40 inches (76 to 102 cm) tall. It's equally hardy and dependable, with an identical crop time from seed. This variety will flower freely the first year from seed sown during winter, however.

USES

Once established, *R. fulgida* is a dependable and hardy plant whether it's used in the home garden or commercial landscape. It's especially recommended for those sites needing midsummer color without major maintenance. In the commercial landscape, *R. fulgida* can be staggered in rows 12 to 15 inches (30 to 38 cm) apart.

IN THE HOME LANDSCAPE

Plant in a full-sun location with adequate drainage. *R. fulgida* doesn't require either staking to remain upright or mulching to maintain its hardiness. Once planted and established in the garden, Goldsturm will be a long-lived, reliable performer. Plants don't need regular division, nor do they die out in the center like some perennials. Plants can be left in the same spot for years without spreading beyond the measurements described above. At the risk of sounding trite, I'd recommend this plant as the strong, silent type that won't encroach upon its neighbors.

REFERENCES

[1] Fay, A.M., S.M. Still, and M.A. Bennett. 1993. Optimum germination temperature of *Rudbeckia fulgida*. *HortTechnology*. Oct./Dec.

■ RUDBECKIA HIRTA

(also labeled ***Rudbeckia hirta* var. *pulcherrima***)

FAMILY: Asteraceae

COMMON NAME(S): Gloriosa Daisy, Black-Eyed Susan

DESCRIPTION

Rudbeckia hirta is a native plant growing 2½ to 3 feet (75 to 90 cm) tall in flower. While the wild forms are widely seen growing across the great plains eastward, it's the seed strains that are what's commonly grown in the garden today (see **Varieties**). Plants range in height from 10 to 40 inches (25 to 102 cm) tall and spread 10 to 36 inches (25 to 91 cm) across. The single and semidouble flowers are shades of yellow or orange and measure 3 to 5 inches (7 to 13 cm) across depending on the variety. Notorious for their sensitivity to powdery mildew, gloriosa daisies often succumb to the disease, and many die by summer's end.

HARDINESS

The species is hardy to Zone 4, but the seed strains, especially any of the dwarf varieties, are best treated as short-lived perennials or annuals. The crop can reseed, however.

SEASON OF BLOOM: June to frost.

PROPAGATION: *R. hirta* is propagated by seed.

GERMINATION OVERVIEW

27 to 80,000 seeds per ounce (0.9 to 2,800 per gram) depending on the variety.

Rudbeckia hirta germinates readily—no pretreatments will be necessary to get a 70% plus seedling stand. Seeds germinate in five to 10 days at 70F (21C) without covering. Seedlings can be transplanted in 20 to 28 days after sowing.

GROWING ON

January sowings of any of the dwarf pot plant varieties (Marmalade, Goldilocks, Becky Mix or Toto) will flower in May in a 4-inch (10 cm) or quart container. Goldilocks flowers approximately 10 days earlier than Marmalade, although both have similar habits and performance. The remaining two varieties haven't been trialed yet since they've only recently entered the market. Taller varieties like Rustic Mixture, Double Gold, Indian Summer, and Single Mix should be sold as either green packs or 6-inch (15 cm) pots. Green packs are salable in eight to 10 weeks when grown at 55F to 58F (13C to 15C) nights. Allow 14 to 16 weeks at the same temperatures for 6-inch (15 cm) pots. Plants flower in July from both winter and spring sowings.

VARIETIES

All the following are **seed propagated**. In general, the taller varieties are hardier than shorter selections—through at least one winter. The taller varieties are also not as sensitive to powdery mildew as the dwarf pot plant and border varieties.

Becky Mix is a simple mix with two predominant flower colors—orange and orange red. Occasionally a golden yellow color pops up. Becky is a pot plant variety growing only 10 inches (25 cm) tall in the pot 12 to 14 inches (30 to 35 cm) tall in the garden. Flowers are single, measuring 2½ to 3½ inches (6 to 8 cm) across.

Double Gold is 24 to 29 inches (61 to 74 cm) tall with double, golden orange, 3½-inch (19 cm) flowers with a large black center. This variety blooms later; spring sowings seldom flower until August.

Goldilocks is an intermediate-flowering variety similar to Marmalade. It tends to flower seven to 10 days earlier than Marmalade, blossoming in June from an early April sowing. Plants will be 10 inches (25 cm) tall in the pot—especially if a growth retardant is used—but 15 to 18 inches (38 to 46 cm) tall in the garden. Flowers are golden orange with dark centers. Blooms are semidouble to double.

Indian Summer is an All-America Selections Award winner with huge, 5- to 9-inch (13 to 23 cm), single to semidouble, golden orange flowers on plants 30 to 36 inches (76 to 91 cm) across.

Irish Eyes has 3½-inch (8 cm), single, golden yellow flowers with green centers on plants from 3 to 3½ feet (90 to 105 cm) tall.

Marmalade is an intermediate variety, excellent for pot sales in May from a January sowing. Flowers are golden orange, single to semidouble, and measure up to 3 inches across. Like Goldilocks, Marmalade will be 10 inches (25 cm) tall in the pot—especially if a growth retardant is used—but 18 to 20 inches (46 to 51 cm) tall in the garden. This variety is very sensitive to powdery mildew. Plants often succumb to the disease before late August.

Rustic Mixture is primarily made up of two colors: light orange and an orange-red

R

bicolor. Flowers are 3 to 4½ inches (7 to 11 cm) across on plants from 15 to 20 inches (38 to 51 cm) tall.

Single Mix. As the name implies, the flowers are mostly single, but some semidouble blooms do occur. Flower colors include golden yellow, deep mahogany or crimson, and golden yellow with a mahogany ring around the center. Flowers range 4½ to 5 inches (11 to 13 cm) across. Plants can grow 27 to 31 inches (68 to 79 cm) tall.

Toto is the most dwarf, smallest flowering variety available at the time of this writing. This pot plant variety has single, 2- to 3-inch (5 to 7 cm), golden yellow flowers on plants 8 to 10 inches (20 to 25 cm) tall in the pot; 12 inches (30 cm) tall at most in the garden.

IN THE HOME GARDEN

Rudbeckia hirta is described here as an annual or short-lived perennial that will last, on the average, through only one winter. This is especially true of the taller varieties; dwarf and intermediate varieties seldom make it through our hot and humid summers, let alone our winters.

Rudbeckia hirta performs best in a full-sun, open location where its foliage is allowed to dry quickly from morning dew or a summer storm. Extended periods of high heat and humidity encourage severe cases of transparent white powdery mildew. Under prolonged exposure, the plants usually die before summer ends.

The more dwarf varieties perform best as a pot plants, edgings, or borders. Intermediate varieties can be grouped in "threes" or "fours" toward the middle of the garden for best visual effect. The tall varieties, however, are the real show. The blossoms are usually large, well formed, and appear from July to frost, depending on when sown. These taller types don't usually require staking, but if well fed and watered, the plants can become weak stemmed.

In the garden, space dwarf and intermediate varieties 10 to 12 inches (25 to 30 cm) apart; space taller selections 12 to 15 inches (30 to 38 cm) apart.

S

▬ SAGINA SUBULATA
(syn. *Spergula pilifera*)

FAMILY: Caryophyllaceae

COMMON NAME(S): Irish Moss, Corsican Pearlwort

DESCRIPTION

Low growing and mosslike, *Sagina subulata* develops in evergreen tufts that are 2 to 4 inches (5 to 7 cm) tall. The leaves are small, only one-quarter-inch (6 mm) long and close to the crown. The single white flowers are one-half-inch (1 cm) wide, borne aloft on 1-inch (2.5 cm) or slightly longer stalks. See Color Plate 62 for photo of *Sagina subulata*.

HARDINESS: Zones 4 to 7.

It's the summer heat—not the winter—that limits *Sagina subulata's* potential. High heat and humidity will kill this plant. Near Chicago we seldom have a crop that survives from one season to the next, so we treat the plants as short-lived perennials. Read additional comments under **In the home garden**.

SEASON OF BLOOM: June and July.

PROPAGATION

Sagina is usually grown from seed, but home gardeners can divide the developing mat in either spring or fall.

GERMINATION OVERVIEW: 1,000,000 seeds per ounce/35,000 per gram.

Sagina germinates in five to eight days at 70F (21C), and seed doesn't need to be covered. Seedlings can be transplanted 18 to 24 days after sowing.

GROWING ON

Crop time: From seed, sow several seeds to a plug tray (290 or larger), and then transplant directly to the final 4-inch (10 cm) or quart pot. Plants grow and spread quickly. When grown in a 32-cell pack, the plants can become matted together, requiring a knife to separate them for sales or transplanting.

S

If cell packs are required, allow 10 to 12 weeks when grown on at 55F to 60F (13C to 15C) nights; 4-inch (10 cm) pots require 13 to 15 weeks. As plants become established in packs or other containers, transfer them to a cold frame and finish off at 50F (10C) to keep the plants short. Sowings made in February will produce plants that start to flower in March and April before they increase their size in any container. The plants will continue to flower as long as temperatures are cool.

Commercial propagators offer *Sagina subulata* in small pots or, less frequently, as liners/plugs. From autumn and winter shipments, either size can be potted up into quarts and gallons and sold in spring.

VARIETIES

Sagina subulata is available in the United States from both seed and nursery companies.

RELATED MATERIAL

Sagina subulata Aurea is a golden-yellow leaved form of the above, often called Scotch moss. Plants are 2 inches (5 cm) tall, with flowers in June and July. It is not as readily available as *S. subulata* nor as hardy.

USES

Plants perform their best when grown in the small crevices of a rock wall or between stepping stones. They have limited value in commercial landscapes, particularly in locations viewed from a distance. *Sagina* is an "up close and personal" plant—not an impact landscape plant in the Midwest. Instead, it is recommended for herb gardens and any cool, moist, but well-drained location where it can spread.

IN THE HOME GARDEN

Sagina needs space to grow. Don't plant it near any slow or low growing perennials where it may be smothered. Plants are often short lived here in Chicago, but they endure longest in morning sun locations with high shade, that is, not heavily covered by trees. Dense shade can cause them to die out. The plants are not long-term performers for us, regardless.

■ SALVIA × SUPERBA

(*S. nemorosa, S. sylvestris* **var.** *superba*)

FAMILY: Lamiaceae

COMMON NAME(S)

No common names are usually used. It is sometimes called Perennial Salvia.

DESCRIPTION

Bushy growth, excellent basal branching, and a superb garden performance highlight this tried-and-true perennial. Plants grow from 15 inches to over 2 feet (38 to 60 cm) tall and spread from 15 to 18 inches (38 to 46 cm) across depending on the cultivar. The flowers have violet-blue, sometimes rose, spikes from 6 to 10 inches (15 to 25 cm) long. Tubular in shape, they're small, single, and one-eighth to one-quarter inch (3 to 6 mm) across. As a class, salvias are easy to propagate and grow. They provide reliable performance year after year.

HARDINESS: Zones 4 to 8.

SEASON OF BLOOM: May and June.
If trimmed back after flowering, plants will flower again in late July or August.

PROPAGATION

This perennial can be seed propagated, but the clones are propagated by cuttings or divisions (see **Varieties**). The easiest method is to take cuttings in spring before flowering or in the summer after flowering is over. This latter method is difficult since you have to trim the foliage back on the plant after flowering and wait for growth to begin again. Plants can be divided in spring or autumn.

GERMINATION OVERVIEW: 25,000 seeds per ounce/875 per gram.
Salvia from seed doesn't require any pretreatments and readily germinates in four to eight days at 72F (22C). Seed will germinate uncovered. Seedlings can be transplanted 15 to 22 days after sowing.

GROWING ON

Crop time: From seed, plants grow quickly; green cell packs are ready to sell nine to 11 weeks after sowing when finished off at 50F to 55F (10C to 13C) nights. Plants form rosettes and will only measure about 1 inch (2.5 cm) tall at this point. If hardening the plants off in a cold frame, you may notice the leaves turning purple as temperatures drop. This is a cold temperature response that fades as plants establish themselves in the garden.

February sowings, transplanted to cell packs or 4-inch (10 cm) pots and then sold in May, will flower reliably in the summer without a cold treatment. As for greenhouse or cold frame temperatures, avoid night temperatures of 60F (15C) and higher during active growth to keep the plants more compact. Instead, after transplanting, keep the plants at 50F to 55F (10C to 13C) temperatures during the night and only 10F to 15F (5C to 9C higher) higher during the day to keep plant height controlled.

You can take cuttings in April and May prior to the plants budding up and flowering. Three-inch-long (7 cm long) vegetative shoots will root easily and be ready to pot up after the spring rush is over. Transplant into quart or gallon containers and grow on for late summer sales or overwinter for next spring sales.

Spring divisions are easy: Plants can be dug, divided, and potted during April and May. These can be allowed to acclimate to the pot or sold immediately—salvias will tolerate this type of propagation with ease. Be sure you know what your customers

S

prefer, however. A plant dug the day before it is sold will have very few roots and may not meet the buyer's expectations.

Purchased roots potted one root to a gallon container in March, moved to a cold frame and grown on at 50F to 55F (10 C to 13C) nights, will be salable green in seven to nine weeks. If potting in February, add one to two weeks. In Chicago, roots potted up in mid-March produced ready-to-sell plants in either early or mid-May. If you prefer flowering plants, the variety East Friesland flowered for us in a 1-gallon pot by the first of June, using the same conditions.

VARIETIES

Salvia × superba from seed is a variable crop. Depending on your seed source and whether the production company was scrupulous about keeping fields clean of rogues and interspecific crosses, plants may or may not be uniform. Some growers select better performing strains of the seed selections and then vegetatively propagate the crop in the future. Seed, under names like Blue Queen, Stratford Blue, and Blue Princess, is available on the market. Blue Queen and Stratford Blue are the same plant, between 15 and 20 inches (38 to 51 cm) tall with violet-blue spikes. Both flower uniformly, and extra care has been taken to select as uniform a growth habit as possible.

Rose Queen is also a seed-propagated variety, although it's often taller than Blue Queen, ranging in height from 18 to 24 inches (46 to 61 cm) tall. The flowers are medium rose in color.

The remaining varieties result from a number of crosses between species including *S. nemorosa*, *S. pratensis* and *S. villicaulis*. This collection is offered commercially under either *S. × superba* or *S. nemorosa*. All of these should be **vegetatively propagated**; seed sold under these names will not come true.

East Friesland (Ostfriesland) has deep violet-purple flowers on plants reaching 18 to 24 inches (46 to 61 cm) tall. It flowers from June to August.

May Night (Mainachet) has dark violet-purple flowers on plants from 18 to no more than 24 inches (46 to 61 cm) tall. Plants seem more compact than other varieties, often not growing above 20 inches (51 cm) in our gardens. Plants flower June and July.

USES

Salvia has a place in the perennial border, the home flower garden, or in commercial landscapes due to its violet-blue flower color and dark foliage. In any commercial uses, avoid large blocks of this plant due to its limited flowering period. It can be used in small quantities, however, especially when combined with other seasonal perennials that will provide color after salvia blooms have faded. If pinched, salvias will flower

again in several weeks though not with the full color seen in spring or early summer.
The flowers make good cut flowers for home use.

IN THE HOME GARDEN

For best performance, plant in full sun in any moist, but well-drained, location. Stems and leaves will darken under cool night temperatures in May and June and put on their strongest flowering and brightest colors when exposed to cooler temperatures during budding. Plants don't require staking here in our Chicago location, although in zones farther south and in rich soils, the plants can become robust.

Trim dead flower spikes back after blooming to help retain the plants' shape. The varieties listed don't fall open in the middle after they flower as do a number of perennials.

■■■ SANGUINARIA CANADENSIS

FAMILY: Papaveraceae

COMMON NAME(S): Bloodroot, Puccoon

The common name, bloodroot, describes the plant's red sap. During propagation or rhizome division, sap will ooze from the open wound. In Colonial days this sap was used to make dye.

DESCRIPTION

Sanguinaria canadensis is a native perennial prized in woodland landscapes and wildflower gardens. Low-growing plants reach 6 inches (15 cm) in height when flowering and spread up to 10 inches (25 cm) across when mature and established. Flowers are pure white, with eight to 12 anemone-like petals. Blooms can be either single or double, measuring 2 to 3 inches (5 to 7 cm) across. Double-flowering plants have both larger blooms and a longer flowering period than single-flowered types. When flowering, plants bloom from 10 days to three weeks, depending on the duration of cool spring weather. High daytime temperatures shorten the period of continual color. Flowers open on sunny days but close on cloudy days and at night. Plants are suited for shady locations, not full sun.

The rhizomes are fleshy, semibranching, and a reddish-brown color. They enable the plant to spread across the forest floor. Plants are not invasive, however, and require several years to fill in. Leaves are blue green with a gray-green underside. The leaves develop with the flowers. Plants go dormant in mid to late summer, earlier if stressed by hot weather.

HARDINESS: Zones 4 to 9.

S

SEASON OF BLOOM: May.

PROPAGATION

Division and seed are the common ways to propagate *Sanguinaria*, but division is most common for mass production and quick turnaround. Seed can be sown for single-flowering plants only; double-flowering specimens require division.

GERMINATION OVERVIEW

If you're searching for new varieties or prefer to grow more challenging plants, this particular crop may pique your interest. On a commercial basis, seedling success is exacting and time consuming and seldom fits easily into a grower's program. Specialty nurseries are more adept at this.

A word of caution about this crop: Don't plan on routinely buying seed from seed companies, since a stored seed results in a prolonged germination process. Fresh seed doesn't germinate immediately but can start within a year after sowing. I suggest you maintain your own stock plants from which to gather seed. If you must buy seed, consider using seed exchanges where growers have the seed seasonally available, usually over a short period of time. *Sanguinaria* is definitely not the type of seed crop you buy in February, sow immediately, and expect any kind of quick results. Following this method, you'll probably have no germination.

Allow seed to fall from the plants. Lightly mix it into the soil, and cover it with soil plus leaves and other organic material to keep it moist and protected. Seedlings will emerge the following spring. If you prefer to gather seed instead, sow immediately in a peat-lite mixture, subjecting it to temperatures of 72F to 78F (22C to 25C) for two to four weeks, and then a cold-moist period—just above freezing—for six weeks. After this, gradually raise temperatures for over a week to 60F (16C) to encourage germination. This method works more often than not depending on the seed, but it isn't always reliable. Additional details on moist chilling seed are provided in the **Propagation Techniques** chapter.

GROWING ON

Crop time: Plants will start to flower two years after sowing fresh seed. Plants are usually fully established after three years, with a stronger, more free-flowering performance.

Divisions work best when taken from summer-dormant plants (usually in August), although they can also be taken in early spring. This year's divisions will be salable the following year, depending on their size and whether your production schedule requires flowering plants the same year. In general, the plants flower sporadically—usually 40 to 60%—the spring following division.

VARIETIES

Numerous reference books describe this crop as being monospecific or monotypic, meaning this crop has only one species.

S. canadensis. Most U.S. seed firms won't carry this variety, although specialty seed houses and seed exchanges may offer it seasonally. As previously stated, the single-flowering variety is available from seed only; the double-flowering one is vegetatively propagated.

S. canadensis Flore Pleno (Multiplex) is a double-flowering form. Similar to the description provided above, it bears white double blossoms to 3 inches (7 cm) across. With this double-flowering selection, petals number 30 to 50 per flower and last one to two weeks longer than single-flowering types, longer if the weather is cool. Flore Pleno is propagated vegetatively since its flowers are sterile.

USES

The value of this plant in wildflower, native perennial, or woodland gardens cannot be overstated. Although not an easy plant to establish, it's at home in these environments as long as its requirements are met.

IN THE HOME GARDEN

Plant in any partially to heavily shaded area in the rich humus at the base of trees and shrubs. When working with newly created "forests" or woodlands, be sure that organic material is present to successfully grow *Sanguinaria* and other similar plants such as trilliums, ferns, etc. While these plants can grow in other soil types, they thrive when grown as suggested here.

Plants don't grow tall enough for staking, nor do they need winter protection if trees and shrubs have been allowed to drop their leaves around the plants in autumn. *Sanguinaria* doesn't usually need irrigation unless recently planted or if weathering a dry season.

As a rule, plants go dormant in August or September, dying back to the ground. Plants can be divided at this time, watered, and allowed to establish before cold weather. In dry periods, especially when combined with sunny exposures, *Sanguinaria* will often go dormant one to two weeks earlier than usual.

■ SANGUISORBA OBTUSA

FAMILY: Rosaceae

COMMON NAME(S): Japanese Burnet, Bottlebrush Flower

DESCRIPTION

An uncommon perennial, *Sanguisorba obtusa* is prized for its airy, bottle-brush-like plumes of rose-pink flowers with elongated stamens. Its multitude of scentless flowers are arranged along 3- to 4-inch (7 to 10 cm) arching spikes. The blooms become top heavy as they open and gracefully nod to and fro on windy days. Plants grow from creeping rhizomes but are noninvasive and easily maintained. The foliage is a light gray green on plants that grow 3 to 4 feet (90 to 120 cm) tall and spread 18 to 30 inches (46 to 76 cm).

HARDINESS: Zones 4 to 8.

SEASON OF BLOOM: July.

PROPAGATION

Rhizome division is the most common way to propagate this plant. It can be done in the spring or in late summer. Seed can also be used. Germination usually begins within one to two weeks. If germination results are low or nonuniform, subject the sowing tray to two to four weeks of 38F to 40F (3C to 4C) to improve germination.

GROWING ON

Crop time: Commercial propagators have bare root transplants ready for potting up during autumn and winter. Potting the roots as late as March will still produce green, salable plants in mid to late May when grown at 50F (10C) nights or warmer. The roots should be potted into 3- or 4-quart containers in which they'll quickly establish, producing a rosetting crown of individual leaf stalks. The 10 or 11 leaflets are arranged in pinnate form. In general, allow nine to 11 weeks for finishing, depending how well rooted you want the plants to be.

Some additional points: *Sanguisorba obtusa* is broader than it is tall, growing 8 to 10 inches (20 to 25 cm) tall in the pot but spreading up to 18 inches (46 cm) across the crown. Space plants accordingly. In our trials, plants flowered in 13 to 15 weeks when the roots were potted up in mid-March and grown at 50F (10C) nights.

Besides bare root transplants, small pots are usually available, but liners aren't normally sold. The pots can be purchased in winter and transplanted to larger containers for spring sales. In some cases, the plants will be flowering when sold.

VARIETIES

Sanguisorba obtusa is available as a bare-root transplant or a small or prefinished pot. Seed isn't typically used in North America, although seed exchanges and plant societies may offer it.

USES

While not overly showy, *Sanguisorba obtusa* is a plant worth considering. Few plants can reach 3 or 4 feet (90 to 120 cm) in height, offer both foliage and flower attributes, and not be a rampant menace or demand coddling in the garden—but *S. obtusa* is just that. Its soft pink, bottle-brush flowers are eye-catchers when combined with deeper colored or pastel plants.

Interplanting with artemisias and other gray-leaved plants, or plants with blooms of soft blue, rose, or light yellow, will highlight this perennial's attributes.

IN THE HOME GARDEN

S. obtusa is at home in woodland gardens, preferring moist, though well-drained, soils in a morning sun location. Our plants are in a sunny location, but we've mulched their roots with at least 2 inches (5 cm) of cypress bark to protect them during dry spells. Thus protected, they've thrived despite the exposure.

Sanguisorba doesn't require any special treatments or winter protection for long-lived performance nor does it require staking.

■ SANTOLINA CHAMAECYPARISSUS

(syn. *S. incana*)

FAMILY: Asteraceae

COMMON NAME(S): Lavender Cotton

DESCRIPTION

Prized for its evergreen, gray-green, finely divided foliage, *Santolina chamaecyparissus* is considered a subshrub. It develops a woody base the first year regardless of how it is propagated. The plants are aromatic but not overpowering, with the scent more prevalent after a rain shower. *Santolina* grows 18 to 24 inches (46 to 61 cm) tall and spreads about the same. The golden yellow flowers are rather unattractive but are appreciated by some for their brightening effect in herb gardens. The blooms are single, one-half to three-quarter-inch (1 to 2 cm) across, and globed shaped.

HARDINESS: Zones 6 to 8.

Plants are only marginally hardy here in Chicago, often dying out within three years. With mulch however, the plants are more dependable.

SEASON OF BLOOM: August and September.

PROPAGATION

Cuttings are the preferred way to propagate, though seed can be used as well. Cuttings root readily when taken during the summer. Overwinter them in quart pots for sales the following season.

GERMINATION OVERVIEW: 56,000 seeds per ounce/1,960 per gram.

Seed germinates in four to eight days at 72F (22C); cover lightly or not at all during germination. Seedlings can be transplanted 18 to 24 days after sowing.

GROWING ON

Crop time: Cuttings root easily and can be transplanted to a quart container within several weeks.

S

From seed, it's best to start six months to a year prior to sales in 4-inch or quart containers. February sowings grown in a 32-cell pack will be salable green 10 to 12 weeks after germination when grown at 60F (15C). Once plants are established when containers, grow them on at 50F (10C) nights until salable. Plants will look like small pine trees.

At this stage *Santolina* grows erect—about 8 inches (20 cm) tall—without basal branching, and its roots fill a cell pack. If space and time don't permit growing a year in advance, offer the plants in a 4-inch (10 cm) pot to allow for more developed growth prior to sales.

The plants will not flower the same season from seed but will reach 10 inches (25 cm) in height and spread about the same.

Commercial propagators offer *Santolina* as a bare-root transplant or as a plug/liner. Primarily available during the autumn and winter, either of these can be potted up into quart and gallon containers and sold in spring.

VARIETIES

Santolina chamaecyparissus is more readily available as started plants than from seed in the U.S. trade, although seed can be found. If growing from seed, be prepared for a number of off-types. Plants develop uniformly but can vary in foliage color, ranging from dusty miller gray to light green.

USES

Plants are short lived in locations with frequent overhead waterings and high humidity. Combined, these two are the death of this plant. It is at home in herb gardens for its scented foliage, in perennial borders as an edging, or in small groups.

In commercial landscapes, it has value but needs more individual attention than the factory-approach to care and maintenance that commercial landscapes often receive.

IN THE HOME GARDEN

Plant into any well-drained, sunny location, avoiding sites that receive frequent overhead watering. When mulching in winter, try to protect the plant's base without piling materials around the foliage. The hairy foliage can hold water and introduce disease into the plant's crown, which ultimately leads to death. No staking is required, but an occasional trimming to maintain the rounded appearance may be necessary.

■ SAPONARIA OCYMOIDES

FAMILY: Caryophyllaceae

COMMON NAME(S): Rock Soapwort

DESCRIPTION

An easily grown perennial, *Saponaria ocymoides* displays one-quarter-inch, single, bright pink blooms. The flowers are five-petaled. The sprawling, sometimes rampant, plants are borderline evergreen and grow to between 5 and 9 inches (13 to 23 cm) tall. They can spread up to 2 feet (60 cm) across. See Color Plate 63 for photo of *Saponaria ocymoides*.

HARDINESS: Zones 3 to 9.

SEASON OF BLOOM: May.
Plants flower only once, although some scattered blooms may appear later, especially if the summer is cool.

PROPAGATION
Saponaria is commonly propagated by seed, although cuttings and divisions can also be taken. Plants can be divided just about any time during the warmer months, while terminal cuttings are taken in the spring prior to bud set or in summer after flowering.

GERMINATION OVERVIEW: 16,000 seeds per ounce/560 per gram.
Pretreatments: Stored seed benefits from a chilling to maintain germination rates. If using old seed, consider sowing into an open flat or plug tray and chilling the sown, moistened seeds at 40F (4C) for up to four weeks or until germination begins. If using fresh or recently harvested seed within several months of collecting, the germination rates will be 60% or above, and pretreatments aren't necessary.

Seeds will germinate in four to eight days at 70F (21C) and should be covered during germination. Seedlings can be transplanted 18 to 25 days after sowing.

GROWING ON
Crop time: From seed you can sell the plants green, in a 32-cell pack, 10 to 11 weeks after sowing when grown at 50F to 55F (10C to 13C) nights. The plants don't have much of a shape, however, and their scrawny, rambling habit will make your uninformed customers think they're buying weeds. Instead, start from seed the previous summer by sowing two or three seeds to a plug tray (390 or larger). These plugs can be transplanted directly to a quart by midsummer for overwintering dormant. They will be more filled out and have a better presentation than green packs. If February sown, the plants won't flower the same year. *Saponaria* requires a cold treatment before it will flower.

Commercial propagators offer plants as bare-root transplants in small pots or as liners/plugs. Purchased in autumn and winter, any of these can be potted up into quarts or gallons and sold in spring.

VARIETIES
Saponaria ocymoides is sold by numerous U.S. seed and nursery companies.

S. ocymoides var. *alba* is a white-flowering version of the species growing to 8 inches (20 cm) tall. Plants flower in May and June. Seed is more difficult to find.

S

RELATED MATERIAL

Saponaria officinalis (known as Bouncing Bet) is a rather common but increasingly unimportant plant with 1-inch (2.5 cm), single, dull pink flowers on plants between 15 and 30 inches (38 to 76 cm) tall. Plants were a staple in American gardens of the past, but now it's the double-flowering varieties that are gaining interest in the trade.

S. officinalis var. *roseo-plena* is a double-flowering, light rose plant to 24 inches (61 cm) tall. The fragrant flowers appear from June through August. Plants are vegetatively propagated by either cuttings or division. Seed is seldom available on the U.S. trade, although it may be found from European sources. Sowing from seed seldom provides acceptable results, however, and vegetative methods are preferred.

USES

If you're reviewing sources to find out how to use this plant effectively, you may encounter more comments on how to remove it than preserve it. While the plants are sprawling and can get rather rampant if planted in fertile soils, *Saponaria* can also be utilized as a trailing plant in poor soils. The plants don't lend themselves to commercial landscapes due to their short blooming season and unkempt habit (unless shaped by trimming), although they should be considered for wildflower gardens where they'll have some room to spread.

IN THE HOME GARDEN

Plants are long lived in the garden with limited die-out from year to year. We've never seen any reseeding. Plants don't spread readily; they keep to themselves without becoming invasive. Once flowering is over, the plants can be trimmed back to encourage more uniform growth during the summer.

Plant in any full-sun location where water drains off and allows the plants to become established.

■■ SAXIFRAGA × ARENDSII

FAMILY: Saxifragaceae

COMMON NAME(S): Saxifrage, Mossy Saxifrage

DESCRIPTION

The rock garden plant *Saxifraga × arendsii* grows up to 6 inches (15 cm) tall in flower, with rounded, rosetting tufts that are mosslike in appearance and spread via stolons. These rosettes are evergreen except in the coldest climates. The leaves are shaped like palm fronds—deeply dissected and dark green in color. Flowers are single, three-quarter-inch (2 cm) across, appearing at the terminal end of each flowering stalk. Rose, white, pink, or red blooms are available.

HARDINESS: Zones 5 to 9.

Be sure to read about conditions for hardiness under **In the home garden**.

SEASON OF BLOOM: April and May, sometimes June.

PROPAGATION

Seed, rosettes, and basal cuttings are frequently used to propagate this crop. Seed can be sown anytime of the year while cuttings are taken in early spring before flowering. Offsets are removed from around the outer edge of the mother plant, along with a portion of their roots. Saxifrage can also be propagated by divisions.

GERMINATION OVERVIEW: 700,000 seeds per ounce/24,500 per gram.

Pretreatments: Seed germinates readily. Some perennial manuals providing germination information, however, have indicated that seed needs to be stored cold or stratified before sowing. While cold storage is recommended for stored seed, it's not necessary when using fresh seed that is less than a year old.

Seedlings will emerge eight to 10 days after sowing but are extremely slow growing in the pretransplant stage. This is a critical time since the seedlings are small and cannot be left under mist for fear of algae growth. Also, direct overhead watering, especially with a breaker, can often wash seedlings away. To be safe, be prepared to handle the seedlings with added care for at least four to five weeks after sowing before they can be transplanted.

GROWING ON

Crop time: From seed, plants are slow to develop into salable green transplants in a 4-inch (10 cm) or quart container. Even when transplanted to a 32-cell pack, the plants are slow to fill out.

I suggest you sow during the spring, transplant to cell packs to size up the plants, and move them to quart containers for growing on during the summer. Since plants can die out in the center, protect them from high humidity and direct sun for best performance. Overwinter in a cold frame or similar structure with overhead protection.

February sowings will not fill out a 32-cell pack until June or July. If sowings are necessary for spring sales, then sow the previous year, pot up into 4½-inch (11 cm) pots and overwinter dormant.

Leo Jelitto and Wilhelm Schacht suggest that cuttings are best taken in fall, rooted in a sand-based media, and covered with glass [1]. During the following year, the plants can be transplanted to quarts for late spring or summer sales depending on how fast they fill out the container. They can also be transplanted to 4-inch pots to fill in sooner. We've taken basal cuttings in the spring rather than in the fall and have had good results.

S

Divisions are best made in the spring on two-year-old plants. The plants are lifted, the stolons cut, and the plant potted into quarts for sales later that year or grown on and overwintered for sales next year.

Active growing temperatures need to be cool or warm but not hot. Make your sowings during the spring while nights are still cool. If sown in April or May, seedlings will be big enough to transplant before the onset of hot weather. Night temperatures of 50F to 65F (10C to 18C) are suggested. At 80F (20C) night temperatures and above, especially with high humidity, the plants will often falter and grow more slowly.

VARIETIES

Flower Carpet (Blutenteppich) has carmine and red-shaded blossoms on plants no taller than 8 inches (20 cm) in bloom, but they may be taller when grown in areas with only several hours of sun a day. Many commercial plant catalogs in the eastern United States refer to a variety called Blood Carpet. This may be misconstrued from the German word "blute," which means blood. The German word for flower or bloom, "bluten," is only slightly different. Allan Armitage, however, says that there is a difference between the two varieties, with Blood Carpet deeper in flower color than Flower Carpet.

Purple Carpet (Purpurteppich) has deep purple-rose blossoms on plants up to 9 inches (23 cm) tall in flower. It looks similar to Purple Robe. The flower color shades or lightens as the flowers age.

Purple Robe. See Purple Carpet. See Color Plate 64 for photo of *Saxifraga × arendsii* Purple Robe.

Spring Snow is a white-flowering variety not unlike Snow Carpet. Plants grow to 9 inches (23 cm) in flower. Snow Carpet is also sold as Schneeteppich.

IN THE HOME GARDEN

Use this perennial in a rock garden or other raised, moist, but well-drained location. In humid summer locations, plant in shady places where the plants are protected from high summer temperatures. Without shielding, the plants and their roots heat up, causing center brown-outs and a quick death if the conditions persist. Soils with a gravel or sandy base are best for long-term performance.

If planting in a border or edging, be sure to keep the plants raised. Flat surfaces cause the plants to fight for position, and consequently they'll be short lived. Plants will fill in between rocks by producing short stolons that anchor them in place. Saxifrage flowers only in the spring but will remain green all summer long.

REFERENCES

[1] Jelitto, L., and W. Schacht. 1990. *Hardy herbaceous perennials*. Vol. II. Portland, Ore.: Timber Press.

■ SCABIOSA CAUCASICA

FAMILY: Dipsacaceae

COMMON NAME(S): Pincushion Flower

DESCRIPTION

Scabiosa caucasica is an erect-growing perennial with long, linear basal leaves that arch and curve toward the ground, creating a wispy appearance. Leaves that develop along the stems are more lobed than the basal leaves but look similar. Plants don't have a full habit in our Chicago climate, although in less hot and humid areas of the country, they perform better. *Scabiosa* flowers are blue or white, single, usually scentless, and open on long stalks above the plant. The striking flower heads are 2 to 3 inches (5 to 7 cm) across and composed of large, slightly cupped or flat petals at the outer margin with a tufted center cluster. The prominent pinlike stamens give this perennial the name of "pincushion flower." In bloom, it grows 2 to 2½ feet (60 to 75 cm) tall and 12 to 14 inches (30 to 35 cm) across.

HARDINESS: Zones 4 to 7.

While *Scabiosa* is usually winter hardy, stress from summer heat and humidity usually results in short-lived plants in Chicago. They last two to four seasons at best.

SEASON OF BLOOM: June.

When continuously deadheaded, plants have flowered for us sporadically, until late July or August. If night temperatures rise above 80F (26C), flowering is less.

PROPAGATION

Scabiosa is usually propagated by seed or cuttings, although some experts suggest divisions are possible. Our plants never get big enough to warrant divisions. In cooler summer locations, plants are longer lived and grow large enough for dividing. I personally feel this type of propagation is more for home gardeners than commercial growers. Basal cuttings are most common. Additional information is provided in the front of this book.

GERMINATION OVERVIEW: 2,400 seeds per ounce/84 per gram.

Pretreatments: None are needed. The normal germination percentages range from 68 to 80% the first year after harvesting.

Sow seed into a peat-lite media, cover lightly with vermiculite or leave exposed, and germinate between 65F and 70F (18C to 21C). Seed easily germinates at 72F (22C), but don't allow it to dry out. Seed germinates in about 10 to 18 days at 65F (18C); five to eight days at 72F. Seedlings can be transplanted in 20 to 29 days.

GROWING ON

Crop time: From seed, plants in 32-cell packs will be large enough to sell in 10 to 12 weeks. They can be sold as green packs or moved up into larger containers for

S

late-season sales or for the next spring. If grown during the spring, night temperatures of 48F to 55F (9C to 13C) yield the best growth. Summer production is possible with light shade and cool night temperatures. If you're growing for pack sales, winter sowings made until March will be salable in spring and, if planted in the garden by late May, will be in flower by July. Second-year plants will resume their normal flowering in June.

Occasionally we're asked if August flowering will stress and winterkill the plants because of inadequate root development and/or food storage. If *Scabiosa* is planted in the ground by April or May and allowed to root before blooming, it should return the following year. If the summer is too hot, the plants may die no matter when they were planted.

Beware of warm temperatures during the seedling and small plant stages. Plants will respond accordingly, producing more open crowns with elongated leaves. Try to keep the plants cool, with night temperatures of 55F (13C) and less. A night/day temperature combination of of 58F/70F (14C/21C) will yield soft, wispy growth. Another production method is to autumn sow for quart pot sales in May. The plants are grown cold, but not dormant, during the winter for spring sales. These plants stay more compact and uniform because of the cool nights.

Commercial propagators offer *Scabiosa* in small pots or as plugs/liners. Primarily available during the autumn and winter, either of these can be potted up into quarts and gallons for spring sales.

VARIETIES

All of the following are **seed propagated**:

Compliment is a dark lavender variety to 2 feet (60 cm) tall. It's darker in color than Fama.

Fama has lavender-blue flowers on plants 2 to 3 feet (60 to 90 cm) tall. Its habit is more uniform than House Hybrids, but it is available in only one color.

House Hybrids (House Mix) is a common variety found across the United States through a number of seed companies. It's known outside the United States as Isaac House Hybrids in honor of its selection at the Issac House in England. The hybrids are a mixture of blue- and white-flowering varieties, 2 to 3 feet (60 to 90 cm) tall.

Perfecta series. Perfecta is a lilac-flowering variety to 2 feet (60 cm) tall, while Perfecta White is the white-flowering counterpart.

RELATED MATERIAL

S. atropurpurea. Every year we're asked about the "other" colors besides blue and white and how these varieties can be obtained. *Scabiosa atropurpurea* is similiar in height and habit to *S. caucasica*, and while it does bloom in brighter colors of burgundy, carmine, pink, plus white and blue, it's an annual—the plants won't return the following year. If this species is to your liking, look for it in seed catalogs under the cultivar name, Imperial Giants Mix.

USES

These flowers can be sold commercially, but they're a traditional favorite as a home-garden cut flower. In commercial landscapes, these plants are seldom used in hot summer areas where they're weaker in stature. In coastal areas and cool summer locations, they'll fill in, be more free flowering, and generally look better than elsewhere.

IN THE HOME GARDEN

Scabiosa prefers a full-sun, well-drained location with a neutral pH for best performance. We've planted Fama in various locations where it gets light shade in the afternoon; the plants haven't had problems with flowering or weak stems due to the exposure.

Plants don't require staking but will bend severely in wind and storms. During calm periods, however, the plants regain their upright habit, although they may be a little weakened at the tops.

■ SEDUM SPURIUM

FAMILY: Crassulaceae

COMMON NAME(S)

Stonecrop is the common name for the whole genus. Note: Read the information under **Varieties** to avoid confusion.

DESCRIPTION

An excellent ground cover, *Sedum spurium* can become invasive in moist and fertile locations. Plants reach 4 to 6 inches (10 to 15 cm) tall in or out of bloom and spread 12 to 24 inches (30 to 61 cm) across from a single clump. The foliage is dark green. The single, one-half-inch (1 cm) blooms are rose, white, or dull red, often atop reddish tinged flowering stems.

HARDINESS: Zones 3 to 9.

SEASON OF BLOOM: July and August.

PROPAGATION

Sedum is generally propagated by cuttings, divisions, or seed. Basal cuttings are taken in the spring, while stem cuttings can be taken any time the plant is not in flower. Divisions can be taken any time of the year when warm growing conditions are likely.

GERMINATION OVERVIEW: 400,000 seeds per ounce/14,000 per gram.

Sedum will germinate under various soil temperatures. Most cultural references, including the *Ball Culture Guide*, 2nd edition, and the *Ball RedBook*, 15th edition, recommend alternating germination temperatures of 85F days/75F nights (29C/24C). This method will yield the best results when using old seed, improperly stored seed, or seed that, for no apparent reason, germinates erratically or with a limited seedling stand.

In most cases, however, fresh *Sedum* seed will germinate at 60% or better at 72F (22C). Seed doesn't need to be covered to germinate. Seedlings will emerge in eight to 14 days and can be transplanted 20 to 29 days after sowing.

GROWING ON

The cultivars or seed strains noted under **Varieties** are the preferred types in the market, not the species. Therefore the culture noted below is based on these selections.

Sedum spurium roots quickly from cuttings, within seven to 10 days, and can be transplanted to the final 4-inch (10 cm) or quart container within two weeks after they are placed in the propagation bench. If propagated during the summer, the plants can be grown on and then overwintered dormant to sell the following spring. Commercial propagators offer many cultivars in various plug and liner sizes that can be purchased during autumn or winter. These are potted up into 4-inch (10 cm) or quart containers for spring sales.

From seed: Sowings made in the winter or spring can be sold green in packs 11 to 14 weeks later when grown at 58F to 60F (14C to 16C) nights. The plants will grow together between the cell packs, however, and while not overly difficult to pull apart, they are cumbersome to handle. For 4½-inch (11 cm) pot sales in May, sow seed in December, and grow warm at 60F (16C) during the winter and early spring until plants have become well rooted. Then drop the night temperatures to 50F (10C) to keep the plants short. This cooler temperature will also help to deepen the foliage color.

S. spurium will flower the same season from seed, usually in late July or August from a midwinter sowing. The best bloom, however, comes the second season from seed.

A number of cultivars are available as bare-root transplants for autumn and winter delivery. These should be potted when received, grown at no lower than 55F (13C) nights, and sold in the spring in gallon containers.

VARIETIES

Sedum cultivars can be confusing. In the American market, Dragon's Blood has sometimes been used as the common name for *Sedum spurium*, although it's actually a cultivar name.

S. spurium itself isn't typically offered by either seed firms or companies specializing in vegetatively propagated plants. Instead, the following varieties are the ones most commonly found in the American market. However, only one is available from seed.

S. spurium var. *coccineum* is the more commonly available seed-propagated cultivar within the United States. The variety has green foliage highlighted in reddish or bronzed shades. The foliage isn't as intense in color as the vegetatively propagated varieties noted below, however. The flowers are rose red on plants 4 to 6 inches (10 to 15 cm) tall.

Bronze Carpet has bronzed foliage with bright rose-pink flowers in July and August. The foliage, however, isn't as dark as Dragon's Blood plants. This is a vegetatively propagated cultivar.

Dragon's Blood (Schorbuser Blut) has richly colored, bronzed foliage with deep carmine-red flowers. This cultivar is vegetatively propagated.

Fuldaglut (Fulda Embers) has dark red leaves with carmine-red flowers on plants 4 to 6 inches (10 to 15 cm) tall. It's vegetatively propagated.

Red Carpet has bright bronze-crimson foliage to 4 inches (10 cm) tall in flower. Flowers are crimson to red, with foliage similar to Bronze Carpet. It is vegetatively propagated.

Tricolor has variegated cream, green, and pink foliage on low-growing plants 3 to 5 inches (7 to 13 cm) tall in flower. The flowers are light to medium pink. Occasionally an all-green rosette will develop. Since these are more persistent than the tricolored foliage, they should be removed, otherwise they could grow large enough to smother the tricolored form. Tricolor is vegetatively propagated.

RELATED VARIETIES

S. acre isn't as common as *S. spurium* in the American market, although the plants' low-growing, trailing habit makes them an excellent choice for rock gardens, borders, edging, or mass plantings. Widely available from seed companies, *Sedum acre* has small, single, one-half-inch (1 cm) yellow flowers on 2- to 4-inch (5 to 10 cm) tall plants. This species has a smaller habit than *S. spurium* var. *coccineum*. The plants have small, one-quarter-inch (6 mm) long, needlelike leaves. The variety is often sold as Golden Carpet, either from seed or vegetative propagation. Those vegetatively propagated have a more uniform appearance. *S. acre* flowers in June and can be sown and grown on as described under *S. spurium*.

Sedum × Autumn Joy (also called Indian Chief and Herbstfreude). Most often listed as a cultivar of *S. spectabile*, Autumn Joy resulted from a cross between *S. spectabile* and *S. telephium* (*Hylotelephium telephium*). Autumn Joy flowers in late August and September on well-branched and mounded plants to 2 feet (61 cm) tall. The flowers are bright pink, borne in flat clusters to 5 inches (13 cm) across. They often turn bronze about the time of the first frost here in Chicago. Propagate Autumn Joy by stem cuttings or division in spring or fall.

Sedum reflexum also has needlelike foliage similar to *S. acre*, except the foliage is bluish green and "sprucelike" in its appearance. Flowers are yellow on plants to 8 inches (20 cm) tall. Propagate by seed or vegetatively, and treat as you would *S. spurium*. See Color Plate 66 for photo of *Sedum reflexum*.

S

Sedum × Ruby Glow (also called Rosy Glow) is a cross between *S. cauticola* and *S.* × Autumn Joy. Ruby-red flowers appear in August and September on plants 6 to 8 inches (15 to 20 cm) tall. The foliage has a purplish gray cast. Propagate by division or cuttings.

Sedum spectabile Brilliant has carmine flowers appearing in August. Plants are 15 to 18 inches (38 to 46 cm) tall with gray-green foliage. This plant looks similar to Autumn Joy, although Brilliant flowers about two weeks earlier here in the Chicago area. Propagate by cuttings or division. The Royal Horticultural Society's *Dictionary of Gardening* lists this cultivar under the botanical name *Hylotelephium spectabile*, although at the time of this writing that name has yet to gain much footing in the American trade. See Color Plate 67 for photo of *Sedum spectabile* Brilliant.

Sedum × Vera Jameson is a dwarf variety growing 12 inches (30 cm) tall with intense bronze or burgundy leaves. Plants flower in September. Occasionally listed as a variety of *S. spectabile*, Vera Jameson has pink flowers in 2- to 4-inch-wide (5 to 10 cm) clusters. Propagate by cuttings or division. See Color Plate 65 for photo of *Sedum* × Vera Jameson.

Commercial propagators offer all the preceding varieties as bare-root transplants, small pots, or liners to the trade. Available during autumn and winter, any of these can be potted up into quart or larger containers and sold in spring.

USES

Use dwarf, trailing varieties like *S. spurium* and *S. acre* in rock gardens or as border plants in the perennial garden. These two plants are most at home when allowed to cascade to some degree. Because of *S. acre*'s more condensed or restricted habit, it can be planted in gaps between walking stones to provide color and long-lasting greenery.

Sedums work very well in the landscape. Any of the above varieties and related material will provide excellent foliage and flower color. Even though they're taller, *S.* × Autumn Joy or Brilliant are excellent because they keep a uniform habit throughout the summer. Plants won't bud up until July, and the dried flower clusters will stay upright on the plants throughout most of the winter. Use *S. spurium* var. *coccineum*, *S. reflexum*, and *S. acre* together to create a late spring and summer flowering effect on rock walls or as a border. Of the remaining varieties, each cultivar offers a unique addition to the home or professional landscape that's worth evaluating.

IN THE HOME GARDEN

Plant in a warm, well-drained soil in full-sun locations for a long-lived performance. We've established plantings that have survived for years. Space the dwarf, trailing varieties (especially *S. spurium*) 14 to 16 inches (35 to 41 cm) apart and the taller upright varieties 15 to 18 inches (38 to 46 cm) apart. No staking is required, although some plants will need to be tied up by August if grown in fertile, shady areas. Plants tolerate dry soils. *Sedum* is recommended for xeriscaping.

■ SEMPERVIVUM TECTORUM

Sempervivum is a variable species. A number of cultivars listed below are the result of hybridization between one or more species and may be of questionable heritage. The resulting progeny can be unique.

FAMILY: Crassulaceae

COMMON NAME(S): Hen and Chicks, Houseleeks

DESCRIPTION

A dwarf, compact, rock garden plant, *Sempervivum tectorum*'s versatility makes it adaptable to a number of other uses as well (see the additional information under **Uses**). Plants grow no more than 10 inches (25 cm) in flower, seldom above 3 inches (7 cm) otherwise. Plants spread 3 to 6 inches (7 to 15 cm) or more depending on the number of offsets that develop around the mother plant. Plants are succulent with fleshy leaves tightly clustered in rosettes, each with a deep red, pointed leaf tip. They are valued more for their rosetting habit than their blooms. The flowers are single, purple red, and less than an inch wide. They're starlike in appearance and scentless.

HARDINESS: Zones 4 to 8.

SEASON OF BLOOM: June to August.

PROPAGATION

The easiest way to propagate *S. tectorum* is to remove the offsets that develop at the base of the mother plant. These are small rosettes that can be separated, along with a portion of their roots, from the mother plant.

Seed is also available but seldom found in the U.S. market. However, seed is available primarily as a mix rather than separate colors. Additional details are provided under **Varieties**.

GERMINATION OVERVIEW: 368,000 seeds per ounce/12,880 per gram.
Seed will germinate in five to 10 days at 72F to 75F (22C to 24C) with limited problems. It can be germinated at higher temperatures but not higher than 85F (29C) in the greenhouse. Watch for emergence and move the seedlings away from the heat before they stretch. Also, *Sempervivum* is more susceptible to damping-off diseases than other crops, and higher germination temperatures can increase the spread of disease.

We experienced equal germination results with peat-lite mixtures with vermiculite and peat/sand mixtures. We did incur more damping off diseases (*Rhizoctonia* and *Pythium*), however, with the peat/vermiculite mixture. In our opinion, it was due to

S

overwatering. To compensate, we sowed into a damp but not wet peat/sand mixture. We covered the top of the flat with a glass pane and placed it in indirect light.

While quick to germinate, *Sempervivum* develops slowly into seedlings large enough to handle. *Sempervivum*, and succulents in general, will require six to nine weeks to fill a germination tray so that they can be transplanted. If you're using a plug tray, avoid large cell trays (72s, 96s, etc.) and work with smaller ones (220 or a comparable size). If you're double sowing only, the tendency is to overwater larger cells, which encourages damping off.

GROWING ON

Crop time: The keys to success when sowing from seed are warmth and a well-drained media. Crop time is slow, requiring 14 to 17 weeks at no lower than 60F (15C) nights for salable green 2½-inch (6 cm) pots or 32-cell packs. Though well rooted, these plants will grow only 2 to 3 inches (5 to 7 cm) in diameter their first season in the garden. Numerous secondary rosettes will develop around the outer edge of the mother plant during this first summer.

If you prefer to sell in 4-inch (10 cm) containers, sow seed in late summer or the previous autumn and grow on at 60F (15C) nights or warmer for best performance until established. Sowings are best handled in plug trays (220 cells per flat or smaller), then transplanted to the final pot. If larger containers are preferred (1- to 3-quart), then either sow seed the previous spring or summer and overwinter in a cold frame or cold greenhouse, or order liners for potting up during early winter. These, too, are initially grown at 58F (14C) nights or warmer for best rooting and quickest growth.

Seed-propagated varieties will not flower until the second or third year after sowing. The plants are most often prized for their foliage, however, rather than their flowers and will form small clusters by the first midsummer after planting. Obviously, those started from seed during the winter will be smaller than those grown from liners.

Offsets can be removed from the mother plant in the spring. Try to include as much of the root as you can. If you remove only the root directly beneath the soil surface, you seldom get enough root hairs on the offset for fast rooting. Root the offsets first before transplanting them into larger containers. When taken in the spring, the plants have enough time to become established in the final pot during the summer and early fall before cold weather. Offsets can be removed during late summer as well, but a warm greenhouse is necessary to assure rooting and good development with minimum rot.

One final comment regarding temperatures. *Sempervivum* tolerates temperatures below 60F (16C). However, when growing from seed or liners, allow warmer temperatures during the first few weeks until roots have started to form. Cold and overwatering can lead to other problems.

VARIETIES

Since the various species cross so readily, seed-propagated cultivars are mostly sold as mixes. It's difficult to ensure that seed will produce only one type of plant. Our experience, however, is that most of the seed-propagated plants develop and grow uniformly, appearing surprisingly similar. However, the flower color can vary and the habit can be limited in spread, depending on how the mother plants were handled, where they were grown, and the opportunity for natural cross-pollination.

Clones or hybrids are propagated vegetatively since they don't come true from seed. Most nurseries only offer mixtures of these types, but some U.S. companies offer separate colors, and a few offer a wide variety.

RELATED MATERIAL

S. arachnoideum (cobweb houseleek) is an unusual plant with each red-tipped leaf point covered with silvery, web-like strands. Plants grow 2 to 4 inches (5 to 10 cm) across and about 1 to 2 inches (2.5 to 5 cm) tall. The flowers are red, but blooms are insignificant compared to the foliage. In bloom, the flower stalks reach 5 to 7 inches (13 to 18 cm) tall. Cobweb houseleek's hardiness is questionable, but plants will survive in Zone 5. It's our experience, however, that they're not as hardy as *S. tectorum* and more sensitive to overwatering, hot/humid summers, and wet and cold winters.

Primarily propagated by separating secondary rosettes from the mother plant, cobweb houseleek is also available from seed, but that can produce mixed results. It's usually easy to germinate, but if seedlings fail to emerge in three weeks, moist chill the seedling tray two to four weeks to encourage germination.

This crop is available in bare-root transplants and liners and can be treated like *S. tectorum*.

USES

A premier plant for the home or rock garden, *Sempervivum* has other uses, too. The plants will fit snugly into rock wall crevices containing a little bit of soil. For best growth, position them in the rocks at a 45-degree angle where rain water will reach the roots. *Sempervivum* performs best where the foliage can get morning sun but the plants and the rocks are shaded by midafternoon. Avoiding full-sun locations decreases the heat absorbed by the rocks, and this also minimizes the chances of the root ball drying out.

S

IN THE HOME GARDEN

Plant into a well-drained, preferably raised, location in full sun. Avoid heavy clay-loam soils since the plants often winterkill when water is held close to the roots. If a heavy soil is all you have, mix in sharp or coarse sand to improve drainage, or plant in large, shallow containers that can be moved to a cold, but not frozen, area during winter. An attached garage is ideal. Keep temperatures at 35F (2C) during winter for best results.

Sempervivums don't like exposures that receive frequent overhead watering or extremely shady locations. Instead, plant them where they get full sun in an arid or xeriscape-like environment. They can work in commercial landscapes, but be cautious about automatic irrigation systems. If water collects in the crown of the leaves and isn't able to drain away, it can lead to rot and premature death.

▬ SIDALCEA MALVIFLORA

FAMILY: Malvaceae

COMMON NAME(S): Checkerbloom, Checkermallow, Prairie Mallow

DESCRIPTION
A clump-forming North American native perennial with numerous radiating stems, *Sidalcea malviflora* grows 2 to 4 feet (60 to 120 cm) tall and 2 to 3 feet (60 to 90 cm) wide. The leaves are rounded and slightly lobed at the base while the stem foliage is deeply lobed. The flowers are single, medium to deep pink or lilac colored, and 1½ to 2½ inches (3 to 6 cm) wide. Plants resemble a smaller flowered, less ruffled hollyhock.

HARDINESS: Zones 5 to 7.
Plants are hardy in Chicago, but our combined high heat and late summer humidity usually take a toll on this plant. Plants visibly weakened during August and September will not return the following year. In our garden, we generally expect three to four summers of color, with losses anticipated every year.

SEASON OF BLOOM: Summer.

PROPAGATION
The species can be sown from seed, though the hybrids (several of which are listed under **Varieties**) are propagated by divisions in spring or fall.

GERMINATION OVERVIEW: 9,000 seeds per ounce/315 per gram.
This information is based on germinating Party Girl.
Pretreatments: Seed can be either easy or difficult to germinate depending on its age. If germination is slow, chill the tray for one to two weeks at 40F to 50F (4C to 10C), and then move it to a germination bench with 55F to 65F (13C to 18C) bottom heat. Seedlings emerge in 14 to 21 days and can be transplanted six to eight weeks after sowing.
With seed harvested during the past six months, however, germination should be rapid with limited problems. Seed will germinate in five to nine days at 72F (22C) and can be lightly covered with coarse vermiculite for more uniform emergence. Seedlings can be transplanted 18 to 25 days after sowing.

GROWING ON

Crop time: From seed, plants will fill out a 32-cell pack in 10 to 11 weeks when grown at 50F (10C) night temperatures. At that time, you can either move plants up into larger containers for same year sales or pot them up for overwintering. Seed sown during winter or early spring will still produce plants large enough to flower sporadically their first year when planted into the garden by late May.

Commercial propagators usually offer *Sidalcea malviflora* as a liner/plug or in a small pots. Finished containers are also available. Bare-root transplants, however, aren't common—few companies will offer these. If divisions are preferred, you will probably have to take your own.

Divisions are obtained from the crown. The individual plantlets are potted up for sales later in the year if taken in spring. Autumn dug and divided crops can be potted up and overwintered for sales the following year.

VARIETIES

Sidalcea isn't all that common in the American perennial trade, partly due to its short-lived nature as well as its similarities to malvas and hollyhocks. Of the few varieties offered, however, most are propagated by seed. Party Girl and Stark's Hybrids Mix are the most common in the U.S. trade.

Elsie Heugh has lacy, light pink flowers on plants to 3 feet (90 cm) tall. Only propagate it vegetatively.

Party Girl is often listed as *S. hybrida*. Growing 2½ to 3 feet (75 to 90 cm) tall, it has medium pink flowers with a prominent white eye. Propagated by seed, this variety is relatively new in the United States but has been sold in Europe for several years.

Stark's Hybrids Mix is also seed propagated, with rose-red flowers on plants as tall as 5 feet (1.5 m) once they are established.

William Smith has salmon-pink flowers on plants up to 3 feet (90 cm) tall in bloom. Plants are propagated vegetatively only.

USES

Sidalcea plants can be used where smaller versions of hollyhocks or malvas are wanted in the garden. *Sidalcea* is less vigorous and neater in appearance. Plants can be grouped or used singly; they work best in home perennial gardens rather than commercial landscapes. The cultivars noted can be massed around office buildings and other locations but aren't recommended for unprotected and abrasive sites such as flower islands in the center of busy highways, etc.

IN THE HOME GARDEN

Plant to any well-drained, full-sun location for best results. As the previous information notes, these plants don't live long in hot, humid climates, usually four years at best. Instead, they prefer 70F (21C) night temperatures or lower, in a drier climate.

Plants don't require staking unless they've been overfed, well-watered, or are a taller variety. Plants will tolerate some light shade for a short time each day. However, plants grown in shade all summer will be weak, will require staking, and will seldom be free flowering.

■■ SILPHIUM PERFOLIATUM

FAMILY: Asteraceae

COMMON NAME(S): Cup Plant
So named because the leaves fuse together at the base and flare up and out, leaving a depression that will hold water after a rainstorm.

DESCRIPTION
Silphium perfoliatum is a large, impressive, clumping perennial to 8 feet (2.4 m) tall in full bloom. It spreads 4 to 5 feet (1.2 to 1.5 m) wide. The scentless, single, 3-inch (7 cm) yellow flowers are reminiscent of sunflowers since both the ray and disc florets are the same color, although much smaller. The plants reseed readily and are native to the central and southeastern United States.

HARDINESS: Zones 3 to 8.

SEASON OF BLOOM: July and August.

PROPAGATION
Two propagation methods are seed and divisions. Seed should be collected and sown in the nursery row in autumn, although for green transplants, seed can be sown in the winter or spring. Divisions can be taken in spring or fall. Divisions are more useful for home gardeners than the professional grower, however. See additional notes under **In the home garden**.

GERMINATION OVERVIEW
Pretreatments: Collect the seed from your stock plants since it'll be difficult to find for sale. Sow fresh seed, less than six months after harvest, for best germination results.

We have seen variable germination rates with seed collected in the late summer and autumn and then sown in a greenhouse during winter. In most cases, germination rates of 55%—plus or minus 10%—are common using the following methods.

Silphium will germinate in eight to 10 days at 72F (22C) after sowing. The seed can be lightly covered for germination, but avoid heavy coverings that inhibit germination. Seedlings can be transplanted 25 to 35 days after sowing. If germination is low, treat the seed with a moist-chill period as described in the **Propagation** chapter.

GROWING ON

Crop time: From seed, seedlings will take from 14 to 16 weeks to be large enough to fill out a 32-cell pack. Seed sown anytime from December to March can be sold green in a 4-inch (10 cm) pot or quart container from May to July. Earlier sowings yield similar results if you allow 19 to 22 weeks to finish 4-inch (10 cm) or quarts for spring sales. Any sowings made during the winter and spring, however, won't produce flowering plants until the following year.

For flowering plants from seed, sow in summer and transplant to the final container before cool weather. Once rooted in a gallon pot, grow on cool/cold until November here in the North. Then allow the plants to go dormant, to be sold green the following spring. These plants will flower during July.

If you're growing plants in a nursery row, you'll probably never have to collect any seed if you dig out the small seedlings that proliferate around the base of the plants. If the seed heads are allowed to ripen and disseminate their seed, numerous green seedlings will sprout the following spring.

Silphium isn't readily available as anything but a started plant in the United States. Cell packs, small pots, and possibly liners (although I haven't seen any available for several years now) are usually available during the winter. These can be sold as is or potted up for spring sales. Additional notes on divisions are provided under **In the home garden**.

VARIETIES

Silphium perfoliatum is seldom available from seed on the U.S. trade and is more apt to be found at various nurseries as a liner or cell pack.

RELATED MATERIAL

Silphium laciniata is another tall selection (to 7 feet/2.1 m), but it is a slower grower than *S. perfoliatum*. Flowers are bright yellow, and the plant is more free flowering than *S. perfoliatum*. The plant is commonly called "compass plant," a reference to the north-south arrangement on the lower leaves. The variety is native to the central and southeastern United States.

The variety is propagated and produced similarly to *S. perfoliatum*.

USES

This is an excellent plant for herbaceous hedges or backgrounds that die back to the soil line in fall. Plants are erect and won't cascade or arch, so stagger plants by spacing them 2 feet (60 cm) apart to fill in.

Silphium can also be used to advantage in commercial landscapes or in wildflower gardens. Remember that the plants resow themselves readily and will have to be weeded out during the summer.

IN THE HOME GARDEN

Plant in areas with full sun and ample room to grow. Don't place in small gardens where the large habit and height will be too overwhelming. Plants do not require any staking to keep them upright.

Their reseeding habit should not be underestimated. This isn't a plant to place among weak or slow-growing perennials since these seedlings often outgrows surrounding plants to the point of killing them.

For divisions, use one- to three-year-old plants so that the roots are firmly established. You'll have to take an axe to cut the roots up in old plantings. Regardless, many times the resulting division dies. Instead, the best divisions are made from plants that have been through one or two winters. Plants will wilt immediately after being dug up and divided. If divided in spring and quickly replanted to another spot, plants will take hold in two to three weeks, but they should be watered frequently until established. Leaf edges frequently burn, but plants will survive. If taken late in the spring or in early summer, shade the crop to avoid excessive leaf burn once day temperatures are above 75F (24C).

■■ SOLIDAGO SPP.

Botanically, this group of commonly marketed goldenrod varieties results from numerous crosses between species. Unfortunately, the exact crosses aren't known for all the cultivars. Incorrectly listed as cultivars of *S. canadensis*, "the taller hybrids resulted from *S. canadensis* and *S. virgaurea* while the shorter ones originated from × *Solidaster lutens* (a intergeneric cross descended from *S. missouriensis* and *Aster ptarmicoides*) and *S. brachystachys*," explains Allan Armitage in his book, *Herbaceous Perennial Plants*.

FAMILY: Asteraceae

COMMON NAME(S): Goldenrod

DESCRIPTION

Solidago is a perennial whose day has yet to come. Wrongly accused of causing hayfever—ragweed is the true cause—this plant is infrequently used in the American perennial garden. Plants are commonly seen across the eastern and central United States, flowering along roadsides and open areas during mid to late summer. Their golden yellow color, appearing in midwestern and eastern fields in late summer, represents the "dog days" of summer to many.

Goldenrods form clumps with a small base and a wide crown. The stems are strong, erect to slightly arching, and void of secondary branches until they set flower buds. The blooms are small and scentless and appear in multitudes on the many branched flowering stalks. The plants grow 18 inches to 3 feet (46 to 90 cm) tall, depending on species, with a spread of 15 to 24 inches (38 to 61 cm) on the broader varieties.

HARDINESS: Zones 4 to 8.

S. canadensis is hardy to Zone 3.

SEASON OF BLOOM: July and August.

PROPAGATION

Seed is available for the species varieties and Golden Baby, a listed cultivar of *S. canadensis*, which isn't as invasive or as tall as the species. Most cultivars in the trade are propagated by divisions and cuttings.

GERMINATION OVERVIEW

The following information is based on Golden Baby only: 220,000 seeds per ounce/7,700 per gram.

Seed germinates in five to eight days at 70F (21C). We cover the seed lightly with a coarse vermiculite. Seedlings can be transplanted 18 to 25 days after sowing.

GROWING ON

Crop time: From seed, seedlings develop a single stem and are ready to transplant or sell green from a 32-cell pack in 10 to 12 weeks when grown at 50F (10C) nights. Plants will be about 5 inches (13 cm) tall without growth regulators and can be transplanted to quarts or gallons for late-season sales or the next year after overwintering. While in the cell pack, plants are fairly uniform although they may vary an inch or two in height.

If started from seed in February, sold green in packs, and planted into the garden in May, *Solidago* develops a single stem the first summer and is often uneven in height and flowering performance. From a winter sowing, you can expect 50 to 75% blooming plants in mid to late July, the remainder flowering either later or the following year.

For 4-inch (10 cm) pot sales, allow 13 to 15 weeks from seed when grown at no less than 50F (10C) nights. These plants can be sold green but will flower—some better than others—during July and August.

The crown can be divided during spring or autumn with minimal rooting problems. Depending on the size of the division taken, plants will often root in three to four weeks in a quart container, one to three weeks longer for gallons. The night temperatures should be 50F (10C) and warmer for active root development.

As for cuttings, use 3- to 4-inch-long (7 to 10 cm) terminal shoots, stuck in sand at 70F (21C) bottom heat. Select your cutting material by early June since plants begin to bud up in mid to late June before flowering in July. Basal cuttings can also be taken as the plants emerge in spring. This method isn't usually suggested since spring propagation is difficult for most growers.

S

Commercial propagators offer *Solidago* as bare-root transplants, in small pots, or as liners during winter and early spring. These can be potted up into quarts and gallons and sold in April, May, and June.

VARIETIES

Seed varieties

Baby Gold (Golden Baby) is a common cultivar available from many U.S. seed companies. It grows 20 to 26 inches (51 to 66 cm) tall with golden yellow plumes.

From vegetative propagation

A number of cultivars are mentioned in various perennial reference books. Only a limited number are commercially available, however. The following can be obtained as liners, small pots, bare-root transplants, and/or prefinished containers.

Crown of Rays (Strahlenkrone, Radiant Crown) has golden yellow flowers on 18- to 24-inch-tall (46 to 61 cm) plants. This variety has a columnar habit. It's easily found here in the United States.

Golden Fleece is one of the most commonly available clones seen in North America. This cultivar is listed in nursery catalogs under *S. sphacelata*, a species not recognized by the popular references. It flowers freely and grows 14 to 18 inches (35 to 46 cm) tall with golden yellow flowers. It's an excellent cultivar.

Goldenmosa has deep yellow flowers on 24- to 30-inch-tall (61 to 76 cm) plants.

Lemore is a buff or light yellow flowering variety to 3 feet (90 cm) tall in bloom. The plant is sometimes listed as a variety of × *Solidaster*, but many experts claim it's a clone.

USES

This perennial makes an excellent cut flower for either the commercial market or in the home. Flowers can be used fresh or dried. It also is recommended for commercial landscaping and home gardens. Plants have handsome foliage with a layered look and a symmetrical habit. The golden yellow color can be rather garish, so mass plantings are only suggested for large, open expanses such as golf courses. Two or three in a clump will work better in a small garden. *Solidago* is especially suggested for any wildflower plantings.

IN THE HOME GARDEN

Plant in any full-sun location that's well drained, avoiding waterlogged or boggy conditions. Plants don't require staking unless they've been heavily fed or watered. Even then, it's only the taller varieties—and most often the species—that require staking.

Depending on the selection you have, plants can be short lived in the garden. In our clay loam soils, we've seen some varieties last for at least three years but have seldom seen a clump survive longer than five years without dividing. If the plants are dug, divided, and replanted, longevity improves. Plants can be divided every three or four years.

■ STACHYS BYZANTINA
(formerly *S. lanata, S. olympica*)

FAMILY: Lamiaceae

COMMON NAME(S): Lamb's Ear, Woolly Betony

DESCRIPTION
A long-lived perennial, *Stachys byzantina* has woolly gray foliage similar to dusty miller. Plants grow 20 to 28 inches (51 to 71 cm) tall when flowering, but the carpet of foliage is only about 8 to 10 inches (20 to 25 cm) tall without blooms. The erect floral spikes measure 18 to 24 inches (46 to 61 cm) long with the top half dotted with one-half-inch (1 cm) rose or rose-purple flowers. The foliage is more sought after than the flowers, although both make an excellent show.

HARDINESS: Zones 4 to 9.

SEASON OF BLOOM: June.

PROPAGATION
Seed, basal cuttings, and division are the common methods used to propagate lamb's ear. Divisions are more common in the spring. Basal cuttings can be taken during the spring or summer months from the spreading crown. Seed can be sown anytime.

GERMINATION OVERVIEW: 16,000 seeds per ounce/560 per gram.
Stachys will germinate in eight to 15 days at 70F (21C); the seed should be continuously exposed to light during germination. Transplanting can begin 18 to 24 days after sowing.

GROWING ON
From seed: Seed sown during the winter or spring won't produce flowering plants the same season. Winter-sown seed will make green, salable 32-cell packs in 11 to 13 weeks, at 50F to 55F (10C to 13C) nights. For 4½-inch (11 cm) pots, allow 12 to 14 weeks. For larger, more robust quart or gallon pots, sow seed during summer for sales the following spring. *S. byzantina* requires a cold period before it will flower.

Cuttings taken during spring or summer months will root readily, but you should avoid excess water on the hairy foliage. Under excessive heat and humidity, it can rot, although it isn't as sensitive to rot as other woolly foliage plants.

Once rooted, the cuttings can be potted up into larger containers and grown on in

S

spring for mid to late summer sales. Otherwise, the plants can be overwintered for spring sales.

Commercial propagators offer this perennial in small pots or as liners, occasionally as bare root. Any of these can be potted up into quarts or gallons and sold in spring.

VARIETIES

Your variety choices should be based on what your market requires. For the home gardener, either of the two varieties listed below will be fine. Both are long lived and are excellent performers. If you're selling both retail and wholesale, however, Silver Carpet will be preferred because it's nonflowering. Some prefer a smooth border or edging plant all summer long over the upright, gray-flowering spikes of the species. Home gardeners may likewise select the species for just this purpose, adding a unique spike-type cut flower to their arrangements. You may need both selections.

S. byzantina is easily available as seed from a number of commercial seed and nursery companies. The plants flower the second year from seed.

Silver Carpet is a vegetatively propagated variety growing 6 to 8 inches (15 to 20 cm) tall. It, too, has deep gray foliage but on nonflowering plants.

USES

Especially useful in perennial gardens where gray or silver-leaved plants highlight other colors, *Stachys* is not known for its flowers. Plants work well as edgings and will fill in heavily once established.

This is an excellent choice for landscaping. Use nonflowering Silver Carpet or the species, and cut the flowers off when they appear, or use the spikes as cut flowers. Plants will fill in on 15-inch (38 cm) centers and provide a dramatic accent.

IN THE HOME GARDEN

Plants have been long lived for us with few problems. When planting lamb's ears in the perennial border, be sure to clean out the matted, dead foliage that develops annually under the leaf canopy at the plant base. If this layer is left in place, the roots often suffocate and die, causing the center of the crown to brown out. Plants can also be divided once every three or four years to prevent center browning.

Plant in full sun or partial shade, spacing on 15- to 18-inch (38 to 48 cm) centers in a well-drained but moist garden location. Seed varieties will need deadheading after flowering to avoid looking unkempt and wild. In areas with extended high humidity and heat, lamb's ears can rot as the foliage holds moisture. This is especially true in the southern United States.

■ STOKESIA LAEVIS

FAMILY: Asteraceae

COMMON NAME(S): Stokes' Aster

DESCRIPTION

Stokesia laevis is a native North American perennial with large, lavender-blue flowers up to 4 inches (10 cm) across. The outer ring of petals are large, strap-shaped and broader than the tubular center florets. Blooms, which appear in summer, are positioned atop upright, stiff stems to 15 or 18 inches (38 to 46 cm) long. Plants spread 12 to 18 inches (30 to 46 cm) across in a rounded form.

HARDINESS: Zones 5 to 9.
Read **In the home garden** for additional information.

SEASON OF BLOOM: June and July.

PROPAGATION

Seed, divisions, and stem cuttings are the usual methods to propagate Stokes' aster. Root cuttings can also be taken while the plants are dormant in winter; divisions are often taken in spring but work equally well if taken in autumn.

GERMINATION OVERVIEW: 3,000 seeds per ounce/105 per gram.
Pretreatments: Seed germination is usually rapid and without problems. Seed will sprout in seven to 12 days at 70F (21C) and doesn't need covering. The resulting seedlings can be transplanted 14 to 18 days after sowing, in most cases.

If seedlings emerge slowly, or if germination is erratic, place the moistened seed tray in a refrigerator at 40F (4C) for four to six weeks, watering as needed. Then remove the tray and place on the bench for germination. Watch the flat in the refrigerator for early signs of germination, and remove it if you see a number of shoots.

GROWING ON

Crop time: Seed can be sown any time of the year, although spring sowing and transplanting will produce green plants in quart containers by midsummer. These can be sold in late summer, but in our Chicago climate, the plants seldom produce a strong enough root in the garden to survive a normal winter. In colder climates, overwinter quart or larger containers for spring sales. If seeds have been slow to germinate and plants don't develop uniformly, overwintering will produce a more consistent crop the next year.

S

Commercial propagators offer *Stokesia* in either small pots or as liners. Available in autumn and winter, either of these can be potted up into quarts or gallons and sold in spring.

For more on root cuttings, see the additional information in the front of this book under **Propagation Techniques**.

VARIETIES

Stokesia laevis is available from a number of commercial seed companies and wild-flower or native seed firms. Numerous commercial propagators and plug companies offer started plants. Although a native plant, *Stokesia laevis* rises above the reputation many native seed crops have for commonality, weediness, and the "wild" wildflower syndrome.

The following cultivars are vegetatively propagated only and will not come true from seed. In all cases, the plant heights are shorter in our Chicago location; their listed height is more accurate the farther south they're grown.

Blue Danube is a lavender-blue flowering variety, 15 to 20 inches (38 to 51 cm) tall. It is a very popular selection found in many commercial catalogs.

Silver Moon is a white-flowering variety that grows 15 to 18 inches (38 to 46 cm) tall in bloom.

Wyoming is a darker flowering variety than Blue Danube on plants of similar height and habit.

USES

This is an excellent perennial for the home garden as a specimen planting or as a cut flower. Commercially, it isn't a common cut flower. Although it is short stemmed, it is a respectable cut flower for home use. The plants have often been shunned in the landscape due, in part, to their limited blooming. I suggest that you use groupings of three or more to fill in the planting and make it appear more aesthetically pleasing. Avoid large mass plantings and concentrate on smaller groupings instead.

IN THE HOME GARDEN

It's important to note that in Chicago, we're on the northern boundaries of winter hardiness for *Stokesia*. We have plants that have been well established for years, but we also lose a plant or two every few years.

Stokesia performs best in warm, sunny locations where it is well drained, especially in winter. If the soil is frequently moist or if there's standing water around the plant crown, it may be short lived.

No special care is required. Staking isn't necessary to keep the plants upright, nor should you overfertilize these plants in the garden. During the winter, we place an "open" mulch of evergreen boughs over the tops of the crowns to keep them from drying out, although this is more important in exposed plantings away from foundations or other protection. If planted in the open, a winter mulch is suggested for the colder areas of the country.

S

T

■ TANACETUM COCCINEUM

The genus *Chrysanthemum* has recently been divided between new and existing genera, including *Pyrethrum*. This crop was formerly called *Chrysanthemum coccineum*.

FAMILY: Asteraceae

COMMON NAME(S): Pyrethrum, Painted Daisy

DESCRIPTION

Pyrethrums are a well-known favorite in the perennial garden. The flowers can be single, semidouble or fully double, measure from 2 to 3 inches (5 to 6 cm) across and have no flower scent. The pastel flower colors include red, rose, pink, and shades in between. Plants range from 18 to 24 inches (46 to 61 cm) tall with fernlike foliage similar to the millefolium types of *Achillea*. Plants are taller than they are wide, spreading from 12 to 18 inches (30 to 46 cm). *T. coccineum* is the source of pyrethrum, an insecticide widely used in greenhouses and gardens.

HARDINESS: Zones 4 to 9.

Here in our Midwest gardens, the plants look good for two years at most before they decline, so they're treated as short-lived perennials.

SEASON OF BLOOM: May and June.

Like many plants related to *Chrysanthemum*, pyrethrums will flower repeatedly during the summer if they're cut back.

PROPAGATION

Pyrethrums are usually seed propagated, except for the fully double varieties and the hybrids. These are propagated by cuttings or division, but are short lived and seldom sold in the United States. Divisions can be made in either the spring or late summer.

GERMINATION OVERVIEW: 17,000 to 35,000 seeds per ounce/595 to 1,225 per gram.

Pyrethrums germinate readily without pretreatments to get ample seedling stands.

Seed doesn't need to be covered and germinates in 14 to 21 days at 60F to 70F (16C to 21C). Transplant 20 to 35 days after sowing.

GROWING ON

From seed: For green, 4-inch (10 cm) pot sales in the spring, allow 12 to 14 weeks at 55F (13C) nights. These plants will flower sporadically during July and August from seed sown during January or February. If you prefer green, 32-cell packs, allow 10 to 12 weeks to finish off at 55F (13C) nights.

Commercial propagators offer pyrethrum as bare-root transplants, small potted plants, and liners/plugs. Primarily available during the autumn and winter, any of these can be potted up into quart and gallon containers and sold in spring.

VARIETIES

Note: You may find commercial varieties listed as varieties of *Chrysanthemum coccineum* or, less commonly, as pyrethrum rather than *Tanacetum coccineum*. Since the nomenclature just recently changed to *Tanacetum*, many companies may leave the former name intact so buyers will recognize it.

One additional comment: Seed lots of double-flowering varieties are usually only 20 to 40% double. The remaining 60 to 80% will be either semidouble or single. The double-flowering varieties will require a full summer after being planted to the garden before they'll put on their best show.

Robinson's series. This series is made up of several separate flower colors including red and rose, plus a mix. The mix is the most popular in the U.S. market. The flowers are 3 inches (7 cm) across and either single or double.

One additional note regarding Robinson's series: Occasionally the variety will be listed as double flowering. This selection was originally a clone and propagated vegetatively. Seed propagated plants are primarily single, though double-flowering plants are common.

IN THE HOME GARDEN

In the home perennial garden, pyrethrums seldom live longer than three years. However, it helps to plant them close to the home or in other locations that protect them from the severity of both summer and winter weather. While they'll probably live only one more year, the plants will look healthier and more robust, with stronger, more upright growth.

Plant to a well-drained location with full or half-day sun. Avoid areas with puddling water, which can lead to crown rot. Space pyrethrums 12 to 15 inches (30 to 38 cm) apart. Once planted to the garden, they seldom require dividing more than every two or three years, if at all. Some staking will be necessary if the plants are not growing along a fence or next to other tall plants. Use pyrethrums as home cut flowers and treat as you would chrysanthemums.

T

■ TANACETUM PARTHENIUM
(formerly *Chrysanthemum parthenium*, *Matricaria capensis*, and *M. exima*)

FAMILY: Asteraceae

COMMON NAME(S): Matricaria, Feverfew

DESCRIPTION
An erect plant 15 to 24 (38 to 61 cm) inches tall, *Tanacetum parthenium* spreads 10 to 15 inches (25 to 38 cm). Many shorter varieties are used primarily as bedding plants, but they seldom survive a northern winter. The freely branching plants have deeply divided, aromatic leaves. Plants often fill out rapidly as they develop. The flowers are mostly white, sometimes cream colored, and either single or double in appearance. Flowers are one-half to 1 inch (1 to 2.5 cm) across and held in an open cluster at the top of the plant. Numerous bloom types are available including pompon, anemone, and fully double forms.

HARDINESS: Zones 5 to 8.
Tanacetum parthenium works best treated as a hardy annual here in our Chicago-area gardens and isn't reliably hardy without winter cover. Plants may live through one winter, but 100% return isn't probable. Remarkably, the plants are hardier if self-sown and left undisturbed.

SEASON OF BLOOM: July and August.

PROPAGATION
Seed, divisions, and cuttings are the three propagation methods that are always reliable. Seed can be sown anytime, while both cuttings and divisions work best when taken in the spring.

GERMINATION OVERVIEW: 200,000 seeds per ounce/7,000 per gram.
Seed germinates in seven to 10 days at 70F (21C) and doesn't need covering. Seedlings can be transplanted 16 to 26 days after sowing.

GROWING ON
Crop time: From seed, seedlings develop quickly, and green, salable 32-cell packs will be ready 10 to 12 weeks after sowing when grown at 50F (13C) nights after establishing. These plants will be in full garden bloom between late June and the end of July as long as they're planted by May.

A better method is to sow seed in early winter and transplant to 4½-inch (10 cm) or quart containers for green plant sales in May. These plants will flower in June as well, but are larger, more vigorous, and give better results than those grown in a cell pack. If the temperatures get to the upper 60s (19C to 20C) at night, stretching may occur on plants grown in cell packs.

Divisions establish quickly and can be sold several weeks after digging. Plants can be potted up into quarts or gallons for same season sales.

As for cuttings, tip cuttings root quickly and can be treated as you would garden mums. Cuttings stuck into moistened peat moss or sand with a 65F to 70F (19C to 21C) soil temperature will root within a week or two.

VARIETIES

All of the following are propagated from seed.

Ball Double White is an old variety developed by the late George J. Ball, founder of the Ball Seed Co. It's an upright variety with fully double, three-quarter-inch (2 cm) white flowers on plants to 2 feet (60 cm) tall. Mr. Ball developed the variety for the cut flower trade, and it's still a premier variety some 50 years after its introduction.

Golden Ball has cream white to light yellow flowers on plants from 10 to 12 inches (25 to 30 cm) tall. This variety is not as reliable to overwinter as the taller types and often dies out.

Santana is a dwarf bedding plant variety with single anemone flowers on 8- to 10-inch-tall (20 to 25 cm) plants. Plants aren't winter hardy and are best treated as an annual in the United States.

White Pompon is a 2-foot (60 cm) flowering variety with three-quarter-inch (2 cm) single white blooms. It makes an excellent cut flower.

USES

Matricaria is useful in wildflower gardens, in small clumps in the perennial garden, and as a cut flower. The plant may be too "wild" in its appearance and remind customers of its relatives in the open meadows.

IN THE HOME GARDEN

Plant matricaria where it can get full sun and good drainage. Plants will be more prolific in moist, sandy loams than in clay soils and require staking only if grown in fertile and moist locations. If cultivating as a cut flower, harvest the blooms when color first shows. For dried flowers, wait until the flower almost fully opens.

Plants don't require special treatment, but they don't respond well to excess water in their crowns. Under prolonged exposure, especially during the winter, the plants often rot and can die. Plant in well-drained locations or in raised beds for best performance. To protect the plants in the winter, provide a layer of mulch in areas with cold weather but limited snowfall. If planted in open, unprotected areas where the winter winds hound the plants frequently, higher losses can be expected.

T

■ THALICTRUM AQUILEGIFOLIUM

FAMILY: Ranunculaceae

COMMON NAME(S): Columbine Meadow Rue
The common name refers to *Thalictrum's* columbine-like foliage.

DESCRIPTION
Thalictrum aquilegifolium is a graceful and decorative perennial with small, rose-lavender flowers arranged in open flower heads similar to baby's breath, but not as large or as branched. The plants are dioecious (male and female flowers on separate plants), and the male flowers tend to be showier, with elongated stamens that make the flowers look like small puff-balls. The blue-green foliage has numerous leaflets like a columbine. Plants are open and airy in form and sway gently in the breeze. The plants grow from 2 to 3 feet (60 to 90 cm) tall and spread from 1½ to no more than 3 feet (45 to 90 cm) in Zone 5 climates.

HARDINESS: Zones 5 to 8.

SEASON OF BLOOM: May and June.
Numerous reference books on perennials suggest June and July as the blooming season, but our plants often fade out of bloom before the end of June.

PROPAGATION
Although it's a member of the *Ranunculus* family (collectively, a difficult genus to germinate), this seed germinates quickly and easily.

Once a planting has become established, it's possible to remove the small seedlings as they emerge at the base of the mother plant in the spring. These can be potted up and easily grown on.

GERMINATION OVERVIEW: 11,000 seeds per ounce/385 per gram.
This number reflects cleaned seed, not seed directly harvested from the plant.

Pretreatments: None usually are needed. If seed has been stored for over a year, erratic germination may be noted. Conditioning the seed in a cool, moist environment can increase chances of germination on older seed. Additional information is provided under moist chilling in the front of the book.

Seed germinates in five to 10 days at 70F (21C) and doesn't need to be covered. Seedlings can be transplanted 15 to 24 days after sowing.

GROWING ON
Crop time: From seed, growth is relatively quick, although the resulting plants will seldom flower the first year if sown after March 1. Sowings before March 1 aren't guaranteed to flower either, but we've had greater percentages of flowering plants the first year when seed is sown earlier—in January or February. Flowering may not be that important the first year, however.

Transplant seedlings into large cell packs or small pots for moving into larger containers at a later date. We usually transplant to a 32-cell pack and allow 10 to 13 weeks from sowing for the roots to fill out (when grown at 50F/10C nights). The plants are then transplanted to quarts and overwintered for spring planting the following year. The first season from seed, plants will reach 9 to 12 inches (23 to 30 cm) tall in the pot, depending on fertilizer, temperature, and watering.

Commercial propagators offer this perennial in either small pots or liners. Primarily available during the autumn and winter, either of these can be potted up into quarts and gallons and sold in spring.

VARIETIES

Thalictrum aquilegifolium isn't usually available from U.S. commercial seed houses because seed is easily gathered from your own plants. You can locate the variety from some domestic and European seed firms, as a mixture of lavender, rose-purple and white, although separate colors are also available.

T. aquilegifolium var. *album* is a pure-white-flowering selection available as seed. Plants are from 3 to 4 feet (90 to 120 cm) tall.

T. aquilegifolium var. *purpureum* is similar in habit and performance to var. *album*, only with lilac-colored flowers. This variety is also seed propagated.

RELATED MATERIAL

T. minus (*T. adiantifolium*) has maidenhair fernlike foliage with one-half-inch (1 cm) yellow-green flowers on 12- to 20-inch-tall (30 to 51 cm) plants. It's a variable species, however, and often yields interesting plant forms from seed. If a particular variety piques your interest, division is the key to maintaining the variety. Seed is often more troublesome to germinate than *T. aquilegifolium*. If you encounter problems, moist chill the seed for several weeks for better results. *T. minus* var. *adiantifolium* is a taller selection that can be found from seed mostly in Europe. Plants grow 2 to 3 feet (60 to 90 cm) tall, although the plants vary in height, with inconspicuous yellow-green flowers. This variety is the most commonly grown of the species but is prized more for its foliage than its flowers.

T. delavayi (Yunnan Meadow Rue) is a beautiful specimen usually growing to 5 feet (150 cm) when established in the garden, although it can range from 3 to 5 feet (90 to 150 cm) depending on exposure, watering, and fertilizer. The flowers are lavender with yellow stamens and one-half to 1 inch (1 to 2.5 cm) across. The foliage is blue green. According to Ruth Clausen in *Perennials for American Gardens*, this species is the only one that's long lived in warm climates. Plants are hardy to Zones 4 through 7 and can be treated like *T. aquilegifolium*. The noted exception is Hewitt's Double.

T. delavayi album is the white-flowering form of the above plant. Growth is similar to the species. The variety can be propagated from seed.

Hewitt's Double is a double-flowering plant with one-half-inch (1 cm), lavender-rose flowers. This particular variety is more temperamental than the species and dies out where other selections might be long lived. It is commercially propagated by tissue culture; seed does not come true on this variety. In his *Propagation of Hardy Perennials*, Richard Bird writes that "Hewitt's Double is always considered difficult but can easily be increased by lifting the cylindrical rootstock in March and cutting vertically down through it. This can be further sectionalized, creating up to eight thin sections that can be potted up. There is no need to have visible buds at the top of each section as these will quickly form. Plants can be set out in August in a rich, moisture-retentive soil in sun."

T. dipterocarpum closely resembles *T. delavayi*, and the cultivated varieties are often interchangeably used with either botanical name. To the naked eye the differences are hard to discern.

As for the species itself, it's available from a limited number of U.S. seed companies. It grows to about 3 feet (90 cm) tall and bears rose-lavender flowers with yellow stamens. *Thalictrum dipterocarpum* is hardy to Zones 5 to 7. It can be propagated as suggested for *T. aquilegifolium*.

T. rochebrunianum resembles the previous two varieties with blue-green foliage on plants 3 to 5 feet (90 to 150 cm) tall in flower. Plants can be propagated from either seed or division and are hardy down to Zones 5 to 7. One cultivar, Lavender Mist, is commonly sold, and while the species can be seed propagated, Lavender Mist is vegetatively propagated. Blooms are purple with yellow stamens. Plants can tolerate more sun than other species within this genus.

USES

This is an underused perennial in both commercial and home landscapes. Only a few plants are necessary to provide a backdrop; they can also be used as a home cut flower, providing open sprays similar to baby's breath. Remember to showcase the foliage as well as the flowers. Some varieties have rather lackluster blooms—a short blooming season only compounds this effect. Companion plantings that contrast with the blue-green foliage work very well.

IN THE HOME GARDEN

Due to their rather tall habits, the plants should be spaced 3 feet (90 cm) apart for the more vigorous selections, slightly closer on shorter cultivars. The plants don't necessarily require any staking, but when planted in fertile locations, the growth may be more wiry and weak than normal. In these cases, staking is beneficial.

Plants do best in morning and late-day sun here in our Chicago-area gardens. Plants will tolerate full sun but often wilt during the late afternoon in sunnier exposures. If plants are small and only recently planted before hot weather sets in, they often die out by late summer. Likewise, plants grown in heavy shade are short lived.

■ TRADESCANTIA × ANDERSONIANA

T. virginiana is probably the most widely known *Tradescantia* within the horticultural trade. Many varieties sold under this name in garden centers and nurseries have resulted from breeding various species together; however, *T. × andersoniana* represents the many crosses. Read the information under of **Varieties** for more detail.

FAMILY: Commelinaceae

COMMON NAME(S): Spiderwort

DESCRIPTION

Tradescantia × andersoniana is a grasslike plant with succulent stems ranging in height from 12 to 30 inches (30 to 76 cm) tall and 20 to 30 inches (51 to 76 cm) wide, depending on the species. Many species in this genus are native to either North or South America and bear three-petaled blossoms in blue, rose, purple, or white. Flowers last only one day or a fraction thereof, often wilting prior to dying in the afternoon. Once in full bloom, however, subsequent buds open at the same time. Flowers measure between 1 and 3 inches (2.5 to 7 cm) across.

HARDINESS: Zones 4 to 9.

SEASON OF BLOOM: June to August.

PROPAGATION

Tradescantia is increased by seed, division and, rarely, stem cuttings. Seed can be sown anytime, but it's difficult to find and cultivars don't come true from seed. Rather, divisions are the primary method for propagating *Tradescantia*.

Divisions can be taken in spring until flowers set—even then, plants can be divided if the flowering stems are cut back and they're protected from direct sun. Cuttings are taken anytime during the growing season, although they root and grow with greater ease and better eventual performance if taken prior to full flower. For cuttings, choose stems with closely spaced internodes and then cut into sections, leaving two nodes per section. Cuttings taken in July will set roots under mist within seven to 14 days and can be potted up two to three weeks after being stuck into the propagating media.

GERMINATION OVERVIEW: 10,000 seeds per ounce/350 per gram.
Germination temperatures of 70F to 72F (21C to 22C) work well, and seed can be left exposed or lightly covered during germination. Seedlings will emerge in seven to 14 days and can be transplanted 20 to 30 days after sowing.

GROWING ON

Crop time: Seed-propagated crops are slow growing and are more often the option when cultivating native species. While not inferior plants, seed-grown types are

T

difficult to find and are usually available only in blue, rose, white, or mixtures. From seed to established 32-cell packs takes anywhere from 13 to 15 weeks from an early February sowing. *Tradescantia* doesn't grow evenly from seed, however, and you may have to pot up the transplants over a period of two weeks or more. Plants will flower the same season from seed; February sowings will yield plants starting to flower by mid-June, although it will be mid-July before all plants have at least one flower on them.

Plants that are divided with foliage trimmed back will start to flower in about four to six weeks depending on when the division was taken. Spring dug and divided plants can be salable the same year, although well-rooted containers and ample shoot development are only possible if overwintered from divisions taken the previous summer or early autumn. Divisions taken in spring will only send up a few new shoots until the roots have reestablished themselves in either the nursery bed or container. This is especially true of divisions taken after flowering has begun.

Commercial propagators like DeVroomen and Walters Gardens will have bare-root transplants available in the fall and winter for potting into 2- to 4-quart containers. Depending on the root size, one to four shoots will develop from the crown. Visually, many varieties won't fill out the top of the pot for 10 to 12 weeks when grown at 50F to 55F (10C to 13C) nights. Salability is in the eyes of the beholder, however. Roots potted up in late February and after will bud up and flower in eight or nine weeks even though the rootball will not yet be dense. However, the plants can be sold and will grow on without difficulty. For more visually acceptable plants, allow 10 weeks or more at no lower than 50F (10C) nights.

A comment on temperatures: After germination, drop night temperatures to no lower than 58F to encourage root development. Plants often grow slowly—regardless of propagation methods—under cool temperatures and short days. As for summer-grown plants in containers, it's only necessary to shade newly taken divisions, cuttings, or seedlings. Once established, allow them more light since temperatures will be difficult to control.

VARIETIES

Tradescantia species cross-pollinate readily, giving rise to the many garden hybrids commercially available today. *T. × andersoniana* reflects the complex interbreeding among these plants over the years. It's the result of crosses between *T. virginiana*, *T. subaspera*, and *T. ohiensis*. Plants of *T. × andersoniana* tend to have larger flowers but can vary in height depending on their genetic makeup. Each species noted is still available but if grown in areas where other species prevail, purity of seed-propagated selections cannot be guaranteed.

There are no named seed varieties in the trade. When available from seed houses, the most common selection is *T. virginiana*. Numerous species will be available through native perennial seed firms, however. Seed offers the grower the opportunity to select varieties of merit, then propagate them vegetatively since they seldom breed true due to crossbreeding. In the U.S. trade, few seed houses carry *Tradescantia* since seed can be gathered easily in the wild, or the varieties can be propagated readily by other means. The following are **seed-propagated** varieties.

T. ohiensis reaches a height of 2 to 3 feet (60 to 90 cm). Sold primarily through seed and plant houses offering native plant material. Flowers grow to slightly over 1 inch (2.5 cm) across and come in blue or rose and sometimes white. Plants can become rank growing, which is fine for large areas, but its habit and size may be out of proportion with foundation plantings. From seed, 60% or more of the plants will often flower blue, although the shades can differ from plant to plant.

T. virginiana reaches a height of 18 to 36 inches (46 to 91 cm). This is the most common *Tradescantia* sold in the United States. Flowers are purple or deep blue—rose and white are less common.

The following seven varieties must be propagated **vegetatively**.

Cultivars sold under the name of *T. virginiana* are most often *T. × andersoniana*.

Blue Stone (also Bluestone). Midblue flowers on plants to 18 inches (46 cm) tall.

Innocence. Pure white flowers to 2½ inches (6 cm) across on plants from 20 to 24 inches (51 to 61 cm) tall.

Pauline. Orchid or lavender-pink flowers (sometimes described as mauve) on plants 18 to 24 inches (46 to 61 cm) tall.

Red Cloud. Deep rose-red blooms on plants 15 to 18 inches (38 to 46 cm) tall.

Snowcap. Pure white flowers on plants 18 to 24 inches (46 to 61 cm) tall.

Zwanenberg. Large-flowering variety with blooms 3 inches (7 cm) across in a rich violet-based vibrant blue. Grows 18 to 24 inches (46 to 61 cm) tall. See Color Plate 68 for photo of *Tradescantia × andersoniana* Zwanenberg.

USES

Tradescantia is a versatile plant beneficial to either landscape or home garden locations. By keeping several key points in mind when landscaping with this plant, you'll enjoy it in the garden for years to come. *Tradescantia* is often found growing across the Midwest and eastern United States in woodlands, alongside roads and in between railroad ties on abandoned lines. It can take full sun to bright shade. If placed in an area with ample water and nutrients, it will become weedy and easily fall open.

Avoid fertilizer-enriched soils and allow for good drainage. Feed only to establish the plants in the spring and/or after trimming them back after flowering. Set plants into areas that receive either full sun or exposures with morning or afternoon sun only. Full-shade areas yield tall plants that fall open, require staking, and bear a fraction of the flowers seen on plants grown in brighter locations.

In the landscape, plants will flower in the Chicago area a week before Memorial Day and continue blooming all summer. The prime flowering period is June and early July, although scattered color will remain after this time. Once flowering is over, the stems tend to get top heavy on most varieties and should be trimmed back to 10 to 12 inches (25 to 30 cm). Grown all over the country, *Tradescantia* is best during early summer. It often falters during the hottest weather by falling open and stalling in bloom. If trimmed back, the plants will flower again in four or five weeks. No winter protection or staking is needed.

V

■ VERBASCUM PHOENICEUM

FAMILY: Scrophulariaceae

COMMON NAME(S): Purple Mullein

DESCRIPTION

Although commonly called purple mullein, *Verbascum phoeniceum* can also have white, rose, and red flowers, as well as shades in-between. The scentless flowers are single, 1 inch (2.5 cm) across, and open in upright racemes to 26 inches (66 cm) tall when blooming. When not in bloom, the rosetting, grey-green basal foliage is about 3 to 4 inches (7 to 10 cm) tall. *V. phoeniceum* is a plant with limited attributes to be used sparingly as a novelty. Plants spread from 10 to 20 inches (25 to 51 cm) across.

HARDINESS: Zones 5 to 8.

SEASON OF BLOOM: June.
If cut back to the rosetting foliage after flowering, plants will flower again in three to four weeks.

PROPAGATION

The species can be easily grown from seed, although many cultivars listed below will have to be propagated by root cuttings or, less frequently, by dividing the secondary rosettes in spring. Additional detail of propagating by root cuttings is available in the **Propagation Techniques** chapter.

GERMINATION OVERVIEW: 200,000 seeds per ounce/7,000 per gram.
Pretreatments: None are necessary. *Verbascum* germinates readily. Seeds sprout in four to seven days at 72F (22C), and covering isn't necessary. Seedlings can be transplanted in 14 to 16 days after sowing.

GROWING ON

Crop time: From seed, plants grow quickly and can be sold green as either 4-inch (10 cm) pots or cell packs in the spring. Plants will rosette, growing 3 to 5 inches (7 to

V

435

13 cm) wide but no more than 1 inch (2.5 cm) tall. Green transplants are salable in a 32-cell pack nine to 11 weeks after sowing; 18-cell packs will be ready in 10 to 12 weeks and 4-inch (10 cm) pots about the same. These crop times are based on growing on at no lower than 50F (10C) nights.

As an alternative method, try sowing to a large plug tray (290 or larger) and then transplant directly into a 4-inch (10 cm) pot for same season sales, or into quarts for overwintering. Regardless of the method used, the plants will flower the same season from seed. The bloom is often insignificant and the blooming time short; however, better color can be expected the second season from seed.

Divisions aren't difficult—they simply involve removing secondary rosettes from the mother plant and potting them up for sales the next spring. The plants aren't consistent in setting and developing rosettes, however. In cases where the plants are vigorously growing and have ample light and fertility, secondary rosettes will develop at the base and can be removed along with a portion of the root. But for commercial growers, root cuttings and seed offer the greatest opportunity to meet volume demand at sales time.

VARIETIES

Verbascum phoeniceum is available on a limited basis from U.S. seed suppliers; it's
  more common in the European trade.

In Europe there are numerous varieties that have resulted from crosses between *V. phoeniceum* and other species. Collectively these are often listed under the designation *Verbascum × hybridum*, although they're also sold as Cotswold Hybrids. You can only propagate these varieties by root cuttings to maintain the original colors. Seed-propagated plants will revert back to one of the parents. They aren't commonly available in the United States and will require perseverance to find them.

RELATED MATERIAL

Verbascum bombyciferum is a biennial form with stately, pubescent (covered with fine
  hairs), gray-green stems and leaves. The plants look gray in overall appearance.
  The flowers are single and clustered in upright spikes growing 12 to 20 inches
  (30 to 51 cm) long. The individual blooms are yellow and about 1 inch (2.5 cm)
  across. Plants reach 6 feet (180 cm) tall in bloom when grown under ideal conditions, although they seldom grow over 3 feet (90 cm) tall for us here in Chicago
  and are short lived. *V. bombyciferum* isn't fond of our hot and humid summers and
  wet winters and often dies out before flowering the second year. Plants are susceptible to crown rot and should be planted in raised beds.

These are very dramatic looking when in full bloom, but they won't tolerate frequent overhead watering because it often leads to fatal crown rot and foliar diseases. Plants flower in June and July.

Plants have a similar culture to *V. phoeniceum*. Allow nine to 11 weeks for salable plants in a 4-inch (10 cm) pot from winter-sown seed. For larger container sales, sow earlier in the year, although plants won't flower until the following year. *V. bombyciferum* is a true biennial, requiring a cold period prior to flowering.

Verbascum chaixii is similar in its growth and performance to *V. phoeniceum*, but it has woolly gray-green leaves with 1-inch (2.5 cm), light yellow flowers. Plants grow to 3 feet (90 cm) tall.

V. chaixii var. *album* is a white-flowering version of the species similar in height and form.

Both of the above crops can be propagated and grown on as indicated for *V. phoeniceum*.

USES

Of all the different species noted above, only *V. bombyciferum* has a major impact as a garden or landscape plant. The plant performs better in California and other temperate locations than it does in either Chicago or Atlanta winters and summers. Since it's a biennial, it should be planted sparingly, but it's extremely interesting when in the full regalia of bloom.

For the remaining species, I would suggest trying them but realize they're not spectacular in flower and are more of a novelty than a prerequisite for perennial borders. In England and similar favorable climates, *Verbascum*'s numerous spikes and low-growing foliage are striking.

IN THE HOME GARDEN

V. phoeniceum is a long-lived variety that we've had in our gardens for well over seven years. The plants will reseed themselves but aren't aggressive and are easily weeded out. Plants don't require any staking and, while not overly attractive, they do have their merits in their reliable flowering two or three times a season.

Once flowering is finished in June, cut the flower stalk all the way down to the foliage rosette at the base, and the plants will flower again in several weeks. If you let the plants go to seed, however, the rosettes will die and leave only the maturing seed pods on naked stalks sticking out of the ground. If these stalks are cut down to the soil line, new rosettes will develop in two to three weeks and flower a second time within two to three weeks after that.

Plants prefer full sun in well-drained locations.

▄▄ Veronica incana

Family: Scrophulariaceae

Common name(s): Woolly Speedwell

Description

Prized for its woolly foliage, *V. incana* has soft, pubescent (hairy), gray-green leaves similar in appearance to dusty miller. The plants are basal branching, producing numerous upright or slightly arching stems that end in flower spikes. In bloom, the plants grow from 15 to 20 inches (38 to 51 cm) tall, although *V. incana* is only 4 to 6 inches (10 to 15 cm) tall when not in flower. The single, one-quarter inch (6 mm), violet-blue flowers are held on 4- to 8-inch-long (10 to 20 cm) flowering spikes.

Hardiness: Zones 4 to 8.

Season of bloom: June and July.

Propagation

Seed, division, and cuttings are the usual propagation methods. Clumps can be divided in the spring or fall, while tip cuttings are taken during late spring or early summer.

Germination overview: 221,000 seeds per ounce/7,735 per gram.
Pretreatments: Woolly speedwell can be one of the more difficult veronicas to grow from seed. Germination rates will decrease if the seed is covered. Once the seedlings have emerged, reduce the temperatures to 60F (16C). Remember, like most woolly-leaved plants, *Veronica incana* can succumb to high humidity and heat, even during the germination stage.

Germinate seed at temperatures of 65F to 75F (18C to 24C), and leave it exposed to light during germination. Germination occurs in seven to 14 days; seedlings can be transplanted 16 to 25 days after sowing.

Growing on

Crop time: From seed, allow 12 to 14 weeks from sowing for salable, green 32-cell packs. When grown at 50F to 55F (10C to 13C) nights, 4½-inch (11 cm) pots are salable in 14 to 16 weeks. *V. incana* will not flower readily from seed sown anytime after early January.

For larger plants, in quart or gallon containers, sow seed the previous summer and transplant to the final container before cool weather sets in. Overwinter dormant and sell in the spring. These plants will flower in June.

Commercial propagators offer *Veronica incana* in either small pots or liners. Primarily available during the autumn and winter, either of these can be potted up into quarts and gallons and sold in spring.

VARIETIES

V. incana is available from many commercial seed and nursery companies and should be easy to locate.

RELATED MATERIAL

Crosses made between *V. incana* and either *V. spicata* or *V. longifolia* have resulted in a number of excellent selections. These include:

Barcarolle, a rose-pink variety with dusty gray foliage on plants to 12 inches (30 cm) tall.

Minuet, a pink-flowering variety to 15 inches (38 cm) tall, also with gray foliage. Flowers June to August.

These varieties are vegetatively propagated only but can be grown like *V. incana*.

USES

In the commercial landscape, there have been problems planting *V. incana* in areas with hot and humid summers. Plants love full sun, but with overhead irrigation they're not long lived and are poor performers. In some cases, they die off rapidly. Selected sites with well-drained soil and no overhead irrigation are the best guarantee that this variety will thrive.

IN THE HOME GARDEN

Space plants 12 inches (30 cm) apart in full-sun locations that offer afternoon shade. Excess water will shorten this crop's life. Staking isn't necessary.

▬ VERONICA SPICATA

FAMILY: Scrophulariaceae

COMMON NAME(S): Spike Speedwell

DESCRIPTION

One of the more popular border perennials, *V. spicata* bears blue flowers on basal branching plants 18 to 24 inches (46 to 61 cm) tall and 15 to 24 inches (38 to 61 cm) across. The single, one-quarter-inch (6 mm) flowers develop on upright spikes measuring 8 to 15 inches (20 to 38 cm) long. Additional flower colors include white and rose pink.

HARDINESS: Zones 4 to 8.

SEASON OF BLOOM: June and July.

PROPAGATION

Seed, division, and cuttings are the most common ways of propagation. Clumps can be divided in the spring or fall, while tip cuttings are done during late spring or early summer.

GERMINATION OVERVIEW: 221,000 seeds per ounce/7,735 per gram.

Veronica spicata germinates in seven to 14 days at 65F to 75F (18C to 24C), with the seed left exposed to light. The seedlings can be transplanted 16 to 25 days after sowing.

GROWING ON

Crop time: From seed, allow 10 to 13 weeks from sowing for salable, green 32-cell packs. When planted in June, this size plant will flower during July of the same year. For 4-inch (10 cm) pot sales, allow 12 to 15 weeks when growing at 50F to 55F (10C to 13C) nights.

For larger containers, such as quarts or gallons, sow seed the previous summer and transplant to the final container before the onset of cool weather. These plants can be overwintered dormant for spring sales.

Commercial propagators offer a wide variety of *Veronica* cultivars that are the result of breeding between species. These are frequently available as bare-root transplants, in small pots or as liners. Primarily available during the autumn and winter, any of these can be potted up into quart and gallon containers and sold in spring.

VARIETIES

Note: Of the following, the only **seed-propagated** selections are the species and Blue Bouquet. The remainder are all **vegetatively produced**.

V. spicata is available from many commercial seed and nursery companies through-out North America. When grown from seed the species will vary in habit, intensity of flower color, and crop time. While colors are predominantly blue and shades of blue, off-types can produce other colors. Due to this variable performance, the species is seldom grown.

Some of *Veronica*'s parentage isn't known, although many were the result of crosses between *V. spicata* and *V. longifolia*. Others are the result of crosses with *V. teucrium* (*V. latifolia*), as well as *V. incana*. These probably include:

Blue Bouquet, the newest variety, was introduced in 1994. It is a seed-propagated selection with dark green foliage and medium blue flowers on plants 12 to 15 inches (30 to 38 cm) tall in bloom. From seed sown in mid-January, the plants flower in late May and June after a growing regime of 50F to 55F (10C to 13C) nights. This is the best seed-propagated variety on the market.

Blue Charm has dark green foliage with violet-blue flowers. Blue Charm is a result of a number of crosses and can only be propagated vegetatively. It reaches 15 to 18 inches (38 to 46 cm) tall.

Crater Lake Blue has midblue flowers on plants to 15 inches (38 cm) tall. The flower-

ing spikes are short and numerous, making this one of the most well-known cultivars on the market. Maximum height is 15 inches (38 cm).

Icicle is a white-flowering cultivar reaching 24 inches (61 cm). It flowers from June to
late summer.

Red Fox (Rotfuch) is a deep rose-pink-flowering variety from 12 to 15 inches (30 to
38 cm) tall. Plants flower in June through August. Propagate this selection
vegetatively.

Sunny Border Blue is probably the most well-known cultivar and a former Perennial
Plant Association plant of the year. Introduced by Robert Bennerup, founder of
Sunny Border Nurseries in Kensington, Connecticut, Sunny Border Blue has an
upright, erect habit with violet-blue flowers on plants measuring from 15 to
20 inches (38 to 51 cm) tall.

RELATED MATERIAL

Veronica repens is a prostrate, creeping species to 1½ inches (4 cm) tall and 12 to
18 inches (30 to 46 cm) in spread. An excellent performer, this is one of the most
underused and underrated plants in the perennial trade. Plants are excellent in the
rock garden. While they won't flower the same season from seed, it's their creeping habit that makes them valuable. Flowers are small—about one-quarter inch
(6 mm)—and lavender blue in color. They develop in early spring and show color
in late April or May.

Propagate and grow as you would *V. spicata*.

USES

This is one of the main perennial performers for long-term color and repeat performance. It's also one of the primary blue-flowering perennials available. The shorter
cultivars are excellent for front of the border while the taller ones can be used as cut
flowers. For cuts, harvest when the lower one-quarter inch (6 mm) of the spike
begins to show color.

In the commercial landscape, all of the above will work in those areas with full
sun (*V. repens* should be given some shade) and well-drained soils. Allow *V. repens* to
trail over rock walls in a cascading fashion.

IN THE HOME GARDEN

Space plants 12 inches (30 cm) apart in a well-drained, full-sun or part-shade location. Excess water around the crown during autumn or winter leads to crown rot
and, probably, death.

The cultivars and *V. spicata* itself require minimal care and will be long lived in the
garden. In our gardens outside Chicago, the cultivars usually outlive the species and
are more adaptable. Winter mulching and staking aren't necessary.

■ VERONICASTRUM VIRGINICUM

(syn. *Veronica virginica*)

FAMILY: Scrophulariaceae

COMMON NAME(S): Culver's Root, Black Root

DESCRIPTION

Veronicastrum virginicum is an imposing, native North American perennial with whorled leaves on upright, branchless stems from 4 to 5 feet (1.2 to 1.5 m) tall. In our gardens, the plants can reach 6 feet (1.8 m) if well fertilized and watered. The flowers are off-white (sometimes a blush-lavender color), tubelike in appearance and held in 4- to 9-inch-long (10 to 23 cm) racemes. The individual flowers can grow to one-eighth inch (3 mm) across, with a length of one-quarter to three-quarter inch (6 mm to 2 cm). See Color Plate 69 for photo of *Veronicastrum virginicum*.

The plants arise from a clump that lacks basal leaves during the summer. The clump measures as wide as 3 feet (90 cm), although in natural plantings they can be larger.

HARDINESS: Zones 3 to 8.

SEASON OF BLOOM: July and August.

PROPAGATION

Division and stem cuttings are most common methods of propagation. Divisions can be cut in spring or late summer, while stem cuttings are taken during spring or summer prior to flowering. Propagation is also possible by seed, but it will be hard to find. It may be easier to grow the plants and harvest your own seed.

GERMINATION OVERVIEW

Since it's so easy to take divisions, I haven't grown this variety from seed. After referring to various authors and talking with some of the growers who are familiar with this practice, I can offer the following advice:

1. It will be a challenge to find seed for this variety offered commercially in the United States. Contact seed companies that specialize in native perennial plants, or consult the seed exchanges listed in various horticultural magazines. This will work if you're looking for only a limited amount of seed. If commercial quantities are desired, contact the wildflower seed companies first.
2. Once you locate seed, keep in mind that germination slows with length of storage. It's best to sow seed immediately upon receipt.

Veronicastrum has optimum germination at 70F (21C) when sown on the surface of the media but not allowed to dry out. It does appear that the seed germinates better if exposed to light. Germination appears to be uneven, and flushing (multiple emergence dates) is common.

GROWING ON

Crop time: Divisions taken in the spring will root easily within a few weeks. Take late summer divisions after flowering, but remember that there is limited—if any—crown foliage then. Plants will also root easily at that time and be ready for spring sales.

Concentrate on taking cuttings in May and early June prior to bud set. In our Chicago location, plants emerge in a ground bed in late April. The erect, nonbranching shoots are about 12 to 18 inches (30 to 46 cm) tall by the middle of June, so we're able to take the cuttings early.

Commercial propagators offer *Veronicastrum*, but it's not as easily found as other perennials noted in this book. Not commonly available as a bare-root perennial, *Veronicastrum* usually is offered in small pots or cell packs.

VARIETIES

Veronicastrum virginicum var. *alba* features 3- to 4-inch (7 to 10 cm), pure white spikes composed of single blooms. If you're growing from seed, contact wildflower seed sources here in the United States or in Europe. Commercially, it's probably easier to find started plants than seed.

V. virginicum var. *rosea* has softly colored, rose-pink blossoms on plants 4 to 5 feet (1.2 to 1.5 m) tall in flower.

USES

Don't underestimate the potential for this native perennial. It's definitely worthy of your attention and its longevity is assured. In commercial landscapes the plants do best in the center of large, open displays where surrounding material will hide the long stalks. Capitalize on its elongated stems in the landscape, where the upright flower spikes can protrude and spire above lower growing plants. Since it's a midsummer flowering plant, companion plantings of spring and late summer blooming plants will complement its performance.

Veronicastrum is a natural as a cut flower. With the branchless stems, there is little cleaning required, and once the primary color spike is gone, secondary flowering spikes will start. Although not yet commercially popular, *Veronicastrum* has potential.

IN THE HOME GARDEN

A long-lived perennial in the full sun, *Veronicastrum* tolerates moist to well-drained locations but will often burn in prolonged dry soil conditions. Plants don't normally require staking, but heavy feeding and/or shade will often encourage weaker, more spindly growth that might need support.

When planting *Veronicastrum* in the garden, remember that the plants lack any secondary branches. The stems growing from the crown will emerge, grow erect, and terminate with flowers, with no branching along the stem. I would suggest planting a dwarf perennial crop at the base. Unlike some native plants that are sometimes referred to as "weeds," *Veronicastrum* is not invasive nor known to reseed. It has all

V

the merits of a true garden performer but is little known to either amateur or professional gardeners.

■ VINCA MINOR

FAMILY: Apocynaceae

COMMON NAME(S): Common Periwinkle, Common Myrtle, Myrtle

DESCRIPTION

A trailing, woody perennial, *Vinca minor* has the attributes that all gardeners and landscapers look for—evergreen foliage, easy maintenance, and a manageable, uniform habit. Plants can grow 6 to 8 inches (15 to 20 cm) tall, although I have seen established clumps all the way up to 10 inches (25 cm) tall. Plants can spread several feet away from the original crown and root at every node. The lavender-blue flowers are single and three-quarters to 1 inch (2 to 2.5 cm) across. *Vinca* flower petals are fused into a tubelike structure. The glossy, dark green foliage measures from three-quarter to 1 inch (2 to 2.5 cm) wide and 1½ inches (4 cm) long, and is persistent throughout the year.

HARDINESS: Zones 4 to 9.

SEASON OF BLOOM: May and June.
Plants can flower sporadically during the summer, but the main flush of color is in the spring.

PROPAGATION

Vinca is commercially propagated from tip cuttings taken anytime during active growth (any time of year when maintaining stock plants in a greenhouse). Obviously, the amount of cutting material decreases during the coldest and darkest days of the year the farther north you go. Stock plants kept actively growing will continue to produce as long as the temperatures stay warm.

Divisions can also be taken in either spring or fall. Many varieties easily root at the nodes. Cut the stems and use a trowel or shovel to remove the rooted pieces. This method is preferred by home gardeners.

Vinca minor seed is not propagated by seed.

GROWING ON

Crop time: If you're purchasing liners for potting up into larger containers, crop time will vary based on your plug or liner size, and the time of year that you're potting these up. Commercial propagating companies offer a choice of containers including 2¼-inch (5.7 cm) pots or 72 cells per tray (often considered liners). These can be transplanted into larger containers during autumn or winter for sales the following spring. They can also be purchased the previous summer, potted up into gallons, then overwintered for sales the following spring.

If you're taking your own cuttings, shoot tip cuttings work best, although almost any part will root (stem, heel, lateral, etc.). Be sure you're taking uniform cuttings to encourage a consistent crop.

Two- to 2½-inch-long (5 to 6 cm) cuttings are best to produce plants that will be salable in five to six weeks in a 135-tray with mist and bottom heat. To reduce water loss, some growers cover their cuttings with a row cover or similar material for the first week or so after sticking. If the resulting transplants are to be sold, trim or pinch the crowns one time prior to shipping so there is uniformity across the tray. You can use removed shoots as cutting material.

Transplants from a 135 tray potted into 4-inch (10 cm) or quart containers in winter will be salable in spring. Four-inch pots take eight to 10 weeks, and quarts take one to two weeks longer at 50F (10C) nights.

VARIETIES

All of the following are vegetatively propagated and, unless otherwise stated, are about the same height and habit as the species.

V. minor is available from many commercial propagators. While the species is still popular, the following varieties have gained more attention in recent years:

V. minor var. *alba* is the white-flowering version of the above. It's similar in all respects other than flower color.

Aureola (probably *V. minor Variegata*) is sold by several nurseries across the country. Each leaf center features a cream-yellow coloring. (The Royal Horticultural Society calls this *V. minor* var. *aureovariegata*.)

Bowles Variety (also listed *V. minor* var. *bowlesii*) bears deep blue flowers to 1¼ inches (3 cm) across on plants that are less vigorous than the species. Bowles Variety mounds more toward the crown and has glossier, thicker foliage than the species. This is an excellent variety.

Miss Jekyll (also listed as Jekyll's White) is a pure white flowering variety with smaller blooms, usually three-quarter to 1 inch (2 to 2.5 cm) across. The plants are dwarf with smaller leaves than Bowles Variety. Even though it is smaller, it's considered by some to be the best white flowering variety.

Sterling Silver is a variegated variety with cream-yellow veins down the center of each leaf. The flowers are single, blue, and 1 inch (2.5 cm) across.

RELATED MATERIAL

Vinca major is very similar to *V. minor* except, as implied by the name, it has larger leaves on more robust and fuller plants. The flowers are blue, measuring 1 to 2 inches (2.5 to 5 cm) across. Like *V. minor*, *V. major* leaves stay evergreen in warm

V

winter climates. *V. major* is faster growing than *V. minor* and is often used as a filler for hanging baskets and containers as well as in the landscape, where it can be quite vigorous. Not hardy in Zone 5, the variety is reliably hardy in Zone 7 and selected parts of Zone 6. Propagate as you would *V. minor*.

Many *V. major* cultivars are available, although the species is used most often. *V. major* Variegata is also commonly used but more often in baskets and other containers where its straight, vertical stems are appreciated. If planted into a garden, the stems, as with all vinca varieties, grow parallel to the soil surface, rooting along the nodes.

USES

If you're not already familiar with *Vinca minor* as a landscape plant, be aware that it grows and establishes quickly. This crop is often overused in commercial plantings since it's so well proven. To expand vinca's uses, concentrate on combining it with other flower colors or variegated foliage.

IN THE HOME GARDEN

Vinca minor can be used as a ground cover or tucked in at the edge of the border. However, it's unsurpassed as a mass planting on sloping embankments or on hillsides. Newly established plants will require from one to two years to fill in completely but once they do, the effect will be long lasting.

Since they trail, *Vinca minor* plants are thought to choke out any weeds or other surrounding plants. While the canopy of stems and foliage over the soil surface is several layers deep, it isn't enough to completely shade out all germinating seeds in the soil. Therefore, it will be necessary to pull out any unwanted developing seedlings that poke through the mat. Likewise, companion plants that are transplanted in-between the various strands of vinca stems and foliage will survive, although it's best to trim away stems from the crown of the new transplant to avoid competition for food and moisture.

Plant in any partially shaded, well-drained garden location for best performance. Plants can tolerate full sun for a period of time, but it's best to plant them where they get some shade, especially during the hottest parts of the day. This is particularly true of first year plantings, if they have been planted in mid-June or after, to ensure adequate rooting.

A word about *Vinca*'s evergreen characteristics. After establishing *Vinca minor* here in our Chicago-area garden with the stems cascading across the landscape, plants are a medium green color by early to mid-March. Once the snow melts, the darker green color returns quickly. The foliage remains intact on stems from the previous year. Plants in south- and east-facing locations do better than those that are west facing or those exposed to drying winter winds. We don't use any mulch on our plants other than throwing snow on them after a storm.

▰ VIOLA TRICOLOR

FAMILY: Violaceae

COMMON NAME(S): Johnny Jump-Up, Viola

DESCRIPTION

Viola tricolor plants are known for their unusual tricolored blooms and free-flowering performance, although the bloom itself is rather small. Despite the species name "tricolor," some flowers will appear to have only one color. On closer inspection, however, you'll find each bloom has a "face" towards the flower center. Both the white- and yellow-flowering varieties may be pure in color, or possess dark violet lines or "whiskers" in the lower petal radiating out away from the center.

In nature, the flowers are usually combinations of deep purple, purple-black, yellow, white, and/or blue. These colors also predominate in commercially offered varieties. The breeder's attention has brought *V. tricolor* into the limelight recently, and F$_1$ hybrids are now available. As new varieties enter the market, it's possible that more pure colors will be available. The blooms are usually less than 1 inch across, and the flowers are often sweetly scented.

Though this low growing, rosetting plant generally reaches only 7 inches (18 cm) tall in full bloom, it grows up to 10 inches (25 cm) in cool, prolonged springs or falls. The leaves are heart shaped and sprout in rosette fashion around the plant's crown. Violas spread no more than 7 or 8 inches (18 to 20 cm) in our Chicago climate but can spread more in other areas of the country.

HARDINESS: Zones 6 to 8.

This crop isn't hardy throughout most of the United States, but plants will live from year to year in areas where they aren't subjected to severe weather changes. This omits most of the central, eastern and southern United States. The West Coast and mountainous regions, on the other hand, can get perennial performance from *Viola tricolor*. Regardless of climate, the plants can easily reseed and sometimes do so with a vengeance. Plants are best treated as an annual or short-lived perennial.

SEASON OF BLOOM: From May or June on.

High heat and humidity limit flowering. If plants aren't subjected to long durations of either, they'll flower as long as temperatures are above 40F (5C).

PROPAGATION

Viola tricolor is usually propagated by seed.

GERMINATION OVERVIEW: 30,000 to 40,000 seeds per ounce/1,050 to 1,400 per gram. Seed germinates readily in seven to 14 days at 65F to 70F (19C to 21C); cover lightly after sowing. Seedlings can be transplanted in 15 to 26 days.

V

GROWING ON

Crop time: Since these plants aren't truly hardy, they're most often produced in packs or small pots for spring sales and treated as a bedding plant. Winter sowings will start to flower in 11 to 12 weeks in a 32-cell pack. Grow on at no less than 45F (7C) nights with bright light (no artificial lights are necessary), and the plants will be strong, hardy, and ready for planting. If you prefer more free-flowering cell packs, add an additional one to two weeks.

If 4-inch (10 cm) pots fit your market better, pot up one to two plants per pot when ready, and they'll be salable 13 to 15 weeks after sowing. Obviously with two plants per pot, they'll fill out faster and bloom a week earlier.

If you're growing *V. cornuta* types (see **Related material**) side by side with these, *V. tricolor* varieties will flower as much as two weeks earlier than *V. cornuta* or *V. wittrockiana* (garden pansy) varieties, depending on the color.

VARIETIES

All of the following are propagated from seed.

Alpine Summer is the F_1 hybrid counterpart to Helen Mount. It has the true tricolored blooms of deep purple on the upper two petals with lavender and yellow on the lower three petals. Plants are more prostrate than Helen Mount with slightly smaller flowers, three-quarters-inch (2 cm) across.

Blue Elf (also called King Henry or Prince Henry) is a vivid purple variety with lavender and white shading toward the flower center. The blooms are three-quarters-inch (2 cm) across.

Helen Mount is the standard variety of the species, known as Johnny Jump-Up, with violet or purple upper petals and lavender and yellow lower petals. Flowers are three-quarters to just under 1 inch (2 to 2.5 cm) across. Plants grow from 6 to 8 inches (15 to 20 cm) tall.

RELATED MATERIAL

Viola cornuta (Horned Violet) is closely allied to *V. tricolor* in appearance and culture. One major difference is that *V. tricolor* will look tidier and more dwarf than *V. cornuta* cultivars. From personal experience I feel that *V. tricolor* varieties are more uniform in both appearance and flowering performance than the older *V. cornuta* varieties. The newer selections, however, are another story, and they are noted as follows.

In culture and development, *V. cornuta* varieties usually require one to two weeks longer to start flowering when growing side by side with *V. tricolor*. They're equally easy to sow, germinate, and grow, requiring little care. Several additional points: This crop is also only marginally hardy and is best treated as an annual or short-lived perennial. Also, *V. cornuta* has traditionally been available as an open-pollinated crop, although F_1 varieties have been released into the trade recently.

V. cornuta has been highlighted over the years with such old-time varieties as Chantreyland, with orange blossoms; Jersey Gem, with violet-blue flowers; and Yellow Perfection, a bright yellow. There are additional individual varieties plus several mixtures. Improved lines are being introduced at a record rate. The following is only a sampling of these improved lines:

Jewel is an F_1 hybrid series with four separate colors at the time of this writing. Its cornerstone was the variety Yellow Jewel (formerly Baby Yellow until the new colors became available), but blue, purple, and white varieties have been added as well. Additional colors are in the works. Plants grow 6 to 8 inches (15 to 20 cm) tall with 1-inch (2.5 cm) blooms.

Princess Series has a number of separate colors available including blue, purple and white, cream, white, and yellow. There is also a mix. Plants grow from 6 to 8 inches (15 to 20 cm) tall with 1-inch (2.5 cm) flowers.

Viola odorata is the true perennial violet that overwinters dependably for us in Chicago year after year, although it depends on the variety. Some—like the species—are hardy to Zones 6 or 7 and south while others will winter kill readily. White Czar, for example, will be hardy here in our Zone 5 winters. In all fairness, however, a cold wet autumn followed by a severe, cold winter can be challenging to this plant.

Viola odorata is the violet of writings and romance. The species can be extremely fragrant (hence the "odorata" part of its name), but some varieties are scentless. The plants can also be evergreen in less severe winter areas. *V. odorata* is a soloniferous plant able to fill in between plants more readily than either of the other two violas, which only form rosettes. Plants may also appear larger due to their ability to spread easily. Plants may be either the same height or only several inches taller than either of the other two species. The flowers are most often purple, lavender, or white, or sometimes yellow. Blooms measure up to 1 inch (2.5 cm) across.

Since they're true perennials, the plants can be propagated by offsets (cuttings) or division as well as from seed. Remove the offsets in the spring, root and pot them up for late summer sales. These offsets, as well as the divisions, usually don't flower until the second year, although they may flower in the fall—especially in areas where fall pansies prosper.

Seed of *V. odorata* will be more challenging than the seed of the other two violas noted here. Many times a winter sowing of Queen Charlotte will yield 0% germination. Seed given a moist chilling will yield more favorable results. See the information provided in the **Propagation Techniques** chapter for additional details.

Some varieties will come true from seed, while others need to be vegetatively propagated to maintain the cultivar's integrity. Selections include:

Queen Charlotte (Konigin Charlotte), a fragrant, violet-blue flowering variety that

V

comes true from seed. It is not common here in the United States. Be prepared to call your favorite seed supplier to inquire whether they carry it.

White Czar has 1-inch (2.5 cm) white flowers on plants to 6 inches (15 cm) tall in bloom. The flowers are pure in color, although they have several deep purple lines or "whiskers" on the lower petal radiating out from the flower center. The flowers aren't fragrant. White Czar is vegetatively propagated. See Color Plate 70 for photo of *Viola odorata* White Czar.

USES

Unlike their garden pansy cousins, violas have not shared fall sales popularity in the southern United States for home and landscape use. They should be promoted for their steadfast performance in woodland settings as well as the garden border or edge.

IN THE HOME GARDEN

Depending on your reference source, violas are described as both sun- and shade-loving plants. In our experience in Chicago, the plants perform better in shaded exposures with a well-drained but moist soil. This is especially true in our hot and humid summers. Under these conditions plants often succumb by August to powdery mildew or *Botrytis* with continued exposure. Plant violas where they'll get morning sun and afternoon shade. Plant violas on the north side of trees and shrubs. Instead of planting them at the base of tree trunks, however, try planting them out closer to the drip-line where they'll receive more air circulation and brighter light.

W

▬ WALDSTEINIA FRAGARIOIDES

FAMILY: Rosaceae

COMMON NAME(S): Barren Strawberry

Description

Waldsteinia looks similar to both *Fragaria* (common strawberry) and *Duchesnea* (mock strawberry) but, unlike both of these plants, it doesn't produce any fruit after flowering. Although *Waldsteinia* is rhizomatous and creeps, it's not invasive and usually won't overpower other plants. Also, the plant is slower to fill in than either *Fragaria* or *Duchesnea* when grown side by side with them.

The bright yellow, saucer-shaped, single flowers measure up to one-half inch (1 cm) across or less, and are usually sterile. Plants are seldom free flowering. There's a sharp contrast between the deep green foliage and the bright yellow flowers but, due to the small flower size plus the spreading habit, the flowers are dotted across the mat of foliage instead of clustered in a mass. The foliage may bronze during cold weather but is commonly evergreen. Plants grow 4 to 6 inches (10 to 15 cm) tall with a 24-inch (61 cm) spread. The first several years after planting in warmer and more well-drained locations, the plants often spread 12 to 18 inches (30 to 46 cm).

HARDINESS: Zones 5 to 7.

SEASON OF BLOOM: June and July.

PROPAGATION

Waldsteinia is propagated by rhizome divisions in spring or terminal cuttings taken during spring before flowering.

It can also be seed propagated, although this isn't common. Seed will seldom be found commercially here in the United States, but plant societies and seed exchanges usually offer fresh seed.

GERMINATION OVERVIEW

I haven't propagated this variety myself so I am including comments from other authorities here. Methods differ among propagators depending on their experience.

W

451

I've been shown the results of fall-sown seed, left to overwinter between freezing and 40F (4C) for several months. The germination rate attained was of 60 to 65% in two to four weeks at 68F (20C). Visually, the seedlings sized up well and were of good quality.

Norman Deano in his book, *Seed Germination Theory and Practice*, 2nd edition, saw similar results at 70F (21C) instead of 68F (20C). He also got 95% germination in four to 14 weeks after sowing at 70F (21C) when the seed was exposed constantly to light. Additionally, he found that no seeds germinated if it was kept dark during the germination process [1].

GROWING ON

Crop time: You can divide *Waldsteinia* by removing rooted runners from the plant in spring and summer and potting them up into the final container. If the rootlets aren't well formed, the rhizomes can be placed in a propagation chamber to encourage better rooting.

Terminal tip cuttings are taken in spring and placed in a peat/sand rooting media at 70F. Rooting starts in two to four weeks. Plantlets can be shifted to their final container during summer, grown on until cold, overwintered, and sold in spring.

Regardless of the propagation method, resulting plantlets taken from divisions, cuttings, or started from seed should be potted up the previous summer for sales the following spring. Plants taken from divisions are occasionally sold the same year as taken, but these seldom root throughout the container nor do they appear as aesthetically pleasing as divisions overwintered in the pot.

VARIETIES

Waldsteinia fragarioides is not as commonly found in the commercial trade as *W. ternata* (formerly *W. sibirica*). It's excellent as a ground cover, however.

RELATED MATERIAL

W. ternata (formerly *W. sibirica*) is the Siberian barren strawberry, a rampant grower that has been used instead of *W. fragarioides* due to its ability to hold embankments together readily. Its vigor, however, also allows it to literally run over smaller, weaker plantings unless pruned back or watched.

W. ternata has yellow flowers either equal in size or slightly larger than *W. fragarioides*. Flowers are yellow but have been cream or white with yellow shading as well. Plants have a more vigorous but similar appearance to *W. fragarioides*. *W. ternata* is propagated by rhizome divisions and from seed.

USES

The barren strawberry is especially suitable for mass planting in rock gardens for an appealing effect. This isn't a plant to only have one or two of. An area covered with a mat of these plants is more interesting and effective. Plants can be used for borders or edgings but also look good in woodland settings among ferns, anemones, and other similar plants.

IN THE HOME GARDEN

Plants will tolerate full- or part-day sun where the soil is well drained but constantly moist. An exposure of several hours of sun a day is preferred to full-day sun, especially in hot, humid weather where the soil is allowed to dry out.

When flowering, the plants often produce more flowers at the growing edge of the mat rather than across the top of the foliage canopy. This is especially true in areas where the plants are grown in heavy shade, next to tree trunks, or under the arching branches of low-growing shrubs.

REFERENCES

[1] Deano, N. 1993. *Seed germination theory and practice*. 2nd ed. Personally published.

W

APPENDIX 1

USDA PLANT HARDINESS ZONE MAP

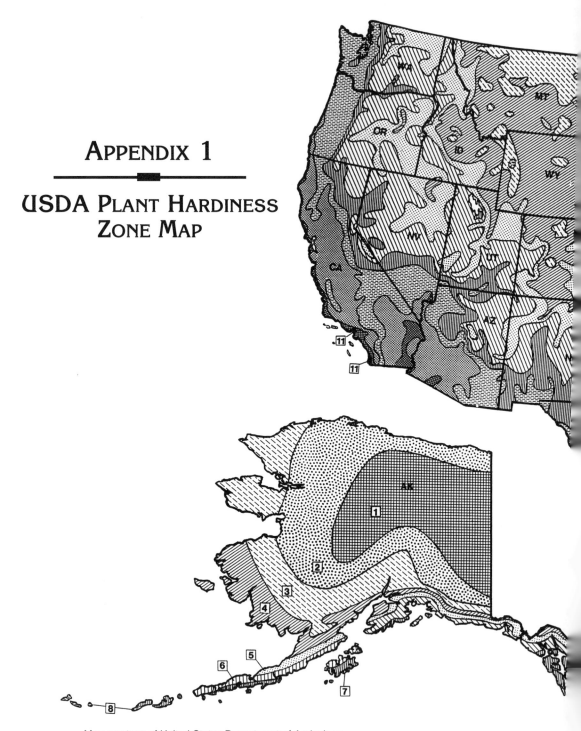

Map courtesy of United States Department of Agriculture.

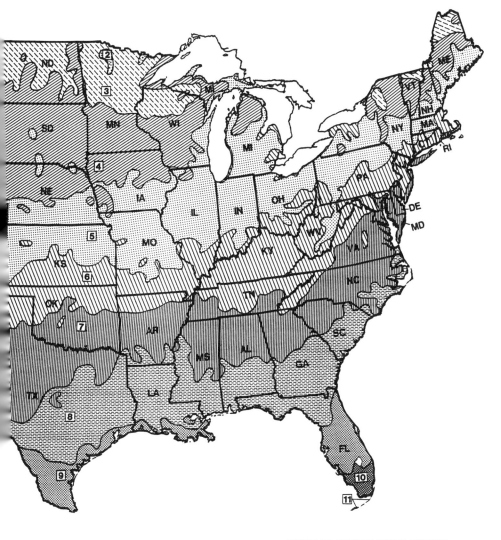

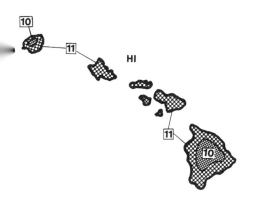

RANGE OF AVERAGE ANNUAL MINIMUM TEMPERATURES FOR EACH ZONE

ZONE 1	BELOW −50°F	
ZONE 2	−50° TO −40°	
ZONE 3	−40° TO −30°	
ZONE 4	−30° TO −20°	
ZONE 5	−20° TO −10°	
ZONE 6	−10° TO 0°	
ZONE 7	0° TO 10°	
ZONE 8	10° TO 20°	
ZONE 9	20° TO 30°	
ZONE 10	30° TO 40°	
ZONE 11	ABOVE 40°	

APPENDIX 2

PERENNIALS PROPAGATED FROM SEED

The following is a list of seed-propagated perennials and their expected response the first summer after sowing during winter or spring. This list is based on seed sowings from January to early March, and the notations under each heading are described at the end of the table.

While the best performing seed-grown plants in the garden come from seed sown the previous year, first-time growers and gardeners often ask what to expect from seed sown after the first of the year. Sowings made anytime the previous year to October will usually have had sufficient time to root into a quart container or gallon pot for sales by spring, depending on the crop's growth habit and whether a pretreatment is necessary for germination.

If sown January through April, most of these plants will be large enough to sell in gallon pots by the latter part of the summer. Sowings made the previous year, overwintered dormant or kept in a cold greenhouse produce stronger flowering plants than those plants sown during winter.

Note: The plants listed here are generally grown from seed and may include genera and species not covered elsewhere in this book. **Legend follows table listing**.

Crop	Time of bloom	Notes
Achillea filipendulina	F	1
Achillea millefolium	E	1
Achillea ptarmica	E	1
Aethionema cordifolium	G	3
Alcea rosea	I	
Alchemilla mollis	F	2
Alyssum montanum	G	1, 8
Amsonia tabernaemontana	H	4

Crop	Time of bloom	Notes
Anacyclus depressus	F	1, 7
Anaphalis margaritacea	G	1
Anchusa azurea	G	1, 11
Anchusa capensis	A, E	1, 7
Anthemis tinctoria	E	1, 11
Aquilegia spp.	G	2
Arabis alpina	G	1
Armeria maritima	G	3
Asclepias tuberosa	F	4, 6, 12
Aster alpinus	G	1
Aster novae-angliae	E	1
Aster novi-belgii	E	1
Astilbe × *arendsii*	G	3
Aubrieta deltoidea	G	1
Aurinia saxatilis	G	1, 8
Baptisia australis	G	3
Belamcanda chinensis	G	4
Bellis perennis	D, E	7
Bergenia cordifolia	G	2
Buddleia davidii	E	1, 11, 12
Buphthalmum salicifolium	E	1
Campanula carpatica	E	1
Campanula cochleariifolia	D	1
Campanula glomerata	G	1
Campanula medium	B, G	4
Campanula persicifolia	G	1
Campanula pyramidalis	G	1
Carlina acaulis	G	4, 8, 10
Catananche caerulea	E	1
Centaurea macrocephala	G	1, 11
Centaurea montana	F	1
Centranthus ruber	E	1
Cephalaria gigantea	G	1, 11
Cerastium tomentosum	G	1, 9
Chrysanthemum leucanthemum	See *Leucanthemum*	
Chrysanthemum × *morifolium*	See *Dendranthema*	
Chrysanthemum parthenium	See *Tanacetum*	
Coreopsis grandiflorum Early Sunrise	D, E	1
Coreopsis grandiflorum	G	1

Crop	Time of bloom	Notes
Delphinium × *belladonna*	E	4
Delphinium chinense	D, E	1, 4
Delphinium × *cultorum*	E	4
Dendranthema × *grandiflora*	E	1, 5
Dianthus arenarius	G	1
Dianthus barbatus	B, G	1
Dianthus caryophyllus	F	1
Dianthus deltoides	E, F, J	1
Dianthus plumarius	G	1
Digitalis × *mertonensis*	G	4, 11
Digitalis purpurea	B, G	4, 11
Doronicum caucasicum	G	1
Echinacea purpurea	E, F	1
Echinops ritro	G	4
Erigeron speciosus	G	1, 4
Eriophyllum lanatum	G	1
Eryngium spp.	G	3
Euphorbia myrsinites	C, F	3
Euphorbia polychroma	C, F	3
Filipendula vulgaris	G	1, 4
Gaillardia × *grandiflora*	E, F	1
Gaura lindheimeri	E	1, 7
Geum quellyon	G	1, 8
Goniolimon tataricum	H	2, 3
Gypsophila paniculata	F	1
Gypsophila repens	C, F	1, 9
Helenium autumnale	E	1
Helianthemum nummularium	G	2, 3
Heliopsis helianthoides	E	1, 12
Hesperis matronalis	G	1
Heuchera micrantha	C, G	2, 3
Heuchera sanguinea	G	2, 3
Hibiscus moscheutos	E	4, 12
Hypericum calycinum	G	2, 7
Iberis sempervirens	G	1
Kniphofia uvaria	H	2, 3
Lathyrus latifolius	G	1, 4, 9
Leontopodium alpinum	G	2, 7

Crop	Time of bloom	Notes
Leucanthemum × *superbum*		
Single/semidoubles		
Alaska	E	1
Silver Princess	F	1
Snow Lady	D, E, A	1
White Knight	E	1
Doubles	G	1
Liatris spicata	F	1
Limonium latifolium	H	1
Linum perenne	F	2
Lobelia cardinalis	E, F	4, 7
Lunaria annua	B, G	1
Lupinus polyphyllus	B, G	4
Lychnis chalcedonica	E	1
Malva spp.	E	1
Monarda didyma	G	1
Myosotis sylvatica	E	1, 7
Oenothera missouriensis	F	1
Oenothera speciosa	E	1
Papaver orientale	G	1, 4
Physalis franchetii	E	1
Physostegia virginiana	E, F	1
Platycodon grandiflorus	E	1, 4, 6, 12
Polemonium caeruleum	E	1
Pyrethrum	See *Tanacetum*	
Rudbeckia fulgida	G	2
Rudbeckia hirta	E	1
Salvia × *superba*	E	1
Saponaria ocymoides	G	1
Saxifraga × *arendsii*	G	2
Scabiosa caucasica	F	1
Sedum acre	F	1, 9
Sedum spurium var. *Coccineum*	E	1, 9
Sempervivum spp.	C, G	2, 3
Sidalcea malviflora	F	1
Solidago canadensis	E, F	1
Spergula pilifera	C, E	4, 7, 9
Stachys lanata	C, G	1

Crop	Time of bloom	Notes
Tanacetum coccineum	G	1
Tanacetum parthenium	E	1
Tradescantia spp.	E	1, 4
Verbascum bombyciferum	B, G	4, 7, 11
Verbascum phoeniceum	E, F	1, 4
Veronica incana	G	1
Veronica repens	G, C	4, 9
Veronica spicata	E, F	1
Viola cornuta	A, E	1, 7
Viola tricolor	A, E	1, 7

LEGEND

Time of bloom:

A Best treated as an annual or bedding plant and not as a perennial.

B A biennial that forms rosettes the first year, flowers the second.

C Plants sold for their foliage, growth habit, or other trait rather than their flowers.

D Plants that will be in flower in the cell pack or 4-inch (10 cm) pot 10 to 14 weeks after sowing.

E Will flower the first year from seed after planting to the garden from a cell pack or 4-inch (10 cm) pot.

F Will flower some the first year, better the second year.

G Will flower the second year.

H Will flower some the second year and will flower better the third year from seed.

I *Alcea rosea* (hollyhock) is divided into two groups—those that are annual flowering and those that are biennial, flowering the year after seeding. Both types are sold in the perennial trade. Read the information under *Alcea* for clarification.

J In *Dianthus deltoides*, some varieties like Brilliant and Brillancy will not flower the first year after a winter or spring sowing. Zing Rose, by contrast, will flower the same year from seed in less than 20 weeks in a 4-inch (10 cm) pot.

Notes:

1 Plants are salable green in April and May from a January to early March sowing (10 to 14 weeks) for retail or commercial sales in a 32-cell pack. Plants can be sold as is or transplanted to 4-inch (10 cm) pots, quart or gallon containers as the plants are ready to be moved out of the cell packs. For 4-inch (10 cm) pot sales, crop times until salable range from 13 to 20 weeks. The information under each crop within the book provides additional details.

2 Plants that require a longer crop time. If you prefer green pack sales, seed should be sown from late November or December to fill out a 32-cell pack by April or May. For 4-inch (10 cm) or quart container sales, sow the previous summer or early autumn and overwinter.

3 Plants are very slow to grow and a full year may be necessary before they look aesthetically pleasing. These plants can be sown from December to April for sizing up in a quart or larger container during the summer, then overwintered for sales the following year.

4 These crops have more developed root systems or require a longer crop time and may become restricted in a cell pack. Instead, offer these plants in nothing smaller than a 4-inch (10 cm) or quart container to allow for ample root formation and development. Some, like lupine, digitalis and hibiscus, need a 5- or 6-inch (12 or 15 cm) pot for best performance.

5 *Dendranthema grandiflora* (formerly *Chrysanthemum* × *morifolium*) can be grown in a cell pack for spring sales from a winter sowing. However, the U.S. market demands 4-inch (10 cm) pots in the spring followed by quart or larger containers for late summer sales. More than 90% of this market is for vegetatively propagated varieties.

6 These plants are late to emerge in the spring. Here in Chicago most perennials are visible after winter from April to May. Those crops noted as #6 will wait until the soil is warmer (mid-May to June) before they emerge.

7 Not truly hardy for us in Chicago. Plants grown in open areas without winter protection had numerous losses the following spring. Plants may be more hardy when used as foundation plantings or when given winter protection.

8 Plants will survive several winters but often die out by the third or fourth year. Plants in the #8 category seldom make it through the second year.

9 Trailing or vining plants that should be grown in individual pots rather than cell packs. If grown in cell packs, the stems from one plant will root in the cell of another.

10 Implies that the plant possesses small, needlelike protrusions that will hurt if handled inappropriately.

11 Vigorous growers. These varieties will often be large or vigorous in habit as they are growing.

12 Most perennials propagated from seed are grown cool to cold at 45F to 50F (7C to 10C) during the production phase after transplanting. However, perennials in this group should be grown warm at night temperatures of 55F to 60F (13C to 16C) to prevent plants from producing yellow foliage and/or going dormant.

APPENDIX 3

---◼︎---

PERENNIAL PLANTS AND HOW THEY ARE PROPAGATED

The following is a table of perennials common to the commercial trade listed with their methods of propagation. Remember that many cultivars usually require vegetative propagation methods to remain true to type.

The following propagation methods are for the genus and not crosses between species. Refer to the appropriate crop and its related varieties for further information. Not all the species noted under a genus will be propagated in the same manner. Since the members of a species can occur in different regions of the world and may grow differently, their propagation methods may vary as well. Review the information under the crop cultures. If a crop is listed below but not detailed in the book, use the following only as a guideline. **Legend follows table listing.**

Crop	Seed	Division	Cuttings	Other
Acanthus	A	H=I, K	P	
Achillea	A	I, J	L, N, O	
Aconitum	C	I, K		
Adenophora	A	H=I	L	
Adonis	C, E	H=K, I		
Aegopodium		I, K		T
Aethionema	B		L, N	
Agastache	A	I	L	
Ajuga reptans		J, K	L, N	S, T
Alcea rosea	A			
Alchemilla	A	I		
Althaea	A			
Alyssum (also *Aurinia*)	A, F		L, N	
Amorpha	G		N	

Crop	Seed	Division	Cuttings	Other
Amsonia	A	I	L	
Anacyclus	A			
Anaphalis	A	I, K	L	
Anchusa	A	I, K	L, P	
Anemone	C, E	H=I	P	
Angelica	A			
Anoda	A			
Antennaria	A	I, J	P	
Anthemis	A	I, K	L	
Aquilegia	A, C, F	H=I, K		
Arabis	A		L, M	
Arenaria	A	I, K		
Armeria	A	I, K		Q
Artemisia		I, K	L, N, O	
Aruncus	A, B, D	I, K		
Asarum	E	J		U
Asclepias	E, F	H=I	L, P	
Asphodeline	A	I		
Aster alpinus	A, C, F	I, K	L, N	
Aster × frikartii			L, N	
Aster novae-angliae	A	I, K	M, N	
Aster novi-belgii	A	I, K	M, N	
Astilbe × arendsii	A	I, K		
Astrantia	E, F	J		T
Aubrieta	A	I	L, N	
Aurinia	A	I	M	
Baptisia	A, E, G	H=I		
Begonia grandis	A		M, N	R
Belamcanda	A, F	I		T
Bellis	A	I, K		
Bergenia	A, E	I, J	L	T, V
Boltonia	A	I, K	M, N	
Brunnera	A	I, J	P	
Buddleia	A		N, O	
Buphthalmum	A	I		
Caltha	C, E	I		
Campanula	A, F	I, J	L, M	
Carlina	A, E, F	H=I	P	
Catananche	A	K	P	

Crop	Seed	Division	Cuttings	Other
Centaurea	A	I, K	L, M, P	
Centranthus	A	I	L	
Cephalaria	A	I	P	
Cerastium	A	I, K	L, N	
Ceratostigma	A	I	L, M, N	
Chelone	A, F	I, J	L, M	
Chrysanthemum × morifolium, see *Dendranthema*				
Chrysanthemum parthenium, see *Tanacetum*				
Chrysanthemum × superbum, see *Leucanthemum*				
Chrysogonum	A	I		T
Chrysopsis	A, E	I		
Cimicifuga	C, E	I, K		
Clematis	A, F		M	
Coreopsis	A	I, J	L, M, N	
Crambe	A	H=I	P	
Crepis	E	H=I	P	
Crocosmia	A			W
Delphinium	A	I	L	
Dendranthema	A	I, J	L, M, N	
Dianthus	A		M, N	Q
Dicentra	A, E, F	I, J	M, P	
Dictamnus	A, C, E	H=I		
Digitalis	A	I		
Dodecatheon	A, E	I		
Doronicum	A, E	I, K		
Duchesnea		I, J, K		S
Echinacea	A	I, K	L	
Echinops	A	I, J	P	
Epimedium	A, C, F	I, K		T
Erigeron	A	I, J	L	
Eriophyllum	A	I		
Eryngium	A, C	H=I	P	
Eupatorium	A	I, K	M	
Euphorbia	A, F	I, K	L, N, O	
Filipendula	A	I, J, K		
Fragaria	A	I, J		S

Crop	Seed	Division	Cuttings	Other
Gaillardia	A	I, J	L, N, P	
Galium	A	I		
Gaura	A		M, N	
Geranium	A	I	L, M, N, P	T
Geum	A	I, K		
Goniolimon	A	H		
Gunnera	A, E	I		T
Gypsophila	A	I	L, M, N	V
Helenium	A	I, K	L, M, N	
Helianthemum	A, E	H=I	N	
Helianthus		I, K	L, N	
Heliopsis	A	I	L, N	
Helleborus	C, E	I		
Hemerocallis	A, E	I, K		V
Hesperis	A	I	N	
Heuchera	A	I, K		
Hibiscus	A	I, K	M	V
Hosta	A	I, J		V
Houttuynia		I		T
Hypericum	A	I	M, N, O	
Iberis	A		N, O	
Iris		I, J		
Kniphofia	A	I, J		
Lamiastrum	A	I, K	L, M	S
Lamium	A	I	L, N	
Lathyrus	A		M, O	
Leontopodium	A, F	I		
Leucanthemum	A	I, K	M	
Liatris	A	I, K		W
Ligularia		I, K		
Limonium latifolium	A	I	P	
Limonium tataricum, see *Goniolimon*				
Linum	A	H=I		
Liriope		I, K		
Lobelia	A	I, J	M	Q
Lunaria	A			
Lupinus	A, G	H=I	L, M	

Crop	Seed	Division	Cuttings	Other
Lychnis	A	I, J		
Lysimachia		I, K	L, M	T
Lythrum	A	I, K	L, M	
Macleaya	A	I	L, P	T
Malva	A	I, K	L, M	
Monarda	A	I, K	L, M, O	
Myosotis	A	J, K	L, N	
Oenothera	A	I	L	
Paeonia	C, E	J, K		
Papaver	A	J	P	
Penstemon	A	I	M	
Perovskia	A	H	L, M	
Phlox	F	I, J	L, M, N, P	
Physalis	F	I, K		
Physostegia	A	I, J	L, M	
Platycodon	A	H=I		
Plumbago	A	I	L, M, N	
Polemonium	A	I, K		
Polygonatum	A, E	I, K		
Polygonum	A	I, K		T
Potentilla	A	I, K	M, N	
Prunella		I, K	L	
Pulmonaria		I, K		V
Pulsatilla	C	I, K		
Pyrethrum, see *Tanacetum*				
Rudbeckia	A	I, K	L, M	
Sagina subulata	A	I, K		
Salvia	A	I, K	L, M, N, P	
Sanguinaria	A, E	I, J		
Sanguisorba	A	I, K		
Santolina	A		N	
Saponaria	A, F	I	L	
Saxifraga	A, B	I, J	L, M	Q
Scabiosa	A	H=I	L	
Sedum	A	I, K	L, N	
Sempervivum	A			Q
Sidalcea	A	I, K		
Silphium	A, E	I, K		

Crop	Seed	Division	Cuttings	Other
Solidago	A	I, K	L	
Stachys lanata	A	I	L	
Stokesia	A	I	P	
Tanacetum	A	I	L, M	
Thalictrum	A, E	I		
Tiarella	A, E	I, K		
Tradescantia	A	I, K		
Trollius	C, E	I, J		
Verbascum	A	I	P	
Verbena	A, F	I	L, O	
Veronica	A	I, K	M, N	
Veronicastrum	A	I, J	M, N	
Vinca		I, K	M, N, O	
Viola	A		M	
Waldsteinia	A	I, K	L, M	

LEGEND (Details are provided in the **Propagation Techniques** chapter.)

Seed (See Appendix 2 for seed propagation details.)

A Easy to germinate, yielding 50% and higher germination.

B Needs moist chilling.

C Needs a warm-moist period.

D Dioecious—produces male and female flowers on separate plants. Both parents are needed to produce seed.

E Fresh seed mandatory, otherwise may take up to a year to germinate.

F Older seed may need prechilling of 38F to 40F (3C to 4C) for several weeks. Sometimes seed doesn't need to be old to require a prechilling to improve germination.

G Seed with a hardened outer coat as in the case of legume family members. Scarification or soaking are suggested to increase germination.

Division

Divisions can be taken anytime the soil can be worked and the plant is vegetative.

H Careful division. Plants have fleshy, brittle, or easily wounded roots that can be damaged while dividing. When a division is taken, some plants die and others remain weak for the rest of their lives. Some roots are taproots and do not appreciate transplanting of any kind, especially on older, more well-established plantings. Plantings of two years or less are more agreeable to division than their older counterparts.

I Spring dug.

467

J Summer divisions. In some cases, the divisions are not done in June but in August. Many references separate these two classes as summer and late summer or autumn divided plants. Additional information is provided under crop culture.

K Fall dug.

Cuttings

Cuttings can be taken any time the plant is vegetative.

L Basal stem or tip cuttings taken in spring or summer, depending on the crop. These are taken from the crown of shoots developing at the base of the plant just above the soil line. In some cases, a portion of the root can also be taken.

M Spring cuttings. Spring cuttings are stem or tip cuttings taken anytime during the spring when there is active, vegetative growth. Unlike basal cuttings, spring cuttings are taken from more upright plants, though there are times the two practices overlap. Basal cuttings often root faster.

N Stem or tip cuttings taken in the summer. Cuttings may be taken before or after flowering. If taken before flowering, be sure that the flower buds have yet to form. If taken after flowering, be sure the plant does not produce woody stems.

O Stem or tip cuttings taken in the fall. This implies that plants will be vegetative again after flowering. Take cuttings as long as it is worth your time and interest, giving some thought as to how the resulting plants will be overwintered.

P Root cuttings.

Other

Q Offsets. Rosette forming plants can be either tightly held with a tuftlike appearance such as *Armeria* or more open as in *Saxifraga*. Many of these plants produce a number of shoots either singly held or clustered with two or three stems. These are often complete with roots.

R Bulbils—small, round bulbs that develop around the base of the root system. These can be removed and planted to develop new plants.

S Runners or stolons. Remove a portion of the stem along with its accompanying root.

T Rhizome producing plants where a vegetative shoot emerges from the soil away from the crown. These can be treated as "cuttings"—the rhizome, some attached roots, and the shoot are removed, allowed to root fully in a propagation area and then are transplanted.

U Stems that are already rooted. Once removed, treat as you would a basal cutting.

V Tissue cultured plants.

W Corms.

Appendix 4

Perennial Source List

The following is a partial list of perennial companies in the United States and Canada specializing in either plants, seeds, or both. You may contact these and other perennial companies for product listings and availability.

Addison Gardens
Rd. 1, Box 1865
Vergennes, Vermont 05491
Tel: (802) 759-2529

Andre Viette Farm & Nursery
Rte. 1, Box 16
Fishersville, Virginia 22939
Tel: (703) 943-2315
Fax: (703) 943-0782

Arnold's Greenhouse
RR #1, Box 232
LeRoy, Kansas 66857
Tel: (316) 964-2463

Babikow Greenhouses
7838 Babikow Road
Baltimore, Maryland 21237
Tel: (800) 835-7617
Fax: (301) 574-7582

Bailey Nurseries Inc.
1325 Bailey Road
St. Paul, Minnesota 55119
Tel: (800) 829-8898
Fax: (612) 459-5100

Ball Seed Company
622 Town Road
West Chicago, Illinois 60185
Tel: (708) 231-3500
Fax: (800) 234-0370

Ball Superior, Ltd.
c/o Ball Seed Company
622 Town Road
West Chicago, Illinois 60185
Tel: (708) 231-3500
Fax: (800) 234-0370

Behnke Nurseries Company
P.O. Box 290
Beltsville, Maryland 20705
Tel: (301) 937-1100
Fax: (301) 937-8034

Bill Kolvek Perennials
28 Wierimus Road
Hillsdale, New Jersey 07642
Tel: (201) 664-6963

Bio Propagation Inc.
20835 Broze Road
Humble, Texas 77338
Tel: (800) 843-9031
Fax: (713) 446-8616

Bluebird Nursery
519 Bryan Street
Box 460
Clarkson, Nebraska 68629
Tel: (402) 892-3457
Fax: (402) 892-3738

Bluemount Nurseries Inc.
2103 Blue Mount Road
Monkton, Maryland 21111
Tel: (410) 329-6226
Fax: (410) 329-8120

Bluestone Perennials Inc.
7211 Middle Ridge Road
Madison, Ohio 44057
Tel: (800) 852-5243
Fax: (216) 428-7198

Borbeleta Gardens
15980 Canby Avenue
Faribault, Minnesota 55021
Tel: (507) 334-2807

Busse Gardens Company Inc.
13579 10th Street N.W.
P.O. Box N
Cokato, Minnesota 55321
Tel: (612) 286-2654
Fax: (612) 286-2654

C. Raker & Sons Inc.
10371 Rainy Road
Litchfield, Michigan 49252
Tel: (517) 542-2316

Caprice Farm Nursery
15425 S.W. Pleasant Hill
Sherwood, Oregon 97140
Tel: (503) 625-7241
Fax: (503) 625-5588

Center Greenhouse, Inc.
1550 East 73rd Avenue
Denver, Colorado 80229
Tel: (303) 288-1209
Fax: (303) 288-4522

Colorado Cuttings
10500 Isabelle Road
P.O. Box 337
Lafayette, Colorado 80026
Tel: (303) 665-5725
Fax: (303) 665-5769

County Lane Wholesale Nursery, Inc.
2979 North Highway 83
Franktown, Colorado 80016
Tel: (303) 688-2442
Fax: (303) 688-5978

Cramers' Posie Patch
740 High Ridge Road
Columbia, Pennsylvania 17512
Tel: (717) 684-0777
Fax: (717) 393-3295

D'Angelo Farms
546 Washington Avenue
Dumont, New Jersey 07628
Tel: (201) 385-7788
Fax: (201) 385-9040

Donahue's Clematis Specialists
420 S.W. 10th Street
P.O. Box 366
Faribault, Minnesota 55021
Tel: (507) 334-8404
Fax: (507) 334-0485

Dunvegan Nursery
1001 South New Street
West Chester, Pennsylvania 19382
Tel: (215) 344-7566

Germania Seed Company
5952 North Milwaukee Avenue
Chicago, Illinois 60646
Tel: (312) 631-6631
Fax: (312) 631-4449

Green Leaf Enterprises
17 West Main Street
Leola, Pennsylvania 17540
Tel: (717) 656-2606
Fax: (717) 656-0465

Gro `N Sell
307 Lower State Road
Chalfont, Pennsylvania 18914
Tel: (215) 822-1276
Fax: (215) 997-1770

Growing On
Rte. 1, Box 392
Wallace, Virginia 26448
Tel: (304) 796-4790

H.R. Talmage & Son
36 Sound Avenue
Riverhead, New York 11901
Tel: (516) 727-0124
Fax: (516) 727-0326

Heitman Place
3304 Heitman Drive
Winston-Salem, North Carolina 27107
Tel: (919) 784-7777

Iverson Perennials
Box 2787 RFD
Long Grove, Illinois 60047
Tel: (708) 359-3500
Fax: (708) 359-0155

Iwasaki Bros. Inc.
2555 S.E. Minter Bridge Road
Hillsboro, Oregon 97123
Tel: (503) 640-2734
Fax: (503) 640-9626

Jackson & Perkins
2518 South Pacific Highway
P.O. Box 1028
Medford, Oregon 97501
Tel: (503) 776-2000
Fax: (503) 776-2194

Jelitto Staudensamen GmbH
P.O. Box 1264
Schwarmstedt D-29685
Germany
Tel: 011 (49) 5071-4085
Fax: 011 (49) 5071-4088

Jost Greenhouses
12340-48 Eckelmann Lane
Des Peres, Missouri 63131
Tel: (314) 821-2834
Fax: (314) 821-4950

J. Van Hoorn & Company Inc.
27617 Rte. 176
P.O. Box 814
Island Lake, Illinois 60042
Tel: (708) 526-1811
Fax: (708) 526-7668

Klehm Nursery
Rte. 5, Box 197, Penny Road
South Barrington, Illinois
60010
Tel: (708) 551-3710
Fax: (708) 551-3722

Kurt Bluemel, Inc.
2740 Greene Lane
Baldwin, Maryland 21013
Tel: (410) 557-7229
Fax: (410) 557-9785

Les Vivaces Duquette Inc.
579 Grande Allee
St. Hilaire, Quebec J36 456
Canada
Tel: (514) 464-8198

**Les Vivaces Quebecoises
Inc.**
412 Chemin du Bas de Ste-
Therese
Blainville, Quebec J7E 4H4
Canada
Tel: (514) 621-7810
Fax: (514) 621-1204

Matterhorn Nursery Inc.
227 Summit Park Road
Spring Valley, New York
10977
Tel: (914) 354-5986
Fax: (914) 354-4749

Millcreek Gardens
15088 Smart-Cole Road
Ostrander, Ohio 43061
Tel: (614) 666-7125
Fax: (614) 666-1234

Moss Seedlings
269 South 300 East
Jerome, Idaho 83338
Tel: (208) 324-8325
Tel: (208) 324-7391

Mount Arbor Nurseries
400 North Center
P.O. Box 129
Shenandoah, Iowa 51601
Tel: (800) 831-4125
Fax: (712) 246-1841

Mouse Creek Nursery
276 County Road 67
Riceville, Tennessee 37370
Tel: (615) 462-2666

**North Creek Nurseries,
Inc.**
RR #2, Box 33
Landenberg, Pennsylvania
19350
Tel: (215) 255-0100
Fax: (215) 255-4762

Peppergrove Nursery
1076 Maple Grove Road
P.O. Box 641
Lapeer, Michigan 48446
Tel: (313) 664-2223
Fax: (313) 664-1669

Piccadily Farm
1971 Whippoorwill Road
Bishop, Georgia 30621
Tel: (706) 769-6516

Plantage Inc.
P.O. Box 28
Cutchogue, New York 11935
Tel: (516) 734-6832
Fax: (516) 734-7550

Prairie Nursery
P.O. Box 306
Westfield, Wisconsin 53964
Tel: (608) 296-3679
Fax: (608) 296-2741

Saul Nurseries Inc.
P.O. Box 190403
Atlanta, Georgia 31119
Tel: (404) 458-0058
Fax: (404) 458-0172

Skagit Gardens
1719 Old Highway 99 South
Mount Vernon, Washington
98273
Tel: (206) 424-6144
Fax: (206) 424-8644

Springbrook Gardens, Inc.
6776 Heisley Road
P.O. Box 388
Mentor, Ohio 44061
Tel: (216) 255-3059
Fax: (216) 255-9535

**Stacy's Greenhouses &
Garden Center**
2009 Highway 321 North
York, South Carolina 29745
Tel: (803) 684-2331
Fax: (803) 684-0472

**Summersun Greenhouse
Company Inc.**
4100 East College Way
Mount Vernon, Washington
98273
Tel: (206) 424-8553
Fax: (206) 424-6722

Sunbeam Gardens
3332 Center Road (Rte. 83)
Avon, Ohio 44011
Tel: (216) 934-5778
Fax: (216) 934-6078

**Sunny Border Nurseries,
Inc.**
1709 Kensington Road
Kensington, Connecticut
06037
Tel: (203) 828-0321
Fax: (203) 828-9318

Swift Greenhouses Inc.
2724 300th Street
Gilman, Iowa 50106
Tel: (515) 478-3217
Fax: (515) 478-3226

T & Z Nursery Inc.
28 West 571 Roosevelt Road
Winfield, Illinois 60190
Tel: (708) 293-1040
Fax: (708) 293-7835

Tideland Gardens
10040 Perkins Hill Road
Chestertown, Maryland
21620
Tel: (410) 778-5787
Fax: (410) 778-0135

Valleybrook Gardens, Ltd.
1896 Hollow Road RR1
Fonthill, Ontario L0S 1E6
Canada
Tel: (416) 892-1661
Fax: (416) 892-1662

**Vandenberg Bulb
Company Inc.**
1 Black Meadow Road
P.O. Box 532
Chester, New York 10918
Tel: (914) 469-9161
Fax: (914) 469-2015

Walters Gardens Inc.
P.O. Box 137
Zeeland, Michigan 49464
Tel: (616) 772-4697
Fax: (616) 772-5803

Yoder Brothers, Inc.
Box 230
Barberton, Ohio 44203
Tel: (216) 745-2143
Fax: (216) 753-5294

Zelenka Nursery
16127 Winans Street
Grand Haven, Michigan
49417
Tel: (616) 842-1367
Fax: (800) 253-3743

GLOSSARY

Alpine plants—dwarf plants native to or associated with cool, rocky growing environments.

Annual—a plant that completes its life cycle of growth, flowering and death in one year. Many plants that are perennials in warmer climates are annuals in cold winter environments.

Apomixis—production of seed without pollination. The resulting seed produces plants identical to the parent plant.

Biennial—a plant with a two-year life cycle that produces only foliage the first year, then blooms and dies the second year.

Bract—a modified leaf growing at the base of a flower.

Bulbil—a small bulb that forms alongside an established bulb. Bulbils can be separated from the parent bulb to propagate certain plants.

Callus—plant cells that form as a result of wounding. Cells divide and differentiate to form roots, shoots, and specific plant organs. Callus formation is the first indication that cuttings are beginning to root.

Calyx—the group of sepals below a flower.

Cation exchange capacity (CEC)—the quantity of positively charged ions (cations), such as magnesium and calcium ions, that can be held and exchanged by a given amount of soil. CEC is a measure of soil fertility.

Corolla—the group of petals present as part of a flower.

Crown—the part of a plant at the soil surface from which new shoots are produced.

Damping-off—disease and death of young plant tissues as a result of infection by *Botrytis*, *Pythium*, *Rhizoctonia*, *Phytophthora*, or other fungi. Damping-off is of most concern in warm, high humidity environments.

Dioceious—a plant that produces male and female flowers on separate plants. A given plant that produces only male or only female flowers.

Diploid—a plant with two sets of chromosomes. In daylilies, diploid varieties generally have smaller flowers than tetraploid varieties, which have acquired four sets of chromosomes through hybridizing.

Glaucous—covered with a white substance that can be rubbed off. Plants with glaucous leaves display a bluish or gray cast.

Hardening off—process of slowing the growth of greenhouse grown plants prior to shipping or planting by reducing moisture and temperature and increasing exposure to outdoor conditions.

Internodal cutting—a cutting that includes the stem area between two adjacent nodes. Such a cutting includes at least two nodes.

Internode—the area on a plant stem between two adjacent nodes.

Margin—the outer edge of a plant part, usually a leaf.

Monoecious—a plant that produces male and female flowers separately on the same plant. A given flower is either male or female.

Nodal cutting—a cutting that includes one node and a small amount of stem above and below the node.

Node—a point along the stem where leaves are attached.

Offset—a lateral shoot or branch produced at the crown of a plant. Offshoots are often already rooted when removed from the parent plant.

Panicle—an indeterminate branching inflorescence.

Pubescent—plant parts, usually leaves, covered with short hairs.

Raceme—a simple, indeterminate inflorescence with pedicilled flowers.

Radicle—the initial root to emerge from a germinating seed.

Scarification—any process of mechanically weakening a seed coat to make it more permeable to water and gases to encourage germination.

Sepals—leaflike flower parts that protect a developing flower bud and are usually visible at the base of the flower when it opens.

Tetraploid—a plant with four sets of chromosomes. In daylilies, tetrapoild varieties generally have larger flowers than diploid varieties, which have only two sets of chromosomes.

Tomentose—describes a plant part that is densely covered by woolly hairs.

Umbel—an indeterminate inflorescence, usually but not necessarily flat-topped, with the pedicels and peduncles arising from a common point and resembling the stays of an umbrella.

Vegetative growth—the production of roots, stems, and leaves before initiation of flower buds begins.

Vegetative propagation—using an existing plant part, such as a cutting, offset, leaf, or root, to produce a plant that is identical to the parent plant.

Vernalization—exposure of seed to a period of cold temperature to encourage germination or promote flowering.

Wetting agent—a substance added to a liquid chemical or water to decrease the cohesion within the liquid and allow it to stick better, especially to oily surfaces. Wetting agents are often added to pesticide sprays or liquid solutions of rooting hormone to increase coverage on plant surfaces.

REFERENCE LIST

—————■—————

The following is a list of references that I used in compiling the information for the *Ball Perennial Manual*. The culture information came primarily from our own research with input and clarification from a wide number of growers, including the ones noted in the front of this book and at the end of a number of the crop chapters.

Aden, P. 1988. *The Hosta book.* Portland, Ore.: Timber Press, Inc.

Allen, C.L. 1893. *Bulbs and tuberous rooted plants.* New York: Orange Judd Publishing Co.

American Peony Society, 1983. *Handbook of the Peony.* 4th ed.

Arkansas bans *Lythrum* as a noxious weed. 1990. *Greenhouse Manager.* April.

Armitage, A.M. 1989. *Herbaceous perennial plants.* Athens, Ga.: Varsity Press Inc.

————. 1993. *Specialty cut flowers.* Portland, Ore.: Timber Press, Inc.

Bagust, H. 1992. *The gardener's dictionary of horticultural terms.* London: Cassell, Villiers House.

Bailey Hortorium. 1976. *Hortus third.* New York: MacMillan Publishing Co.

Bailey, L.H. 1925. *The nursery manual.* New York: MacMillan Publishing Co.

————. 1942. *The standard cyclopedia of horticulture.* 3 vols. New York: MacMillan Publishing Co.

————. 1951. *Manual of cultivated plants.* New York: MacMillan Publishing Co.

Bales, S.F. 1991. Perennials. In *Burpee American gardening series.* New York: Prentice Hall Press.

Ball, G.J. 1948. *Ball redbook.* 7th ed. West Chicago, Ill.: George J. Ball Inc.

Beckett, K. 1981. *Growing hardy perennials.* London: Croom Helm.

Biles, R.E. 1961. *The complete book of garden magic.* Chicago: J.G. Ferguson Publishing Co.

Bird, R. 1993. *The propagation of hardy perennials.* London: B.T. Batsford, Ltd.

Bond, S. 1992. *Hostas.* London: Ward Lock Ltd.

Bush-Brown, L. and J. 1939. *America's garden book.* New York: Charles Scribner's Sons.

Clarke, G., and A. Toogood. 1992. *The complete book of plant propagation.* England: Ward Lock.

Clausen, R.R., and N.H. Ekstrom. 1989. *Perennials for American gardens.* New York: Random House.

Coombes, A.J. 1985. *Dictionary of plant names*. Portland, Ore.: Timber Press.

Cornell perennial guidelines for New York. 1987. Cornell Cooperative Extension. Cornell University, New York.

Correvon, H. 1930, 1993. *Rock garden and Alpine plants*. New York: The MacMillan Publishing Co.

Cox, J. and M. 1985. *The perennial garden*. Emmaus, Pa.: Rodale Press.

Cumming, R.W., and R.E. Lee. 1960. *Contemporary perennials*. New York: Macmillan Publishing Co.

Dana, Mrs. W. S. 1916. *How to know the wild flowers*. New York: Charles Scribner's Sons.

Deano, N. 1993. *Seed germination theory and practice*. 2nd ed. Personally published.

Dirr, M.A. 1977. *Manual of woody landscape plants*. Champaign, Ill.: Stipes Publishing Co.

————. 1983. *Manual of woody landscape plants*. 3rd. ed. Champaign, Ill.: Stipes Publishing Co.

Domoto, T. 1983. Digging and shipping tree peonies. In *Handbook of the Peony*. 4th ed. American Peony Society.

Erwin J., and D. Schwarze. *Factors affecting Clematis rooting*. Minnesota Commercial Flower Growers Association Bulletin 41(4).

Fay, A.M., S.M. Still, and M.A. Bennett. 1993. Optimum germination temperature of *Rudbeckia fulgida*. HortTechnology. Oct./Dec.

Foster, H.L. 1968. *Guide to rock gardening*. Portland, Ore.: Timber Press.

Fretwell, B. 1989. *Clematis*. Deer Park, Wis.: Capability Books.

Giles, F.A., R. M. Keith, and D. C. Saupe. 1980. *Herbaceous perennials*. Reston, Va.: Reston Publishing Co.

Gillette, R. 1983. Propagating perennials. *GrowerTalks* 47 (December).

Gorer, R. 1978. *Growing plants from seed*. London: Faber and Faber.

Halliwell, B. 1992. *The propagation of Alpine plants and dwarf bulbs*. Portland, Ore.: Timber Press.

Harding. Mrs. E. 1923. *Peonies in the little garden*. Boston: The Atlantic Monthly Press.

Hardy perennials From seed. 1987. Benary Seed Company, Hann-Muenden, Germany.

Harper, P., and F. McGourty. 1985. *Perennials, how to select, grow and enjoy*. Tucson, Ariz.: HP Books.

Hartman, H.T., and D.E. Kester. 1983. *Plant propagation: principles and practices*. 4th ed. Englewood Cliffs, New York: Prentice Hall.

Hartman, H. T., D.E. Kester, and F.T. Davies, Jr. 1990. *Plant propagation: principles and practices*. 5th ed. Englewood Cliffs, New York: Prentice Hall.

Hayward, G. 1990. The elegant Epimedium. *Fine Gardening*. March/April.

Henderson, P. 1884. *Garden and farm topics*. New York: Peter Henderson and Company.

Hill, L. and N. 1991. *Daylilies: the perfect perennial*. Pownal, Vt.: Garden Way Publishing.

Hottes, A.C. 1924. *A little book of climbing plants*. New York: A.T. De La Mare Co.

————. 1945. *Book of shrubs*. New York: A.T. De La Mare Co.

———. 1947. *Plant propagation.* New York: A.T. De La Mare Co.

———. 1949. *Garden facts and fancies.* New York: Dodd, Mead & Company.

Howells, J. 1990. *A plantsman's guide to clematis.* Villiers House, London: Ward Lock Ltd.

Ingwersen, W. 1978. *Manual of Alpine plants.* Villiers House, London: Cassell Publisher.

Jelitto, J. and W. Schacht. 1990. *Hardy herbaceous perennials.* 2 vols. Portland, Ore.: Timber Press.

Jones, S.B. Jr., and L.E. Foote. 1990. *Gardening with native wild flowers.* Portland, Ore: Timber Press.

Laurie, A., and L.C. Chadwick. 1934. *Commercial flower forcing.* Philadelphia: P. Blakiston's Son & Co. Inc.

Lewis, P. and M. Lynch. 1989. *Campanulas.* Portland, Ore.: Timber Press.

Lima, P. 1989. *The Harrowsmith perennial garden.* Ontario, Canada: Camden House Publishing, Firefly Books.

Lloyd, C. 1989. *Clematis.* Deer Park, Wis.: Capability Books.

Mahlstede, J.P., and E.S. Haber. 1957. *Plant propagation.* New York: John Wiley & Sons.

McEwen, C. 1981. *Siberian irises.* Hanover, New Hampshire: University Press of New England.

———. 1990. *The Japanese Iris.* Hanover, New.Hampshire: University Press of New England.

Mitchell, S.B. 1949. *Iris for every garden.* New York: M. Barrows and Company, Inc.

Nau, J., and M. Levy. 1991. *Up and coming perennials.* GrowerExpo Presentation.

Nau, J. 1983-1944. Ball Seed Company perennial and field trial notes from 1983 to 1994.

———. 1988. *Ball culture guide.* West Chicago, Ill.: Geo. J. Ball Inc.

———. 1993. *Ball culture guide.* 2nd ed. Batavia, Ill.: Ball Publishing.

Nehrling, A., and I. Nehrling. 1964. *The picture book of perennials.* New York: Hearthside Press Inc.

The New Royal Horticultural Society dictionary of gardening. 1992. New York: The Stockton Press.

Perennial Plant Association. In *Proceedings.* Bulletin 717. Herbaceous Perennial Symposium.

Phillips, E., and C. C. Burrell. 1993. *Rodale's illustrated encyclopedia of perennials.* Emmaus, Pa.: Rodale Press.

Phillips, H. R. 1985. *Growing and propagating wild flowers.* Chapel Hill, N.C.: University of North Carolina Press.

Phillips, R., and M. Rix. 1991. *Random House book of perennials.* Vol. 1. (Early). New York: Random House.

———. 1991. *Random House book of perennials.* Vol. 2. (Late). New York: Random House.

Pinnell, M.M., A.M. Armitage, and D. Seaborn. 1985. *Germination needs of common perennial seed.* Research Bulletin No. 331, University of Georgia.

Reilly, A. 1978. *Park's success with seeds.* Greenwood, South Carolina: Geo. W. Park.

Rock, H.W. 1981. *Prairie propagation handbook.* 6th ed. Franklin, Wisconsin: Wehr Nature Center.

Rockwell, F.F. 1933. Peonies. In *The home garden handbooks.* New York: MacMillan Publishing Co.

Seymour, E.L.D. 1970. *Wise garden encyclopedia*. New York: Grosset & Dunlap.

Still, S. 1988. *Manual of herbaceous ornamental plants*. 3rd ed. Champaign, Ill.: Stipes Publishing Co.

Stout, A.B. 1986. *Daylilies*. New York: Saga Press.

Swift, S., and D. Koranski. 1987. A how-to guide to producing perennials. *Greenhouse Grower*. April.

Tayama, Harry. Ed. 1989. *Tips on growing potted perennials and biennials*. Ohio Cooperative Extension Service. Bul. FP-766. The University of Ohio.

Taylor's guide to perennials. 1986. Ed. G.P. DeWolf Jr. Boston: Houghton Mifflin Co.

Taylor, Norman. 1956. *Taylor's encyclopedia of gardening*. Cambridge, Mass.: The Riverside Press.

———. 1958. *The guide to garden flowers*. Boston: Houghton, Mifflin Co.

Thomas, G.S. 1990. *Plants for ground cover*. Portland, Ore.: Timber Press.

———. 1990. *Perennial garden plants*. 3rd ed. Portland, Ore.: Sagapress, Inc., Timber Press, Inc.

Thompson, P. 1992. *Creative propagation*. England: B.T. Batsford, Limited.

Trehane, Piers. 1989. *Index hortensis*. Vol. 1. Perennials. Hampreston Manor, Wimborne, Dorset: Quarterjack Publications.

Van Hees, G., and C.D. Hendricks. 1987. Summer Cutting Propagation Workshop. Perennial Plant Symposium. Baltimore, Maryland.

Voigt, T.B., B.R. Hamilton, and F.A. Giles. 1983. *Ground covers for the Midwest*. Publication 65. University of Illinois.

Weaver, R.E., Jr. 1987. In praise of Epimediums, Part I. *Perennial Plant Association Quarterly Newsletter*. Vol. XI.

———. 1987. In praise of Epimediums, Part II. *Perennial Plant Association Quarterly Newsletter*. Vol. XII.

Weiler, T.C., and P.K. Markham. 1986. Eight steps to better Bleeding Hearts. *Greenhouse Grower*. January.

Welch, W.C. 1989. *Perennial garden color: For Texas and the South*. Dallas, Texas: Taylor Publishing Company.

Wells, J.S. 1985. *Plant propagation practices*. Chicago: American Nurseryman Publishing.

Western garden book. 1988. Sunset Books. Menlo Park, Calif.: Lane Publishing Co.

Wister, J.C., ed. *The Peonies*. 1962. Washington, D.C.: American Horticulltural Society.

———. 1947. *Woman's home companion garden book*. New York: Doubleday and Company.

Young, J.A., and C.G. Young. 1986. *Seeds of wildland plants (collecting, processing, germininating)*. Portland, Ore.: Timber Press.

INDEX TO SCIENTIFIC NAMES

INDEX TO COMMON NAMES

SUBJECT INDEX

About the Author

Since 1982, Jim Nau has been the Trials Manager for Ball Seed Company, West Chicago, Illinois, where he has coordinated their six-acre trial gardens. He has had several accompanying positions with Ball Seed—all related to the seed field. Most recently, he was promoted to resource person for the entire seed and vegetative line of the Ball Seed Company.

His writing accomplishments include magazine articles, variety and cultural descriptions for the *Ball Seed Catalog*, various crops in the *Ball Redbook*, 16th Edition, as well as three editions of the *Ball Culture Guide*.

Jim has taught horticulture for five years, first with the DuPage Horticulture School and then with the College of DuPage. He is a member of various horticultural societies including the Perennial Plant Association, and he is the past president of the Association of Specialty Cut Flower Growers, Oberlin, Ohio.